AF089512

Pathfinder for

Olympiad and JEE Advanced

Physics

Arvind Tiwari

Sachin Singh Ajay Jangid

Universities Press

All rights reserved. No part of this book may be (i) modified, reproduced or utilised in any form, or by any means, electronic or mechanical, including photocopying, recording or by any information storage and retrieval system, in any form of binding or cover other than in which it is published, without permission in writing from the publisher; or (ii) used or reproduced in any manner for the purpose of training, development or operation of artificial intelligence (AI) technologies and systems, including generative AI technologies, without permission in writing from the copyright holder.

PATHFINDER FOR OLYMPIAD AND JEE ADVANCED PHYSICS

UNIVERSITIES PRESS (INDIA) PRIVATE LIMITED

Registered Office
3-6-747/1/A & 3-6-754/1, Himayatnagar, Hyderabad 500 029, Telangana, India
info@universitiespress.com; www.universitiespress.com

Distributed by
Orient Blackswan Private Limited

Registered Office
3-6-752 Himayatnagar, Hyderabad 500 029, Telangana, India

Other Offices
Bengaluru / Chennai / Guwahati / Hyderabad
Kolkata / Mumbai / New Delhi / Noida / Patna

© The Authors and Universities Press (India) Private Limited 2025
First published 2025
Reprinted 2025

Cover and book design
© The Authors and Universities Press (India) Private Ltd 2025
ISBN: 978-93-49750-06-7

Typeset in Century Schoolbook by the Authors

Printed in India by
B.B Press, Tronica City, Ghaziabad, U.P. 201103

Published by
Universities Press (India) Private Limited
3-6-747/1/A & 3-6-754/1, Himayatnagar, Hyderabad 500 029, Telangana, India

Disclaimer
Care has been taken to confirm the accuracy of the information presented in this book. The author and the publisher, however, cannot accept any responsibility for errors or omissions or for consequences from application of the information in this book, and make no warranty, express or implied, with respect to its contents.

> "If I had an hour to solve a problem and my life depended on the solution, I would spend the first 55 minutes determining the proper question to ask, for once I know the proper question, I could solve the problem in less than five minutes."
>
> **Albert Einstein**

Preface

Philosophy behind the work

Applying intuitive thinking together with acquired subject knowledge while dealing with problems in physics is certainly very rewarding. This not only helps in developing a better understanding of the physical processes involved in a problem but also enhances capabilities of making a proper physical model of the physical situation at hand and then applying subject knowledge with an utmost clarity.

This work is an effort to cultivate the above-mentioned philosophy that also happens to be an essential prerequisite for aspirants of national and international Physics Olympiads as well as of JEE Advanced.

Structure of the work

In every chapter, very fundamental ideas of the subject are introduced in a section 'Back to Basics' followed by four sections of exercises that are 'Multiple Choice Questions', 'Build up your understanding', 'Check your understanding' and 'Challenge your understanding'. These sections are structured in gradually increasing level of difficulty as well as in accordance with usual teaching sequences.

The first two sections of the exercises are primarily for aspirants of JEE Advanced and along with these the next two sections are for aspirants of national and international Physics Olympiads.

Acknowledgements

We are humbled by the gracious guidance and support of Mr. Brajesh Maheshwari, a great teacher and motivator, without which even the conception of this work would not have been possible. We also like to thank Mr. Ajay Pratap Singh, Mr. Anish Srivastava, Mr. Sanjay Srivastava, Mr. Kamal Kishore Sharma, Mr. Harsh Kumar Sharma for their valuable suggestions.

We always welcome corrections and suggestions from the readers.

Arvind Tiwari (atphysics@hotmail.com)
Sachin Singh (physicsachin@hotmail.com)
Ajay Jangid (aj.iitk@yahoo.com)

Photo Credits

Chapter Openers

Chapter 1
Page 1.1: iStock: nullplus

Chapter 2
Page 2.1: iStock: stanley45

Chapter 3
Page 3.1: iStock: umdash9

Chapter 4
Page 4.1: iStock: dima_zel

Chapter 5
Page 5.1: iStock: AnatolEr

Chapter 6
Page 6.1: Wikimedia Commons: George Eastman House Collection

Chapter 9
Page 9.1: iStock: bjdlzx

Chapter 10
Page 10.1: iStock: jpgfactory

Chapter 11
Page 11.1: iStock: cturtletrax

Chapter 12
Page 12.1: iStock: mishooo

Chapter 13
Page 13.1: iStock: RuudMorijn

Chapter 14
Page 14.1: iStock: nemoris

Chapter 15
Page 15.1: iStock: Zvesta

Chapter 16
Page 16.1: iStock: itsmejust

Scientists

Chapter 1
J Robert Oppenheimer: Wikipedia: Unknown

Chapter 3, 16
Albert Einstein: Library of Congress

Chapter 4
Paul Dirac:
Wikimedia Commons: Nobel Foundation

Chapter 5
Sir Lord Kelvin:
Wikipedia: T. & R. Annan & Sons

Chapter 6
Neils Henrick David Bohr:
Wikimedia Commons: ETH-Bibliothek

Chapter 7
James Clark Maxwell:
Wikimedia Commons: Unknown

Chapter 8
Sir William Henry Bragg:
Wikimedia Commons: Nobel Foundation

Chapter 9
James Prescott Joule:
Wikimedia Commons: Henry Roscoe

Chapter 11
Galileo Galilei:
Wikimedia Commons: Unknown

Chapter 12
Sir Isaac Newton:
Wikimedia Commons: Isaac Newton Institute

Chapter 13
René Descartes: Library of Congress

Chapter 15
Michael Faraday: Wikipedia: Unknown

Exercise Openers

Multiple Choice Questions
iStock: alexsl

Build-up Your Understanding
iStock: koun

Check Your Understanding iStock: abluecup

Challenge Your Understanding
iStock: Duan ZeFan

Contents

1.	Kinematics of Translational Motion	1.1 – 1.28
2.	Newton's Laws of Motion	2.1 – 2.36
3.	Methods of Work and Energy	3.1 – 3.20
4.	Methods of Impulse and Momentum and System of Particles	4.1 – 4.26
5.	Rotational Motion	5.1 – 5.32
6.	Gravitation	6.1 – 6.8
7.	Fluid Mechanics	7.1 – 7.21
8.	Thermal Physics	8.1 – 8.33
9.	Properties of Matter	9.1 – 9.12
10.	Waves and Oscillations	10.1 – 10.17
11.	Ray and Wave Optics	11.1 – 11.19
12.	Electrostatics	12.1 – 12.31
13.	Electric Current	13.1 – 13.27
14.	Magnetic Effects of Electric Current	14.1 – 14.16
15.	Electromagnetic Induction and Alternating Current	15.1 – 15.21
16.	Modern Physics	16.1 – 16.11

Chapter 1

Kinematics of Translational Motion

Ideas of space and time, reference frame, position vector, instantaneous and average velocities, speeds and accelerations; types of motion: rectilinear motion, curvilinear motion in a plane and in three dimensions; Cartesian and polar co-ordinate systems and their use in analysing rectilinear and curvilinear motions; angular motion variables: angular position, angular velocity and angular acceleration, kinematics of circular motion; constrained or dependent motion.

"There are children playing in the streets who could solve some of my top problems in physics, because they have modes of sensory perception that I lost long ago."

BACK TO BASICS

Average velocity $\vec{v}_{av}$ and average acceleration $\vec{a}_{av}$ of a particle:

$$\vec{v}_{av} = \frac{\Delta \vec{r}}{\Delta t} \qquad \vec{a}_{av} = \frac{\Delta \vec{v}}{\Delta t}$$

Here $\vec{r}$ is position vector of the particle.

Instantaneous velocity $\vec{v}$ and instantaneous acceleration $\vec{a}$ of a particle:

$$\vec{v} = \frac{d\vec{r}}{dt} \qquad \vec{a} = \frac{d\vec{v}}{dt}$$

Usually the term "instantaneous" is dropped and in practice, we simply speak and write velocity and acceleration instead of instantaneous velocity and instantaneous acceleration.

Displacement $\Delta \vec{r}$ and distance travelled s in a time interval $[t_1, t_2]$:

$$\Delta \vec{r} = \int_{t_1}^{t_2} \vec{v} dt = \vec{v}_{av}(t_2 - t_1) \qquad s = \int_{t_1}^{t_2} |\vec{v}| dt$$

J. Robert Oppenheimer
(22 April 1904 - 18 February 1967)

Angular Motion Variables:

Angular position θ is an angle made by position vector from a fixed direction.

Average angular velocity ω_{av} and average angular acceleration $\vec{\alpha}_{av}$

$$\omega_{av} = \frac{\Delta\theta}{\Delta t} \qquad \vec{\alpha}_{av} = \frac{\Delta\vec{\omega}}{\Delta t}$$

Instantaneous angular velocity $\vec{\omega}$ and instantaneous angular acceleration $\vec{\alpha}$

$$\vec{\omega} = \frac{d\vec{\theta}}{dt} \qquad \vec{\alpha} = \frac{d\vec{\omega}}{dt}$$

Acceleration $\vec{a}$ of a particle: normal and tangential components:

Tangential component of acceleration:
It accounts for change in speed.

$$a_\tau = \frac{dv}{dt} = v\frac{dv}{ds} \qquad \vec{a}_\tau = \left(\frac{\vec{a}\cdot\vec{v}}{v}\right)\frac{\vec{v}}{v} = \vec{\alpha}\times\vec{\rho}$$

Normal Component of Acceleration:
It accounts for change in direction of motion.

$$a_n = v\omega_v = \frac{v^2}{\rho} = \omega_v^2\rho \qquad \vec{a}_n = \vec{a} - \vec{a}_\tau = \vec{\omega}_v \times \vec{v}$$

Here ω_v is time rate at which velocity vector rotates and ρ is radius of curvature of the trajectory at the point under consideration.

In circular motion, this component of acceleration is usually called centripetal acceleration and radius of curvature ρ becomes radius r of the circular path.

Angular motion and linear motion variables in circular motion:

$$s = \theta r \qquad v = \omega r \qquad a_\tau = \alpha r$$

Here centre of the circular path is taken as the origin of the coordinate system.

Kinematics of translational motion in polar coordinate system:

$$\vec{r} = r\hat{e}_r$$

$$\vec{v} = \frac{d\vec{r}}{dt} = \frac{dr}{dt}\hat{e}_r + r\frac{d\theta}{dt}\hat{e}_\theta = \dot{r}\hat{e}_r + r\dot{\theta}\hat{e}_\theta$$

$$\vec{a} = \left\{\ddot{r} - r\left(\dot{\theta}\right)^2\right\}\hat{e}_r + \left(r\ddot{\theta} + 2\dot{r}\dot{\theta}\right)\hat{e}_\theta = \left\{\ddot{r} - r\omega^2\right\}\hat{e}_r + \left(r\alpha + 2\dot{r}\omega\right)\hat{e}_\theta$$

Here components along base unit vectors $\hat{e}_r$ and $\hat{e}_\theta$ are known as radial and transverse components respectively.

The first derivative of a variable with respect to time is generally denoted by putting a single dot (˙) and double derivative by putting a double dot (¨) over the variable.

Multiple Choice Questions

1. From a town, cars start at regular intervals of 30 s and run towards another town with a constant speed of 60 km/h. At some point of time, all the cars simultaneously have to reduce their speeds to 40 km/h due to bad weather conditions. What will be the time interval between arrivals of the cars at the second town during the bad weather?
   (a) 20 s (b) 30 s
   (c) 40 s (d) 45 s

2. Sam used to walk to school every morning, and it takes him 20 min. Once on his way, he realized that he had forgotten his homework notebook at home. He knew that if he continued walking to school at the same speed, he would be there 8 min before the bell, so he went back home for the notebook and arrived at the school 10 min after the bell. If he had walked all the way with his usual speed, what fraction of the way to school had he covered till the moment he turned back?
   (a) 8/20 (b) 9/20
   (c) 10/20 (d) 12/20

3. A particle moving continuously in the positive x-direction passes the positions $x = 9$ m and 17 m at the instants $t = 1$ s and 3 s respectively. Its average velocities in the time intervals [1 s, 3 s] and [0 s, 6 s] are equal. Which of the following statements is/are correct?
   (a) It was at $x = 5$ m at $t = 0$ s.
   (b) It is moving at a uniform speed.
   (c) Average velocity in the interval [3 s, 6 s] is 4 m/s.
   (d) Information is insufficient to decide any of the above.

4. When a car passes mark-A, the driver applies brakes. Thereafter reducing speed uniformly from 160 km/h at A, the car passes mark C with a speed of 40 km/h. The marks are at equal distances on the road as shown below.

   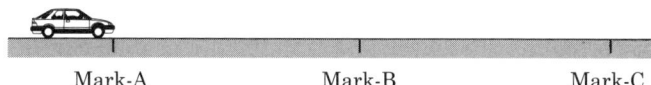

   Where on the road was the car moving at a speed of 100 km/h? Neglect the size of the car as compared to the distances involved.
   (a) At mark-B (b) Between mark-A and mark-B
   (c) Between mark-B and mark-C
   (d) Information is insufficient to decide.

5. A material particle is chasing another one and both are moving on the same straight line. After they pass a particular point, their velocities (v) vary with time t as shown in the figure. When will the chase end?
   (a) 4.0 s (b) 6.0 s
   (c) 12 s (d) Insufficient information.

   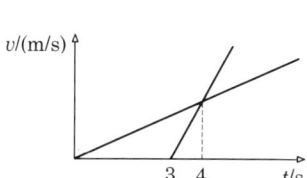

1.4 Chapter-1

6. Two particles A and B start from the same point and move in the positive x-direction. In a time-interval of 2.00 s after they start, their velocities (v) vary with time t as shown in the following figures. What is the maximum separation between the particles during this time interval?

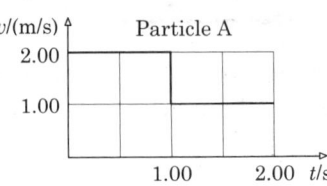
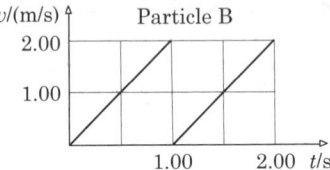

(a) 1.00 m (b) 1.25 m
(c) 1.50 m (d) 2.00 m

7. Two cars A and B simultaneously start a race. Velocity v of the car A varies with time t according to the graph shown in the figure. It acquires a velocity of 50 m/s a few seconds before $t = 100$ s and thereafter moves with this speed. Car B runs together with car A till both acquire a velocity 20 m/s; after this, car B moves with zero acceleration for one second and then follows velocity-time profile identical to that of A with a delay of one second. In this way, car B acquires a velocity of 50 m/s one second after car A acquires it. How much more distance Δs does car A cover in the first 100 s as compared to car B?

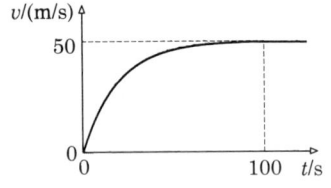

(a) $\Delta s = 30$ m (b) $\Delta s < 30$ m
(c) $\Delta s = 20$ m (d) Insufficient information.

8. A model rocket fired from the ground ascends with a constant upward acceleration. A small bolt is dropped from the rocket 1.0 s after the firing and fuel of the rocket is finished 4.0 s after the bolt is dropped. Airtime of the bolt is 2.0 s. Acceleration of free fall is 10 m/s². Which of the following statements is/are correct?

(a) Acceleration of the rocket while ascending on its fuel is 8.0 m/s².
(b) Fuel of the rocket was finished at a height 100 m above the ground.
(c) The maximum speed of the rocket during its upward flight is 40 m/s.
(d) Total airtime of the rocket is 15 s.

9. Drag force of water on a body is proportional to the velocity of the body relative to the fluid. A student drops several small identical stones from different heights over a deep lake and prepares graphs between speed v of every stone in the water and time t. The graphs can be divided into three categories as shown here. Which of the following explanations of these graphs appear reasonable?

(a) The first graph is for a stone dropped from a small height, and the second is for a stone dropped from a large height.
(b) The first graph is for a stone dropped from a large height, and the second is for a stone dropped from a small height.
(c) The third graph is for a stone dropped from a height sufficient to acquire the speed v_0 at the instant it enters the water.
(d) The third graph is not possible.

10. From a place on the ground that is 20 m away from a wall, a bullet is fired aiming at a 50 m high mark on the wall. The location of the bullet is shown by a circular dot at some point of time. Where on the wall will the bullet hit?

   (a) 20 m mark (b) 25 m mark
   (c) 30 m mark (d) 35 m mark

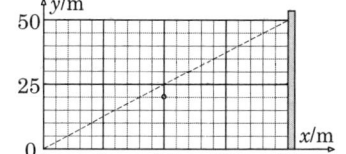

11. A cylindrical pipe of radius r is rolling towards a frog sitting on the horizontal ground. Centre of the pipe is moving with a constant velocity v. To save itself, the frog jumps off and passes over the pipe touching it only at the top. Denoting airtime of the frog by T, horizontal range of the jump by R and acceleration due to gravity by g, which of the following conclusions can you make?

   (a) $T = 4\sqrt{\dfrac{r}{g}}$ (b) $T \geq 4\sqrt{\dfrac{r}{g}}$

   (c) $R = 4(\sqrt{gr} - v)\sqrt{\dfrac{r}{g}}$ (d) $R \geq 4(\sqrt{gr} - v)\sqrt{\dfrac{r}{g}}$

12. Seven buoys A, B, C, D, E, F and G are released in a lake at regular intervals in a manner to make a square pattern as shown in the figure. The buoys A, C, E and G are on the vertices and the buoys B, D and F are at the midpoints of the sides of the square. If the buoys were released in a uniformly flowing river in the same manner, the buoy G falls on A. What pattern would they make in the river?

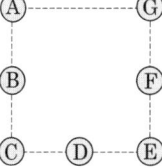

(a) 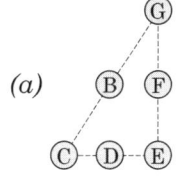 (b)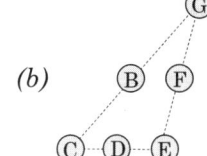

(c) 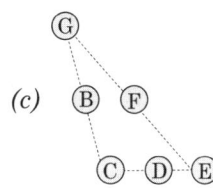 (d)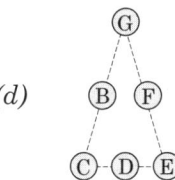

13. Two motorboats that can move with velocities 4.0 m/s and 6.0 m/s relative to water are going upstream in a river. When the faster boat overtakes the slower boat, a buoy is dropped from the slower boat. After a lapse of a time interval, both the boats turn back simultaneously and move at the same speeds relative to the water as before. Their engines are switched off when they reach the buoy again. If the maximum separation between the boats is 200 m after the buoy is dropped and the water flow velocity in the river is 1.5 m/s, find distance between the places where the faster boat passes by the buoy.

   (a) 75 m (b) 150 m
   (c) 300 m (d) 350 m

14. On a road going out of a city, lights of the last traffic signal glow green for 1.0 min and red for 2.0 min. After the traffic signal, the road is straight, and vehicles run at their constant speeds that lie in the range 60 km/h to 80 km/h. This mode of operation of traffic lights causes the vehicles to come out of the city in groups. Some distance away from the traffic signal, these groups merge and become indistinguishable. If the vehicles acquire their constant speeds after the traffic signal in negligible time, which of the following conclusions can you make?

   (a) The groups become indistinguishable 4.0 km after the traffic signal.
   (b) The groups become indistinguishable 8.0 km after the traffic signal.
   (c) Wider is the range of speed of the vehicles; greater is the distance where the groups become indistinguishable.
   (d) The larger the number of fast-moving vehicles, the shorter the distance, where the groups become indistinguishable.

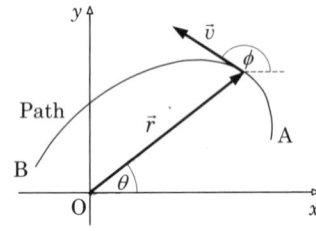

15. Two students simultaneously start from the same place on a circular track and run for 2 min. In this time, one of them completes three and the other four revolutions. Due to thick vegetation in a circular area as shown in the figure, either of the boys can see only one third of the track at a time. How long do they remain visible to each other during their run?

   (a) 20 s (b) 40 s
   (c) 80 s (d) 160 s

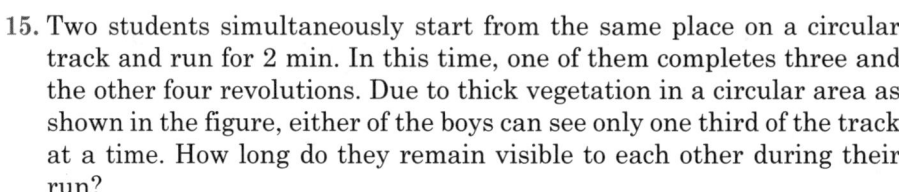

16. At a particular instant of time, position vector $\vec{r}$, velocity vector $\vec{v}$ and angular position θ of a particle traversing a path AB are shown in the figure. Here ϕ is the angle made by the velocity vector with the positive x-axis. Which of the following statements is/are correct?

   (a) Modulus of angular velocity is $\dfrac{d\theta}{dt} = \dfrac{v\sin(\phi-\theta)}{r}$.

   (b) Modulus of tangential component of acceleration is $r\dfrac{d^2\theta}{dt^2}$.

   (c) Modulus of normal component of acceleration is $v\dfrac{d\theta}{dt}$.

   (d) Modulus of normal component of acceleration is $v\dfrac{d\phi}{dt}$.

17. A boy takes 60 min to swim across a river, if his goal is to minimize time; and takes 180 min, if his goal is to minimize to zero the distance that he is carried downstream. In both these attempts, the boy swims at the same speed relative to the river current. Which of the following statements can be true?

   (a) He can swim relative to water faster than the river current.
   (b) He cannot swim relative to water faster than the river current.
   (c) If the width of the river is $3\sqrt{2}$ km, the speed of the river current must be 4 km/h.
   (d) If he crosses a $3\sqrt{2}$ km wide river in $60\sqrt{2}$ min, he will be carried $\sqrt{2}$ km downstream.

18. Two balls A and B are simultaneously released on two frictionless inclined planes from the positions shown. The inclined planes have equal inclinations. The balls pass through a particular horizontal level 12 s and 4 s after they are released. How long after they were released will they be closest to each other?

    (a) 6 s
    (b) 8 s
    (c) 12 s
    (d) 16 s

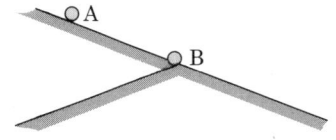

19. A horizontal wax bar B rests between a wedge and a vertical wall as shown in the figure. The wedge starts moving towards the wall with a constant acceleration 0.5 mm/s². The moment the wedge starts moving, a continuous supply of heat from the wall starts melting 1.0 mm length of the wax bar per second. If the bar always remains horizontal, which of the following conclusions can you make?

    (a) The bar first moves downwards and then upwards.
    (b) The bar stops for a moment after 2.0 s from the beginning.
    (c) The modulus of the displacement of the bar in the first 4 s is 1.5 mm.
    (d) The distance travelled by the bar in the first 4 s is 1.5 mm.

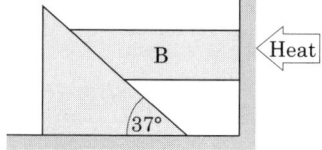

20. Particle A moves with a constant speed 2 m/s on a circular path of radius 4 m, whereas particle B moves on a straight-line coinciding with a diameter of the circular path, maintaining a constant distance 4 m from the particle A. Which of the following conclusions can be drawn?

    (a) Maximum speed of B is 4 m/s.
    (b) Maximum acceleration of B is 2 m/s².
    (c) During one revolution of A, distance travelled by B is 32 m.
    (d) Modulus of velocity of a particle relative to the other is constant.

21. Three ants A, B and C are crawling on a large horizontal tabletop always occupying vertices of an equilateral triangle, size of which may vary with time. If at an instant, the speeds of A and B are v_A and v_B, which of the following conclusions can you make for speed v_C of C?

    (a) $v_C < 0.5(v_A + v_B)$
    (b) $v_C \leq 0.5(v_A + v_B)$
    (c) $v_C < v_A + v_B$
    (d) $v_C \leq v_A + v_B$

22. Components along and perpendicular to a position vector are known as radial and transverse components respectively. A particle is projected horizontally from the top of a tower. Assume acceleration due to gravity to be uniform and the origin of the coordinate system at the point of projection.

Column-I	Column-II
(a) Radial component of velocity	(p) Always increases.
(b) Transverse component of velocity	(q) Always decreases.
(c) Radial component of acceleration	(r) First increases then decreases.
(d) Transverse component of acceleration	(s) First decreases then increases.

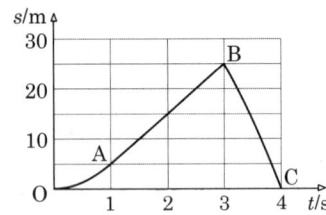

Questions 24 and 25 are based on the following physical situation.

A stone is dropped from the top of a tower and before it hits the ground another stone is also dropped. Assuming the stones do not bounce from the ground, the separation s between the stones is plotted against time t. Portions OA and BC of the graph are parabolic, while portion AB is a straight line. Acceleration due to gravity is 10 m/s².

23. The height of the tower is
    (a) 25 m (b) 30 m
    (c) 40 m (d) 45 m

24. When the first stone hit the ground, the second stone was moving with
    (a) 10 m/s at a height 40 m. (b) 10 m/s at a height 25 m.
    (c) 20 m/s at a height 20 m. (d) 20 m/s at a height 25 m.

Questions 26 to 28 are based on the following physical situation.

In a convoy on a long straight level road, 50 identical cars are at rest in a queue at equal separation 10 m from each other as shown.

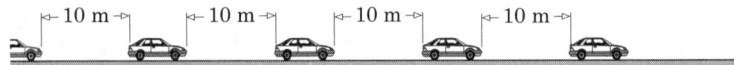

The engine of a car provides a constant acceleration of 2 m/s² and the brakes can provide a maximum deceleration of 4 m/s². When an order is given to start the convoy, the first car starts immediately, and each subsequent car starts when its distance from a car that is immediately ahead becomes 35 m. The maximum speed limit on this road is 72 km/h. When an order is given to stop the convoy, the driver of the first car applies brakes immediately and the driver of each subsequent car applies brakes with a certain time delay after noticing the brake lights of the car in front of his car turned red.

25. When all the cars are moving at the maximum speed, what is the separation between two adjacent cars?
    (a) 35 m (b) 85 m
    (c) 100 m (d) 110 m

26. During the time when motion is building up in the convoy, some of the cars are moving and others are resting. What is the average rate of change in length of the segment consisting of stationary cars?
    (a) Decreasing at 0.5 m/s (b) Decreasing at 1 m/s
    (c) Decreasing at 2 m/s   (d) Decreasing at 5 m/s

27. When all the cars are moving at the maximum speed, an order is given to stop the convoy. If all the cars decelerate at equal constant rates and separation between every two adjacent cars again becomes 10 m after the whole convoy stops, what can be the deceleration of the cars during braking?
    (a) 2 m/s² (b) 4 m/s²
    (c) ≤ 4 m/s² (d) Insufficient information

Questions 29 to 31 are based on the following physical situation.

A hot air balloon of constant ascent velocity can be used to investigate wind velocities at various altitudes. Employing this idea, one day a hot air balloon was released at a distance $l = 100$ m from a point where a telescope was installed to track the balloon. Since wind velocity was almost zero up to a height of approximately 30 m that day, the balloon first rose upwards and then due to horizontal drift caused by the wind it followed a plane curvilinear path. During continuous tracking of the balloon, the telescope has been rotated in a vertical plane without any change in azimuth. A graph depicting how the angle of elevation varies with time thus obtained is shown in the figure.

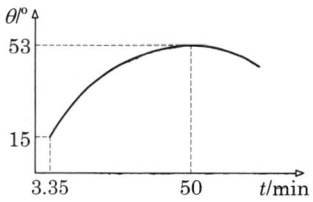

28. Ascent velocity of the balloon is closest to

    (a) 2.67 m/min (b) 6 m/min
    (c) 8 m/min (d) Information is insufficient to decide.

29. Wind velocity at the altitude of the balloon, where the angle of elevation acquires its maximum value is closest to

    (a) 4 m/min (b) 6 m/min
    (c) 8 m/min (d) 10 m/min

30. Horizontal drift of the balloon, when angle of elevation acquires its maximum value is closest to

    (a) 180 m (b) 200 m
    (c) 300 m (d) Insufficient information.

Questions 32 to 35 are based on the following physical situation.

Two particle A and B are moving towards each other on a straight line with equal speeds 5 m/s. At an instant that is assumed $t = 0$ s, distance between the particles is 100 m. It is desired to move another particle C, always maintaining a distance of 40 m from particle A and 30 m from particle B.

31. When and for how long can particle C fulfil the given condition?

    (a) $3 \text{ s} \leq t \leq 9 \text{ s}$ (b) $9 \text{ s} \leq t \leq 11 \text{ s}$
    (c) $11 \text{ s} \leq t \leq 17 \text{ s}$ (d) $3 \text{ s} \leq t \leq 17 \text{ s}$

32. What is the speed of particle C at the instant $t = 5$ s?

    (a) 3.5 m/s (b) 4.8 m/s
    (c) 5 m/s (d) 6 m/s

33. What is modulus of acceleration of particle C at the instant $t = 5$ s?

    (a) 2.3 m/s² (b) 0.58 m/s²
    (c) 0.90 m/s² (d) 3.30 m/s²

34. At the instant, when the line joining locations of A and B is perpendicular to the line joining locations of B and C, what are the magnitudes of velocities of C relative to A and B respectively?

    (a) 0 m/s and 5 m/s (b) 0 m/s and 10 m/s
    (c) 3.75 m/s and 0 m/s (d) 3.75 m/s and 10 m/s

Build up your understanding

1. In an announcement at a railway station, a passenger hears that the last train has passed $\Delta t_1 = 30$ min earlier than his train. At the next station that is $s = 20$ km away, in another announcement he hears that the first train arrived $\Delta t_2 = 20$ min earlier than his train. Reading time from his watch, he calculates the average speed of his train to be $v_p = 60$ km/h. Relying on the announcements and the passenger's calculations, determine the average speed of the first train.

2. One day you were on a picnic with your class. During the return journey from the picnic spot to your school, it began to rain, therefore the driver reduced the speed of the bus and drove with an average speed $v_1 = 60$ km/h instead of the scheduled average speed $v_0 = 70$ km/h. After the rain stopped, the driver drove the bus at an average speed $v_2 = 75$ km/h and covered the remaining $s = 40$ km exactly in scheduled time. How long did it rain?

3. There is a narrow bridge somewhere on a road connecting two towns. Two cars travel from one of the towns to the other at a constant speed v_1 everywhere on the road, except on the bridge, where they travel at another constant speed v_2. How the separation s between the cars varies with time t is shown in the following graph.

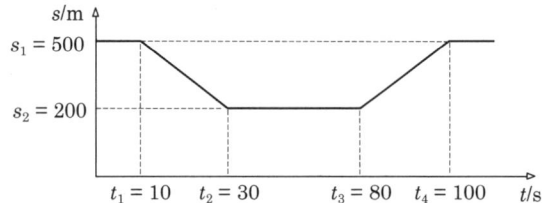

(a) What is the speed v_1 of the cars on the road?
(b) What is the speed v_2 of the cars on the bridge?
(c) What is the length of the bridge?

4. Traffic signals are installed at every $s = 1.00$ km on a long straight road. Every signal remains red for $\tau = 30$ s and green for next $\tau = 30$ s. The signals are synchronized in such a way that at a time, alternate signals remain red and the other remain green. The scheme is shown in the following figure.

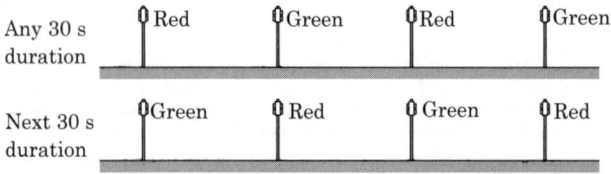

Suggest possible constant speeds at which a vehicle can run on this road without a stop.

5. A traffic officer receives complaints about frequent traffic jams at a traffic signal on the main street of a busy market. He studied the traffic pattern and to simplify calculations made some reasonable assumptions that all the vehicles are identical in size and move at identical speeds. At present, durations of red and green signals are equal, and the average speed of traffic advancement is $v_1 = 1.5$ m/s. For improvement in the situation, if he makes duration of green signals $\eta = 2$ times and to leave that of red signals unchanged, what would be average speed v_2 of the traffic advancement?

6. An engineer designs a robot that can climb stairs. If the robot climbs with a constant speed v, the battery of the robot discharges completely in a time interval τ. This dependence is shown in the following graph.

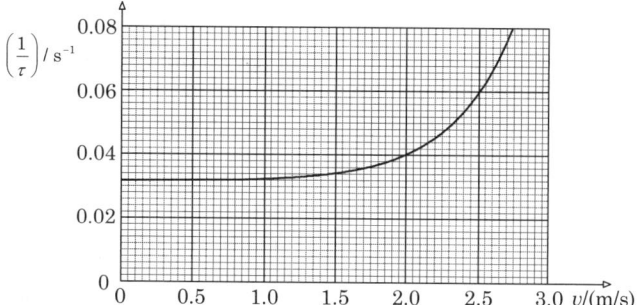

With the help of the graph, determine the maximum length of a staircase, which the robot can climb with a constant velocity.

7. A semi-cylindrical groove of radius $r = 20$ cm is made on a horizontal floor. An ant wants to cross the groove. A boy decides to help the ant making a bridge consisting of straight wire segments. But all the wires available are of length $l = 38$ cm, so the boy rigidly connects two wires at right angle and places the bridge in the groove as shown in the figure. If the ant can crawl up a wire segment at speed $v = 0.5$ cm/s and down a wire segment at speed $2v$, in what minimum time can the ant cross the groove with the help of this bridge?

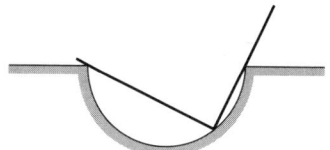

8. A particle covers a distance unidirectionally with uniform acceleration. If its average velocity is v_{av}, what could be range of modulus of its instantaneous velocity at the midpoint of the path?

9. Relation between average velocity v_{av} of a body and time t is shown in the graph. If during the time interval considered, the body did not change direction of motion, draw a graph between instantaneous velocity of the body and time.

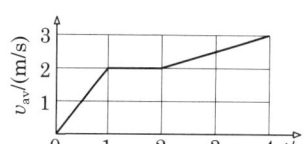

10. A passenger is standing on the platform at the beginning of nth (= 3rd) coach of a train. If the train starts moving with constant acceleration, the third coach passes by the passenger in $\Delta t_1 = 5.0$ s and rest of the train including the 3rd coach in $\Delta t_2 = 20$ s.

(a) How many coaches does the train consist of?
(b) In what time interval did the last coach pass by the passenger?

11. A ball is thrown vertically upwards. Its distance s from a fixed point varies with time t according to the following graph. Calculate the velocity of projection of the ball.

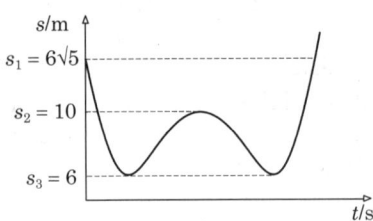

12. A clown in a circus, juggles n balls. He throws each ball vertically upwards at the same speed at equal time intervals τ. The acceleration of free fall is g.

    (a) Find expressions for the speed of projection and height of the ith ball above his hand when he throws the nth ball.

    If he uses $n = 4$ balls, distance between the second and third ball is $d = 50$ cm at the instant the fourth ball is projected.

    (b) Where is the first ball when the juggler throws the fourth ball?
    (c) What is the maximum height attained by each ball above the hands of the juggler?

13. To study effect of air resistance, a rubber ball was shot vertically upwards from a spring gun from 20th floor of a tall building. Velocity of the ball was recorded at regular intervals of time and the data obtained were plotted on a graph paper. Some labels on the axes are erased as shown in the following figure. With what speed did the ball strike the ground?

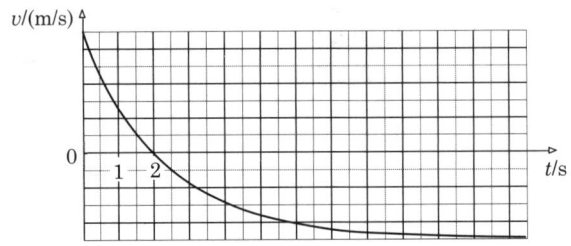

14. A student throws large number of small pebbles in all possible directions with equal speeds u out of a window. The pebbles hit the horizontal ground moving at an angle θ or greater with the ground. Air resistance is negligible and acceleration due to gravity is g. Deduce suitable expression for the height of the point of projection above the ground.

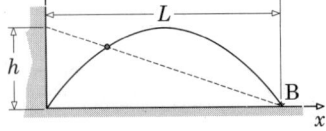

15. A small ball is thrown from the foot of a wall at the minimum possible velocity to hit bulb B on the ground a distance L away from the wall. Find expression for height h of shadow of the ball on the wall as a function of time t. Acceleration due to gravity is g.

16. The maximum range of a shell fired from a gun is $R = 22.5$ m. This gun is mounted on a platform that can move horizontally at a constant speed $v = 15.0$ m/s. At what angle above the horizontal, must the gun be aimed at to achieve maximum horizontal range? Neglect air resistance as well as height of the gun. Acceleration of free fall $g = 10.0$ m/s².

17. A cannon installed at the top of a hill can fire shells in all directions at the same speed u. There is an enemy bunker at an angle of elevation ϕ and a distance d from the cannon. All the shells explode in the air in time T before they reach the bunker. At what angle above the horizontal, should a shell be fired to explode closest to the bunker? Acceleration due to gravity is g.

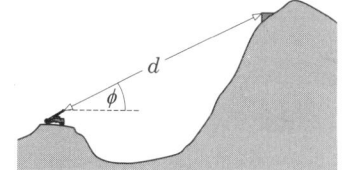

18. A boy while watering a garden keeps outlet of the hose $h = 0.8$ m above the ground. Water is continuously flowing out of the hose with a constant velocity $u = 6$ m/s at an angle $\theta = 30°$ above the horizontal. Cross section area of the outlet is $A = 1.5$ cm², density of water is $\rho = 1000$ kg/m³ and acceleration of free fall is $g = 10$ m/s². Find mass of water in the water stream?

19. The angle of projection for the maximum horizontal range of a projectile is 45°, if the point of projection and the point of landing are in the same horizontal level. Determine the angle of projection for the maximum horizontal range of a projectile, if

    (a) the point of landing is at a height h above the point of projection.
    (b) the point of landing is at a depth h below the point of projection.

20. A ball dropped bounces repeatedly on a large, inclined plane. Every bounce is perfectly elastic i.e. there is no loss of speed and lines of motion make equal angles with the inclined plane before and after the bounce. Find the ratio of distance R_{12} between the first and the second bounce to distance R_{23} between the second and the third bounce.

21. A marble is projected in a viscous fluid, with an initial speed u at an angle θ above the horizontal. Drag force of the fluid results in an acceleration $\vec{a}_D = -k\vec{v}$ in addition to that of gravity, where k is a positive constant and $\vec{v}$ is the velocity of the marble. Determine position coordinates and x (horizontal) and y (vertical) components of velocity of the marble as functions of time t. What is the terminal velocity?

22. In a battlefield in ancient times, a soldier with a catapult stationed on the top of an extremely high cliff notices camps of enemy close to the bottom of the cliff as shown in the figure. Stones can be launched from the catapult with a speed $u = 40$ m/s at an angle $\theta = 60°$ above the horizontal. If the air resistance reduces speed of the stone at a rate $k = 0.1$ (m/s)/m and there is no wind, at what horizontal separation from the enemy camps should the soldier install the catapult to hit the enemy camps?

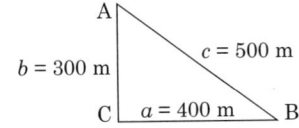

23. Two bikers simultaneously start a race with constant speeds from point A to traverse a triangular track ABC, one in clockwise and the other in anticlockwise sense. They simultaneously cross at B first time after a time interval $\Delta t_1 = 4$ min. If they continue the race, how long after they cross at B first time, will they again simultaneously cross at B?

24. On a straight section of a highway, sensors are installed to measure traffic density. For each lane of the highway, a sensor runs on an overhead wire. On a particular day, a sensor running with a speed $u = 5$ km/h opposite to the flow of traffic underneath, counts $N = 360$ vehicles in a length $L = 1$ km of the highway. If all the vehicles are moving with the same constant speed $v = 40$ km/h and density of the vehicles is uniform, calculate the number of vehicles per $l = 100$ m of the lane.

25. A train passes a platform with a uniform speed. A boy standing on the platform decides to estimate the length of a coach and speed of the train. For this purpose, he first runs with a constant speed of $u = 10$ km/h in the direction of the motion of the train and passes by a coach in $n_1 = 30$ steps. Then he turns back, runs at the same constant speed and passes by a coach in $n_2 = 20$ steps. If the boy covers a distance $l = 1.0$ m in each step, answer the following questions.
    (a) What is the speed of the train?
    (b) What is the length of a coach?

26. A ship of length $l = 150$ m moving with velocity $v_s = 36$ km/h on the sea suddenly discovered a sinking boat straight ahead. A rescue boat has been lowered from the mid of the ship, which went to the sinking boat with speed $v_b = 72$ km/h. When the rescue boat overtook the leading edge of the ship, the sinking boat was $x_0 = 3.0$ km away. The rescue boat reaches the sinking boat, spends there $t_0 = 1.0$ min to take the people on board and then returns with the same speed. Determine the time taken in the whole rescue operation from the moment the rescue boat was lowered to the moment the rescue boat returned to the mid of the ship from where it was lowered.

27. At the initial instant, two particles are observed at different locations moving towards each other with velocities u_1 and u_2. If they are subjected to constant accelerations a_1 and a_2 in directions opposite to their initial velocities, they will meet twice. If the time-interval between these two meetings is Δt, find a suitable expression for their initial separation.

28. At a particular instant, a particle moving with a constant velocity is approaching a fixed point with a velocity $u = 3$ m/s and after a time interval $\Delta t = 6$ s the particle passes the position closest to the fixed point with a velocity $v = 5$ m/s. Find the closest distance between the fixed point and the particle.

29. Two particles, A and B, are moving in free space. How their position coordinates x, y and z vary with time t is shown in the following graphs.

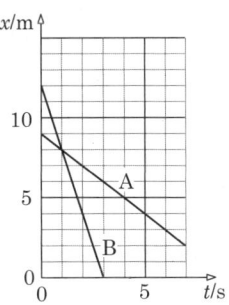
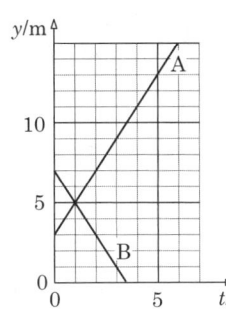
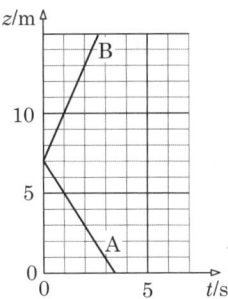

Determine at what instant of time the particles are closest to each other and the closest separation.

30. Consider two steamers, A and B, on a calm sea. Steamer A moves towards the north with a constant speed $v_A = 30$ km/h and steamer B moves towards the south with a constant speed $v_B = 10$ km/h. If smoke ejected by steamer A spreads in a straight line from the steamer towards the west and smoke ejected by steamer B spreads in another straight line from the steamer towards the north-west, determine magnitude and direction of the wind velocity.

31. Two identical boats are moving relative to the water current with equal speed $v_{b/w} = 1.0$ m/s. To a boy standing on the ground, the first boat appears moving perpendicular to the river current and to another boy standing on a raft in the river, the second boat appears moving perpendicular to the shoreline. In a certain time interval, distances of the boats from the shoreline increase by $\Delta y_1 = 4.0$ m and $\Delta y_2 = 5.0$ m respectively. Calculate speed of the river current.

32. A man in a boat starts from a point A and wants to reach a point C on the other bank of a river of width b. Point C is at distance a downstream from point B, which is directly opposite to point A. The water current velocity v_w is uniform everywhere. Find the minimum speed of the boat relative to the water-current and corresponding direction at which the boat must be steered.

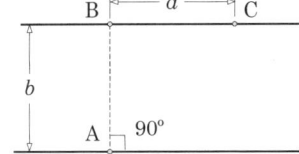

33. Three particles A, B, and C are on a straight horizontal line at equal distances between adjacent one. At an instant all the three particles start moving, particle A begins to move vertically upwards with a constant velocity u and particle C vertically downwards with a constant acceleration a without any initial velocity. How should particle B move vertically so that the three particles always remain collinear?

34. Three blocks A, B and C are suspended with the help of three pulleys and two threads with equal horizontal separation between adjacent blocks. Initially the blocks are held at rest at the same level and then released. The blocks move in such a way that they always remain in a straight line. If at an instant, block B is observed moving downwards with a velocity of 4 cm/s relative to block A, find velocities of all the blocks at this instant.

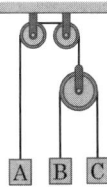

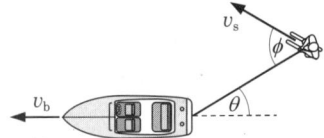
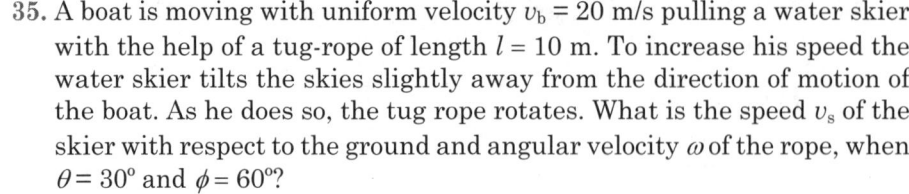

35. A boat is moving with uniform velocity $v_b = 20$ m/s pulling a water skier with the help of a tug-rope of length $l = 10$ m. To increase his speed the water skier tilts the skies slightly away from the direction of motion of the boat. As he does so, the tug rope rotates. What is the speed v_s of the skier with respect to the ground and angular velocity ω of the rope, when $\theta = 30°$ and $\phi = 60°$?

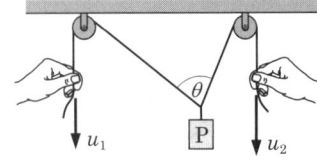

36. A load P is being pulled with the help of two inextensible strings that pass through two fixed pulleys as shown in the figure. At an instant, the velocities of the ends of the string being pulled are u_1 and u_2 and the angle between the strings connected to the load is θ, what is the speed of the load?

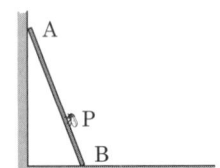

37. A stick AB of length l stands vertically on a horizontal floor leaning on a wall. A beetle P starts climbing the stick from the floor. When the beetle starts climbing, the lower end B of the stick is made to move away from the wall with a constant velocity v. The beetle climbs the stick with a constant speed u relative to the stick. If the upper end A does not leave the wall, what maximum height can the beetle rise?

38. A spacecraft is moving in space, where all the external forces can be neglected. Any change in its speed and direction of motion can be accomplished by rockets installed on it. At an instant when it is moving with a speed $v = 100$ m/s, the crew inside decides to take a 90° turn and then move in the new direction with the same speed v. The rockets installed can provide a maximum acceleration $a = 5\sqrt{2}$ m/s². Find the minimum time spent and shape of the path followed during the turn.

39. A dog running with a constant speed v is chasing a cat that is running with a constant velocity $\vec{u}$. During the chase, the dog always heads towards the cat. At an instant, direction of motion of the dog makes angle θ with that of the cat and the distance between them is r. Find magnitude of acceleration of the dog at this instant.

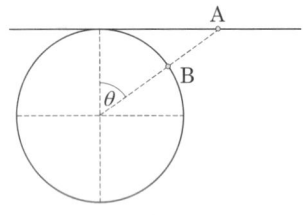

40. A straight track is tangent to a circular track of radius r. Two material points A and B start simultaneously from the common point of the tracks. The point A moves with uniform velocity u on the straight track whereas the point B on the circular track always keeping itself collinear with the centre of the circular track and the point A. Find suitable expression for magnitude of acceleration of the point B when it is at angular position θ.

Check your understanding

1. A 10 km long straight road connects two towns A and B. Two cyclists start simultaneously, one from town A and the other from town B. On reaching the opposite town a cyclist immediately returns to his starting town whereas the other cyclist takes some rest and then returns to his starting town. Both can ride at a speed of 20 km/h in absence of wind but during their whole journey, uniform wind from town A to B increases the speed of a cyclist going with the wind by the same amount as it decreases the speed of the cyclist going against the wind. Both the cyclists meet twice, first 2 km and then 6 km away from one of the towns. In which town and for what period a cyclist rests.

2. Imagine a change in the famous story of the hare and the tortoise. In this new story, when the hare wakes up, he finds the tortoise $x_0 = 10.0$ km ahead moving with a constant velocity. The hare not ready to give up starts running again with a constant velocity. In its effort to win, it overcomes this distance in time t_1, but during this time the tortoise crawls further a distance x_1, the hare overcomes x_1 in time t_2, but the tortoise in this time crawls further a distance x_2. This situation continues repeatedly. A monkey, who was the referee measures only distance $x_3 = 0.08$ m and time $t_7 = 1.28 \times 10^{-7}$ s. Assuming the hare and the tortoise as particles, find their speeds. How long after the hare wakes up, will it win?

3. A train is moving at a constant speed of $v = 90$ km/h on a straight level track. From a railway station P on the track, there is a village Q at a distance $y = 1.2$ km in a direction perpendicular to the track. When the engine E is $x = 1.6$ km away from the station, the driver honks a horn of duration $\tau = 44$ s. Calculate durations of the honking τ_P and τ_Q heard at the station and in the village. Speed of sound in still air is $c = 350$ m/s and there is no wind.

4. A material point moving along a straight line enters an 87.5 m segment with speed 5.0 m/s and leaves with speed 10 m/s. The particle crosses the segment with unidirectional acceleration that never exceeds 1.0 m/s². Find range of average acceleration of the point on this segment?

5. Two balls are dropped from the top of a cliff at a time interval $\Delta t = 2$ s. The first ball hits the ground, rebounds elastically (reversing direction instantly without losing speed), and collides with the second ball at a height $h = 55$ m above the ground. How high is the top of the cliff?

6. A ball released from a certain height, falls in the influence of gravity, strikes the ground and repeatedly rebounds elastically. During a time interval $t = 8$ s from the instant it is released, it covers a distance $s = 20$ m. How many collisions during this time did the ball make with the ground? Acceleration of free fall is $g = 10$ m/s².

7. During the last second of its flight, a ball thrown vertically upwards covers one-half of the distance covered during the whole flight. The point of projection and the point of landing may or may not be in the same horizontal level. What maximum possible duration of the flight can be obtained? Neglect air resistance and assume acceleration of free fall to be 10 m/s².

8. A boy starts from point A and passes point C of a track ABC shown in the figure. Portion AB of length l is straight, and portion BC is a semicircle of radius r ($r < l$). Anywhere on the track, the modulus of the maximum acceleration of the boy is a. Find minimum transit time of the boy from A to C.

9. A fun drive in an amusement park runs between two spots that are 2.0 km apart. For safety reasons, acceleration of the drive is limited to ±4.0 m/s², and the jerk, i.e. the rate of change in acceleration, is limited to ± 1.0 m/s³. If the drive can achieve a maximum speed of 144 km/h, find the shortest transit time of the drive between the spots.

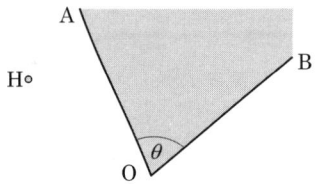

10. House H of an angler is at a distance d from bank OA of a bay AOB and at a distance l from the corner O? The angler can walk on the ground at a constant speed v and swim in the bay with a constant speed u ($u < v$) relative to the water. One day he decides at his house to fish somewhere on the bank OB. Find the minimum time in which he can reach the desired fishing spot.

11. A biker is moving with constant velocity v away from a long straight wall at an angle θ with the wall. He honks a short beep of horn when he is at a distance l from the wall. After how long from the instant he has honked, will he again hear an echo of the honking? Speed of the sound in air is c.

12. A grasshopper is sitting on the horizontal ground, and the sun is shining at an angle φ above the horizon. The grasshopper jumps towards the sun with an initial velocity u at an angle θ with the ground. Find expression for speed of shadow of the grasshopper on the ground. Acceleration due to gravity is g.

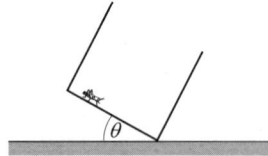

13. A grasshopper on the bottom of a cubical box has to jump out of the box. If each side of the box is $h = 52$ cm and the grasshopper can jump with a maximum initial velocity $u = 3$ m/s, what should the minimum tilt angle θ the box be so that the grasshopper can jump out of the box. Acceleration due to gravity is $g = 10$ m/s².

14. Water flows out in all directions with the same speed from a sprinkler consisting of a perforated spherical shell fixed at the end of a hose. When the sprinkler is fixed at the ground, maximum height attained by a water stream is h. If the sprinkler is shifted to height h above the ground, by what factor will the watered area on the ground change? Neglect diameter of the spherical shell as compared to the height h.

15. A particle projected from the ground passes two points, which are at heights $h_1 = 12$ m and $h_2 = 18$ m above the ground and a distance $d = 10$ m apart. What could be the minimum speed of projection? Acceleration due to gravity is $g = 10$ m/s².

16. A stone projected from edge A of a high cliff strikes the ground at point C moving almost vertically. The reason for this strange behavior is air resistance that is proportional to the speed of the stone. The points A and B on the trajectory are in the same horizontal level. Time taken by the stone in its upward and downward motions above the level AB differ by Δt and moduli of vertical component of velocities at points A and B differ by Δv_y. Horizontal component of velocity at point A is u_x and horizontal displacement of the stone from A to C is R. Denoting acceleration due to gravity by g, find suitable expression for the maximum height of the stone above the horizontal level AB.

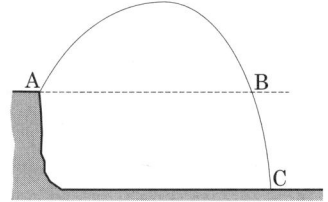

17. Three boys A, B and C decide to walk on straight tracks parallel to a powerline in which poles are 18 m apart. Boys A and B walk on the same track while C on a different track in the same direction with velocities 4 m/s, 2 m/s and 2 m/s respectively. The track of boys A and B is equidistant from the power line and from the track of boy C. In the beginning, all the boys and one of the poles are in a line that is perpendicular to the powerline. Draw a graph to show how does number of poles that the boy C can see through the space between boys A and B vary with time.

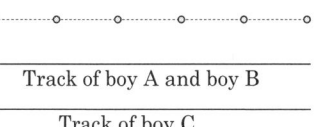

18. Two boys enter a running escalator on the ground floor of a shopping mall. The first boy repeatedly follows a cycle of $p_1 = 1$ step up and then $q_1 = 2$ steps down whereas the second boy repeatedly follows a cycle of $p_2 = 2$ steps up and then $q_2 = 1$ step down. Both move relative to escalator with a speed $v_r = 50$ cm/s. If the boys take $t_1 = 250$ s and $t_2 = 50$ s respectively to reach the first floor in complete numbers of cycles, how fast is the escalator running?

19. Two boys are standing near the ends of a 100 m long conveyor belt that is running with a constant velocity of 1.0 m/s. The boys step on the conveyer belt on its opposite ends and start walking towards each other. After meeting, they immediately return towards the ends of the belt and then continue the process repeatedly. The boys walk with a constant speed of 3 m/s relative to the conveyer belt. What distance relative to the ground do the boys walk in the first 300 s?

20. Two cyclists, Mike and Josh, simultaneously started toward each other from two towns $d = 24$ km apart. Josh rode at $v_J = 25$ km/h, and Mike at $v_M = 15$ km/h. The moment they start, a fly also starts from Josh towards Mike and after reaching Mike, immediately returns towards Josh. The fly continues back and forth between the cyclists till the cyclists meet. The air speed of the fly is $v_F = 30$ km/h and the wind blows always towards Mike with a constant velocity $u = 10$ km/h. Find the total distance s flown by the fly.

21. A speedometer shows speed, and an odometer shows distance travelled, both relative to the surface on which the vehicle moves. Two conveyor belts each of length $L = 500$ m are arranged along a line one after the other with a negligible gap. The belts are running in the same but unknown direction with constant speeds $u_1 = 20$ km/h and $u_2 = 30$ km/h. A toy car installed with both the instruments runs on the belts one after the other spending $\tau = 72$ s on them. The speedometer shows constant reading on each of the belts and the odometer shows a total reading of $s = L = 500$ m. Find the speedometer readings on each of the belts.

22. When a deer was 48 m from a leopard, the leopard starts chasing the deer and the deer immediately starts running away from the leopard with constant velocity. A leopard cannot run at high speeds for a long time and has to slow down due to fatigue. If we assume that the leopard starts with an initial speed of 30 m/s and reduces its speed by equal steps of 5 m/s after every 2 s interval, at what minimum speed must the deer run to escape from the leopard?

23. On a large slippery ground, a boy left his dog sitting and walks away with a constant velocity $v_b = 2.0$ m/s. When he is $x_0 = 199$ m away from the dog, the dog decides to catch him and thereafter move together. The dog cannot develop acceleration more than $a = 2.0$ m/s² in any direction. In what minimum time will the dog meet the boy?

24. On a straight highway, two cars A and B are running at the same speed $u = 108$ km/h in the same lane. In the best efforts of braking, at this speed the car A can stop in $t_{sA} = 7.0$ s and the car B in $t_{sB} = 10$ s. In an emergency when driver of the front car applies brakes, in response the driver of the rear car also has to apply brakes to avoid accident. However, braking of the rear car begins after a delay $t_d = 1.0$ s from the instant its driver notices the brake light signal of the front car.
  (a) If car A is running ahead of car B, what should be the minimum separation between them before driver of the car A applies brake?
  (b) If car B is running ahead of car A, what should be the minimum separation between them before driver of the car B applies brake?

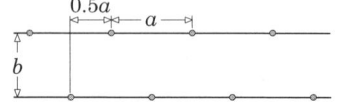

25. A large number of pedestrians are walking in the same direction in queues on each side of a road of width $b = 3.0$ m. Distance between two adjacent pedestrians on either side of the road is $a = 2.0$ m and pedestrians on one side are displaced by a distance $0.5a$ with respect to pedestrians on the other side as shown in the figure, depicting the pedestrians by small circles. A boy distributing advertisement leaflets bypasses all the pedestrians. The boy and the pedestrians are all walking with the same constant speed $v = 1.5$ m/s. Starting from a pedestrian if the boy handovers leaflets to all the pedestrians he comes across, how much length l of the road will he cover in 2.0 minutes?

26. Two cars A and B are running in the same direction with constant speeds $v_A = 25$ m/s and $v_B = 27$ m/s on a straight road. Another car C is running with a constant speed $v_C = 30$ m/s on another straight road. If the car C always remains equidistant from the cars A and B, find moduli of velocities of the car C relative to the car A and the car B.

27. A beetle carrying a food-grain rests on a small platform, which is moving with uniform velocity u parallel to a uniform frictionless slope as shown in the figure. At some point of time, the food-grain fell out of the grip of the beetle. After a collision with the slope, the food-grain stops for a moment and then starts sliding down the slope. The moment when the food-grain collides with the slope, the beetle jumps off horizontally backwards with a velocity $3u$ relative to the platform for the food-grain. If the beetle grabs the food-grain exactly when it lands on the slope, find a suitable expression for the height h of the platform above the slope.

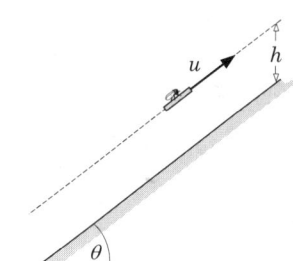

28. A honeybee is flying parallel to a tabletop at a height $h = 2.0$ m with a constant velocity $v = 20\sqrt{2}$ m/s. With its wings, it can achieve a maximum acceleration $a = 400\sqrt{3}$ m/s². At an instant when the honeybee is vertically above a honey drop on the tabletop, it decides to reach the honey drop. Neglect the reaction time of the honeybee and find the minimum time in which the honeybee can reach the honey drop.

29. A boy crosses a river twice on a straight path at an angle $\phi = 30°$ with the downstream direction, first time in two minutes and second time in four minutes. If his speed relative to river current is $v_{b/w} = \sqrt{3}$ m/s in both attempts, find speed of the river current.

30. To cross a river of width $b = 320$ m, a boatman steers his boat always aiming toward a point that is directly opposite to the starting point. The velocity of the boat relative to the river current is $v_{b/w} = 2.5$ m/s and river current velocity is $v_w = 1.5$ m/s everywhere. Determine the time which the boat will take to cross the river.

31. Two ships A and B can establish mutual communication when they are not more than 50 km apart. At midnight, the ship B moving towards the north with a velocity 4 km/h passes a location 80 km east of ship A that is moving with velocity $16\sqrt{2}$ km/h towards the northeast. Find the time interval during which they were in communication.

32. An aircraft is flying at a level height in a straight line. When you see it at an elevation $\alpha = 53°$ above the horizontal, you hear its sound coming from an elevation $\beta = 37°$ above the horizontal. When the aircraft passes a location vertically above your head, its angular velocity relative to you is $\omega = 0.125$ rad/s. Speed of sound in air is $v_s = 330$ m/s. If the transit time of light from the aircraft to you is negligible as compared to that of the sound, calculate altitude of the aircraft.

33. In a particular scene of a science fiction movie, a UFO is flying horizontally at a very high altitude with a speed u that is η (< 1) times of speed c of light. The UFO is emitting sharp light pulses at regular and very small intervals. Find the speed of the UFO recorded by an observer on the ground at point O when the UFO appears at an angle θ with the vertical. Ignore relativistic corrections.

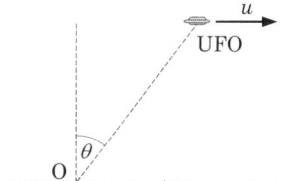

A UFO (un-identified flying object) is believed to be a spaceship used by aliens.

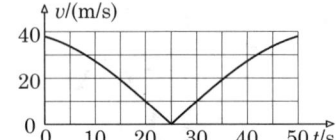

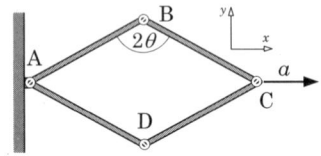

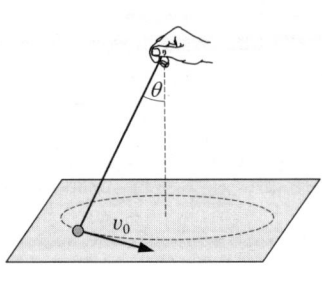

34. Two cars are moving at constant speeds: one on a circular path of radius $R = 200$ m and the other on a straight road. Magnitude v of velocity of one car relative to the other has been recorded at regular intervals of time and data thus obtained is represented in a graph as shown in the figure. Calculate speeds of both the cars relative to the ground.

35. A stone is projected from the ground with a velocity of 10 m/s and its trajectory is drawn to an unknown scale on a graph paper. The horizontal range and the maximum height on the graph are 1.0 m and 0.25 m respectively. The graph paper is glued on a horizontal tabletop. If an insect moves along the trajectory on the graph paper with a uniform speed of 1.0 cm/s, what should the modulus of its maximum acceleration be? Acceleration due to gravity is 10 m/s².

36. Four identical rods are hinged at their ends to make a parallelogram ABCD. The hinged joint A is rigidly attached to a wall and the opposite joint C is pulled away from the wall with a constant acceleration a as shown in the figure. Initially, joints A and C were coincident. Find the acceleration vector of joint B at the instant shown.

37. A particle P is moving with a constant speed u on a straight line that makes an angle θ with the positive x-direction of a coordinate system. When P crosses the y-axis at a point $(0, l)$, another particle Q starts from the origin and chases P with a uniform speed v ($v > u$). The chaser Q always maintains its velocity vector towards the chased P.

   (a) How long after Q starts from the origin, will it catch P?
   (b) If both the chaser Q and the chased P move with equal speeds (i.e. $u = v$), what will be the minimum distance between them and what will be the maximum magnitude of acceleration of the chaser Q?

Challenge your understanding

1. When you start your stopwatch, a particle moving with constant velocity on the x-axis is observed somewhere between the positions $x = 10$ m and $x = 12$ m. Sometime during the fourth second, it passes the position $x = 22$ m and at the instant $t = 12$ s it is observed somewhere between the positions $x = 55$ m and $x = 60$ m. If the particle is moving with uniform velocity, when do you expect its arrival at the position $x = 88$ m?

2. One end of a light inextensible thread of length l is held stationary over a frictionless horizontal floor while a small bead tied at the other end of the thread is describing a circular path with a uniform speed v_0 on the floor as shown in the figure.

   The upper end of the thread is suddenly pulled vertically upwards with a constant acceleration a_0. If the bead does not leave the floor, find magnitude of its acceleration immediately after the upper end of the thread is pulled.

3. Starting from the centre of a circular path of radius R, a particle P chases another particle Q that is moving with a uniform speed v on the circular path. The chaser P moves with a constant speed u and always remains collinear with the centre and the location of the chased Q.

   (a) On which path will P eventually move and how long will it take to reach on this path? Consider the cases $u < v$, $u = v$ and $u > v$.

   (b) If speeds of the particles are $v = 4$ m/s and $u = 8$ m/s and radius of the circular path is $R = 84$ m, how long P will take to reach Q. Use $\pi = 22/7$.

4. An $L = 70$ m long thin tape wound on a spool of radius $r_0 = 10$ mm makes a tape roll of outer radius $R = 25$ mm. A motor used to wind the tape rotates the spool at a constant angular velocity and takes $T = 165$ s to complete the winding. Calculate length of the tape, which has been wound in $t = 110$ s from the beginning of the winding.

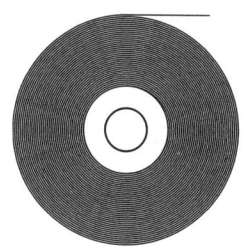

ANSWERS AND HINTS

Multiple Choice Questions

1. (d)
2. (b)
3. (d)
4. (c)
5. (b)
6. (b)
7. (a)
8. (a), (b), (c) and (d)
9. (b) and (c)
10. (c)
11. (a) and (d)
12. (d)
13. (c)
14. (b)
15. (b)
16. (a) and (d)
17. (a), (c) and (d)
18. (b)
19. (a), (b) and (d)
20. (a), (b), (c) and (d)
21. (d)
22. (a) → (p)
    (b) → (p)
    (c) → (p)
    (d) → (q)
23. (d)
24. (d)
25. (d)
26. (c)
27. (a), (b) and (c)
28. (c)
29. (b)
30. (b)
31. (a) and (c)
32. (c)
33. (a)
34. (b)

Build up your understanding

1. $\dfrac{sv_p}{s + v_p(\Delta t_1 - \Delta t_2)} = 40$ km/h

2. $\dfrac{s(v_2 - v_0)}{v_2(v_0 - v_1)} = 16$ min

3. (a) $v_1 = \dfrac{s_1}{t_2 - t_1} = 25$ m/s (b) $v_2 = \dfrac{s_2}{t_2 - t_1} = 10$ m/s

   (c) $\dfrac{s_2(t_3 - t_1)}{(t_2 - t_1)} = 700$ m

   Hint: The front and the rear cars travel the distances s_2 and s_1 respectively in the interval $[t_1, t_2]$. The front and the rear cars spend the intervals $[t_1, t_3]$ and $[t_2, t_4]$ respectively on the bridge.

4. $\dfrac{s}{\tau(1+2n)} = 120$ km/h, 40 km/h, 24 km/h, ...

   Here $n = 0, 1, 2, 3....$

5. $v_2 = \dfrac{2\eta v_1}{\eta + 1} = 2$ m/s

   Hint: Average speed of traffic advancement remains constant in the absence of the traffic signal. The traffic light schedule controls how long the traffic keeps on moving and how long it remains standstill thus controls the average speed of traffic advancement.

6. 50 m

7. $\dfrac{l}{2v} + \dfrac{\sqrt{4r^2 - l^2}}{v} \approx 63$ s

8. $v_{av} \leq v \leq \sqrt{2} v_{av}$

9.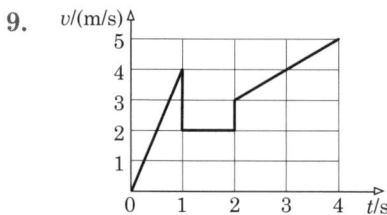

10. (a) $n + \left(\dfrac{\Delta t_2^2 - \Delta t_1^2}{\Delta t_1^2}\right) = 18$

    (b) $\Delta t_2 - \sqrt{\Delta t_2^2 - \Delta t_1^2} = 0.64$ s

11. $\sqrt{2g\left(\sqrt{s_1^2 - s_3^2} + \sqrt{s_2^2 - s_3^2}\right)} = 20$ m/s

    Hint: The fixed point cannot be on the line of motion of the ball.

12. (a) $\tfrac{1}{2} gn\tau$ and $\tfrac{1}{2} g\tau^2 \{i(n-i)\}$

    (b) 1.5 m   (c) 2.0 m

    Hint: Airtime of each ball must be equal to product of number of balls and interval between projections of two consecutive balls for the successful juggling.

13. 25 m/s

14. $\dfrac{(u \tan \theta)^2}{2g}$

    Hint: Pebbles that strikes the ground at angle θ, were thrown horizontally.

15. $h = t\sqrt{\dfrac{gL}{2}}$

    Hint: The ball has been thrown at an angle 45° with the horizontal.

16. $\cos^{-1}\left|\dfrac{v - \sqrt{v^2 + 8Rg}}{4\sqrt{Rg}}\right| = 60°$

    Hint: Horizontal movement of the gun can affect only the horizontal component of velocity of the shell but not the vertical component and hence the air time.
    Horizontal range is product of horizontal component of velocity and the airtime.

17. $\tan^{-1}\left(\tan\phi + \dfrac{gT^2}{2d\cos\phi}\right)$

18. $\dfrac{\rho Au}{g}\left(u\sin\theta + \sqrt{u^2 \sin^2\theta + 2gh}\right) = 720$ g

19. (a) $\sin^{-1}\left(\dfrac{u}{\sqrt{2(u^2 - gh)}}\right)$

    (b) $\sin^{-1}\left(\dfrac{u}{\sqrt{2(u^2 + gh)}}\right)$

20. 1 : 2

21. Position coordinates: $x = \dfrac{u_x}{k}(1 - e^{-kt})$;

    $y = \left(\dfrac{u_y}{k} + \dfrac{g}{k^2}\right)(1 - e^{-kt}) - \dfrac{g}{k}t$

Velocity components: $v_x = u_x e^{-kt}$;

$$v_y = \left(u_y + \frac{g}{k}\right)e^{-kt} - \frac{g}{k}$$

Here $u_x = u\cos\theta$ and $u_y = u\sin\theta$

Terminal Velocity: $\frac{g}{k}$ downwards.

Hint: Resolve acceleration vector $\vec{a}_D = -k\vec{v}$ into its Cartesian components.

22. $\dfrac{u\cos\theta}{k} = 200$ m

23. $\dfrac{n_1(a+b+c)\Delta t_1}{a+b} = \dfrac{n_2(a+b+c)\Delta t_1}{c} = 48$ min

Here n_1 and n_2 are the smallest integers satisfying the equation $n_1 c = n_2(a+b)$.

24. $\dfrac{luN}{L(u+v)} = 4$

25. (a) $u\left(\dfrac{n_1 - n_2}{n_1 + n_2}\right) = 2$ km/h (b) $\dfrac{2n_1 n_2 l}{n_1 + n_2} = 24$ m

26. $\dfrac{l}{2(v_b - v_s)} + \dfrac{1}{(v_b + v_s)}\left(\dfrac{l}{2} + 2x_0 + v_b t_0\right) = 250$ s

27. $\dfrac{(u_1 + u_2)^2}{2(a_1 + a_2)} - \dfrac{(a_1 + a_2)(\Delta t)^2}{8}$

Hint: Both the particles first meet during their forward motion and second time they meet in their return motion.

28. $\dfrac{v\Delta t \sqrt{v^2 - u^2}}{u} = 40$ m

29. 0.5 s; $2.5\sqrt{2}$ m

30. $\sqrt{(v_A + v_B)^2 + v_A^2} = 50$ km/h and

$\tan^{-1}\left(\dfrac{v_A + v_B}{v_A}\right) \approx 53°$ west of north

Hint: The smoke-line will spread in the direction of wind velocity relative to the ship.

31. $\dfrac{v_{b/w}\sqrt{\Delta y_2^2 - \Delta y_1^2}}{\Delta y_2} = 0.6$ m/s

32. $\dfrac{b}{\sqrt{a^2 + b^2}} v_w$ at angle $\tan^{-1}\left(\dfrac{b}{a}\right)$ upstream from the line AB

33. Point B moves upwards with initial velocity $u/2$ and constant downwards acceleration $a/2$.

34. $v_A = 3$ cm/s $\uparrow$, $v_B = 1$ cm/s $\downarrow$ and $v_C = 5$ cm/s $\downarrow$

35. $v_s = \dfrac{v_b \cos\theta}{\cos\phi} = 20\sqrt{3}$ m/s and

$\omega = \dfrac{v_b \sin(\phi - \theta)}{l \cos\phi} = 2$ rad/s

36. $\dfrac{\sqrt{u_1^2 + u_2^2 - 2u_1 u_2 \cos\theta}}{\sin\theta}$

37. $= \begin{cases} \dfrac{lu}{2v}; & \text{If } u \leq v\sqrt{2} \\ l\sqrt{1 - \dfrac{v^2}{u^2}}; & \text{If } u \geq v\sqrt{2} \end{cases}$

38. $\dfrac{v\sqrt{2}}{a} = 20$ s, parabola

Hint: To realise a change in velocity vector in a minimum time with an acceleration of constant modulus, in every infinitesimal time interval, changes in velocity vectors must be in the same direction. Therefore, the acceleration vector throughout the process of change in the velocity vector must be a constant and in the direction of the change in the velocity vector.

39. $\dfrac{uv\sin\theta}{r}$

40. $\dfrac{v^2}{r}\left(\sqrt{1 + 3\sin^2\theta}\right)\cos^3\theta$

Hint: Both the particles have the same angular velocity and particle B has tangential as well as centripetal acceleration.

Check your understanding

1. In town B for 18.75 minutes

2. $v_H = \dfrac{x_3^2}{x_0 t_7} = 5.00$ m/s, $v_T = \dfrac{x_3^{7/3}}{t_7 x_0^{4/3}} = 0.10$ m/s

   and $t \approx 2041$ s

3. $\tau_P = \tau\left(1 - \dfrac{v}{c}\right) = 40.86$ s

   and $\tau_Q = \tau + \dfrac{\sqrt{(x-v\tau)^2 + y^2}}{c} - \dfrac{\sqrt{x^2 + y^2}}{c} = 42$ s

   Hint: The beginning and the end of the honking travel different distances to reach the listener with the same speed that is speed of sound, therefore they would reach the listener with different delays.

4. 0.33 m/s² $\leq a_{av} \leq 0.5$ m/s²

   Hint: Under the given conditions, sooner the particle increases its speed, lesser is the time taken by it to cross the segment.

5. $\dfrac{\{8h + g(\Delta t)^2\}^2}{32g(\Delta t)^2} = 180$ m

   Hint: Both the balls spend equal time in downward motion from the top of the cliff to the place of their collision, therefore the total time spend by the first ball in its downwards and upwards motions between the place of the collision and the ground must be equal to the time interval Δt.

6. $\dfrac{gt^2 + 2s}{4s} = 8$

   Hint: Average speed of any one-way motion of the ball whether upwards or downwards can be approximately taken as the average speed for the given interval without appreciably sacrificing accuracy. Using this idea, you may find an integral or non-integral solution for the number of collisions. If you find a non-integral solution, the number of collision must be its integral part, because the fractional part corresponds to the last incomplete trip.

7. 4 s

   Hint: The ball must be thrown upwards from a certain height above the ground, in addition in the last second of its flight, it must be below the point of projection.

8. $(\pi - 1)\sqrt{\dfrac{r}{a}} + 2\sqrt{\dfrac{2l+r}{2a}}$

9. 64 s

   Hint: To simplify calculations you may use velocity-time graph exploiting symmetries in its shape.

10. $\dfrac{d(u^2 - v^2 \sin^2\theta)}{uv\sqrt{u^2 - v^2 \sin^2\theta}} + \left(\dfrac{\sin\theta}{u}\right)\sqrt{l^2 - d^2}$

11. $2l\left\{\dfrac{v\sin\theta + \sqrt{c^2 - v^2\cos^2\theta}}{c^2 - v^2}\right\}$

    Hint: Laws of reflection for sound and light are the same, in addition, to listen an echo, sound reflected from the wall and the biker must simultaneously reach at the same point. For this, projections of velocities of the sound and the biker along the wall must be equal.

12. $\dfrac{u\sin(\varphi - \theta)}{\sin\varphi} + gt\cot\varphi$, here $t < \dfrac{2u\sin\theta}{g}$

13. $\theta = \cos^{-1}\left(\dfrac{u^2}{2gh}\right) = 30°$

14. 2

15. $\sqrt{g(h_1 + h_2 + d)} = 20$ m/s

    Hint: If the line joining the given points is assumed as an inclined plane and the length of the line as the maximum range, corresponding velocity at the lowest point will be the minimum velocity of a projectile for this range.

16. $\approx \dfrac{R}{u_x}\left(\dfrac{\Delta v_y + g\Delta t}{2}\right)$

17.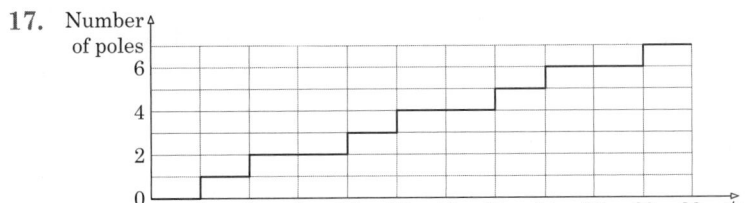

18. $\dfrac{v_r}{(t_1-t_2)}\left\{\dfrac{(p_2-q_2)t_2}{(p_2+q_2)}-\dfrac{(p_1-q_1)t_1}{(p_1+q_1)}\right\} = 25$ cm/s

    Hint: Product of average speed and time taken equals the distance travelled.

19. 800 m each

20. $s = \dfrac{d(v_F^2+uv_J-u^2)}{v_F(v_J+v_M)} = 21$ km

    Hint: For the whole journey, the displacement of Josh and that of the fly are the same.

21. On the first belt: $u_2\left(\dfrac{L-u_1\tau}{u_2\tau-L}\right) = 30$ km/h

    On the second belt: $u_1\left(\dfrac{L-u_2\tau}{u_1\tau-L}\right) = 20$ km/h

    Hint: Since $s = L$, the car must run on both the belts in directions same as that of motion of the belts.

22. 17 m/s

23. $\dfrac{v_b}{a}+\sqrt{\dfrac{4ax_0+2v_b^2}{a^2}} = 21$ s

24. (a) $u\left(t_d+\dfrac{t_{sB}-t_{sA}}{2}\right) = 75$ m

    (b) $\dfrac{ut_d^2}{2(t_{sB}-t_{sA})} = 5.0$ m

    Hint: To avoid accident, when separation between the cars vanishes, speed of the rear car cannot exceed that of the front car.

25. $l = \left(\dfrac{4b^2-a^2}{4b^2+a^2}\right)vt = 144$ m

    Hint: The boy must reach all the pedestrians to handover the leaflets. It is possible only when the advancement of the boy along the road is in the direction of motion of the pedestrians.

26. $v_{C/A} = v_{C/B} = \sqrt{v_C^2-v_Av_B} = 15$ m/s

    Hint: The road of car C is not parallel to the road of cars A and B. In addition, projection of velocity of the car C on the road of the cars A and B is arithmetic mean of velocities of the cars A and B.

27. $h = \dfrac{2u^2(3-\cos\theta)(3\cos\theta-1)}{g\sin^2\theta\cos\theta}$

28. $\dfrac{\sqrt{2(v^2+\sqrt{v^4+h^2a^2})}}{a} = 0.1$ s

    Hint: Since the time interval between two events is independent of frame of reference in non-relativistic domain, it is better to use a frame moving with the initial velocity of the honeybee. In this frame, the honey drop appears moving with a constant velocity equal in magnitude and opposite in direction to that of initial velocity of the honeybee and when the honeybee is above the honey drop, it appear at rest, therefore to minimize time the honeybee must move straight towards the honey drop with its maximum acceleration.

29. $v_{b/w}\cot\phi = 3$ m/s

30. $\dfrac{bv_{b/w}}{v_{b/w}^2-v_w^2} = 200$ s

    Hint: To simplify calculations, you may use a reference frame moving with the river current. In this frame, the destination point appears moving with a constant velocity equal in magnitude and opposite in direction to that of the river current and the boat appears chasing the destination point always heading towards it.

Chapter-1

31. 2:30 A.M. to 3:54 A.M.

    Hint: When the ships start communicating with each other, a ship relative to the other ship appears entering a circle of radius equal to the range of communication with centre at the other ship.

32. $\dfrac{v_s \sin\beta}{\omega}(\cot\beta - \cot\alpha) = 924$ m

33. $\dfrac{u}{1+\eta\sin\theta}$

    Hint: Light pulses emitted from the UFO at two different instants travel different distances, thus reach the observer with different delays. Due to this fact, time intervals between two consecutive pulses recorded by the observer will differ from that recorded in the UFO.

34. $\approx \sqrt{R\left(\left|\dfrac{dv}{dt}\right|_{t=25^\pm}\right)} = 20$ m/s each

    Hint: Modulus of change in velocity of the car on the circular path in the interval $[25$ s, 25^+ s$)$ is equal to the modulus of relative velocity of the car at the instant $t = 25^+$ s. Therefore, slope of the graph in this interval is equal to the modulus of the acceleration of the car on the circular path. Similarly you may consider the interval $(25^-$ s, 25 s$]$.

35. 2×10^{-4} m/s²

36. $a\left\{\dfrac{1}{2}\hat{i} + \left(\dfrac{3}{2}\tan\theta + \tan^3\theta\right)\hat{j}\right\}$

37. (a) $l\left(\dfrac{v + u\sin\theta}{v^2 - u^2}\right)$

    (c) $l\left(\dfrac{1+\sin\theta}{2}\right)$ and $\dfrac{3\sqrt{3}v^2}{4l(1+\sin\theta)}$

Challenge your understanding

1. Between $t = 19.5$ s to $t = 21$ s

    Hint: Try to find the least and the greatest speeds satisfying all the three conditions.

2. $\dfrac{v_0^2}{l\sin\theta} + a_0\cot\theta$ towards the centre of the circular path

3. (a) On a circular path of radius $\dfrac{u}{v}R$ and after a time interval: $\dfrac{\pi R}{2v}$

    Hint: Distance of particle P from the centre of the circular path of particle Q increases due to the radial component of velocity of P. In addition, this component is continuously decreasing, therefore it will eventually become vanishingly small, making path of particle P a circle. Moreover, since angular velocities of both the particles are equal, they will eventually move on concentric or the same circular paths. Radius of the path of P will be smaller, equal or greater than R depending on $u < v$, $u = v$ and $u > v$.

    (b) $\dfrac{R}{v}\sin^{-1}\left(\dfrac{v}{u}\right) = 11$ s

4. $L\left[\dfrac{\left\{\dfrac{(R-r_0)t}{T} + r_0\right\}^2 - r_0^2}{R^2 - r_0^2}\right] = 40$ m

    Hint: Rate of increase in volume of the tape wound on the roll is equal to the rate of volume added from unwound portion of the tape.

Chapter 2

Newton's Laws of Motion

Ideas of linear momentum, inertia, force, inertial and non-inertial reference frames, physical and pseudo forces, the three laws of Newton, applications of these laws in analysing translational equilibrium and translational motion, concept of friction and resistive forces, laws of dry friction, applications of Newton's laws in analysing dynamics of circular and curvilinear translation.

"I learned very early the difference between knowing the name of something and knowing something."

BACK TO BASICS

Linear momentum:

It is the amount of translational or linear motion of a body.

Linear momentum $\vec{p}$ of a body in translational motion is equal to product of mass m and velocity vector $\vec{v}$ of the body.

$$\vec{p} = m\vec{v}$$

Usually, the term linear is dropped and we use the term momentum.

Inertia:

Inertia of a material body is its tendency to oppose any change in its momentum.

Mass of a body is the measure of its inertia to translational motion.

Force:

The concept of force explains mutual interaction between two material bodies as the action of one body on another in the form of push or pull.

Richard P. Feynman
(11 May 1918 – 15 February 1988)

A mutual interaction between two bodies, which creates force on one body, also creates force on the other body. Force on the body under study is known as *action* and that on the other body is known as *reaction*.

The first law:

Every material body preserves its state of rest or of uniform motion in a straight line, unless it is compelled to change that state by external forces impressed on it.

The second law:

The rate of change in momentum of a body is equal to and occurs in the direction of the net applied force.

A body of mass m in translational motion with velocity $\vec{v}$, if acted upon with a net external force $\Sigma \vec{F}$, the second law suggests:

$$\Sigma \vec{F} = \frac{d}{dt}(m\vec{v})$$

If mass of the body is a constant, the above equation relates acceleration $\vec{a}$ of the body with the net force $\Sigma \vec{F}$ **acting on it**.

$$\Sigma \vec{F} = m\vec{a}$$

The third law:

The action and reaction originating from a mutual interaction between two bodies are equal in magnitude, opposite in direction and identical in kind.

These laws are fundamental in nature. The first law tells us under what conditions there is no net external force, the second law shows how to measure a force when it exists, and the third law reminds us that a force is interaction between two bodies.

Inertial and non-inertial reference frames:

A reference frame that is in the state of absolute rest or of uniform motion in a straight line is an inertial reference frame and a reference frame that is in the state of accelerated motion is a non-inertial reference frame.

The three laws of Newton are valid only in inertial reference frames.

Physical and pseudo force:

A physical force or real force is result of interaction between two bodies, whereas a pseudo force is a false force. The idea of pseudo force is used to account for the observed acceleration of a body in a non-inertial frame due to acceleration of the non-inertial frame.

Pseudo force on a body equals the product of the mass of the body and negative of acceleration vector of the non-inertial frame.

Translational equilibrium:

An un-accelerated body is said to be in the state of translational equilibrium.

For a body to be in translational equilibrium, no net force must act on it i.e. vector sum of all the forces acting on it must be a null vector.

$$\Sigma \vec{F} = \vec{0}$$

Friction:

Whenever surfaces in contact and pressing each other slide or tend to slide over each other, opposing forces acting tangentially to the surfaces in contact are generated. These tangential forces opposing sliding or tendency of sliding between the surfaces, are called *frictional forces*. Frictional forces on both the bodies constitute a third law action-reaction pair.

Frictional force between two solid un-lubricated surfaces is known as dry friction or Coulomb friction.

Static friction:

When a force of normal reaction N exists between two surfaces, and there is tendency of sliding between them, the force of static friction f_s acts before sliding initiates. It balances the net available force F creating the tendency of sliding and can have a value up to a limiting value known as limiting friction f_{sm}.

$$f_s = F \leq f_{sm}$$

The limiting friction is proportional to the normal reaction.

$$f_{sm} = \mu_s N$$

The constant of proportionality μ_s is known as *coefficient of static friction*.

Kinetic friction:

It opposes sliding between the surfaces. When a force of normal reaction N exists between the two surfaces that are sliding on each other, the force of kinetic friction f_k acts on a surface opposite to its velocity relative to the other surface. Kinetic friction is proportional to the normal reaction.

$$f_k = \mu_k N$$

The constant of proportionality μ_k is known as *coefficient of kinetic friction*.

Dynamics of curvilinear translation and circular motion:

Components of the net external force towards the centre of curvature of a path and along the tangent to the path are known as the normal component F_n of the force and the tangential force F_τ respectively. The normal component of the force is responsible for change in direction only whereas the tangential force is responsible for change in speed only.

$$F_n = ma_n = \frac{mv^2}{\rho} = m\omega_v^2 \rho \quad \text{and} \quad F_\tau = ma_\tau = m\frac{dv}{dt}$$

Here ω_v is the time rate of rotation of the velocity vector.

In circular motion, normal component of the force is usually called centripetal force.

Multiple Choice Questions

1. A bead released from one end of a frictionless rigid wire frame fixed in a vertical plane, slides periodically on the frame. Size of the bead is negligible as compared to the radius of curvature of the turns, which is negligible as compared to the length of straight portions of the frame. If linear dimensions of the frame are made four times, by what factor will frequency of periodic motion of the bead change?

   (a) 4 (b) 2
   (c) 1/4 (d) 1/2

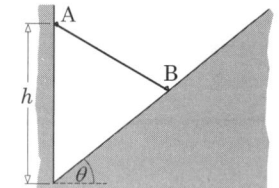

2. In the setup shown a thread is taut between nail A on a wall and nail B on an inclined plane as shown in the figure. You can change the length of the thread by changing location of nail B. A bead that can slide on the thread without friction is released from nail A. What should the length of the thread be so that the bead reaches the nail B in shortest time?

   (a) h (b) $h\cos\theta$
   (c) $h\sec(0.5\theta)$ (d) $h\cos\theta\sec(0.5\theta)$

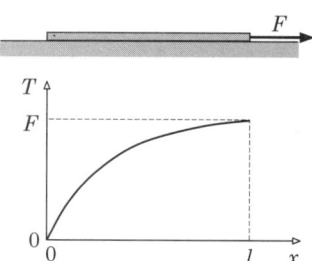

3. A rope of length l placed straight on a frictionless horizontal floor is pulled longitudinally by a force F from one of its ends. Tensile force T developed in the rope at a distance x from the rear end varies with x as shown in the graph. What can you certainly conclude about density of the rope?

   (a) It is uniform.
   (b) It decreases with distance x from the rear end.
   (c) It increases with distance x from the rear end.
   (d) It is maximum in the middle and decreases towards the ends.

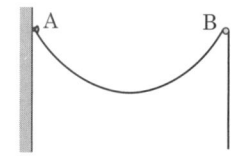

4. A uniform rope of length 13 m tied on peg A on a wall passes over a frictionless peg B fixed in level with peg A as shown in the figure. If in equilibrium, length of the rope hanging between the pegs is 8 m, the angle which the rope makes with the wall at peg A is closest to

   (a) 30° (b) 37°
   (c) 45° (d) 53°

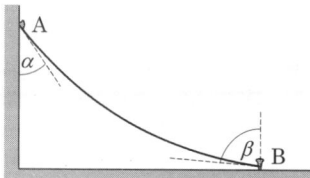

5. A uniform rope is tied between nail A on the wall and another nail B on the ground. The rope without touching the ground anywhere assumes a curved shape known as "catenary". Tangents at the ends A and B of this catenary make angles α and β with the vertical respectively. Which of the following conclusions can you make?

   (a) Horizontal component of the tensile force in the rope is uniform.
   (b) Vertical component of the tensile force increases with height.
   (c) Angle α can be greater than angle β.
   (d) Angle α cannot assume a value of 0°.

6. A light inextensible string of length 15 m is hanging between two pegs that are 9 m horizontally apart as shown. A small frictionless pulley of weight W_p = 4.8 N supporting a block of weight W_b = 8.0 N is gently placed on the string and allowed to move gradually to a place on the string, where it can stay in equilibrium. Radius of the pulley-wheel is negligible as compared to the length of the string. Which of the following conclusions can you make when the pulley is in equilibrium?

   (a) Level difference of the pegs is 4.0 m.
   (b) Tensile force in the string depends on the level difference of the pegs.
   (c) Tensile force in the string is 8.0 N irrespective of the level difference of the pegs.
   (d) Lengths of string segments on left and right sides of the pulley are 10 m and 5.0 m respectively.

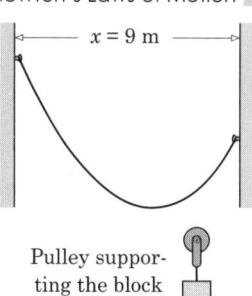

Pulley supporting the block

7. A small metal ball is being pulled gradually on a fixed frictionless hemisphere as shown in the figure. Radii of the ball and that of the pulley are much smaller than that of the hemisphere. As the ball slides from the bottom to a position close to the top of the hemisphere, how do the magnitudes of pulling force F and contact force R between the ball and the hemisphere change?

   (a) F increases and R decreases.
   (b) F decreases and R increases.
   (c) F decreases and R remains unchanged.
   (d) F remains unchanged and R decreases.

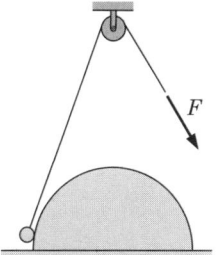

8. A block is suspended from a uniform rope that passes through two ideal pulleys. The other end of the rope is tied to a fixed support as shown in the figure. If the pulleys are pulled vertically with forces F_1 = 110 N and F_2 = 90 N, the system stays at rest. Assuming linear mass density of the rope 0.25 kg/m and the acceleration of free fall 10 m/s², find the length of the rope. Pulleys are not small.

   (a) 4 m   (b) 6 m
   (c) 8 m   (d) Insufficient information.

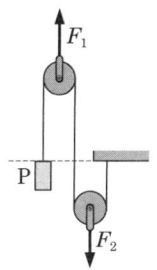

9. Two blocks A and B of masses 3 kg and 6 kg respectively are suspended at the ends of a light inextensible cord. The cord passes over an ideal pulley P fixed to the ceiling. Ends of another light inextensible cord are attached at the bottoms of the blocks. This cord supports another ideal pulley Q from which a block C of mass 4 kg is suspended as shown in the figure. Initially the system is held motionless and then released. Which of the following conclusions can you make? Acceleration due to gravity is 10 m/s².

   (a) All the blocks remain motionless.
   (b) Acceleration magnitudes of blocks A and B is 10/3 m/s² while C remains motionless.
   (c) Tensile forces in the upper and the lower cords are 40 N and 20 N respectively.
   (d) Tensile forces in the upper and the lower cords are 60 N and 20 N respectively.

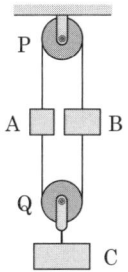

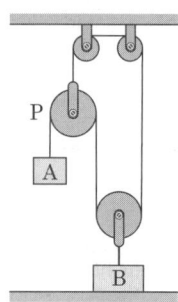

10. In the setup shown, the string is inextensible and light, there is no friction at the axles of the pulleys but friction between the string and the pulley wheels is sufficient to prevent slipping. All the pulleys are light except pulley P, which has whole of its mass m concentrated in its axle. Initially block B of mass M is on the ground and block A is held at rest. How much minimum mass should block A have, so that after releasing it, block B starts rising?

   (a) $0.5M$
   (b) $0.5M - m$
   (c) Whatever mass the block A has, the block B will not rise.
   (d) Pulley P moves downwards without rotation of its wheel while wheels of all the other pulleys rotate.

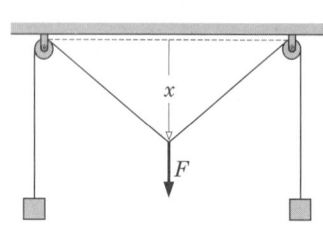

11. A light inextensible cord supporting two identical loads at its ends passes over two ideal small pulleys fixed to a horizontal ceiling. If the midpoint of the cord between the pulleys is gradually pulled downwards, the pulling force F varies with displacement x of the midpoint according to the following graph. Acceleration of free fall is 10 m/s². The distance between the pulleys is closest to

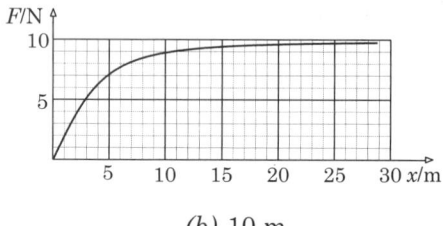

   (a) 5 m
   (b) 10 m
   (c) 15 m
   (d) 20 m

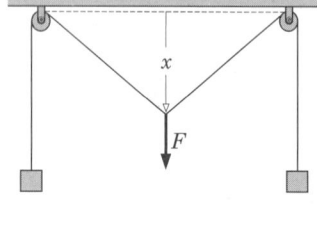

12. Consider three identical massless springs. The left ends of the first, second and the third springs are affixed to a wall, to a block of mass m placed on a horizontal floor (not frictionless) and to a block of mass m placed on a horizontal frictionless floor respectively as shown in the figures. The right end of each spring is pulled by a gradually increasing force. When magnitude of the force becomes F, extensions in these springs become x_1, x_2 and x_3 respectively. Which of the following statements is correct?

   (a) $x_1 = x_2 = x_3$
   (b) $x_1 > x_2 > x_3$
   (c) $x_1 > x_2 = x_3$
   (d) $x_1 = x_2 > x_3$

13. Length of a one-metre-long uniform spring of mass 50.0 g increases by 2.00 cm due to its own weight, if it is suspended from a fixed support. How much load should be suspended from the lower end of this spring, so that total extension becomes 10.0 cm.

   (a) 100 g
   (b) 125 g
   (c) 200 g
   (d) Insufficient information

14. A light uniform spring is tied between the ceiling and the floor keeping the spring vertical as shown in the figure. A bead of finite mass is glued at a distance l from the upper end of the spring and then allowed to move gradually downwards. The bead shifts a distance y to come in equilibrium. This experiment is repeated for different values of l. Which of the following graph shows the best dependence of y on l?

(a)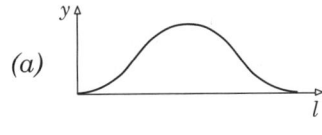

(b)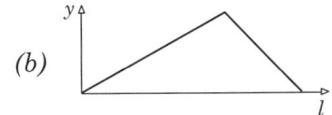

(c)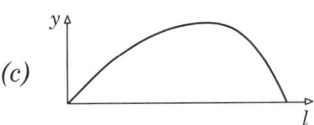

(d)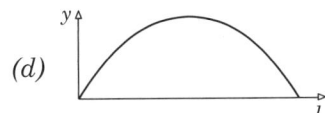

15. A light spring of force constant 1.00 N/cm is stretched between two fixed supports A and B. A point P on the spring is pulled parallel to the spring towards the support B by a gradually increasing force. When this force becomes 5.00 N, what is magnitude of displacement of the point P?

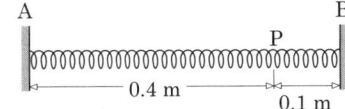

(a) 8.00 mm
(b) 22.2 mm
(c) 40.0 mm
(d) Relaxed length of the spring is required.

16. Three rubber cords of force constants k_A, k_B and k_C and relaxed lengths l_A, l_B and l_C are joined with each other at one of their ends. The free ends of the cords are pulled maintaining them always in a plane. For a particular set of pulling forces, an arrangement shown in the figure-I is obtained and for another set of pulling of forces, arrangement shown in the figure-II is obtained. In the arrangement of figure-I, extended length of each cord is L_1; and in the arrangement of figure-II, extended length of each cord is $L_2 > L_1$.

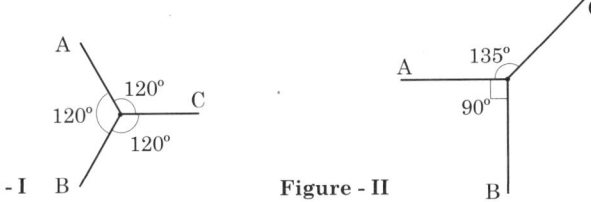

Figure - I   **Figure - II**

With the help of the given information, check validity of the following statements.

(a) $l_A = l_B < l_C$ and $k_A = k_B < k_C$
(b) $l_A = l_B < l_C$ and either $k_A = k_B > k_C$ or $k_A = k_B < k_C$
(c) $l_A = l_B < l_C$ if $k_A = k_B > k_C$ or $l_A = l_B > l_C$ if $k_A = k_B < k_C$
(d) $l_A < l_B < l_C$ if $k_A > k_B > k_C$ or $l_A > l_B > l_C$ if $k_A < k_B < k_C$

17. Two blocks A and B each of mass m are connected by an ideal string that passes over two fixed ideal pulleys. The blocks are also connected with the ground by springs of force constants k_1 and k_2 ($k_1 > k_2$). When both the springs are relaxed, the block A is pulled down a distance x and released. Acceleration magnitudes of the blocks A and B immediately after the release are a_1 and a_2 respectively. Mark the correct options.

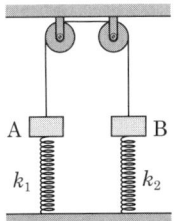

(a) $a_1 > a_2$
(b) $a_1 \le a_2$
(c) $a_1 > a_2$ if $k_1 > k_2 + 2mg/x$
(d) $a_1 = a_2$ if $k_1 \le k_2 + 2mg/x$

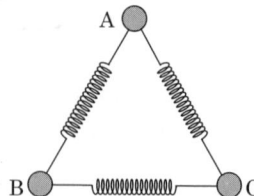

18. Three identical balls A, B and C each of mass *m* connected by three identical springs when placed on a frictionless horizontal floor occupy corners of an equilateral triangle as shown in the figure. This assembly is suspended by attaching the ball A to the ceiling with the help of a light thread. What can you predict regarding accelerations of the balls immediately after the thread is cut? Acceleration of free fall is *g*.

 (a) All the balls will have downward acceleration *g*.
 (b) All the balls have acceleration greater than *g* in different directions.
 (c) Acceleration of the upper ball is 3*g* downwards and the accelerations of the lower balls are vanishingly small.
 (d) Acceleration of the upper ball is 3*g* downwards and the lower balls move apart with finite accelerations.

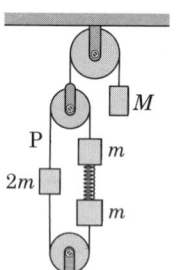

19. In the setup shown, the pulleys, the cords and the spring are ideal, and masses of the loads are indicated in the figure. Initially the system is in equilibrium. What should be the range of mass *M* so that acceleration of the load of mass 2*m* becomes greater than acceleration of free fall immediately after the cord is cut at point P?

 (a) $M > 4m$ (b) $M > 6m$
 (c) $M > 8m$ (d) $M > 14m$

20. While a block is sliding on a horizontal floor, a constant horizontal force is applied on it opposite to its direction of motion. Which of the following can be a correct velocity-time graph for the ensuing motion of the block?

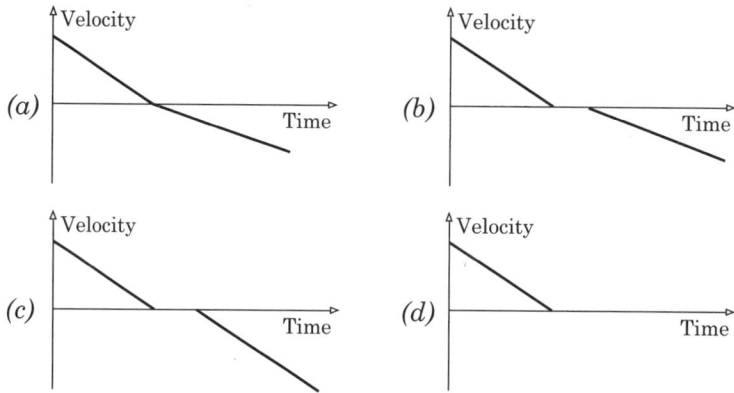

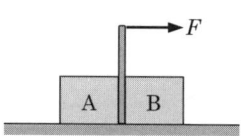

21. A rod is inserted between two identical blocks A and B placed close to each other on a horizontal floor, which is not frictionless. If the upper end of the rod is pulled horizontally by a gradually increasing force *F*, which of the blocks will start sliding first?

 (a) Block A
 (b) Block B
 (c) Both will start sliding simultaneously.
 (d) It is a matter of chance and hence either one may start sliding first.

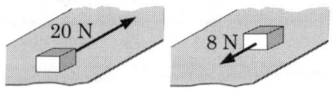

22. A force of 20 N along the line of the greatest slope is required to slide a block upwards with constant speed and a force of 8 N along the line of the greatest slope is required to slide the block downwards with constant speed on an inclined plane. The force of kinetic friction between the block and the plane is

(a) 8 N (b) 12 N
(c) 14 N (d) None of these

23. A block of mass 5 kg rests on a horizontal floor. When a constant horizontal force is applied on the block for a time interval 5 s, the block slides on the floor a distance 5 m under the action of the force and after the removal of the force, it further slides a distance 1 m before coming to a stop. Acceleration due to gravity is 10 m/s².

(a) Magnitude of the applied force is 12 N.
(b) The maximum speed acquired by the block is 2 m/s.
(c) Coefficient of friction between the block and the floor is 0.2.
(d) The block continues to move for 1 s after the removal of the force.

24. Near a station, a train is retarding at 2.0 m/s² to stop. When its speed is 36 km/h a passenger standing in the corridor of a bogie, puts his suitcase on the floor. The floor was a little bit slippery, so the suitcase began to slide and finally stopped in the train after sliding 12 m on the floor relative to the train. According to this situation, which of the following statements are correct?

(a) The train stopped before the suitcase stopped sliding.
(b) Speed of the suitcase relative to the bogie decreases monotonically.
(c) Speed of the suitcase relative to the bogie first increases then decreases.
(d) Coefficient of friction between the suitcase and the floor of the bogie is close to 0.135.

25. A block rests on a long plank that is moving with a constant velocity 2.0 m/s on a horizontal floor. Coefficient of friction between the block and the plank is 0.10. If the plank starts decelerating uniformly and stops in 0.50 s, what is the distance slid by the block on the plank? Acceleration of free fall is 10 m/s².

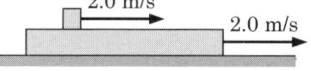

(a) 0.50 m (b) 0.75 m
(c) 1.0 m (d) 1.5 m

26. A pair of scissors is used to cut a wire of circular cross section held vertically. To reduce required force the wire must be placed close to the hinge; but if it is placed close to the hinge, it slides away from the hinge until the angle between the blades becomes θ. Find the coefficient of friction between the blades and the wire.

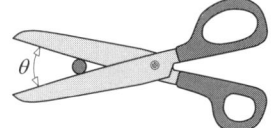

(a) $\cot(0.5\theta)$ (b) $\tan(0.5\theta)$
(c) $0.5\tan\theta$ (d) Insufficient information

27. A homogeneous bar of mass m is released from rest on a fixed inclined plane of inclination θ above the horizontal as shown. The upper part of the plane shown in dark grey is not frictionless and the lower part shown in light grey is frictionless. Coefficient of friction between the bar and the upper part of the plane is μ. What will be the maximum tensile force in the bar while it is sliding on the plane? Acceleration of free fall is g.

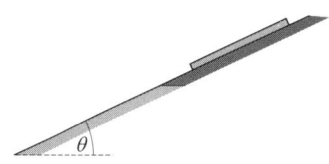

(a) Zero (b) $0.25\mu mg \cos\theta$
(c) $0.5\mu mg \cos\theta$ (d) $\mu mg \cos\theta$

28. Two balls of equal volume and masses m_1 and m_2 ($m_2 > m_1$) connected with a thin light thread are dropped from a certain height. Viscous drag of air on a ball depends on its velocity and buoyant force is equal to the weight of air displaced by the ball. When the balls acquire a uniform velocity after a sufficient time from the instant they were dropped, what is the tensile force in the thread? Acceleration due to gravity is g.

    (a) Zero
    (b) $(m_2 - m_1) g$
    (c) $0.5(m_2 + m_1) g$
    (d) $0.5(m_2 - m_1) g$

29. A block of mass 1.0 kg is given an initial velocity 20 m/s by a sharp hit on a horizontal floor lubricated with oil. The block moves in a straight line and stops due to viscous drag of the oil film. How the force F of viscous drag varies with velocity v of the block is shown in the following graph for a velocity interval [14 m/s, 0.0 m/s]. However, the experimenter forgot to label the ordinate.

    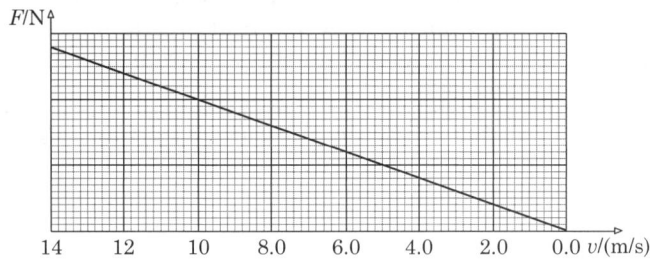

    After an instant, when the block was moving with 8 m/s, it slides 20 m and stops. How far does the block slide from the beginning to the instant it stops sliding?

    (a) 50 m
    (b) 75 m
    (c) 100 m
    (d) More information is required.

30. A massive bead is threaded on a long light rod, one end of which is pivoted to a fixed-point O. Initially, the rod is held horizontally, and the bead is at a distance l from the pivot. Coefficient of friction between the rod and the bead is μ. Which of the following statements correctly describe relation between angle θ that the rod makes with the horizontal after the rod is released and time t?

    (a) If μ is negligible, $\theta \to \tan^{-1}\left(\dfrac{gt^2}{2l}\right)$.

    (b) If μ is finite, $\theta \to \tan^{-1}\left(\dfrac{gt^2}{2l}\right)$.

    (c) If μ is finite, θ is smaller than $\tan^{-1}\left(\dfrac{gt^2}{2l}\right)$ by a finite amount.

    (d) None of the above statements is correct.

31. A ball dropped from a high altitude acquires a terminal velocity before hitting the ground, where it bounces off elastically. If air resistance depends on the speed of the ball, what will its acceleration be immediately after the first bounce?

    (a) Zero
    (b) $g \downarrow$
    (c) $2g \downarrow$
    (d) $3g \downarrow$

32. In the setup shown, blocks of masses 3m and 2m are placed on a frictionless horizontal ground and the free end P of the thread is being pulled by a constant force F. Find acceleration of the free end P.

(a) $F/(5m)$ (b) $2F/m$
(c) $3F/m$ (d) $5F/m$

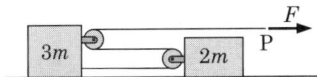

33. A small block is sliding on a frictionless inclined plane that is moving upward with a constant acceleration. If the block remains at a level height, what is the acceleration of the inclined plane? Acceleration due to gravity is g.

(a) $g\tan\theta$ (b) $g\cot\theta$
(c) $g\sin^2\theta$ (d) $g\tan^2\theta$

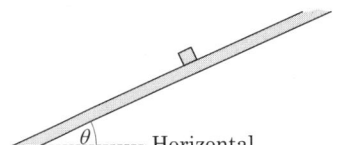

34. In the arrangement shown, the springs are light and have stiffness k_1 =100 N/m and k_2 = 200 N/m and the pulleys are ideal. An 8.0 kg block suspended from the lower pulley is initially held at rest maintaining the strings straight and springs relaxed. Now the force supporting the block is gradually reduced to zero. How far does the block descend during the process of reduction of the force? Acceleration due to gravity is 10 m/s².

(a) 10 cm (b) 15 cm
(c) 1.6 m (d) None of these

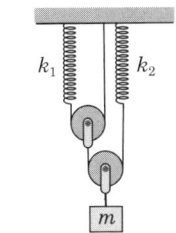

35. In the setup shown, a block is placed on a frictionless floor, the cords and pulleys are ideal, and each spring has stiffness k. The block is pulled away from the wall. How far will the block shift, while the pulling force is increased gradually from zero to a value F?

(a) $\dfrac{2F}{5k}$ (b) $\dfrac{10F}{3k}$
(c) $\dfrac{8F}{9k}$ (d) $\dfrac{10F}{9k}$

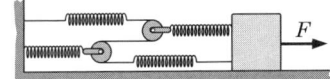

36. A large parking place has uniform slope of angle θ with the horizontal. A driver wishes to drive his car in a circle of radius R, at constant speed. Coefficient of static friction between the tyres and the ground is μ. What greatest speed can the driver achieve without slipping? Assume entire load of the car on the front wheels.

(a) $\sqrt{gR\tan\theta}$ (b) $\sqrt{gR\cot\theta}$
(c) $\sqrt{gR(\sin\theta+\mu\cos\theta)}$ (d) $\sqrt{gR(\mu\cos\theta-\sin\theta)}$

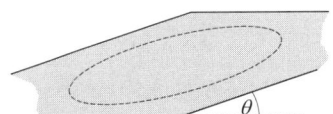

37. Consider a circular turn on a highway, where angle of banking is more than angle of repose. A car on this turn can move with a constant speed v_0 without help of friction. Taking advantage of friction, it can achieve a maximum speed v_{max} but cannot reduce its speed lower than a minimum speed v_{min}. Which of the following conclusions can you draw from the given information?

(a) $v_0 < 0.5(v_{max} + v_{min})$ (b) $v_0 = 0.5(v_{max} + v_{min})$
(c) $v_0 > 0.5(v_{max} + v_{min})$ (d) It depends on coefficient of static friction.

2.12 Chapter-2

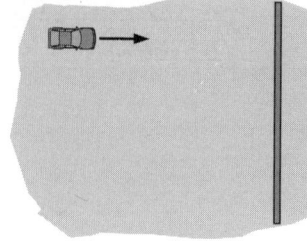

38. A car is moving with speed 108 km/h on a large uniform horizontal pavement perpendicularly towards a wall. To avoid collision, the driver takes a turn and finally runs the car parallel to the wall with the same speed. Coefficient of friction between the tyres and the pavement is 0.6, acceleration of free fall is 10 m/s² and all the load of the car is concentrated on the front axle. If the turning process is the fastest one on this pavement, check validity of the following statements.

(a) The car follows a circular path during the turn.
(b) The car follows a parabolic path during the turn.
(c) Minimum radius of curvature of the path is 75 m.
(d) Initial distance of the wall must be greater than 75√2 m.

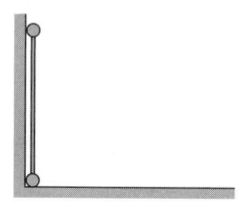

39. A dumbbell is constructed by fixing small identical balls at the ends of a light rod of length l. The dumbbell stands vertically in the corner formed by a frictionless wall and frictionless floor. After the bottom end is slightly pushed towards the right, the dumbbell begins to slide. The value of which of the following quantities vanishes when the upper ball is leaving the wall.

(a) Tensile force in the rod
(b) Acceleration of the lower ball
(c) Acceleration of the upper ball
(d) Normal reaction from floor on the lower ball

40. A particle is moving with constant angular velocity on a circular path of radius R in the x-y plane. If observed from a reference frame moving with constant velocity along the z-axis, the particle will appear moving on a helical path of constant pitch h. Making use of the given information, what expression can be deduced for radius of curvature of the helical path.

(a) $\sqrt{R^2 + \dfrac{h^2}{4\pi^2}}$

(b) $R + \dfrac{h^2}{4\pi^2 R}$

(c) $\sqrt{R^2 + h^2}$

(d) Cannot be calculated from the given information.

41. Imagine that mass, which governs acceleration of the bodies and their mutual gravitational interaction, might sometimes be negative. Two particles A and B of masses m_1 and m_2 are initially at rest some distance apart in free space relative to an inertial frame. What would happen after they are released?

The masses	Observation
(a) $m_1 < 0$ and $m_2 < 0$	(p) They move towards each other.
(b) $m_1 > 0$, $m_2 < 0$ and $|m_1| = |m_2|$	(q) They move away from each other.
(c) $m_1 > 0$, $m_2 < 0$ and $|m_1| > |m_2|$	(r) Eventually B will escape away from A.
(d) $m_1 < 0$, $m_2 > 0$ and $|m_1| > |m_2|$	(s) B follows A and finally collides with A.
	(t) B follows A with a constant separation.

Newton's Laws of Motion

Questions 42 to 44 are based on the following physical situation.

A horizontal conveyor belt is running at a constant speed $v_b = 3.0$ m/s. A small disc enters the belt moving horizontally with a velocity $v_0 = 4.0$ m/s that is perpendicular to the velocity of the belt. Coefficient of friction between the disc and the belt is 0.50.

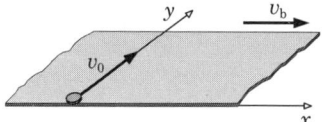

42. What can you predict regarding the path of the disc?
    (a) It is a parabola relative the belt.
    (b) It is a straight line relative to the belt.
    (c) It is a parabola relative to the ground.
    (d) It is a straight line relative to the ground.

43. What should the minimum width of the belt be so that the disc always remains on the belt?
    (a) 0.9 m   (b) 1.6 m
    (c) 2.0 m   (d) 2.5 m

44. What is the minimum speed of the disc relative to the ground?
    (a) 0.0 m/s   (b) 1.8 m/s
    (c) 2.4 m/s   (d) 3.0 m/s

Questions 45 to 47 are based on the following physical situation.

Lower end of a uniform inextensible rope of mass 2 kg and length 4 m is attached to a block of mass 7.5 kg placed on a horizontal floor. Coefficient of friction between the block and the floor is 0.5. The upper end of the rope is held 2 m above the lower end so that the tangent at the lower end remains horizontal as shown in the figure. In this situation, the block stays standstill on the floor. Acceleration due to gravity is 10 m/s².

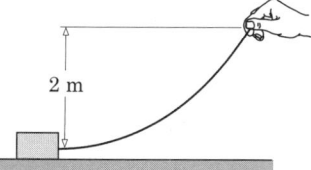

45. The upper end must be pulled at an angle that is closest to
    (a) 60° above the horizontal   (b) 53° above the horizontal
    (c) 45° above the horizontal   (d) Insufficient information

46. Frictional force between the block and the floor is closest to
    (a) 15 N   (b) 20 N
    (c) 30 N   (d) 37.5 N

47. The upper end of the rope is now slowly shifted downwards and simultaneously away from the block maintaining the tangent at lower end horizontal. When the block begins sliding, at what height above the lower end is the upper end?
    (a) 0.5 m   (b) 0.75 m
    (c) 1.0 m   (d) 1.5 m

Questions 48 to 50 are based on the following physical situation.

Velocity-time relation of a four-wheel drive car running without any gearshift on a straight level road is shown in the following graph. The engine is running at constant throttle, and the wheels are maintained always at the verge of slipping. Air drag on the car depends on its speed; therefore, it can be neglected for initial few seconds. The graph can satisfactorily be treated as a straight line in every 10 s interval.

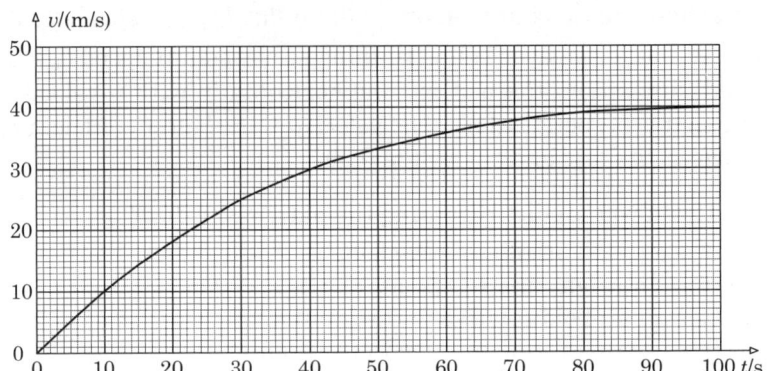

The driver shifts gears once after acquiring some speed. Gear shifting requires a period of 0.5 s, during which the engine remains declutched so that the car decelerates due to air drag. After the gearshift, clutches are released, and the car follows the same velocity profile as shown in the graph with a delay of 1.0 s. Therefore, the car acquires the final velocity 1.0 s later than that acquired without a gearshift. Acceleration of free fall is 10 m/s².

48. Coefficient of friction between the tyres and the road is closest to
    (a) 0.04
    (b) 0.05
    (c) 0.10
    (d) 0.20

49. Minimum time after the car starts, when the gear was shifted is closest to
    (a) 10 s
    (b) 25 s
    (c) 30 s
    (d) 35 s

50. Due to gearshift, how much lesser distance does the car cover during the first 100 s, as compared to the case of no gearshift?
    (a) 12.5 m
    (b) 15 m
    (c) 18 m
    (d) 30 m

Build up your understanding

1. Under simultaneous action of two forces, a stationary particle starts moving parallel to a vector $\hat{i} - \hat{j}$. If one of the forces is $(3\hat{i} - \hat{j} - \hat{k})$ N and the other has smallest possible magnitude, find the other force.

2. Two small discs A and B of masses 1 kg and 2 kg are connected by a light cord that is connected at its midpoint to another light cord. This assembly is placed on a frictionless horizontal floor in such a way that the segments of the cord connecting the disc and the new cord remain straight making angles of 90°, 120° and 150°. For this description, following four arrangements are suggested.

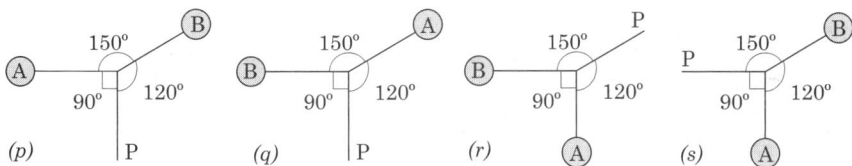

(p) (q) (r) (s)

The free end P of the new cord is pulled by a 10 N force, and both the discs begin to move with accelerations of equal magnitudes.

(a) Which of the above arrangements satisfy the given condition?
(b) What is the magnitude of the acceleration?

3. A light and inextensible string of length $l = 20$ m tied between two nails, supports a frictionless pulley of weight $W_p = 10\sqrt{2}$ N from which a block of weight $W_b = 10\sqrt{2}$ N is also suspended as shown in the figure. The nails are fixed in a level a distance $x = 10\sqrt{2}$ m apart. Radius of the pulley is $r = 10$ cm. How much normal reaction per unit of its length does the string apply on the pulley?

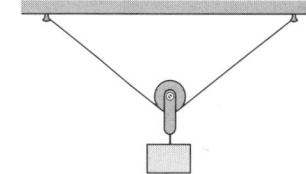

4. Two identical elastic cords of negligible relaxed lengths are tied at one of their ends to fixed nails A and B that are equidistant from the origin O. The other ends of the strings are tied to a small ball. To hold the ball in equilibrium at a point P (4 m, 3 m), a force of magnitude $F = 1000$ N is required. Assuming free space conditions, find force constant of the cords?

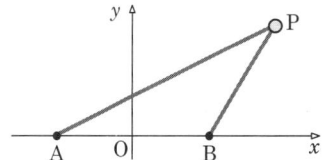

5. A wide container filled with water is suspended with the help of a light spring of stiffness 1000 N/m, a light inextensible cord and an ideal pulley. Initially, when the system is in equilibrium, the plug inserted in an orifice at the centre of the bottom of the container is pulled out. The extension in the spring is recorded and shown in the adjoining graph. Find the time rate of flow of water from the orifice.

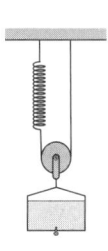 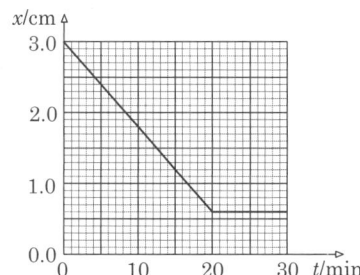

6. Two light discs A and B are attached at the ends of a spring of force constant 100 N/m. The assembly is placed on a rubber pad C, which is placed on the floor. When a load D is placed on the disc A, the disc shifts downwards and stays there in equilibrium simultaneously the rubber pad is compressed, and the disc B shifts downwards by a distance x. The restoring force F of the rubber pad varies with its compression x according to the given graph. Acceleration due to gravity is 10 m/s². Find mass of the load, so that when equilibrium is established, the disc A shifts 10 cm downwards.

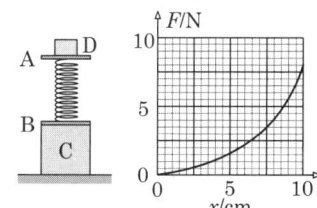

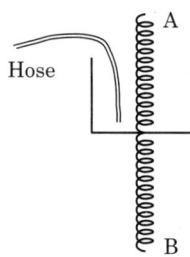

7. Two identical springs each of force constant $k = 10$ N/m are attached at the midpoint of the bottom of an inertia-less cup, one from the inside and the other from the outside. Free ends A and B of the springs are held maintaining the springs vertical. The ends A and B of the springs are made to move simultaneously with constant velocities $v_A = 10.0$ cm/s upwards and $v_B = 8.0$ cm/s downwards respectively. The moment when the ends start moving, the cup starts collecting water at the rate $r = 1.0$ g/s from a hose with a negligible velocity relative to the cup. Find velocity of the cup. Acceleration due to gravity is $g = 10$ m/s².

8. An assembly placed on a frictionless floor, consists of two light bars A and B, four light springs and a block C of mass m. Stiffness of each spring is shown in the figure. Initially all the springs are relaxed, and the bars are parallel to each other. The bar A is pulled from its midpoint towards the right by a force that increases gradually from zero. When the block acquires an acceleration a, by what amount will the separation between the bars increase?

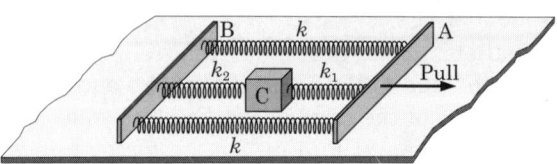

9. A uniform massless spring if extended or compressed, distance between every two consecutive turns (pitch) changes by the same amount. A spring obeying this property and Hooke's law is called a linear spring.

    (a) A linear spring of relaxed length $l_0 = 30$ cm is attached at one end to a wall. If the other end is pulled away from the wall with a force $F = 60$ N, $p = 6^{th}$ turn from the wall reaches a position, where $q = 8^{th}$ turn of relaxed spring was. Find force constant of the spring.

    (b) The ends A and B of a linear spring of relaxed length l_0 are so pulled that the ends shift by distances $\Delta l_A = 5$ cm and $\Delta l_B = 25$ cm as shown in the figure. Find shift of a point of the spring that was at a distance l_0/n ($n = 3$) from the end A in relaxed spring.

10. Three segments cut from a long elastic light cord are knotted at point P. The other ends of the cords are attached to the ceiling so that all the segments are in a vertical plane and angles between the outer and the middle segments each being θ as shown in the figure. A load of mass m is suspended from the knot P. If extensions in the cords are negligible as compared to their relaxed lengths, find the tensile force T developed in the middle cord. Acceleration due to gravity is g.

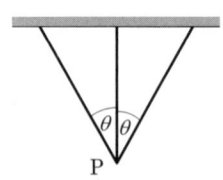

11. A light elastic cord is tied between two nails in the same level 100 cm apart. Distance between the nails is equal to the relaxed length of the cord. A bead is glued somewhere on the cord and then released. When equilibrium is established, elongated sections of the cord make angles 37° and 53° with the horizontal. At what distance from the left nail was the bead glued?

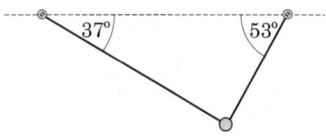

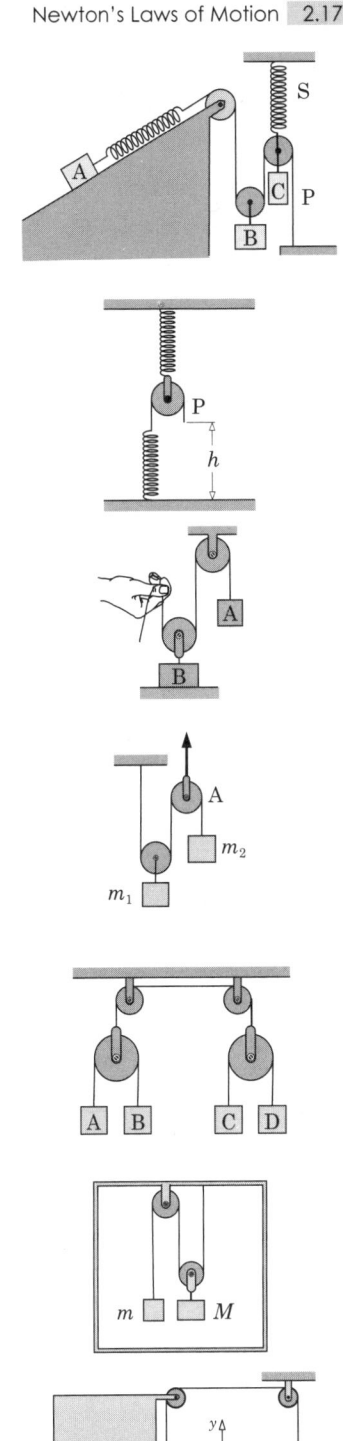

12. The system shown in the figure is in equilibrium. The blocks A, B and C are of equal masses, the inclined face is frictionless, the pulleys are light and frictionless, the thread is light and inextensible, the springs are light, and the blocks B and C are connected to the axles of the respective pulleys by rigid links. Find accelerations of the blocks A, B and C, immediately after

    (a) the thread is cut at point P.   (b) the spring S is cut.

13. A light frictionless pulley is suspended with the help of a light spring. One end P of a light inextensible thread that passes over the pulley is free and the other end is tied to another light spring that is affixed to the ground at its lower end as shown in the figure. Stiffness of both the springs is $k = 500$ N/m. The free end P is $h = 10.0$ cm above the ground. What minimum pull at the end P will bring it to the ground?

14. In the system shown, initially the block A of mass m is hanging at rest and the block B of mass $2m$ is on the ground. The pulleys have negligible masses and negligible friction, and the thread is extremely light and almost inextensible. Acceleration due to gravity is g. The free end of the thread is pulled upwards with a constant force. When it acquires a speed v, find speeds of both the blocks.

15. In the system shown, thread is inextensible, masses of the thread and that of the pulleys are negligible as compared to the loads to be lifted and friction at the axles of the pulleys is absent. Masses of the loads are $m_1 = 1.0$ kg and $m_2 = 2.0$ kg. Acceleration of free fall is $g = 10$ m/s². If axle of the pulley A is pulled upwards with a force $F = 20$ N, how much acceleration will it acquire?

16. The system shown in the figure consists of four blocks A, B, C and D of masses m, $2m$, $2m$ and $4m$ respectively. The threads are inextensible, masses of the threads and the pulleys are negligible, and friction is absent at the axles of the pulleys. Initially the system is held motionless. Find accelerations of all the blocks after the system is set free. Acceleration of free fall is g.

17. An arrangement setup inside a lift is shown in the figure. The pulleys and threads are ideal, and masses of the blocks are m and M ($M > 2m$). Find minimum acceleration of the lift for which the thread remains taut, and both the blocks accelerate in the same direction relative to the ground. Acceleration due to gravity is g.

18. In the system shown, the blocks A, B and C are of equal mass, the pulleys are ideal, and the cord is light and inextensible. There is no friction between the blocks B and C as well as between the horizontal floor and the block C. If the system is set free, find acceleration vectors of all the blocks. Acceleration of free fall is $g = 10$ m/s².

19. In the given arrangement, masses of the blocks A, B, C and D are M_1, M_2, m_1 and m_2 respectively, pulleys are ideal, and cords are light and inextensible. There is no friction between any pair of surfaces in contact. If the system is set free, find x-components of accelerations of all the blocks. Acceleration of free fall is $g = 10$ m/s².

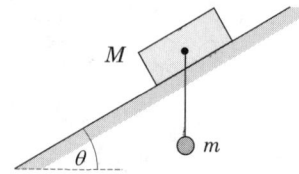

20. A ball of mass m is suspended from a bar of mass M with a light inextensible cord. The bar can slide on a frictionless slope of inclination θ. Initially the bar is held motionless so that the ball also stays motionless as shown in the figure. Find accelerations of the bar and of the ball relative to the ground immediately after the bar is released. Acceleration due to gravity is g.

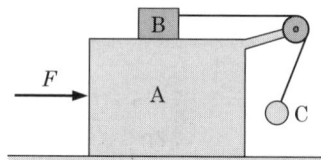

21. In the setup shown, magnitude of the force F exerted on the block A is so adjusted that the block B and the ball C remain motionless relative to the block A without contact between A and C. All surfaces in contact are frictionless. Masses of these bodies are $m_A = 12$ kg, $m_B = 5$ kg and $m_C = 3$ kg respectively. Acceleration of free fall is $g = 10$ m/s². Find expression for the necessary force F.

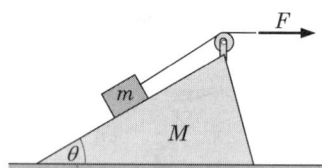

22. A block of mass m placed on a wedge of mass M is attached at one end of a light inextensible cord that passes over an ideal pulley affixed on the top of the wedge as shown in the figure. The free end of the thread is pulled by a constant horizontal force F. If friction between the block and the wedge as well as between the wedge and the floor is absent, find acceleration of the wedge. Acceleration due to gravity is g.

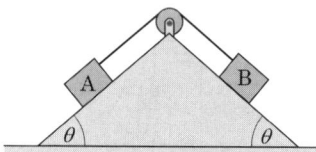

23. In the system shown, blocks A and B of masses m_1 and m_2 ($m_2 > m_1$) are placed on the frictionless inclined surfaces of a triangular wedge of mass m_0. The blocks are connected by a light inextensible cord that passes over an ideal pulley affixed at the top of the wedge. The wedge is placed on a horizontal frictionless floor. Initially the system is held motionless and then set free. Find acceleration of the wedge. Acceleration due to gravity is g.

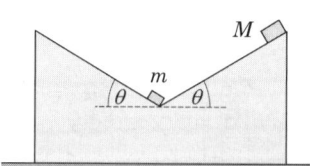

24. Top of a wedge made of a very light material has two frictionless inclined planes. A block of mass m is placed at the bottom of the inclined planes and another block of mass M is held motionless at the top of one of the inclined planes as shown in the figure. Find range of values of m in terms of M and the angle of inclination θ so that when the upper block is released, the lower block starts sliding up the wedge.

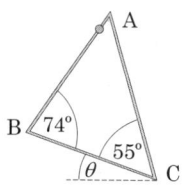

25. A rigid triangular frame ABC made of a thin rod is fixed in a vertical plane. Angles between the rod segments at the corner B and C are 74° and 55° respectively. A small bead starting from rest from corner A takes equal time to slide down the arms AB and AC. There is no friction between the bead and the arms. Find angle θ, which the arm BC makes with the horizontal.

26. To drag a block up an inclined plane with a constant speed, a force F_1 has to be applied along the line of fastest descent, whereas to drag the block down the plane with a constant speed, a force F_2 has to be applied along the line of fastest descent as shown in the following figure. Find the minimum horizontal force F parallel to the plane required to slide the block.

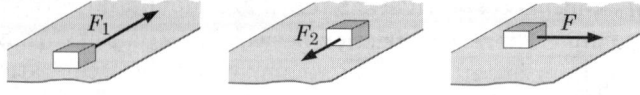

27. A small block is kept on an inclined plane of adjustable inclination. Coefficients of static and kinetic frictions between the block and the plane are μ_s and μ_k respectively. The angle of inclination of the plane is gradually increased from zero until the block starts sliding. How much speed will the block acquire in sliding down a distance l? Acceleration due to gravity is g.

28. One end of a spring of stiffness k is attached to a nail O on an inclined plane and the other end to a small disc of mass m placed on the inclined plane. Inclination of the plane with the horizontal is α and coefficient of friction between the disc and the plane is slightly less than $\tan\alpha$. Find suitable expression for deformation Δr in the spring when the disc is in equilibrium at an angular position θ from the line of greatest slope as shown in the figure. Acceleration due to gravity is g.

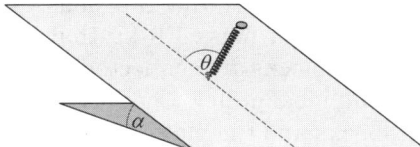

29. A catapult placed on horizontal ground can launch blocks at angle θ above the horizontal with the help of a spring as shown in the figure. Mass of a block to be launched is m, mass of the catapult is much smaller than m, the maximum force F of the spring on the block is much greater than the gravitation pull of the earth on the block and coefficient of friction between the catapult and the ground is μ. How much maximum horizontal acceleration can the block be imparted by the catapult?

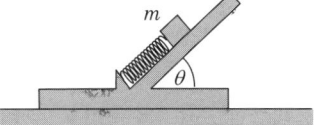

30. A light block P on a horizontal tabletop placed equidistant from the pulleys supports a load with the help of a cord as shown in the figure. If the minimum and the maximum forces applied by hand to keep the system in equilibrium are $F_{min} = 40$ N and $F_{max} = 90$ N, calculate mass m of the load. Acceleration due to gravity $g = 10$ m/s².

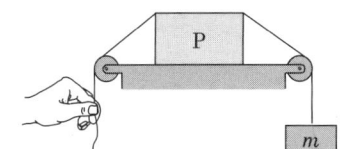

31. A block given a velocity u on horizontal ground (not frictionless) is observed a distance s away a time τ later. Find coefficient of kinetic friction between the floor and the block. Acceleration of free fall is g.

32. A block of mass m made of chalk is projected with velocity u along a horizontal floor. Coefficient of friction between the block and the floor is μ. If due to wear, mass of the block decreases at a constant rate r (a unit of mass in every unit of distance travelled), find expression for total distance travelled by the block. Acceleration due to gravity is g.

33. A block of mass $m = 5.0$ kg is sliding eastwards on a horizontal floor. When its velocity is $u = 8.0$ m/s, in addition to frictional force from the floor a westward force F starts acting on it. Magnitude of this force varies with time according to equation $F = kt$, where $k = 5.0$ N/s and t is time in seconds. Coefficient of friction between the block and the floor is $\mu = 0.3$. Draw a graph to show how the frictional force f on the block varies with time. Acceleration of free fall is $g = 10$ m/s².

2.20 Chapter-2

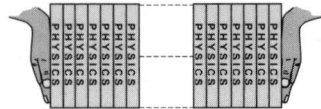

34. A boy lifts a stack of several identical books pressing hard with his hands. Coefficient of static friction between hand and a book is $\mu_{hb} = 0.40$, between the books is $\mu_{bb} = 0.25$ and mass of a book is $m = 400$ g. Now the boy starts decreasing the pressure gradually. When the horizontal component of the force applied by the boy becomes $F = 120$ N, the books are about to fall. Acceleration of free fall is $g = 10$ m/s².

(a) How many books are there in the stack?
(b) Find frictional force between the third and the fourth book.

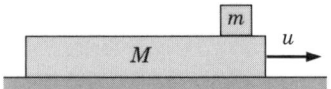

35. A large plank of mass M is moving with a velocity u on a horizontal frictionless floor. A block of mass m is gently placed on the plank without any velocity. If the block slides a distance l on the plank before it stops sliding, find coefficient of friction between the block and the plank.

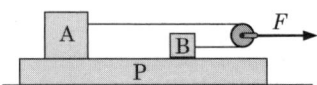

36. In the setup shown, blocks A and B of masses 4.0 kg and 1.0 kg are placed on a platform P of mass 1.0 kg that is placed on a horizontal frictionless floor. The blocks are connected by a light inextensible string that passes round an ideal pulley. Coefficients of static and kinetic friction between the blocks and the platform are 0.16 and 0.10. On applying a horizontal force F on the pulley, acceleration of the platform becomes 2.0 m/s². Find magnitude of the force F, frictional forces on the blocks and their accelerations. Acceleration due to gravity is 10 m/s².

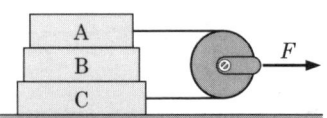

37. In the given setup, a bar B is sandwiched between bars A and C that are connected by a light inextensible thread, which passes round an ideal pulley. Mass of each bar is m, coefficient of friction between the bars is μ and the floor is frictionless. Acceleration due to gravity is g. If a horizontal force F is applied on the pulley, find acceleration of the bar B.

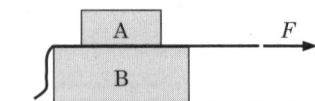

38. On a horizontal frictionless floor, a block A of mass m rests on another stationary block B of mass M ($m < M$) with a thin paper sheet of negligible mass inserted between them. The paper sheet is wide enough to prevent direct contact between the blocks. Coefficient of friction between each block and the paper sheet is μ. Find necessary horizontal force F applied on the paper sheet as shown in the figure to fulfil the following conditions. Acceleration due to gravity is g.

(a) The block B does not slide relative to the paper sheet.
(b) The paper sheet slides relative to B but does not slide relative to A.

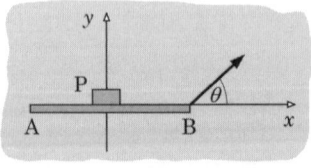

39. A bar AB and a block P are placed on a frictionless horizontal floor with their adjacent vertical faces in contact as shown in the figure by a top view. Here the x-y plane of a coordinate frame is in the plane of the floor. The bar is made to move horizontally along the floor in a straight line with a constant acceleration without rotation. Direction of motion of the bar makes an angle $\theta = \sin^{-1}(0.6)$ with the positive x-axis. Coefficient of friction between the block and the bar is $\mu = 0.75$. Find distance travelled by the block until the plank moves a distance $l = 40$ cm.

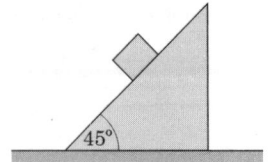

40. A block is released on the slant face of a wedge of equal mass placed on a horizontal floor. The slant face of the wedge makes an angle of 45° with the floor. Coefficient of friction between all surfaces in contact is the same. Find range of coefficient of friction μ for the following cases.

(a) Both the bodies remain motionless.
(b) The wedge remains motionless and the block slides down.
(c) The block slides down the wedge and the wedge slides on the floor.
(d) The block does not slide on the wedge but the wedge slides on the floor.

41. A wedge of mass $M = 3$ kg rests on a horizontal floor. Slant face of the wedge makes an angle $\theta = \sin^{-1}(0.6)$ with the horizontal. A block of mass $m = 5$ kg is released on the slant face. Coefficient of friction between the floor and the wedge is $\mu = 1/3$ and the slant face is friction-less. Find the force of normal reaction between the block and the slant face. Acceleration of free fall is $g = 10$ m/s².

42. One end of a uniform rope of mass $m = 3.0$ kg placed on the ground is pulled by a force $F = 10\sqrt{2}$ N in such a way that $\eta = 2/3$ of length of the rope remains at rests on the ground in a straight line and rest of the rope in the air in the vertical plane containing the portion of the rope on the ground. Find range of values of coefficient of friction between the rope and the ground. Acceleration of free fall is $g = 10$ m/s².

43. A train of mass $M = 1000$ ton is running with a uniform velocity on a level track. Resistance to motion is proportional to the mass being pulled and pulling force of the engine is a constant. The last carriage of mass $m = 200$ ton gets decoupled. The driver discovers it after travelling a distance $l = 100$ m and instead of applying brakes, he immediately shuts off the engine. When both the parts of the train come to rest, what is the distance s between them?

44. A student starts an experiment with a stack of three identical sheets of paper. He crumples the stack against his fist as shown in the figure, then separates a single sheet from the other two without altering their crumpled (pseudo-conical) shape. This yields two objects of the same shape, but of different masses. He releases these objects simultaneously and records their motion in still air. After the two objects acquire their terminal velocities, the heavier one moves $\eta = \sqrt{2}$ times farther than the lighter one in a particular time interval. If the force of air resistance is proportional to v^x, where v is velocity and x is a constant exponent, what should be value of the exponent x?

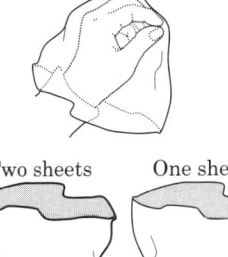

Two sheets   One sheet

45. A ball projected vertically upwards with a velocity 20 m/s returns back on the ground with a velocity 16 m/s. If the air resistance is proportional to the speed of the ball, find airtime of the ball. Acceleration of free fall is 10 m/s².

46. A cricket ball during its motion in the air experiences a drag force proportional to square of its speed relative to the air. Immediately before a batsman hits a ball, the ball was moving horizontally in the air with speed $u = 20$ m/s and acceleration $a = \sqrt{164}$ m/s². After the hit, the ball starts rising vertically upwards with an initial velocity $v = 10$ m/s. Neglecting buoyant force, calculate acceleration of the ball immediately after the hit? Assume acceleration of free fall $g = 10$ m/s².

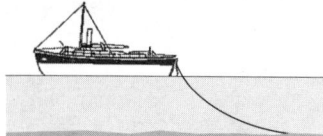

47. A boat of mass m is anchored in the middle of a river, which is flowing with a constant velocity v_0. Horizontal component of the force exerted on the boat by the anchor chain is T_0. If the anchor chain suddenly breaks, determine time required for the boat to attain a velocity equal to $0.5v_0$. Assume that the drag force of the water is proportional to the velocity of the boat relative to the water and neglect air drag.

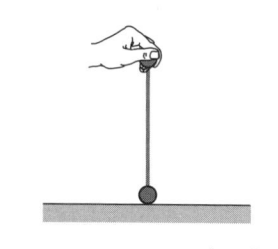

48. The given figure shows how forces of air resistance F_a and water resistance F_w on a sailboat vary with velocity v of the boat relative to the respective media.
   (a) What speed a sailboat will acquire in stagnant water, when the wind speed is 5 m/s everywhere? The direction of motion of the boat coincides with the direction of the wind.
   (b) What speed a sailboat will acquire in stagnant air, when the water is flowing with velocity 5 m/s everywhere? The direction of motion of the boat coincides with the direction of the water current.

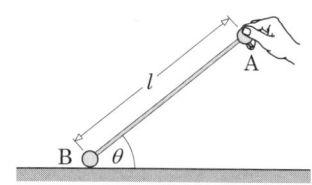

49. A dumbbell is constructed by affixing small balls each of mass m at the ends of a light rod of length l. The dumbbell is held vertically with the lower ball resting on a horizontal floor as shown in the figure. The upper ball is released and given a horizontal velocity v_0 by a sharp hit. If the bottom ball immediately loses contact with the floor, what should be the maximum length l of the dumbbell be? Acceleration due to gravity is g.

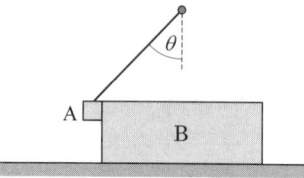

50. A dumbbell consists of two very small size balls A and B of masses m and M fixed at the ends of a light rigid rod of length l. The dumbbell is held motionless on a horizontal floor making an angle θ with the floor as shown in the figure. Find range of coefficient of friction μ between the floor and the ball B, so that the ball starts sliding immediately after the dumbbell is released.

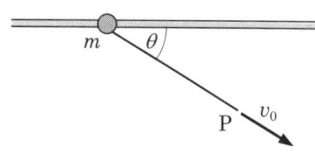

51. In the setup shown, a small block A of mass m suspended from a peg with the help of a light inextensible cord rests on a vertical face of a block B of mass M, which is held motionless on the horizontal ground. Inclination of the cord with the vertical is θ and all the surfaces in contact are frictionless. Find acceleration of the block B immediately after it is released. Acceleration due to gravity is g.

52. A bead of mass m, which can slide on a straight horizontal frictionless rod, is being pulled with the help of a light inextensible thread of length l in such a manner that the end P of the thread, which is being pulled moves with a constant speed v_0 always directed along the thread. Find an expression for the tensile force T in the thread at an instant when the thread makes angle θ with the rod.

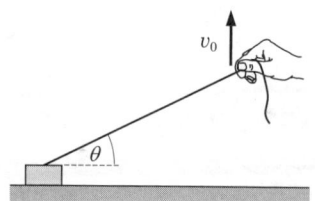

53. A light inextensible straight thread of length $l = 3.2$ m is placed on a frictionless horizontal floor. A small block of mass $m = 3$ kg placed on the floor is attached at one end of the thread. With how much constant speed v_0 the free end of the thread must be lifted vertically upwards so that the block leaves the floor, when the thread makes an angle $\theta = 30°$ with the floor. Acceleration of free fall is $g = 10$ m/s².

54. In a gravity free space, a long uniform cylinder of radius $r = 30$ cm wears a thin uniform ring that can slide on the cylinder. When the ring is given an angular velocity $\omega = 10$ rad/s, it stops in $t_0 = 3.0$ s. Now the ring is given the same angular velocity and simultaneously projected along the rod with speed $u = 4.0$ m/s. How far will the ring move along the rod before it stops?

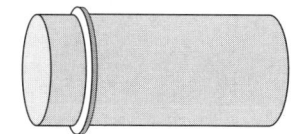

55. A motor is installed at the top of a pole rigidly fixed on a platform. A light rod of length $r = 1$ m is rigidly attached to the motor shaft at its one end and at the other end a small ball of mass m is attached. The rod can be rotated in a vertical plane with the help of the motor. Total mass of the platform, the pole and the motor is $\eta = 4$ times the mass of the ball. The motor rotates the rod at a constant angular velocity. The platform is placed on a horizontal surface, where coefficient of friction is $\mu = 1/\sqrt{3}$. At which minimum angular velocity ω_0 of the rod, will the platform start sliding?

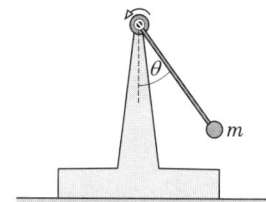

56. A disc D of mass $m = 4.0$ kg is tied at one end of a cord of length $l = 1.0$ m, the other end of which is fixed at the centre of a large circular platform. The platform is maintained horizontal and rotated about its vertical axis of symmetry. The disc is placed on the platform as shown. How long after the disc is placed, will the cord break? The maximum tensile force the cord can withstand is $T_{max} = 100$ N and coefficient of kinetic friction between the disc and the platform is $\mu_k = 0.1$.

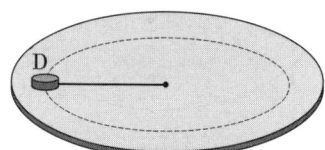

57. Consider a hollow cylinder of radius r fixed in a laboratory with its axis horizontal. A small block is placed inside the cylinder as shown in the figure. Coefficient of friction between the block and the inner surface of the cylinder is μ. Find the angular velocity at which if the cylinder is rotated about its axis, the block does not slide. Acceleration due to gravity is g.

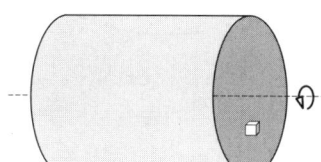

58. A small block of mass m is placed on a platform that has a rectangular protrusion. The block is connected to one end of a light inextensible cord that passes over an ideal pulley fixed on the corner of the rectangular protrusion and finally attached to the wall. Segment of the cord between the pulley and the wall is horizontal and is at a height h above the top face of the platform as shown in the figure. The platform is on a horizontal frictionless floor. Coefficient of friction between the block and top face of platform is μ. The platform is pulled away from the wall so that it moves with a constant velocity v. Find the force F pulling the platform when segment of the cord between the block and the pulley makes angle θ with the horizontal. Denote acceleration of free fall by g and assume that the block does not leave the platform.

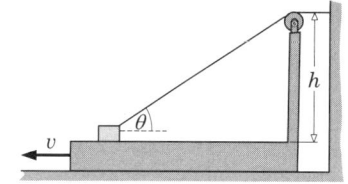

Check your understanding

1. As shown in the following figure, consider three arrangements A, B and C, where the pulleys are ideal, strings are light and inextensible, balls attached at the ends of the strings are identical and surfaces where the balls rest are frictionless. Identify nature of equilibria (i.e. stable, unstable or neutral) of the arrangements.

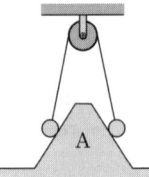
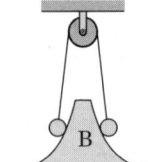
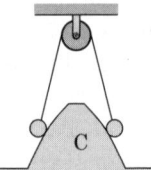

2. A long elastic cord obeying Hooke's law is stretched considerably due to its own weight. In one such case, a cord is held from one of its ends and hung vertically and in another case that is shown in the figure, the ends are attached to separate nails A and B in the same level so that the cord assume shape of a catenary. In which case is the cord stretched longer?

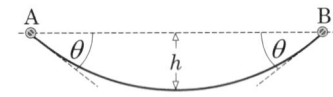

3. A uniform rope of length $l = 12$ m is suspended between two fixed nails A and B that are in the same horizontal level. If the rope makes an angle $\theta = \sin^{-1}(0.6)$ with the horizontal at the nails, find depth h of the lowest point on the rope below the nails and radius of curvature ρ of the rope at the lowest point.

4. If you hang vertically some length of a long uniform inextensible rope, the longest hanging length is $l_0 = 2$ m that does not break due to its own weight. Now you cut a length of the rope and place it straight on a horizontal frictionless table with a little length hanging over the edge so that it begins to slide down when released. What maximum length can this piece have so that it does not break during sliding?

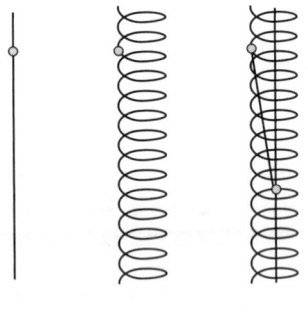

5. A bead slides down a height h on a rigid thin vertical rod in time T_1, and the same height on a rigid helix in time T_2. Now the rod is rigidly fixed along the axis of the helix and the bead that can slide on the helix is tied with a light inextensible thread to another identical bead that can slide on the rod as shown in the figure. The assembly consisting of the beads and the thread is released from rest. How long will this assembly take to slide down the same height h? Neglect friction as well as air resistance and assume radius of the helix so small as compared to the length of the thread that the thread can be assumed almost vertical.

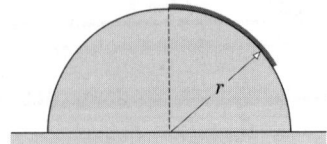

6. A uniform rope of length l is held motionless on a frictionless hemisphere of radius r with one end of the rope at the top of the hemisphere. The hemisphere is made immobile by gluing it on a horizontal floor. Find where on the rope, maximum tensile force is developed immediately after the rope is released.

7. A block of mass $m = 15$ kg is suspended in an elevator with the help of three identical light elastic cords stretched vertically. One of them is tied to the ceiling and the other two are tied to the floor of the elevator as shown in the figure. When the elevator is stationary, the tensile force in each of the lower cords is $F = 7.5$ N. Acceleration due to gravity is $g = 10$ m/s².

   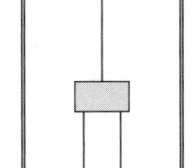

   (a) For what acceleration of the lift, will the lower cords become relaxed?
   (b) If the elevator moves with an upward acceleration $a = 1.0$ m/s², how much tensile force will develop in the upper cord?
   (c) If the elevator moves with an upward acceleration $a = 2.0$ m/s², how much tensile force will develop in the upper cord?
   (d) For what acceleration of the lift will the upper cord become relaxed?

8. An elastic cord that obeys Hooke's law is stretched along the y-axis in the x-y plane of a coordinate frame so that its ends A and B occupy positions (0, 2) and (0, –8) respectively. A point of the cord that coincides with the origin is marked by a permanent ink; let us call this mark C. Now both the ends are made to move simultaneously; the end A in positive x-direction with constant velocity 1.0 m/s and end B in the negative y-direction with a constant acceleration. If the mark C passes the point (4, –2), find acceleration of the end B. All the coordinates are in metres.

9. Turns of a uniform spring of relaxed length $l = 1.00$ m and force constant $k = 500$ N/m almost touch each other. A light glue is applied evenly between every adjacent turn. Breaking strength of the glue is $F_b = 100$ N. The spring is placed on a frictionless horizontal floor and pulled from one of its ends. If the pulling force is gradually increased to a value $F = 200$ N, how much will the length of the spring become?

10. Two beetles are hanging from the lower end of a light elastic cord suspended from the ceiling. Stiffness of the cord is k, its relaxed length is l_0, mass of each beetle is m and acceleration due to gravity is g. One of the beetles starts climbing the cord with a constant velocity u relative to the ceiling while the other one keeps on hanging from the lower end. With what velocity and in which direction will the lower beetle be shifted? Ignore all disturbances caused by the initial acceleration of the beetle that is climbing the rope.

11. A small block placed at the bottom of an empty container is attached at its top with one end of an elastic cord of relaxed length 80 cm and force constant 100 N/m. The force constant of the cord increases with decrease in temperature. Its value at 0 °C becomes 4 times of its value at room temperature. The other end of the cord is attached to a fixed hook at height 100 cm above the top of the block as shown in the figure. In this situation, the cord is extended but its elastic force is not sufficient to lift the block. Up to what minimum height cold water of temperature 0 °C should be filled into the container so that the block leaves the bottom. Weight of the block in the cold water is 40 N. Assume no heat conduction in the cord along its length and no heat loss to the surroundings.

    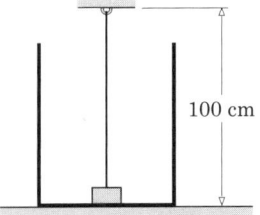

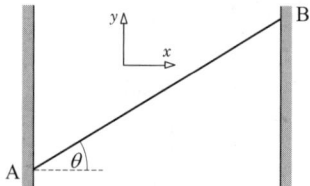

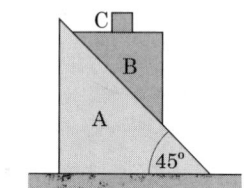

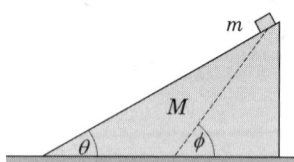

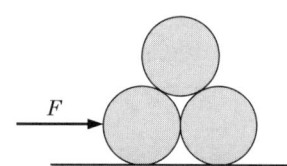

12. A cobweb thread of negligible relaxed length is stretched between points A and B on two opposite walls as shown in the figure. In this state, the thread makes an angle θ with the horizontal and its length and force constant are l and k respectively. A spider of mass m crawls gradually from end A to B on this thread. Representing the horizontal by x-axis, the vertical by y-axis and point A as the origin, find equation of path followed by the spider assuming that the thread obeys Hooke's law.

13. A wedge A of mass M and base angle 45° is placed on a horizontal floor. Another wedge B of the same mass and base angle is set on the wedge A and a small block C of mass m is placed on the upper horizontal face of the wedge B. Initially the system is held motionless as shown in the figure. All the surfaces in contact are frictionless. Find acceleration of the block C after the system is released. Acceleration of free fall is g.

14. The wedge shown can slide without friction on a horizontal floor. Mass of the wedge is M and its angle of inclination is $\theta = 30°$. A block of mass m slides down the wedge without friction when released on its inclined face. If path of the block relative to the ground makes an angle of $\phi = 60°$ with the horizontal, find the ratio of mass of the block to that of the wedge.

15. Three identical cylinders, each of mass $m = 10\sqrt{3}$ kg, are arranged on a horizontal floor as shown in the figure with their axes horizontal. The floor as well as the cylinders are frictionless. You apply a constant horizontal force (directed to the right) on the left cylinder. For what range of F will all three cylinders remain in contact with each other. Acceleration of free fall is $g = 10$ m/s².

16. Having lost his way, a hunter reached bank of a frozen river of width l. However, due to extremely low friction he was unable to walk on the icy river. If a large horizontal area near the riverbank exists where the friction coefficient between the shoes of the hunter and the ground is μ; deduce suitable expression for the minimum time in which the hunter can reach the other bank of the river. Acceleration of free fall is g.

17. A horizontal conveyor belt reverses its velocity almost instantly after every $\tau = 1.0$ s. Speed of the belt in each direction is $v_0 = 1.0$ m/s. The coefficient of friction between the belt and a block placed on the belt depends on the direction of sliding. When the block slides to the right on the belt, the coefficient of friction is $\mu_r = 0.25$ and when it slides to the left on the belt, the coefficient of friction is $\mu_l = 0.50$. Find the average velocity of the block relative to the ground during a complete cycle of motion of the belt long time after the block is placed.

18. On a fixed inclined plane place a thin paper sheet of negligible mass and then a block on the paper and hold them motionless. The coefficient of friction between the block and paper is μ_1 and the coefficient of friction between the paper and the incline plane is μ_2. Now release them simultaneously.
    (a) If $\mu_2 \geq \mu_1 < \tan\theta$, find accelerations a_b of the block and a_p of the paper.
    (b) If $\mu_1 > \mu_2 < \tan\theta$, find accelerations a_b of the block and a_p of the paper.

19. A well-known experiment to demonstrate property of inertia is to pull out a cloth without letting a glass placed on it to fall. The cloth spreads up to a length l from an edge of a table and the glass is placed on the cloth at a distance x ($x \leq l$) from this edge. Coefficient of friction between the cloth and the glass is μ and that between the glass and the table is sufficient to prevent slipping of the glass on the table. The glass can be considered as a point particle and the cloth light. If the cloth is pulled with a constant speed, find range of this speed for a successful demonstration of the experiment.

20. Two identical books each of $n = 400$ pages are so meshed that their alternate papers overlap each other. Mass of overlapped portion of each paper is $m = 0.5$g and coefficient of static friction between the papers is $\mu = 0.1$. The arrangement is placed on a frictionless horizontal table and the books are pulled apart horizontally without rotation. Find minimum pulling force F required. Acceleration due to gravity is $g = 10$ m/s².

21. One end of a light inextensible cord is attached to a nail A on the ceiling. The cord passes through frictionless hole of a small bead P thereafter it passes round two ideal pulleys and finally the other end is attached to the bead. Initially the bead is held at rest with the cord segments AP and BP making angles α and β with the horizontal while keeping the segment CP vertical as shown in the figure. Find acceleration of the bead immediately after it is released. Acceleration due to gravity is g.

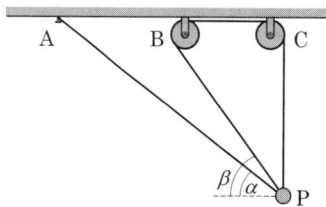

22. A rod of mass m and length L is suspended from the ceiling with the help of two light inextensible cords each of length l so that the rod is horizontal. The rod is given an angular velocity ω about its central vertical axis. Find increment in the tensile force in a cord immediately after the rod is given the angular velocity.

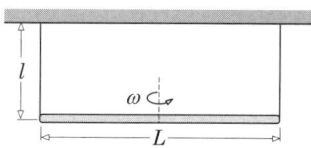

23. A cylinder is being pulled slowly with the help of a long uniform rope lying on a horizontal floor as shown in the figure. The pulling force applied at the end A is so adjusted that the length BC of the rope touching the cylinder always subtends angle $\theta = \sin^{-1}(0.8)$ at the centre of the cylinder and the length of the hanging portion CD always remains half of the length DE being dragged on the floor. Find coefficient of friction between the rope and the floor.

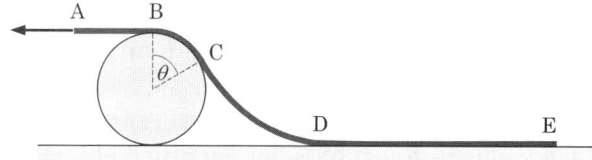

24. A disc of radius R inclined at an angle θ with the horizontal is evenly covered with a thin layer of sand. Coefficient of friction between the sand and the disc is μ. The disc is made to rotate about its central axis of symmetry with gradually increasing angular velocity. The angular velocity is increased so gradually that tangential acceleration of any of the sand particle is practically negligible. What is the angular velocity of the disc, when η fraction of the sand has fallen off the disc? Acceleration due to gravity is g.

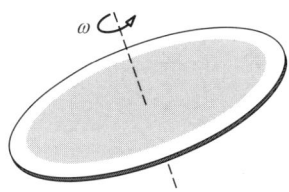

2.28 Chapter-2

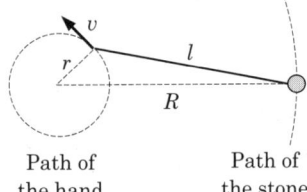

Path of the hand   Path of the stone

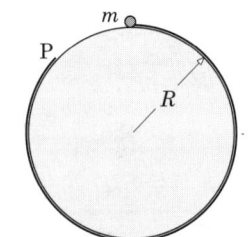

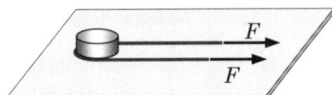

25. To whirl a stone tied to a cord, one has to move the free end of the cord on a circular path pulling the stone on a larger circular path. In this way a stone of mass m is whirled on a horizontal circular path of radius R with the help of a light inextensible cord of length l by moving the free end on a circular path of radius r with a uniform speed v as shown in the figure. At sufficiently great speed v, tensile force in the cord becomes so large that the effect of gravity can be neglected but at this speed air resistance becomes considerable. Find suitable expression for the force of air resistance. Acceleration due to gravity is g.

26. A light inextensible cord is wrapped around a frictionless cylinder of radius R fixed vertically on a floor that is lubricated with oil. A bead of mass m is tied at one end of the cord and the other end P is free as shown by the top view of the situation. Force of viscous drag on the bead due to layer of the lubricating oil is proportional to the speed of the bead and the proportionality constant is k. If the free end of the cord is pulled with a constant speed u along the cylinder, the bead eventually acquires a steady motion on a circular path. Find expressions for speed of the bead and radius of its circular path in its steady motion.

27. A uniform rope of mas m and length l is spread out on a horizontal frictionless surface, wrapping half turn around a fixed vertical frictionless cylinder of radius $r \ll l$. Initially, both the ends of the rope are pulled by equal forces each F in magnitude keeping both the unwrapped segments parallel to each other and equal in length as shown in the figure. Suddenly pulling force at one end is removed without any change in the pulling force at the other end. After how much time from removal of the pulling force at an end, will the rope start losing contact with the cylinder?

28. A small disc of mass $m = 100$ g is placed on a large horizontal floor lubricated with oil. Force of viscous drag due to layer of lubricating oil is given by equation $\vec{f} = -k\vec{v}$, here $\vec{v}$ is velocity of the disc and $k = 0.04$ kg/s. If a force of constant magnitude $F = 0.06$ N rotating with a constant angular velocity $\omega = 0.3$ rad/s is applied on the disc, the disc eventually acquires a steady motion on a circular path. Find speed of the disc in its steady motion.

29. A small bead starts sliding down a frictionless rigid helical wire frame. The axis of the helix is vertical, radius is R and pitch is h.
    (a) In how much time, will the bead descend by a height H?
    (b) How much force will the wire frame exert on the bead when the bead has descended by a height H? Acceleration of free fall g.

30. A small bead slides down a helical wire frame with a constant speed v due to gravity. Axis of the helix is vertical, and its turns are inclined at angle θ with the horizontal and its radius is R. Find expression for the coefficient of kinetic friction between the wire and the bead.

31. Starting from rest a motorcyclist moves on a horizontal un-banked circular track of radius $R = 28$ m. Coefficients of friction between the tyres and the track is uniform everywhere. How much minimum

distance must the motorcycle cover to achieve the maximum allowable speed? Treat the motorcycle as a point particle and use $\pi = 22/7$.

32. A small block is placed inside a hollow cylinder of radius r, axis of which is inclined at an angle θ with the horizontal as shown in the figure. Coefficient of friction between the block and the inner surface of the cylinder is μ. Find angular velocity of the cylinder about its axis, so that the block does not slide. Acceleration due to gravity is g.

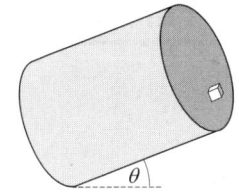

33. A block is placed on a large, inclined plane that makes an angle θ with the horizontal. Coefficient of kinetic friction between the block and the plane is $\mu > \tan\theta$. The block is given a velocity v_0 at an angle ϕ_0 with the line of fastest descent. Find expression for the time interval during which the block remains in motion. Acceleration due to gravity is g.

Challenge your understanding

1. A wedge of mass M can slide on two parallel rails A and B inclined at an angle θ to the horizontal. In the middle of the rails and parallel to them runs a frictionless rod C that wears a light ring D. The rod does not touch the wedge. A light inextensible cord attached with the ring runs through a hole in the wedge without touching it, then runs through an ideal pulley on the top of the wedge and finally attached to a block of mass m that can slide on the vertical face of the wedge without friction as shown in the figure. Coefficient of friction between the wedge and the rails is μ. Initially the system is held motionless and then released. Find the acceleration of the block. Acceleration due to gravity is g.

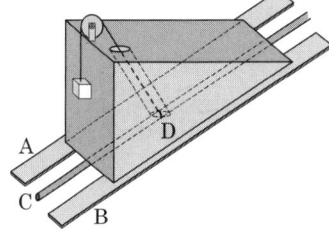

2. A boy is driving a model aircraft of mass m with the help of a light inextensible cord of length L. He does so by moving the free end of the cord with a constant speed in a horizontal circle of radius r. As a result, the aircraft moves in another horizontal circle of radius $R > r$ with a constant speed v at an altitude h above the plane containing circular path of the end held. The centres of both the circular paths lie on a vertical line. Considering the air drag, find lift force of air on the aircraft.

3. Two small identical discs A and B are tied to a nail P on a large horizontal platform with the help of identical light inextensible strings each of length $l = 25\sqrt{2}$ cm. The nail is fixed at distance l from the centre O of the platform. Initially the threads tying the discs A and B are straight and make angles $\theta_0 = 45°$ as shown in the figure. Coefficient of friction between the discs and the platform is $\mu = 0.40$. Acceleration of free fall is $g = 10$ m/s². Now the platform starts rotating with gradually increasing angular velocity ω about its vertical central axis. Find expression to describe angle θ between the threads PA and PB as function of angular velocity of the platform and draw an approximate graph to show this relationship.

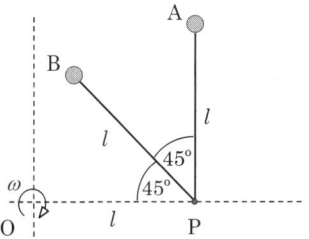

Answers and Hints

Multiple Choice Questions

1. (d)
2. (d)
3. (b)
4. (b)
5. (a), (b) and (d)
6. (c)
7. (c)
8. (c)
9. (b) and (d)
10. (c) and (d)
11. (b)
12. (a)
13. (a)
14. (d)
15. (a)
16. (a)
17. (c) and (d)
18. (c)
19. (b)
20. (a) and (d)
21. (b)
22. (c)
23. (a), (b), (c) and (d)
24. (a), (c) and (d)
25. (d)
26. (b)
27. (b)
28. (d)
29. (a)
30. (a) and (b)
31. (c)
32. (d)
33. (d)
34. (b)
35. (d)
36. (d)
37. (a)
38. (b), (c) and (d)
39. (a) and (b)
40. (b)
41. (a)→(q) and (r), (b)→(t), (c)→(s), (d)→(r)
42. (b) and (c)
43. (c)
44. (c)
45. (b)
46. (a)
47. (c)
48. (c)
49. (c)
50. (b)

Build up your understanding

1. $\left(-\hat{i} - \hat{j} + \hat{k}\right)$ N

2. (a) s (b) $\dfrac{10}{\sqrt{3}}$ m/s²

3. $\dfrac{(W_p + W_b)l}{2r\sqrt{l^2 - x^2}} = 200$ N/m

   Hint: Since the pulley is ideal and the string is light, modulus of tensile force at every point of the string in contact with the pulley is the same. Therefore, modulus of normal reaction between the pulley and the string at every point in contact must be uniform in magnitude.

4. $\dfrac{F}{2|\overrightarrow{OP}|} = 100$ N/m

   Hint: To simplify calculations make use of vector notations.

5. 4.0 g/s

6. 300 g

   Hint: Compression in the spring equals the difference of the downward shift of disc A say h and compression x of the rubber pad. Express the spring force that is equal to the weight mg in terms of h and x. Substitute given values in the equation obtained and plot it on the given graph.

7. $\dfrac{k(v_A - v_B) - rg}{2k} = 0.95$ cm/s ↑

   Hint: Since the cup is inertia-less, resultant of all the forces acting on it must be a null vector.

8. $x = \dfrac{mak_2}{2k(k_1 + k_2) + k_1 k_2}$

9. (a) $k = \dfrac{pF}{(q-p)l_0} = 600$ N/m

   Hint: Uniformity of change in length of every turn suggests that the fractional change in the length i.e. longitudinal strain of any portion of the spring is equal to that of the whole spring.

(b) $\Delta x = \dfrac{\Delta l_B - (n-1)\Delta l_A}{n} = 5$ cm

In the direction of $\Delta \vec{l}_B$

Hint: Displacement of a point P on a linear spring relative to one of its ends is proportional to the length of the segment of the spring between the point P and that end of the spring.

10. $T = \dfrac{mg}{1 + 2\cos^3 \theta}$

Hint: Since product of force constant of a segment of an elastic cord or spring and length of the segment is a constant, therefore force constant of the middle cord differs from that of the outer cords.

11. 59.17 cm

12. (a) $g/2$ down the plane, $g\downarrow, g\uparrow$

(b) $0, 0, 2g\downarrow$

Hint: No material body at rest can change its position by a finite amount in an infinitesimally small interval of time due to its inertia. Therefore, force of a spring connected with stationary material bodies at both of its ends cannot change by a finite amount in an infinitesimally small interval of time.

13. $\dfrac{kh}{5} = 10.0$ N

Hint: Since the pulley has vanishingly small inertia, net forces on it must be vanishingly small; in addition, the pulley can acquire a finite velocity as well as can be stopped almost instantaneously.

14. $v_A = v_B = \dfrac{v}{3}$

Hint: While the free end is speeding up, accelerations of the blocks are equal, therefore both the blocks will always have equal speeds.

15. $\dfrac{(m_1 + 4m_2)F}{4m_1 m_2} - \dfrac{3g}{2} = 7.5$ m/s² ↑

16. $a_A = \dfrac{7g}{9} \uparrow$; $a_B = a_C = \dfrac{g}{9} \downarrow$; $a_D = \dfrac{5g}{9} \downarrow$

17. $a > \dfrac{(M - 2m)g}{6m} \uparrow$ and $g > a > \dfrac{2(M - 2m)g}{3M} \downarrow$

18. $\vec{a}_A = -2\hat{j}$ m/s², $\vec{a}_B = (4\hat{i} - 2\hat{j})$ m/s², $\vec{a}_C = 4\hat{i}$ m/s²

19. For blocks A and C:

$$\dfrac{2g\hat{i}}{(M_1 + m_1)\left(\dfrac{1}{M_1 + m_1} + \dfrac{1}{M_2 + m_2} + \dfrac{1}{m_1} + \dfrac{1}{m_2}\right)}$$

For blocks B and D:

$$\dfrac{-2g\hat{i}}{(M_2 + m_2)\left(\dfrac{1}{M_1 + m_1} + \dfrac{1}{M_2 + m_2} + \dfrac{1}{m_1} + \dfrac{1}{m_2}\right)}$$

20. $\dfrac{(m + M)g \sin\theta}{M + m\sin^2\theta}$ down the slope

and $\dfrac{(m + M)g \sin^2\theta}{M + m\sin^2\theta} \downarrow$

Hint: The bar, which accelerates from rest, cannot change its position in a vanishingly small time due to its inertia, hence immediately after the bar is released the cord remains vertical and tensile force in it decreases causing the ball to accelerate vertically downwards. Moreover, vertical component of acceleration of the bar cannot exceed the acceleration of free fall; the inextensible cord remains taut making acceleration of the ball equal to the vertical component of acceleration of the bar.

21. $F = \dfrac{(m_A + m_B + m_C)m_C g}{\sqrt{m_B^2 - m_C^2}} = 150$ N

22. $\dfrac{F(1 - \cos\theta) + mg\sin\theta\cos\theta}{M + m\sin^2\theta} \rightarrow$

23. $\dfrac{(m_2 - m_1)g\sin\theta\cos\theta}{m_0 + (m_1 + m_2)\sin^2\theta} \rightarrow$

24. $m < M\cos 2\theta$

25. 19°

26. $F = \sqrt{F_1 F_2}$

27. $\sqrt{\dfrac{2(\mu_s - \mu_k)gl}{\sqrt{1+\mu_s^2}}}$

28. $\Delta r = \dfrac{2mg \sin \alpha}{k} \cos \theta$

29. $a_{max} = \dfrac{\mu F}{m\sqrt{1+\mu^2}}$

30. $m = \dfrac{\sqrt{F_{min} F_{max}}}{g} = 6$ kg

Hint: Limiting friction depends on the normal reaction, therefore a change in the pull on the rope changes the normal reaction and hence the limiting friction.

31. $\mu = \begin{cases} \dfrac{u^2}{2gs}; & 0 \leq s \leq \dfrac{u\tau}{2} \\ \dfrac{2(u\tau - s)}{g\tau^2}; & \dfrac{u\tau}{2} \leq s \leq u\tau \end{cases}$

And $s > u\tau$ is impossible.

32. $x = \dfrac{m}{r}$ or $x = \dfrac{u^2}{2\mu g}$ whichever is smaller

Hint: The block slides with a uniform retardation and its size gradually reduces due to wear. Therefore, it may completely vanish before it stops or may stop before it completely vanishes.

33.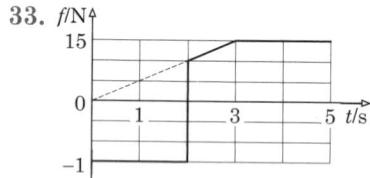

34. (a) $2\left(1 + \dfrac{\mu_{bb} F}{mg}\right) = 17$

Hint: The limiting friction between the hand and book is greater than that between any two books, therefore slipping will occur between the end books and the stack of the inner books.
(b) 22 N

35. $\mu = \dfrac{Mu^2}{2gl(m+M)}$

36. 18 N, 1.0 N, 1.0 N, 2.0 m/s² and 8.0 m/s² respectively

Hint: Since pull of string on both the blocks are equal and limiting friction on the block B is smaller than that on block A, the block B slides whereas block A does not slide on the plank under the given conditions.

37. $= \begin{cases} \dfrac{F}{3m}; & F \leq 6\mu mg \\ \dfrac{F + 2\mu mg}{4m}; & 6\mu mg \leq F \leq 10\mu mg \\ 3\mu g; & F \geq 10\mu mg \end{cases}$

38. (a) $F < \mu mg\left(1 + \dfrac{m}{M}\right)$

(b) $\mu mg\left(1 + \dfrac{m}{M}\right) < F < 2\mu mg$

Hint: The paper is almost massless, therefore the net force on it must be vanishingly small.

39. $s = l \sin \theta \sqrt{1+\mu^2} = 30$ cm

Hint: Friction is not sufficient to prevent slipping between the block and the bar and normal reaction between the bar and the block is a constant, therefore a constant total contact force (resultant of the normal reaction from the bar and kinetic friction) acts on the block by the bar. In addition, starting from rest, the block moves in a straight line.

40. (a) $\mu > 1.0$ (b) $\sqrt{5} - 2 < \mu < 1.0$
(c) $\mu < \sqrt{5} - 2$ (d) The event is not possible.

41. $N = \dfrac{mMg(\cos\theta + \mu \sin\theta)}{M + m\sin\theta(\sin\theta - \mu\cos\theta)} = 37.5$ N

Hint: The wedge will also accelerate.

42. $\mu \geq \dfrac{1}{\eta}\sqrt{\left(\dfrac{F}{mg}\right)^2 - (1-\eta)^2} = \dfrac{1}{2}$

Hint: Horizontal component of the force F balances the frictional force, which cannot exceed the limiting friction. Vertical component of the force F equals the weight of the hanging portion.

Newton's Laws of Motion   2.33

43. $s = \dfrac{Ml}{M-m} = 125$ m

44. 2

45. 3.6 s

46. $g + \left(\dfrac{v}{u}\right)^2 \sqrt{a^2 - g^2} = 12$ m/s^2

   Hint: Immediately before the ball is hit, force of air resistance and of gravity are mutually perpendicular and after the hit, both the forces are vertically downward.

47. $\dfrac{mv_0 \ln 2}{T_0}$

48. (a) 3.0 m/s

   Hint: As the boat speeds up, its velocity relative to water increases and that with respect to wind decreases. Therefore, curve representing the air resistance must be inverted about a suitable line parallel to the ordinate to make it suitable for decreasing speed relative to air.

   (b) 2.0 m/s

   Hint: As the boat speeds up, its velocity relative to air increases and that with respect to water decreases. Therefore, curve representing the water resistance must be inverted about a suitable line parallel to the ordinate to make it suitable for decreasing speed relative to water.

49. $\dfrac{v_0^2}{2g}$

   Hint: Immediately after the hit, the upper ball is in circular motion around the lower ball.

50. $\mu < \dfrac{m \sin 2\theta}{2(M + m \sin^2 \theta)}$

51. $\dfrac{mg \sin\theta \cos\theta}{m + M \cos^2 \theta}$

   Hint: The block A will move on circular path and initially it has only tangential acceleration, whose horizontal component is equal to the acceleration of block B.

52. $T = \dfrac{mv_0^2 \sin^2 \theta}{l \cos^4 \theta}$

53. $v_0 = \left(\sqrt{\dfrac{gl}{\sin\theta}}\right) \cos^2 \theta = 6$ m/s

   Hint: When the block is leaving the floor, vertical component of the tensile force balances weight of the block and horizontal component provides necessary acceleration to the block.

54. $x = \dfrac{ut_0 \sqrt{u^2 + (\omega r)^2}}{2\omega r} = 10$ m

   Hint: Friction at a point of the ring acts opposite to velocity of the point relative to the rod.

55. $\omega_0 = \sqrt{\dfrac{\mu(1+\eta)g}{r\sqrt{1+\mu^2}}} = 5$ rad/s

56. $t = \dfrac{1}{\mu_k g} \sqrt{\dfrac{T_{max}}{ml}} = 5.0$ s

   Hint: The tensile force in the cord and the frictional force provide the centripetal and the tangential accelerations respectively.

57. $\omega \geq \sqrt{\dfrac{g\sqrt{1+\mu^2}}{\mu r}}$

58. $F = m \left\{ \dfrac{v^2 \tan^3 \theta + \mu gh}{h(\cos\theta + \mu \sin\theta)} - \dfrac{v^2 \tan^3 \theta}{h} \right\}$

Check your understanding

1. Arrangements A and B are in stable, whereas C is in unstable equilibrium.

2. In the second case.

   Hint: You may use the idea of average tensile force developed in the cord.

3. $h = \dfrac{l(1-\cos\theta)}{2\sin\theta} = 2$ m, $\rho = \dfrac{l \cot\theta}{2} = 8$ m

4. $4l_0 = 8$ m

Hint: Tensile force in the sliding rope acquires its maximum value at the edge of the table when half of the rope has slid.

5. $\sqrt{\dfrac{T_1^2 + T_2^2}{2}}$

6. From the top at angular position
$\sin^{-1}\left[\dfrac{r}{l}\left\{1 - \cos\left(\dfrac{l}{r}\right)\right\}\right]$

7. (a) $\dfrac{3F}{m} = 1.5 \text{ m/s}^2 \uparrow$

   (b) $m\left(g + \dfrac{a}{3}\right) + 2F = 170 \text{ N}$

   (c) $m(g + a) = 180 \text{ N}$

   (d) $3g + \dfrac{6F}{m} = 33 \text{ m/s}^2 \downarrow$

8. 0.8 m/s^2

   Hint: Ratio of lengths of segments AC and CB as well as ratios of their x and y-components is a constant.

9. $l + \dfrac{F^2 - F_b^2}{2kF} = 1.15 \text{ m}$

10. $\dfrac{mgu}{kl_0 + 2mg} \uparrow$

11. 60 cm

    Hint: Denoting the relaxed length of the cord by l, its force constant by k, height of the hook above the block by H, relaxed length of the portion of cord above water by l_1 and height of water level by h, the following equations can be written.
    For portion of string above water:
    $\dfrac{kl}{l_1}(H - h - l_1) = F$
    For portion of string under water:
    $\dfrac{4kl}{(l - l_1)}(h - l + l_1) = F$

12. $y = \left(\tan\theta - \dfrac{mg}{kl\cos\theta}\right)x + \dfrac{mg}{kl^2 \cos^2\theta}x^2$

13. $\dfrac{2(m + M)g}{(3M + 2m)}$

    Hint: Vertical component of acceleration of wedge B is equal to acceleration of block C and horizontal component of acceleration of wedge B is equal in magnitude and opposite in direction to acceleration of wedge A.

14. $\dfrac{m}{M} = \dfrac{\tan\phi - \tan\theta}{\tan\theta} = 2$

    Hint: Express $\tan\phi$ in terms of acceleration of the block relative to the wedge a and acceleration of the wedge b.
    $$\tan\phi = \dfrac{a\sin\theta}{a\cos\theta - b}$$
    Since there is no net force in horizontal direction on the system, you can write
    $$m(a\cos\theta - b) = Mb$$

15. $\dfrac{mg}{\sqrt{3}} \leq F \leq mg\sqrt{3} \Rightarrow 100 \text{ N} \leq F \leq 300 \text{ N}$

    Hint: For the given condition, the force F has a range of values. At its minimum value, the lower cylinders tend to lose contact from each other and at the maximum value, the upper cylinder tends to lose contact from the front cylinder.

16. $2\sqrt{\dfrac{(\sqrt{2} + 1)l}{\mu g}}$

17. $\dfrac{v_0^2}{\tau g}\left(\dfrac{1}{\mu_r} + \dfrac{1}{\mu_1}\right) = 0.2 \text{ m/s} \rightarrow$

18. (a) $a_b = g(\sin\theta - \mu_1 \cos\theta)$ and $a_p = 0$

    (b) $a_b = a_p = g(\sin\theta - \mu_2 \cos\theta)$

    Hint: The paper sheet is almost massless, therefore, the net force on it must be vanishingly small.

19. $v_c : \begin{cases} v_c > \sqrt{\dfrac{\mu g l^2}{2x}}; & x < \dfrac{l}{2} \\ v_c > \sqrt{2\mu g(l - x)}; & x > \dfrac{l}{2} \end{cases}$

    Hint: For successful demonstration of the experiment, average velocity of the glass should not be greater than half the constant velocity of the cloth and hence displacement of the glass cannot exceed half the displacement of the cloth.

20. $F \geq n(2n-1)\mu mg = 39.9$ N

    Hint: One paper has two pages.

21. $a = g\sin\theta$

    Here $\theta = \tan^{-1}\left(\dfrac{\cos\alpha + \cos\beta}{1 + \sin\alpha + \sin\beta}\right)$

22. $\dfrac{m\omega^2 L^2}{8l}$

23. $\mu = \dfrac{\cot\theta}{2} = \dfrac{3}{8}$

    Hint: The event described in the problem is possible only when, either the rope slides on the cylinder and the cylinder rolls on the floor or the cylinder slides on the floor without rotation and the rope does not slide on the cylinder, making the whole rope in state of pure translational motion. In addition, at the point C, vertical component of the tensile force equals the weight of the portion CD and horizontal component equals the force of kinetic friction on the portion DE.

24. $\omega = \sqrt{\dfrac{g(\mu\cos\theta - \sin\theta)}{R\sqrt{1-\eta}}}$

    Hint: Sand particle at the lowest position has maximum tendency to slide off the disc.

25. $\dfrac{mv^2 R}{r^2}\sqrt{\dfrac{4R^2 l^2}{(R^2 + l^2 - r^2)^2} - 1}$

    Hint: Components of the tensile force in the cord towards the centre of the path of the stone provides the necessary centripetal force and the component along the tangent to the path counterbalances the force of air resistance.

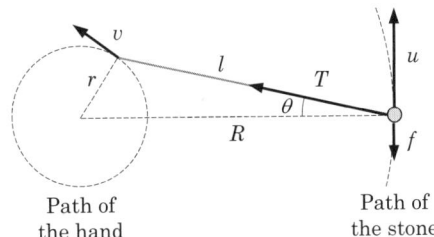

Path of the hand   Path of the stone

26. $u\sqrt{1+\left(\dfrac{mu}{kR}\right)^2}$ and $R\sqrt{1+\left(\dfrac{mu}{kR}\right)^2}$

27. $\sqrt{\dfrac{ml}{3F}\left(1-\dfrac{\pi r}{l}\right)}$

28. $\dfrac{F}{\sqrt{(m\omega)^2 + k^2}} = 1.2$ m/s

29. (a) $\sqrt{\dfrac{2H(4\pi^2 R^2 + h^2)}{gh^2}}$

    (b) $\dfrac{2\pi mgR\sqrt{4\pi^2 R^2 + h^2 + 16\pi^2 H^2}}{(4\pi^2 R^2 + h^2)}$

30. $\dfrac{gR\tan\theta}{\sqrt{g^2 R^2 + v^4 \cos^2\theta}}$

31. $\dfrac{\pi R}{4} = 22$ m

32. $\geq \begin{cases} \sqrt{\dfrac{g\sqrt{1+\mu^2}}{\mu r}}; & \mu > \tan\theta \\ \sqrt{\dfrac{g(\mu\cos\theta + \sin\theta)}{\mu r}}; & \mu < \tan\theta \end{cases}$

33. $\dfrac{v_0(\mu\cos\theta + \sin\theta\cos\phi_0)}{g(\mu^2\cos^2\theta - \sin^2\theta)}$

    Hint: Assume line of the fastest descent as y-axis and horizontal as x-axis and express tangential and y-component of accelerations. Integrate these equations over the limits considering speed change from v_0 to zero and time change from zero to the desired time.

Challenge your understanding

1. $= \begin{cases} g\left\{\dfrac{(m+M)(\sin\theta - \mu\cos\theta) - \mu m}{m + M - \mu m \sin\theta}\right\}; & \mu < \dfrac{(m+M)\sin\theta}{m+(m+M)\cos\theta} \\ 0 & \mu > \dfrac{(m+M)\sin\theta}{m+(m+M)\cos\theta} \end{cases}$

2. $m\left(g + \dfrac{2v^2 h}{R^2 + L^2 - r^2 - h^2}\right)$

3. $\theta = \begin{cases} \dfrac{\pi}{4}; & 0 < \omega < \omega_1 \\ \dfrac{\pi}{4} + \sin^{-1}\left(\dfrac{\mu g}{l\omega^2}\right); & \omega_1 < \omega < \omega_2 \\ 0; & \omega_2 < \omega \end{cases}$

Here $\omega_1 = \sqrt{\dfrac{\mu g}{l}} = \sqrt{8\sqrt{2}}$ rad/s and

$\omega_2 = \sqrt{\dfrac{\mu g}{l \sin\theta_o}} = 4$ rad/s

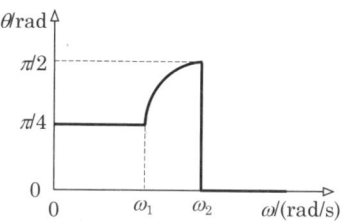

Hint: Since the discs can move on a circular path of radius l with centre at the point P, therefore frictional force on them can only be along the tangent to this path.

Conditions of motion of the discs can be analysed with more convenience relative to a frame attached with the platform. Now you can find angular velocities ω_1 and ω_2 at which the disc A and B begins to slide respectively.

Till the angular velocity of the disc reaches the value ω_1 none of the discs slide and angular separation between them remains $\pi/4$ radians. Since $\omega_1 < \omega_2$, the disc A begins to slide first and very slowly the thread attached to it turns through angle $\pi/4$ radians in clockwise direction and remains there almost motionless. When the angular velocity of the platform reaches value ω_2, the disc B begins to slide and catches the disc A thereafter both of them move together.

Chapter 3

Methods of Work and Energy

Concepts of energy, mechanical energy and power, work of a force, the work energy theorem, conservative and non-conservative forces, potential energy and associated conservative force, the law of conservation of mechanical energy.

"The words of language, as they are written or spoken, do not seem to play any role in my mechanism of thought. The physical entities, which seem to serve as elements in thought are certain signs and more or less clear images."

BACK TO BASICS

Concept of energy:

Energy is an entity stored in motion of a material particle due to its inertia or in stresses developed in a force creating mechanism that may be a material body or a force field. The first form is kinetic energy and the second is potential energy.

All forms of energy, which we know by different names as mechanical energy, thermal energy, electromagnetic energy, chemical energy, energy in waves etc. fundamentally consists of any one or both of the above two forms.

Mechanical energy of a system is the sum of kinetic energies due of some sort of regular motion of all the material particles of the system and potential energy due to configuration of the system.

Concept of mechanical work and power:

Work is transfer of mechanical energy to a material body.

When a material particle moves under action of a force $\vec{F}$, work of the force during an infinitesimal displacement $d\vec{r}$ is defined as scalar product of $\vec{F}$ and $d\vec{r}$.

$$dW = \vec{F} \cdot d\vec{r}$$

Albert Einstein
(14 March 1879 – 18 April 1955)

If a particle moves from a position $\vec{r}_i$ to a position $\vec{r}_f$, work of a force $\vec{F}$ acting on the particle over the entire path is expressed by the following equation.

$$W_{i \to f} = \int_{\vec{r}_i}^{\vec{r}_f} \vec{F} \cdot d\vec{r}$$

Work done by several simultaneous forces:

When several forces $\vec{F}_1$, $\vec{F}_2$, ... $\vec{F}_i$ .... $\vec{F}_n$ act simultaneously, the total work done by all these forces is algebraic sum of individual work of each force.

$$W_{i \to f} = \sum_{i=1}^{n} \int \vec{F}_i \cdot d\vec{r}$$

Power

Power of a force is defined as time rate at which the force does work.

$$p = \frac{dW}{dt} = \vec{F} \cdot \vec{v}$$

Work energy theorem:

When a particle moves from one position to another, total work of all the forces acting on the particle is equal to change in kinetic energy of the particle between the positions.

$$W_{i \to f} = \tfrac{1}{2} m v_f^2 - \tfrac{1}{2} m v_i^2 = K_f - K_i$$

Here the terms $\tfrac{1}{2} m v_i^2$ and $\tfrac{1}{2} m v_f^2$ are kinetic energies K_i and K_f of the particle at the initial and final positions.

Work energy theorem is applicable in all reference frames whether they are inertial or non-inertial.

While making use of the work energy theorem in a particular reference frame, consider velocities and displacement relative to the frame; moreover, if the frame is a non-inertial one, consider work of pseudo force in addition to the work of physical forces.

Conservative and non-conservative forces:

A conservative force has a property that if it does work in moving a particle from a position to another, the work must be independent of the path followed or equivalently the net work done by a conservative force around a closed path is zero.

$$\oint \vec{F} \cdot d\vec{r} = 0$$

- A conservative force must be a function of position and not of velocity or time.
- All uniform time independent forces are conservative forces.
- All the central time independent forces are conservative forces.

A central force at any point acts always towards or away from a fixed point and its magnitude depends on the distance from the fixed point.

Potential energy:

For an infinitely small change in configuration of a two-particle system, change in potential energy dU is equal to the negative of work done dW_c by internal conservative forces.

$$dU = -dW_c$$

Because only change in potential energy has significance, we can assign an arbitrary value to potential energy of a particular configuration and treat it as a reference value. This enables us to assign definite potential energies to other configurations.

The potential energy of a system consisting of a large number of particles is the sum of potential energies of all possible pairs of particles interacting through conservative forces.

Potential energy and associated conservative force:

The conservative force associated with a potential energy is equal to negative of gradient of the potential energy function.

$$\vec{F} = -\vec{\nabla} U = \begin{cases} -\left(\hat{i}\dfrac{\partial U}{\partial x} + \hat{j}\dfrac{\partial U}{\partial y} + \hat{k}\dfrac{\partial U}{\partial z} \right); & \text{Cartesian coordinates} \\ -\left(\hat{e}_r\dfrac{\partial U}{\partial r} + \hat{e}_\theta\dfrac{\partial U}{r\partial \theta} \right); & \text{Polar coordinates} \end{cases}$$

Potential energy and nature of equilibrium:

Depending on the nature of equilibrium of a system as stable or unstable, total potential energy of the system must be a local minima or a local maxima. If the system is in neutral equilibrium, the potential energy must be uniform over the range of change in configuration under consideration.

Law of conservation of mechanical energy:

Change in mechanical energy of a system is equal to the net work done by external forces ($W_{\text{ext, i}\to\text{f}}$) and internal non-conservative forces ($W_{\text{nc int, i}\to\text{f}}$).

$$W_{\text{ext, i}\to\text{f}} + W_{\text{nc int, i}\to\text{f}} = E_f - E_i = (K_f + U_f) - (K_i + U_i)$$

Mechanical energy of a system remains conserved, if total work of all the external forces and internal non-conservative forces is zero.

$$K_i + U_i = K_f + U_f$$

Multiple Choice Questions

1. Greater is the range, longer should be length of barrel of a gun. What is the reason behind this belief?

    (a) To allow better cooling of the gun due to increased surface area.
    (b) To allow the force of the expanding gases to act for a longer distance.
    (c) To increase the force exerted on the shell due to the expanding gases.
    (d) To provide a more favourable ratio of kinetic energy to potential energy.

2. You are in a paddleboat that is floating alongside a wooden block in a river. You are asked to perform following three experiments.
   I. Row your boat 20 m downstream ahead of the wooden block.
   II. Row your boat upstream to go 20 m away from the wooden block.
   III. Row your boat to move along the stream together with the block and simultaneously shift 20 m towards a bank.

   In all these experiments, you row your boat at a constant speed relative to water expending energies E_1, E_2 and E_3 respectively. Which of the following statements is correct?
   (a) $E_1 < E_2 < E_3$
   (b) $E_2 < E_1 < E_3$
   (c) $E_1 = E_2 = E_3$
   (d) It depends on reference frame you choose.

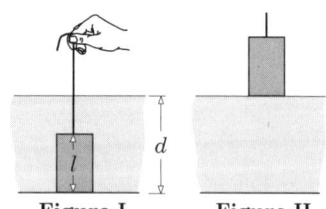

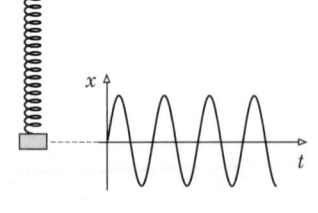

3. Two men move identical heavy boxes through equal distances on a horizontal floor (not frictionless) as shown. The first man is pushing, while the second is pulling the box with forces of equal magnitudes.
   I. Both the men deliver equal power.
   II. Both the men do equal amount of work.
   III. First man does more work than the second does.
   IV. First man delivers more power than the second one.
   V. Second man delivers more power than the first one.

   Which one of the following represents correct statements?
   (a) I and II   (b) II only
   (c) II and V   (d) III and IV

4. A solid right cylinder of length l stands upright at rest on the bottom of a large water reservoir, where depth is d as shown in the figure-I. Density of material of the cylinder is equal to that of water. Now the cylinder is slowly pulled out of water with the help of a thin light inextensible cord as shown in figure-II. Find the work done by the pulling agency.
   (a) $0.5mgl$ (b) mgl
   (c) mgd (d) $mg(0.5l + d)$

5. A spring-mass system oscillating in uniform gravity is shown in the figure. If we neglect all dissipative forces, it will keep on oscillating endlessly with constant amplitude and frequency. Accompanying graph shows how displacement x of the block from the equilibrium position varies with time t.

   Now at a certain instant when the block reaches its lowest position, gravity is switched off by some unknown mechanism. Which of the following graphs would correctly describe the changes taking place due to switching off the gravity?

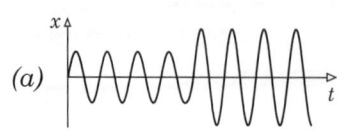
(a)

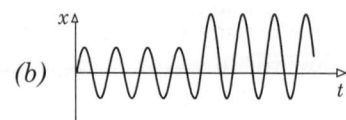
(b)

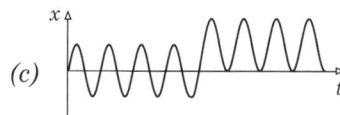 (c)

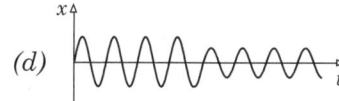 (d)

6. A potential energy function is shown in the graph. A particle moving in this potential field in the positive x-direction, if possesses 1.0 J of kinetic energy at $x = 1.0$ m, where will it reverse its direction of motion?
   (a) $x = 1.0$ m
   (b) $x = 2.0$ m
   (c) $x = 5.0$ m
   (d) $x = 6.0$ m

7. A ball of mass m is suspended from the ceiling with the help of an elastic cord. An additional downward force applied on the ball, if increased gradually to a value F_0, the cord would break. What should be the additional minimum constant force F that will break the cord?
   (a) $F = \frac{1}{2} F_0$
   (b) $F = \frac{1}{2} F_0 + mg$
   (c) $F = \frac{1}{2}(F_0 - mg)$
   (d) $F = \frac{1}{2}(F_0 + mg)$

8. A raindrop of mass m at a height h starts from rest and initially accelerates under gravity. Due to viscous drag of air, its motion is resisted and finally it acquires a constant terminal velocity v_T and hits the ground. Neglect the buoyancy; denote acceleration due to gravity by g and assume no wind. The magnitude of average viscous force on the raindrop during the entire downward trip is
   (a) $m\left(g + \dfrac{v_T^2}{h}\right)$
   (b) $m\left(g - \dfrac{v_T^2}{h}\right)$
   (c) $m\left(g + \dfrac{v_T^2}{2h}\right)$
   (d) $m\left(g - \dfrac{v_T^2}{2h}\right)$

9. Two identical ropes A and B of uniform mass per unit length are suspended from the ceiling and are made to pass through an almost inertia-less metallic tubular structure C as shown in the figure. The structure is made by welding two identical bent tubes. There is no friction between the ropes and the tubes. Initially the structure is held at rest and then released. What will happen?

   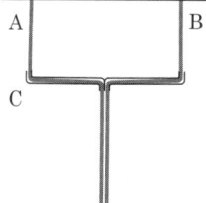

   (a) It will not move at all.
   (b) It will move downwards with speed decreasing at the rate 0.5g.
   (c) It will move downwards with speed increasing at the rate 0.5g.
   (d) The rope will heat up.

10. A slider is released from a point P on a frictionless track, which bends into a circular loop at its bottom. Height of the point P above the ground is selected such that the slider is just capable of moving round inside the circular loop without breaking contact anywhere. The circular loop is now made elliptical without altering its height. The slider is now released from a point Q as shown in the figure. If the slider again rounds the complete elliptical loop, the minimum height of Q above the ground

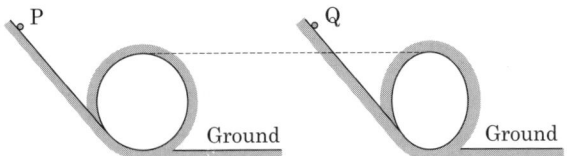

(a) should be less than that of P.
(b) should be equal to that of P.
(c) should be more than that of P.
(d) cannot be determined with the given information.

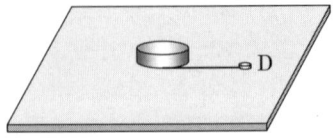

11. A small disk placed on a frictionless horizontal floor is attached at one end of a light inextensible cord, the other end of which is attached on a vertical cylinder fixed on the floor. The disc is projected with a certain velocity perpendicular to the cord and along the floor. How will the tensile force in the cord and speed of the disc change during the ensuing motion?

    (a) Both will increase.
    (b) Both will remain constant.
    (c) Tensile force will increase, and speed will decrease.
    (d) Tensile force will increase, and speed will remain constant.

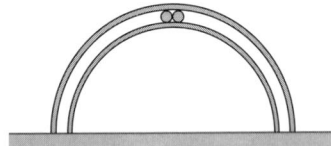

12. A semicircular rigid cylindrical tube is placed on a horizontal floor. Two identical balls that loosely fit inside the tube are simultaneously released from the top of the tube. Each ball moves down the tube on either side. Which of the following statements best describe the total force of normal reaction between the tube and the floor?

    (a) It decreases continually.
    (b) It increases continually.
    (c) It first decreases, acquires a minimum value then increases.
    (d) The tube may leave the ground.

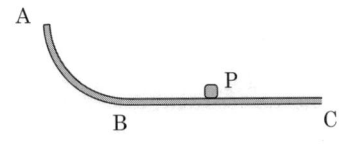

13. A frictionless rod ABC and a particle P of mass m are lying on a frictionless horizontal floor as shown in top view of the situation. The portion AB of the rod is bent to form a quarter of a circle. The rod is suddenly made to move with a constant velocity v towards the right along portion BC. What is the work done by the rod on the particle till it leaves the rod?

    (a) $0.5mv^2$ (b) mv^2
    (c) $2mv^2$ (d) None of these.

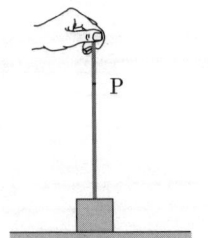

14. One end of an elastic cord is attached to a block of mass m and the other end is held keeping the cord relaxed and vertical. Relaxed length of the cord is l and there is a mark P at a height $0.8l$ from the lower end. If the upper end is slowly raised, the block leaves the ground, when the mark P reaches the point where the upper end of the relaxed cord initially was. Expression for the work done by the force applied by the hand is

    (a) $\dfrac{mgl}{16}$ (b) $\dfrac{mgl}{8}$
    (c) $\dfrac{mgl}{5}$ (d) $\dfrac{mgl}{4}$

15. A small block starts sliding down from point A on a slide of irregular shape as shown in the figure. Here x and y-axes represent the horizontal and the vertical directions respectively. Coefficient of friction between the slide and the block is 0.6 everywhere. Radius of curvature of the slide everywhere is large enough and speed of the block is small enough so that normal component of acceleration becomes negligible as compared to acceleration of free fall. At which point may the block stop?

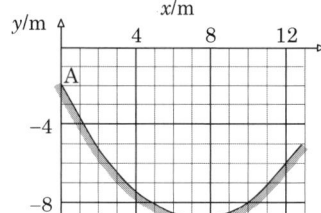

  (a) (5, −8) (b) (10, −8)
  (c) (12, −6) (d) Insufficient information

16. A spherical object of mass 60 kg is dropped from a very large height. Its speed at every 1.0 s interval is recorded and is represented in the velocity-time graph, but the experimenter forgot marking velocities. Line AB is a tangent to the graph at an instant $t = 5.0$ s. What is power of air resistance at the instant $t = 5.0$ s. Acceleration due to gravity is 10 m/s^2.

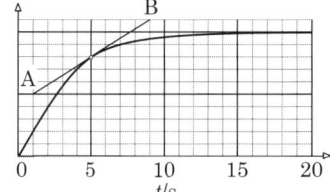

  (a) 0.6 kW (b) 10.24 kW
  (c) 15.0 kW (d) 24.0 kW

17. A light thin rod is bent into a right angle and a massive bead is affixed at the bend. The structure thus formed is placed on two frictionless platforms of different heights as shown in the figure. When the structure stays in equilibrium, what can you conclude regarding position of the ball relative to the vertical faces of the platforms?

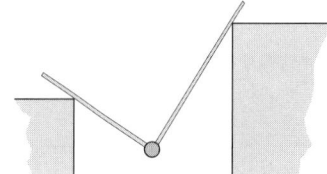

  (a) The ball is closer to the lower platform than the higher one.
  (b) The ball is closer to the higher platform than the lower one.
  (c) The ball is equidistant from both the platforms irrespective of their heights.
  (d) The ball is equidistant from both the platforms only when both the platforms are of the same height.

18. Two identical sleeves A and B each of mass m can slide without friction on a fixed horizontal rod. A load C of mass $2m$ is suspended from the mid-point of a light inextensible cord of length $l = 3\sqrt{3}$ m connecting the sleeves A and B. Initially the sleeves are at a separation l and the load is held motionless. What can you conclude for subsequent motion after the load is released? Acceleration of free fall is 10 m/s^2.

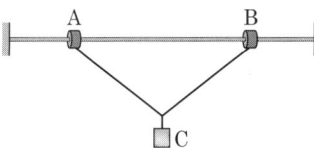

  (a) Maximum speed of the sleeves is $\sqrt{10}$ m/s.
  (b) Maximum speed acquired by the load C is $2\sqrt{5}$ m/s.
  (c) The load descends a height 1.5 m to acquire maximum speed.
  (d) Before the sleeves collide, the net force on the system consisting of the sleeves, the cord and the load becomes zero once.

19. A box of mass 1.0 kg moving horizontally with a velocity 10 m/s towards the left, is gently placed on a conveyor belt that is moving horizontally with a velocity 10 m/s towards the right. Coefficient of kinetic friction between the belt and the block is 0.5. Some physical quantities and their possible value in SI units are mentioned in the given table. Suggest suitable matches.

3.8 Chapter-3

Immediately after the block is placed on the conveyor (figure: block with 10 m/s leftward on conveyor belt moving 10 m/s rightward)

Modulus in SI	Physical Quantity
(a) zero	(p) Work of friction on the block with respect to the ground
(b) 20	(q) Work of friction on the block with respect to the belt
(c) 40	(r) Work of friction on the belt with respect to the ground
(d) 200	(s) Distance slid by the block on the belt with respect to the belt
	(t) Change in momentum of the block with respect to the ground

20. A particle moves from point A to point B then to point C and finally back to A under action of a force. Magnitudes of the work done by the force in these displacements are W_{AB}, W_{BC} and W_{CA} respectively. Suggest suitable match or matches.

Column I	Column II
(a) The force is conservative and $W_{AB} = W_{BC} \neq 0$	(p) W_{CA} may be zero
(b) The force is non-conservative and $W_{AB} = W_{BC} \neq 0$	(q) W_{CA} may be > zero
(c) The force is conservative and $\|W_{AB}\| > \|W_{BC}\|$	(r) W_{CA} may be = W_{BC}
(d) The force is non-conservative and $\|W_{AB}\| > \|W_{BC}\|$	(s) $\|W_{CA}\|$ may be > $\|W_{BC}\|$

Questions 21 to 23 are based on the following physical situation

A conveyor belt collects sand and transports it to a height h as shown in the figure. The sand falls on the belt with negligible speed at constant rate μ (mass per unit time). Friction between the belt and the sand particle is so high that the sand particles stop sliding almost instantaneously after they hit the belt. Acceleration due to gravity is g.

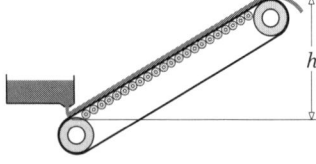

21. What should speed of the belt be for the least possible driving force on the belt applied by the motor?

(a) $\sqrt{0.5gh}$ (b) $\sqrt{gh}$
(c) $\sqrt{2gh}$ (d) A speed however small is possible.

22. What is the power delivered by the motor to the belt, when the motor is applying least possible driving force?

(a) $0.5\mu gh$ (b) μgh
(c) $1.5\mu gh$ (d) $2\mu gh$

23. What is the power dissipated by the sand-belt system, when the motor is applying least possible driving force?

(a) Zero   (b) $0.25\mu gh$
(c) $0.5\mu gh$ (d) μgh

Build up your understanding

1. Efficiency of an engine is measured to be 24% in an experiment running the engine at constant throttle. After the experiment, it was found that 4% of the fuel used in the experiment had actually leaked through a faulty gasket. Find efficiency of the engine after repair of the gasket.

2. Two uniform hemispheres A and B are concentrically fixed to each other and the composite body thus formed is placed on a horizontal floor as shown. Masses of the hemisphere A and B are m_A and m_B and their radii are r_A and r_B respectively. Find conditions for stable, unstable and neutral equilibria of the composite body in the situation shown.

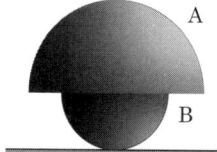

3. Two small identical discs each of mass $m = 1.0$ kg placed on a frictionless horizontal floor are connected by a light inextensible cord of length $l = 1.0$ m. Now the midpoint of the cord is pulled perpendicular to the line joining centres of the discs by a constant force $F = 2.0$ N. What is velocity of approach of the discs, when they are about to collide?

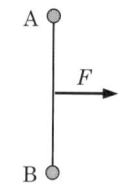

4. On a horizontal surface of non-uniform texture, friction varies from point to point. On this surface a small disc projected with speed 5 m/s covers 10 m along a straight path before it stops. Variation in speed v of the disc with distance s covered is shown in the figure. If the disc is projected with speed 4 m/s from the same initial point in the same direction, how much total distance will it cover?

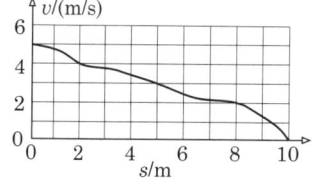

5. A small block when released on an inclined plane, it first slides down and then stops after sliding down a height h. This strange behavior is due to the coefficient of friction that is here proportional to the distance slid by the block. Find the maximum speed of the block during this motion. Acceleration due to gravity is g.

6. An experimenter throws a ball of mass $m = 1.0$ kg vertically upwards with a velocity $u = 4.0$ m/s from the top of a high tower. During the flight of the ball, modulus of the force of air resistance on the ball is given by equation $F = kv$, here $k = 0.41$ kg/s and v is the speed of the ball. The tower is so high that the ball achieves a constant speed before striking the ground. Find the velocity of the ball when its kinetic energy changes most rapidly. Acceleration due to gravity is $g = 10$ m/s².

7. A piston of mass M with a ball of mass m rests inside a fixed long vertical tube due to frictional forces acting between the periphery of the piston and the inner surface of the tube. The ball is raised to height h above the piston and then released. All the collisions of the ball with the piston are perfectly elastic. Net frictional force on the piston has a constant value F that is more than the total weight of the ball and the piston. How far will the piston eventually move down in the tube? Acceleration due to gravity is g and air resistance is negligible.

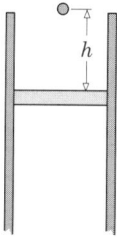

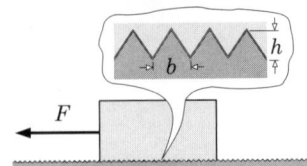

8. In a very simple experiment suggested to understand contribution of surface irregularities on the force of dry friction, a portion of a floor in a laboratory and bottom of a block are knurled by cutting V-shape parallel grooves of very small dimensions (height h and width b). The block is placed on the floor so that their grooves exactly fit into each other as shown in the figure and then the block is pulled with a constant velocity perpendicular to the grooves. Assuming faces of the grooves frictionless and collisions between them completely inelastic, suggest a suitable expression for an effective coefficient of kinetic friction.

9. A plank is being pushed on a frictionless horizontal floor with a constant velocity $u = 1.5$ m/s. When a block is gently placed on the plank, it slides for a while, acquires velocity of the plank and then moves together with the plank. If the agency pushing the plank has to do a work $W = 11.25$ J during the sliding of the block, find mass of the block.

10. A boy is holding one end of an inextensible cord supporting a block of mass m at its lower end. From this block, another block of mass M is suspended with the help of a light spring of stiffness k. The boy brings the assembly over a table and lowers it until the lower block touches the tabletop and then releases the cord. How far will the upper block move before coming to an instantaneous rest first time?

11. A ball of mass m is suspended in a box of mass M with the help of a light spring of force constant k and the setup is placed on a horizontal floor as shown in the figure. With what maximum amplitude can the ball oscillate up and down so that the box remains standstill? Acceleration of free fall is g.

12. A spring is inserted in a 2.0 m long transparent pipe held vertically on a floor and then the lower ends of the spring and the pipe are glued on the floor. Inner surface of the pipe is frictionless. A ball is dropped into the pipe. Kinetic energy of the ball is recorded at various heights above the floor and the data thus obtained are shown in the following graph.

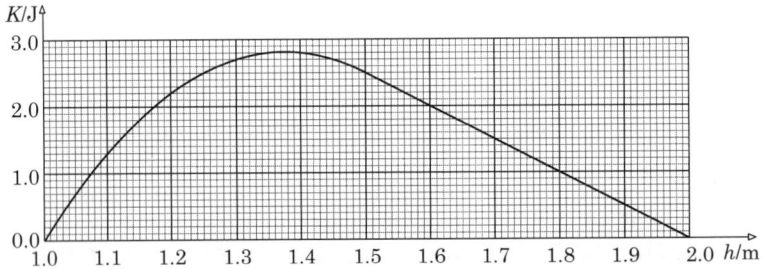

Determine length of the relaxed spring, stiffness of the spring and mass of the ball. Assume the collision of the ball with the upper end of the spring to be lossless, the Hooke's law to be valid for deformations of the spring under consideration and acceleration of free fall to be 10 m/s².

13. A bar of mass M rests in equilibrium on a vertical spring, lower end of which is affixed on the ground. Now a block of mass m is held on the bar without exerting any force on it and then the block is released. How much maximum force the bar will apply on the block during the subsequent motion? Acceleration of free fall is g.

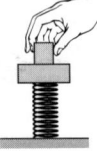

14. A bar supporting a block on its top is placed on a frictionless plank that rests on a horizontal floor. The bar is attached to a nail driven into the plank with the help of a spring as shown in the figure. Coefficient of friction between the bar and the block is μ. What maximum acceleration parallel to the spring can the plank be given preventing sliding between the block and the bar? Acceleration due to gravity is g.

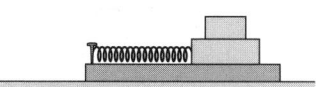

15. A block of mass $m = 1.0$ kg placed on a floor is connected at one end of a long spring of stiffness $k = 100$ N/m. Coefficient of kinetic friction between the floor and the block is $\mu_k = 0.47$. The free end of the spring is pulled gradually away from the block until the block begins to slide. If the block stops after sliding a distance $s = 0.6$ cm in one stroke, find coefficient of static friction between the block and the floor.

16. In the arrangement shown, the blocks have masses m_1 and m_2, the spring constant is k and coefficient of friction is μ. Initially the lower block is held at rest keeping the spring relaxed and the vertical and horizontal segments of the cord straight. Find maximum possible speeds of the blocks after the lower block is released.

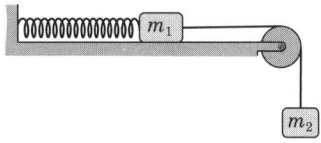

17. In the setup shown, an almost inertia-less bar is suspended horizontally with the help of two identical springs each of stiffness k, two light inextensible cords that pass over fixed ideal pulleys and two counterweights each of mass m. A small disc of mass $0.01m$ is placed at the midpoint of the bar. A block of mass $1.99m$ is suspended from the disc with the help of a light cord that passes through a hole in the bar. If this cord is cut, up to what maximum height will the disc jump?

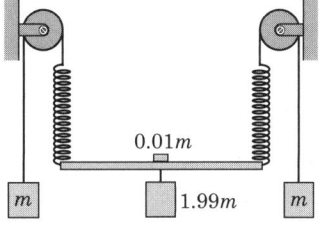

18. In bungee jumping, a performer ties one end of an elastic cord with his feet and the other end to a fixed support on a very high place and then jumps off. A bungee jumper of height $h = 1.5$ m and mass $m = 66$ kg has to jump from a tower of height $H = 62.5$ m. The bungee cord available is $l_0 = 30$ m long and has a force constant $k = 33$ N/m. If the minimum safe clearance from the ground is $d = 1.0$ m, what maximum length of this cord can the bungee jumper use?

19. An elastic light cord of length 10 m is taut between two nails that are in the same level. A load suspended at the midpoint of the cord, if allowed to move gradually, stops after descending a height $y_1 = 1$ cm. If the same load is dropped from a height above the midpoint of the cord, the load on striking the midpoint sticks there and then descends a maximum height $y_2 = 2$ cm. Assuming collision of the load with the cord to be lossless, estimate the height above the cord from where the load was dropped.

20. A horizontal frictionless thin rod wearing a sleeve of mass m is being rotated at a constant angular velocity ω about a stationary vertical axis through one of its ends. The sleeve is held stationary with respect to the rod at a distance $r = r_1$ from the axis with the help of a light cord as shown in the figure. At some instant of time, the cord is cut. Find work done by the external agency in maintaining the angular velocity of the rod constant until the sleeve slides to a distance $r = r_2$.

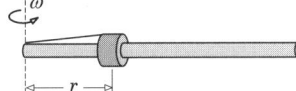

21. A disc placed on a large horizontal floor is connected from a vertical cylinder of radius r fixed on the floor with the help of a light inextensible cord of length l as shown in the figure. Coefficient of friction between the disc and the floor is μ. The disc is given a velocity u parallel to the floor and perpendicular to the cord. How long will the disc slide on the floor before it hits the cylinder?

22. A marble is being whirled on a circular path in a vertical plane with the help of a light inextensible cord of length $l = 50$ cm around a fixed center O. If the cord is cut when the ball is at the bottom of the circular path, the ball hits the horizontal ground at point A and if the cord is cut when the ball is at top of the circular path, the ball hits the ground at point B a distance $d = 4.8$ m away from the point A. If points A and B are equidistant from centre O, find the height of centre O above the ground. Ignore effects of air resistance.

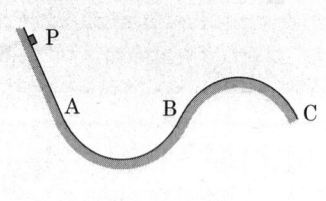

23. A point mass can slide in a vertical plane on a frictionless curvilinear track as shown in the figure. Sections AB and BC of the track are circular arcs each of angular span 120° and radius r. From what minimum height above the bottom of section AB should a small block P be released so that it certainly loses contact with the track?

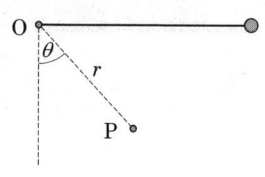

24. A small ball P is suspended from a fixed nail O with the help of a light inextensible cord of length l. There is another nail P at a distance r from O. The ball is pulled aside stretching the cord horizontal and released. In the ensuing motion, the cord clings to the nail P and the ball begins to turn around nail P. Find range of values of r, so that the ball makes a complete circular turn around the nail P. Ignore air resistance and radii of the nails.

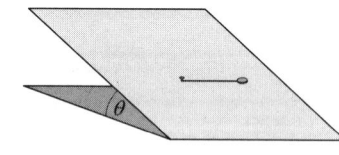

25. A small disc of mass m placed on a plane of inclination $\theta = \cos^{-1}(0.8)$ with the horizontal is connected from a nail driven into the plane with the help of a light inextensible cord of length $l = 1.0$ m. Coefficient of friction between the plane and the disc is $\mu = 3/8$. The disc is held on the plane stretching the cord horizontal as shown in the figure and released. Find maximum speed of the disc and angular displacement where tensile force in the cord becomes maximum during subsequent motion

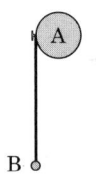

26. A light cord of length l is attached to a nail driven into curved surface of a cylinder A of radius r ($l > \pi r$). The cylinder is fixed with its axis horizontal. A small ball B of mass m is hanging at the lower end of the cord. How much horizontal velocity must be imparted to the ball B so that the cord will certainly slack during the subsequent motion?

27. A prototype train of length $l = 168$ m is running at a constant speed v with its engine off on horizontal portion of a track that has a hilly portion as shown in the figure. Dimensions of the hilly portion are $a = 60$ m, $b = 80$ m and $c = 100$ m respectively.

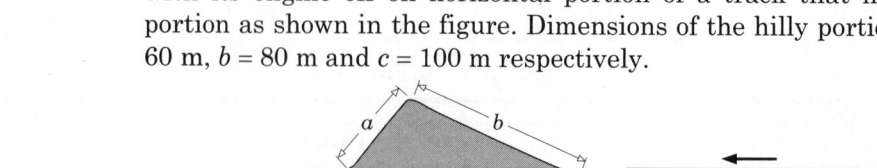

What should the minimum speed of the train be to pass over the hill? For simplicity, assume size of a bogie negligible as compared to the rounded portions of the hill and size of the rounded portions as compared to the straight portions. All kinds of resistive and frictional forces are absent. Use acceleration of free fall $g = 10$ m/s².

28. A system of blocks A and B of masses m_1 and m_2 connected by a spring of force constant k_1 is placed on a spring of force constant k_2, which rests on the ground. Both the springs are vertical and the whole system is in equilibrium. Find increment in gravitational potential energy of the system in lifting the block A upwards until the lower spring becomes relaxed.

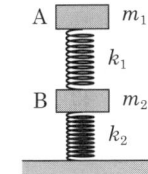

29. When a particle passes a point (x, y) in a force field created by stationary sources, potential energy of the system associated with the force field is given by equation $U = kx/(x^2 + y^2)^{3/2}$. If at a position $\vec{r} = r_0(\hat{i} + \hat{j})$, the particle is observed moving perpendicular to $\vec{r}$, find the tangential and normal components of acceleration of the particle at this point.

30. A ball of mass m projected horizontally from the top of a tower with kinetic energy K flies in the air for a time interval τ before it hits the horizontal ground. If force of air drag is proportional to the speed, and the proportionality constant is k, find horizontal range of the ball.

31. Two long and four half as long light rods are hinged at their ends to form a pantograph consisting of two identical rhombi. The pantograph is suspended from the ceiling, the lowest hinge of the pantograph is connected to the hinge above it by a light inextensible cord and a load of mass m is suspended from the lowest hinge as shown in the figure. Find the tensile force developed in the cord connecting the two hinges.

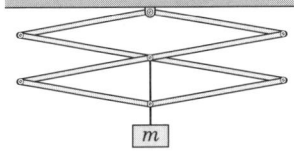

Check your understanding

1. A stone of mass $m = 5$ kg is fixed at one end of a uniform flexible chain of linear mass density $\lambda = 0.5$ kg/m. Assembly thus formed is placed on the ground. If the stone is projected vertically upwards with a velocity $v_0 = 20\sqrt{6}$ m/s, how high will the stone rise for the following two given lengths of the chain? Assume air resistance negligible and acceleration due to gravity $g = 10$ m/s².

    (a) Length of the chain is 60 m. (b) Length of the chain is 30 m.

2. A particle like ball is connected to one end of a light inextensible cord, the other end of which is connected to a very thin frictionless fixed vertical rod. The entire length of the cord is wound around the rod into a large number of closely spaced turns and the ball is held touching the rod. When the ball is released, the cord gradually unwinds, and the ball starts circling the rod. What angle does the cord make while it is unwinding the rod?

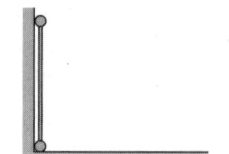
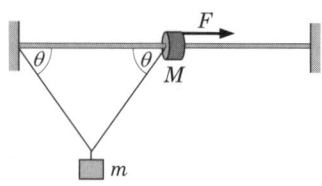
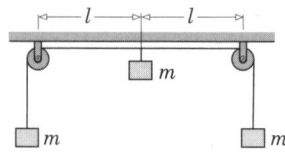
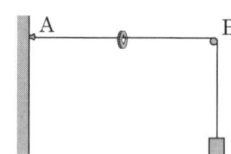

3. A dumbbell constructed by affixing small identical balls each of mass m at the ends of a light rod of length l stands vertically on a frictionless floor touching a frictionless wall as shown in the figure. If the lower ball is gently pushed away from the wall, the dumbbell begins to slide. Denoting acceleration due to gravity by g, find expression for speed of the lower ball, when the upper ball is leaving the wall.

4. A sleeve of mass $M = 10$ kg can slide on a horizontal frictionless rod. A block of mass $m = 2.0$ kg is suspended at the mid-point of a light inextensible cord of length $l = 102.5$ cm, one end of which is attached to the sleeve and the other to one end of the rod. Initially the sleeve is held at rest and the angle between the rod and a cord segment is $\theta = \theta_0 = \sin^{-1}(0.8)$ as shown in the figure. If a constant horizontal force $F = 50$ N is applied on the sleeve, find its speed when the angle between cord segments and the rod becomes $\theta = \sin^{-1}(0.6)$?

5. In the arrangement shown, the middle block is initially held at rest keeping the portion of cord between the pulleys straight and then released. Find its acceleration when the two segments of the cord between the pulleys make a right angle. Neglect friction everywhere and denote acceleration of free fall by g.

6. A light inextensible cord tied at on one end to peg A on a wall, passes over a frictionless peg B fixed in level with the peg A and supports a load at the other end. Between the pegs, the cord is wearing a small ring of mass equal to that of the load. Initially the ring is held in level with the pegs as shown in the figure and then released. Determine acceleration of the ring when the block passes an equilibrium position. Acceleration of free fall is g.

7. A boat installed with two engines commutes between two towns P and Q connected by a river. The boat takes $t_1 = 50.00$ min on its way from P to Q with only one engine on and $t_2 = 25.00$ min with both the engines on. Force of water resistance is proportional to velocity of the boat relative to the water. Assume water flow velocity to be uniform and the boat always moves with respect to water with its maximum possible velocity.

(a) What minimum time will the boat take on its way from Q to P with one engine on?

(b) What minimum time will the boat take on its way from Q to P with both the engines on?

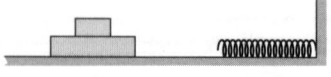

8. A block of mass m is placed on a bar of mass M, which rests on a frictionless horizontal floor. The floor terminates into a wall where an ideal spring is attached as shown in the figure. When the spring is compressed by an amount l, all inter-turn spacing of the spring vanishes. Coefficient of friction between the bar and the block is μ. If the bar is pushed towards the wall so that it strikes the spring with a velocity u, what should be range of spring constant so that the block does not slide relative to the bar?

9. A portion of the floor in a laboratory is made frictionless. A homogeneous bar of length $l = 1.0$ m placed on the frictionless portion perpendicular

its boundary is being dragged by pulling it with the help of a light spring of force constant $k = 4.0$ N/m as shown in the figure. If the pulling agency drags the entire bar out of the frictionless portion by performing minimum amount of work that is $W_{min} = 17.5$ J, how much energy is lost as heat in this pulling process?

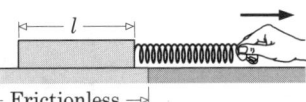

Frictionless

10. A block of mass 1.0 kg placed on a horizontal floor is attached to a fixed nail with the help of a spring of stiffness 5.0 N/cm. Coefficient of friction between the block and the floor is 0.25. The block is pulled away from the nail stretching the spring by an amount 8.5 cm and released. Find the final deformation of the spring when the block stops. How many times did the spring become relaxed during this process? Acceleration of gravity is 10 m/s².

11. A light elastic cord of force constant k and relaxed length l is suspended from the ceiling. A bead of mass m threaded on the cord is held motionless close to the ceiling and released. If the bead slides down the cord with a constant speed v relative to the ceiling, find expression for thermal power dissipated during sliding of the bead.

12. A special box used to store several plate-like articles contains a light spring loaded piston inside it. When the box is empty, the piston touches the top inner surface of the box. The plates can be inserted or pulled out through an opening at the top of the box as shown in the figure. Initially the box contains $n = 20$ identical square plates each of edge length $l = 5$ cm. Coefficient of friction between all the surfaces in contact is $\mu = 0.5$. All the plates are pulled out one by one in two different trials, in the first trial the opening was at the top and in the second trial the box was inverted. If difference of work done by the agent pulling the plates in both these trials is $\Delta W = 10$ J, calculate mass of a plate.

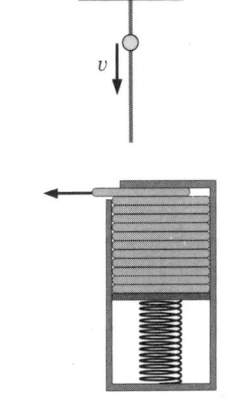

13. A light elastic cord of length $l_0 = 5.0$ m and stiffness $k = 50$ N/m is inside a fixed box with a small portion of length $x_0 = 20$ cm left out of a hole on a wall of the box as shown in the figure. If the cord is pulled out of the box, a frictional force $F = 25$ N acts on the cord. How much work has to be done in slowly pulling out the entire length of the cord?

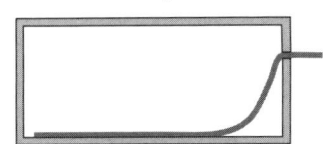

14. A small disc of mass m on an inclined plane of inclination θ with the horizontal is connected to a nail driven into the plane with the help of a light inextensible cord of length l. Coefficient of friction between the plane and the disc is $\mu = \tan\theta$. The disc is given such a horizontal velocity at the lowest position that it moves on a complete circular path around the nail without wrapping the cord on the nail.

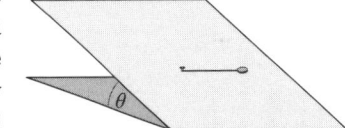

(a) Where is the disc when tensile force in the cord becomes minimum?
(b) How much minimum velocity should be given to the disk at the lowest position to round a complete circle?

15. A particle like ball is projected horizontally from a point at a height h above the centre of a hemispherical dome of radius $R = 10\sqrt{2}$ m. The height h is greater than the radius of the dome. The ball touches the dome and thereafter strikes the ground. Find the minimum speed of the ball when it hits the ground, corresponding velocity of projection and the height h. Acceleration due to gravity is $g = 10$ m/s².

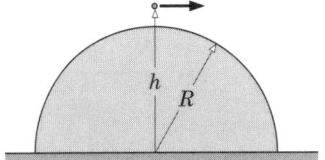

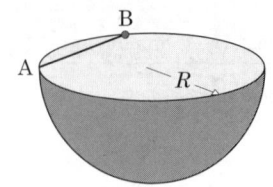

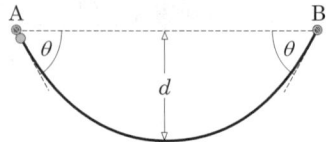

16. Consider a fixed hemispherical bowl of radius R with its opening horizontal. One end of a light rod of length $l = R$ is hinged at a point A on the brim of the bowl. A small bead of mass m is attached at the other end the rod. Initially the bead is held at a point B also on the brim and then released. Find the tensile force in the rod when the bead passes the lowest position. Acceleration of free fall is g.

17. A massive homogeneous rope of length l is suspended between two nails A and B driven in the same horizontal level. The rope makes angle θ with the horizontal at the nails and its lowest point is at a depth d below the nails. A bead threaded in the rope released from the nail A slides down the rope without friction. If the bead is so light that the shape of the rope remains unaffected, find acceleration of the bead when it passes the lowest point of the rope.

Challenge your understanding

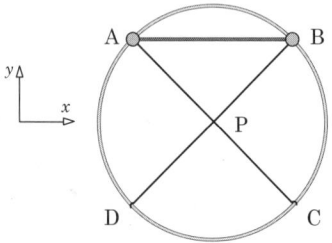

1. Two identical beads A and B each of mass m connected by a light rod of length $r\sqrt{2}$ can slide without friction on a fixed ring of radius r. The beads are also connected to fixed points C and D with identical elastic cords each of force constant k and relaxed length $r\sqrt{2}$ as shown in the figure. Initially the cords coincide with diameters of the ring and the system is in equilibrium. Now the bead-rod assembly is displaced slightly aside and released. Find acceleration of the point of intersection P of the cords immediately before a cord becomes relaxed.

2. A ball dropped from a certain height, bounces off the ground repeatedly and losing some of its energy in every bounce, it stops bouncing after a certain number of hits. Consider a ball of mass $m = 0.2$ kg and radius $r = 10$ cm. When it hits the ground, it gets deformed and while leaving the ground, it completely regains its shape and in one collision half of the elastic potential energy stored during deformation is lost. In addition, assume that during a collision with the ground, the part not touching the ground remains spherical and the bottom flat creating a uniform pressure of $p = 0.2$ atm. If the ball is dropped from a height $h = 1.0$ m, how many times will it bounce off (i.e. leave) the ground?

Answers and Hints

Multiple Choice Questions

1. (b)
2. (c)
3. (c)
4. (a)
5. (b)
6. (d)
7. (a)
8. (d)
9. (c)
10. (a)
11. (d)
12. (c) and (d)
13. (b)
14. (b)
15. (b)
16. (c)
17. (c)
18. (b), (c) and (d)
19. (a) → (p)
    (b) → (t)
    (c) → (s)
    (d) → (q) and (r)
20. (a)→(q) and (s)
    (b)→(p), (q), (r) and (s)
    (c)→(q), (r) and (s)
    (d)→(p), (q), (r) and (s)
21. (b)
22. (d)
23. (c)

Build up your understanding

1. 25%

2. For stable equilibrium: $m_A r_A < m_B r_B$
   For unstable equilibrium: $m_A r_A > m_B r_B$
   For neutral equilibrium: $m_A r_A = m_B r_B$

3. $\sqrt{\dfrac{2Fl}{m}} = 2.0$ m/s

   Hint: Component of tensile force in the cord along the direction of the pull is always $F/2$.

4. 5 m

   Hint: In the given situation, even though the coefficient of friction depends on location, yet it remains constant with time at a particular location. Therefore, work done by friction on a body sliding on the surface in a segment of path remains unchanged.

5. $\sqrt{\dfrac{gh}{2}}$

6. ≈ 12.2 m/s

7. $\dfrac{mgh}{F-(m+M)g}$

   Hint: Gravitational potential energy lost has been consumed in doing work against the friction.

8. $\dfrac{h}{b}$

   Hint: Kinetic energy gained every time falling a distance h is lost in the inelastic collisions. The work done by average force pulling the upper block horizontally is continuously supplying the losses.

9. $\dfrac{W}{u^2} = 5.0$ kg

   Hint: The work done by the pushing agency is partly utilized in increasing kinetic energy of the block and partly consumed in losses. Furthermore, the losses are independent of reference frame.

10. $\dfrac{2(m+M)g}{k}$ downwards

11. $\dfrac{(m+M)g}{k}$

    Hint: At the time of maximum compression, the spring force must be equal to the weight of the box.

12. 1.5 m, 40 N/m, 0.5 kg

13. $mg\left(\dfrac{M+2m}{M+m}\right)$

14. $\dfrac{\mu g}{2}$

   Hint: The only force providing acceleration to the block-bar system is the spring force. Therefore, if the block does not slide on the bar acceleration provided by the spring force at the instant of its maximum elongation must not exceed μg.

15. $\mu_s = \mu_k + \dfrac{ks}{2mg} = 0.50$

   Hint: During sliding, change in stored potential energy in spring is consumed into work done against force of kinetic friction.

16. $\dfrac{(m_2 - \mu_k m_1)g}{\sqrt{k(m_1 + m_2)}}$

   Hint: After the block m_1 begins sliding, it speeds up, till the resultant spring force and force of kinetic friction balances the weight of m_2.

17. $\approx \dfrac{100 mg}{k}$

18. $(H - h - d)\left\{\left(1 + \dfrac{mg}{kl_0}\right) - \sqrt{\left(1 + \dfrac{mg}{kl_0}\right)^2 - 1}\right\} = 20$ m

   Hint: Speed of the performer must vanish as he approaches the safe clearance height above the ground.

19. $\approx \left(\dfrac{1}{4}\left(\dfrac{y_2}{y_1}\right)^3 - 1\right) y_2 = 2$ cm

   Hint: Find force constant by analysing equilibrium in the first case and then use work-energy theorem in the second case. Take care of suitable approximations.

20. $m\omega^2 (r_2^2 - r_1^2)$

   Hint: During the process, the radial (along the rod) as well as the transverse component of velocity of the sleeve increases.

21. $= \begin{cases} \dfrac{u}{\mu g}; & \text{If } u \leq l\sqrt{\dfrac{\mu g}{r}} \\ \dfrac{u}{\mu g}\left(1 - \sqrt{1 - \dfrac{\mu g l^2}{u^2 r}}\right); & \text{If } u \geq l\sqrt{\dfrac{\mu g}{r}} \end{cases}$

22. $\sqrt{l^2 + \dfrac{d^2}{16}} = 1.3$ m

23. $0.75 r$

   Hint: The sliding mass moving at the smallest possible speed will leave contact immediately after it crosses point B.

24. $r \geq \dfrac{3l}{2\cos\theta + 3}$

   Hint: No energy will be lost in the collision of the cord with the nail and after this collision; the ball has to follow a circular path.

25. $\sqrt{(6\sqrt{3} - 2\pi)}$ and $\cos^{-1}\left(\dfrac{2\mu}{3\tan\theta}\right) = \cos^{-1}(1/3)$

   Hint: When speed acquires its maximum value, tangential acceleration vanishes.

26. $\sqrt{2g(l - r)} < v < \sqrt{g(5l - 3\pi r)}$

   Hint: At every instant, the point of contact of the cord with the cylinder is at rest, therefore the ball can be thought moving on a path of radius of curvature equal to unwound length of the cord and with its velocity vector always perpendicular to the unwound length. Therefore, power of tensile force of the cord at every instant is zero, and hence work done by this tensile force over any length of path must be zero.

27. $\sqrt{g\dfrac{(a+b)ab}{cl}} = 20$ m/s

   Hint: In the configuration of maximum gravitational potential energy, the maximum portion of the train must be elevated above the ground.

   Since length of the train is more than the segment of the track on the hill, therefore in maximum potential energy configuration, the train must cover the whole segment of the track on the hill.

28. $\dfrac{(m_1+m_2)\{k_1(m_1+m_2)+m_1k_2\}g^2}{k_1k_2}$

29. $\dfrac{k}{4\sqrt{2}mr_0^3}(-\hat{i}+\hat{j})$ and $\dfrac{k}{2\sqrt{2}mr_0^3}(\hat{i}+\hat{j})$

30. $\dfrac{\sqrt{2Km}}{k}\left\{1-\exp\left(-\dfrac{k\tau}{m}\right)\right\}$

31. $2mg$

Check your understanding

1. (a) $\sqrt{\left(\dfrac{m}{\lambda}\right)^2+\dfrac{mv_0^2}{\lambda g}}-\dfrac{m}{\lambda}=40$ m

   Hint: The chain is partially in air and partially on the ground.

   (b) $\dfrac{mv_0^2+\lambda gl^2}{2g(m+\lambda l)}=41.25$ m

   Hint: The chain is completely hanging with the stone in air.

2. $\approx \tan^{-1}\sqrt{2}$

   Hint: As the rod is very thin, the path of the ball can be assumed to be almost a horizontal circle expanding as well as descending at negligible speeds. Under these reasonable assumptions, write kinetic energy of the ball at an instant and equate it with work done by gravity till that instant without appreciable loss in accuracy.

3. $\sqrt{\dfrac{8gl}{27}}$

   Hint: The moment when the upper ball is leaving the wall, the speed of the lower ball acquires its maximum value.

4. $\sqrt{\dfrac{4l\{2F(\cos\theta-\cos\theta_0)-mg(\sin\theta_0-\sin\theta)\}}{4M+m\operatorname{cosec}^2\theta}}$

   $=1.2$ m/s

5. $\dfrac{g}{4}$ upwards

6. $\dfrac{3(2\sqrt{3}-3)}{8}g$

7. (a) $\dfrac{t_1t_2(\sqrt{2}-1)}{2t_1-(\sqrt{2}+1)t_2}=13.06$ min

   (b) $\dfrac{t_1t_2(\sqrt{2}-1)}{(\sqrt{2}+1)t_1-2\sqrt{2}t_1}=10.35$ min

   Hint: Maximum speed of the boat with both the engines on is √2 times the maximum speed with one engine on. This information together with the time intervals t_1 and t_2 suggests that the river is flowing from the town Q towards the town P.

8. $= \begin{cases} \dfrac{(m+M)u^2}{l^2}\leq k\leq\dfrac{(m+M)\mu^2g^2}{u^2}; & u<\sqrt{\mu gl} \\ k=\dfrac{(m+M)g}{l}; & u=\sqrt{\mu gl} \\ \text{Phenomenon is not possible}; & u>\sqrt{\mu gl} \end{cases}$

9. $\dfrac{l\sqrt{k^2l^2+8kW_{\min}}-kl^2}{4}=5$ J

   Hint: To minimize the work, the bar must be pulled at negligible speed. When the bar leaves the frictionless portion, its kinetic energy is almost zero and spring is extended under the applied force, which is equal to the frictional force. Therefore, the minimum work done equals the sum of magnitudes of stored potential energy in the spring and the heat lost, which is the work against the frictional forces.

10. 4.5 cm and 4

11. $mgv\left\{\dfrac{mg+2kl}{2(mg+kl)}\right\}$

12. $\dfrac{\Delta W}{2\mu n^2 lg} = 5 \times 10^{-2}\,\text{kg}$

Hint: Normal reaction and hence the friction force between any pair of surfaces sliding on each other is partly contributed by spring force and partly by gravity. Work done by the part of friction forces contributed by the spring force cancels out in the given difference operation.

13. $F(l_0 - x_0) + \dfrac{F^2}{k}\left(1 - \dfrac{x_0}{2l_0}\right) = 132.25\,\text{J}$

Hint: The agency pulling the cord first has to extend it till the pulling force becomes slightly greater than the frictional force and thereafter continue pulling the free end with a constant force till the last end of the cord comes out of the hole.

14. (a) At angular displacement $\sin^{-1}(2/3)$ after it crosses the top point on the line of the greatest slope through the nail.

(b) $\sqrt{4\pi gl \sin\theta}$

15. $\sqrt{\dfrac{gR}{\sqrt{2}}} = 10\,\text{m/s}$ and $\dfrac{3R}{2\sqrt{2}} = 15\,\text{m}$

Hint: The ball would strike the ground with minimum speed only when it was projected with minimum mechanical energy.

16. $mg\sqrt{3}$

17. $\dfrac{4gd\tan\theta}{l}$

Hint: Resultant of vertical components of the tensile force at two infinitely close points on both sides of the bottom equals the weight of the portion of the rope between these points. Make use of this fact to find the radius of curvature at the bottom.

Challenge your understanding

1. $-\hat{i}\left\{\dfrac{k(2-\sqrt{2})^2 r}{m\sqrt{2}}\right\}$

Hint: The intersection point P will move on a circular path with centre at the mid-point of chord DC.

2. $\dfrac{h}{2^n} \geq \dfrac{mg}{2\pi rp} \Rightarrow n = 12$

Hint: Vertical displacement ($h/2^n$) of centre of the sphere after the nth bounce when becomes smaller than static deformation (decrease in radial dimension at the contact with ground) due to weight in equilibrium position, the sphere will not be able to lose contact with the ground.

Chapter 4

Methods of Impulse and Momentum and System of Particles

Concept of impulse of a force, the impulse momentum principle, conservation of linear momentum, collision, system of particles and concept of centre of mass, dynamics of a system of particles from centre of mass frame, variable system of particles.

"I consider that I understand an equation when I can predict the properties of its solutions, without actually solving it."

BACK TO BASICS

Impulse of a force:

Linear impulse or simply impulse of a force $\vec{F}$ over a time interval from t_i to t_f of action of the force is defined by the following equation.

$$\vec{I}_{mp} = \int_{t_i}^{t_f} \vec{F} dt$$

Impulse momentum principle:

If all the forces applied on a particle, change its momentum from $\vec{p}_i$ to $\vec{p}_f$ during a time interval from t_i to t_f, the total impulse of all the forces is equal to change in momentum of the particle.

$$\vec{I}_{mp} = \int_{t_i}^{t_f} \vec{F} dt = \vec{p}_f - \vec{p}_i$$

Principle of conservation of linear momentum:

If net external force on a system is a null vector in a time interval, the total linear momentum of the system in that time interval remains conserved.

$$\Sigma \vec{p}_i = \Sigma \vec{p}_{\text{during the time interval}} = \Sigma \vec{p}_f$$

Paul Dirac
(8 August 1902 - 20 October 1984)

Collision between two bodies:

Collision or impact is interaction of a short duration between two bodies in which the bodies apply relatively large forces on each other.

Duration of the interaction is as short in comparison to the time scale of interest as to permit us only to consider the states of motion immediately before and after the impact and not during the impact. Duration of an impact ranges from 10^{-23} s for impacts between elementary particles to millions of years for impacts between galaxies. The impacts we observe in our everyday life last from 10^{-3} s to a few seconds.

Head–on (Direct) central collision:

Process of collision between two bodies 1 and 2 is shown in the figure.

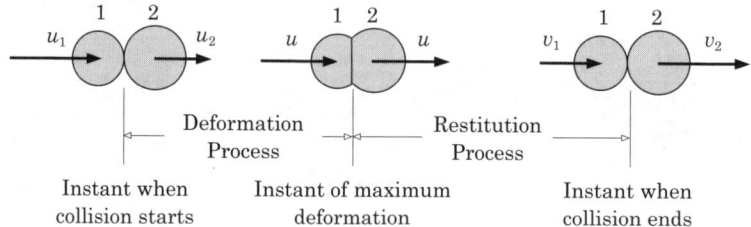

Conservation of momentum:

$$m_1 u_1 + m_2 u_2 = (m_1 + m_2) u = m_1 v_1 + m_2 v_2$$

Coefficient of restitution:

Ratio of magnitude of impulse on a body from the other body, during period of restitution to that during period of deformation is called coefficient of restitution and is denoted by e.

$$e = \frac{\int R dt}{\int D dt} = \frac{v_2 - v_1}{u_1 - u_2} = \frac{\text{Velocity of separation}}{\text{Velocity of approach}}$$

Coefficient of restitution depends on various factors such as elastic properties of materials forming the bodies, velocities of the contact points before impact, state of rotation of the bodies and temperature of the bodies etc. In general, its value ranges from *zero to one*.

For a perfectly inelastic collision, $e = 0$ and for a perfectly elastic collision $e = 1$.

Oblique central collision:

Consider two bodies 1 and 2 undergoing an oblique impact. Their velocity components along the tangent and the normal axes at the point of contact immediately before and after the impact are shown in the following figures.

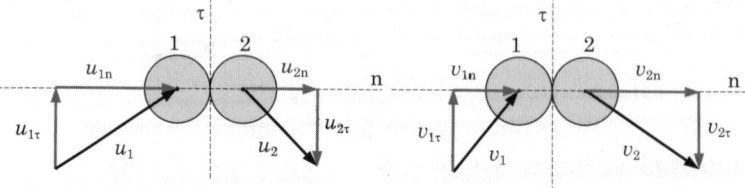

Immediately before collision   Immediately after collision

Along the τ-axis: $v_{1\tau} = u_{1\tau}$ and $v_{2\tau} = u_{2\tau}$

Along the n-axis: For components of velocities along the n-axis, the collision can be treated as a head-on central collision.

$$m_2 v_{2n} + m_1 v_{1n} = m_2 u_{2n} + m_1 u_{1n}$$

$$v_{2n} - v_{1n} = e(u_{1n} - u_{2n})$$

Concept of mass centre:

Mass centre of a system of particles is a mathematical point, translational motion of which is the same as that of a particle of mass equal to that of the system under the action of the unbalanced forces. In addition, if different forces having a net resultant are applied at different particles of a rigid body, the body may rotate but the mass centre translates as if it were a particle of the mass same as that of the body and the net resultant were applied on it.

The concept of mass centre is used to represent gross translational motion of a system. Therefore, total linear momentum of a system must be equal to the linear momentum of the system due to translation of its mass centre.

Centre of mass of a system of discrete particles:

Position vector $\vec{r}_c$ of mass centre of a system consisting of several particles of masses $m_1, m_2, \ldots m_i, \ldots m_n$ at locations $\vec{r}_1, \vec{r}_2, \ldots \vec{r}_i, \ldots \vec{r}_n$ respectively is given by the following expression.

$$\vec{r}_c = \frac{\Sigma m_i \vec{r}_i}{\Sigma m_i}$$

Centre of mass of a continuous mass distribution:

Position vector $\vec{r}_c$ of mass centre of a continuous distribution of mass is given by the following expression.

$$\vec{r}_c = \frac{\int \vec{r} dm}{\int dm}$$

Centre of mass frame:

In a centre of mass frame or centroidal frame of a system, mass centre of the system remains at rest but not necessarily at the origin. A centre of mass frame is a reference frame in which the mass centre remains at the origin.

Sum of mass moments as well as total linear momentum of the system in centroidal frame vanishes.

$$\Sigma m_i \vec{r}_{i/c} = \vec{0} \qquad \text{and} \qquad \Sigma m_i \vec{v}_{i/c} = \vec{0}$$

Application of Newton's laws of motion to a system of particles

Sum of all internal forces between all the particles of a system must be a null vector. Keeping this fact in mind and denoting the mass of the system by M and acceleration of the mass centre by $\vec{a}_c$ relative to an inertial frame, Newton's second law representing translational motion of the system can be represented by the following equation.

$$\Sigma \vec{F}_i = \Sigma(m_i \vec{a}_i) = M\vec{a}_c = \frac{d\vec{p}_c}{dt}$$

Here in the above equation $\vec{p}_c = \Sigma m_i \vec{v}_i$ is total linear momentum of the system.

Kinetic energy of a system of particles:

Kinetic energy of a system of particles is the sum of kinetic energies of all the particles of the system.

$$K = \Sigma\left(\tfrac{1}{2} m_i v_i^2\right)$$

If the system consists of a continuous distribution of mass instead of discrete particles, expression of kinetic energy becomes

$$K = \int\left(\tfrac{1}{2} v^2 dm\right)$$

Kinetic energy of a system of particles using centre of mass frame:

$$K = \Sigma\left(\tfrac{1}{2} m_i v_c^2\right) + \Sigma\left(\tfrac{1}{2} m_i v_{i/c}^2\right)$$

Here the first term on the right-hand side is kinetic energy due to translation of the mass centre and the second term is kinetic energy of the system relative to the centre of mass frame.

For a two-particle system, the above equation reduces to

$$K = \tfrac{1}{2}(m_1 + m_2) v_c^2 + \tfrac{1}{2} \mu v_{rel}^2$$

Here μ is reduced mass of the two-particle system and v_{rel} is magnitude of velocity of either of the particles relative to the other.

$$\mu = \frac{m_1 m_2}{m_1 + m_2} \quad \text{and} \quad v_{rel} = |\vec{v}_1 - \vec{v}_2| = |\vec{v}_2 - \vec{v}_1|$$

Impulse-momentum principle for a system of particles:

Sum of internal forces between all pairs of interacting particles of a system must be a null vector, so is their total impulse in a time interval. Therefore, the net impulse of all the external forces in a time interval must be equal to change in total momentum of the system in that time interval.

Variable system of particles:

Variable system of particles is a system that continually exchanges particles with its surroundings.

While applying energy and momentum methods in analysing dynamics of these systems, consider the same set of particles in the beginning, during and in the end of a time interval under consideration.

Multiple Choice Questions

1. A box of mass 4 kg placed on a horizontal floor, is acted upon by a horizontal force F that varies with time t as shown in the given graph. If coefficients of static and kinetic frictions are 0.25, on which of the following conclusions can you arrive?

   (a) The box starts moving at an instant $t = 2.0$ s.
   (b) The maximum velocity acquired by the box is 5.0 m/s.
   (c) The box stops at an instant $t = 9.0$ s.
   (d) Modulus of average power of force F is more than that of the frictional force.

   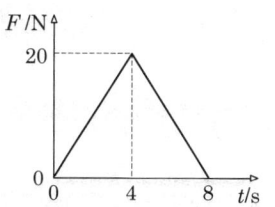

2. A mountain climber is sliding down a vertical rope. Her total mass, including equipment, is 65 kg. By adjusting frictional force of the rope, she controls the force that the rope exerts on her. For a 2.0 s interval, this force T is shown as a function of time t in the given graph. What is change in her speed in this interval? Assume acceleration of free fall to be 10 m/s² and neglect air resistance.

   (a) 5 m/s (b) 10 m/s
   (c) 15 m/s (d) 20 m/s

   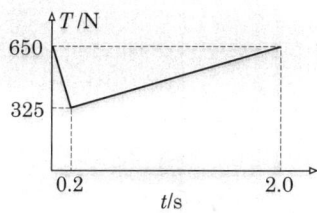

3. A boy of mass 50 kg is standing at one end of a 9.0 m long boat of mass 100 kg that is floating motionless on a calm lake. The boy walks to the other end of the boat and stops there. The boat also moves and finally stops due to water resistance. If force of water resistance is proportional to velocity of the boat relative to the water. What is the magnitude of the net displacement s of the boat?

   (a) $s = 0.0$ m (b) $s = 3.0$ m
   (c) $s < 3.0$ m (d) $s > 3.0$ m

4. A block of mass 2.0 kg is sliding on a frictionless horizontal floor with a velocity of 5.0 m/s due east. It is subjected to a variable net force for 10 seconds resulting in an impulse of 6.0 N·s in the north and 18.0 N·s in the west. What is the total work done by this force?

   (a) 0.0 J (b) 90 J
   (c) 100 J (d) 200 J

5. An astronaut leaves his spaceship for some experiment and floats freely in space at rest relative to his spaceship. His friend in the spaceship ignites a rocket installed on the spaceship for a very short duration. Which of the following observations can you make relative to a reference frame moving together with the astronaut outside the spaceship?

   (a) The spaceship has lesser kinetic energy than the ejected gases.
   (b) The spaceship and the ejected gases have equal kinetic energies.
   (c) The spaceship has greater kinetic energy than the ejected gases.
   (d) Magnitudes of momenta of spaceship and ejected gases are equal.

4.6 Chapter-4

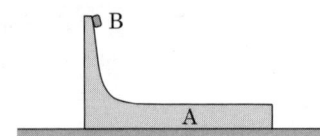

6. Top of a large block A of mass 4 kg consists of a frictionless slope of height 40 cm which smoothly merges into a horizontal flat portion. The block rests on a frictionless horizontal floor. When a small block B of mass 1.0 kg is released on the top of the slope, it slides down the slope and then stops after sliding a distance 1.0 m on the horizontal portion of the top of the block A. Find coefficient of friction between the block B and horizontal portion of the top of the block A.

   (a) 0.2 (b) 0.3
   (c) 0.4 (d) 0.5

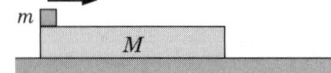

7. A small block of mass m is placed on a plank of mass M, which rests on a frictionless horizontal floor. Coefficient of friction between the block and the plank is μ. The block is given a sharp impulse, so that it starts sliding on the plank with an initial velocity u. Due to friction between the block and the plank, the block slows down and finally stops sliding on the plank. What average thermal power is dissipated in this process?

   (a) $\dfrac{\mu m g u}{2}$ (b) $\dfrac{\mu M g u}{2}$
   (c) $\dfrac{\mu(m+M)gu}{2}$ (d) $\dfrac{\mu m (m+M)gu}{M}$

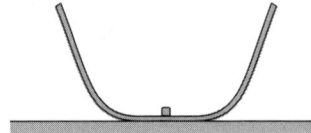

8. A small block rests on the flat bottom of a deep bowl that is placed on a horizontal floor. There is no friction between the block and the bowl as well as between the bowl and the floor. Total mass of the bowl and the block is M. If the bowl is given a horizontal velocity by a sharp hit, the block rises to a maximum height h sliding on the walls of the bowl. Which of the following statements are correct?

   (a) Maximum kinetic energy of the bowl is Mgh.
   (b) If the bowl is lighter than the block, minimum kinetic energy of the bowl is zero.
   (c) To predict the minimum kinetic energy of the bowl, we must know the ratio of the masses.
   (d) To predict the maximum as well as the minimum kinetic energy of the bowl, we must know the ratio of the masses.

9. A sledge on which you are riding is given an initial push to slide on a straight level frictionless track. Snow is falling vertically on the sledge in the frame of the track. You have to adopt any one of the following three strategies to keep your sledge moving fastest.

   I: You sweep the snow off the sledge so that it leaves the sledge perpendicular to the track, as seen by you in the frame of the sledge.
   II: You sweep the snow off the sledge so that it leaves the sledge perpendicular to the track, as seen by someone in the frame of the track.
   III: You do nothing

   Order the strategies from the best to the worst.

   (a) II, III and I (b) III, II and I
   (c) I, II, and III (d) II, I, and III

10. A particle of mass m moving with velocity v makes a head-on elastic collision with a stationary particle of mass $2m$. Kinetic energy lost by the lighter particle during period of deformation is

(a) $\frac{1}{2}mv^2$
(b) $\frac{1}{18}mv^2$
(c) $\frac{4}{9}mv^2$
(d) $\frac{8}{9}mv^2$

11. A block of mass m is given a velocity towards another block of mass M kept at rest on a frictionless horizontal floor some distance apart from a wall as shown in the figure. If all the collisions are elastic, under which of the following conditions, will the blocks collide only once?

(a) $m \leq M$
(b) $M \leq 3m$
(c) $M \geq 3m$
(d) $M \leq 3m \leq 3M$

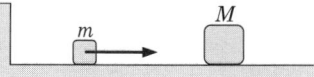

12. Two bodies A and B of masses 5.00 kg and 10.0 kg moving in free space in opposite directions with velocities 4.00 m/s and 0.50 m/s respectively undergo a head-on collision. The force F of their mutual interaction varies with time t according to the given graph. What can you conclude from the given information?

(a) The period of deformation is 0.20 s.
(b) The coefficient of restitution is 0.5.
(c) Body A will move at a velocity of 0.5 m/s in the original direction.
(d) Body B will move at a velocity of 1.75 m/s in the reverse direction.

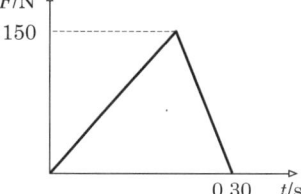

13. A particle projected at an angle θ with the horizontal from the centre of the floor of a cylindrical room of radius r returns to the point of projection after three elastic collisions with the walls and the ceiling. If the particle remains in air for time T, find the speed of projection.

(a) $\dfrac{3r}{T\cos\theta}$
(b) $\dfrac{4r}{T\cos\theta}$
(c) $2\sqrt{\dfrac{gr}{\sin 2\theta}}$
(d) $> 2\sqrt{\dfrac{gr}{\sin 2\theta}}$

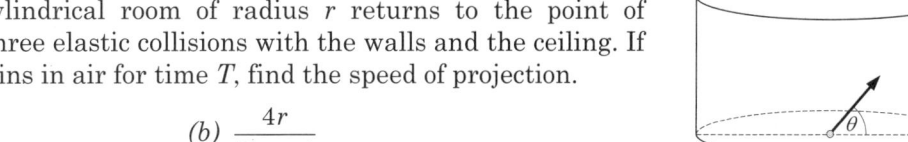

14. Travelling a distance on a bicycle is less toiling than running the same distance in equal time. Which of the following factors is responsible for this well-known fact?

(a) Gravity
(b) Friction force
(c) Mechanical advantage of the bicycle
(d) All the above

15. An expert juggler, carrying five identical balls, has to cross a swing bridge, maximum safe load rating of which is 50 kgf. The juggler weighs 47 kgf and each ball weighs 2 kgf. He believes that he can cross the bridge safely by juggling the balls in such a way that he never has more than one ball in his hands. His skill enables him to juggle smoothly without any jerk. What can you say about his belief?

(a) Correct, as total load on the bridge never exceeds 49 kgf.
(b) Correct, as total load on the bridge slightly exceeds 49 kgf.
(c) Incorrect, as average load on the bridge is 47 kgf + 5×2 kgf = 57 kgf.
(d) I am indecisive, as more information is needed.

16. A shell fired from the ground explodes into two fragments A and B somewhere before the highest point of its trajectory. The fragment A immediately comes to an instantaneous rest and then falls. Knowing that horizontal range of the shell would have been R, if it were not exploded, predict location of mass centre of the two fragments relative to the location of firing, when the fragment A hits the ground.

   (a) On the ground at a distance that is equal to R.
   (b) In the air at a horizontal distance that is equal to R.
   (c) In the air at a horizontal distance that is less than R.
   (d) In the air at a horizontal distance that is more than R.

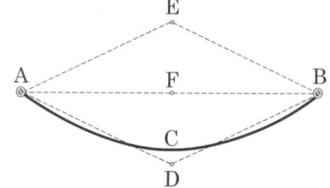

17. A uniform rope suspended between two level nails A and B assume a curved shape ABC as shown in the figure. The midpoint C of the rope is pulled vertically down to a position D to make a V shape and released. When the rope again acquires the curved shape ACB, the midpoint is pulled vertically up to a position E to make an inverted V shape. If in these two pulling processes, total work done by the pulling agency is W, how much work will be done by the pulling agency in lifting vertically the midpoint from equilibrium to a position F in level with the nails?

   (a) W/4 (b) W/3
   (c) W/2 (d) None of these

18. Total mass of a system consisting of several particles is 10 kg. To apply Newton's laws of motion in centroidal frame, you have to assume a pseudo force of $(4\hat{i} - 2\hat{j})$ N acting on a particle of mass 2 kg of the system. What is the net external force acting on the whole system?

   (a) $(10\hat{i} - 20\hat{j})$ N (b) $(-10\hat{i} + 20\hat{j})$ N
   (c) $(20\hat{i} - 10\hat{j})$ N (d) $(-20\hat{i} + 10\hat{j})$ N

19. Consider two particles A and B of masses m and 2m at rest in an inertial frame. Each of them is acted upon by net forces of equal magnitudes F in the positive x-direction for equal amounts of time t. Momenta of the particles A and B in centre of mass frame respectively are

   (a) $\dfrac{2Ft}{3}\hat{i}$ and $-\dfrac{2Ft}{3}\hat{i}$. (b) $-\dfrac{2Ft}{3}\hat{i}$ and $\dfrac{2Ft}{3}\hat{i}$.
   (c) $\dfrac{Ft}{3}\hat{i}$ and $-\dfrac{Ft}{3}\hat{i}$. (d) $-\dfrac{Ft}{3}\hat{i}$ and $\dfrac{Ft}{3}\hat{i}$.

20. Water is flowing through two rigidly connected coplanar U tubes. In the left tube of cross-sectional area A, speed of water flow is u and in the right tube of cross-sectional area A/2 speed water flow is unknown. If the net force on the tube assembly due to water flow is zero, what must be the speed of the water flow in right tube? Neglect effect of gravity.

   (a) $\dfrac{u}{2}$ (b) $\dfrac{u}{\sqrt{2}}$
   (c) $u\sqrt{2}$ (d) $2u$

Questions 21 and 22 are based on the following physical situation

A plank of mass 1.5 kg is placed on a horizontal floor that is lubricated with oil. Top of the plank is in level with a platform as shown in the figure. Force of viscous drag on the plank due to layer of lubricating oil, when the plank slides is given by equation $\vec{f} = -k\vec{v}$, where $\vec{f}$ is in N, $\vec{v}$ is velocity of the plank in m/s and $k = 2.0$ kg/s. A small block of mass 0.5 kg lands from the platform on the plank with a velocity 10 m/s and after sliding some distance on the plank, the block stops on the plank.

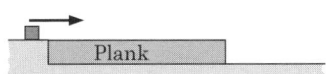

21. How far does the plank slide on the floor?
    (a) 1.0 m   (b) 1.5 m
    (c) 2.5 m   (d) 3.0 m

22. Which of the following graphs best describes the relation between the magnitude of frictional force F between the block and the plank with time t?

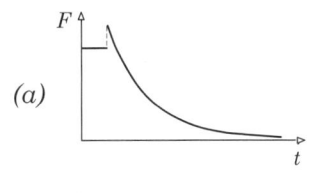
(a)

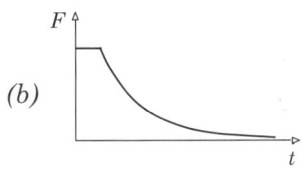
(b)

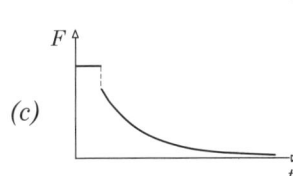
(c)

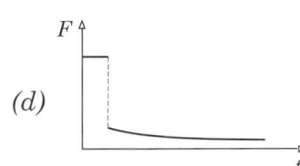
(d)

Questions 23 and 24 are based on the following physical situation

Ends of three light identical rods each of length l are connected to a light pivot that enables them to rotate in any direction. At the other ends of the rods, three particles A, B and C of masses m, $2m$ and $3m$ respectively are affixed. Initially, the rods are coplanar, angle between any two adjacent rod is 120° and the particles are at rest. Now the particle C is given a velocity u perpendicular to the rod connected to it and in the plane of the rods as shown in the figure. Ignore gravitational interaction between the particles.

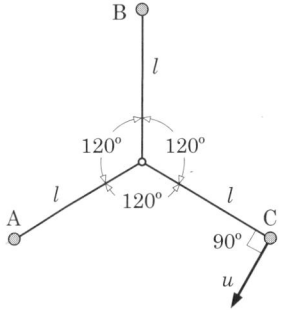

23. Denoting acceleration vectors of the particles A, B and C by $\vec{a}_A$, $\vec{a}_B$ and $\vec{a}_C$ respectively, which of the following conclusion can you make?
    (a) $\vec{a}_A + \vec{a}_B + \vec{a}_C = \vec{0}$
    (b) $3\vec{a}_A + 2\vec{a}_B + \vec{a}_C = \vec{0}$
    (c) $\vec{a}_A + 2\vec{a}_B + 3\vec{a}_C = \vec{0}$
    (d) None of these

24. What are moduli of acceleration vectors of the particles A, B and C immediately after the particle C is given velocity u?
    (a) All equal to $\dfrac{u^2}{l}$.
    (b) $\dfrac{3u^2}{l}$, $\dfrac{3u^2}{2l}$ and $\dfrac{u^2}{l}$
    (c) $\dfrac{6u^2}{11l}$, $\dfrac{3u^2}{11l}$ and $\dfrac{2u^2}{11l}$
    (d) $\dfrac{12u^2}{13l}$, $\dfrac{6u^2}{13l}$ and $\dfrac{4u^2}{13l}$

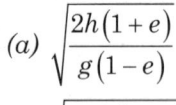

Questions 25 to 27 are based on the following physical situation

A marble is bouncing down a stair in a regular manner, hitting each step at identical points and then rising the same height H above each step. Height and depth of a stair each are equal to h as shown in the figure. Coefficient of restitution for each bounce is e.

25. Airtime between two successive bounces is

(a) $\sqrt{\dfrac{2h(1+e)}{g(1-e)}}$ (b) $\sqrt{\dfrac{2h(1-e)}{g(1+e)}}$

(c) $\sqrt{\dfrac{1.5h(1+e)}{g(1-e)}}$ (d) $\sqrt{\dfrac{1.5h(1-e)}{g(1+e)}}$

26. Horizontal component of velocity of the marble is

(a) $\sqrt{\dfrac{2gh(1-e)}{(1+e)}}$ (b) $\sqrt{\dfrac{2gh(1+e)}{(1-e)}}$

(c) $\sqrt{\dfrac{gh(1-e)}{2(1+e)}}$ (d) $\sqrt{\dfrac{gh(1+e)}{2(1-e)}}$

27. The height H attained by the marble after a bounce is

(a) $\dfrac{eh}{1-e}$ (b) $\dfrac{2eh}{1-e}$

(c) $\dfrac{2h}{1-e}$ (d) $\dfrac{e^2 h}{1-e^2}$

Questions 28 and 29 are based on the following physical situation

A 30 kg shell in free space explodes into three identical fragments. After the explosion, the fragments rush apart. Forces of mutual interaction between the fragments are long range attractive conservative forces. Immediately after the explosion, velocities of the fragments relative to an inertial frame are $(3\hat{i}+2\hat{j})$ m/s, $-2\hat{i}$ m/s and $(5\hat{i}-5\hat{j})$ m/s.

28. If entire energy released in the explosion is converted into kinetic energy of the fragments, how much energy has been released in the explosion?
(a) 260 J (b) 290 J
(c) 335 J (d) 410 J

29. After sufficiently long time, when the forces of mutual interactions cease to act, what can be minimum total kinetic energy of all the fragments?
(a) 15 J (b) 45 J
(c) 75 J (d) More information required

Build up your understanding

1. A wooden bar of thickness $d = 20$ cm is symmetrically placed on a hole made in a horizontal tabletop. A bullet of mass $m = 20$ g shot vertically up through the hole, pierces the wooden bar. Within the bar, speed of the bullet reduces uniformly from $u = 100$ m/s at the bottom to $v = 80$ m/s at the top. What should the minimum mass of the bar be so that it will not leave the tabletop? Acceleration of free fall is $g = 10$ m/s².

2. A plank of length $l = 2.0$ m rests on a calm water close to a frictionless platform A that is a distance $b = 17$ m from another platform B as shown in the figure. A block of mass $m = 25$ kg sliding on the platform A lands on the plank and stays on it. Force of water resistance on the plank is given by equation $\vec{F} = -k\vec{v}$, where $\vec{F}$ in N is the force of water resistance, $\vec{v}$ in m/s is velocity of the plank and $k = 15$ N·s/m. Calculate the minimum speed of the block on the platform A so that the plank reaches the platform B.

3. A thin light inextensible frictionless cord of length l wearing a small bead is tied between two nails that are in the same level a distance $0.5l$ apart. Initially the bead is held close to a nail and released. Find speed of the bead immediately after the cord becomes taut.

4. A remote-controlled car of mass m can move on a long plank of mass M that rests on a horizontal floor. The mechanism of the car is so designed that it always moves on the plank with a constant velocity v with respect to the plank. Coefficient of friction between the plank and the floor is μ and acceleration of free fall is g. How will velocity of the car with respect to the floor vary with time t after it is switched on?

5. A shell projected vertically upward explodes into three identical fragments at the top of its flight. After the explosion, one fragment moves vertically downwards and hit the ground in time t_1, while the other two hit the ground in time t_2. Denoting acceleration due to gravity by g, find the height above the ground where the shell exploded.

6. Two identical frictionless slides A and B each of height h and mass M are placed on a horizontal frictionless floor. A small disc C of mass $m \ll M$ is released on the top of the slide A. Find expressions for the speeds eventually acquired by both the slides when interaction of the slides with the bead ceases.

7. Two particles A and B repel each other by a force $F = 6.0$ N when distance between them is less than $r_0 = 1.0$ m and apply no force on each other when distance between them is greater than r_0. Mass of particle A is $m = 1.0$ kg and mass of particle B is $\eta = 3$ times the mass of A. If the particle B is projected with velocity $u = 2.0$ m/s towards the particle A kept at rest in free space, find the minimum distance between them.

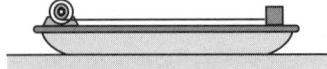

8. A barge stays motionless on a lake. An electric motor affixed on the deck can pull a block with the help a light inextensible string as shown in the figure. Coefficient of friction between the block and the deck is 0.2 and water offers no resistance to motion of the barge. Mass of the barge including the motor is 200 kg and mass of the block is 50 kg. When the motor is switched on, it pulls the block by a constant force of 150 N. If the motor is switched off after 4 s, determine displacement of the block on the deck and draw velocity-time (v-t) graph for the barge. Acceleration due to gravity is 10 m/s².

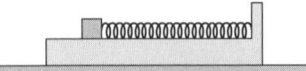

9. A block of mass $m = 1.0$ kg is placed on a plank of mass $M = 15$ kg that rests on a frictionless floor. The block is connected to an obstruction on the plank with the help of a light spring of stiffness $k = 500$ N/m as shown in the figure. Coefficient of friction between the plank and the block is $\mu = 0.5$. Initially when the spring is relaxed, the block is given a velocity v_0 towards the obstruction. If the block stops on the plank before reversing its direction of motion relative to the plank, find the velocity v_0. Acceleration due to gravity is $g = 10$ m/s².

10. Two cubes each of mass $M = 240$ g are placed a distance $d = 90$ cm apart on a frictionless horizontal floor. A bullet of mass $m = 12$ g hits the first cube moving horizontally with a speed $u = 180$ m/s, emerges with a speed $0.5u$, hits the second cube and gets embedded there. How long after the bullet emerges from the first cube, will the cubes collide? Neglect time of interaction of the bullet with the first cube.

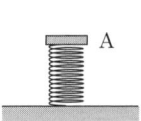

11. A thin plate A of mass m is affixed on the upper end of a spring, lower end of which is affixed on the ground. In equilibrium, the spring is compressed by an amount x_0. Another thin plate B of mass $2m$ dropped from a height $3x_0$ above plate A hits the plate A, moves downwards together with the plate A and after reaching a lowest position, both the plates rebound upwards. What maximum height above the initial position of plate A will plate B rise?

12. A frictionless inclined plane terminates smoothly into a frictionless vertical circular loop mounted on a plank that can slide on a frictionless horizontal floor. This assembly has a total mass of 0.8 kg. A small ball P of mass 0.2 kg is released on the inclined plane from a height that is triple of the radius of the circular loop. Find force of normal reaction between the ball and the circular loop, when the ball is at its topmost position in the circular loop.

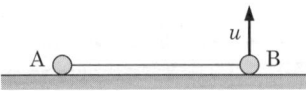

13. Two identical small balls A and B each of mass m connected by a light inextensible cord of length l are placed on a frictionless horizontal floor. With what velocity u must the ball B be projected vertically upwards so that the ball A leaves the floor? Acceleration of free fall is g.

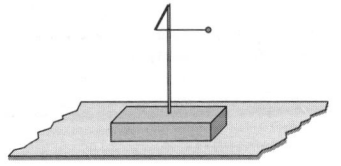

14. A block of mass M can slide without friction on a horizontal floor. A small ball of mass m is suspended by a light inextensible cord of length l from a hanger fixed at the top of a vertical pole mounted on the block so that the ball can swing freely in a vertical plane. The ball is released from a horizontal position as shown. Find the maximum tensile force in the string during the subsequent motion.

15. A small ball of mass m_0 is suspended from a thread of length l attached at the top of a pole, which is mounted on a block A of mass m_1. The block A and the ball both are moving with a velocity u when the block A strikes another block B of mass m_2 and sticks to it. If the ground is frictionless, find the minimum velocity u so that the ball can move on a complete circular path. Assume that the blocks A and B are much heavier than the ball.

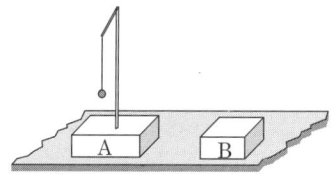

16. A block of mass 2 kg is sliding on a horizontal floor towards another block of mass 4 kg placed at rest on the floor. When the blocks are a distance 16 cm apart, velocity of the first block is 1 m/s as shown in the figure. Coefficient of friction between the floor and the blocks is 0.2 and the collision is perfectly elastic. Find separation between the blocks, when they come to rest. Acceleration due to gravity is 10 m/s².

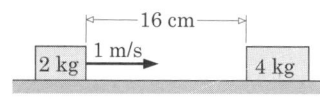

17. A small disc sliding on a frictionless horizontal floor with an unknown velocity collides head on with another identical disc kept at rest on the floor. If during a time interval τ, the first and the second discs cover distances s_1 and s_2 respectively, find possible values of initial velocity u of the first disc and initial distance l between the discs.

18. Two blocks A and B of masses m_A and m_B placed on a frictionless horizontal floor are connected by a light and almost inextensible cord. The block A is given a velocity u away from the block B. If coefficient of restitution defined for the cord has a value e, find velocity with which block B begins to move.

19. In gravity free space, a small ball is placed at the centre of a box of the same mass. The ball and the box both are moving with a velocity v towards a wall. Assume all collisions to be perfectly elastic.
    (a) How many collisions are possible?
    (b) Find velocities of the box and the ball and position of the ball relative to the box after all possible collisions.

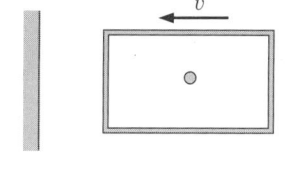

20. A box of length 22 cm and mass 100 g rests on a horizontal frictionless floor. A small bead of mass 10 g is placed at the centre of the bottom of the box. There is no friction between the bead and the bottom of the box. The bead is projected with a velocity 11 cm/s parallel to the length of the box. If all the collisions are perfectly elastic, find displacement of the box in a time interval 60 s after the bead was projected.

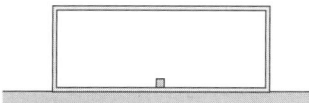

21. Four identical small blocks marked 1, 2, 3 and 4 with separations a, b and c as shown in the figure are moving on a frictionless floor in a line all with a velocity v towards a wall. If all the collisions are perfectly elastic, with what velocities and separations will the blocks move after all possible collisions?

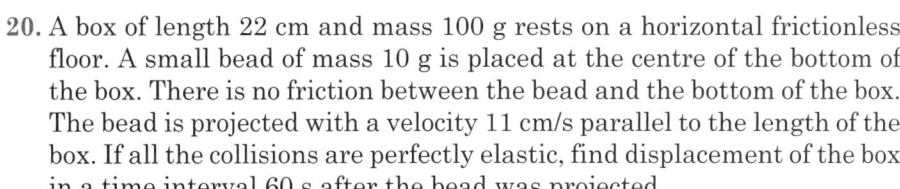

22. Is it possible that after an elastic oblique collision between two identical uniform balls, one of them will stop? If yes, find necessary conditions.

23. Three identical small discs rest on a frictionless horizontal floor. One of them is projected along the floor to successively collide elastically with the other two and thereafter to move in its original direction with half of its initial speed. Assume the floor in the x-y plane and initial velocity of the first disc u in the positive x-direction, find velocities of the other two discs after the collisions.

24. A shell of mass $m = 100$ kg explodes at some point on its trajectory into two fragments that fly with momenta $p_1 = 3.6 \times 10^4$ kg·m/s and $p_2 = 2.4 \times 10^4$ kg·m/s making angle $\theta = 60°$ from each other. Determine the ratio of masses of the fragments for which kinetic energy released in the explosion will be minimal. How much is this kinetic energy?

25. A ball moving with a uniform velocity in free space collides with another stationary identical ball and thereafter each of them move at angle 30° from the initial direction of motion of the first ball. Find fraction of the initial kinetic energy lost in the collision and coefficient of restitution?

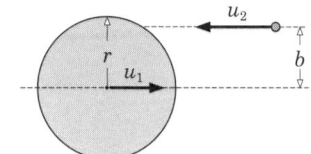

26. A massive frictionless cylinder of radius r, moving with a constant velocity u_1 collides elastically with a small light ball moving with a velocity u_2 towards the cylinder perpendicular to its axis as shown in the figure. The distance between the lines of motion (impact parameter) of the bodies is b. Find speed of the ball after the collision. Assume gravity free conditions.

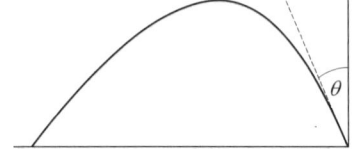

27. A ball is dropped from a certain height on a straight horizontal road and its motion is recorded from a car that starts moving with a uniform acceleration when the ball is dropped. Path of the ball relative to the car between the first and the second bounce is shown in the figure. The dashed line shown is a tangent to the path and makes and angle $\theta = \tan^{-1}(0.4)$ with the vertical. If collision of the ball with the road is perfectly elastic and duration between the first and the second bounce is 2.0 s, find displacement of the car between the first and the second bounce of the ball. Acceleration due to gravity is 10 m/s².

28. A ball projected horizontally from a large, inclined plane, collides successively with the plane. Coefficient of friction between the plane and the ball during these collisions is μ. What should be inclination of the plane and coefficient of restitution for the collisions so that between every two successive bounces the ball follows identical trajectories?

29. A container of mass $M = 10.0$ kg, containing $m = 1.0$ kg of an ideal gas is released without initial velocity from a height $h_0 = 12.1$ m. If collision of the container with the ground is perfectly elastic, how high above the ground will the container bounce? Neglect air resistance and assume that all the internal fluctuations in the gas damp out almost in no time. Acceleration of free fall is $g = 10$ m/s².

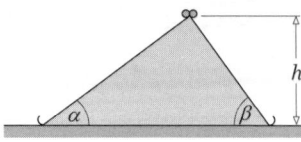

30. Two identical small balls each of mass m are held on the top of a triangular wedge of mass M and height h that is at rest on a frictionless horizontal floor. When the balls are released, they roll down the inclined faces of the wedge and at the bottom get stuck in special traps. How far will the wedge shift during movement of the ball relative to the wedge?

31. In the setup shown, the block B can slide on a vertical guide rigidly fixed to the wedge C. Masses of the block A, the wedge C and the block B are m, $2m$ and $3m$ and cosine of angle of inclination θ of the inclined face of the wedge with the horizontal is 2/3. The pulley and the thread are ideal and there is no friction between any of the surfaces in contact. The block B is released from a height 27 cm above the floor. Find displacement of the wedge when the block B touches the floor.

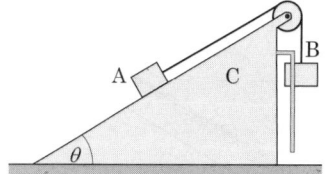

32. A shell projected horizontally with a velocity of 165 m/s from the top of a 15 m high wall explodes into two identical fragments in the air. One of the fragments strikes the ground 1.5 s after the shell was projected at a distance of 240 m from the foot of the wall and 7 m to the right of the x-axis. Determine position of the other fragment at this instant. Neglect air resistance and assume acceleration of free fall to be 10 m/s².

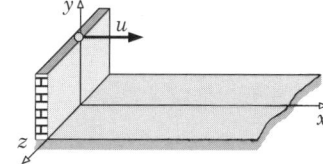

33. In free space, a shell is flying with a speed u towards a large stationary plane along its normal. When the shell is at a distance l from the plane, it explodes into an infinitely large number of fragments that fly apart in all directions such that speed of each fragment relative to the mass centre is v. Find area on the plane in which all the fragments strike.

34. A small bead of mass $m = 4.0$ kg is threaded on a homogeneous frictionless ring of mass $M = 6.0$ kg and radius $R = 0.5$ m. Initially the system rests in free space. Now the bead is struck to impart it a velocity $u = 5.0$ m/s along the tangent to the ring. Find magnitude of force of interaction between them and the minimum kinetic energy of the bead in subsequent motion.

35. Two balls of unequal masses, moving in opposite directions with equal speeds collide elastically. Thereafter, the heavier particle is observed deviated from its original direction of motion by an angle $\alpha = 30°$ in the laboratory frame and by an angle $\beta = 60°$ in the centre of mass frame. How many times of the mass of lighter ball is the mass of heavier ball?

36. When an empty freight train of mass m_0 starts, loading of coal in the train begins at a constant rate r from a stationary hopper. If the track is horizontal and engine pull F is a constant, deduce expression for speed of the train as a function of time t. Neglect all resistive forces.

37. A uniform thread of linear mass density $\lambda = 2.0$ g/m passes through a fixed ideal pulley. At its ends, the thread is stacked into two heaps that do not interfere with the motion of the thread. A beetle of mass $m = 80$ g tries to manage itself at a constant height on the thread by adjusting its speed relative to the thread. At a steady speed of the thread, the beetle succeeds in doing so. Find this steady speed of the thread. Acceleration due to gravity is $g = 10$ m/s².

38. Ends of a thin uniform inextensible rope of mass $m = 1.0$ kg and length $l = 2.0$ m are fastened to the ceiling close to each other. If one of the ends is released and allowed to fall freely as shown in the figure, find the largest force that the fastening at the other end must be capable of bearing so that rope remains fastened there. Acceleration of free fall is $g = 10$ m/s².

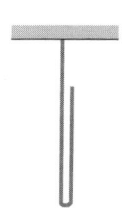

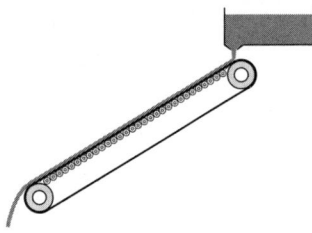

39. A conveyor belt is inclined at an angle θ with the horizontal. Length of a straight portion of the belt is l, resistive forces in the belt mechanism are negligible and radii of the end cylinders are negligible as compared to the length l. Sand falls on the belt with a negligible speed at a constant rate at the top and leaves at the bottom. Friction between the belt and the sand is high enough to stop sliding of sand particles almost in no time. Inertia of the belt mechanism is negligible as compared to that of the total sand on it. Find the steady speed acquired by the belt. Acceleration due to gravity is g.

40. The fan of a remote-operated model helicopter of mass m has diameter d. Denoting density of air by ρ and acceleration of free fall by g, deduce expression for the minimum power required for take-off.

Check your understanding.

1. A small disc A placed on a frictionless tabletop is connected to a small protrusion B on the tabletop with the help of an almost inextensible elastic cord of relaxed length l. There is a trap C in the table at distance $\eta = 0.5$ times of l from the protrusion. Initially the disc, the protrusion and the trap are in a line and the cord is straight and relaxed as shown in the top view of the setup. At what angle with the line AC must the disc be projected along the tabletop so that it enters the trap? Diameter of the protrusion is negligible as compared to the length of the thread.

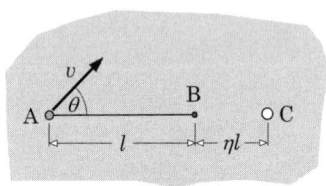

2. Three identical long metal bars each of mass m are placed in a stack on a horizontal floor as shown in the figure. Surfaces of the plates as well as of the floor are lubricated with oil. Force $\vec{F}$ of viscous drag from lubricating oil on a surface is given by equation $\vec{F} = -k\vec{v}_{rel}$, where k is a positive constant and $\vec{v}_{rel}$ is velocity of the surface relative to the other. If the upper bar is given a velocity u towards the right by a sharp hit, find displacement of each of the bars when all of them stop.

3. A disc of mass $M = 2.0$ kg is connected with two identical discs each of mass $m = 1.0$ kg with the help of two light inextensible threads each of lengths $l = 50$ cm. Initially the system rests on a frictionless horizontal floor with centres of the discs in a straight line and the threads straight. Now the middle disc is projected along the floor with a velocity $u = 2$ m/s perpendicular to the threads. Find tensile forces in the threads when the end discs are about to collide.

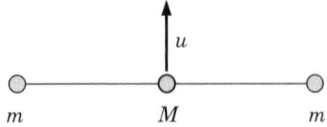

4. When a flexible bag filled with sand is dropped on the pan of a spring balance from a height of $h = 4$ cm above the pan, pointer of the balance suddenly shoots to a reading $m_1 = 6.0$ kg and after several oscillations finally settles to a reading $m_2 = 2.0$ kg. If force constant of the spring is $k = 1.5$ kN/m and dry friction is absent, find mass of the pan. Assume acceleration of free fall $g = 10$ m/s².

5. Inclined face of a wedge is frictionless, and its inclination is θ with the horizontal everywhere except at the bottom, where it increases gradually from a vanishingly small value to θ in a very small region. The wedge is placed on a frictionless horizontal floor and a small disc is projected towards the wedge with an initial velocity u. Mass of the disc is equal to that of the wedge. The disc slides up the inclined face and then slides down. Assuming transit time of the disc on the curved entry to be negligible, find displacement of the wedge when the disc is at the highest point on the wedge.

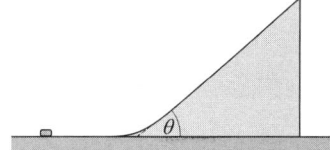

6. A bar is placed with a slight offset l_0 on another identical bar that rests on a horizontal frictionless floor. Coefficient of friction between the bars is μ. Initially both the bars are moving towards a wall with a velocity u. The wall is parallel to the front face of the bars. If collision of the bars with the wall is perfectly elastic, find final velocities of both the bars long time after collisions with the wall.

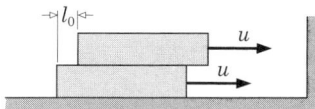

7. A small block of mass 490 g rests close to the left wall of a box of equal mass. Length of the box is 40 cm. The box is placed on a horizontal floor lubricated with oil. Force of viscous friction of the lubricating oil is given by equation $\vec{F} = -k\vec{v}$, where $k = 0.5$ kg/s and $\vec{v}$ is velocity of the box relative to the floor. There is no friction between the block and the floor of the box. If the block is given a velocity 10 m/s towards the right, how many times will the block collide with walls of the box and how far will the box move?

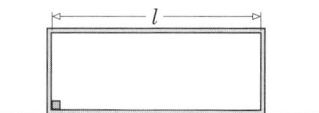

8. A ball is placed on a stationary horizontal plate. At an instant when the ball is projected upwards with a velocity u, the plate is made to move upwards with a constant speed $v_P < u$ in such a way that immediately after every collision with the ball, direction of the motion of the plate is reversed without a change in speed. If collisions between the ball and the plate are elastic, find average velocity of the plate over a large interval of time.

9. A ball is dropped from a height h above a massive platform that is moving upward with a constant speed u. If the ball collides with the platform elastically, find height above its initial position the ball will rebound. Acceleration of free fall is g.

10. A small ball of mass $m = 1.0$ kg is placed in a closed box of mass $M = 2.0$ kg and height $h = 80$ cm that is placed on a pan of a weighing machine as shown. The ball is projected upwards with a velocity $u = 5.0$ m/s. If all the collisions are perfectly elastic, find average forces F_T and F_B exerted by the ball on the top and on the bottom of the box and the reading W of the weighing machine. Assume that the box does not lose contact with the pan. Acceleration of free fall is $g = 10$ m/s^2.

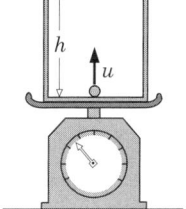

11. Between two parallel walls n identical balls each of mass m and radius r are arranged in a line perpendicular to the walls. Distance between the walls is l. The balls are simultaneously given unequal speeds randomly towards any of the walls. If total kinetic energy of all the balls is K, all the collisions are perfectly elastic and the floor is frictionless, find average force on either of the walls exerted by the balls.

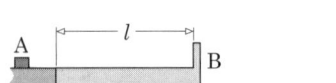

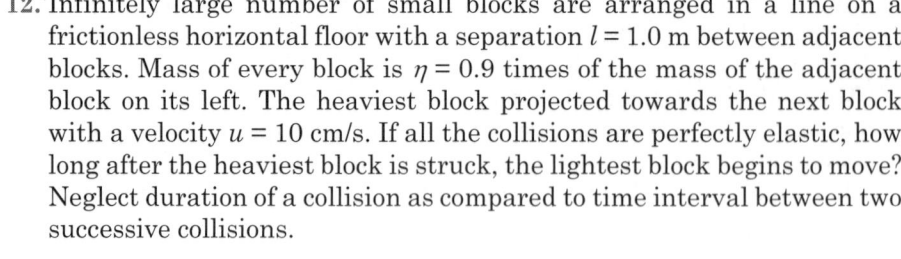

12. Infinitely large number of small blocks are arranged in a line on a frictionless horizontal floor with a separation $l = 1.0$ m between adjacent blocks. Mass of every block is $\eta = 0.9$ times of the mass of the adjacent block on its left. The heaviest block projected towards the next block with a velocity $u = 10$ cm/s. If all the collisions are perfectly elastic, how long after the heaviest block is struck, the lightest block begins to move? Neglect duration of a collision as compared to time interval between two successive collisions.

13. A small block A of mass $m = 2.0$ kg sliding on a platform, lands on a cart B of mass $M = 8.0$ kg that is placed on a frictionless horizontal floor. Distance between left end of the cart and an obstruction at the right end is $l = 1.0$ m. Coefficient of friction between the cart and the block is $\mu = 0.5$ and collision between the block and the obstruction is perfectly elastic. If the speed with which the block lands on the cart is so adjusted that the block stops on the cart at its rear end, find time spent by the block on the cart and loss of mechanical energy during this time.

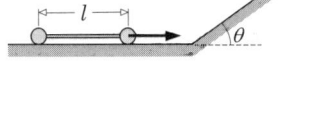

14. A toy similar to letter H in shape is made by fixing two identical cylinders at the ends of a light rod of length l. The toy is placed on a frictionless horizontal floor, which terminates into a uniform frictionless slope of inclination θ. Cylinders are parallel to the line joining the floor and the slope. Find range of velocity given to the toy towards the slope so that it can rise completely on the slope. Collisions of the cylinders with the slope are perfectly inelastic.

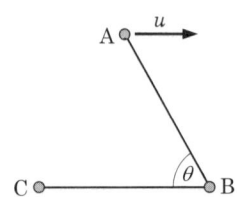

15. Three particle-like balls A, B and C of masses $m_1 = 1.0$ kg, $m_2 = 1.0$ kg and $m_3 = 2.0$ kg connected by identical elastic and almost inextensible threads are placed on a frictionless horizontal floor. The threads are straight and the angle between them is $\theta = 60°$ as shown in the figure. The ball A is projected with a velocity $u = 6$ m/s parallel to the thread connecting the balls B and C. With what velocity will the ball C begin to move?

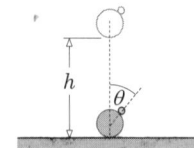

16. A heavy steel ball held in contact with an extremely light steel ball at a height $h = 5\sqrt{3}$ m above a hard horizontal floor. The line joining the centres of the balls makes angle $\theta = 30°$ with the vertical. If all the collisions are elastic and sizes of the balls are negligible as compared to the height h, find the horizontal range of the lighter ball.

17. A ball of mass m is dropped from a height $h = 9.0$ m and after a time interval, another ball of mass $m/2$ is dropped from the same place. If all the collisions are perfectly elastic, what maximum height can one of the balls rise?

18. A cylindrical beaker is held at rest with its bottom horizontal and inside it, a large number of identical elastic balls are moving up and down continuously colliding with each other and with the bottom. In this way, the balls fill the beaker up to 750 ml mark. At a random moment, the beaker is made to move downwards with an acceleration of $0.5g$. Here g denotes the acceleration due to gravity. What fraction of the total number of balls will now fill the beaker up to 1125 ml mark?

19. Two prisms A and B of masses $m_A = 9.0$ kg and $m_B = 16.0$ kg are placed on a frictionless horizontal floor touching each other at their bottom edges. The slant faces of the prisms are frictionless and inclined at angles $\alpha = 53°$ and $\beta = 37°$. A horizontal cylinder of mass $m = 25$ kg is gently placed on the prisms as shown. The cylinder comes down due to gravity pushing the prisms apart. Find ratio of speed of prism A to that of prism B immediately before the cylinder touches the floor.

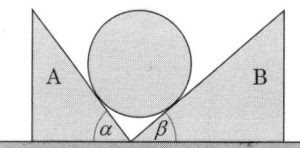

20. Two small discs A and B of masses m_1 and m_2 connected by a light inextensible thread of length l are placed on a frictionless horizontal floor. The disc A is held at rest and the disc B is projected to move around the disc A with a constant speed u on a circular path. If the disc A is now released, the disc B will move on a path shown in the figure.

(a) Which disc has more mass?
(b) Find suitable expressions for the step-lengths p and q.

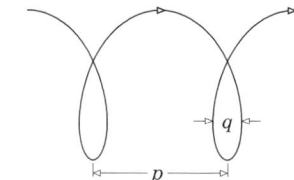

21. A shell of mass m moving with a velocity u in free space explodes into two identical fragments. If mass of the explosive material is negligible as compared to the mass of the shell and due to the explosion total kinetic energy increases by an amount ΔW, find the maximum angle between the directions of motion of the fragments.

22. A shell fired vertically upwards explodes at the highest point of its trajectory into three fragments A, B and C of masses $2m$, $3m$ and $4m$ respectively and the fragments begin to move at equal speeds. At an instant after the explosion, when distance between the fragments A and B is l_{AB}, what is the distance between the fragments A and C? Assume all the fragments are in the air.

23. In free space, a 4.0 kg shell passes the origin of an inertial frame at the instant $t = 0$ moving with a velocity 2.5 m/s in the positive x-direction relative to the frame. Thereafter it explodes into three fragments A, B and C of masses 2.0 kg, 1.0 kg and 1.0 kg respectively. At the instant $t = 10$ s, the fragment A is observed at position (85, 80, 64) moving with velocity $\left(10\hat{i} + 10\hat{j} + 8\hat{k}\right)$ m/s and fragment B at position (−35, 0, −64) moving in the x-z plane. Find velocity vector of the fragment C. All the coordinates are given in metres.

24. A spaceship of mass m with its engine off moving in free space with a velocity u enters a cloud of uniform density ρ and length l. Particles forming the cloud strike the spaceship and stick to it. How much time will the spaceship take to cross the cloud? For simplicity, assume the spaceship as a cylinder of circular section area S.

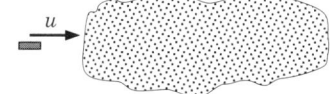

25. In rocket propulsion, kinetic energy imparted to the burnt fuel as ejected gases is wasted as far as propelling is concerned. If at an instant v is the speed of the rocket and u is the speed of the ejected gases relative to the rocket, develop suitable expression for efficiency of propulsion.

Challenge your understanding

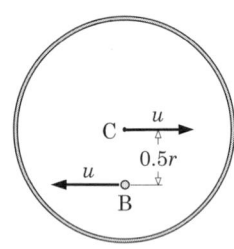

1. A ring of radius r and a small ball of the same mass are placed on a frictionless horizontal floor. The ball is at a distance $0.5r$ from centre of the ring. Now both of them are given opposite velocities of equal moduli in directions perpendicular to the line joining the centre C of the ring and location B of the ball. All the collisions between them are perfectly elastic.

   (a) Draw trajectories of the ball and the centre of the ring.

   (b) Find the minimum and maximum separations between them during process of their motion.

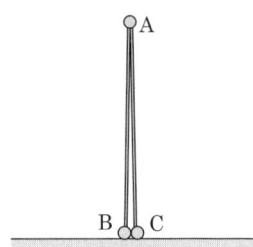

2. Two light rigid rods, each of length l are connected by a hinged joint. A particle A of mass m is attached at the joint and two thin cylinders B of mass m and C of mass $2m$ are attached at the free ends of the rods perpendicular to the rods. The assembly is held motionless with rods vertical and cylinders B and C touching each other on a frictionless horizontal floor as shown in the figure. After the assembly is released, the rods rotate, the cylinders move apart and finally the particle A hits the floor. Find velocity of the particle A when angle between the rods becomes θ.

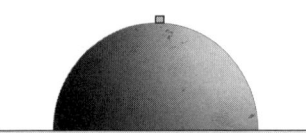

3. A hemispherical bowl is placed on a frictionless horizontal floor and a small disc is placed on the top of the bowl as shown in the figure. The disc and the bowl are of equal mass and there is no friction between them. The disc is slightly pushed horizontally so that it starts sliding down the bowl with a negligible speed. At what angular displacement of the disc measured from a vertical line through the centre of the bowl will the disc lose contact with the bowl?

Answers and Hints

Multiple Choice Questions

1. (a), (b), (c) and (d)
2. (a)
3. (a)
4. (a)
5. (a) and (d)
6. (c)
7. (a)
8. (a), (b), (c)
9. (a)
10. (c)
11. (b)
12. (a), (b) and (d)
13. (b) and (d)
14. (a)
15. (c)
16. (c)
17. (a)
18. (d)
19. (c)
20. (c)
21. (c)
22. (d)
23. (c)
24. (c)
25. (a)
26. (c)
27. (d)
28. (a)
29. (c)

Build up your understanding

1. $\geq \dfrac{m(u^2 - v^2)}{2gd} = 18$ kg

2. $\dfrac{k(b-l)}{m} = 9.0$ m/s

   Hint: Impulse of water resistance stops the block-plank system at the platform B, therefore must be equal to the initial momentum of the block.

3. $\sqrt{\dfrac{3gl}{20}}$

4. $= \begin{cases} \dfrac{Mv}{m+M} + \mu g t; & 0 \leq t \leq \dfrac{mv}{\mu g(m+M)} \\ v; & t \geq \dfrac{mv}{\mu g(m+M)} \end{cases}$

5. $\dfrac{gt_1 t_2}{2}\left(\dfrac{t_1 + 2t_2}{2t_1 + t_2}\right)$

   Hint: Fragments, which take time t_2 follow symmetrical parabolic trajectories after the explosion.

6. $\approx \sqrt{\dfrac{mgh}{M}}$ (Same for both the slides)

   Hint: Finally, kinetic energy of the disc will be negligible in comparison to kinetic energies of the slides.

7. $r_0 - \dfrac{\eta m u^2}{2(\eta + 1)F} = 0.75$ m

   Hint: Total kinetic energy of both the particles in a frame moving with their mass centre will completely be utilized into the work done by forces of their mutual interaction.

8. 15 m ←

   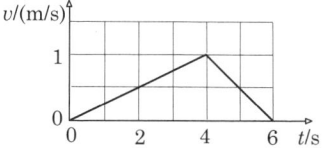

9. $v_0 = \mu g \sqrt{\dfrac{3m(m+M)}{kM}} = 0.4$ m/s

   Hint: Consider a reference frame moving with the velocity of the plank at the instant when the block is reversing its direction of motion (it is also the frame of mass centre). In this frame, initial kinetic energy of the block is completely consumed into the work done by the frictional force and the spring force.

10. $\dfrac{2d}{u}\left(\dfrac{M}{m}\right)^2 = 4.0$ s

11. $\dfrac{3x_0}{2}$

12. 3 N

13. $u \geq \sqrt{3gl}$

14. $\left(3 + \dfrac{2m}{M}\right)mg$

    Hint: Tensile force in the thread has its maximum value when the ball is at the lowest point.

15. $u = \dfrac{(m_1 + m_2)}{m_2}\sqrt{5gl}$

16. 5 cm

17. $u = \dfrac{s_1 + s_2}{\tau}; (s_1 - s_2) \leq l \leq s_1$

    Hint: Mass centre of the discs moves with a constant velocity that remains unaffected by the collision, therefore we get

    $$u = \dfrac{s_1 + s_2}{\tau}$$

    If x is the distance between the discs at the end of interval τ, we can write

    $$l = s_1 - (s_2 - x)$$

The above equation suggests that $l_{max} = s_1$ for a perfectly elastic collision and $l_{min} = s_1 - s_2$ for a perfectly inelastic collision.

Alternatively, by expressing the distances in term of initial velocity and coefficient of restitution, you can also solve the problem.

18. $v_B = \dfrac{m_A(1+e)}{m_A + m_B} u$

   Hint: During the very short time interaction of the blocks through the cord, the cord first becomes straight, and then it becomes slightly extended and after acquiring a maximum extension, it comes to a relaxed state. These processes of extension and of return to relaxed state are similar to processes of deformation and restitution respectively of a head-on collision. At the end of deformation or in the beginning of restitution, length of the thread is maximal, and both the blocks have the same velocity.

   Apply impulse momentum principle for the blocks separately for deformation and restitution processes and then use the following definition of coefficient of restitution e.

   $e = \dfrac{\text{Impulse of tension in restitution process}}{\text{Impulse of tension in deformation process}}$

   In this way, you observe that the event gives result similar to a head-on collision.

19. (a) Three; the first is between the box and the wall, the second is between the ball and left wall of the box and the third is between the box and the wall.

   (b) Both will move with velocity v away from the wall and the ball will be at the centre of the box.

20. 60 cm

21.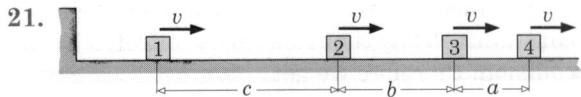

   Hint: In an elastic head-on collision, two identical bodies exchange their velocities. Therefore, it can be thought that these bodies pass through each other without change in their velocities and during an elastic head-on collision with a stationary wall the colliding body goes into the wall and another identical body comes out with opposite velocity without change in speed. Following the above reasoning for the elastic collision with the wall as well as between the blocks, we can say that the given row of blocks enters into the wall and a reversed row comes out of the wall.

   Otherwise, you can consider each collision in its strict sequence and place and then find the same result.

22. Yes, both the balls must be moving in mutually perpendicular directions and line of velocity vector of one of them must pass through the centre of the other at the time of collision.

23. $0.5u(\hat{i} - \hat{j})$ and $0.5u\hat{j}$

   or $0.5u(\hat{i} + \hat{j})$ and $-0.5u\hat{j}$

   Hint: Consider the following two possibilities.

   Possibility-I

   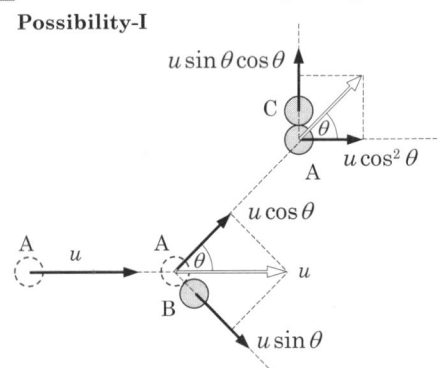

   Possibility-II

   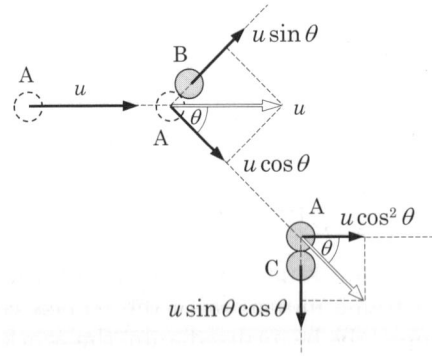

24. $\dfrac{m_2}{m_1} = \dfrac{p_2}{p_1} = \dfrac{2}{3}$ and $\dfrac{p_1 p_2 (1 - \cos\theta)}{M} = 4.32 \times 10^6$ J

25. $\dfrac{\Delta K}{K} = \dfrac{1}{3}$ and $e = \dfrac{1}{3}$

26. $\sqrt{u_2^2 + 4u_1(u_1+u_2)\left(1-\dfrac{b^2}{r^2}\right)}$

   Hint: Since the cylinder is very massive as compared to the ball, its velocity will remain almost unchanged in the collision.

27. 16 m

28. $\tan^{-1}(\mu)$ and 1.0

29. $h_0\left(\dfrac{M-m}{M+m}\right)^2 = 8.1$ m

   Hint: Internal fluctuations produced in motion of the gas molecules due to sudden change in velocity of the container die out very rapidly, causing the gas molecules to acquire the velocity of the container in addition to their random motion in a vanishingly small time-interval. During this time impulse of the only external force on the gas container system that is their weight, is so insignificant that momentum can be assumed almost unchanged.

30. $\dfrac{mh}{M+2m}(\cot\alpha - \cot\beta)$

   Hint: Initially mass centre of the system consisting of the wedge and both the balls is at rest and there is no external horizontal force on the system, therefore the mass centre will not shift in the horizontal direction.

31. 3 cm towards the left

32. (255 m, 7.5 m, –7 m)

   Hint: The first fragment strikes the ground in a time that is smaller than the airtime of un-exploded shell. It suggests that when the first fragment strikes the ground, the second fragment is in the air.

33. If $v < u$, the area is a circle of radius $r = vl/\sqrt{u^2-v^2}$; and if $v \geq u$, the area covers the entire plane.

   Hint: Velocity vector $\vec{v}_f$ of a fragment moving with speed v ($v < u$) at the largest angle θ from the direction of motion of unexploded shell is shown in the figure. These fragments will strike the plane at the farthest places.

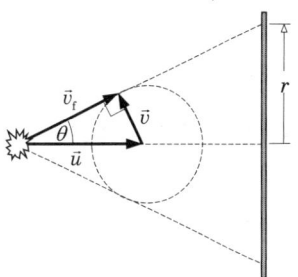

34. $\dfrac{mMu^2}{(m+M)R} = 120$ N and $\dfrac{mu^2}{2}\left(\dfrac{M-m}{M+m}\right)^2 = 2.0$ J

   Hint: Mass centre of bead-ring system will move with a constant velocity. In the frame of mass centre, the bead and centre of the ring both will keep on moving with constant speeds on circular paths around the mass centre. Moreover, the ring will have no rotational motion.

   When the bead is moving in direction opposite to motion of mass centre, it has minimum speed in laboratory frame and hence minimum kinetic energy.

35. 3

36. $\dfrac{Ft}{m_0 + rt}$

37. $\sqrt{\dfrac{mg}{\lambda}} = 20$ m/s

38. $2mg = 20$ N

39. $\sqrt{gl\sin\theta}$

40. $\dfrac{(mg)^{3/2}}{d\sqrt{\pi\rho}}$

   Hint: The fan of the helicopter collects motionless air above it and blows it downwards. Momentum imparted to air blown per unit time is the lifting force and kinetic energy imparted per unit time to this air is the power requirement.

   It is reasonable to assume the air above the fan almost motionless and its density above and below the fan uniform.

Check your understanding

1. $\theta = \cos^{-1}\sqrt{\dfrac{1+\eta}{4\eta}} = 30°$

   Hint: Since the cord is elastic and almost inextensible, kinetic energy of the disc remains unchanged when cord slackens again. Component of velocity perpendicular to the cord remains unchanged and component of velocity along the cord is reversed.

   This event is analogous to a perfectly elastic collision of the disc with a circular wall of radius equal to the length of the thread and centre at the protrusion.

2. Upper bar $3mu/k$, middle bar $2mu/k$ and the lowest bar mu/k all towards the right.

3. $\dfrac{m(Mu)^2}{(M+2m)^2 l} = 2.0 \text{ N}$

   Hint: Use the fact that in the reference-frame moving together with the middle disc, both the disc are in circular motion and this frame is a non-inertial frame.

4. $\dfrac{2km_2^2 h}{m_1(m_1 - 2m_2)g} - m_2 = 2.0 \text{ kg}$

   Hint: Weight of the pan corresponds to zero reading of the balance.

5. $\dfrac{u^2}{8g\sin\theta}\{2\sqrt{1+\sin^2\theta} - \cos\theta\}$

6. $= \begin{cases} 0; & u^2 \leq 2\mu g l_0 \\ \sqrt{u^2 - 2\mu g l_0}; & u^2 \geq 2\mu g l_0 \end{cases}$

   Hint: Immediately after the first collision between the upper bar and the wall, direction of motion of the upper bar is reversed and both the bars are moving with their initial speeds in opposite directions. Now slipping between the bars causes loss in their kinetic energies and equality of masses and absence of friction at the floor makes rate of this loss equal for both the bars, therefore losing equal speeds in equal time, both the bars have equal speed at every instant before the lower bar collides with the wall.

7. 49 and 9.8 m

   Hint: In every collision, the box and the block will exchange their velocities. When the block was projected the box was at rest, therefore, only one of them will move at a time. In addition, the block cannot stop sliding on frictionless bottom of the box and every time the box moves, it does so with an exponentially decreasing velocity. Therefore, eventually the box will move with a vanishingly small velocity making its collision with the block practically impossible.

   Collision of moving block and stationary box is always an odd numbered collision and collision of moving box with stationary block is always an even numbered collision.

   Since viscous force is proportional to speed, every time the box moves, its momentum decreases by amount kl.

   Therefore, total number of collisions is $2n+1$, where n is the greatest integer satisfying the following equation.

   $$n < \dfrac{mu}{kl}.$$

8. $\dfrac{v_P^2}{u} \downarrow$

9. $\dfrac{2u\sqrt{u^2 + 2gh}}{g}$

10. $F_T = mg\left(\dfrac{\sqrt{u^2 - 2gh}}{u - \sqrt{u^2 - 2gh}}\right) = 15 \text{ N} \uparrow$

    $F_B = mg\left(\dfrac{u}{u - \sqrt{u^2 - 2gh}}\right) = 25 \text{ N} \downarrow$

    $W = (M+m)g = 30 \text{ N}$

    Hint: Average force exerted by colliding ball on any of the surfaces is equal to ratio of change in

11. $\dfrac{2K}{l-2nr}$

Hint: Follow the reasoning applied in problem 21 of "Build up your understanding".

12. $\dfrac{2l}{u(1-\eta)} = 200$ s

Hint: Speed acquired by the nth block after collision with the $(n-1)^{\text{th}}$ block assuming the heaviest as the first block is given by the following expression.

$$v_n = u\left(\dfrac{2}{1+\eta}\right)^{n-1}$$

Therefore, the required time is $T = \sum\limits_{n=1}^{n\to\infty}\left(\dfrac{l}{v_n}\right)$

13. $2\sqrt{\dfrac{Ml}{(m+M)\mu g}} = 0.4$ s and $2\mu mgl = 20$ J

Hint: For simplicity consider a frame moving with the cart. It is a non-inertial frame. In this frame, the block is always retarded by the same magnitude during its to and fro motion and ultimately stops after covering a total distance $2l$.

Alternatively, you can use an inertial frame attached with the platform. In this frame, total impulse of the friction force equals the decrease in momentum of the block.

14. $\geq \sqrt{\dfrac{gl\sin\theta(1+\cos^2\theta)}{2\cos^2\theta}}$

Hint: Total momentum component of the toy along the inclined plane remains unchanged during collision of the first cylinder.

15. $\dfrac{4m_1 m_2 u \cos^2\theta}{(m_1+m_2)(m_2+m_3)} = 1.0$ m/s $\rightarrow$

Hint: Use the idea developed in problem 18 of "Build up your understanding", first with pair of balls A and B and then with the pair of balls B and C.

16. $16h\sin(2\theta)\left(\cos 2\theta + \dfrac{1}{2}\right) = 120$ m

17. $\dfrac{25h}{9} = 25$ m

18. 0.5

Hint: In steady state, number of balls crossing every horizontal section of beaker in the region filled with the balls must be equal.

19. $\dfrac{m\tan\beta + m_B(\tan\alpha + \tan\beta)}{m\tan\alpha + m_A(\tan\alpha + \tan\beta)} = 1$

Hint: While coming down, the cylinder shifts horizontally too. Total momentum component of the prisms and the cylinder in horizontal direction remain conserved.

20. (a) The disc A,

(b) $p = \dfrac{2\pi m_2 l}{m_1 + m_2}$ and

$q = \dfrac{2l}{m_1+m_2}\left\{\sqrt{m_1^2 - m_2^2} - m_2\cos^{-1}\left(\dfrac{m_2}{m_1}\right)\right\}$

21. $\cos^{-1}\left(\dfrac{mu^2 - 2\Delta W}{mu^2 + 2\Delta W}\right)$

Hint: Energy released in the explosion will impart equal and opposite momenta to the fragments in the frame moving with initial velocity of the shell. Moreover, for the fragments to fly apart with maximum angle included between their directions of motion in laboratory frame, the momenta components received due to explosion in the frame moving with the initial velocity must be perpendicular to the velocity of the frame.

22. $1.5 l_{AB}$

23. $-(5\hat{i} + 20\hat{j} + 8\hat{k})$ m/s

Hint: It may be helpful to find where the shell exploded with the help of velocity vector of the fragment A after the explosion, location of fragment A at $t = 10$ s and the information that explosion occurred on the x-axis.

24. $\dfrac{l}{u}\left(1 + \dfrac{\rho Sl}{2m}\right)$

25. $\dfrac{2vu}{u^2 + v^2}$

Challenge your understanding

1. (a) Both of them follow equilateral triangular trajectories confined in a circle of radius $0.5r$ with its centre at the stationary mass centre of the system.

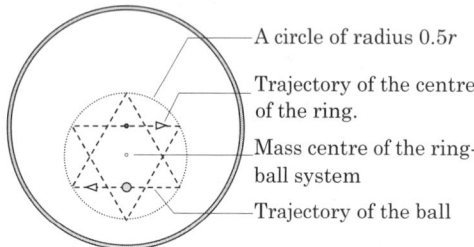

 — A circle of radius $0.5r$
 — Trajectory of the centre of the ring.
 — Mass centre of the ring-ball system
 — Trajectory of the ball

   (b) $0.5r$ and r

2. $\sqrt{\dfrac{gl}{2}(1-\sin\theta)\left(\dfrac{\sin^2\theta + 16\cos^2\theta}{11\sin^2\theta + 4\cos^2\theta}\right)}$

3. $\cos^{-1}\left(\sqrt{3}-1\right)$

   Hint: In a reference frame moving with the bowl, till the moment the disc breaks off the surface of the bowl, the horizontal component of velocity of the disc increases, acquiring its maximum value at the time of breaking contact and thereafter becomes a constant.

Chapter 5

Rotational Motion

Kinematics of rotational motion: rotation about fixed axis, rotation about axis in translation and rotation about axis in rotation; concept of torque, equilibrium of rigid bodies, concept of moment of inertia, concept of angular momentum, rotational equivalent of Newton's laws of motion, use of methods of work and energy, angular impulse and angular momentum, law of conservation of angular momentum, eccentric impacts.

"I am never content until I have constructed a mechanical model of what I am studying. If I succeed in making one, I understand; otherwise, I do not."

BACK TO BASICS

Rigid body:
A rigid body is an assemblage of a large number of material particles, which do not change their mutual distances under any circumstance or in other words, a rigid body is not deformed under any circumstance.

Sir Lord Kelvin
(26 June 1824 – 27 December 1907)

Rotational motion of a rigid body:
Motion of a rigid body is identified by a change in location or a change in orientation or change in both. Change in orientation during motion is rotational motion and change in location is translational motion.

Axis of rotation:
A mathematical straight line parallel to the angular velocity vector of the body is an axis of rotation.

Instantaneous axis of rotation (IAR):
It is a mathematical straight line about which a body in general plane motion (rotation about an axis in translation) can be considered in state of only rotational motion at an instant.

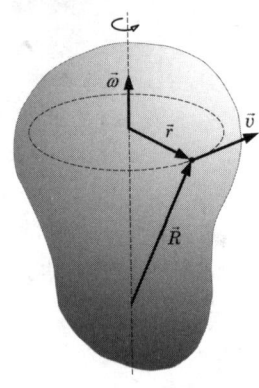

Kinematics of rotation about fixed axis:

Consider a particle of a rigid body in rotation about a fixed axis. In an infinitesimal time interval dt, this particle covers a distance ds along a circular path of radius r and radius vector $\vec{r}$ turns through angle dθ. There is a point on the axis from where position vector of the particle is $\vec{R}$.

$$d\vec{s} = d\vec{\theta} \times \vec{r} = d\vec{\theta} \times \vec{R}$$

$$\vec{v} = \frac{d\vec{s}}{dt} = \frac{d\vec{r}}{dt} = \frac{d\vec{R}}{dt}$$

$$\vec{v} = \vec{\omega} \times \vec{r} = \vec{\omega} \times \vec{R}$$

$$\vec{a} = \frac{d\vec{v}}{dt} = \frac{d\vec{\omega}}{dt} \times \vec{r} + \vec{\omega} \times \frac{d\vec{r}}{dt} = \vec{\alpha} \times \vec{r} + \vec{\omega} \times \vec{v}$$

Kinematics of general plane motion:

General plane motion of a rigid body can be conceived as well as analysed as superposition of translation of any of its particle and simultaneous rotation about an axis through that particle.

According to the above idea, we have the following useful equations for any two particles A and B of a rigid body.

$$\vec{v}_B = \vec{v}_A + \vec{v}_{B/A} = \vec{v}_A + \vec{\omega} \times \overline{AB}$$

$$\vec{a}_B = \vec{a}_A + \vec{a}_{A/B} = \vec{a}_A + \vec{\alpha} \times \overline{AB} + \omega^2\left(-\overline{AB}\right)$$

Torque: Moment of a force

Torque is rotational analogue of force and accounts for time rate of change in amount of rotational motion.

Torque of a force acting on a particle of a body about a point is defined as the cross product of position vector of the particle relative to the point about which torque is sought and the force vector.

$$\vec{\tau} = \vec{r} \times \vec{F}$$

Concept of moment of inertia or rotational inertia:

Moment of inertia is inertia to rotational motion in the same way as mass is inertia to translational motion.

Moment of inertia of a system of discrete particles:

$$I = \sum_{i=1}^{n}\left(m_i r_i^2\right)$$

Moment of inertia of a continuous mass distribution of mass:

$$I = \int dI = \int r^2 dm$$

Theorem of perpendicular axes:

For a laminar body, moment of inertia about an axis perpendicular to the plane of the body is sum of the moment of inertias about any two mutually perpendicular axes in the plane of the body provided that all the three axes are concurrent.

$$I_z = I_x + I_y$$

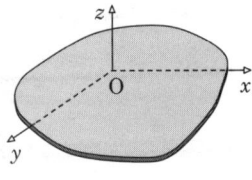

Sum of moment of inertias of a body of any shape about three concurrent mutually perpendicular axes is equal to the term $2\int r^2 dm$. Here r is distance of an infinitesimal mass dm of the body from the point of concurrency of the three axes.

$$I_x + I_y + I_z = 2\int r^2 dm$$

Theorem of parallel axes (Steiner's theorem):

The moment of inertia about any axis parallel to an axis through the mass centre C is given by sum of moment of inertia about the axis through the mass centre and product term of mass of the body and square of the distance between the axes, provided that angular velocity of rotation of the line OC equals the angular velocity of intrinsic rotation of the rigid body.

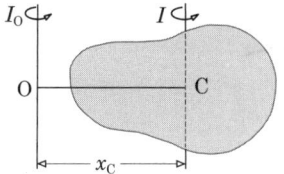

$$I_O = I_C + M x_C^2$$

Among all the parallel axes the moment of inertia of a rigid body about an axis through the mass centre is the minimum moment of inertia.

Radius of gyration:

If the mass m of a body were assumed concentrated at a distance k from the axis, the moment of inertia I of the body about that axis would be mk^2. Here k is radius of gyration of the body about the axis under consideration.

$$k = \sqrt{\frac{I}{m}}$$

Dynamics of a rigid body as a system of particles:

The net torque of all the external forces acting on a body about the origin of an inertial frame equals the sum of moment of effective force due to translation of mass centre and moments of effective forces on all the particles due to their motion with respect to the mass centre.

$$\sum_{i=1}^{n} \vec{\tau}_O = \vec{r}_C \times M\vec{a}_C + \sum_{i=1}^{n} (\vec{r}_{i/C} \times m_i \vec{a}_{i/C})$$

For a rigid body in rotation about a fixed axis or in general plane motion, the second term in the above equation reduces to $I_C \vec{\alpha}$.

$$\sum_{i=1}^{n} \vec{\tau}_O = \vec{r}_C \times M\vec{a}_C + I_C \vec{\alpha}$$

Methods of work and energy:

Since definition of work, power and potential energy do not consider type of motion; they have their usual meaning in rotational motion as they have in translational motion.

Kinetic energy of a rigid body in general plane motion:

Kinetic energy of a rigid body equals the sum of kinetic energy due to translation of the mass centre and kinetic energy due to intrinsic rotation about the mass centre.

$$K = \tfrac{1}{2} M v_C^2 + \tfrac{1}{2} I_C \omega^2$$

These two terms of the above equation are sometimes known as translational kinetic energy and rotational kinetic energy respectively.

Kinetic energy of a rigid body in general plane motion can be expressed in a single term of kinetic energy due to rotation about instantaneous axis of rotation.

$$K = \tfrac{1}{2} I_{\text{IAR}} \omega^2$$

Work-energy theorem and mechanical energy conservation:
Work energy theorem and the law of conservation of mechanical energy are applicable in analysing rotational motion in the same way as they are applicable in translational motion.

Angular momentum:
Angular momentum is the measure of amount of rotational motion.

Angular momentum of a particle about the origin is the moment of its linear momentum i.e. cross product of position vector of the particle with its linear momentum.

Angular momentum of a system of particles is the sum of angular momenta of all the particles of the system.

Angular momentum of a rigid body in general plane motion:

$$\vec{L}_O = \vec{r}_C \times (M\vec{v}_C) + I_C \vec{\omega}$$

The first term of the above equation represents angular momentum due to translation of the mass centre and the second term represents angular momentum due to intrinsic rotation about the mass centre.

Rotational analogue of Newton's second law:
For a rigid body in general plane motion:

$$\Sigma \vec{\tau}_O = \frac{d\vec{L}_O}{dt} = \vec{r}_C \times M\vec{a}_C + I_C \vec{\alpha}$$

Angular impulse:
Angular impulse $\vec{J}_{O, i \to f}$ of a torque $\vec{\tau}_O$ about an axis through a point O during a time interval from t_i to t_f is given by the following equation.

$$\vec{J}_{O, i \to f} = \int_{t_i}^{t_f} \vec{\tau}_O \, dt$$

Angular impulse-momentum principle:
The angular impulse-momentum principle states that the net angular impulse of all the external forces about an axis during a time interval equals the change in angular momentum of the body about the same axis in that time interval.

$$\Sigma \vec{J}_{O, i \to f} = \vec{L}_{Of} - \vec{L}_{Oi}$$

Conservation of angular momentum:
In the absence of torque of external forces about a point or an axis, total angular momentum of a system of particles about that point or axis remains conserved.

Multiple Choice Questions

1. An object is rotating at an angular velocity ω_0 about an axis that passes from the origin and is directed in the x-y plane at 45° from the y-axis as well as from the negative x-axis. What is velocity of a point on the body located on the positive z-axis at a distance z from the origin?

   (a) $\dfrac{\omega_0 z}{\sqrt{2}}(\hat{i}+\hat{j}+\hat{k})$
   (b) $\dfrac{\omega_0 z}{\sqrt{2}}(-\hat{i}+\hat{j}+\hat{k})$
   (c) $\dfrac{\omega_0 z}{\sqrt{2}}(\hat{i}+\hat{j})$
   (d) $\dfrac{\omega_0 z}{\sqrt{2}}(-\hat{i}+\hat{j})$

2. A disc placed on a frictionless horizontal plank is rotating with a constant angular velocity ω about its central vertical axis. Now the plank is made to move with a constant acceleration a on a straight path. If you assume initial location of the centre of disc as origin, direction of motion of the plank in negative y-axis of the coordinate system attached with the plank, which of the following equations represent trajectory of instantaneous centre of rotation of the disc.

   (a) If $\vec{\omega}=\omega\hat{k}$, then $y=\dfrac{\omega^2 x^2}{2a}$ and $x \leq 0$.
   (b) If $\vec{\omega}=-\omega\hat{k}$, then $y=\dfrac{\omega^2 x^2}{2a}$ and $x \geq 0$.
   (c) If $\vec{\omega}=\omega\hat{k}$, then $y=-\dfrac{\omega^2 x^2}{2a}$ and $x \leq 0$.
   (d) If $\vec{\omega}=-\omega\hat{k}$, then $y=-\dfrac{\omega^2 x^2}{2a}$ and $x \geq 0$.

3. Two uniform triangular plates ABC and ABD of the same thickness, height and made of the same material are shown in the figure. If moment of inertias of these plates about the axis PQ are I_C and I_D, which of the following statements is true?

   (a) $I_C > I_D$
   (b) $I_C < I_D$
   (c) $I_C = I_D$
   (d) More information needed.

   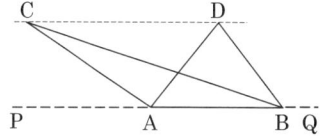

4. A uniform equilateral triangular lamina of side l has a mass m. Its moment of inertia about the axis through the centroid and perpendicular to its plane is

   (a) $\frac{1}{3}ml^2$
   (b) $\frac{1}{6}ml^2$
   (c) $\frac{1}{12}ml^2$
   (d) None of these

   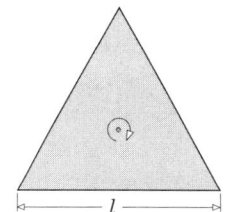

5. A light beam suspended with the help of two ropes supports two loads as shown in the figure on the next page. The load at the left end is of 75 kg and the load P at the right end is unknown. The maximum tension that either of the rope can bear is 1200 N. In an experiment, mass of the

load P is gradually increased from zero. If the rod remains horizontal in equilibrium, which of the following conditions must be satisfied?

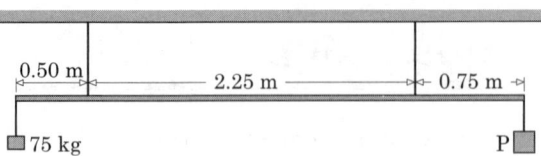

(a) Minimum mass of load P can be 12.5 kg.
(b) Maximum mass of load P can be 102.5 kg.
(c) When the mass of load P is minimum, tension in one of the ropes vanishes.
(d) When the mass of load P is maximum, tension in one of the ropes vanishes.

6. A uniform right-angled triangular lamina is suspended from the ceiling with the help of three light strings. The plane of the lamina is horizontal, and the strings are vertical as shown in the figure. In which of the following options, tensile forces T_A, T_B and T_C developed in the strings connected to the vertices A, B and C respectively of the lamina are arranged in correct order of their magnitudes?

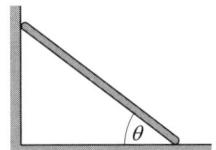

(a) $T_A > T_B > T_C$
(b) $T_B > T_A > T_C$
(c) $T_C > T_A > T_B$
(d) $T_A = T_B = T_C$

7. A uniform steel rod leans against a frictionless wall in static equilibrium. Frictional force between the lower end and the floor is less than its limiting value by a finite amount. The rod is supplied with some amount of heat so that it expands. Assume that the coefficient of friction does not change on heating. What can you conclude regarding contact forces from the wall and from the floor?

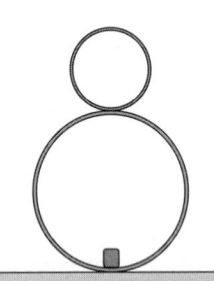

(a) From the wall it decreases and from the floor it increases.
(b) From the wall it increases and from the floor it decreases.
(c) From the wall as well as from the floor it increases.
(d) From the wall as well as from the floor it decreases.

8. A toy "roly-poly" consists of two rigidly attached hollow uniform plastic balls. The upper and the lower balls are of radii 6 cm and 9 cm respectively. A small load of mass 250 g is glued at the bottom of the lower ball. This toy has a property that if it is tilted to one side by any angle and then set free, it oscillates and finally settles in vertical orientation. Which of the following statements are correct?

(a) More is the mass of the load, faster is the response.
(b) More is the mass of the lower ball, more sluggish is the response.
(c) Mass of the upper ball should be less than 150 g and that of the lower ball should be more than 150 g.
(d) Mass of the upper ball should be less than 150 g and that of the lower ball may have any value.

9. It is easier to break a wooden bar by bending it as compared to pulling it. To break a wooden bar a man holds the bar in his fists and then tries to twist his fists as shown in the figure, where b is width of his fists and l is a characteristic distance between places where he holds the bar.

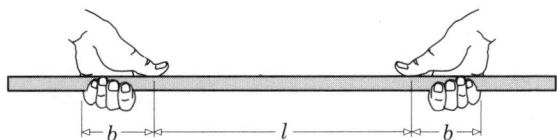

To break the bar most easily, the best strategy is to

(a) increase l and keep b unchanged.
(b) increase b and keep l unchanged.
(c) increase b and l both.
(d) It is the strength of the bar, which matters. The quantities b and l have no effect.

10. A squirrel of mass m climbs slowly on a thin straight vertical rod of length L. Mass of the rod is negligible as compared to that of the squirrel and size of the squirrel is negligible as compared to the length l that it climbs on the rod. Due to weight of the squirrel, the rod bends at its lower end through an angle θ and due to elasticity of the material of the rod a restoring torque $C\theta$ is developed. If $C = 2mgL$, find the maximum length the squirrel can climb on the rod.

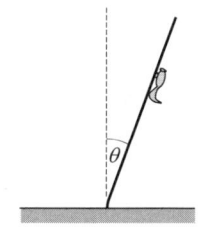

(a) $L/2$ (b) $3L/4$
(c) L (d) $2L$

11. A uniform bar AB is placed asymmetrically on two identical wedges P and Q that can slide on a frictionless horizontal tabletop as shown in the figure. Centre of the bar is C. Coefficient of static friction between the bar and the wedges is more than that of kinetic friction. If the wedges are shifted slowly with equal speeds on the tabletop towards each other, what will you observe?

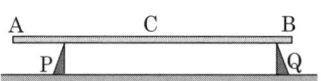

(a) The wedges meet below the centre C.
(b) The wedges meet somewhere between the centre C and end B.
(c) The wedges always slide relative to the bar until they meet.
(d) At a time, only one wedge that is farther away from the centre C slides relative to the bar.

12. A rigid body is observed in equilibrium in a particular non-rotating non-inertial frame. What can you conclude, if the body is observed from an inertial frame?

(a) The body is in rotational equilibrium but not in translational equilibrium.
(b) Net torque of all the forces on the body about its mass centre is a null vector.
(c) Net torque of all the forces on the body about any point that is collinear with line of the acceleration of the mass centre is a null vector.
(d) Net torque of all the forces on the body about all the points of a line that is parallel to the line of the acceleration of the mass centre is a null vector.

13. A cylinder P of radius r_P is being rotated at a constant angular velocity $\omega_P \hat{j}$ with the help of a motor about its axis that is fixed. Another cylinder Q of radius r_Q free to rotate about its axis that is also fixed is touched

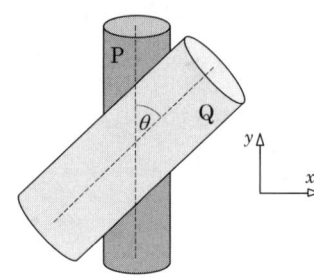

with and pressed on P making an angle θ between their axes. Soon after the cylinders are pressed against each other, a steady state is reached, and the cylinder Q acquires a constant angular velocity. What can you conclude when the steady state is reached?

(a) Angular velocity of cylinder Q is $\vec{\omega}_Q = -\dfrac{\omega_P r_P}{r_Q \cos\theta}\left(\sin\theta \hat{i} + \cos\theta \hat{j}\right)$.

(b) Angular velocity of cylinder Q is $\vec{\omega}_Q = -\dfrac{\omega_P r_P \cos\theta}{r_Q}\left(\sin\theta \hat{i} + \cos\theta \hat{j}\right)$.

(c) Unit vector of frictional force on cylinder Q is $\left(\sin\theta \hat{i} + \cos\theta \hat{j}\right)$.

(d) Frictional force on each cylinder becomes vanishingly small.

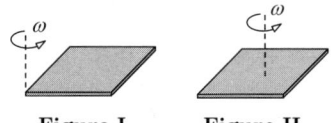

Figure-I   Figure-II

14. A uniform square plate is placed on a horizontal floor. When it is given an angular velocity ω about a vertical axis through one of its corners as shown in figure-I, it takes time t_1 to come to a complete stop. Now the same square plate is given the same angular velocity to rotate about another vertical axis through its centre as shown in figure-II. How long will it take to come to a complete stop now?

(a) $t_1/2$
(b) $2t_1/3$
(c) $3t_1/2$
(d) $2t_1$

15. A particle of mass m at a distance r from a fixed point is attracted towards the fixed point by a force given by equation $F = k/r^2$, where k is a positive constant. If L be its angular momentum with respect to the fixed point, which of the following equations is correct?

(a) $\Delta\left(\dfrac{L^2}{2mr^2} - \dfrac{k}{r}\right) = 0$

(b) $\Delta\left(\dfrac{1}{2}m\left(\dfrac{dr}{dt}\right)^2 + \dfrac{k}{r} + \dfrac{L^2}{2mr^2}\right) = 0$

(c) $\Delta\left(\dfrac{1}{2}m\left(\dfrac{dr}{dt}\right)^2 - \dfrac{k}{r}\right) = 0$

(d) $\Delta\left(\dfrac{1}{2}m\left(\dfrac{dr}{dt}\right)^2 - \dfrac{k}{r} + \dfrac{L^2}{2mr^2}\right) = 0$

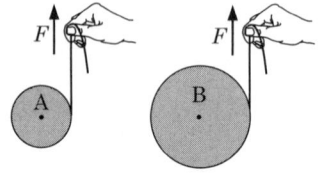

16. Two uniform discs A and B of equal masses and different radii r_A and r_B are mounted on fixed horizontal axles passing through their centres. On each of the discs, a light inextensible long cord is wound, and the discs are held motionless. If free ends of both the cords are pulled with equal forces for equal amounts of time, lengths of the cord unwound from the discs l_A and l_B bear the relation

(a) $l_A > l_B$
(b) $l_A < l_B$
(c) $l_A = l_B$
(d) More information needed.

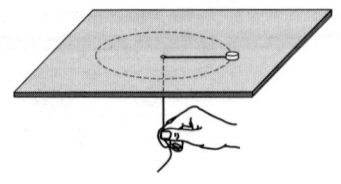

17. A small disc is attached at one end of a light inextensible string that passes through a hole in a frictionless horizontal tabletop. Initially the disc moves on a circle of radius R with kinetic energy K_0. The other end of the string is slowly pulled so that the disc finally moves on a circle of radius R/η. What is the work W done by the pulling agency?

(a) $W = 0$
(b) $W = \eta^2 K_0$
(c) $W = (\eta^2 - 1) K_0$
(d) $W = (\eta - 1) K_0$

18. A horizontal disc of mass 1.0 kg mounted on a fixed vertical axle through its centre can rotate without friction. On the disc a semicircular groove OP is cut. A small ball B of mass 1.5 kg when pushed on the disc towards the centre O, the ball enters the groove with a speed 2.0 m/s and moves through the groove without friction. With what speed will the ball leave the disc? Neglect loss of mass due to cutting the groove.

(a) 1.0 m/s
(b) 1.5 m/s
(c) 3.0 m/s
(d) Insufficient information

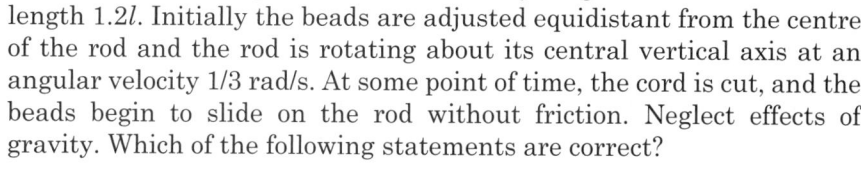

19. Two identical small beads A and B threaded on an almost inertia-less horizontal rod of length $2l$ are connected by a light inextensible cord of length $1.2l$. Initially the beads are adjusted equidistant from the centre of the rod and the rod is rotating about its central vertical axis at an angular velocity $1/3$ rad/s. At some point of time, the cord is cut, and the beads begin to slide on the rod without friction. Neglect effects of gravity. Which of the following statements are correct?

(a) Path of a bead in an inertial frame is a spiral.
(b) Path of a bead in an inertial frame is a straight line.
(c) To leave the rod, the beads take 4 s after the cord is cut.
(d) To leave the rod, the beads take more than 4 s after the cord is cut.

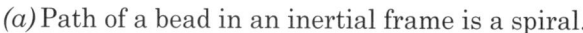

Questions 20 to 22 are based on the following physical situation.

A typical conveyor belt used to transport luggage is shown in the figure. Strip of the conveyer belt is moving with a constant velocity v_0 towards the east. A stationary homogeneous sphere of radius R and mass M is gently placed on the conveyor belt. Assume coefficient of static and kinetic friction to be μ_s and μ_k respectively.

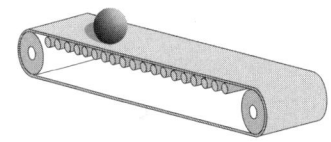

20. Which of the following statements are correct?

(a) It will appear rotating clockwise, if seen facing due north.
(b) It will appear rotating anticlockwise, if seen facing due north.
(c) Its linear speed relative to the ground as well as relative to the belt decreases.
(d) Its linear speed relative to the ground increases and relative to the belt decreases.

21. After a time t from the instant the sphere was placed on the belt, it starts pure rolling and moves with a velocity v relative to the ground. Which of the following are correct expressions for t and v?

(a) $t = \dfrac{2v_0}{5\mu_k g}$
(b) $t = \dfrac{2v_0}{7\mu_k g}$
(c) $v = \dfrac{2v_0}{5}$
(d) $v = \dfrac{2v_0}{7}$

22. Work done by the kinetic friction on the sphere relative to the ground is W_G and relative to the belt is W_B. Which of the following are correct expressions for W_G and W_B?

(a) $W_G = \dfrac{1}{7}Mv_0^2$
(b) $W_G = -\dfrac{1}{7}Mv_0^2$
(c) $W_B = \dfrac{1}{7}Mv_0^2$
(d) $W_B = -\dfrac{1}{7}Mv_0^2$

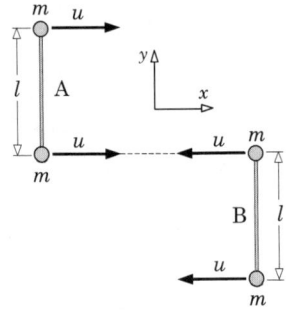

Questions 23 and 24 are based on the following physical situation.

Two identical dumbbells are fabricated by welding small identical particles each of mass m at the ends of light identical rods each of length l. The dumbbells are moving in free space with equal speeds u towards each other without rotation as shown in the figure. Collisions between the particles are perfectly elastic.

23. Angular velocity of each dumbbell after the first collision is

    (a) $\dfrac{u}{2l}$ (b) $\dfrac{u}{l}$

    (c) $\dfrac{2u}{l}$ (d) $\dfrac{4u}{l}$

24. How many times will the dumbbells collide?

    (a) One (b) Two
    (c) Three (d) Four

Build up your understanding

1. A rigid lamina is sliding on a horizontal floor with one of its flat faces on the floor. The floor is represented by x-y plane of a coordinate system. At an instant, some of the velocity components of three particles A, B and C of the lamina, when they occupy positions (0, 0), (1 m, 2 m) and (2 m, 1 m) are $v_{Ax} = 2$ m/s, $v_{Bx} = 4$ m/s and $v_{Cy} = -2$ m/s. Find coordinates of the instantaneous centre of rotation at this instant.

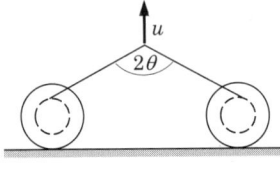

2. A thread is wound on two identical bobbins placed on a horizontal floor with their axes parallel. Radius of the outer flanges of the bobbins is η times of that of the inner spools. The midpoint of the thread is pulled vertically upwards with a constant velocity u. If the bobbins roll on the floor without slipping, find velocity of approach of their centres when angle between thread segments becomes 2θ.

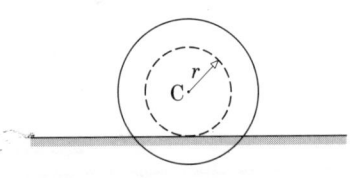

3. Spool of a bobbin rolls without slipping on a horizontal track. The radius of the spool is r and that of the flanges is significantly more than r. At some instant speeds of two diametrically opposite points on the spool are v_1 and v_2.

   (a) What is the speed of the centre of the bobbin?
   (b) Locate points on the flange that are moving vertically either upwards or downwards with a speed equal to that of the centre.

4. A sphere is rolling without slipping on two horizontal and parallel rails that are not in the same level. Distance between the rails is equal to radius of the sphere. If speed of the centre of the sphere is v, find greatest speed of a point on the sphere.

5. A toy is made by affixing coaxially two thin discs of radii $r_1 = 9.95$ cm and the other $r_2 = 10.05$ cm at the ends of a rod of length $l = 1.00$ cm. When this toy rolls on a horizontal ground without slipping, it rotates about the rod, advances on a circular path and also rotates about a vertical axis. If centre of the rod moves with a speed $v_C = 10.0$ cm/s, find angular velocity of the toy about the vertical axis.

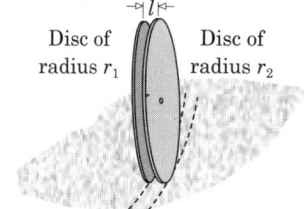

6. A car is moving on a circular path of radius $R = 20$ m and its wheels are rolling without slipping. Wheels of the car are of radius $r = 25$ cm and length of an axle that is distance between the wheels on the same axle is $l = 1.5$ m. If speed of midpoint of an axle is $v_C = 36$ km/h, find amount with which angular velocity of the outer wheel on this axle exceeds that of the inner wheel.

7. Two identical wheels each of radius R are harnessed by connecting their axles with a rigid rod and pivotally connecting midpoints of two parallel spokes with a bar. A box is placed on the bar and the assembly is made to move on a horizontal track with a gradually increasing speed maintaining rolling without slipping. Coefficient of friction between the bar and the box is μ and acceleration due to gravity is g. Find speed of the centre of the wheels at which the box begins sliding with respect to the bar.

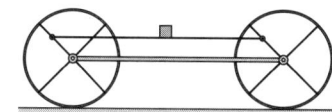

8. A uniform rod of length 100 cm and mass 1.0 kg is supported between two walls with the help of frictional forces. If maximum frictional force between an end of the rod and the wall is 20 N, where on the rod can a kitten of mass 2.0 kg sit safely?

9. If a load A of unknown mass is suspended at one end of a rod of length l and another load B of mass $m = 30$ kg at the other end, the rod stays horizontal provided that the rod is pivoted l/p away from its centre O towards the load B as shown in the first figure. In the absence of the load A, the rod stays horizontal, if it is pivoted l/q away from the centre towards the load B as shown in the second figure. If $p = 4$, $q = 3$, find mass of the load A.

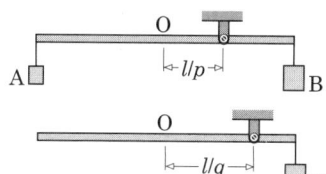

10. A balance consists of a straight light rod A, a right-angled light rod B rigidly welded with rod A and a fixed fulcrum F. Four loads are suspended from the balance with the help of light threads as shown in the figure. The rods have equidistant marks on them. If the masses of three loads are known ($m = 6$ kg), find the mass of the load C.

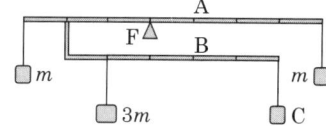

11. A uniform bar of mass $m_0 = 10$ kg is placed on a frictionless horizontal floor and its ends are fixed. If midpoint of the bar is pulled by a gradually increasing force F applied perpendicular to the bar as shown in the first figure, the bar breaks at its midpoint when the force F becomes $F_0 = 150$ N. Now another identical bar is placed on the floor and identical blocks of masses $m = 5$ kg are attached at the ends with the help of light inextensible cords as shown in the second figure. What maximum force F can be applied perpendicular to the bar at its midpoint so that the bar does not break?

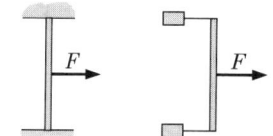

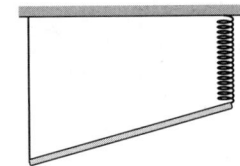

12. A rod of mass $m = 4.0$ kg is suspended from the ceiling with the help of an inextensible cord and a spring. In equilibrium, the cord and the spring are vertical and the rod stays at an angle 15° above the horizontal as shown in the figure. When an unknown load is suspended from the rod at the end connected with spring, the rod turns clockwise and stays at angle 15° below the horizontal. If in the second case extension in the spring is $\eta = 2$ times of that in the first case, find mass of the unknown load.

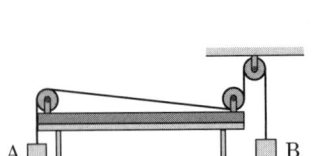

13. A uniform bar is placed on a horizontal frictionless tabletop. Two pulleys are rigidly attached at the ends of the bar and two loads A and B of masses m_1 and m_2 are suspended with the help of a light inextensible cord as shown in the figure. The pulleys attached to the bar and on the ceiling are to be considered ideal. If the bar stays horizontally on the tabletop in equilibrium, find its mass.

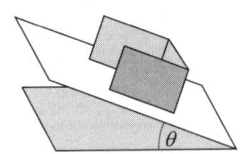

14. A cardboard strip, folded in U shape, is placed on an inclined plane, as shown in the figure. Length of the two parallel sections is $\eta = 1.5$ times of the length of the middle section, that is a square. At what minimum angle of inclination θ of the inclined plane with the horizontal, will the cardboard topple? Friction is sufficient to prevent sliding.

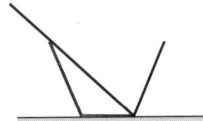

15. A cup having shape of a frustum of a cone is placed on a horizontal tabletop. Mass of the cup is $m = 20$ g and diameter of its bottom is $d = 5$ cm. A uniform rod of mass $M = 10$ g is placed in the cup as shown. The rod is inclined at an angle $\theta = 60°$ to the horizontal. Find maximum length l of the rod so that the system will not turn over.

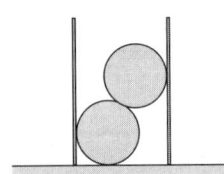

16. A cylindrical pipe of radius R and mass M is placed vertically on a horizontal floor. Two identical spheres each of radius r and mass m are inserted in the cylinder as shown in the figure. Radius of the spheres is more than $0.5R$. At what minimum value of m/M will the arrangement topple? There is no friction between the spheres and between a sphere and inner wall of the cylinder.

17. In a circus show, several clowns stand on wooden boards arranged in a queue. Each board can rotate about a fixed fulcrum that divides its length in ratio 2:1. A portion of the scheme is shown in the figure. A small load of mass 30 kg is placed on the end of the leftmost board and the clowns stand keeping their feet at the ends of adjacent boards. If mass of a clown is 80 kg and that of a board is negligible, find the maximum number of clowns that can keep balance in this way.

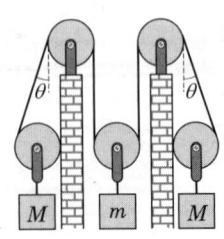

18. In the arrangement shown three loads are suspended in equilibrium from three pulleys. The segment of the rope between each of the uppermost pulleys and the outermost pulleys leans at angle θ with the vertical.
    (a) What is the ratio of masses $m:M$?
    (b) Find range of coefficient of friction between the walls and the outermost pulleys.
    (c) What is the nature of the equilibrium?

19. Upper edges of two identical uniform planks each of mass $M = 87$ kg and length $l = 1.0$ m are hinged to a horizontal axle affixed to the ceiling. A cylinder of mass $m = 20$ kg and radius $r = 0.30$ m is inserted horizontally between the planks as shown. The cylinder touches the planks at a distance $\eta = 0.75$ times the length of the plank from the hinge. Find range of coefficient of friction between the planks and the cylinder to keep the system in equilibrium.

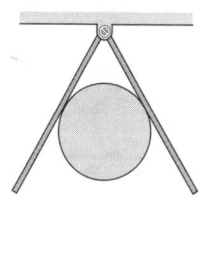

20. A structure consisting of two identical square plates of side $l = 40$ cm hinged to a common axle at one of their edges is placed on a fixed horizontal cylinder of radius $r = 10$ cm as shown in the figure. There is no friction between the cylinder and the plates. At what angle with vertical will the plates lean in equilibrium?

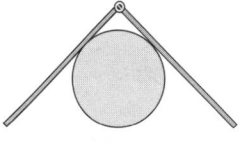

21. A cylinder of mass $M = 2.0$ kg is placed on two parallel rails inclined at an angle $\theta = 37°$ to the horizontal (side view shown in the figure). A load of unknown mass is suspended from a light inextensible cord wound on the cylinder. The cylinder is held initially at rest and then released. If the cylinder starts rolling up the rails without slipping, what should mass of the load be?

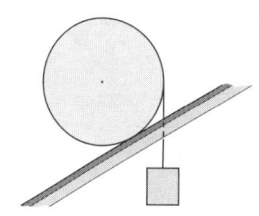

22. A thin uniform rod of mass m stays in equilibrium on the top of a fixed horizontal cylinder perpendicular to the axis of the cylinder. Length of the rod is equal to circumference of the cylinder. A beetle of mass $0.2m$ starts crawling slowly from the centre of the rod and reaches an end of the rod. As the beetle crawls on the rod, the rod rotates slowly without slipping on the cylinder. Find coefficient of friction between the cylinder and the rod for which the above movement is possible.

23. A rear-wheel-drive car moves with a constant speed $v = 20$ m/s on a circular path of radius $r = 200$ m on a horizontal ground. Centre of gravity of the car is close to the ground and equidistant from all the four wheels that have negligible mass as compared to rest of the car.

   (a) What should the minimum coefficient of friction between the tyres and the ground be to make this movement of the car possible?
   (b) If coefficient of friction is made double, in how much minimum time can the driver of the car increase speed from 20 m/s to 20.5 m/s on the circular path?

24. A metal pipe bent at right angle at its midpoint is pivoted to a fixed support at one of its ends so that it can rotate freely in its plane about a horizontal axis through the pivoted end. A flexible hose is connected at the pivoted end. When water is fed at a particular rate into the pipe, the upper arm of the pipe makes an angle α with the vertical as shown in the figure. If the rate of feeding water is gradually made η times, find an expression for the angle β, which the upper arm of the pipe will make with the vertical.

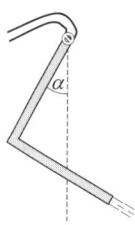

25. A light rigid rod is placed on a frictionless horizontal floor and blocks of masses of m and $3m$ are attached to the ends of the rod with the help of light inextensible cords. If a horizontal force F is applied perpendicular to the rod at its midpoint as shown in the figure, what will acceleration of the midpoint of the rod be?

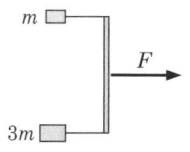

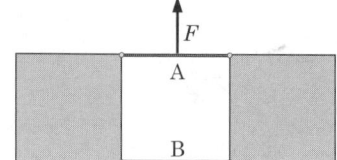

26. Two identical square laminae connected by two rods A and B are placed on a frictionless horizontal floor with their flat faces on the floor. The rods are free to rotate at the joints where they are connected with the laminae. Rod A is pulled horizontally at its midpoint perpendicular to the rod by a constant force F as shown in the figure. Find moduli of the reaction forces F_A and F_B between one of the laminae and the rods A and B respectively. Consider the following cases.

   (a) Mass of each rod is negligible as compared to that of a lamina.
   (b) Mass of each rod is equal to that of a lamina.

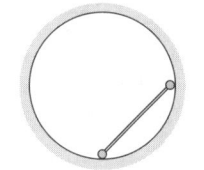

27. Inside a fixed frictionless spherical cavity of radius r, a dumbbell is held touching the bottom of the cavity at its lower end. The dumbbell consists of two identical small balls each of mass m affixed at the ends of a light rod of length $r\sqrt{2}$. What will the force of interaction between the lower ball and the cavity be immediately after the dumbbell is released?

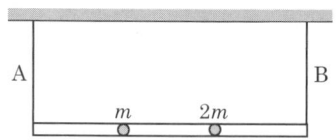

28. A light rigid pipe is suspended with the help of two light inextensible vertical threads. Inside the pipe, two balls one of mass m and other of mass $2m$ can slide without friction. Initially the pipe is horizontal, and the balls stay equidistant from each other and from the ends of the pipe as shown in the figure. How many times will the tension force in the thread A change, immediately after the thread B is cut?

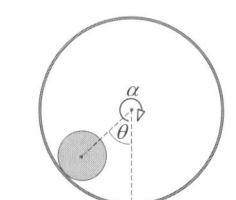

29. A uniform cylinder is held motionless in a horizontal stationary pipe at an angular position $\theta = 30°$ touching inner surface of the pipe. Radii of the cylinder and the pipe are $r = 0.2$ m and $R = 2.0$ m respectively. The pipe is now made to rotate about its fixed horizontal axis with a constant angular acceleration and the cylinder is released. If the axis of the cylinder remains motionless, find the angular acceleration of the pipe.

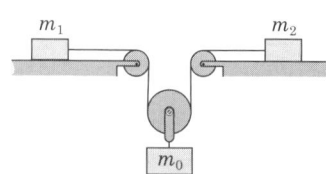

30. In the arrangement shown, masses of blocks are $m_0 = 5$ kg, $m_1 = 5$ kg and $m_2 = 10$ kg and radius of the movable pulley is $r = 10$ cm. The threads and the pulleys are ideal and friction between the blocks and the horizontal surface is negligible. Find change in angular velocity of the movable pulley in a time interval $\Delta t = 0.22$ s. Acceleration of free fall is $g = 10$ m/s².

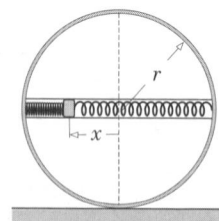

31. A light rigid tube is welded along a diameter of a uniform cylindrical pipe of mass M and radius r. A bead of mass m connected by two identical light springs each of force constant k can slide inside the tube. Other ends of the springs are connected to the pipe as shown in the figure. The pipe is held motionless on a horizontal floor, the bead is pulled aside a distance x away from the centre of the pipe and then the pipe and the bead both are released simultaneously. If the cylinder rolls without slipping on the ground, find acceleration of its centre immediately after the system is released.

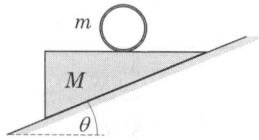

32. A uniform hollow cylinder of mass m rests on a wedge of mass M that is held on a frictionless slope of inclination θ as shown in the figure. Friction between the cylinder and the top horizontal surface of the wedge is sufficient to prevent sliding of the cylinder after the wedge is released. Find acceleration of the wedge after it is released.

33. In the setup shown, masses of the pulleys and the thread are negligible as compared to mass m of the load hanging from the lower pulley. The radius of the smaller drum of the two-step pulley (drums of a two-step pulley are coaxially fixed preventing them from rotating independently) is r and that of the larger drum is R. There is no friction at the axles of the pulleys whereas friction between the thread and peripheries of the pulleys is sufficient to prevent slipping. The acceleration of free fall is g. If the free end P of the thread is pulled horizontally with a constant velocity v, find power delivered by the pulling agency.

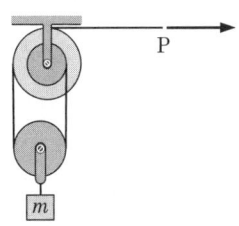

34. In the setup shown, the pulley and the threads are ideal, the spring of force constant k is massless, the wheel has all its mass m uniformly distributed in its rim, the harness used to connect wheel axle with the spring and with the thread is massless and the loads A and B are of masses m and 3m respectively. Initially the harness is held motionless keeping the spring relaxed and then released. If the wheel rolls on the horizontal tabletop without slipping, find maximum tension developed in the thread connecting the loads.

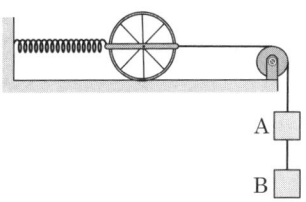

35. A uniform wheel of mass m and radius r is free to rotate about a horizontal massless axle that passes through its centre. A horizontal conveyor belt is running underneath the wheel with the help of a motor at a constant velocity u perpendicular to the axle of the wheel. Radius of gyration of the wheel is k.

(a) The wheel is lowered on the belt and then pressed down holding the axle stationary. Find additional energy delivered by the motor during the process of slipping.

(b) The wheel is gently released on the belt. Find additional energy delivered by the motor during the process of slipping.

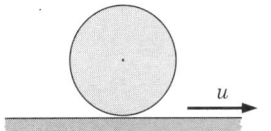

36. A cart consists of a box of mass m mounted on four identical wheels. Total mass of all the four wheels is also m. When released from rest on a uniform slope of inclination $\theta = 30°$, the cart rolls down a distance $l = 15$ m in time $t_0 = 3.0$ s. Now a load of mass m is put in the box of the cart and the cart is again released on the slope. If the load does not slide in the box, calculate time taken by the cart to roll down the same distance again. Acceleration due to gravity is $g = 10$ m/s².

37. A rear-wheel drive car of mass m, engine of which delivers a constant power p starts from rest on a straight level road. Coefficient of friction between tyres and the road is μ. If centre of gravity of the car is close to the road and equidistant from all the four wheels and masses of the wheels are negligible as compared to mass of the rest of the car, how does speed of the car vary with time?

38. A particle of mass m placed on a frictionless horizontal floor is connected with the help of a light elastic cord to a nail O driven in the floor. The particle is pulled stretching the cord to a point A on the floor at a distance $l_0 = 12$ cm from the nail and projected horizontally perpendicular to the cord. If the particle is observed moving with a velocity $v = 24$ m/s at a point B a distance $l = 10$ cm away from the nail at an angle $\theta = 37°$ with the cord as shown, find the velocity of projection of the particle.

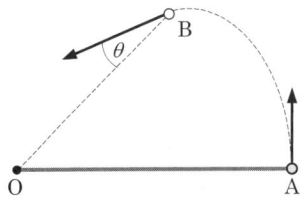

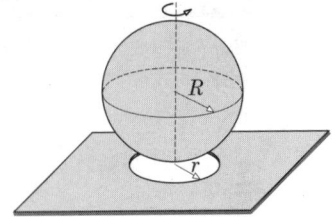

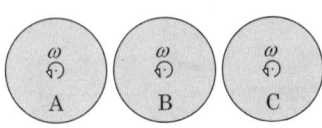

39. A homogeneous sphere of radius $R = 10$ cm rotating about its vertical diameter is gently released on a hole of radius $r_1 = 8.0$ cm made in a fixed horizontal slab. Centre of the hole is vertically below the centre of the sphere. The sphere stops in a time interval $\Delta t_1 = 9.0$ s. Calculate time interval required to stop the same sphere, if it is placed rotating with the same angular velocity on a hole of radius $r_2 = 6.0$ cm made in another identical horizontal slab.

40. Three identical uniform cylinders are mounted on frictionless horizontal axles passing through their centres. They are given equal angular velocities ω_0 each and then gradually brought into contact preventing any vertical movement and rotation of their axles.

    (a) Find angular velocities of the cylinders after they stop slipping.
    (b) Can you use principle of conservation of angular momentum to analyse the situation?

41. Two insects each of mass m are at opposite ends of a diameter of a turntable, moment of inertia of which is I about its central vertical axis. The turntable is rotating freely, and both the insects start crawling slowly towards each other on the turntable. At what distance r from the centre of the turntable, do the insects have to apply maximum horizontal force on the turntable?

Check your understanding

1. Two identical thin rigid rods AB and CD each of length L touching each other at point P rotate in a plane about their stationary ends A and C that are a distance h apart. Velocities of their ends B and D have constant moduli v_1 and v_2 respectively. Find component of velocity of their point of intersection P along the rod AB when the rods make angles α and β with the line AC.

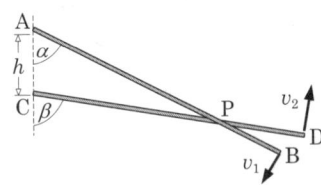

2. Free ends of two inextensible cords wrapped around a massive disc of radius $r = 10\sqrt{3}$ cm are affixed to the ceiling at two different points. Both the cords and the disc are in the same vertical plane. At an instant after the disc is released, angles made by the cords with the ceiling are $\theta = 67°$ and $\phi = 53°$ and angular velocity of the disc is $\omega = 5.0$ rad/s. Find magnitude of velocity of the centre of the disc at this instant.

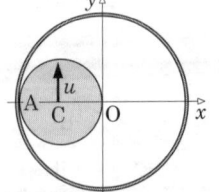

3. A disc of radius R is rolling on the inner surface of a stationary coplanar ring of radius $2R$. If speed u of the centre C of the disc is a constant, write coordinates of the point A of the disc as a function of time t. At instant $t = 0$ s, the point A is in contact with the ring as shown in the figure.

4. A boy riding a bicycle at a constant speed describes a circular path. Wheels of the bicycle are identical, and axles are a distance l apart. If the front wheel rotates η times faster than the rear wheel, find the radii of the circular tracks traced by both the wheels. Neglect tilting of the bicycle from the vertical and slippage of the wheels.

5. A square lamina ABCD with one of its flat faces on a horizontal floor is sliding on the floor. At an instant velocity vectors of the corners A and B are perpendicular to each other, and the corner C is moving with a velocity v at an angle with vector $\overline{CD}$, tangent of which is 0.5. Find the velocity of the midpoint P of the side AB at this instant.

6. One end of a half ring of mass m is hinged to nail A. When the ring is set free, its diameter makes an angle θ_0 with the vertical as shown in the first figure. Another nail is now driven into the wall, vertically below the former nail at a distance that is equal to radius of the ring and the ring is left resting on the lower nail as shown in the second figure. Assuming friction to be absent everywhere and acceleration due to gravity to be g, find horizontal and vertical components of the reaction force of the upper nail on the ring in the second case.

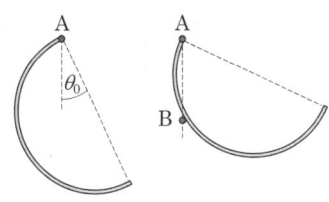

7. A rod of mass $M = 10$ kg is hinged at its midpoint on top of a pedestal of height $h = 50$ cm and mass $m = 250$ g. The ends of the rod are connected to a ceiling with the help of two springs of equal relaxed length $l_0 = 40$ cm and unequal force constants $k_1 = 25$ N/m and $k_2 = 15$ N/m. In equilibrium, the rod stays at an unknown angle from the horizontal and the springs are vertical as shown in the figure. If height of the ceiling above the floor is $H = 1.5$ m, find the force of normal reaction between the pedestal and the floor.

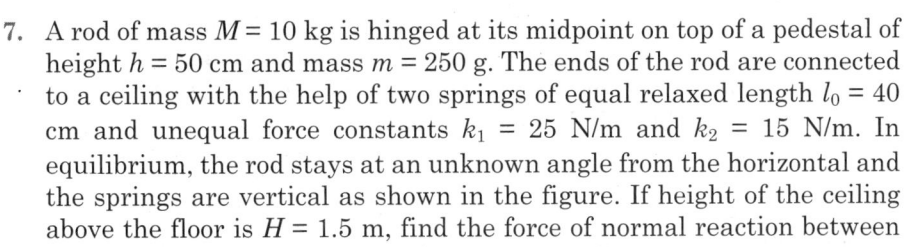

8. A small block is released on the top of a wedge that is placed on a horizontal floor as shown in the figure. Mass of the wedge is M and angle of inclination of its slant face is θ. Friction between the wedge and the floor is sufficient to prevent sliding and coefficient of friction between the wedge and the block is μ. What should the mass of the block be so that the wedge will not topple?

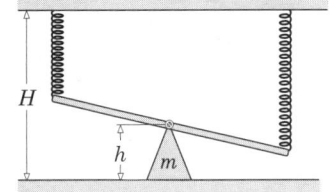

9. A load is suspended from one end of a uniform rod of mass $m = 10$ kg and length l with the help of a light inextensible thin cord and the arrangement is placed on a fixed horizontal frictionless cylinder of radius r as shown in the figure. In equilibrium, the rod stays at angle $\theta = 30°$ with the horizontal and distance between point of contact of the rod with the cylinder and top end of the rod is $\eta = 1/\sqrt{2}$ times the radius of the cylinder. Find mass of the load and ratio of length of the rod to the radius of the cylinder.

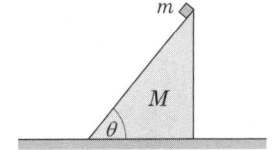

10. A uniform right-angled triangular lamina is placed on a horizontal floor, which is not frictionless. One of the acute angles of the lamina is θ as shown in the figure by the top view of the situation. If F_A and F_B are the minimum forces required to rotate the lamina about stationary vertical axes through the vertices A and B respectively, find the minimum force required to rotate the lamina about a stationary vertical axis through the vertex C.

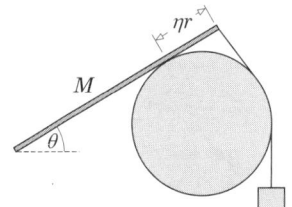

11. Find suitable expression for the moment of inertia of a uniform ring of mass m and radius r about an axis that passes through the centre of the ring and makes an angle θ with the plane of the ring.

5.18 Chapter-5

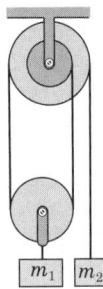

12. In the system shown, masses of pulleys and the thread are negligible as compared to masses $m_1 = 9.0$ kg and $m_2 = 1.0$ kg of the blocks. The upper pulley is a two-step pulley in which radius of the smaller drum is $r = 1/3$ m and that of the larger drum is $\eta = 2$ times of r. At one end, the thread is wrapped on the smaller drum of the two-step pulley and at the other end the block of mass m_2 is attached. There is no friction at the axles of the pulleys whereas friction between the thread and peripheries of the pulleys is sufficient to prevent slipping. Acceleration of free fall is $g = 10$ m/s². When released find acceleration of the block of mass m_1.

13. An attempt is being made to roll a rigid sphere of mass m up a vertical wall. Coefficient of friction between the sphere and the wall is μ. Find the minimum force applied on the sphere to roll it up. Acceleration of gravity is g.

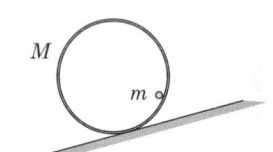

14. A thin rod of mass m is welded on inner surface of a thin-walled pipe of mass M parallel to the axis of the pipe. The composite body thus formed is placed on a uniform slope as shown in the figure. Inclination of the slope is adjustable. Find range of coefficient of friction between the pipe and the slope for which the body slides down without rotation?

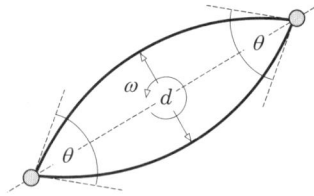

15. In free space, an assembly of two identical particles each of mass m connected by two identical uniform ropes is rotating at a constant angular velocity ω about an axis passing through the centre of the line segment joining the particles and perpendicular to the plane containing the ropes. The ropes fan out due to inertia and assume a curved shape as shown in the figure. If distance between the midpoints of the ropes is d, tensile force at the midpoint of a rope is T and the included angle between the ropes at the particles is θ, find the distance l between the particles.

16. Three small balls A, B and C each of mass m are connected by three thin light rods each of length l to make an equilateral triangular structure. The structure is sliding on a frictionless horizontal floor with all the three balls on the floor. At an instant, the ball A is observed moving with a velocity v along the rod AB and the ball B moving along the rod BC. Find moduli of tensile forces developed in each of the rods.

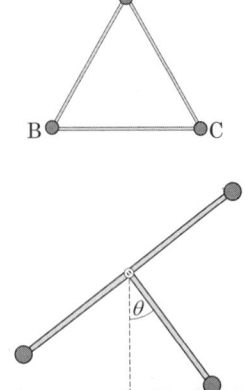

17. Three identical light rods are rigidly connected to frame a T-junction. At the free ends of each rod, identical particle like balls each of mass $m = \sqrt{5}$ kg are affixed and the junction is so pivoted that the frame can rotate without friction in a vertical plane containing the frame. Now the frame is tilted through an angle $\theta = 37°$ and released. Find magnitude of the force exerted by the middle rod on the ball connected to it and the angle made by this force vector with the middle rod immediately after the frame is released. Acceleration of free fall is g.

18. An important criterion in car design is the maximum slope that a car can climb. Consider two cars similar in all parameters; except, one is a rear-wheel drive and the other is a front-wheel drive. Distance between the front and rear axles is $l = 3$ m, mass centre is at a height $h = 0.75$ m above the road and equidistant from all the wheels and coefficient of

friction between the tyres and the road is $\mu = 0.8$. For simplicity, neglect masses of the wheels as compared to the rest of the car.

(a) Which car is better in accordance with mentioned criterion?
(b) What maximum uniform slope can the better car climb?

19. A uniformly filled container of height h and length l is placed on a horizontal plank that can slide on a horizontal floor. Along one of the bottom edge of the container, a small triangular wedge like support is welded and at the other bottom edge extremely light and small rigid wheels are fitted as shown in the figure. There is no friction at the axles of the wheels. If the plank is made to move towards the right with an acceleration a_0, the container begins to slide. Find retardation with which the plank moving towards the right can be stopped preventing the container from sliding and toppling respectively.

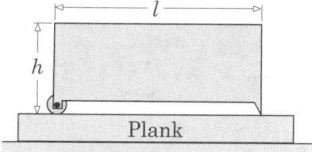

20. A uniform rigid lamina of mass M and area S can rotate about a fixed vertical axis that is in the plane of the lamina. While the lamina is rotating, excess pressure p created by forces of air resistance at a point on the lamina is given by equation $p = kv$, here k is a positive constant and v is speed of the point under consideration. If the lamina is given an angular velocity ω_0, how many revolutions will it make before coming to a complete stop?

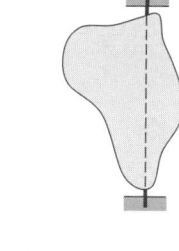

21. To insert into or draw out a cylindrical rod tightly fitted in a circular hole, a usual practice is to apply a necessary axial force (push to insert and pull to draw out) and simultaneously rotate the cylinder. Moreover, we do it in steps because by hands we cannot continuously rotate the rod.

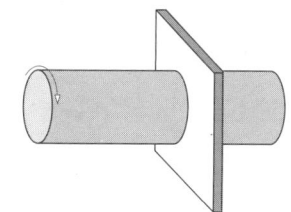

(a) How does this technique work?
(b) Let in each step of duration Δt, the rod rotates at a constant angular velocity ω and advances axially by a constant linear velocity v under action of a constant axial push F. Find the torque applied on the cylinder. Radius of the rod is r.

22. Very often, you have seen an insect dragging an object much larger and heavier than it. The figure is a top view of an ant dragging a straw that is much larger and heavier than the ant. The ant pulls the straw at one end rotating it slightly then it does the same action at the other end and so on.

(a) How does this technique work?
(b) An ant is dragging a straw of mass m on a horizontal floor by this technique. Coefficient of friction between the straw and the floor is μ. How much force F does it have to apply?

23. A uniform disc rotating about its vertical axis of symmetry is gently placed on a horizontal floor with one of its flat faces on the floor. The floor has two portions, where coefficients of frictions between the disc and the floor are $\mu_1 = 0.78$ and $\mu_2 = 0.67$. Consider the line dividing the two portions as y-axis and the point where centre of the disc is placed as the origin of a coordinate system as shown in the figure. Find acceleration of the centre of the disc immediately after it is placed on the floor. Assume acceleration of free fall to be $g = 10$ m/s² and $\pi = 22/7$.

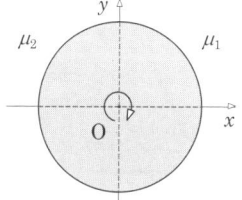

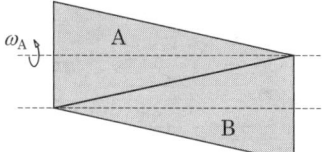

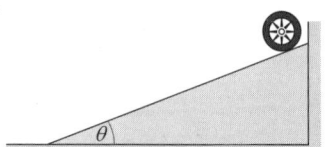

24. A uniform disc of radius R rests with one of its flat faces on a horizontal floor. Coefficient of friction between the disc and the floor is μ. The disc is given an angular velocity ω_0 about its central vertical axis and simultaneously a horizontal velocity v_0 ($v_0 \ll R\omega_0$). Find suitable expression for initial acceleration of the mass centre of the disc.

25. Two identical uniform cones A and B can rotate freely about their fixed central axes, pressing each other uniformly on their entire tapered length as shown in the figure. If the cone A is rotated with a constant angular velocity ω_A, how much angular velocity will the cone B ultimately acquire due to friction between the cones?

26. A right-angled triangular wedge is placed on a frictionless horizontal floor with its vertical face touching a wall. Inclined face of the wedge makes an angle θ with the floor. A wheel of mass M is released near the top of the wedge. During downward movement of the wheel, the wedge exerts a constant force F on the wall. Acceleration of free fall is g.
   (a) How much speed will the centre of the wheel acquire after covering a distance s? Consider both the cases i.e. rolling with slipping and rolling without slipping.
   (b) After covering equal distances, in which case will the centre of wheel acquire higher speed?

27. A dumbbell constructed by affixing of two identical small balls at the ends of a thin light rod rests aligned along a longitude on a frictionless horizontal floor. Now a constant force F always directed towards the east is applied on one of the balls. Find the maximum tensile force developed in the rod.

28. A bead is fixed on a rigid ring of radius r and of mass that is negligible as compared to that of the bead. Assembly thus formed is held motionless on a horizontal floor with the plane of the ring vertical and the bead on the top. Coefficient of friction between the ring and the floor is μ. Now the assembly is given a slight push so that the ring starts rolling. Acceleration of free fall is g.
   (a) By how much angle will the ring rotate before it begins to slide?
   (b) Find speed of the centre of the ring when the ring begins to slide?

29. Motor of a toy car of mass $m = 1.0$ kg delivers a constant power $p = 50$ W. Coefficient of friction between a horizontal floor and the tyres of the car is $\mu = 0.5$. Calculate time required to accelerate the car from rest to a speed $v = 20$ m/s on this floor. Consider both the types: four-wheel drive and rear-wheel drive. For simplicity, ignore masses of the wheels and the air resistance and consider centre of gravity of the cars equidistant from all the wheels and very close to the floor.

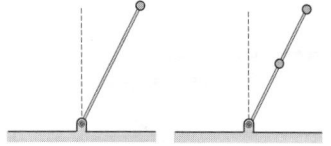

30. A light rigid rod is pivoted at its lower on the ground. The rod is turned to make an angle θ with the vertical and a small bead of mass m is affixed at its upper end as shown in the first figure. When the rod is released, the bead hits the ground in time t_0. Now an additional small bead of mass ηm is affixed at the midpoint of the rod and the rod is again

released from the same angle θ with the vertical as shown in the second figure. In how much time now will the beads hit the ground?

31. A body of circular section rolling on a horizontal track with a velocity u = 5.0 m/s crosses a slightly elevated curved section AB of the track in time Δt_1 = 5.0 s without slipping anywhere. On the elevated section, change in gravitational potential energy at any place is much smaller than initial kinetic energy of the body. The length of the section AB is l = 20 m.

Now on the horizontal track consider a slightly depressed section CD, profile of which is a mirror image of the section AB. If the same body enters the section CD rolling with the same velocity u, how much time will it take to move from point C to point D?

32. A homogeneous plank of mass M and length L is released gently on an inclined rolling mill, which consists of a large number of uniform horizontal cylindrical rollers. Axes of the roller are fixed parallel to each other in a plane inclined at an angle θ with the horizontal with a separation l ($l \ll L$) between two adjacent axes. The mass of a roller is m, each roller can rotate about its axis without friction and acceleration due to gravity is g. A long time after the plank is released; it acquires a steady speed v. Find this steady speed.

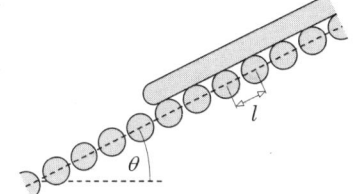

33. A stationary point source creating a potential field is at the origin O of a coordinate frame. Potential energy of interaction of this source and a particle of mass m is given by equation $U = -k/r^4$, where k is a positive constant and r is distance of the particle from the source. The particle is projected with an initial velocity u from an infinitely distant point. Distance between initial line of motion of the particle and the source is b as shown in the figure. What should the minimum value of b for this projection velocity be so that the particle will not hit the source?

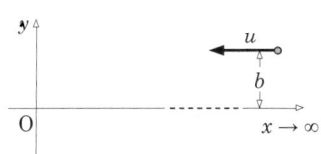

34. A bead of mass m is attached to lower end of a light inextensible thread that passes through a small frictionless hole in a horizontal tabletop. The upper end of the thread is held motionless. The bead is pulled aside and projected horizontally to move on a circular path of radius R with a speed v_0 at a particular depth below the tabletop. Find work done in slowly pulling the thread upwards to reduce the depth of circular path of the bead to half of its previous value.

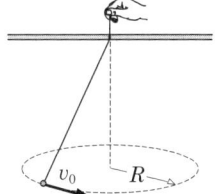

35. An almost inertia-less plank AB can rotate about a stationary horizontal axle O. Its end B rests on a platform where a small block of mass m is placed on it at a distance l from the axle as shown in the figure. A bead of mass m_0 dropped from a height h_0 hits the platform near the end A at a distance l_0 from the axle. If all the collisions are perfectly elastic and every object is perfectly rigid, find height h to which the block will jump.

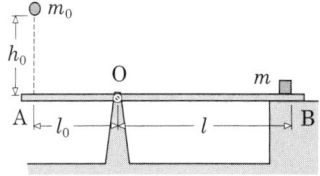

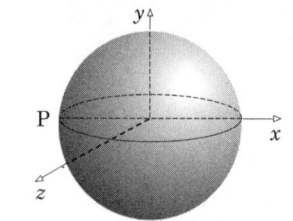

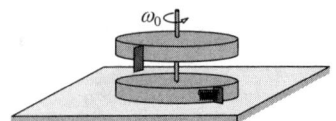

36. A uniform sphere of radius R and mass M is rotating with an angular velocity $\omega_0 \hat{i}$ in free space. A bullet of mass m moving in the positive z-direction hits the sphere at a distance $0.2R$ from the z-axis and comes out almost in no time with a vanishingly small velocity without any appreciable loss of mass of the sphere. As a result, the sphere starts rotating with an angular velocity ω_0 about the y-axis in such a way that point P appears moving in the positive z-direction. Find velocity of the mass centre of the sphere after its interaction with the bullet?

37. Two identical discs each of radius r and mass m having plate-like light protrusions are coaxially mounted on a thin vertical pole that is fixed on a horizontal floor. A small spring of force constant k is affixed on the protrusion of the lower disc as shown in the figure. The upper disc is given an angular velocity ω_0 and gently released on the lower disc. Friction is absent everywhere.
    (a) Find the maximum compression of the spring.
    (b) Find angular velocities of the upper and the lower discs when the spring becomes relaxed.

38. Two identical uniform discs each of mass m and radius r are placed on a horizontal frictionless floor. One of the discs is given an angular velocity ω about its stationary vertical central axis and the other is projected with a horizontal velocity u without rotation for a head-on collision to occur between them. If the collision is perfectly inelastic and slipping between the discs ceases in the end of the collision, find angular velocities of the discs and speeds of their centres after the collision.

39. A uniform cylinder of radius r rolling with a velocity u on a horizontal floor collides elastically with another identical cylinder kept at rest parallel to the former one. Coefficient of friction between a cylinder and the floor is μ, no friction acts between the cylinders during the collision and acceleration of free fall is g. Find separation between the cylinders, when relative acceleration between their centres vanishes.

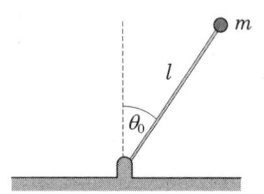

40. A light rod of length l pivoted at its lower end on the ground can rotate is any direction. A particle of mass m is affixed at its upper end and the rod is held and an angle $\theta_0 = 37°$ from the vertical as shown in the figure. Now the particle is given a horizontal velocity $u = \sqrt{2}$ m/s perpendicular to the rod. At an instant in the subsequent motion, when the rod exerts no force on the particle, what is the angle θ made by the rod with the vertical and what is that horizontal component of velocity of the particle which is perpendicular to the rod? Acceleration of free fall is $g = 10$ m/s².

41. A water sprinkler system consists of a tube bent into S shape. This tube rotates in a horizontal plane about a vertical axis through its centre when water flows out from its nozzles. Top view of the tube is shown in the figure. Moment of inertia of the rotating tube including water about the axis is I, cross-section of outlet of a nozzle is S, density of water is ρ, water flow velocity relative to the nozzles is u and length b of the nozzles is much smaller than the length l of the tube arms. Neglect all types of frictional and viscous effects.

(a) Derive an expression for the initial angular acceleration of the tube.
(b) Derive an expression for the angular velocity ω of the tube as a function of time t.

Challenge your understanding

1. A lamp is attached on circumference of a horizontal disc that is sliding on a frictionless horizontal floor in a dark room. The lamp emits sharp light pulses of different colours at regular intervals of $\tau = 1.0$ s. Colours of the pulses repeatedly change in a sequence that is red, green, yellow, blue, and purple. Mass centre of lamp, its power supply and the disc coincides the centre of the disc. In a particular time interval, locations where four pulses are observed are shown in the following graph. Calculate radius R of the disc, velocity v_c of the centre of the disc and angular velocity ω of the disc.

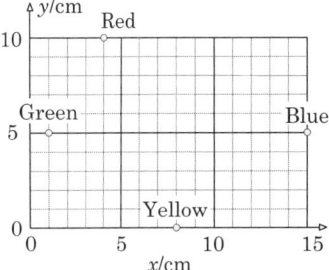

2. You find a table of height $h = 1.0$ m and a square top of side $l = 1.0$ m. One leg of the table is slightly shorter than the other three legs by amount $\Delta h = 1.0$ cm. When the shorter leg is touching the ground, the top is slightly tilted. To make the top horizontal, you have to put a minimum mass $m_0 = 200$ g on the tabletop at the corner opposite to the shorter leg. Find the mass M of the tabletop. Assume perfectly horizontal floor, uniform tabletop and very light thin legs.

3. A light rigid square plate of side l is suspended horizontally with the help of four identical vertical wires affixed at their lower ends on each of the corners of the plate. The upper ends of the wires are affixed to a horizontal ceiling. All these wires are elastic and have very high force constant. Find region of the plate in which if you stick a load much greater than that of the plate, every wire will remain taut. Acceleration of free fall is g.

4. A boy is driving his bicycle at a constant speed on a circular path on a horizontal ground. To do so he turns the handle so that the front wheel makes an angle θ with line joining centres of the axles of the wheels. Distance between the axles is l. Coefficient of friction is the same between both the tyres and the road. Calculate the minimum coefficient of friction between the road and the tyres, so that the cycle does not slip. Assume mass centre of the cycle and the boy equidistant from both the axles and acceleration of free fall is g.

5. Particle-like balls each of mass m are affixed at both the ends of a light rigid rod of length l. The composite body thus formed is suspended from a nail O with the help of two light inextensible cords affixed on each ball. Length of each cord is also l. Now arrangement is pulled aside bringing one ball in level with the nail and keeping both the cords straight and then released. Find maximum tension T_{max} in a cord in the subsequent motion. Acceleration of free fall is g.

5.24 Chapter-5

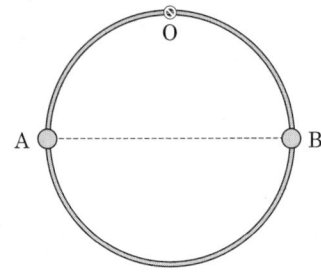

6. A light ring of radius *r* wearing two identical beads A and B each of mass *m* is hinged at its top point O in such a way that it can rotate freely in its plane about a horizontal axis through the hinge O. The bead A is affixed on the ring and the bead B is held so that they occupy positions of the ends of the horizontal diameter of the ring and the system stays motionless. The ring is well lubricated so that the bead B can slide with negligible friction on the ring.

Determine acceleration of the beads immediately after the bead B is released and final angle of rotation of the ring when all motion ceases after a long time due to the little viscous friction between the bead B and the ring. Acceleration due to gravity is *g*.

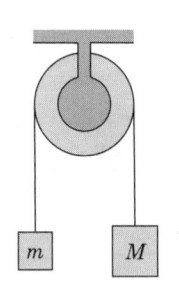

7. A uniform annular disc of outer radius *R* and inner radius *r* is coaxially mounted on a fixed cylinder. Radius of the cylinder is slightly smaller than inner radius of the disc to allow the disc to rotate as a pulley and the fixed cylinder as an axle. Coefficient of friction between the disc and the cylinder is μ. A light inextensible rope supporting two loads of masses *m* and *M* >*m* passes along the upper half periphery of the disc. Find the acceleration *a* of the load *M*. Acceleration of free fall is *g*.

ANSWERS AND HINTS

Multiple Choice Questions

1. (c)
2. (a) and (b)
3. (c)
4. (c)
5. (a), (b) and (c)
6. (d)
7. (d)
8. (b) and (d)
9. (b)
10. (c)
11. (a) and (d)
12. (a), (b) and (c)
13. (b) and (c)
14. (a)
15. (d)
16. (c)
17. (c)
18. (a)
19. (b) and (c)
20. (b) and (d)
21. (b) and (d)
22. (a) and (d)
23. (c)
24. (b)

Build up your understanding

1. (0, −2)

   Hint: Velocity vectors $\vec{v}_P$, $\vec{v}_Q$ of any two particles P and Q of a rigid body and its angular velocity vector $\vec{\omega}$ bear the following relation.

   $$\vec{v}_P = \vec{v}_Q + \vec{\omega} \times \overrightarrow{QP}$$

   Assuming coordinates (*x*, *y*) of instantaneous centre of rotation and assigning it zero speed, use information regarding particles at locations A, B and C together with the abovementioned idea and make necessary equations to find the unknowns.

   Alternatively, you may quicken the process by using the fact that any two particles of a rigid body must have same velocity component along the line joining them. From information of the particle A and B, first find the angular velocity and then by using simultaneously the angular velocity and information of particle at point C, find y-component of velocity of A. Thereafter use abovementioned equation for the particle A and the instantaneous centre of rotation.

2. $\dfrac{2\eta u \cos\theta}{1+\eta \sin\theta}$

3. (a) $\dfrac{\sqrt{v_1^2+v_2^2}}{2}$

(b) Points on the circumference of the flanges to the left and to the right of the instantaneous axis of rotation.

4. $v\left(1+\dfrac{2}{\sqrt{3}}\right)$

Hint: The point of the sphere having greatest speed must be farthest from the chord joining the rails that is also the instantaneous axis of rotation.

5. $\dfrac{2v_C(r_2-r_1)}{l(r_2+r_1)} = 0.10$ rad/s

Hint: Angular velocity of the circular motion of the centre of the axle is equal to the angular velocity of its rotation about the vertical axis.

6. $\dfrac{lv_C}{rR} = 3.0$ rad/s

7. $\sqrt{\dfrac{2\mu gR}{\sqrt{1+\mu^2}}}$

8. Within 25 cm on either side of the mid-point of the rod

9. $m\left(\dfrac{p-q}{p+2}\right) = 5.0$ kg

10. $\dfrac{2m}{3} = 4$ kg

11. $F = 2F_0\left(\dfrac{m_0+2m}{m_0+4m}\right) = 200$ N

12. $\dfrac{(\eta-1)m}{2} = 2.0$ kg

13. $m \geq \dfrac{4m_1 m_2}{m_1+m_2}$

14. $\theta = \tan^{-1}\left(\dfrac{2\eta^2}{1+2\eta}\right) = \tan^{-1}\left(\dfrac{9}{8}\right)$

Hint: At the verge of toppling the mass centre of the U shape structure must be vertically above the bottom edge of its middle section.

15. $l \leq \dfrac{(m+2M)d}{M\cos\theta} = 40$ cm

16. $\left.\dfrac{m}{M}\right|_{min} = \dfrac{R}{2(R-r)}$

Hint: When the pipe is at the verge of toppling, force of the normal reaction on the pipe from the ground must be concentrated at the rightmost bottom point of the pipe. Moreover, at this stage, net torque of forces of normal reactions by the spheres on the inner surface of the pipe and weight of the pipe about the rightmost bottom point of the pipe must be a null vector.

Alternatively, consider increment in gravitational potential energy of the system on slightly tilting the cylinder about an axis through its contact point with the floor located extreme right. For stability of the system, this increment must be a positive quantity and for instability of the system i.e. toppling this increment must be a negative quantity.

17. 3

Hint: By adjusting his posture, a clown can put equal or unequal load on his legs and hence on the planks.

18. (a) $\dfrac{m}{M} = \dfrac{2}{1+\cos\theta}$ (b) $\mu \geq \dfrac{1}{\sin\theta}$ (c) Stable

Hint: Do not forget to consider equilibria of the left-most or the right-most pulleys touching the walls.

19. $\geq \dfrac{m}{M}\left(\dfrac{\eta^2 l^2+r^2}{rl}\right)+\dfrac{r}{\eta l} = 0.9$

20. 45°

21. $m > \dfrac{M\sin\theta}{1-\sin\theta} \Rightarrow m > 3$ kg

Hint: Mass of load must be greater than that required to maintain the system in equilibrium.

22. $\geq \dfrac{1}{\sqrt{3}}$

23. (a) $\dfrac{2v^2}{gr} = 0.4$ (b) 0.125 s

Hint: While a vehicle is executing a curve, frictional forces providing the necessary centripetal force to the vehicle acts only on those wheels that are steered.

24. $\beta = \tan^{-1}\left(\dfrac{1}{3}\right) + \sin^{-1}\left[\eta^2 \sin\left\{\alpha - \tan^{-1}\left(\dfrac{1}{3}\right)\right\}\right]$

Hint: The pipe including the water in it is under action of the forces that are reaction of the pivot, gravity and thrust force imparted by water leaving the lower end. In equilibrium, net torque of all these forces about the pivot must be a null vector.

25. $\dfrac{F}{3m}$

26. (a) $F_A = \dfrac{F\sqrt{5}}{4}$ and $F_B = \dfrac{F}{4}$

(b) $F_A = \dfrac{F\sqrt{10}}{8}$ and $F_B = \dfrac{F\sqrt{2}}{8}$

27. $\dfrac{3mg}{2}$

28. 1/6 times

29. $\dfrac{2g\sin\theta}{R} = 5.0$ rad/s

Hint: The cylinder is in translational equilibrium but not in rotational equilibrium.

30. $\dfrac{(m_2 - m_1)m_0 g \Delta t}{\{m_0(m_1 + m_2) + 4m_1 m_2\}r} = 2$ rad/s

31. $\dfrac{xr(mg + 2kr)}{mx^2 + 2Mr^2}$ ←

Hint: Write equations, first for acceleration of mass centre of the cylinder using Newton's laws and the second for angular acceleration of the given system considering torques of all the external forces about a horizontal axis through centre of the cylinder.

Alternatively, consider torques of all the forces acting on the cylinder-tube structure about the point of contact with the floor that is also the instantaneous centre of rotation.

32. $\dfrac{2(M+m)g\sin\theta}{2M + m(\sin^2\theta + 1)}$

33. $\dfrac{mgv}{2}\left(1 - \dfrac{r}{R}\right)$

34. $5mg$

Hint: The system oscillates and the tension force in the thread becomes maximum when the load B is at the lowest position.

35. (a) $\dfrac{mk^2 u^2}{r^2}$ (b) $\dfrac{mk^2 u^2}{r^2 + k^2}$

Hint: The motor driving the belt has to develop an additional tangential force equal to the frictional force between the belt and the wheel. Therefore, in addition to the power required for normal running of the belt, the motor has to supply an extra power equal to product of the frictional force and speed of the belt during slipping of the wheel.

Since frictional force and speed of the belt both are constant and hence the additional power supplied by the motor during slipping of the wheel, the required additional energy can be obtained by multiplying the additional power with the time during which slipping between the belt and the wheel exists.

36. $\sqrt{\dfrac{2}{3}\left(t_0^2 + \dfrac{l}{g\sin\theta}\right)} = 2\sqrt{2}$ s

37. $= \begin{cases} \dfrac{\mu g t}{2} \; ; & 0 \leq t \leq \dfrac{4p}{m\mu^2 g^2} \\ \sqrt{\dfrac{2p}{m}\left(t - \dfrac{2p}{m\mu^2 g^2}\right)} \; ; & \dfrac{4p}{m\mu^2 g^2} \leq t \end{cases}$

Hint: Immediately after the motor is switched on, the wheels to which the motor delivers power start rotating at very high angular velocities as they have negligible inertia and slip on the road causing forces of kinetic friction to act. These forces of kinetic friction will accelerate the car until these powered wheels continue slipping; thereafter the force of static friction will accelerate the car. During the slipping period of the powered wheels, a portion of power delivered by the motor goes waste into heat and the remaining portion is utilized in increasing kinetic energy of the car. As the car speeds up, the speeds of the contact points of the powered wheels with the floor decrease and so does the rate of heat loss in friction. The moment, when powered wheels acquire the state of pure rolling, heat loss in friction vanishes and the whole power of the motor is now available to increase the kinetic energy and hence to speed up the car.

Since the wheels have negligible inertia, net force required to accelerate their mass centres and net torque required to impart them angular acceleration can be neglected.

38. $\dfrac{vl\sin\theta}{l_0} = 12$ m/s

Hint: Net force on the particle is the elastic force of the cord, which is a central force, therefore angular momentum of the particle about the point O remains conserved.

39. $\Delta t_1 \left(\dfrac{r_1\sqrt{R^2 - r_2^2}}{r_2\sqrt{R^2 - r_1^2}} \right) = 16$ s

Hint: Angular impulse of torque of the frictional forces make the angular momentum zero in the required time interval.

40. (a) $\omega_A = \dfrac{\omega_0}{3}$, $\omega_B = \dfrac{\omega_0}{3}$ and $\omega_C = \dfrac{\omega_0}{3}$

(b) No

Hint: Take care of the forces necessary to prevent vertical movements as well as rotation of the axles.

41. $r = \sqrt{\dfrac{I}{6m}}$

Hint: Angular momentum of the insects-turntable system about the axis of rotation remains conserved. In addition, at every instant horizontal component of the contact force between the legs of the insect and the turntable must be capable of providing the necessary centripetal acceleration.

Check your understanding

1. $\dfrac{h|v_2 \sin(\beta - \alpha)\cos\beta - (v_1 + v_2)\cos(\beta - \alpha)\sin\beta|}{L\sin^2(\beta - \alpha)}$

2. $v = \dfrac{\omega R}{\sin\frac{1}{2}(\theta + \phi)} = 1.0$ m/s

Hint: Since the cords are inextensible, every particle of a cord must be in circular motion about the point where it is affixed to the ceiling. Therefore, the velocities of the points where the cords are leaving the disc are perpendicular to the strings. This information suggests how to locate the instantaneous centre of rotation.

3. $x = -2R\cos\left(\dfrac{u}{R}t\right)$ and $y = 0$

Hint: At every instant in the process of the motion, angle between the position vector of the centre of the disc relative to the centre of the ring and position vector of the point A relative to the centre of the disc is double of the angular displacement of the position vector of the centre of the disc relative to the centre of the ring.

4. $= \begin{cases} \dfrac{\eta l}{\sqrt{\eta^2 - 1}} & \text{Front wheel} \\ \dfrac{l}{\sqrt{\eta^2 - 1}} & \text{Rear wheel} \end{cases}$

5. $\dfrac{\sqrt{5} - 1}{4}v$ or $\dfrac{\sqrt{5} + 1}{4}v$

6. $\dfrac{mg\sqrt{3}}{2}\left(1 - \dfrac{\tan\theta_0}{\sqrt{3}}\right) \leftarrow$ and $\dfrac{mg}{2}\left(1 + \dfrac{\tan\theta_0}{\sqrt{3}}\right) \uparrow$

Hint: The first figure suggests that the angle θ_0 is the angular position of mass centre of the half ring from its diameter.

7. $(m+M)g - \left(\dfrac{4k_1 k_2}{k_1+k_2}\right)(H-h-l_0) = 80$ N

   Hint: The rotational equilibrium of the rod suggests that both the springs are applying equal forces, therefore, the spring having lesser extension must have greater force constant.

8. $= \begin{cases} 0 \le m < \infty; & \mu \ge \tan\theta \\ m < \dfrac{M}{3\sin\theta(\sin\theta - \mu\cos\theta)}; & \mu < \tan\theta \end{cases}$

   Hint: When the block does not slide, its net force on the wedge is equal to its weight and acts vertically downwards creating no torque about the right bottom edge of the wedge and hence there is no possibility of toppling however large is the weight of the block.

   When the block slides, normal reaction remains the same as before but frictional force acting down the plane becomes smaller than its value when the block was not sliding. Hence, net force by the block on the wedge makes some nonzero angle with the vertical towards the right causing a non-zero torque about the right bottom edge.

9. $m\left(\dfrac{1+\eta^2}{1-\eta^2}\right)\sin\theta = 15$ kg and

   $\dfrac{l}{r} = 2\eta\left\{1 + \dfrac{2\eta\tan\theta}{1-\eta^2}\right\} = \dfrac{4+\sqrt{6}}{\sqrt{3}}$

10. $F_A \sin^2\theta \tan\theta + F_B \cos^2\theta$

11. $\dfrac{mr^2}{2}(1+\sin^2\theta)$

12. $(\eta-1)g\left\{\dfrac{m_1(\eta-1) - 2\eta m_2}{m_1(\eta-1)^2 + 4\eta^2 m_2}\right\} = 2.0$ m/s^2

    Hint: Tension forces in the left and the middle vertical segments are equal and that in the right vertical segment is different to satisfy conditions of rotational equilibrium of the two-step pulley. In addition, total length of unwound portion of the thread is not constant.

13. $\dfrac{mg}{\sqrt{1+\mu^2}}$

14. $\le \dfrac{m}{\sqrt{M(M+2m)}}$

    Hint: The external forces are acting on the body are weight of the cylinder, weight of the rod and the total contact force. Net torque of gravitational forces about the mass centre is always a null vector, therefore, to maintain rotational equilibrium, line of action of the total contact force must pass through the mass centre.

    If the slope is frictionless, the rod must be at the point of contact.

    If there is friction between the pipe and the slope, to maintain rotational equilibrium for different values of the coefficient of friction, the rod must be somewhere to the right of the point of contact between the pipe and the slope. In addition, more is the coefficient of friction; farther rightwards must be the rod. Therefore, for maximum value of the coefficient of friction, the rod must be to the extreme right i.e. horizontally rightwards of the axis of the pipe.

15. $l = \dfrac{2}{\omega}\sqrt{\dfrac{Td}{m\tan(0.5\theta)}}$

    Hint: Since the rope has mass, its shape is not changing and it is rotating at constant angular velocity, therefore, it can be considered to be in a state of rotational equilibrium like a rigid body.

16. $\dfrac{mv^2}{l}$ in each rod

17. $mg\sqrt{\cos^2\theta + \dfrac{4}{9}\sin^2\theta} = 20$ N and

    $\tan^{-1}\left(\dfrac{2}{3}\tan\theta\right) = \tan^{-1}\left(\dfrac{1}{2}\right)$

18. (a) The rear-wheel drive car is better.

    (b) $\tan^{-1}\left\{\dfrac{\mu l}{2(l-\mu h)}\right\} = \tan^{-1}\left(\dfrac{1}{2}\right)$

    Hint: Consider inequality created in the normal reactions on the rear and front wheels due to inclination of the slope.

    Since the wheels have negligible inertia, net force required to accelerate their mass centres and net torque required to impart them angular acceleration can be neglected.

19. $\leq \begin{cases} \dfrac{a_0 gl}{gl - 2a_0 h} & \text{to prevent sliding} \\ \dfrac{gl}{h} & \text{to prevent toppling} \end{cases}$

Hint: Consider inequality created in the normal reactions on the support and on the wheels during speeding up and speeding down periods. Since the wheels have negligible inertia, net force required to accelerate their mass centres and net torque required to impart them angular acceleration can be neglected.

20. $\dfrac{M\omega_0}{2\pi kS}$

21. (a) Friction at every point on the rod acts opposite to velocity of that point relative to the point of the hole in contact. When you push and rotate the rod, a component of the friction acts along the periphery and the other component along axis of the rod.

(b) $F\dfrac{\omega r^2}{v}$

22. (a) When the ant pulls the straw at one end, the straw rotates about an off centre point nearer to the other end. Distribution of the frictional forces is shown in the following figure.

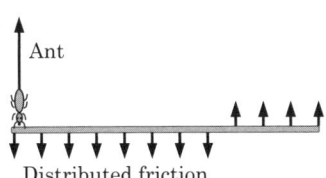
Distributed friction

The net frictional force opposing the pull of the ant is reduced as some friction supports the efforts of the ant.

(b) $F \geq \mu mg(\sqrt{2} - 1)$

Hint: Consider the straw at the verge of rotational as well as translational equilibrium under the action of distributed frictional forces and the pull of the ant.

23. $\hat{j}\dfrac{(\mu_1 - \mu_2)g}{\pi} = (0.35\hat{j})$ m/s²

Hint: Assume the disc composed of infinitely large number of concentric rings. Find net friction force on any of the rings and then sum up all these forces to find net friction force on the whole disc.

24. $\dfrac{2\mu g v_0}{\omega_0 R}$ (retardation)

25. $(\sqrt{2} - 1)\omega_A$

26. (a) $\sqrt{\dfrac{2Fs}{M\cos\theta}}$

The force F is different in both the cases.

(b) When the wheel rolls down with slipping.

27. $1.5F$

28. (a) $\approx 2\tan^{-1}\mu$ (b) $\approx \mu\sqrt{gr}$

29. Four-wheel drive: $\dfrac{mv^2}{2p} + \dfrac{p}{2m(\mu g)^2} = 5.0$ s

Rear-wheel drive: $\dfrac{mv^2}{2p} + \dfrac{2p}{m(\mu g)^2} = 8.0$ s

Hint: Immediately after the motor is switched on, the wheels to which the motor delivers power start rotating at very high angular velocities as they have negligible inertia and slip on the road causing forces of kinetic friction to act. These forces of kinetic friction will accelerate the car until these powered wheels continue slipping; thereafter force of static friction will accelerate the car. During slipping period of the powered wheels, a portion of power delivered by the motor goes waste into heat and the remaining portion is utilized in increasing the kinetic energy of the car. As the car speeds up, the speeds of the contact points of the powered wheels with the floor decrease and so does the rate of heat loss in friction. The moment, when powered wheels acquire the state of pure rolling, heat loss in friction vanishes and the whole power of the motor is now available to increase the kinetic energy and hence to speed up the car.

Since the wheels have negligible inertia, net force required to accelerate their mass centres and net torque required to impart them angular acceleration can be neglected.

In a four-wheel drive car, all the four wheels are powered wheels, in a rear-wheel drive car only rear wheels are powered wheels, and in a front-wheel drive car only front wheels are powered wheels. In addition, due to negligible inertia of the wheels, negligibly small frictional forces are developed between the floor and the unpowered wheels.

In order to solve this question, consider the slipping period only, if the speed required is lesser than the speed at which slipping ceases, and consider the slipping period as well as period of pure rolling, if the speed required is greater than the speed at which slipping ceases.

30. $t_0 \sqrt{\dfrac{\eta+4}{2(\eta+2)}}$

Hint: By making use of work energy theorem, express angular velocities in both the cases as function of angular position.

These angular velocities in both the cases are in the same ratio at every angular position; moreover, this ratio is a constant. Therefore, time taken in both the cases must be in reciprocal ratio of the angular velocities.

31. $\approx \dfrac{2l}{u} - \Delta t_1 = 3.0$ s

Hint: With the help of work energy theorem, write expression for speed v on the elevated track. Now using $v = dl/dt$ and making suitable use of approximations suggested, write expression for time. Do the same for second track and eliminate the unwanted terms from the expressions.

32. $v = \sqrt{\dfrac{2Mgl\sin\theta}{m}}$

Hint: In any time-interval after the plank acquires a steady speed, a part of decrease in the gravitational potential energy of the plank is utilised in increasing total kinetic energy of the cylinders and the remaining part into heat loss setting the cylinders one by one into rotation.

33. $b \geq \left\{\dfrac{8k}{mu^2}\right\}^{1/4}$

Hint: There must be a definite nonzero value of the closest approach between the particle and the source.

34. $\dfrac{mv_0^2}{2}\left(\dfrac{g^2 R^2}{v_0^4} + \sqrt{2} - 1\right)$

35. $h = \dfrac{4h_0(ll_0 m_0)^2}{(m_0 l_0^2 + ml^2)^2}$

36. $2\sqrt{2}R\omega_0 \hat{k}$

37. (a) $\dfrac{\omega_0}{2}\sqrt{\dfrac{mr^2}{k}}$ (b) 0 and ω_0

38. $\omega_1 = \dfrac{2\omega}{3}$, $\omega_2 = -\dfrac{\omega}{3}$ and

$|\vec{v}_1| = |\vec{v}_2| = \dfrac{1}{2}\sqrt{u^2 + \left(\dfrac{\omega r}{3}\right)^2}$

39. $\dfrac{2u^2}{9\mu g}$

40. $\cos^{-1}\left(\dfrac{u^2}{3gl} + \dfrac{2\cos\theta_0}{3}\right) = 53°$ and $\dfrac{3}{2\sqrt{2}}$ m/s

Hint: Angular momentum of the particle about the vertical axis through the hinge is conserved. In addition, the length of the rod is radius of curvature, and the hinge is centre of curvature of the path followed by the particle.

41. (a) $\dfrac{2u^2 \rho Sl}{I}$ (b) $\omega = \dfrac{u}{l}\left\{1 - \exp\left(-\dfrac{2uS\rho l^2}{I}t\right)\right\}$

Hint: Water flowing out of a nozzle exerts a thrust force on the nozzle. Net angular impulse of these thrust forces on both the nozzles in a time interval is equal to increment in angular momentum of the system in that time interval.

Challenge your understanding

1. 5 cm, 2 cm/s, 0.5π rad/s

   Hint: Displacement $\Delta \vec{r}$ of the lamp between two consecutive pulses can be represented by vector sum of two components, one due to displacement of the centre of the disc and the other due to intrinsic rotation of the disc.

   $$\Delta \vec{r} = \vec{v}_c \tau + 2R\sin\left(\tfrac{1}{2}\omega\tau\right)\hat{e}$$

   In the above equation $\hat{e}$ is a unit vector in the direction of the displacement of the lamp relative to the centre of the disc between two consecutive pulses. This unit vector changes its direction by $\omega\tau$ at every flash.

   The above equation represents vector addition of a constant vector $\vec{v}_c \tau$ and another vector $2R\sin\left(\tfrac{1}{2}\omega\tau\right)\hat{e}$ of constant magnitude but for every flash at different angle, therefore tip of the resultant $\Delta \vec{r}$ will lie on a circle. It means that if we draw displacement vectors $\Delta \vec{r}$ of the lamp between every two consecutive pulses as co-initial vectors, the tips of all these $\Delta \vec{r}$ vectors will lie on a circle as shown in the figure.

   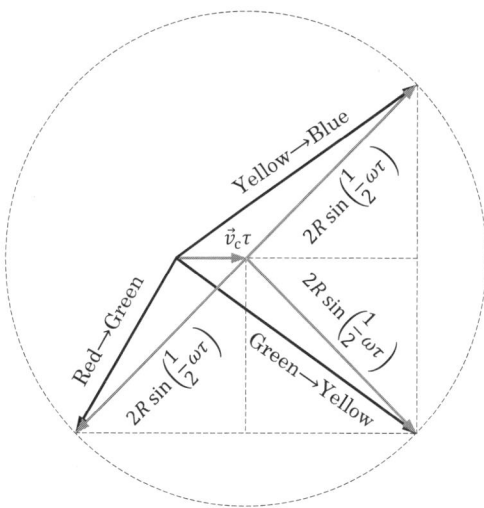

   Now incorporating necessary information from the graph accompanying the problem and knowing $\tau = 1.0$ s into the above geometrical construction, you can find all the required quantities.

2. $M = m_0\left(\dfrac{l^2}{2h\Delta h} - 1\right) = 9.8$ kg

   Hint: In the figure the table is shown with the shorter leg touching the ground. The tabletop ABCD is a square and the view is so selected that corner D is behind the corner B so is not visible. The shorter leg is at the corner A.

   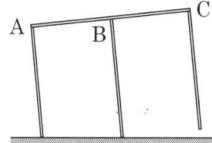

3. Within the square region bounded by lines joining midpoints of the sides shown in the figure in grey shade.

   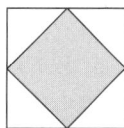

   Hint: Since the plate is light and all the wires must remain taut, all the corners as well as the centre of the plate must shift downwards. Sum of all the tension forces thus developed in the wires equals the load placed on the plate.

   Making torque equations about two axes passing through the point of loading and parallel to the sides of the plate, you will find two equations involving all the four tension forces.

   The mass centre and a pair of diagonally opposite points are always on a straight line; therefore, shift in mass centre must be arithmetic mean of shifts in each pair of diagonally opposite points. Incorporating this fact and by expressing tensions in the wires in terms of force constant and shifts in corner points, you will find that sum of tension forces in each pair of wires attached to diagonally opposite corners are equal.

   Now you can express the four tension forces in terms of the load, side length of the plate and coordinates of the point of loading.

4. $\mu = \dfrac{8v^2 \tan^2 \theta}{gl \sin\theta (4 + \tan^2 \theta)}$

Hint: All the particles of a rigid body in rotation about a stationary axis must move on concentric circular paths, therefore the point O shown in the top view is the centre of circular paths followed by the centres of both the wheel and mass centre of the bicycle.

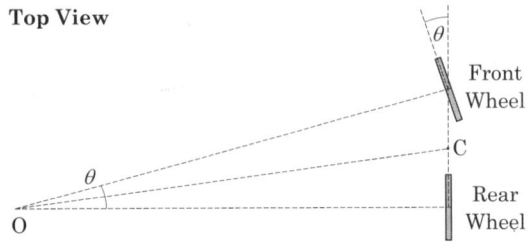

Top View

Express radii of circular paths of the wheels and mass centre in terms of l and θ, then considering circular motion of the mass centre, find expression for the net frictional force on the bicycle. On the front wheel friction force is towards the point O and on the rear wheel friction force is in the forward direction. Component of the net friction force along the line CO provides the necessary centripetal force and the component perpendicular to the line CO vanishes.

5. $T_{max} = \dfrac{mg}{2}\left(\sqrt{\dfrac{103}{3}} - \sqrt{3}\right)$

Hint: Using work energy theorem, find angular velocity of the rod in terms of angular displacement, then by differentiating each term of the equation obtained with respect to the angular position, find angular acceleration of the rod. Now you can find expressions for the tension forces in the cords by considering mass centre in a circular motion and the rod with the particles in rotational motion as a rigid body.

6. $a_A = \dfrac{\sqrt{2}g}{3}$, $a_B = \dfrac{\sqrt{10}g}{3}$ and $\tan^{-1}\left(\dfrac{1}{2}\right)$,

Hint: Vertical component of acceleration of the bead B must be g and horizontal components of accelerations of both the beads must be equal and point towards the right. Acceleration of the bead A must be perpendicular to line OA. With these apparent observations, consider the ring and the bead A as rigid body.

After all motion ceases, the bead B will settle at the lowest point of the ring.

7. $\dfrac{g\{(M-m) - \gamma(M+m)\}}{\{(M+m) - \gamma(M-m)\}}$, where $\gamma = \dfrac{\mu r}{R\sqrt{1+\mu^2}}$

Chapter 6

Gravitation

Newton's law of gravitation, gravitational potential and field, acceleration due to gravity, Kepler's laws of planetary motion, motion of planets and satellites in circular orbits, escape velocity.

"Every great and deep difficulty bears in itself, its own solution. It forces us to change our thinking in order to find it."

Niels Henrik David Bohr
(7 October 1885 – 18 November 1962)

BACK TO BASICS

Newton's law of gravitation:

The magnitude of force of gravitational attraction between two point-masses m_1 and m_2 separated by a distance r is given by the equation

$$F = \frac{Gm_1 m_2}{r^2}$$

Here G is the universal gravitational constant.

$$G = 6.67 \times 10^{-11} \; \frac{\text{N} \cdot \text{m}^2}{\text{kg}^2}$$

Kepler's laws:

The law of orbits:

All planets move in elliptical orbits, one of the foci of which is the Sun.

The law of areas:

The position vector of a planet relative to the sun sweeps equal areas in equal intervals of time. This law finds its explanation in the principle of conservation of angular momentum.

The law of periods:

The square of the time period of revolution of a planet is proportional to the cube of the semi-major axis of the ellipse traced out by the planet.

Gravitational potential energy:

Potential energy due mutual gravitational interaction between particles of masses m_1 and m_2 separated by a distance r is given by the following equation.

$$U_r = -\frac{Gm_1 m_2}{r}$$

When separation between the particles is infinitely large, the potential energy is arbitrarily assumed zero.

Multiple Choice Questions

1. A satellite revolves in an equatorial plane in west to east direction around the earth with a period of 8 hrs. At an instant, it is observed vertically overhead a longitude. After how much minimum time will the satellite again be overhead the same longitude?
   (a) 8 h
   (b) 12 h
   (c) 24 h
   (d) 36 h

2. Assume that the Earth changes its shape and turns into an infinite cylinder whose radius and density are the same as those of our real Earth and the distance of the Moon from the central axis of this cylindrical earth remains unchanged. What can you say about the speed of the Moon (which remains spherical) in its orbit around the cylindrical Earth?
   (a) It will slightly increase.
   (b) It will slightly decrease.
   (c) It will remain unchanged.
   (d) It will increase several times.

3. Suppose the Saturn rings consist of football size particles orbiting in circular orbits. If the maximum speed of these particles is 1.05 times of the minimum speed, find the ratio of radial width to the inner radius of the ring.
   (a) 0.01
   (b) 0.05
   (c) 0.10
   (d) 0.25

4. Two planets A and B are orbiting around their sun in circular orbits of radii r and $4r$. In a quarter year of planet B, how many revolutions will the planet A make?
   (a) 1
   (b) 2
   (c) 4
   (d) 8

5. An asteroid orbiting around a planet in circular orbit suddenly explodes into two fragments in mass ratio 1:4. If immediately after the explosion, the smaller fragment starts orbiting the planet in reverse direction in the same orbit, what will happen with the heavier fragment?

   (a) Fall on the planet.
   (b) Start orbiting the planet in a larger orbit.
   (c) Start orbiting the planet in a smaller orbit.
   (d) Escape from the gravitational interaction with the planet.

6. The sun orbits the centre of the galaxy (Milky-Way) in almost circular path of radius R in a period T and the earth also orbits the sun in an almost circular path of radius r in a period t. Assume whole mass of the galaxy concentrated at its centre and find an expression for the ratio of the mass of the galaxy to that of the sun.

   (a) $\left(\dfrac{R}{r}\right)^3 \left(\dfrac{t}{T}\right)^2$
   (b) $\left(\dfrac{R}{r}\right)^3 \left(\dfrac{T}{t}\right)^2$
   (c) $\left(\dfrac{R}{r}\right)^2 \left(\dfrac{t}{T}\right)^3$
   (d) $\left(\dfrac{R}{r}\right)^2 \left(\dfrac{T}{t}\right)^3$

7. Weight of a body at the equator of a planet is half of that at the poles. If peripheral velocity of a point on the equator of this planet is v_0, what is the escape velocity of a polar particle?

   (a) v_0
   (b) $2v_0$
   (c) $3v_0$
   (d) $4v_0$

8. Consider two identical particles each of mass m held at a separation r_0 in free space. One of them is given a velocity v_0 perpendicular to r_0 and the other one is simultaneously released. For what range of velocity v_0 will the masses be bound in orbital motion under their mutual gravitational forces.

   (a) $v_0 \leq \sqrt{\dfrac{2Gm}{r_0}}$
   (b) $v_0 < \sqrt{\dfrac{2Gm}{r_0}}$
   (c) $v_0 \leq 2\sqrt{\dfrac{Gm}{r_0}}$
   (d) $v_0 < 2\sqrt{\dfrac{Gm}{r_0}}$

9. In free space, two identical particles A and B are rigidly attached at the ends of a light rigid rod of length r_0 and another identical particle C is held at a position in such a way that the locations of the particles make an equilateral triangle. The particle C is given a velocity v_0 tangential to the circumscribing circle of the triangle and the other two are simultaneously released. For what range of velocity v_0 will the particles be bound under their mutual gravitational forces?

   (a) $v_0 \leq \sqrt{\dfrac{3Gm}{r_0}}$
   (b) $v_0 < 3\sqrt{\dfrac{Gm}{r_0}}$
   (c) $v_0 \leq \sqrt{\dfrac{6Gm}{r_0}}$
   (d) $v_0 < \sqrt{\dfrac{6Gm}{r_0}}$

6.4 Chapter-6

10. Consider a thought experiment performed in free space. In the experiment, a small cube C of mass m is placed at the centre of a large and highly massive disc D and a ball B of mass M revolves in circular path of radius R around the centre of the disc. The plane of the circle is perpendicular to the plane of the disc as shown in the figure. Intensity of the gravitational field of the disc near its centre is g. What should be range of coefficient of friction between the cube and the disc so that the cube remains motionless?

(a) $\mu \geq \dfrac{gR^2}{\sqrt{(gR^2)^2 + (GM)^2}}$

(b) $\mu \geq \dfrac{gR^2}{\sqrt{(gR^2)^2 - (GM)^2}}$

(c) $\mu \geq \dfrac{GM}{\sqrt{(gR^2)^2 - (GM)^2}}$

(d) $\mu \geq \dfrac{GM}{\sqrt{(gR^2)^2 + (GM)^2}}$

Build up your understanding

1. Acceleration due to gravity everywhere on the equator of a spherical asteroid of radius R is g_0. A spherical cavity with its centre in the equatorial plane inside the asteroid is made and then acceleration due to gravity is measured everywhere on the equator. The minimum accelerations due to gravity is observed smaller than g_0 by η_1 fraction of g_0 at a point and at its diametrically opposite point, acceleration due to gravity is observed smaller than g_0 by η_2 fraction of g_0. Find radius of the cavity and depth of its centre.

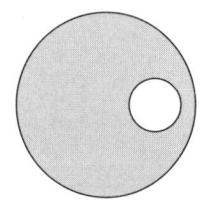

2. A small bead can slide without friction on a wooden rod of length $l = 10.0$ m. Initially the rod and the bead both are held motionless with the rod aligned radially with the earth. The left end of the rod is at a distance $r_0 = 4 \times 10^8$ m from the earth centre and the bead is at a distance $x_0 = 2.0$ cm away from the left end. Both the bodies are released simultaneously. Considering gravitational interaction only with the earth, find how long after the release, will the bead separate from the rod? Radius of the earth is $R = 6400$ km and acceleration due to gravity on the earth is $g = 10$ m/s².

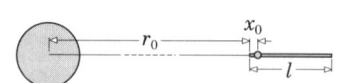

3. An asteroid of mass M explodes into a spherical homogeneous cloud in free space. Due to energy received by the explosion, the cloud expands, and the expansion is spherically symmetric. At an instant, when radius of the cloud is R_0, all of its particles on the surface are observed receding radially away from the centre of the cloud with a velocity v_0. What will the radius of the cloud be, when its expansion ceases.

4. Rockets are used to launch satellites. Draw a graph to show how kinetic energy K imparted to a satellite varies with work done W by the rocket used for all possible circular orbits. Ignore effects of rotation of the earth and resistance of the atmosphere. Denote the mass of the satellite by m,

radius of the earth by R and acceleration of free fall near the earth surface by g.

5. A reconnaissance satellite (spy satellite) of mass m orbiting the earth at very low altitude experiences a retarding force. Assuming magnitude of this retarding force F a constant, find the time rate at which radius of the orbit changes when speed of the satellite is v. Acceleration due to gravity near the earth surface is g.

6. Two space stations A and B are orbiting the earth with speed v in the same orbit of radius R. Station B is a distance s ahead of station A. Two astronauts from station A have to join the station B. For this purpose, they leave station A in a spaceship and move radially to a slightly lower orbit and stay in that orbit and when the station B comes closest to them, they immediately move radially to join the station B. If time spend in the lower orbit is Δt, find separation between the orbits.

7. Astronauts in a spaceship moving with a constant velocity v_0 observe a massive planet at a great distance also moving with velocity v_0 at an angle of 120° with the direction of motion of the spaceship. The astronauts have to reverse the direction of motion of their spaceship. Determine how much maximum speed in reverse direction, the spaceship can acquire without expenditure of fuel with the help of gravitational field of the planet?

8. A spaceship sent to study a binary star system is set into an orbit in order to remain always collinear with the stars. If distances of the spaceship from the stars are r_1 and r_2, find ratio of masses of the stars. Is this orbit a stable one?

9. Three material points of masses m_1, m_2 and m_3 are at the vertices of an equilateral triangle of side d. The system is rotating in free space in such a way that under the mutual gravitational interaction of the three particles, the system is neither expanding nor contracting. Find angular velocity ω of this rotation. Universal gravitational constant is G.

Check your understanding

1. Two asteroids each of mass of mass M and radius R are moving in free space. At an instant, when their velocity vectors are $\vec{v}_1$ and $\vec{v}_2$ respectively, position vector of the second with respect to the first is $\vec{r}_{12}$. Determine the condition under which they will collide.

2. A satellite revolves in the equatorial plane around the earth at an altitude equal to radius of the earth. A very sensitive device can detect its shadow made on the earth surface by the sunrays. Find average velocity of the shadow relative to a non-rotating frame fixed with the centre of the earth. Escape velocity from the earth surface is v_e.

3. A small moon of radius r and mass m is orbiting around a planet of mass M in a circular orbit of radius R ($R \gg r$) always keeping the same face towards the planet. If an object on the moon closest to the planet is in weightlessness, find suitable expression for the radius of the orbit.

4. A spaceship is launched radially away from the earth with the help of a rocket. When the spaceship acquires speed v_0, the rocket used is switched off. As the spaceship proceeds further away from the earth, its speed v decreases with time t as shown in the graph and eventually the spaceship acquires a constant velocity that is one fifth of v_0. How far away from the centre of the earth, was the rocket switched off?

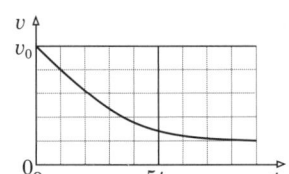

5. A uniform cloud of dust particles approaches a planet from a great distance with a velocity v_0 relative to the planet. Radius of the planet is R and escape velocity from the surface of the planet is v_e. Length of the cloud along its direction of motion is l, cross section of the cloud perpendicular to its direction of motion is very large and its density is ρ. How much mass of the dust particles will the planet collect during its passage through the cloud. Mass of the cloud is negligible as compared to the mass of the planet.

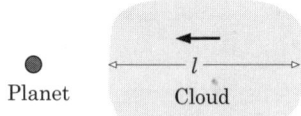

6. Two spacecraft of masses m_1 and m_2 are flying with their engines off in the gravitational field of a star of mass M that is much larger than masses of the spacecraft. Speeds of the spacecraft at great distances from the star are equal to v_1 and v_2, respectively. After passage around the star, when the spacecraft are again at great distances from the star, the spacecraft move with speeds v_1 and v_2 perpendicular to their initial directions of motion. If during passage around the star, the minimum distance of the first spacecraft from the star is r_1, what is the minimum distance of the second spacecraft from the star?

7. In ancient time, the earth was believed to be a flat disc of uniform thickness. Here we adopt the same model and describe the earth as a flat disc of radius sufficiently large say more than 40000 km. Mass density is uniform and is equal to ρ. The disc rotates about a stationary axis through its centre and perpendicular to its plane. Period of rotation equals one earth day. Universal gravitational constant is G.

The centre of the disc is the North Pole, and circular edge is the South Pole. All radial lines on the disc are the longitudes and all concentric circles are the latitudes. Direction along a latitude in the direction of rotation is the East.

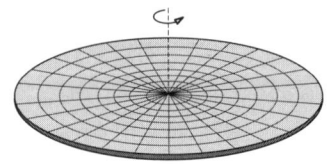

(a) If acceleration due to gravity at the North Pole is g_0, what should thickness of the disc be?
(b) A shell is fired from the ground with velocity u at an angle θ with the longitude containing the place of firing. How far from this longitude, will the shell hit the ground?
(c) A shell is fired from the ground with velocity u at an angle θ with the latitude containing the place of firing. How far from this latitude, will the shell hit the ground?

Answers and Hints

Multiple Choice Questions

1. (b)
2. (d)
3. (c)
4. (b)
5. (d)
6. (a)
7. (b)
8. (d)
9. (d)
10. (c)

Build up your understanding

1. $R\left\{\dfrac{4\eta_1\eta_2}{\left(\sqrt{\eta_1}+\sqrt{\eta_2}\right)^2}\right\}^{1/3}$ and $2R\left(\dfrac{\sqrt{\eta_2}}{\sqrt{\eta_1}+\sqrt{\eta_2}}\right)$

2. $\approx\sqrt{\dfrac{2x_0 r_0^3}{gR^2 l}}=2.5\times 10^4$ s

3. $\dfrac{2GMR_0}{2GM-v_0^2 R_0}$

4.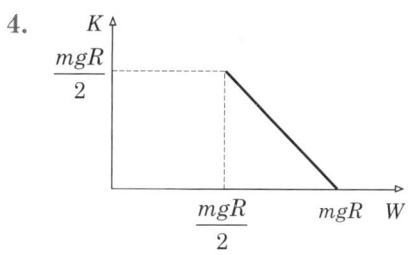

5. $-\dfrac{2Fv}{mg}$

6. $\dfrac{2sR}{3v\Delta t}$

7. $2v_0$

8. $\dfrac{r_1^2}{r_2^2}\left\{\dfrac{(r_1+r_2)^3-r_2^3}{(r_1+r_2)^3-r_1^3}\right\}$, No

9. $\omega=\sqrt{\dfrac{G(m_1+m_2+m_3)}{d^3}}$

   Hint: All the particles move on circular paths with their centres at the mass centre. Since masses are not equal, their mass centre does not coincide with the geometrical centroid.

Check your understanding

1. $\dfrac{\left|\vec{r}_{12}\times(\vec{v}_2-\vec{v}_1)\right|}{16R^2}<\dfrac{(\vec{v}_2-\vec{v}_1)^2}{4}+GM\left(\dfrac{1}{2R}-\dfrac{1}{|\vec{r}_{12}|}\right)$

2. $\dfrac{3v_e}{4}$

3. $R=r\left(\dfrac{3M}{m}\right)^{1/3}$

4. $\dfrac{12v_0 t_0}{5}$

5. $m=\pi\rho lR^2\left\{1+\left(\dfrac{v_e}{v_0}\right)^2\right\}$

6. $r_1\left(\dfrac{v_1}{v_2}\right)^2$

7. (a) $h = \dfrac{g_0}{2\pi\rho G}$

   (b) $(u\cos\theta - \omega r_0)\dfrac{2u\sin\theta}{g}$

   East or west from the longitude depending on whether the shell is fired towards the North Pole or away from it.

   (c) $\dfrac{2(u\cos\theta \pm \omega r)^2 u^2 \sin^2\theta}{r_0 g^2}$

   The "+" and "–" signs correspond to eastwards and westwards directions of horizontal component of velocity of projection respectively.

Chapter 7

Fluid Mechanics

Fluids, fluid statics: concept of pressure, hydrostatic pressure, Pascal's law, buoyant force, Archimedes principle and its applications; fluid dynamics: streamlined and turbulent flow, continuity equation, Bernoulli's theorem and its applications.

"Science appears to us with a very different aspect after we have found out that it is not in lecture rooms only, but that we may find illustrations of the highest doctrines of science in games and gymnastics, in travelling by land and by water, in storms of the air and of the sea, and wherever there is matter in motion."

James Clark Maxwell
(13 June 1831 – 5 November 1879)

BACK TO BASICS

Fluid:

Matter in a state in which it can flow viz. liquids and gases.

An ideal fluid offers negligible resistance to changes in shape, if enough time is allowed for the changes to occur. In other words, ideal fluids are almost non-viscous.

An ideal liquid differs from gases in the sense that they are incompressible whereas gases are not.

Pressure:

Ideal fluids can withstand only distributed forces that act normal to an interface.

Pressure is distributed force per unit area acting along the normal to an interface of two fluids or an interface of a fluid with a solid or an imaginary interface within a fluid.

Fluid Statics

Fluid Statics investigates mechanical behavior of fluids every part of which is at rest relative to its container.

Pressure variation in fluids due to gravity:

Pressure decreases with increase in height. Difference in its value dp between two horizontal levels separated by infinitesimal distance dh is given by the following equation.

$$dp = \rho g dh$$

Here ρ is density of the fluid between the levels and g is acceleration due to gravity there.

In similar fashion, a pressure gradient is established in accelerated fluids. If fluid is accelerated, pressure inside it decreases in the direction of the acceleration. Pressure difference dp between two imaginary surfaces normal to the direction of acceleration a and separated by an infinitesimal distance dl is given by the following equation.

$$dp = \rho a dl$$

Pascal's law:

A pressure increment on any part of an enclosed fluid is transmitted undiminished everywhere in the fluid.

Buoyant force or Archimedes' force:

A fluid exerts an upward force on an object if the object is partially or completely inside the fluid. This force is known as buoyant or Archimedes' force.

Magnitude of buoyant force on a body equals the weight of fluid displaced by the body. This idea was first coined by Archimedes, and we call it Archimedes Principle.

This idea can be extended to an accelerated fluid, where the net Archimedes' force acts in the direction of negative pressure gradient.

Fluid Dynamics

Fluid Dynamics investigates mechanical behavior of fluids in flow.

Equation of continuity:

The rate of flow of a fluid into a fixed closed surface equals the sum of rate of increase in the amount of fluid confined within the closed surface and rate of flow of fluid out of the closed surface.

The above idea suggests that the rate of flow for an incompressible fluid into a completely filled pipe at one end equals the rate of flow out of the pipe at the other end.

$$\int_{\text{inlet}} \vec{v}_i \cdot d\vec{s} = \int_{\text{outlet}} \vec{v}_o \cdot d\vec{s}$$

Bernoulli's theorem:

In steady laminar flow the sum of kinetic energy per unit volume, gravitational potential energy per unit volume and pressure of a fluid remains unchanged everywhere on a streamline.

$$\Delta\left(\tfrac{1}{2}\rho v^2 + \rho g h + p\right) = 0$$

Multiple Choice Questions

1. On a horizontal floor, two identical cylindrical vessels A and B connected by a thin tube near their bottoms contain some water. When an ice block of volume 100 cm³ is gently put inside vessel A, it gets half-submerged in the water. How much water will flow through the connecting tube during the process of melting the ice cube?
   Density of water is 1000 kg/m³ and density of ice is 900 kg/m³.
   (a) 20 g (b) 25 g
   (c) 45 g (d) 50 g

   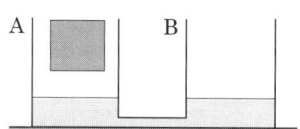

2. A sphere of mass m and radius r rests at the bottom of a large reservoir of water as shown in figure-I. Depth of the reservoir is h. Density of material of the sphere is the same as that of water. Now the sphere is slowly pulled completely out of water as shown in figure-II.
   Which of the following is a correct expression for work done by the agent pulling the sphere?
   (a) mgr (b) $0.5mgr$
   (c) $mg(r+h)$ (d) $mg(0.5r+h)$

   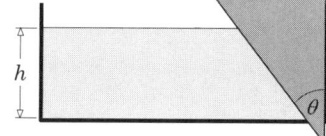
   Figure-I   Figure-II

3. A slit is cut along the right bottom edge of a rectangular tank. The slit is closed by a wooden wedge of mass m and apex angle θ as shown in the figure. The vertical plane surface of the wedge is in contact with the right vertical wall of the tank. The coefficient of static friction between these surfaces in contact is μ. To what maximum height, can water be filled in the tank without any leakage through the slit? The width of tank is b and density of water is ρ.

   (a) $\sqrt{\dfrac{2m}{\rho b(\tan\theta - \mu)}}$ (b) $\sqrt{\dfrac{4m}{\rho b(\tan\theta - \mu)}}$

   (c) $\sqrt{\dfrac{2m}{\rho b(\sin\theta - \mu\cos\theta)}}$ (d) $\sqrt{\dfrac{2m\cos\theta}{\rho b(\tan\theta - \mu\cos\theta)}}$

4. In the setup shown, two identical vessels A and B filled with water up to same level are connected by a horizontal tube equipped with a valve that is closed. There are identical leak proof pistons in contact with the water in both the vessels. The centres of the pistons are connected with the help of two taut elastic cords to the ends of a uniform lever arm supported on a fulcrum C that is fixed somewhere on the right half of the lever arm. The cords are vertical and there is no friction between the pistons and the vessels. If the valve is opened, in which direction will the water flow through the connecting tube?

   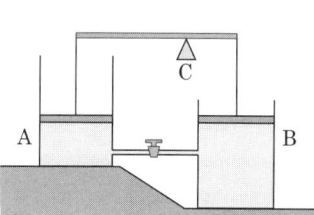

   (a) From A to B (b) From B to A
   (c) Water will not flow (d) Insufficient information

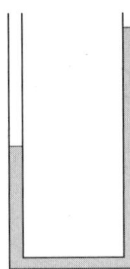

5. Bottom arm of a U-tube of uniform section has length l and the vertical arms have length $3l$ each. The tube is held with its parallel arms vertically and filled with a liquid of density ρ to occupy a total length of $4l$ of the tube and then it is made to accelerate horizontally in the plane of the tube with an acceleration g that is modulus of acceleration of free fall. What will gauge pressure at the midpoint of the bottom arm be immediately after acceleration of the tube is made abruptly zero?

   (a) $\rho g l$
   (b) $2\,\rho g l$
   (c) $1.5\rho g l$
   (d) $1.375\rho g l$

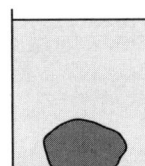

6. An object of volume 0.5 m³ and density 500 kg/m³ is glued to the flat bottom of a vessel containing water. The flat base of the object glued to the bottom has an area of 100 cm² and the density of water is 1.0 g/cm³. If the maximum force that the glue can withstand is 2000 N, to what maximum height above the base can water be filled in the vessel so that the object is not torn apart from the base?

   (a) 5 m
   (b) 10 m
   (c) Up to any height
   (d) Insufficient information

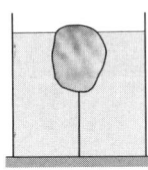

7. A piece of ice tied with the help of a thread to bottom of a cylindrical container having some amount of water. Length of the thread is so adjusted that the ice is not fully submerged. Tension force in the thread is 1.0 N. How much and in what way will the water level in the container shift, when all the ice melts? Area of the bottom of the vessel is 400 cm², density of water is 1.0 g/cm³ and density of ice is 0.9 g/cm³.

   (a) 2.5×10^{-3} m upwards
   (b) 2.5×10^{-3} m downwards
   (c) 2.8×10^{-3} m upwards
   (d) 2.8×10^{-3} m downwards

8. A ball is suspended with the help of two threads inside an empty cylindrical vessel without touching its walls, from two points on the walls of the vessel. If the vessel is filled with water up to such a height that the ball remains submerged and both the threads become taut, tension forces in the threads remain the same as they were in the empty vessel. Density of water is 1000 kg/m³. Which of the following is a correct statement?

   (a) Density of the ball is 500 kg/m³, if threads are of equal length.
   (b) Density of the ball is 500 kg/m³, if the threads are of equal length and affixed on walls of the vessel at equal heights.
   (c) Density of the ball is 500 kg/m³, if the threads are of equal length and affixed on walls of the vessel at equal heights on diametrically opposite points.
   (d) Density of the ball is 500 kg/m³, irrespective of lengths of the threads and location of point of suspension.

9. A wooden plank is floating on water in a pool. It is tethered to the bottom of the pool by a string attached at mid-point of an edge of its bottom face, which causes it to float with a diagonal of one of its vertical cross-sections coinciding with the level surface of the water, as shown in the figure. What is the specific gravity of the wood?

   (a) 1/5
   (b) 1/4
   (c) 1/3
   (d) 1/2

10. A semicircular glass tube filled with water containing an air bubble is sealed at its ends. If the tube is held with its plane vertically and made to move in its plane with a constant acceleration, the bubble stays aside of the highest point as shown in the figure. What can you conclude about the acceleration vector of the tube?

    (a) It points towards the left. (b) It points towards the right.
    (c) Its magnitude is $g\tan\theta$. (d) Its magnitude is $g\cot\theta$.

11. A cylinder of length 10 cm, made of a material of density 0.65 g/cm³, floats half submerged in an ideal liquid kept in closed vessel. The air in the vessel has a density of 1.30 kg/m³. If the pressure of air in the vessel is made 100 times the initial value, what will you observe?

    (a) The cylinder moves upwards.
    (b) The cylinder moves downwards.
    (c) Displacement of the cylinder is 0.56 cm.
    (d) Displacement of the cylinder is 0.60 cm.

12. A wooden cube of mass 2048 g is attached to the bottom of a cylindrical vessel with the help of a spring. The vessel is filled with some amount of water so that the cube floats half submerged, and the spring is relaxed. Area of the bottom of the cylinder is 600 cm², density of water is 1000 kg/m³ and acceleration of free fall is 10 m/s². Now additional water is slowly poured in the vessel until the cube is fully submerged. In this process, the water level rises by 20.48 cm. Which of the following statements are correct?

    (a) The length of a side of the cube is 16 cm.
    (b) The amount of additional water is 10.24 L.
    (c) Spring force when the cube is fully submerged is 20.48 N
    (d) Displacement of the cube when it is fully submerged is 12.48 cm.

Question 13 and 14 are based on the following physical situation

An ideal liquid of density ρ is filled in a horizontally fixed syringe fitted with piston. There is no friction between the piston and the inner surface of the syringe. The cross-section area of the syringe is A. An orifice is made at one end of the syringe. When the piston is pushed into the syringe, the liquid comes out of the orifice and then following a parabolic path falls on the ground.

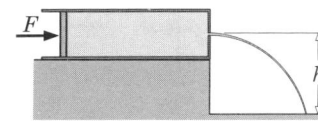

13. With what velocity does the liquid come out of the orifice?

    (a) $\sqrt{\dfrac{F}{\rho A}}$ (b) $\sqrt{\dfrac{2F}{\rho A}}$

    (c) $\sqrt{\dfrac{F+2\rho ghA}{\rho A}}$ (d) $\sqrt{\dfrac{F+\rho ghA}{\rho A}}$

14. With what velocity does the liquid strike the ground?

    (a) $\sqrt{\dfrac{F+\rho ghA}{\rho A}}$ (b) $\sqrt{\dfrac{F+2\rho ghA}{\rho A}}$

    (c) $\sqrt{\dfrac{2F+\rho ghA}{\rho A}}$ (d) $\sqrt{\dfrac{2(F+\rho ghA)}{\rho A}}$

Build up your understanding

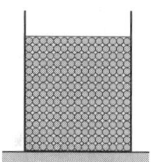

1. A cylindrical vessel is filled with water up to a height $h_0 = 1.0$ m and then a large number of small iron balls are gently dropped in it until the topmost layer of the balls becomes completely submerged in water as shown in the figure. Density of iron is $\rho_i = 7140$ kg/m³ and density of water is $\rho_0 = 1000$ kg/m³. If the average density of the contents is $\rho = 4070$ kg/m³, find the height of the water level in the vessel with the iron balls.

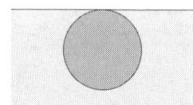

2. A plastic sphere of radius r floats almost fully submerged in a liquid as shown in the figure. Density of the liquid is ρ, acceleration of free fall is g. Find the force exerted by the liquid on the lower half of the sphere excluding contribution of the atmospheric pressure.

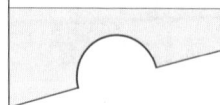

3. The bottom of a vessel is inclined at an angle θ and has a hemi-spherical dent of radius r as shown in the figure. If a liquid of density ρ is filled in the vessel to a height h above the highest point of the dent, find a suitable expression for magnitude of force of liquid pressure on the dent excluding contribution of the atmospheric pressure.

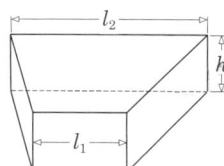

4. Walls and base of an open trapezoidal tank each are of mass m. Some of the dimensions of the tank are shown in the figure. The tank is placed on a frictionless horizontal floor and filled with water completely. At some point of time, the front and the back walls are removed. Find acceleration of the tank immediately after removal of the walls. Density of water is ρ and acceleration due to gravity is g.

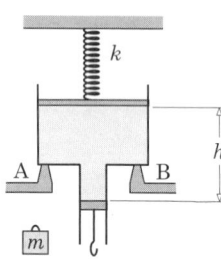

5. In a vessel that consists of two vertical portions of unequal sections, some water is trapped between two airtight light pistons that can slide without friction. The vessel is placed on two fixed supports A and B. The upper piston is suspended from the ceiling with the help of a spring of force constant k and a hook is attached to the lower piston. The area of the upper and the lower sections are S_1 and S_2 respectively, the distance between the pistons is h, the density of water is ρ and the acceleration due to gravity is g. Find the change in extension of the spring after a block of mass m is suspended from the hook.

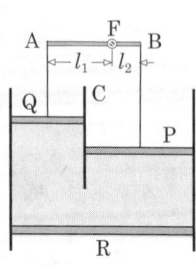

6. A volume V of water is trapped in a fixed vertical pipe of uniform section having a fixed partition C with the help of three light pistons P of area S, Q and R that can slide without friction. The piston Q and R are connected to a light lever arm AB with the help of two vertical light cords. The lever arm has a fixed fulcrum that divides it into two portions of lengths l_1 and l_2 as shown in the figure. If the system is in equilibrium, find the height of the water column between pistons P and R.

7. Two vertical cylindrical vessels containing water are connected by a thin horizontal tube at their bottom. Water in the vessels is enclosed by

pistons P and Q of masses m and αm that stay in equilibrium in the same level. A gradually increasing downward force is applied on the piston P. When the magnitude of this force becomes F, piston Q moves to a height h above its initial level. Now the force on piston P is gradually removed and applied on piston Q. How high will piston P move above its initial equilibrium level when magnitude of the force on piston Q becomes βF? Neglect all dissipative effects.

8. In a real hydraulic press, frictional forces between the piston and the inner surface of tubes cannot be neglected. In a particular real hydraulic press shown in the figure, piston in the wider arm can stay in equilibrium above the piston in the narrower arm at any height that ranges from $h_{min} = 1.0$ cm to $h_{max} = 2.0$ cm. Density of material of the pistons is $\eta = 3$ times of that of the fluid used. If the thickness of the piston in the narrower arm is $t = 5.0$ cm, find the thickness of the piston in the wider arm.

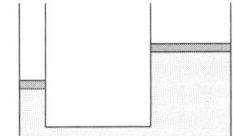

9. Two identical vessels each of height 36 cm are filled with water and oil each to a height 27 cm. A thin U tube equipped with a valve at its centre is filled with water and the valve is closed. The tube is held vertically and lowered in the vessels until its open ends reach a depth 18 cm in each liquid as shown in the figure. Density of water is 1.0 g/cm³ and that of the oil is 0.8 g/cm³. At what heights will the water and the oil levels settle in the vessels after the valve is opened?

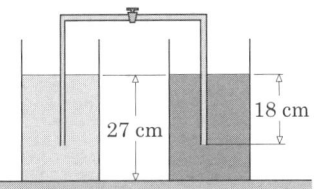

10. Vertical arms of a special U-tube are connected by a thin transparent rubber tube that has a piston inside. The tube contains three immiscible liquids A, B and C of densities ρ_A, ρ_B and ρ_C ($\rho_C > \rho_A > \rho_B$). Initially when the piston is held in the middle, the lengths of columns of liquid C in both the arms are equal, length of column of liquid A in the left arm is h, the connecting tube meets liquid A in the middle and in the right arm is liquid B. If after release, the piston stops before reaching an end of the connecting tube, find by what amounts will the liquid levels in both the arms change?

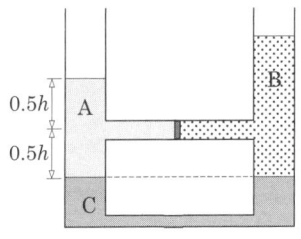

11. A specially designed glass tube has a rectangular loop and only one opening through a tube extending from centre of a longer arm of rectangular loop. It is filled with mercury and held with its plane vertical, and its opening is dipped in mercury filled in a large vessel. There is some air in the middle of upper horizontal arm of the tube. When the tube is stationary, ends of the air packet are at distance l from the axis of symmetry of the tube. Pressure in the air packet is p and density of mercury is ρ. At what angular velocity must the tube be rotated about its vertical axis of symmetry so that pressure in the air packet becomes η times of its value in stationary tube?

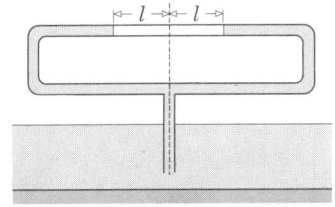

12. In a vessel there is a liquid, density of which increases with depth y from its surface according to the law $\rho = \rho_0 + ky$, where $\rho_0 = 1.0$ g/cm³ and $k = 0.01$ g/cm⁴. Two balls connected with an inextensible thread of length 15 cm are dropped in the liquid. The volume of each ball is 1.0 cm³ and their masses are 1.2 g and 1.4 g. At what depth will these balls settle in equilibrium?

7.8 Chapter-7

13. Consider two identical cylindrical vessels, one filled up to a height $h = 1.0$ m with several plastic beads and the other filled up to the same height with water. The total mass of the beads is $m = 500$ kg and that of the water is $M = 1000$ kg. If all the water is gradually transferred in the first vessel, find height attained by the top layer of the beads. Density of the plastic is $\rho = 800$ kg/m³ and that of water is $\rho_0 = 1000$ kg/m³.

14. At every metre on a very thin rod, small air-filled balloons are attached except at the top end. The length of the rod is integral multiple of a metre and mass of every metre of the rod including balloons is 2.7 kg. The rod is lowered vertically into water. Volume of a balloon in air is 0.003 m³ and it reduces by 100 cm³ for every 10 kPa increase in pressure. What maximum length of the rod can float in water with its upper end in level with the water surface? Density of water is 1000 kg/m³.

15. A uniform rod of length l is lying on horizontal bottom of an empty container, and one end of the rod is hinged there. The container is now slowly filled with water. Draw a graph to show how length l_i of rod immersed in water varies with height h of the water level in the container. Density of material of the rod is ρ and that of water is $\rho_w > \rho$.

16. One-half of a rod of length $l = 100$ cm has density $\rho_1 = 0.50$ g/cm³ and the other half has density $\rho_2 = 2.50$ g/cm³. The rod is placed on the horizontal bottom of a large tub and then water is gradually poured in the tub. Find the depth of water in the tub, when the rod makes angle $\theta = 53°$ with the horizontal. Density of water is $\rho = 1.00$ g/cm³.

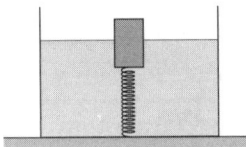

17. A wooden cylinder of cross-section area S is connected with the bottom of a large vessel by a spring of stiffness $k = 10$ N/m. When some water is filled in the vessel, the cylinder floats partially submerged and extension in the spring becomes x_0. Density of water is ρ_w and acceleration of free fall is g. If the vessel is given an upwards acceleration a, by what amount will the length of the submerged portion of the cylinder change?

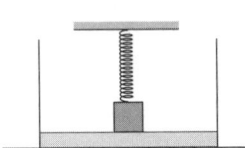

18. A light iron cube of side l suspended from a spring of stiffness k touches water level in a vessel as shown in the figure. If more water is added in the vessel at such a rate that water level in the vessel rises with a small and steady speed u, how will speed of the iron cube vary with time t? The density of water is ρ_w and acceleration of free fall is g.

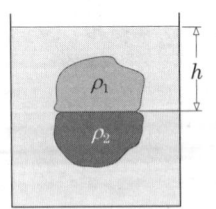

19. Two objects of equal volume $V = 1.0$ m³ and densities $\rho_1 = 400$ kg/m³ and $\rho_2 = 600$ kg/m³ have identical flat portions of area $S = 100$ cm² on their surfaces. These flat portions are glued to each other. The composite body thus formed; floats fully submerged in a liquid with the common flat portion horizontal as shown in the figure. If the glue can withstand a maximum force $F = 500$ N, at what minimum depth h in the liquid can the common flat portion be in equilibrium keeping the objects intact? The acceleration of free fall is g.

20. A tube made of very thin glass-sheet has mass m, length l and cross section area S. Its lower end is closed. Up to what height h should water be filled in the tube so that it can float vertically in water in stable equilibrium? The water is ρ_0.

21. Two steel loads A of mass $m_A = 0.68$ kg and B of unknown mass are suspended from an ideal fixed pulley with the help of a light inextensible cord. An unknown amount of ice C is affixed on the bottom of the load B and the setup is in equilibrium with the load A in air and half volume of the load B submerged in water of a large tank as shown in the figure. When all the ice melts, the setup still remains in equilibrium, but the load B is now completely submerged in water. Find mass of the load B as well as initial mass of the ice C. Density of water is $\rho_w = 1000$ kg/m³, density of ice is $\rho_i = 900$ kg/m³ and density of steel is $\rho_s = 7800$ kg/m³.

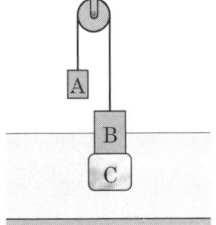

22. A glass sphere of volume V is placed in a vessel filled with water. A sidewall of the vessel is inclined at an angle θ with horizontal bottom of the vessel. The container is moving with uniform leftward acceleration a. Find force of normal reaction between the bottom of the vessel and the glass sphere. Density of water is ρ_w, density of the glass is ρ and acceleration of free fall is g.

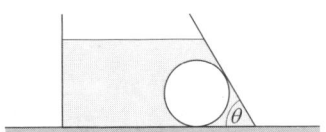

23. A closed tube of length l filled completely with water has a small air bubble trapped in it. When the tube is held at an angle θ with the vertical and rotated at a constant angular velocity ω about the vertical axis through its lower end, the bubble settles at some intermediate position in the tube. What fraction η of length of the tube is the distance of the bubble from the lower end? The acceleration due to gravity is g.

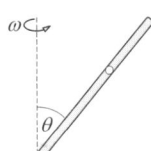

24. Two balls A and B, made of materials of densities $\rho_A = 7140$ kg/m³, and $\rho_B = 1740$ kg/m³ are affixed at the ends of a rod of length $l = 40$ cm. A thread is tied at the middle of the rod. When holding the thread, the balls are lowered in water, both the balls get fully submerged, and the rod remains horizontal. When the thread is pulled upwards and both the balls come out of water, the rod does not stay horizontal. By what distance should ball B be shifted on the rod to make the rod horizontal when both the balls are in air? Density of water is ρ_0.

25. A uniform sphere of mass m and another uniform hemisphere of the same material and radius r are placed in a vessel. In the vessel water is filled up to height $r = 30.0$ cm as shown. There is no water or air under the hemisphere. The sphere and the hemisphere both are connected with vertical threads to the ends of a light rod AB of length $l = 116$ cm having a hinge O. Find the distance of the hinge from the end A so that when an upward minimum pull is applied at the hinge, the sphere and the hemisphere both will simultaneously leave the bottom of the vessel. Density of the material of the sphere is $\rho = 5.0$ g/cm³ and that of water is $\rho_0 = 1.0$ g/cm³.

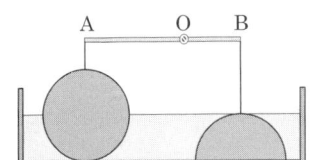

26. A uniform cylinder made of a material of density $\rho = 250$ kg/m³ is held at rest in a pool so that its upper circular surface is in level with the water surface. The length of the cylinder is $l = 20$ cm and radius is $r = 3.0$ cm. When released, the cylinder jumps out of water moving vertically. Find the velocity with which the cylinder leaves the water surface. Density of water is $\rho_0 = 1000$ kg/m³ and acceleration due to gravity is $g = 10$ m/s². Neglect all dissipative effects.

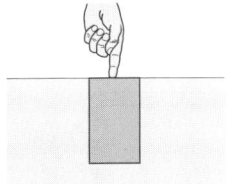

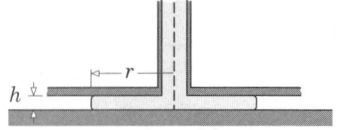

27. A homogeneous beam of length l and square section of side length a is held horizontally so that one of its long faces touches the water in a large reservoir. Density of material of the beam ρ is equal to density of water. The beam is released. Find the amount of heat developed until all the perturbations cease. The acceleration of free fall is g.

28. A cylindrical tube is fitted coaxially at one of its ends into a hole made at the centre of a large disc. The structure is held firmly at a height h above a horizontal floor, keeping plane of the disc horizontal. When an incompressible non-viscous fluid of density ρ is fed at a constant rate μ (kg/s) into the tube completely filling the tube, the fluid spreads evenly in all directions in the gap between the disc and the floor. Find radius r of the fluid spreading in the gap as a function of time t.

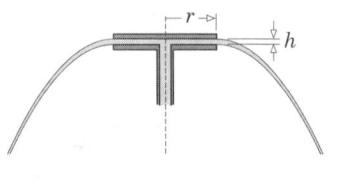

29. One end of a long cylindrical tube is fitted coaxially into a hole made at the centre of a thin disc of radius r. The structure is held firmly under another horizontally fixed disc of the same radius. Gap between the discs is h. Water fed into the tube comes out evenly everywhere from the opening between the discs and spreads in a dome-like shape. If water is fed into the tube at a rate μ (kg/s), find the radius of the dome at a depth H below the opening between the discs. Neglect capillary effects and the distance h between the discs as compared to the depth H. Acceleration of free fall is g.

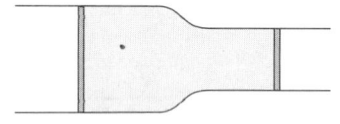

30. A horizontal cylindrical pipe consists of two coaxial sections, the section to the left has radius r_1 and that to the right has radius r_2. Inside the pipe, there is a piston in each section trapping an incompressible fluid of density ρ filled in the complete space between them. Constant pressures p_1 and p_2 ($p_1 > p_2$) are maintained outside the pistons in the sections to the left and to the right respectively. When both the pistons acquire constant speeds towards the right, find their speeds.

31. A spherical air bubble of radius 0.5 mm made under water moves up with a velocity of 0.5 cm/s. Another spherical air bubble of double radius moves up in water four times faster than the smaller bubble. A metal ball of radius 1.0 mm and density 5.0 g/cm³ when released in water sinks down with a velocity 8.0 cm/s. Knowing that the force of water resistance on a spherical body is proportional to the product $r^\alpha v^\beta$, where α and β are real numbers, r is radius of the body and v is its speed, find the constant velocity with which another plastic ball of density (2/3) g/cm³ and radius 3.0 mm will move in water. Density of water is 1.0 g/cm³ and density of the air in the bubbles is negligible as compared to the density of water. The acceleration of free fall is $g = 10$ m/s².

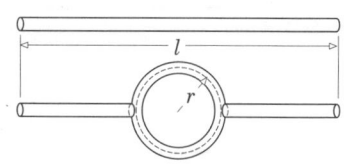

32. A pump circulates water at a time rate q_0 through a straight pipe of length l. Now a ring-shape section of mean radius r is connected in the middle of the pipe. The inner section of the ring is equal to that of the pipe as shown in the figure. If the same pump is connected to this new pipe, how much time rate q of water flow will the pump maintain? Assume that the pressure difference at the ends of the tube remains unchanged.

Check your understanding

1. A rubber tube AB is connected to a glass tube BC. The glass tube consists of $n = 5$ identical inverted U-sections. Diameter of the tubes are negligible as compared to height $h = 10$ cm of these sections.

   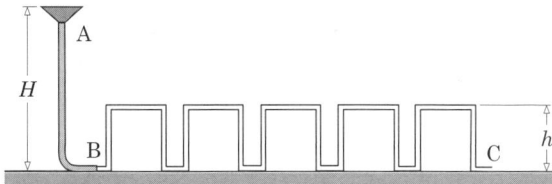

   Now water is poured very slowly through a funnel into the rubber tube at its open-end A. What should be the minimum height H of the end A, so that water starts flowing out of the end C of the glass tube? Neglect capillary action and viscosity.

2. Some amount of water is trapped between two pistons, which can slide without friction in the vertical arms A and B of an S-shape tube. The area of horizontal cross-section of arm B is $\eta = 5$ times the area $S_A = 100$ cm² of arm A. The piston in arm B is supported on a spring of force constant $k = 1000$ N/m. In the equilibrium, the length of tube below the piston in arm B is $l = 20$ cm. What maximum additional mass can be gently placed on the piston in arm A so that piston in arm B will remain inside the tube? Density of water is $\rho = 1000$ kg/m³ and acceleration due to gravity is $g = 10$ m/s².

   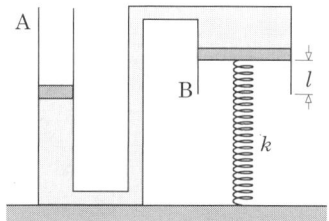

3. Two cylindrical vessels A and B containing oil of density $\rho = 0.5$ g/cm³ are connected by a thin tube at their bottom and are placed on a horizontal floor. Horizontal cross-sectional area of vessel A is $\eta = 4$ times that $S = 10$ cm² of the vessel B. A light piston fitted in the vessel B is connected at one end of a light inextensible cord and the other end of the cord is attached to the ceiling. The cord passes under a moveable light pulley and then over a fixed pulley. An empty box is attached to the movable pulley and the system is in equilibrium as shown in the figure. Now a mass $\Delta m = 100$ g of sand is gradually added in the box and simultaneously an equal mass Δm of the oil in vessel A maintaining the system almost in equilibrium. Find the distance that the box will move. There is no friction anywhere.

   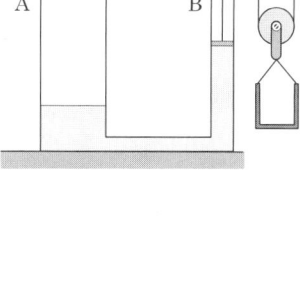

4. Vertical arms of a special U-tube are connected by a thin glass tube equipped with a valve. Initially the valve is closed, and the tube contains three immiscible liquids A, B and C of densities ρ_A, ρ_B and ρ_C ($\rho_C > \rho_A > \rho_B$). Lengths of columns of liquid C in both the arms are equal, length of column of liquid A is h in the left arm, the connecting tube meets liquid A in the middle and in the right arm is liquid B. After the valve is opened, by what amount do the liquid levels in both the arms change?

   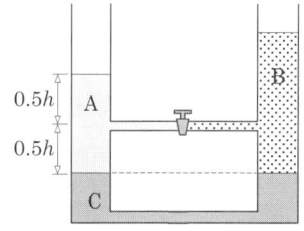

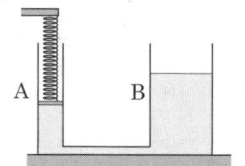

5. Two cylindrical vessels A and B connected by a thin tube at their bottom containing a liquid of density $\rho = 2.5$ g/cm³ are placed on a horizontal floor. The horizontal cross-sectional area of vessel B is $S = 1.0$ m². A light piston that can slide without friction in vessel A is connected at one end of a light spring, the other end of which is attached to a movable support. If the movable support is shifted downwards, the piston shifts down a distance that is $a = 0.5$ times of shift in the movable support and water level in vessel B moves up a distance that is $b = 0.1$ times of shift in the movable support.

   (a) Find the force constant of the spring.
   (b) If a volume $V = 120$ L of water is added to vessel B maintaining the movable support stationary, by what distance will the water level rise in vessel A?

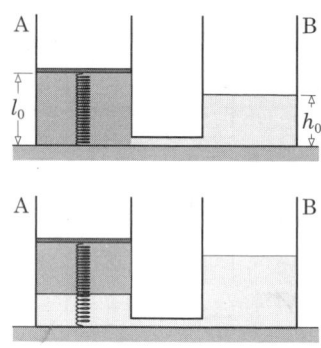

6. Two identical cylindrical vessels A and B of horizontal section area 0.5 m² each are interconnected at their bottom with a thin tube. Vessel A is filled with an ice block of height $l_0 = 100$ cm in which is embedded a relaxed spring of stiffness 2.5 kN/m. One end of the spring is connected to a light piston covering the ice and the other end to the bottom of the vessel. Water at room temperature is filled in the vessel B up to a height $h_0 = 70$ cm. Suppose the ice melts in horizontal layers reducing thickness of the ice block uniformly and the ice-piston block slides inside the vessel A without friction. Find the height of the water level in vessel B when thickness of the ice block becomes 0.5 times its initial thickness. The density of ice is 900 kg/m³ and that of water is 1000 kg/m³.

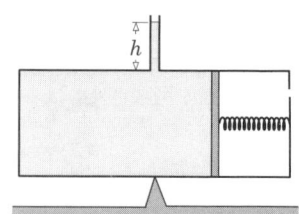

7. A cylinder of radius $r = 10.0$ cm and length $l = 33.0$ cm has a thin tube connected at its middle. In the right side of the cylinder is a piston connected to the circular wall with the help of a spring of force constant $k = 400\pi$ N/m and relaxed length $l_0 = 15.0$ cm. The piston is airtight and can slide inside the cylinder without friction. There is an orifice in the right circular wall of the cylinder. A fulcrum supports the cylinder exactly at its middle as shown in the figure. When the mass of water in cylinder equals the mass of the piston, the cylinder stays horizontal. What length h of the tube is filled with water? Acceleration due to gravity is $g = 10$ m/s².

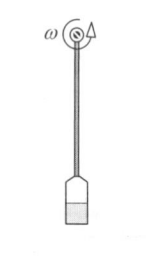

8. A cylindrical vessel of radius r and height h is affixed coaxially at one end of a rod of length l, the other end of which is pivoted to a fixed support so that it can rotate in a vertical plane. The vessel is half filled with water and its dimensions are much smaller than the length of the rod. With what minimum constant angular velocity ω must the rod be rotated so that water does not spill out of the vessel anywhere in its circular path? Acceleration due to gravity is $g = 10$ m/s².

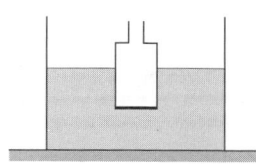

9. A thin empty glass bottle floats in a cylindrical vessel containing some amount of water as shown in the figure. Area of the bottom of the vessel is $S = 250$ cm². When $m = 300$ g of water is added in the bottle, the bottle begins to sink and when all the air comes out of the bottle, water level in the vessel changes by $\Delta h = 0.6$ cm from its initial level. Calculate volume of the bottle. Density of water $\rho = 1.0$ g/cm³.

10. A long cylindrical vessel of radius $R = 10$ cm placed on a horizontal table is filled with water up to a height $h = 8$ cm. A disc of radius $r = 5$ cm, thickness $t = 1$ cm and made of material of density $\rho = 0.8$ g/cm^3 when put on the water it floats. When another identical disc is coaxially placed on it the former shifts further down and now both of them float. If we keep on putting more identical discs in this manner one above the other, eventually the lowest disc will touch the bottom of the vessel. How much minimum number of these discs is needed so that the lowest disc touches the bottom of the vessel? Density of water is $\rho_0 = 1.0$ g/cm^3.

11. A U shape vessel shown consists of two cylindrical vertical arms A and B of cross-sectional area $S_A = 300$ cm^2 and $S_B = 500$ cm^2. A very light piston can slide without friction in arm A and confines water below it. A thin light thread attached to the piston at one of its ends, passes under two ideal pulleys fixed at the bottom of the vessel and then attached at the other end to the bottom of a very light cube C of side $l = 10$ cm. Initially, when a block of mass m is placed on the piston, the cube floats with negligible portion inside the water and the thread is not slack. How high will the piston move if the block is gradually lifted off the piston? Density of water is $\rho_0 = 1000$ kg/m^3.

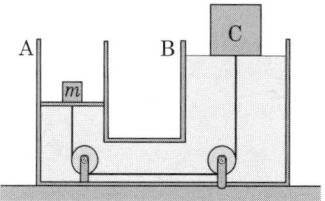

12. A cylindrical vessel has a narrow horizontal tube of cross-section area S at its bottom. A wooden cylinder of cross-section area S_c is suspended inside the vessel with the help of a spring of force constant k. When the vessel is empty, the base of the wooden cylinder is at a height h_c above the base of the vessel. Now some amount of water is added in the vessel so that the cylinder gets partially submerged and piston in the bottom tube is held with a horizontal force F. How much length of the cylinder is submerged in water? Density of water is ρ_w and acceleration of free fall is g.

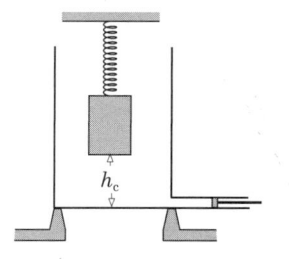

13. A uniform wooden rod of mass m and length l floating in calm water of a tank is being pulled out of water slowly with the help of a light cord attached to one end of the rod. The cord is always kept vertical. Water is so deep that the rod never touches the bottom of the tank. Relative density of the wood is $\gamma = 3/4$. Deduce expression for tensile force T in the cord as a function of height h of the end of rod being pulled above the water level. The acceleration of free fall is g.

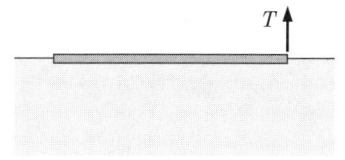

14. In the setup shown four ice blocks A, B, C and D of masses $9m$, $6m$, $3m$ and m suspended from the ceiling with the help of a system of ideal pulleys and ideal threads stay in equilibrium. The blocks A, B and C are partially immersed in water maintained at 0 °C in a vessel placed on a floor and the block D is hanging in air. An amount of heat is supplied to the ice block D. When $\Delta m = 2.5$ kg of ice of the block D melts, water level in the vessel changes by an amount $\Delta h_1 = 1.0$ cm and when complete ice of the block D melts water level in the vessel further changes by an amount $\Delta h_2 = 2.0$ cm. Density of ice is $\rho_i = 900$ kg/m^3 and density of water is $\rho_w = 1000$ kg/m^3. Find area of the bottom of the vessel and the initial tension force supporting the ice block B. The acceleration due to gravity is g.

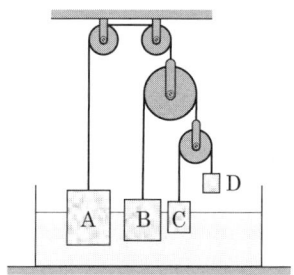

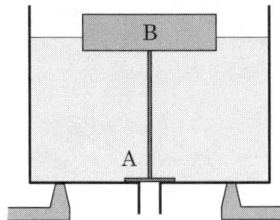

15. A cylindrical tank of horizontal sectional area $S = 25$ cm² has a hole in its bottom. The hole is closed by thin metal plate A of area $S_A = 5.0$ cm² connected with a thin rod of length $l = 10$ cm to a cylindrical float B of horizontal section area $S_B = 10$ cm². This plate-rod-float assembly works as a special valve. Now a tap is opened, and water starts entering the vessel at a constant rate $r = 10$ cc/s. When the water level in the vessel reaches a particular height, the assembly lifts opening the hole through which water drains out at a rate $\eta = 1.5$ times of r. This operation repeats repeatedly. Assuming mass of the assembly to be $m = 100$ g and density of water to be $\rho_0 = 1.0$ g/cm³, find time interval between a closing and a subsequent opening of the hole. Neglect force created by water flow and atmospheric pressure.

16. An open cuboidal tank of height $H = 25$ cm has rectangular bottom of sides $a = 60$ cm and $b = 30$ cm. When it floats in water with the open top upside, a height $h = 5.0$ cm remains out of water. A hole of area $S = 3.0$ cm² is made in the bottom. If water coming into the tank from the hole is not taken out, in how much time t will the tank sink? The acceleration of free fall is g.

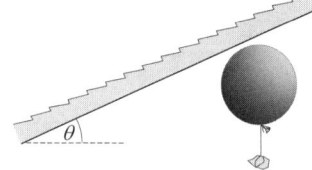

17. A small stone is suspended by a light inextensible cord from a helium-filled balloon of radius r and mass m. When this balloon is released in a hall, it moves up and encounters the ceiling inclined at an angle θ. Friction between the balloon and the ceiling is sufficient to prevent slipping. Find range of values of mass m_0 of the stone so that the balloon stays standstill touching the ceiling. The density of air is ρ_0.

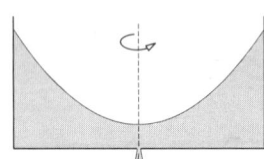

18. A cylindrical vessel of radius R is filled with an ideal liquid of density ρ up to height h above its flat bottom. It is now set into rotation about its vertical axis with constant angular velocity ω. When a steady state is achieved, the liquid does not overflow, and no portion of the bottom is dry. Now at the centre of the bottom a small orifice of radius r is made. How much liquid can flow out of the vessel?

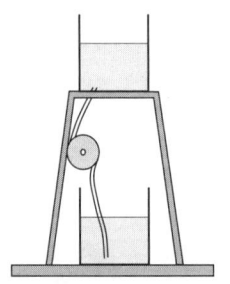

19. A vessel is placed on the pan of a balance and another identical vessel supported on a stand is arranged above the former vessel. The stand is also placed on the pan. Both the vessels are partially filled with water. A pump attached to one leg of the stand can transfer water from any one of the vessels to the other. The total weight of the contents on the pan is W. The base area of the vessels is S and the pump can transfer water at a constant rate of μ (kg/s). How much will the reading of the weighing machine become if the pump begins to transfer water from the lower vessel to the upper one? What will your answer be if the pump transfers water from the upper vessel to the lower one? Density of water is ρ.

20. A small air bubble is in the middle of a long cylindrical tube filled with glycerine. If the tube is held at rest vertically, the bubble moves upward with a constant velocity v_0 and if the tube is held horizontally, the bubble moves up and stops touching the top of the inner curved surface as shown in the figure. When the horizontal tube is given a constant velocity $\bar{v}$ along its axis, by what amount will the bubble shift relative to the tube? The acceleration of free fall is g.

Challenge your understanding

1. A rectangular hole of dimensions $a \times b$ is cut in horizontal bottom of large vessel. To close the hole, a cuboidal block of dimensions $b \times c \times c$ is put on it in such a way that the square faces and a diagonal plane remain vertical as shown in the figure. Now a liquid of density ρ is slowly poured in the vessel. What should the mass m of the block be so that the hole always remains closed irrespective of the level of liquid in the vessel?

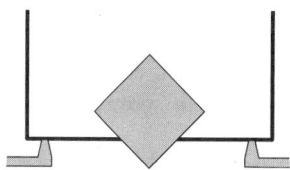

2. To make a candle float stably in water in vertical orientation an aluminium cylinder of radius equal to that of the candle is glued at bottom of the candle. The length of this cylinder is 1.0 cm and the densities of wax, aluminium and water are 0.8 g/cm³, 2.7 g/cm³ and 1.0 g/cm³.

   (a) Find the maximum and the minimum length l of the candle so that it can float in water stably in vertical orientation. The radius of the candle is small enough to ignore horizontal shifting of the point of application of the buoyant force.

   (b) When the candle is lit, it consumes wax. If consumption of wax reduces the length of the candle at a constant rate of 1.0 mm/min and the initial length of the candle is 12.0 cm, how long can the candle be used for lighting always floating vertically.

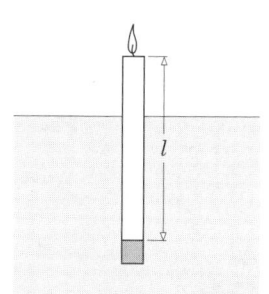

ANSWERS AND HINTS

Multiple Choice Questions

1. (a)
2. (a)
3. (a)
4. (a)
5. (d)
6. (a)
7. (b)
8. (d)
9. (c)
10. (b) and (c)
11. (a) and (c)
12. (a), (b), (c) and (d)
13. (b)
14. (d)

Build up your understanding

1. $h_0 \left(\dfrac{\rho_i - \rho_0}{\rho_i - \rho} \right) = 2.0$ m

2. $\tfrac{5}{3}\pi r^3 \rho g \uparrow$

   Hint: Force of the liquid on the lower hemisphere balances the weight of the sphere and the weight of water above the sphere.

3. $\left[\left(\dfrac{2\pi r^3 \rho g}{3} \right)^2 + \{\pi r^2 \rho g (h+r)\}^2 - 2\left(\dfrac{2\pi r^3 \rho g}{3} \right)\{\pi r^2 \rho g (h+r)\} \cos\theta \right]^{\frac{1}{2}}$

   Hint: Suppose a portion of water identical to the dent in another identical vessel without the dent. This portion of water is in equilibrium under the action of three forces that are the weight of the portion, normal reaction on its bottom and force of water pressure on its hemispherical surface.

Alternatively, you may write expression of the force vector of water pressure on an infinitesimal portion of the dent and then sum up all these force vectors to find the net resultant. This idea is too complex to use.

4. $\dfrac{\rho g h^2 (l_2 - l_1)}{6m}$

5. $\dfrac{mgS_1}{kS_2 - (S_1 - S_2)\rho g S_1}$

6. $\dfrac{Vl_1}{S(l_1 + l_2)}$

7. βh

   Hint: Since the vessels are connected at their bottom, therefore change in pressures at their bottoms between two equilibrium states must be equal.

8. $t - \dfrac{h_{min} + h_{max}}{2\eta} = 4.5$ cm

   Hint: For maximum level difference in pistons, friction force in the narrower arm must be downwards and in the wider arm upwards. For minimum level difference in pistons, directions of frictions must get reversed.

9. 25 cm and 29 cm

10. In the left arm top level rises and in the right arm it dips by the same amount say x and the level of liquid C dips in the left arm and rises in the right arm by an amount say y.

    $x = \dfrac{(\rho_A - \rho_B)h}{2(\rho_A + \rho_B)}$; $y = \dfrac{(\rho_A - \rho_B)h}{2(2\rho_C - \rho_A - \rho_B)}$

    Hint: Initially pressure at the ends of the rubber tube in liquid B is higher than that in liquid A. Therefore, the piston will shift towards the left when released. Due to this, liquid A in the tube flows towards left increasing its amount in the left vertical arm. This shifting increases pressure at the surface of liquid C there, so level of liquid C falls in the left vertical arm and shifts up in the right vertical arm by the same amount. This shifting makes pressures at both the ends of the connecting tube equal.

Now the pressure at the opening of the connecting tube in left vertical arm has been increased from its initial value and pressure at opening in the right vertical arm has been decreased from its initial value. Therefore top level of liquid A must have shifted up and the top level of liquid B must have shifted down.

Incompressibility and immiscibility of the liquids suggests that their total volume remains unchanged; therefore, the top level of liquid A must shift up in the left vertical arm by the same amount as the top level of liquid B shifts down in the right vertical arm.

11. $\dfrac{\eta}{l}\sqrt{\dfrac{2(\eta-1)p}{\rho}}$

12. 22.5 cm and 37.5 cm

13. $h\left(2 + \dfrac{m}{M} - \dfrac{\rho}{\rho_0}\right) = 1.7$ m

    Hint: In the final state, you will find three distinct regions. The lowest region is filled only with water; the middle region filled with a portion of the stack of beads with water filling space between them and the topmost region filled only with the beads. The stack of beads remaining intact shifts upwards due to buoyant forces.

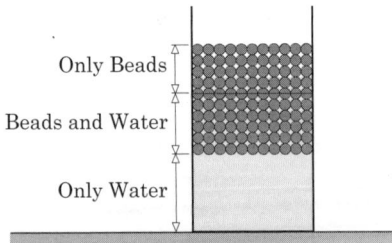

The beads do not absorb water; therefore, total volume occupied by water will not change.

Weight of water of volume equal to volume of beads in the middle region is the buoyant force, which must be equal to the weight of stack of beads.

14. 5 m

   Hint: Pressure change of 10 kPa corresponds to 1.0 m height of water column.

15.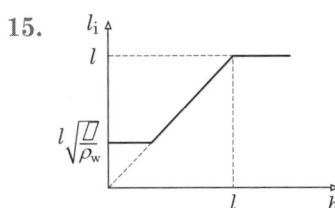

16. $\dfrac{l\sin\theta}{2}\sqrt{\dfrac{3\rho_1+\rho_2}{\rho}} = 80$ cm

   Hint: Since average density of the rod is higher than that of water, the end of the rod on the higher density portion will always remain in contact with the bottom of the tub and the rod will stay inclined under the action of three forces that are the weight of the rod, buoyant force and the normal reaction from the bottom of the tub.

17. Decreases by $\dfrac{kax_0}{g(k+\rho_w S(g+a))}$

18. $= \begin{cases} u\left(\dfrac{\rho_w gl^2}{k+\rho_w gl^2}\right); & 0 \le t \le \dfrac{l}{u}\left(1+\dfrac{\rho_w gl^2}{k}\right) \\ 0; & \dfrac{l}{u}\left(1+\dfrac{\rho_w gl^2}{k}\right) \le t \end{cases}$

19. $\dfrac{(\rho_2-\rho_1)Vg - 2F}{(\rho_1+\rho_2)gS} = 10$ m

20. $\dfrac{1}{2}\left(l - \dfrac{m}{\rho_0 S}\right) < h < \left(l - \dfrac{m}{\rho_0 S}\right)$

   Hint: Tube must float partially immersed and mass centre of the tube and water inside the tube must be below the mass centre of the water displaced.

21. $\dfrac{\rho_s m_A}{\rho_s - \rho_w} = 0.78$ kg and

   $\dfrac{\rho_i \rho_w m_A}{2(\rho_s - \rho_w)(\rho_w - \rho_i)} = 0.45$ kg

22. $(\rho - \rho_w)V(g + a\cot\theta)$

23. $\eta = \dfrac{g\cos\theta}{\omega^2 l\sin^2\theta}$

   Hint: Net force on the bubble by water can be conceived as if it has two components, one of them is the usual buoyant force in the vertically upward direction and the other one acting radially inwards due to radial pressure gradient created by rotating water.

24. $\dfrac{l}{2}\left\{\dfrac{\rho_0(\rho_A - \rho_B)}{\rho_B(\rho_A - \rho_0)}\right\} = 10$ cm

25. $\left(\dfrac{2\rho + \rho_0}{6\rho - \rho_0}\right)l = 44$ cm

26. $\sqrt{\dfrac{(\rho_0 - 2\rho)gl}{\rho}} = 2.0$ m/s

   Hint: Work done by the force of water on the cylinder is utilized in increasing gravitational potential energy as well as kinetic energy of the cylinder.

27. $\dfrac{\rho g l a^3}{2}$

   Hint: Since volume of the beam is negligible as compared to the volume of water in the reservoir, the water displaced by the beam spreads in an infinitely thin layer over the original water surface without any appreciable change in water level.

28. $r = \sqrt{\dfrac{\mu t}{\pi \rho h}}$

29. $r + \dfrac{\mu}{2\pi r \rho h}\sqrt{\dfrac{2H}{g}}$

30. $\sqrt{\dfrac{2r_2^4(p_1-p_2)}{\rho(r_1^4 - r_2^4)}}$ and $\sqrt{\dfrac{2r_1^4(p_1-p_2)}{\rho(r_1^4 - r_2^4)}}$

31. 6.0 cm/s

32. $q = q_0\left(\dfrac{2l}{2l - 4r + \pi r}\right)$

   Hint: Flow rate of water is proportional to the pressure difference between two points and inversely proportional to the flow resistance between the two points.

Flow resistance in a pipe is proportional to length of the pipe and inversely proportional to cross-sectional area of the pipe assuming uniform velocity profile over a cross-section perpendicular to the flow.

Check your understanding

1. $H = nh = 50$ cm

   Hint: Each time water rises up to top right corner of a section, it falls quickly down creating an air packet behind due to very small rate of water supply. In this way, situation shown in the first figure is obtained after some time.

   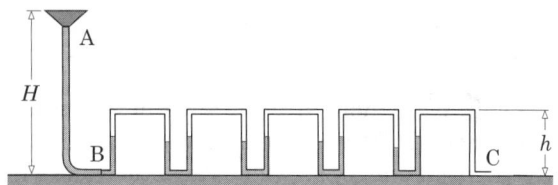

   Now additional quantity of water supplied will force water in each section of the tube to reach top right corners as shown in the next figure. Now any additional supply of water will cause the water in the last section to fall and come out of the tube.

   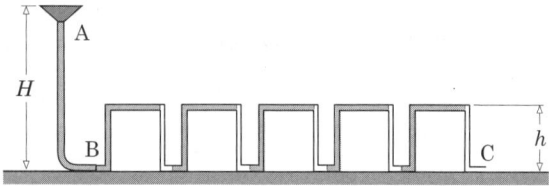

   The pressure at the bottom end B created by the water column in the rubber tube must be equal to total pressure created by water columns in each section up to the end C.

2. $\rho(\eta-1)lS_A + \dfrac{kl}{\eta g} = 12$ kg

3. $\dfrac{(\eta+2)}{4(\eta+1)}\dfrac{\Delta m}{\rho S} = 6.0$ cm

   Hint: The pistons shift upwards due to two factors, one is the increase in tension force in the cord and the other is addition of extra oil. Difference in oil levels in both the arms depends only on the load in the box; therefore, addition of oil will only cause oil level in both the arms to rise by the same amount. The net shift in level of piston is sum of individual contributions of the above two factors. The shift in position of the box is half of the shift in position of the piston.

4. In left arm top-level rises and in right dips by amount x and level of liquid C dips in left arm and rises in the right arm by amount y.

   $$x = \dfrac{(\rho_C - \rho_B)(\rho_A - \rho_B)h}{2\rho_B(2\rho_C - \rho_A - \rho_B)}; \quad y = \dfrac{(\rho_A - \rho_B)h}{2(2\rho_C - \rho_A - \rho_B)}$$

   Hint: Initially pressure at opening of the connecting tube in liquid B is higher than that in liquid A. Therefore, when the valve is opened, the liquid B pushes the liquid A towards the left and at the same time due to lesser density rises above liquid A in the left vertical arm as shown in the first figure and finally when flow through the connecting tube ceases some amount of liquid B settles above the liquid A as shown in the second figure.

   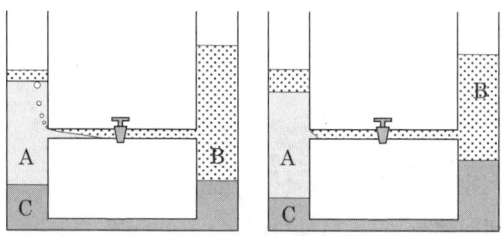

   The extra amount of liquid B in the left vertical arm increases pressure at the surface of liquid C so level of liquid C shifts down in the left vertical arm and shifts up in the right vertical arm by the same amount. This shifting makes pressures at both the ends of the connecting tube equal.

   Incompressibility and immiscibility of the liquids suggest that the total volume remains unchanged; therefore, the top level must shift up in the left vertical arm by the same amount as the top level shifts down in the right vertical arm. In this process, amount of liquid A in the left vertical arm remains almost unchanged due to negligible volume of the connecting tube.

5. (a) $\rho g \dfrac{bS}{a}\left(\dfrac{a+b}{1-a}\right) = 6.0$ kN/m

   Hint: In equilibrium, the unbalanced force on the top levels of the liquids in the two vertical arms must be balanced by the weight of liquid column between the top levels of the liquid in the arms.

   (b) $\dfrac{aV(1-a)}{S(a+b)} = 5.0$ cm

   Hint: Any change in the unbalanced force must create corresponding change in the length of the liquid column between the top levels of the liquid in both the arms.

6. 75 cm

   Hint: In the final state, weight of the remaining ice and force of the extended spring in water is balanced by the weight of the water column equal to height difference of water level in both the vessels. In addition, take care of that the force constant of the extended portion of the spring is not the same as that of the whole spring.

   While accounting for height difference of water level in both the vessels, you must consider addition of water due to melting of ice by using mass conservation.

7. $h = \dfrac{k(3l_0 - l)}{3\rho g \pi r^2} - r = 6.0$ cm

8. $\omega > \sqrt{\dfrac{g\sqrt{h^2 + 4r^2}}{hl}}$

   Hint: Water level in the vessel must tilt as the vessel moves on its circular path and if water does not spill out of the vessel, the water level must rotate through 180° during motion of the vessel from bottom position to the top position.

   When water is about to spill out, the vessel must be tilted and due to a component of gravity along the surface, water layer making the surface starts to accelerate relative to the vessel towards the lowest point of the brim. Therefore, to stop water from spilling out, there must be a force to balance this effect of gravity. In the reference frame of the vessel, this force is the centrifugal force due to the circular motion and in the worst case when the vessel is tilted as shown in the figure, a component of the centrifugal force on an infinitesimal portion of water in the layer making the surface must balance force of gravity. In this state, the horizontal component of the centrifugal force is balanced by force of water on the infinitesimal portion under consideration.

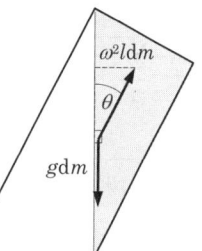

9. $=\begin{cases} \dfrac{2m}{\rho} + S\Delta h = 750 \text{ mL}; & \text{If } \Delta h \downarrow \\ \dfrac{2m}{\rho} - S\Delta h = 450 \text{ mL}; & \text{If } \Delta h \uparrow \end{cases}$

10. $\dfrac{\rho_0 R^2 h}{\rho t(R^2 - r^2)}$

    If the above expression yields an integer, the required number is that integer and if it yields a fraction, the required number is the integer part plus one.

    Here the required number is 14.

11. $\dfrac{m(S_B - l^2)}{\rho\{S_A(S_A + S_B - 2l^2) + l^2(S_B - S_A)\}} = 6$ cm

    Hint: Since the cube is very light, the tension force in the thread will always be equal to the buoyant force on the cube.

    In the initial state, when there is a weight on the piston, negligible portion of the cube is inside the water, therefore the buoyant force on the cube and the tension force in the thread both are almost zero. Thus, pressure of the weight on the pistons equals the pressure of water column in arm B above the level of piston.

    When the weight on the piston is slowly lifted off, the piston shifts upward pulling the cube downwards by the same amount with the help of the thread. Now considering volume of water unchanged you can find relations between shift of water level in the arm B, length of submerged portion of the cube, shift in the piston and the initial difference between level of the piston and water level in the arm B. Now equate pressures under the piston and at a point in the arm B in level with the piston.

12. $h = \dfrac{k(F - \rho_w g h_c S)}{\rho_w g S(k + \rho_w g S_c)}$

13. $T = \begin{cases} mg\left\{1 - \dfrac{1-\sqrt{1-\gamma}}{\gamma}\right\}; & 0 \le h \le \dfrac{l}{2} \\ mg\left\{1 - \dfrac{1}{\gamma}\left(1 - \dfrac{h}{l}\right)\right\}; & \dfrac{l}{2} \le h \le l \\ mg; & h \ge l \end{cases}$

Hint: After analyzing equilibrium conditions, you will find that before the rod becomes vertical, the length of portion of the rod submerged in water is independent of tilt of the rod. It suggests that while the rod is changing its orientation, it rotates gradually about a horizontal axis that passes through a fixed point on the rod and coincides with the water level.

14. $\dfrac{8\Delta m}{\rho \Delta h_1} = 2.0 \text{ m}^2$ and $2\Delta mg\left(1 + \dfrac{\Delta h_2}{\Delta h_1}\right) = 150 \text{ N}$

15. $\dfrac{\eta}{(\eta - 1)r}\left(\dfrac{S_A(S - S_B)}{S_B(S_B - S_A)}\right)\left(lS_B + \dfrac{m}{\rho_0}\right) = 90 \text{ s}$

Hint: The valve opens when such a portion of the float is in water at which resultant of the buoyant force of water on the float and force of water pressure on the metal plate just exceeds the weight of the assembly. The valve closes when such a portion of the float is in water at which the weight of the assembly exceeds the buoyant force of water on the float.

16. $t = \dfrac{abh}{S\sqrt{2g(H-h)}} = 15 \text{ s}$

Hint: Before brim of the tank is above the level of outside water, the height difference between the inside and outside water levels remains unchanged maintaining constant pressure difference between the hole and inside water level, therefore water enters the hole at constant velocity. Water entering from the hole spreads in the tank, thus water level in the tank rises at very small velocity causing the tank to shift downwards at a negligible velocity.

17. $\dfrac{(4\pi r^3 \rho - 3m)\sin\theta}{3(1 + \sin\theta)} \le m_0 < \dfrac{(4\pi r^3 \rho - 3m)}{3}$

Hint: The balloon rises up because of the buoyant force and when it touches the ceiling, the stone is vertically below its centre, thereafter, the balloon rolls up slightly along the ceiling due to static friction and finally settles in a stable stationary state with the stone shifted towards the left of the vertical line through the centre of the balloon.

18. $\approx \pi R^2 h - \dfrac{\pi \omega^2}{4g}(R^4 - r^4)$

Hint: Rotation of water at a constant angular velocity makes the water surface paraboloidal in shape and as the water drains out from the orifice the water surface shifts downwards maintaining its shape intact until it approaches the orifice.

19. Independent of whether the water is pumped up or down, reading of the weighing machine is

$W + \dfrac{2\mu^2}{\rho S}$

Hint: Whether water is pumped up or pumped down, the mass centre of the system consisting of the stand, the pump, the vessels and the total water in both the vessels moves with an upward acceleration.

20. $\dfrac{v_0 \vec{v}}{g}$

Challenge your understanding

1. $m > \rho b \left(c - \dfrac{a}{\sqrt{2}} \right)^2$

   Hint: The buoyant force of water achieves its maximum value in condition shown in the figure.

   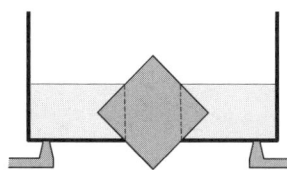

2. (a) $8.5 \text{ cm} \leq l \leq 18.54 \text{ cm}$

   Hint: To float, the depth of immersion cannot exceed the total length of the candle-cylinder structure and to float stably in vertical orientation the force centre of the buoyancy must be vertically above the mass centre of the of the candle-cylinder structure.

   (b) 35 min

Chapter 8

Thermal Physics

Concept of heat and temperature, calorimetry, latent heat, heat transfer: conduction, convection and radiation, Newton's law of cooling, kinetic theory of ideal gases and gas laws, internal energy of a gas, work done by gases, thermodynamic processes, specific heats of gases, the zeroth and the first law of thermodynamics and their applications.

"The important thing in science is not so much to obtain new facts as to discover new ways of thinking about them."

BACK TO BASICS

Heat:
Heat is energy in transit due to temperature difference.

Conduction, convection and radiation are modes of heat transfer between two material bodies.

Internal energy:
Internal energy of a system is total kinetic energy of random motion of all the material particles within the system and total potential energy due to mutual interaction forces between the particles.

Thermal energy:
Thermal energy of a system is a part of its internal energy that results from random motion of all the material particles within the system and is associated with the temperature of the system.

Sir William Henry Bragg
(July 2, 1831 – March 12, 1942)

Calorimetry
Calorimetry is the science of measuring the heat of chemical reactions or physical changes in accordance with the principle of conservation of energy.

Heat given to a material body is utilized either in increasing temperature and doing some mechanical action or in state change and doing some mechanical action.

Here the mechanical action is associated with thermal expansion and is almost negligible for solids and liquids but happens in appreciable amount for gases.

For liquids and solids: $dQ = msd\theta$ (For temperature change)

or

$$dQ = dmL \quad \text{(For state change)}$$

In the above equations, m is mass, s is specific heat capacity, $d\theta$ is change in temperature and L is specific latent heat.

Heat Transfer

Conduction:

Conduction is the flow of heat through an unequally heated body from places of higher to places of lower temperature.

Steady state heat conduction in one dimension:

Heat current H i.e. time rate of flow of amount of heat across a layer of area S and infinitesimal thickness dx with a temperature difference $d\theta$ between its faces is given by the following equation.

$$H = \frac{dQ}{dt} = -kA\frac{d\theta}{dx}$$

Here k is specific thermal conductance or conductivity of the material of the layer and the minus sign (–) indicates that heat flows in the direction of temperature decrease.

Convection:

In convection, hot fluid carrying heat, flows by itself or is made to flow.

Radiation:

Radiation is propagation of heat in the form of electromagnetic waves.

Stefan-Boltzmann law:

Radiant energy P emitted per unit time per unit surface area of a body at absolute temperature T is given by the following equation.

$$P = \sigma e T^4$$

Here σ is the Stefan's constant and e is emissivity of the surface.

$\sigma = 5.67 \times 10^{-8}$ J/(s·m²·K⁴)

$0 \leq e \leq 1$

Prevost's theory of heat exchange:

A body is simultaneously emitting radiation to its surroundings and absorbing them from the surroundings. Therefore, net radiant energy emitted per unit time per unit surface area of a body at absolute temperature T kept in a surrounding of temperature T_0 is given by the following equation.

$$P_{net} = \sigma e \left(T^4 - T_0^4 \right)$$

Wien's displacement law:

Product of wavelength λ_m of the most intense radiation emitted by a black body and the absolute temperature T of the black body is a constant.

$$\lambda_m T = b$$
$$b = 2.897 \times 10^{-3} \text{ m·K}$$

Kinetic Theory of Gases

A gas is modelled as an ensemble of randomly moving tiny particles that are either molecules or atoms. These particles are in incessant random motion continuously colliding with each other and with the walls of container if confined in a container. These collisions are almost perfectly elastic and interaction between the particles is extremely weak except when they are colliding, thus between two collisions the particles move almost freely in straight lines. In this continuous process of random motion, the particles spend negligible time during collisions as compared to the time spent in free motion.

Ideal gas model:

It is a mathematical model in which the particles are assumed like point masses, the collisions are assumed to be perfectly elastic, and the particles move absolutely freely between any two collisions.

Kinetic interpretation of pressure:

Pressure of a gas arises due to collisions between the particles constituting the gas and walls of the container.

Pressure p of an ideal gas is given by the following expression.

$$p = \frac{Nm}{3V} v_{rms}^2$$

Here N is the total number of particles each of mass m in a container of volume V and v_{rms} is the root of mean of squares of velocity magnitudes of the particles.

Kinetic interpretation of temperature:

Temperature of a material body is attributed to the kinetic energies of random motion of its particles. In an ideal gas, the average kinetic energy of a molecule is proportional to the absolute temperature of the gas, and it is independent of pressure and volume of the ideal gas.

Equi-partition of energy:

Kinetic energy associated with each degree of freedom of particles of an ideal gas is equal to $\frac{1}{2}kT$. Here k is the Boltzmann constant, and T is the absolute temperature.

Average kinetic energy of a particle having f degrees of freedom $= \dfrac{f}{2}kT$

$k = 1.38 \times 10^{-23}$ J/K

Ideal gas equation of state:
$$pV = nRT = NkT$$

Here n is number of moles and R is the universal gas constant.

$R = 8.31$ J/(mol·K) $= 1.98$ cal/(mol·K)

Thermodynamics

Thermodynamics investigates heat and its relation to energy and work.

Zeroth law of thermodynamics:

If two systems are each in thermal equilibrium with a third one, they are also in thermal equilibrium with each other.

First law of thermodynamics:

Energy of an isolated system is conserved.

Heat supplied Q to a system is equal to algebraic sum of change in internal energy ΔU of the system and mechanical work W done by the system.

$$Q = \Delta U + W$$

For an infinitesimal change: $\quad dQ = dU + dW$

Molar specific heats of gases:

Molar specific heat of a gas: $\qquad C = \dfrac{dQ}{n\,dT}$

Molar specific heat of a gas at constant volume: $\quad C_V = \left.\dfrac{dQ}{n\,dT}\right|_{dV=0}$

$$= \dfrac{dU}{n\,dT}$$

Molar specific heat of a gas at constant pressure: $\quad C_P = \left.\dfrac{dQ}{n\,dT}\right|_{dp=0}$

Mayer's Relation: $\qquad C_P = C_V + R$

Molar specific heat for processes $d(pV^x) = 0$: $\quad C = C_V + \dfrac{R}{1-x}$

Multiple Choice Questions

1. In colder regions like the poles, two identical open containers one filled with hot water and the other filled with cold water, if left exposed to atmosphere, it is observed that usually the hot water freezes earlier than the cold water.
    - I. The hot water has more heat to lose.
    - II. The hot water initially loses heat at a faster rate.
    - III. More evaporation causes more heat loss in hot water.

    Which of the above reasons can be responsible for this effect?
    (a) Reason II   (b) Reason III
    (c) Reasons II and III (d) All the above reasons

2. Two identical light metal containers filled with equal amounts of water are placed in a room maintained at a constant temperature of 25 °C. A small metal ball suspended by a thin nonconducting string is submerged into one of the containers. Mass of the ball is equal to that of water. Both the containers are heated to a temperature of 40 °C and then allowed to cool. The container with the ball takes k times longer to cool down to the room temperature than the container without the ball. Specific heat of water is s_w. Specific heat of the material of the ball s_b is closest to
    (a) $s_b = k s_w$ (b) $s_b = (k+1)s_w$
    (c) $s_b = (k-1)s_w$ (d) $s_b = (1 - 1/k)s_w$

3. A metal cylinder is placed upright on the horizontal top of a large ice slab of temperature 0 °C. The initial temperature of the cylinder is 50 °C. The vertically curved surface and top of the cylinder are adiabatic while its base is perfectly conducting. Ice below the base of the cylinder melts and the cylinder sinks into the hole thus formed. What fraction of the height of the cylinder will ultimately sink?

    Specific heat of material of cylinder is 400 J/(kg·°C) and density is 9.0 g/cm³. Specific latent heat of melting of ice is 4.0×10^5 J/kg and density is 0.9 g/cm³. Neglect the dip in the melting point of ice due to increase in pressure.
    (a) 30%   (b) 40%
    (b) 50%   (c) 60%

4. A heater of constant power is used to boil water in a pot. During heating, the temperature of water increases from 60 °C to 65 °C in 1.0 min. When the heater is switched off, the temperature of water falls from 65 °C to 60 °C in 9.0 min. If the rate of heat dissipation to the surroundings remains almost constant, what proportion of heat received by water during heating would be dissipated to the surroundings?
    (a) 9%   (b) 10%
    (c) 12.5%   (d) 15 %

5. Two identical calorimeters, one containing water and the other an unknown liquid are left in a room and allowed to cool. Masses of the water, the liquid and the calorimeter are equal. Specific heat of water is 4.20 J/(g·°C) and that of the material of the calorimeters is 0.36 J/(g·°C). If the calorimeter containing water takes 60 s and that containing the unknown liquid takes 40 s in cooling from 50 °C to 45 °C, what is the specific heat in J/(g·°C) of the unknown liquid?

(a) 2.20 (b) 2.68
(c) 2.92 (d) 3.40

6. Speed distribution of molecules of an ideal monoatomic gas trapped in a vessel is given in the following table.

Speeds of the molecules	% number of molecules
100 m/s	10
400 m/s	20
600 m/s	40
800 m/s	20
1000 m/s	10

The temperature of this gas is 324 K. If all the molecules of speed 800 m/s escape from the vessel, by what amount will the temperature of the gas change?

(a) Increase by 47 °C (b) Decrease by 47 °C
(c) Increase by 102.4 °C (d) Decrease by 102.4 °C

7. A balloon filled with 1.0 g of hydrogen is in thermal equilibrium with air in a room. The root-mean-square speed of air molecules at the room temperature is 500 m/s, the average molecular mass of air molecules is 29 g/mol. If hydrogen in the balloon is considered an ideal gas, its total internal energy is closest to

(a) 1813 J (b) 3021 J
(c) 4223 J (d) 6042 J

8. In a container, air is filled and maintained at temperature T_0. The inner surface of walls of the container is maintained at temperature T. At different values of temperatures T that are less than, equal to and greater than T_0, pressure exerted by the air on the container walls are P_1, P_2 and P_3 respectively. Which of the following statements is correct?

(a) $P_1 < P_2 < P_3$ (b) $P_1 > P_2 > P_3$
(c) $P_1 = P_2 = P_3$ (d) $P_1 < P_2 > P_3$

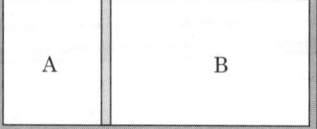

9. A piston can slide without friction inside a horizontal cylindrical vessel, which contains an ideal monoatomic gas. The piston and the inner surface of the cylinder are coated with a thin layer of a perfect heat insulating material. Initially, the piston in equilibrium divides the cylinder into two parts A and B, which are not necessarily equal. The temperatures of the gases in both the parts are equal. Now, the piston is held in its initial position and the gas in part A is supplied with some amount of heat, then the piston is released. What will the piston do in its subsequent motion?

(a) It will execute oscillatory motion of definite amplitude.
(b) It will stop somewhere to the right of its initial position after several oscillations of decreasing amplitude.
(c) After several oscillations of decreasing amplitude, it will stop exactly where it started.
(d) Certainly, it will execute oscillations of decreasing amplitude but the position where it will finally stop depends on the amount of heat supplied.

10. Identical balloons are connected through identical valves with two identical cylinders. One cylinder contains gaseous helium and the other gaseous nitrogen. Both the gases may be assumed ideal, and both the cylinders weigh equally. Which balloon will be inflated faster when the valves are opened, and why?
    (a) The nitrogen balloon will be inflated faster because nitrogen is a heavier element, and so the molecules of nitrogen have greater momentum and thus force the balloon to expand at a greater rate.
    (b) The helium balloon will be inflated faster, because helium is a lighter element and so its atoms move faster and can get into the balloon at a greater rate.
    (c) The helium balloon will be inflated faster because the helium must be at higher pressure and hence the gas will be forced into the balloon at a greater rate.
    (d) It will depend on whether the gases have to flow up or down to enter the balloon. Helium being lighter than air as compared to nitrogen will rise faster than nitrogen. Therefore, if the balloons are at the top of the cylinders, the helium balloon will be inflated faster; and if they are at the bottoms, the nitrogen balloon will be inflated faster.

11. In a two-litre metallic bottle, air is pumped to a pressure of 2.0 atm. A thin plastic bag of large capacity (greater than 10 L) with no air inside is connected to the opening of the bottle that is closed. Bottle together with the bag is placed on one pan of balance and weights are put on the other pan to establish balance. When the opening of the bottle is opened, air flows from the bottle into the bag and the balance may be disturbed. How much additional weight is required to reestablish balance? The density of air is 1.3 kg/m³ at 1 atm pressure, and the acceleration of free fall is 10 m/s².
    (a) 0.0 g (b) 0.6 g
    (c) 1.3 g (d) 2.6 g

12. A cylindrical box is moving at a constant velocity along its axis in a chamber filled with an ideal gas. The velocity of the cylinder is so small that it does not produce any turbulence in the gas. If the absolute temperature of the gas is doubled, in what way must the speed of the cylinder be changed to keep the drag force unchanged?
    (a) It must be made 0.354 times its previous value.
    (b) It must be reduced to half of its previous value.
    (c) It must be made 0.707 times its previous value.
    (d) Drag force does not depend on the temperature of the gas.

8.8 Chapter-8

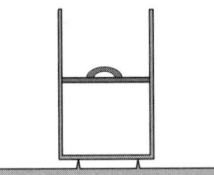

13. A highly conducting cylindrical vessel placed on elevated small supports contains an ideal gas under a piston of mass m. Area of the base of the cylinder is A. The piston is in equilibrium at the mid of the cylinder. Friction force between the cylinder and the piston can be ignored. The total mass of the cylinder and the gas is M. The atmospheric pressure is p_0. If the piston is slowly pulled upwards, find the maximum value of M such that the cylinder can be lifted off the supports.

(a) $\dfrac{p_0 A - mg}{g}$

(b) $\dfrac{p_0 A - mg}{2g}$

(c) $\dfrac{2p_0 A - mg}{2g}$

(d) It is impossible in this way.

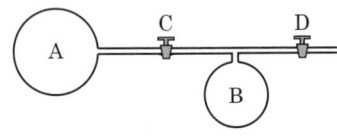

14. Two flasks A and B made of conducting materials are connected by a thin tube. Two valves C and D are installed on the tube as shown in the figure. Initially, both the flasks are evacuated, and the valves are closed. Now valve D is opened, an ideal gas is filled in the flask B at pressure p and then valve D is closed. When valve C is opened, the pressure in flask B drops by amount Δp. If volume of flask B is V_B, what is the volume of flask A?

(a) $\dfrac{\Delta p \, V_B}{p - \Delta p}$

(b) $\dfrac{p V_B}{p - \Delta p}$

(c) $\dfrac{(p - \Delta p) V_B}{p}$

(d) $\dfrac{(p - \Delta p) V_B}{\Delta p}$

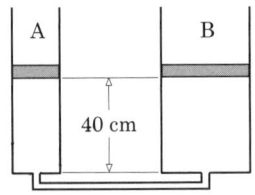

15. Two vertical conducting cylinders A and B of different cross sections are connected by a thin tube as shown. An ideal gas is trapped in the cylinders by two airtight pistons of masses 1.0 kg and 2.0 kg respectively. Initially the pistons are at the same height 40 cm above the base of the cylinders. If an additional mass of 10 g were gently placed on the piston in the cylinder A, which of the following statements correctly describe the new steady state ultimately reached.

(a) Pressure of the gas has been increased.
(b) Pressure of the gas remains unchanged.
(c) Height difference between the pistons becomes 30 cm.
(d) Height difference between the pistons becomes 60 cm.

16. Two rubber balloons filled with the same ideal gas when held at the bottom of a lake in thermal equilibrium with the surrounding water occupy equal volumes. The rubber of the first balloon is a good conductor of heat while that of the second balloon is a good insulator of heat. Both balloons are set free simultaneously. If the temperature of water in the lake is uniform, which balloon will occupy more volume when it comes near surface of the lake?

(a) The first balloon.
(b) The second balloon.
(c) Both balloons will occupy equal volumes.
(d) Decision depends on the adiabatic exponent of the gas.

17. One mole of a monoatomic gas is supplied heat in such a way that its molar specific heat during the heating process is $2R$, here R is the

universal gas constant. If due to heating, the volume of the gas is doubled, by what factor does its temperature change?

(a) 1/4
(b) 1/2
(c) 2
(d) 4

18. In a special quasi-static process, an ideal monoatomic gas is supplied heat in such a way that its volume increases and frequency of collisions of its atoms on unit area of the walls of the container remains constant. What is the molar heat capacity of the gas?

(a) 0
(b) $2R$
(c) $3R$
(d) $4.5R$

19. An ideal monoatomic gas is trapped in a cylinder closed at its right end. The cylinder is divided into two parts by a fixed heat-conducting partition and a piston that is to the left of the fixed partition. The piston and walls of the cylinder cannot conduct heat. Masses of the gas in the left and right parts are m_1 and m_2. A force F applied on the piston is slowly increased, starting from some initial value. What is the molar specific heat of the gas in the left part during this process?

(a) $\dfrac{3m_1 R}{2m_2}$
(b) $-\dfrac{3m_1 R}{2m_2}$
(c) $\dfrac{3m_2 R}{2m_1}$
(d) $-\dfrac{3m_2 R}{2m_1}$

20. If internal energy U of an ideal gas depends on pressure p and volume V of the gas according to equation $U = 3pV$, which of the following conclusions can you make regarding the gas?

(a) The gas is not a monoatomic gas.
(b) The gas can be a di-atomic gas.
(c) The gas can be a tri-atomic gas.
(d) Molar specific heat of the gas in an isobaric process is $4R$.

21. A vessel is divided into two parts, A and B, by a fixed partition. The walls of the vessel and the partition are made of a perfect heat insulating material. There is a hole in the partition, which can be opened and closed. Initially the hole is kept closed, an ideal gas is filled in part A and part B is evacuated. Now the hole is opened for a short time and then closed, as a result some of the gas enters part B. Now the hole is again opened, and gas is allowed to flow through the hole until the net flow of the gas through the hole ceases. How does the temperature of the gas change during the first and the second opening of the hole?

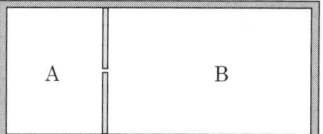

(a) During both the first and the second openings, the temperature decreases.
(b) During the first opening, the temperature remains constant but during the second opening, the temperature decreases.
(c) During the first opening, the temperature remains constant but during the second opening, the temperature increases.
(d) During both the first and the second openings, the temperature remains constant.

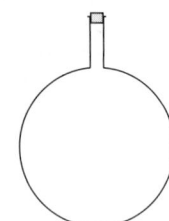

22. A heat-insulated, rigid flask is evacuated, and its opening is sealed with a cork. The flask is held at rest in a large chamber filled with an ideal monoatomic gas at a temperature of 27 °C. The cork is suddenly removed, and air quickly fills the flask. If volume of the flask is negligible as compared to the volume of the chamber, what is the temperature of the air inside the flask immediately after a thermodynamic equilibrium is attained in the flask?

   (a) –93 °C (b) 27 °C
   (c) 227 °C (d) 627 °C

23. An ideal monoatomic gas is confined inside a cylinder with the help of a piston that can slide inside the cylinder without friction. Walls of the cylinder have finite conductivity. Initially the piston is in equilibrium with its external surface exposed to the atmosphere at a pressure of 10^5 Pa. A transient pulse of heat is injected into the cylinder through its walls causing the gas to expand until its volume changes by 0.2 L. How much heat was supplied by the pulse?

   (a) 20 J (b) 30 J
   (c) 50 J (d) 60 J

24. Gaseous helium filled in a horizontal fixed cylindrical vessel is separated from its surroundings by a piston of finite mass, which can move without friction. Inner surface of the vessel as well as of the piston are coated with a perfectly heat insulating material. The external pressure is increased rapidly to triple its initial value without changing the ambient temperature. How many times of its initial value will the volume of helium become, when the piston finally stops?

   (a) $\dfrac{1}{3}$ (b) $\dfrac{3}{5}$

   (c) $\left(\dfrac{1}{3}\right)^{3/5}$ (d) $\left(\dfrac{1}{3}\right)^{5/7}$

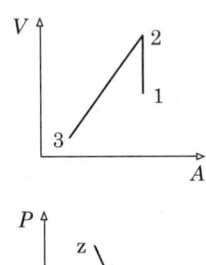

25. A student in an experimental study of a process 1→2→3 on an ideal gas prepares two graphs to show relations between absolute temperature T, pressure P and volume V. Later he found that he had forgotten to specify a coordinate axis in each graph and marking states in the second graph. Unspecified coordinates are shown by letters A and B and unspecified states by letters x, y and z in the second graph. Which of the following combinations best suits these graphs?

   (a) $A \equiv P$, $B \equiv T$, x ≡ 1, y ≡ 2, z ≡ 3
   (b) $A \equiv P$, $B \equiv T$, x ≡ 3, y ≡ 2, z ≡ 1
   (c) $A \equiv T$, $B \equiv V$, x ≡ 3, y ≡ 2, z ≡ 1
   (d) $A \equiv T$, $B \equiv T$, x ≡ 1, y ≡ 2, z ≡ 3

Questions 26 and 27 are based on the following physical situation.

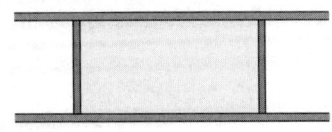

Two heat conducting pistons can slide without friction in a horizontal pipe made of a heat insulating material. Distance between the pistons is 80.0 cm. The space between the pistons is filled completely with water. Densities of water and ice are 1000 kg/m³ and 900 kg/m³ respectively, specific heats of water and ice are 4200 J/(kg·°C) and 2100 J/(kg·°C) respectively, specific latent heat of fusion of ice is 330 kJ/kg and thermal conductivity of ice is four times of that of water. Heat capacity of the pistons and that of the pipe are negligible.

26. The left and the right pistons are maintained at constant temperatures −40 °C and 16 °C respectively. After a sufficiently long time when a steady state is reached, what will the distance between the pistons become?

   (a) 80.5 cm
   (b) 84.2 cm
   (c) 88.0 cm
   (d) 97.5 cm

27. Now the devices maintaining temperatures of the pistons are removed and the pistons are covered with heat insulating materials. After a sufficiently long time when a steady state is reached again, what will the distance between the pistons become?

   (a) 80.0 cm
   (b) 88.9 cm
   (c) 89.2 cm
   (d) 92.7 cm

Questions 28 and 29 are based on the following physical situation.

A hollow cylinder made of a thermally insulating material is equipped with a horizontal piston P of mass m and area A. The piston is also made of a thermally insulating material. There is no friction between the inner surface of the cylinder and the piston. Above the piston, a liquid of density ρ is filled up to brim of the cylinder. The piston is supported at the position shown due to pressure of an ideal gas filled in the lower portion of the cylinder. The number of moles of the gas is n, atmospheric pressure is p_0 and initial temperature of the gas is T_0. The heater H is switched on.

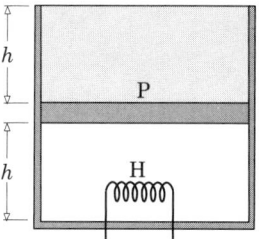

28. Work done by the gas on the piston is

   (a) $\rho g h^2 A + mgh$
   (b) $p_0 hA + \rho g h^2 A + mgh$
   (c) $p_0 hA + 0.5\rho g h^2 A + mgh$
   (d) $0.5(p_0 hA + \rho g h^2 A) + mgh$

29. The final temperature of the gas is

   (a) $2T_0 \left(\dfrac{p_0 + \rho g h}{p_0} \right)$
   (b) $2T_0 \left(\dfrac{p_0}{p_0 + \rho g h} \right)$
   (s) $2T_0 \left(\dfrac{p_0 A + \rho g h A + mg}{p_0 A + mg} \right)$
   (d) $2T_0 \left(\dfrac{p_0 A + mg}{p_0 A + \rho g h A + mg} \right)$

Questions 30 and 31 are based on the following physical situation.

In a long cylindrical vessel made of perfectly conducting walls, an ideal monoatomic gas is confined with the help of a light piston, which can slide inside the cylinder without friction. The number of atoms of the gas in the vessel are N. Initially the piston is kept in equilibrium against the pressure p_i of the gas with the help of a weight placed on the piston. In this state, the temperature of the gas is T. Atmospheric pressure is p_0.

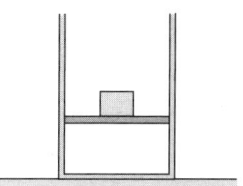

30. When the weight on the piston is removed, the gas expands rapidly and finally the piston settles to a position where the force on the piston due to the gas pressure balances the force due to the atmospheric pressure. Which of the following is a correct description of this process?

(a) The gas does no work.

(b) Work done by the gas is $NkT\left(1 - \dfrac{p_0}{p_i}\right)$.

(c) Work done by the gas is $NkT \ln\left(\dfrac{p_i}{p_0}\right)$.

(d) The process is neither isobaric nor isothermal.

31. In actual practice, considerable frictional forces act between the vessel and the piston. The inner surface of the vessel is lubricated with oil, which makes the frictional forces depend on the velocity of the piston. Now after removal of the weight, the gas expands quasi-statically and finally the piston settles to a position where the force on the piston due to the gas pressure balances the force due to the atmospheric pressure. How much work is done by the frictional forces on the piston during the above movement of the piston?

(a) $-NkT \ln\left(\dfrac{p_i}{p_0}\right)$

(b) $NkT\left\{\left(1 - \dfrac{p_0}{p_i}\right) - \ln\left(\dfrac{p_i}{p_0}\right)\right\}$

(c) $-NkT\left(1 - \dfrac{p_0}{p_i}\right)$

(d) insufficient information to decide.

Build up your understanding

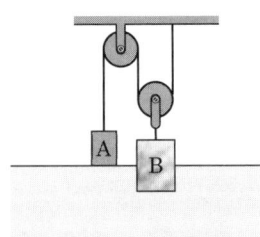

1. In the setup shown, load A of mass 160 g made from aluminium of density 2.7 g/cm³ and load B of mass 400 g made from ice of density 0.9 g/cm³ are suspended from the ceiling with the help of a light inextensible insulating thread and two ideal pulleys as shown in the figure. Specific latent heat of melting of ice is 335 J/g. Initially the setup is in equilibrium with the load A touching the water level and the load B partially submerged in water. How much heat must be given to the load B so that the load A sinks to the bottom of the container? The depth of water is much greater than the liner dimensions of the loads.

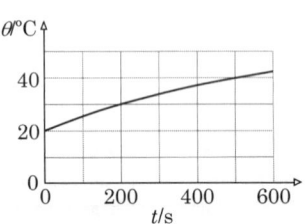

2. Hot water from a reservoir maintained at constant temperature is being added at a very slow and constant rate in a calorimeter initially containing 1.0 kg of water at a temperature of 20 °C. The water in the calorimeter is being stirred continuously to maintain its temperature uniform. The graph shows how the temperature θ of water in calorimeter changes with time t. Assuming heat loss to the surroundings and work done in the stirring process to be negligibly small, find the temperature of the hot water reservoir.

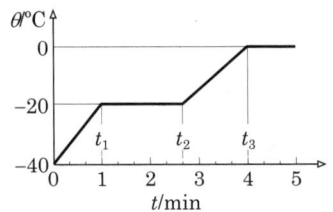

3. Equal masses of an unknown substance in granular form and crushed ice are mixed and kept in an insulated container at –40 °C. Specific heat of ice and the substance in solid state are $s_i = 2.1 \times 10^3$ J/(kg·°C) and $s_s = 900$ J/(kg·°C) respectively. The substance in liquid state is immiscible with water. Now heat is supplied at a constant rate to the contents in the calorimeter and temperature is recorded at regular intervals of time.

The data obtained are shown in the graph. Find specific latent heat L of melting and specific heat s_l in liquid state of the substance.

4. A special container having tilted bottom of uniform slope has one inlet A at top and one outlet B at the lowest place near the bottom. It contains a large amount of crushed ice at $\theta = 0.0\ °C$. From the inlet, water of temperature $\theta_i = 28\ °C$ is continuously fed to the container at a rate $r_i = 3.0$ g/s. Spaces between pieces of the ice permit water to run down and come out from the outlet. The outlet is made wider than the inlet to prevent accumulation of water in the container and the inner surface of the container is adiabatic. Specific heat of water is $s = 4.2$ J/(g·°C) and that of melting of ice is $L = 336$ J/g. Find rate of water coming out from the outlet, if its temperature is $\theta_0 = 1.0\ °C$.

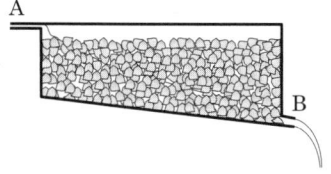

5. Under certain conditions, a mixture of crushed ice and super cooled water at temperature $\theta_1 = -21.0\ °C$ is kept in a calorimeter. The total mass of the mixture is $m = 0.60$ kg. Heat capacities of water and ice in the calorimeter are equal. Specific heat of ice is $s_i = 2.1$ kJ/(kg·°C), specific heat of water is $s_w = 4.2$ kJ/(kg·°C), specific latent heat of fusion of ice is $L = 0.33$ MJ/kg and melting point of ice is $\theta_0 = 0\ °C$. Now heat is supplied at a constant rate by a heater to the mixture. The graph shows temperature of the mixture for a portion of a time interval after the heater is switched on.

Assuming heat loss to the surroundings and heat capacity of the calorimeter to be negligible, find power p delivered by the heater to the mixture, time t_1 elapsed in the process of melting of ice and time t_2 elapsed after complete ice melts until temperature reaches $\theta_2 = 20\ °C$.

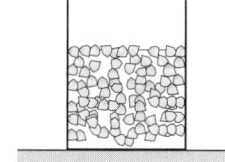

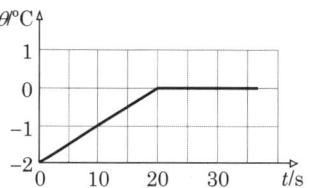

6. You have $m_w = 1.0$ kg of super cooled water at temperature $\theta_w = -10.0\ °C$ kept in a container and crushed ice at temperature $\theta_i = -20\ °C$ kept in another container. How much of this ice would you add to the water so that whole water freezes? Specific heat of water is $s_w = 4.2$ kJ/(kg·°C), specific heat of ice is $s_i = 2.1$ kJ/(kg·°C), specific latent heat of melting of ice is $L = 336$ kJ/kg and melting point of ice is $\theta_0 = 0\ °C$. Heat capacity of the vessel and heat loss to the surroundings are vanishingly small.

7. You have two identical small calorimeters and a very accurate thermometer. In one calorimeter there is 100 g of water at room temperature and in the other is 100 g of boiling water. If you put the thermometer in the first calorimeter, it shows 20.00 °C. When you remove the thermometer from the first calorimeter and put it in the other, it shows 99.20 °C. If you remove the thermometer from the second calorimeter and immediately put it again in the first one, how much would it read? Neglect loss of heat to the environment.

8. Two calorimeters A and B contain equal amounts of water at temperatures 48 °C and 80 °C respectively. Mass of water in each of the calorimeters is 300 g. From calorimeter A, 100 g water is transferred into B and stirred until thermal equilibrium is established, then 100 g water is transferred from B to A and stirred until thermal equilibrium is established. How many times this cycle has to be repeated until, the

difference between the temperatures of the calorimeters becomes less than 1.0 °C. Neglect water equivalent of the calorimeters, work done in transferring the liquid, work done in the stirring and heat loss to the surroundings.

9. A mixture of water and ice is kept in a well-insulated calorimeter of negligible heat capacity. A heater, which can supply heat at a constant rate of 50 W to the mixture, is switched on. At the ends of second, third and fourth minutes after the heater is switched on, temperature of the mixture becomes 0 °C, 2 °C and 7 °C respectively. How many grams of water and ice were initially present in the calorimeter?

Specific latent heat of melting of ice is 390 J/g and specific heat of water is 4.0 J/(g·°C).

10. A pressure cooker on a stove contains m_i = 2.6 kg of water at a temperature θ_i = 120 °C with its lid and pressure vent both closed. Now the cooker is removed from the stove and the lid is opened. How much mass of water will remain in the cooker after the water stops boiling?

Specific latent heat of vaporization is L = 2.1 MJ/kg, specific heat of water is s = 4.2 kJ/(kg·°C). Boiling point of water at atmospheric temperature is θ_b = 100 °C. Neglect the mass of water evaporated, the heat capacity of the cooker and the heat loss to the surroundings.

11. A container of base of area S = 200 cm² and negligible heat capacity contains a mixture of water and ice each of mass m = 1.0 kg and placed on a kerosene stove.

The calorific value of kerosene is q = 7.0×10⁴ kJ/kg. Specific heat of water is s_w = 4.2×10³ J/(kg·°C), specific latent heat of melting of ice is L_i = 3.5×10⁵ J/kg, specific latent heat of vaporization of water is L_v = 2.5×10⁶ J/kg, density of water is ρ = 1000 kg/m³. Boiling point of water is θ_b = 100 °C and melting point of ice is θ_m = 0 °C.

If η = 50% of the heat obtained from burning the kerosene is transferred to the mixture, find the height of water level in the container after burning m_k = 34 g of kerosene.

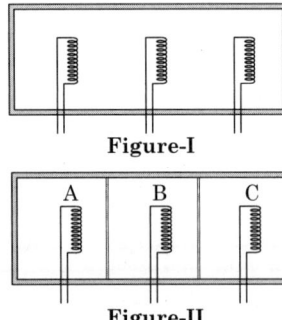

Figure-I

Figure-II

12. Three identical heaters are installed in a chamber that is made of heat insulating walls and is open at one side. The open side is covered with a heat-conducting membrane as shown in figure-I. The outside temperature is 10 °C. If all the heaters are switched on, the steady-state temperature inside the chamber becomes 25 °C. If two more membranes that are similar to the first one were placed between the heaters as shown in figure-II, what would be the steady-state temperatures of the parts A, B and C of the chamber?

13. A closed bowl containing a mixture of equal amounts of water and ice at temperature θ_0 = 0 °C, when left in a room, the whole ice melts in time Δt_0 = 160 min. Room temperature is θ_r = 25 °C, specific heat of water is s_w = 4.2 kJ/(kg·K) and specific latent heat of melting of ice is L = 320 kJ/kg. If the bowl were further left in the room undisturbed, how long would it take to increase the temperature of water in the bowl from θ_1 = 22 °C to θ_2 = 23 °C?

14. Boiling water filled up to the brim in a tub, cools to a desired temperature in a time interval $\Delta t_0 = 20$ min. How long would it take to cool boiling water filled up to the brim in another tub of similar shape having linear dimensions $\eta = 8$ times of those of the former to the same desired temperature? Consider the walls of the tub perfect insulator of heat.

15. Argon in an airtight metal cube of volume V exerts a pressure p_0 only at the bottom at a very low temperature. Find the force exerted on the top of the cube at temperature T when all the argon is in the gaseous state. Acceleration due to gravity is g, molar mass of argon is M and universal gas constant is R.

16. Thin horizontal straight metal pipe of length $l = 80$ m is lying at bottom of a lake that is $h = 100$ m deep. One end of the pipe is closed, and an air packet of length $x_0 = 9.0$ m is trapped in it between the closed end and a light piston. The pipe is now slowly rotated about its closed end. At what height above the closed end will the piston be when the tube becomes vertical? In your calculations, neglect the atmospheric pressure.

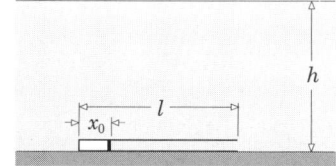

17. A tube of length l closed at lower end is held vertically. If an airtight piston is placed on its mouth, the piston slides down without friction and stops with its upper face at a depth $l/4$ from the mouth of the tube. If the temperature of air inside the tube is halved and the tube is inverted, the piston will settle with its lower face in level with the mouth of the tube as shown in the figure. Find thickness of the piston.

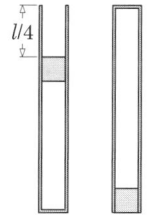

18. A glass tube of length h open at both the ends is held vertically so that half of its length is submerged in mercury kept in a large container. If the top end of the tube is closed and the tube is slowly pulled out, how much length of mercury column will be left in the tube? The atmospheric pressure is equal to the pressure of the column of mercury of height h_0. Assume constant temperature and neglect capillary effects.

19. A volume $V_w = 0.8$ L of water and some dry air at atmospheric pressure $p_0 = 1.03 \times 10^5$ Pa are present at temperature $T_1 = 309$ K in a closed vessel of volume $V = 1.0$ L. A thin layer of oil separates the water from the air and prevents evaporation of water. Density of water is $\rho_w = 1.0$ g/cm^3 and density of ice is $\rho_i = 0.9$ g/cm^3. If the temperature in the container is reduced and maintained at a value $T_2 = 240$ K, find air pressure after all the water freezes.

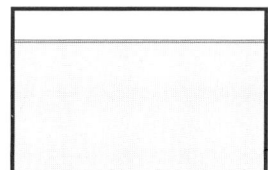

20. A thin tube equipped with a valve is connected at the bottom of a vertical cylinder. A heavy piston is suspended from the top of the cylinder with the help of a spring and the space above the piston is evacuated. If all the air below the piston is pumped out, the piston touches the bottom without exerting any force on the bottom as shown in figure-I. Now an ideal gas at temperature T is introduced under the piston through the tube until the piston slowly rises to a height h and then the valve is closed as shown in figure-II. What will be the height of the piston above the bottom of the container, if the temperature of the gas is increased to $2T$? Assume that the piston moves without friction and the spring obeys Hooke's law.

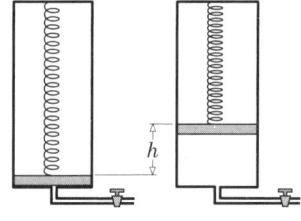

Figure-I   Figure-II

21. Two pistons A and B of masses m_1 and m_2 trapping n moles of an ideal gas between them can slide without friction in a long fixed horizontal pipe of cross-section area S. The pipe and the pistons are perfect conductors of heat; mass of the gas is negligible, outside pressure is p_0 and temperature is T_0. If constant forces F_1 and F_2 are applied on the pistons along the axis of the cylinder as shown in the figure, what will the distance between the pistons ultimately become?

22. An ideal gas is trapped in a stationary container with the help of a piston and there is a small hole in the container through which the gas leaks. If by heating the gas and simultaneously pushing the piston into container, the temperature and pressure of the gas is increased to 4 times and 8 times respectively of their initial values, how many times does the rate of leakage of the gas (i.e. number of molecules leaking per second) change?

23. A diatomic gas is filled in a closed container of constant volume. If temperature of the gas is increased by a significant amount, some of the molecules dissociate into atoms. Do not consider vibrational degrees of freedom while answering the following questions.
    (a) In what way will the specific heat of the mixture change?
    (b) If the specific heat changes by 8%, what fraction of the initial amount of the diatomic gas has been dissociated?

24. A diatomic gas is filled in an adiabatic container at temperature T_1. At this temperature molecules of the gas begin to disassociate. If each molecule absorbs energy ε in disassociation and disassociation process terminates at temperature T_2, find ratio of final pressure to initial pressure of the gas.

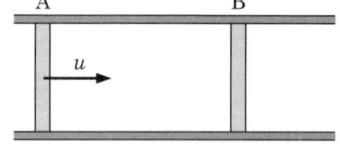

25. In a long fixed horizontal pipe two identical pistons A and B each of mass $m = 415$ g can slide without friction. The pipe and the pistons are made of perfect heat insulating materials. The space between the pistons is filled with $n = 0.1$ mole of gaseous helium. Piston A is given an initial velocity $u = 12$ m/s towards piston B. Find the maximum temperature change of the gas in ensuing motion of the pistons.

26. A monoatomic gas is filled in a heat insulated horizontal cylindrical container at pressure p and temperature T. Density of the gas is ρ. The container is abruptly made to move along its axis with a constant velocity v. Find temperature of the gas when a new steady-state will establish in the container.

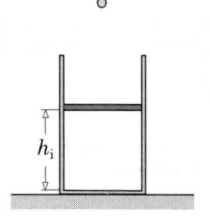

27. A cylindrical container contains hydrogen in gaseous state under a light piston. The container and the piston are both very good heat insulators. Initially the piston stays at a height h_i above the bottom of the container in equilibrium. A ball of mass m dropped from a height above the piston collides elastically with the piston. When all motion ceases and equilibrium is reestablished, the piston again stays at the height h_i. Find work done by the gas on the piston and the height above the piston from where the ball was dropped.

28. Some amount of nitrogen gas is filled inside a vertical cylindrical container under a massive piston that can slide in the cylinder without friction. The inner surfaces of the piston and the container are coated with a perfect heat insulating material. The whole assembly is inside a highly evacuated chamber. If the piston is struck to impart a velocity u downwards, after a large number of oscillations, the piston comes to a complete stop. Find displacement of the piston.

29. An ideal monoatomic gas is confined in a cylinder with the help of a piston that can slide inside the cylinder without friction. The cylinder is placed on a horizontal platform in a vacuum chamber. The walls of the cylinder and the piston are made of heat insulating materials. Initially the temperature of the gas is T_0 and the piston stays in equilibrium as shown in the figure. The temperature of the gas is quickly increased to η times and then the gas is allowed to expand. If the piston rises and again acquires an equilibrium state, find the temperature of the gas in this new equilibrium state.

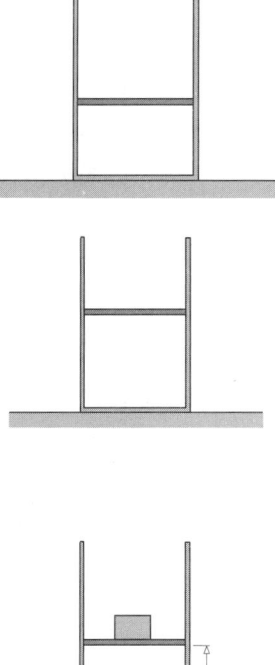

30. Some amount of an ideal gas is confined in a vertical cylinder with the help of a piston of mass m loaded with some extra weight of mass Δm. The walls of the cylinder and the piston are made of heat insulating materials. The piston can slide inside the cylinder without friction. Initially the height of the piston is h_0. The setup is placed in a vacuum chamber. If the extra weight on the piston is removed suddenly, at what height will the piston ultimately settle? Ratio of specific heats of the gas (C_P/C_V) is γ.

31. An ideal monoatomic gas is confined in two portions at the same temperature in an adiabatic cylinder with the help of two pistons of equal masses as shown in the figure. The whole assembly is inside a highly evacuated chamber. The pistons can slide inside the cylinder without friction and initial separation between them as well as between the lower piston and bottom of the cylinder is h. The upper piston is made of a heat insulating material and the lower piston is made of such a material that is an insulator of heat and becomes a permanent conductor of heat once its temperature becomes twice the initial temperature. The heat capacity of both the pistons and of the cylinder is negligibly small compared to that of the gas.

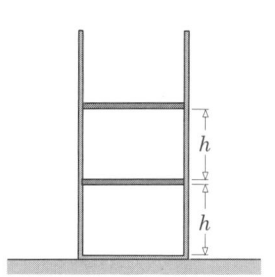

The gas in the lower portion is slowly heated until its temperature becomes double its initial temperature. What will be the separation between the pistons after a long time when thermal equilibrium is re-established between gases in both the portions?

32. In a vertical cylindrical vessel, water is kept at its freezing point T_0 separated by a thin oil film from n moles of a monoatomic gas at temperatures $T < T_0$ under a light piston of area A. The walls of the cylinder and the piston are made of insulating materials and there is no friction between the piston and the cylinder. Initially the piston is in equilibrium. Neglecting heat capacities of the vessel and of the piston, find displacement of the piston after a long time, when temperature of all the contents inside the cylinder settles to T_0. Specific latent heat of melting of ice is L, density of water is ρ_w, density of ice is ρ_i and the atmospheric pressure is p_0.

8.18 Chapter-8

33. A heat insulated cylindrical container is divided into two parts by a piston made from a material of very low thermal conductivity and negligible heat capacity. The cylinder is fixed horizontally, and an ideal monoatomic gas is filled in both the parts to occupy equal volumes V each at equal pressure p_0 but at different temperatures T_1 and $T_2 > T_1$. After a long time, when equilibrium is re-established, what will be the temperature in both the parts? How much heat will pass through the piston from one gas to another?

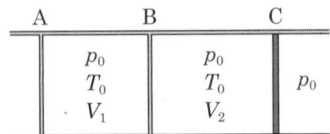

34. A horizontal cylindrical tube is divided into four parts with the help of two fixed partitions A and B and a movable piston C. The tube and the piston C are made from heat insulating materials whereas the fixed partitions A and B are made from a conducting material. Volume between the fixed partitions A and B is V_1 and initial volume between the fixed partition B and piston C is V_2. These volumes are filled with an ideal monoatomic gas at pressure p_0 and temperature T_0. Outside the piston C, pressure is also p_0.

Quantity ΔQ of heat is slowly transferred through the partition A to the gas trapped between the partitions A and B. Find temperatures of the gases on both sides of the partition B and heat transferred through it.

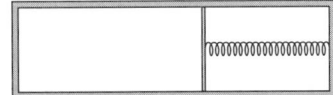

35. Two parts of a heat-insulated container are separated by a piston that can move without friction. The part to the left of the piston is filled with n moles of a monoatomic gas and in the part to the right of the piston is vacuum. The piston is connected to the right end of the container by a spring of relaxed length that is equal to the full length of the container. Find the heat capacity of the system, neglecting the heat capacities of the container, the piston and the spring. Universal gas constant is R.

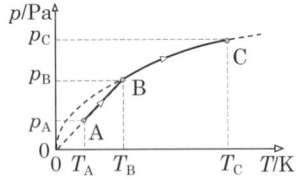

36. One mole of an ideal monoatomic gas undergoes two quasi-static processes A→B and B→C in sequence as shown in the following figure. If in the first process, the pressure p is proportional to the temperature T and in the second process, the pressure p is proportional to $\sqrt{T}$, find the total heat supplied to the gas in both the processes. Universal gas constant is R.

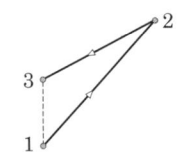

37. In an old record found in a laboratory, a process 1→2→3 was shown. Over the time, ink faded, and it became impossible to see the pressure and volume axes. However, descriptions given there reveal that the states 1 and 3 lie on an isochore corresponding to a volume V, amount of heat supplied during the whole process 1→2→3 is zero and the gas involved is one mole of helium. Find volume occupied by the gas in the state 2.

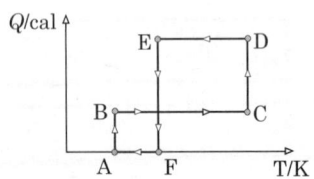

38. As shown in the given figure, an ideal monoatomic gas undergoes a quasi-static process A→B→C→D→E→F→A. Here it is shown how the amount of net heat Q given to the gas varies with temperature T of the gas. Identify the processes in which volume of the gas increases, decreases or remains unchanged, respectively.

39. One mole of an ideal monoatomic gas undergoes quasi-static process A→B→C→A that is shown in the figure, where C is molar heat capacity of the gas and θ is temperature of the gas. Find the amount of heat Q received by the gas from the heater heating the gas, work done W by the gas in the entire cycle and efficiency η of the cycle? Molar gas constant is $R = 8.31$ J/(mol·K).

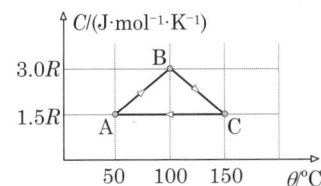

40. Pressure (p)-volume (V) indicator diagram of a cyclic process 1→2→3→1 consists of a straight-line 1→2, an adiabatic 2→3 and an isotherm 3→1. Pressure (p)-volume (V) indicator diagram of another cyclic processes 1→3→4→1 consists of an isotherm 1→3, an isobar 3→4 and an adiabatic 4→1. If efficiencies of these two processes are η_1 and η_2 respectively, determine the efficiency of the cycle 1→2→3→4→1.

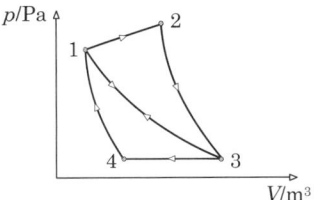

Check your understanding

1. A calorimeter contains a certain amount of a liquid of heat capacity C_1 and a saucer contains a certain amount of a salt of heat capacity C_2. Heat capacity of the solution of the salt and the liquid is C_3, where $C_1 + C_2 < C_3$. It is observed that if the salt is dissolved at temperature T_1, the temperature of the solution increases by ΔT_1. Knowing that the heat released while the salt is dissolving is independent of temperature, find the amount by which the temperature of the solution will change, if the salt is dissolved at temperature T_2.

2. A vessel contains $V_i = 20$ L water at temperature $\theta_i = 20$ °C. When a heater inside the container, which can supply heat at a constant rate, is switched on, the water temperature reached a value $\theta_1 = 60$ °C within a time interval $\Delta t_1 = 40$ min. Now water of temperature $\theta_i = 20$ °C is slowly added into the vessel at a constant rate $r = 200$ cm³/min. Heat capacity of the vessel and heat loss to the surroundings are negligibly small.
   (a) How long after the beginning of the experiment, will the water start boiling? Boiling point of water is $\theta_b = 100$ °C.
   (b) If instead of water, some other liquid having all properties same as those of water except the boiling point that is 150 °C, is used, how long after the beginning of the experiment, will the mixture start boiling? The liquid is miscible in water.

3. Water of equal mass m is filled in each of the two cylindrical containers and then cooled to freeze into ice at 0.0 °C. Area of base of one of the containers is A and that of the other is $2A$. Which vessel must be supplied with a greater amount of heat to melt the whole ice in it? Find the difference of the heats supplied to both the vessels. Heat capacities of the vessels and loss of heat to the surroundings are negligible. Acceleration due to gravity is g. Denote by suitable symbols all the physical characteristics of water or ice you need.

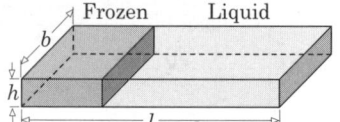

4. A recently designed heater makes use of latent heat obtained in freezing a liquid, which is done by adding a suitable catalyst. This freezing process is possible over a wide temperature range.

The heater shown in the figure is a box of dimensions $l \times b \times h$ made of an insulating material containing a liquid having the above-mentioned property as a working substance. The catalyst is added from the left end in such a controlled manner that the frozen portion grows towards the right at a slow and steady speed v. Find an expression for temperature θ of the heater as function of time t.

Specific latent heat of fusion of the liquid is L, specific heat of the working substance in liquid state is s, in the solid state it is $\eta = 10\%$ less and the initial temperature is $\theta_0 = 0$ °C. In liquid as well as in solid states, the working substance has the same density and very high thermal conductivity. Neglect the heat capacity of the box and heat loss to the environment.

5. A lead pellet is embedded in an ice ball. Mass of ice in the ball is $M = 0.9$ kg and its temperature is $\theta = -42$ °C. When the ice ball is gently released on the surface of water kept at temperature $\theta_0 = 0$ °C in a large container, it first sinks to the bottom and then after some time it comes out and floats partially submerged in water. Find the range of values of mass m of the lead pellet.

Densities of water, lead and ice are $\rho_w = 1.0$ g/cm³, $\rho_p = 11$ g/cm³ and $\rho_i = 0.9$ g/cm³ respectively. Specific heat of ice is $s = 2.4$ J/(g·°C) and specific latent heat of melting of ice is $L = 336$ J/g. Heat capacity of the lead pellet is negligibly small as compared to that of the ice ball.

6. In cold but not freezing weather at temperature $\theta_0 = 0$ °C, it is required to burn $m_d = 34.1$ kg of dry wood of density $\rho_d = 600$ kg/m³ to heat up a large room. Now you are supplied with wet wood of density $\rho_w = 800$ kg/m³, and asked to heat another identical room under identical conditions. How much wet wood will you have to burn to accomplish the task? Smoke produced in burning the wood is taken out of the room through a chimney.

Calorific value of dry wood is $q = 107$ kJ/kg, specific latent heat of vaporization of water is $L = 2.3$ MJ/kg, specific heat of water is $s = 4.2$ kJ/(kg·°C) and boiling point of water is $\theta_b = 100$ °C.

7. A kettle of negligible heat capacity containing $m_i = 1.0$ kg of cold water at $\theta_i = 0.0$ °C is put on a massive plate of an electric heater of constant power. The water starts boiling in a time interval $\Delta t_1 = 15$ min after the heater is switched on. If another 1.0 kg of cold water is added into the kettle, the whole water starts boiling again after a time interval $\Delta t_2 = 10$ min. Now the heater is switched off. If the entire heat stored in the heater plate is transferred to the water, calculate the mass of water evaporated after the heater is switched off.

Specific heat of water is $s = 4.2$ kJ/(kg·°C), specific latent heat of vaporization is $L = 2.1 \times 10^6$ J/kg, boiling point of water is $\theta_b = 100$ °C and heat loss to the environment is negligible.

8. An ice piece at temperature $\theta_i = 0$ °C is affixed at the bottom of an insulated cylindrical vessel. Water equal to that of the ice in mass is now gently poured into the vessel. The area of the base of the vessel is small enough so that water completely covers the ice piece and reaches a level $h = 19.0$ cm above the base. Initially the water level starts coming down and finally settles at level $\Delta h = 0.7$ cm below the initial level. Find temperature θ of the water before it was poured into the vessel.

Heat loss to the environment is negligible. Density of water is $\rho_w = 1.0 \times 10^3$ kg/m³, density of ice is $\rho_i = 0.90 \times 10^3$ kg/m³, specific heat of water is $s_w = 4.2$ kJ/(kg·K), specific heat of ice is $s_i = 2.1$ kJ/(kg·K) and specific latent heat of melting of ice is $L = 3.3 \times 10^5$ J/kg.

9. A block of mass 100 g and temperature 0 °C is immersed in a calorimeter containing 500 g water at temperature 45 °C. Specific heat s of the material of the block depends on temperature θ according to equation $s = s_0(1 + k\theta)$, where $s_0 = 4.2 \times 10^3$ J/(kg·°C), $k = 0.10$ °C⁻¹ and θ is temperature in degree Celsius. Find the final temperature of water in the calorimeter. Neglect heat capacity of the calorimeter and loss of heat to the surroundings. Specific heat of water is 4.2×10^3 J/(kg·°C).

10. Three cylindrical vessels identical in all respects except in their heights are filled completely with water. Volumes of the first, second and the third vessels are $V_1 = 1.0$ L, $V_2 = 2.0$ L and $V_3 = 3.0$ L respectively. A heater can heat water in the first and the second vessels to maximum temperatures of $\theta_1 = 80$ °C and $\theta_2 = 60$ °C in ambience of temperature $\theta_0 = 20$ °C. Up to what maximum temperature can the water in the third vessel be heated by this heater in the same ambience?

11. Thermal conductivity in wood depends on the direction of heat flow and usually it is higher along the fibres of the wood than in other directions. In a wood sample, thermal conductivity along the fibres is η times of that perpendicular to the fibres. Two identical cylinders are cut from this wood; the axis of the first cylinder is parallel to the fibres and that of the second makes an angle θ with the fibres. The curved surfaces of both the cylinders are well insulated from the surroundings. If equal temperature differences are applied across their circular ends, find ratio of heat flux in the first cylinder to that in the second cylinder.

12. One side of a thin metal plate is illuminated by the sun. When the air temperature is T_0, the temperature of the illuminated side is T_1 and that of the opposite side is T_2. What will the temperatures of each side be, if another plate of double thickness is used?

13. A square frame of side $l = 5.0$ m built in a laboratory is rigidly fixed on a frictionless horizontal floor as shown in the figure. Within the frame $N = 50$ identical particle-like balls each of mass $m = 5.0$ g are confined. The balls are moving randomly, all with a constant speed $v = 2.0$ m/s on the floor, colliding with each other and with the walls of the frame. Assuming all the collisions to be perfectly elastic, calculate the average force exerted by the balls on any of the vertical sides of the frame.

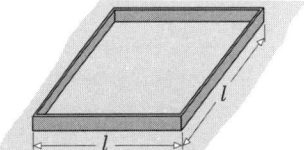

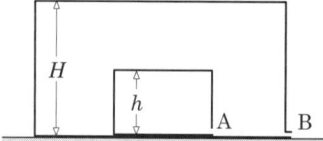

14. A water diver of mass $m = 80$ kg, when breathes in up to his maximum capacity that is $V_{max} = 4.0$ L of air, his body volume becomes $V = 82$ L. If he breathes in up to his maximum capacity and jumps into water, from what maximum depth (measured from the water surface to his chest) can he come to surface of the water without any swimming effort? Assume flesh and the bones in the body of the diver to be almost incompressible as compared to the air in his lungs. Density of water is $\rho = 1000$ kg/m³, atmospheric pressure is $p_0 = 1.0 \times 10^5$ Pa and acceleration due to gravity is $g = 10$ m/s².

15. A weightless box of height h is placed in a larger box of height H. Small holes A and B are made near the bottoms of the boxes as shown in the figure. If water is pumped into the large box through hole B, what will the air pressure be in it, when the smaller box touches the ceiling of the larger box? The process takes place at constant temperature, and the smaller box does not rotate during the process.

16. Temperatures of upper and lower surfaces of a plane horizontal sheet of area S are maintained at T_1 and T_2 respectively. The air pressure on both sides of the sheet is p_0, the ambient temperature is T_0 and acceleration of free fall is g. The air molecules strike a face of the sheet with a kinetic energy that corresponds to the ambient temperature and bounce off the face of the sheet with a kinetic energy that corresponds to the temperature of the face of the sheet. What should the mass of the sheet be so that it stays floating at a level height in the air?

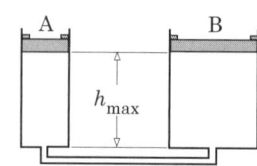

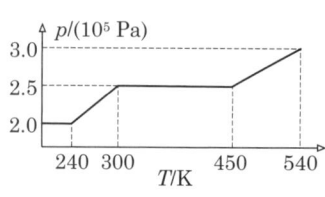

17. Two fixed vertical cylindrical vessels are connected at their bottoms by a thin tube. One mole of gaseous nitrogen is confined in the vessels under pistons A and B that can slide in the vessels without friction. Both the vessels have protrusions near their top on their inner surface to stop further upward motion of the pistons allowing a maximum height $h_{max} = 1.0$ m of columns of nitrogen gas in each of the vessels as shown in the figure. Outside the vessels is air at atmospheric pressure $p_0 = 10^5$ Pa. In an experimental study pressure of the gas is measured over a wide range of temperature and a pressure (p)-temperature (T) graph is prepared. A portion of the graph is shown in the adjacent figure. Calculate masses and areas of the pistons.

18. A bottle of capacity $V_1 = 1.0$ L made of a non-stretchable but flexible plastic contains a monoatomic ideal gas at pressure $p_1 = 2.0p_0$. Here $p_0 = 10^5$ Pa is atmospheric pressure. The bottle is connected to a rigid vessel of capacity $V_2 = 4.0$ L by a thin tube equipped with a valve. The vessel is made of good conducting material. Initially the valve is closed, and the vessel is almost evacuated to pressure $p_2 = 0.1p_0$. The temperature inside the bottle and the vessel is $T_1 = 240$ K that is also the ambient temperature. Now the valve is opened and after pressure in the bottle and the vessel equalizes, the temperature of the gas in the vessel is slowly increased to $T_2 = 600$ K. Construct a graph between the pressure and temperature of the gas inside the vessel during the heating process.

19. An ideal di-atomic gas of molar mass M is filled at temperature T_1 in a large container that is moving with a constant velocity v. The inner

surface of the container is coated with a perfect heat insulating material. At this temperature any sort of rotational motion of the molecules is not present i.e. rotational degrees of freedom of the molecules are frozen. The rotational degrees of freedom become unfrozen at a fixed temperature T_0 of the gas. The container is stopped suddenly. Find the temperature of the gas when a steady state is reached. Assume that no vibrational degrees of freedom are unfrozen.

20. A cylinder of volume $V = 10$ L made by adiabatic walls containing $m = 8$ g of helium gas is divided into two parts by a thin fixed rigid membrane. Volume of the right part is $\eta = 2$ times the volume of the left part. An electric heater of constant power installed in the left part is switched on. Due to finite thermal conductivity of the membrane, heat passes from the left part into the right part. Heat transfer rate through the membrane is $H = 0.2$ W per 1 °C temperature difference across the membrane. Initially the heater was switched off and both the parts were in thermal as well as mechanical equilibria. The membrane can withstand a maximum pressure difference of $\Delta p = 1000$ Pa.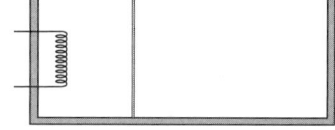

    Find the maximum power P_{max} of the heater so that the membrane remains intact after a long time of heating. Molar mass of the helium is $M = 4$ g. Consider slow heating process.

21. A heat-conducting piston connected with the help of a spring to one end of a horizontal closed insulated cylinder divides the cylinder into two parts. Each part of the cylinder contains equal number of moles of a monoatomic ideal gas. The length of the cylinder is $2l$ and relaxed length of the spring is $l/2$. Initially the temperature of the gas in both the parts is T, extension in springs is x and the piston is in equilibrium. Now a hole is made in the piston. If the heat capacities of the cylinder, the piston and the spring are negligible, find change in the temperature of the gas after establishment of new equilibrium state.

22. A vertical U tube is filled completely with a liquid of density ρ. The inner cross-section area of each of the vertical arms of the U tube is S, the total volume of both the arms is V_0 and volume of bottom arm is negligible. Both the ends of the tube are of the same height. One of them is open to the atmosphere, and the other one is hermetically connected to a flask of volume V_0 filled with an ideal monoatomic gas.

    Find the amount of heat which must be given to the gas to drive slowly half of the liquid out of the tube. The atmospheric pressure is constant and equal to p_0. Pressure of liquid vapors, effects of surface tension and heat loss to the environment are negligible. Acceleration due to gravity is g.

23. An ideal monoatomic gas is trapped in a fixed vertical cylinder under an airtight piston of mass m and area S. Initially, when the piston is held at height h_0 above the bottom of the cylinder, the pressure of the gas is p_0. Outside the cylinder is vacuum, and heat loss to the surroundings is negligible. When the piston is released, it rises and acquires its maximum speed after moving a distance h. Calculate this maximum speed of the piston. The acceleration of free fall is g.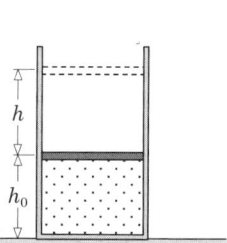

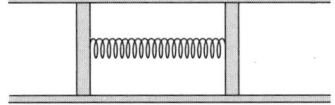

24. A heat-conducting piston that can slide inside an insulated vertical cylinder is held in the middle of the cylinder. In the parts of the cylinder, which are above and below the piston, equal amounts of an ideal monoatomic gas are maintained at temperature T and pressure p. After the piston is released, it moves first and finally stops, when difference of pressures of the gas in both parts of the cylinder becomes Δp. Find the change ΔT in the temperature of the gas. The heat capacity of the piston and the cylinder is negligible.

25. Two heat-insulating pistons connected by a spring can slide without friction inside a horizontal heat insulating tube, which is open at both of its ends. One mole of a monoatomic gas is filled between the pistons at temperature $T_1 = 300$ K. At this temperature of the gas, the spring is not relaxed. If an amount of heat is supplied to the gas, its temperature becomes $T_2 = 400$ K and the length of the spring becomes $\eta = 1.1$ times its initial length. How much heat is supplied to the gas?

26. In a vertical cylindrical container, n_d moles of dry ice (CO_2 in solid state) and n_c mole of CO_2 gas are in thermal equilibrium under a piston. Walls of the cylinder and the piston are insulators of heat. Above the piston is vacuum. When the system is supplied, an amount Q of heat that is greater than heat of sublimation of dry ice, the piston moves up a distance h and a new steady state is reached. Find temperature inside the container in the new steady state.

Sublimation temperature of dry ice is T_c and molar specific heat of sublimation is L.

27. Two cylinders A and B of equal volume V_0 contain the same ideal monoatomic gas at the same temperature T_0 but at different pressures $2p_0$ and p_0 respectively. They are connected by a thin tube installed with a valve that is initially closed. The valve is opened and as the gas leaks from cylinder A to cylinder B, the pressure in cylinder A is maintained $2p_0$ by pushing the piston into the cylinder. The process is continued until the pressure in cylinder B also becomes $2p_0$.

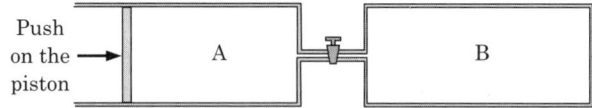

Find the final temperature in terms of T_0 and final volume of gas in cylinder A in terms of V_0. Both the cylinders are in good thermal contact. Neglect heat loss to the surroundings.

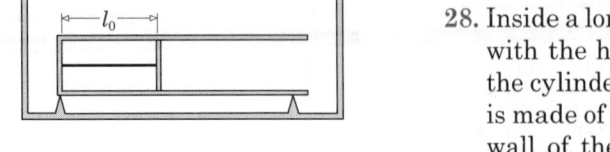

28. Inside a long cylinder, $n = 0.5$ mole of an ideal monoatomic gas is trapped with the help of an airtight heat-insulating piston. The curved wall of the cylinder is made of a heat conducting material and the circular base is made of a heat insulating material. The piston is connected to the left wall of the cylinder with an elastic rubber cord of negligible relaxed length and force constant $k = 25$ N/m. The cylinder is placed in an airtight evacuated oven and then the oven is switched on.

The piston is stopped at a distance $l_0 = 1.0$ m from the left end of the cylinder, the rate of temperature rise of the gas is measured and then the piston is released. If this rate of temperature increase is $r_0 = 0.08$ K/s, find speed of the piston after it is released.

29. One mole of an ideal monoatomic gas is made to undergo a sequence of quasi-static process A→B→C→D→A as shown in the first figure. During one cycle of the process, the gas receives an amount Q of heat and acquires a maximum temperature during the process that is 16 times the minimum temperature. Now consider a somewhat modified process 1→B→C→D→3→2→1 shown in the figure where states B, 2 and D belongs to the same isotherm.

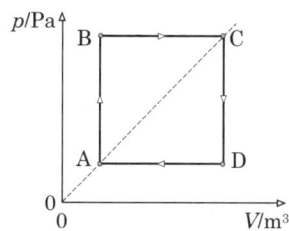
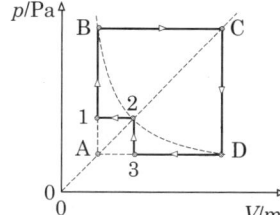

How much heat would the gas receive in one cycle of the modified process? Here the term "heat received by the gas" means the heat supplied to the gas and not the net heat transfer between the gas and the surroundings.

30. An ideal gas undergoes a cyclic process that is shown by a circle in a p-V indicator diagram of the process. What is the ratio of the highest temperature to the lowest temperature attained by the gas during the process?

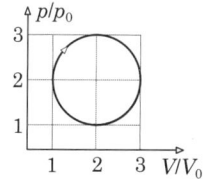

31. One mole of a monoatomic ideal gas is made to undergo a quasi-static cyclic process. During the process A→B, temperature T of the gas varies with its volume V according to the equation $T = bV^2$, where b is a constant. During the whole cycle, the maximum pressure of the gas is two times the minimum pressure. If the gas absorbs 120 J of heat during process A→B, how much heat does the gas liberate during process B→C→A?

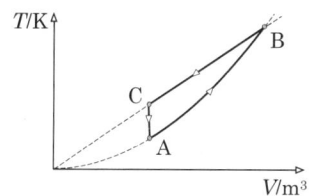

32. If the ratio of efficiencies of the two processes A and B shown in the p-V indicator diagram is k, find the efficiencies η_A and η_B of the processes. The working substance in these processes is one mole of an ideal monoatomic gas.

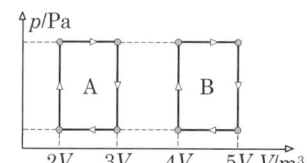

33. One mole of an ideal monoatomic gas undergoes a process A→B that is a straight line on a p-V indicator diagram of the process as shown in the figure. Find volume of the gas when the process turns from an endothermic to an exothermic one.

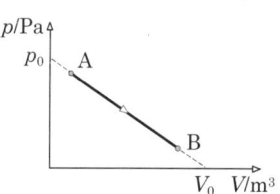

Challenge your understanding

1. Two identical cups are placed on a table. One is filled with hot milk at temperature T_1 and the other one is empty. It is desired to cool the milk to a desired temperature T_2. To quicken the cooling process, you can adopt either of the following methods.
   (a) First, pour the whole milk in the empty cup and wait till temperature falls to T_2.
   (b) First, wait for some time, then pour the whole milk in the empty cup and then wait till the temperature falls to T_2.
   (c) First wait and then pour the milk in the empty cup at such an instant that immediately after pouring the milk its temperature becomes T_2.

   If heat transfer from milk to cup occurs in negligible time, which one of the above strategies will you prefer?

2. A large number of identical elastic balls are moving randomly inside a fixed vertical cylindrical container under a piston that is at a height $h = 1.0$ m above the bottom of the container. The container is kept inside a gravity free chamber. Root-mean-square speed of the balls is of the order of 10^2 m/s and the mean collision time of the balls is of the order of 10^3 s. The piston is suddenly made to move upwards with a constant velocity $u = 1.0$ m/s and stopped at a height $2h$ above the bottom of the container. Find ratio of total internal energy of the balls in the new steady state to that of initial state.

3. The length of the barrel of a gun is $l = 5.0$ m and mass of a shell fired is $m_0 = 45$ kg. During firing, combustion of the gun powder takes place at a constant rate $r = 2.0 \times 10^3$ kg/s, the gun-powder is completely transformed into gas of average molar mass $M = 5.0 \times 10^{-2}$ kg/mol, temperature $T = 1000$ K of the gases remain fairly constant and displacement of the shell inside the barrel is proportional to t^α (t is time and α is a constant). Neglecting all forces other than force of the propellant gases during firing, find the muzzle velocity of the shell.

4. An ideal gas is trapped in a vertical cylinder under a piston. The inner surface of the cylinder is lubricated with oil. The cylinder is made of a material of finite thermal conductivity. Initially the piston stays in equilibrium at a height h above the base of the cylinder and the system is in thermal equilibrium with the surroundings. When a small weight is gently placed on the piston, the piston quickly settles to a new equilibrium position Δh_1 distance below its initial position. After a long time, the piston moves further down by a distance $\Delta h_2 = 0.4\Delta h_1$. If displacements Δh_1 and Δh_2 both are negligibly small as compared to the initial height h of the piston, find molar specific heat at constant volume of the gas and predict atomicity of the gas.

5. A horizontal cylinder with a fixed partition and a piston as its right-side wall is filled with helium gas. In the partition is a valve that opens when pressure in the right part exceeds pressure in the left part. The area of the piston is $A = 100$ cm². Initially the piston is $l_i = 112$ cm away from the partition and lengths of both the parts are equal. The amount of the gas in the left and right parts are $m_1 = 12$ g and $m_2 = 2$ g respectively. The temperature in both parts is $T_i = 0$ °C. Specific heats of helium at constant volume and constant pressure are $c_V = 3.15$ kJ/(kg·K) and $c_P = 5.25$ kJ/(kg·K). Atmospheric pressure is $p_0 = 10^5$ Pa. Walls of the cylinder, the partition and the piston all are made of good heat insulating materials.

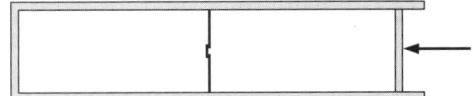

The piston is pushed into the cylinder, stopped for a while when the valve opens allowing thermal equilibrium to establish between both the parts, and then further pushed until it reaches the partition. Find work done by the force pushing the piston.

Answers and Hints

Multiple Choice Questions

1. (c)
2. (c)
3. (c)
4. (b)
5. (b)
6. (b)
7. (b)
8. (a)
9. (c)
10. (c)
11. (d)
12. (c)
13. (b)
14. (a)
15. (b) and (d)
16. (a)
17. (d)
18. (b)
19. (d)
20. (a), (c) and (d)
21. (d)
22. (c)
23. (c)
24. (b)
25. (c)
26. (c)
27. (b)
28. (c)
29. (d)
30. (b) and (d)
31. (b)

Build up your understanding

1. 66.49 kJ
2. 80 °C
3. $L = \left\{ (s_i + s_s) \dfrac{d\theta}{dt} \bigg|_{0 \le t \le t_1} \right\} (t_2 - t_1) = 1.0 \times 10^5 \; \dfrac{J}{kg}$

$s_1 = \dfrac{(s_i + s_s) \dfrac{d\theta}{dt} \bigg|_{0 \le t \le t_1}}{\dfrac{d\theta}{dt} \bigg|_{t_2 \le t \le t_3}} - s_i = 1.9 \times 10^3 \; \dfrac{J}{kg \cdot °C}$

Hint: Since the substance in liquid state is immiscible in water, they can be treated as separate entities with their original specific heats.

4. $r_i\left(\dfrac{L+s(\theta_i-\theta)}{L+s(\theta_0-\theta)}\right) = 4.0$ g/s

Hint: Since ice is a bad conductor of heat, the outer layer of an ice piece in contact with the flowing water will melt and temperature of inner portion will remain almost unchanged.

The flow of water is turbulent enough so that water being cooled is mixed well with hot water.

5. $p = \left(\dfrac{2ms_i s_w}{s_i+s_w}\right)\dfrac{d\theta}{dt}\bigg|_{0\le t\le 20} = 168$ W

$t_1 = \dfrac{L}{2s_i\dfrac{d\theta}{dt}\bigg|_{0\le t\le 20}} = 785.71$ s

$t_2 = \dfrac{(\theta_2-\theta_0)(s_i+s_w)}{2s_i\dfrac{d\theta}{dt}\bigg|_{0\le t\le 20}} = 300$ s

6. $\dfrac{m_w\{L-s_w(\theta_0-\theta_w)\}}{s_i(\theta_0-\theta_i)} = 7.0$ kg

7. 20.79 °C

Hint: Since water is in small quantity, the heat capacity of the thermometer cannot be neglected as compared to that of water and the calorimeter.

8. Five

9. 130 g and 20 g

Hint: The temperature-time graph, if prepared, is not a single straight line, therefore state change must occur at an instant in the given time intervals.

10. $m_i\left\{1-\dfrac{s(\theta_i-\theta_b)}{L}\right\} = 2.5$ kg

Hint: In a short time after opening the lid, temperature of water drops to its boiling point. Heat released in this process is utilized in evaporation of some amount of water.

11. $\dfrac{m\{2L_v+L_i+2s_w(\theta_b-\theta_m)\}-\eta q m_k}{\rho L_v S} = 10$ cm

Hint: Total mass of the contents remaining in the container after burning the given amount of kerosene equals the difference of total mass of the contents initially present and mass of evaporated water.

12. 40 °C, 35 °C and 25 °C

Hint: Since the walls of the chamber are insulating, heat transfer takes place through the membranes only. In addition, the membranes are identical; therefore, rates of heat transfer through them must be in direct ratio of the temperature differences across them.

13. $\dfrac{4s_w(\theta_r-\theta_0)(\theta_2-\theta_1)\Delta t_0}{L(2\theta_r-\theta_1-\theta_2)} = 42$ min

Hint: Due to small difference between the temperatures of the bowl and the room, Newton's law of cooling/heating can satisfactorily be used.

14. $\eta\Delta t_0 = 160$ min

Hint: Mass of water becomes η^3 times whereas surface area from where it dissipates heat becomes η^2 times.

15. $\dfrac{p_0 V^{1/3} RT}{gM}$

16. $\dfrac{h}{2}\left(1-\sqrt{1-\dfrac{4x_0}{h}}\right) = 10$ m

17. $\dfrac{(2-\sqrt{3})l}{4}$

18. $\dfrac{h_0+h-\sqrt{h_0^2+h^2}}{2}$

19. $\dfrac{p_0\rho_i(V-V_w)T_2}{(\rho_i V-\rho_w V_w)T_1} = 1.44\times 10^5$ Pa

20. $\sqrt{2h}$

Hint: Irrespective of state of the spring, whether extended or compressed, the force of the gas pressure equals the product of stiffness of the spring and displacement of the piston from the bottom of the cylinder.

21. $\dfrac{nRT_0(m_1+m_2)}{m_1F_2+m_2F_1+p_0S(m_1+m_2)}$

Hint: Ultimately, the separation will acquire a minimum value, and both the pistons will move with same velocity and acceleration.

22. 4 times

Hint: Under the given conditions, the rate of leakage of the gas at an instant is equal to half of the product of the molecular density in the container, the average speed of the gas molecules perpendicular to the hole inside the container and the area of the hole.

23. (a) increase   (b) 2/5

24. $\left(1+\dfrac{5k(T_1-T_2)}{2\varepsilon+kT_2}\right)\dfrac{T_2}{T_1}$

25. $\approx \dfrac{mu^2}{6nR}=12\text{ K}$

26. $T\left(1+\dfrac{\rho v^2}{3p}\right)$

27. $-mgh$ and $\dfrac{5h_i}{2}$

28. $\dfrac{u^2}{7g}\uparrow$

29. $\left(\dfrac{3\eta+2}{5}\right)T_0$

30. $h_0\left(1+\dfrac{\Delta m}{\gamma m}\right)$

31. $\dfrac{5h}{3}$

32. $\dfrac{nR(T_0-T)}{Ap_0}\left\{1+\dfrac{5p_0(\rho_w-\rho_i)}{2L\rho_w\rho_i}\right\}\approx \dfrac{nR(T_0-T)}{Ap_0}$

Hint: The process takes place at constant atmospheric pressure. Since the initial temperature of the gas is lower than that of water, which is at its freezing point, some amount of water will freeze supplying latent heat released to the gas.

You have to account for an increase in volume of the gas, and net increase in the volume of the remaining water and the ice made.

33. $\dfrac{2T_1T_2}{T_1+T_2}$ and $\dfrac{5}{2}p_0V\left(\dfrac{T_2-T_1}{T_1+T_2}\right)$

34. $T_0\left\{1+\dfrac{2\Delta Q}{p_0(3V_1+5V_2)}\right\}$ and $\dfrac{5V_2\Delta Q}{3V_1+5V_2}$

35. $2nR$

Hint: For the process to be quasi-static, the force of pressure of the gas must always be balanced by the spring force.

36. $\dfrac{R(4T_C-T_B-3T_A)}{2}$

37. $4V$

38. Volume increases in processes A→B, C→D, D→E and F→A.

Volume decreases in processes B→C, E→F.

In none of the processes, the volume remains unchanged.

39. $Q=\dfrac{9R}{4}(\theta_C-\theta_A)=1.9\text{ kJ}$;

$W=\dfrac{3R}{4}(\theta_C-\theta_A)=0.62\text{ kJ}$; $\eta=33\%$

40. $\eta_1+\eta_2-\eta_1\eta_2$

Check your understanding

1. $\Delta T_1+\left(\dfrac{C_1+C_2-C_2}{C_3}\right)(T_2-T_1)$

2. (a) $\Delta t_1\left\{1+\dfrac{V_i(\theta_b-\theta_1)}{V_i(\theta_1-\theta_i)-r\Delta t_1(\theta_b-\theta_i)}\right\}=240$ min

(b) Never

Hint: The maximum attainable temperature θ_{max} in the given conditions is

$$\theta_{max} = \theta_i + \frac{V_i(\theta_1 - \theta_i)}{rt_1} = 120\,°C$$

3. The narrower vessel

$$\frac{m^2 g}{4A}\left(\frac{1}{\rho_i} - \frac{1}{\rho_w}\right)$$

Here ρ_i and ρ_w are densities of ice and water.

Hint: Consider change in gravitational potential energy also.

4. $\theta = \theta_0 - \dfrac{L}{\eta s}\ln\left(1 - \dfrac{\eta v t}{l}\right)$

Hint: Latent heat of freezing released at every instant of time spreads in the liquid as well as in the frozen part of the liquid without any appreciable temperature gradient due to very high thermal conductivity.

5. $M\left\{\dfrac{\rho_p(\rho_w - \rho_i)}{\rho_i(\rho_p - \rho_w)}\right\} < m <$

$M\left(1 + \dfrac{s(\theta_o - \theta)}{L}\right)\left\{\dfrac{\rho_p(\rho_w - \rho_i)}{\rho_i(\rho_p - \rho_w)}\right\}$

$\Rightarrow 110\,g < m < 143\,g$

Hint: Initially when the ice ball containing lead pellet is released into the water, it sinks. Therefore, its weight must be more than the buoyant force.

The initial temperature of the ice ball is lower than that of water, therefore, when it is at the bottom, it absorbs heat from the surrounding water. This causes some amount of surrounding water to freeze and gather an extra layer of ice on the ice ball. In this way, the volume of the ice ball increases and so the buoyant force.

6. $\dfrac{q m_d \rho_w}{\rho_d q - (\rho_w - \rho_d)\{s(\theta_b - \theta_o) + L\}} = 50\,kg$

Hint: Wood absorbs water like a sponge i.e. water goes into pores present in the wood displacing air out of the pores. Thus, in the process of becoming wet, dry wood absorbs water without change in its apparent volume.

Density of a sample of wood equals the ratio of its mass to its apparent volume.

7. $\dfrac{m_i s(\theta_b - \theta_i)(\Delta t_1 - \Delta t_2)}{L\Delta t_2} = 100\,g$

Hint: After the heater is switched on; a part of heat generated is stored in the heater-plate and the remaining part is utilized to increase the temperature of the initial amount of water present in the kettle.

After the heater is switched off, the heat stored in the heater-plate is utilized to vaporize the water present in the kettle.

8. $\theta = \theta_i + \dfrac{\Delta h L}{h s_w}\left(\dfrac{\rho_w + \rho_i}{\rho_w - \rho_i}\right) = 55\,°C$

Hint: Since the ice is fully immersed in water, the height of the water level equals the ratio of total volume of the water and the ice to base area of the container.

If the whole ice were melted, the change in total height would have been greater than the given value of the change in total height.

9. 30 °C

10. $\theta_0 + \dfrac{(\theta_1 - \theta_0)(\theta_2 - \theta_0)(V_2 - V_1)}{(\theta_1 - \theta_0)(V_3 - V_1) + (\theta_2 - \theta_0)(V_2 - V_3)} = 50\,°C$

Hint: In steady state when temperature of a vessel with water achieves its maximum value, the rate of heat delivered by the heater becomes equal to the rate of heat dissipation to the surroundings, which is proportional to the excess temperature and the total surface area of the top and the bottom circular surfaces and the curved surface. The total area of the top and the bottom is identical for all the three vessels and the curved area is proportional to the height and hence to the volume.

11. $\dfrac{1}{\eta \cos^2 \theta + \sin^2 \theta}$

12. $T'_1 = \dfrac{2T_1^2 + T_1 T_2 - T_0(3T_1 - T_2) - T_2^2}{2(T_1 - T_0)}$ and

$T'_2 = \dfrac{T_1 T_2 + T_0(T_1 - 3T_2) + T_2^2}{2(T_1 - T_0)}$

Thermal Physics **8.31**

Hint: In steady state, every plate receives heat at constant rate from the sun; a part of it is radiated to the surrounding from the first face and the remaining part is conducted through the plate to the other face, where it is radiated to the surrounding.

Moreover, the temperatures of the faces of the plates are higher than that of surroundings by such a small amount that Newton's law of cooling can be used to get results within reasonable limits of accuracy.

13. $\dfrac{Nmv^2}{2l} = 0.1$ N

14. $\dfrac{p_0(\rho V - m)}{\rho g\{m - \rho(V - V_{max})\}} = 10$ m

Hint: The condition "without any swimming effort" means that the diver has to come to the surface of the water with the help of buoyancy only; therefore, he can go up to that depth where average density of his body equals the density of water.

Since the density of the flesh and bones remains almost unchanged, all the change in average density is due to reduction in volume occupied by the air in his lungs under the pressure of water.

15. The required condition is impossible to achieve.

Hint: Since the smaller box is weightless, air pressure inside it and inside the large box is always expected to be equal.

16. $\dfrac{Sp_0(T_2 - T_1)}{2gT_0}$

17. Masses and area of one of the pistons are 100 kg and 0.01 m² and that of the other piston are 75 kg and 0.005 m².

18.

$p_A = \dfrac{p_1 V_1 + p_2 V_2}{V_2} = 0.6 p_0$;

$T_B = \dfrac{p_0 V_2 T_1}{p_1 V_1 + p_2 V_2} = 400$ K ;

$T_C = \dfrac{p_0 (V_1 + V_2) T_1}{p_1 V_1 + p_2 V_2} = 500$ K

Process A→B: Isochoric

$p = \left(\dfrac{p_1 V_1 + p_2 V_2}{T_1 V_2}\right) T \Rightarrow p = 250 T$

Process B→C: Isobaric $\quad p = p_0$

Process C→D: Isochoric

$p = \left\{\dfrac{p_1 V_1 + p_2 V_2}{T_1 (V_1 + V_2)}\right\} T \Rightarrow p = 200 T$

Hint: As the bottle is made of a non-stretchable flexible material, its volume depends on the difference of the atmospheric pressure and the pressure inside the bottle. If the pressure inside the bottle is more than the atmospheric pressure, its volume must be V_1 and if the pressure inside the bottle is less than the atmospheric pressure, the bottle shrinks to have vanishingly small volume.

Immediately after the valve is opened, the forces of the atmospheric pressure acting on the walls of the bottle quickly push the gas from the bottle into the vessel. During this transfer, the gas acquires kinetic energy due a unidirectional movement into the tube. Now this kinetic energy of the gas in the vessel is converted into kinetic energy of random motion of molecules of gas in the vessel. This could have increased the temperature of the gas, but the walls of the vessel are conducting, therefore, the gas comes in thermal equilibrium with the surrounding. Now the gas is at its initial temperature and pressure lower than the atmospheric pressure. This state of the gas is designated by letter A.

Now due the heat supplied the gas undergoes an isochoric process (process A→B) until inside pressure becomes equal to the atmospheric pressure. This state is designated by letter B. After acquiring, the state B, the gas undergoes an isobaric expansion (process B→C) in which gas is again gradually transferred into the bottle until the bottle is fully expanded and total volume of the gas becomes equal to sum of the volume of the vessel and initial volume of the bottle. This state of the gas is designated by letter C. If we continue the heating, the gas now again undergoes another isochoric process (process C→D) at volume that is the sum of the volume of the vessel and initial volume of the bottle.

19. $= \begin{cases} T_1 + \dfrac{Mv^2}{3R}; & v \le \sqrt{\dfrac{3R(T_0-T_1)}{M}} \\ T_0; & \sqrt{\dfrac{3R(T_0-T_1)}{M}} < v \le \sqrt{\dfrac{R(5T_0-3T_1)}{M}} \\ \dfrac{3T_1}{5} + \dfrac{Mv^2}{5R}; & \sqrt{\dfrac{R(5T_0-3T_1)}{M}} < v \end{cases}$

20. $P_{max} = \left(\dfrac{\eta+1}{\eta}\right)\dfrac{MV\Delta pH}{mR} = 0.18$ W

Hint: Since the walls of the cylinder are adiabatic, the membrane is conducting and has negligible heat capacity, the total heat supplied by the heater must be distributed between the gases in both the parts of the cylinder. Furthermore, the volume of the gases in each of the parts remains constant during heating, and all the heat they receive must be utilized to increase their internal energies. Therefore, the total heat supplied by the heater is divided between the gases in both the parts in proportion of their amounts.

21. $\dfrac{2xT}{3}\left\{\dfrac{l-2x}{(l+2x)(3l-2x)}\right\}$

Hint: Initially the spring force was balanced by the unbalanced forces of the pressures of the gases on both sides of the piston. This fact provides information about the force constant of the spring and energy stored in the spring.

Since the system consisting of both the parts is a closed system of constant volume, during the process taking place after the hole is made, the total energy stored in the spring is utilized in increasing the internal energy of the gas.

22. $\dfrac{5p_0V_0}{4}\left(1+\dfrac{\rho g V_0}{Sp_0}\right)$

Hint: The gas in flask expands against pressure of level difference of mercury columns augmented by the atmospheric pressure.

Heat supplied to the gas equals the sum of the increase in the internal energy of the gas and work done in expansion of the gas that is equal to work done against gravity by the gas in pushing the liquid out.

23. $\sqrt{\dfrac{3p_0Sh_0}{m} - g(5h+3h_0)}$

24. $\Delta T = \dfrac{T}{5}\left(\sqrt{1+\dfrac{5}{3}\left(\dfrac{\Delta p}{p}\right)^2}-1\right)$

Hint: Since the system consisting of both parts is a closed system of constant volume, during the process taking place after the piston is released, the work done by gravity on the piston is utilized in increasing the internal energy of the gas.

In the final state, the weight of the piston is balanced by the unbalanced forces of pressure difference of the gases in the upper and the lower parts.

The number of moles in both the parts remain unchanged during the process.

25. $\dfrac{R}{2}\left[3(T_2-T_1)+\dfrac{(\eta-1)}{2\eta}(\eta T_1+T_2)\right]=1520$ J

26. $\dfrac{2Q-2n_dL+(5n_d+7n_c)RT_c}{7(n_d+n_c)R}$

Hint: Initially the dry ice and the gaseous CO_2 are in thermal equilibrium at the sublimation temperature.

Sublimation is state change from solid to gaseous state without entering into liquid state. During sublimation, temperature remains unchanged, and heat absorbed is known as heat of sublimation.

27. $\dfrac{17}{15}T_0$ and $\dfrac{7}{10}V_0$

28. $\dfrac{3nr_0R}{8kl_0} = 5$ mm/s

29. $\dfrac{24}{23}Q$

30. $\left(\dfrac{2\sqrt{2}+1}{2\sqrt{2}-1}\right)^2 = 4.39$

31. 130 J

32. $\eta_A = \dfrac{k-1}{3}$ and $\eta_B = \dfrac{k-1}{3k}$

33. $\dfrac{5}{8}V_0$

   Hint: When a process changes from endothermic to exothermic nature or vice versa, it must pass through a stage of extremum of its heat contents.

Challenge your understanding

1. All three will take the same time.
   Hint: Since heat transfer from the milk to the cup is almost instantaneous; therefore, whenever you pour milk into another cup, fall in temperature of the milk must be proportional to the temperature difference between the milk and the surroundings.

2. $\dfrac{3}{4}$

3. $\dfrac{3}{2}\left(\dfrac{4rRTl}{3m_0 M}\right)^{1/3} \approx 550$ m/s

4. $\dfrac{\Delta h_1}{\Delta h_2}R = \dfrac{5}{2}R$; The gas is diatomic.
   Hint: During both the spells of the entire process, the displacements Δh_1 and Δh_2 of the piston are so small that the pressure of the gas can be assumed almost constant and work done by gravity goes partially into the gas and partially into loss in viscous drag. The very small duration of the first spell enables us to ignore energy loss due to viscous drag and at the same time, the finite thermal conductivity of the cylinder does not allow heat to flow out of the gas. In the large time span of the second spell, heat flows out of the cylinder to bring the system into thermal equilibrium with the surroundings.

5. $c_V(m_1 + m_2)T_i\left[\dfrac{m_1}{m_1+m_2}\left\{1+\left(\dfrac{m_2}{m_1}\right)^{1/\gamma}\right\}^{\gamma} - 1\right] - p_0 A l_i$
   = 3674 J
   Hint: As no heat exchange with the surroundings is permitted, the work done by the net external force i.e., the pushing force and the force of atmospheric pressure equals the increase in internal energy of the gas.

Chapter 9

Properties of Matter

Thermal expansion of solids and liquids; elasticity: Hooke's law, modulus of elasticity, elastic potential energy; surface energy and surface tension, capillary phenomenon, excess pressure; viscosity (Poiseuille's equation excluded), Stoke's law, terminal velocity.

"It is evident that an acquaintance with natural laws means no less than an acquaintance with the mind of God therein expressed."

BACK TO BASICS

Thermal Expansion

Most material bodies expand on heating.

Coefficients of thermal expansion

Coefficient of linear expansion: $\alpha = \dfrac{dl}{l \, d\theta}$

Coefficient of area expansion: $\beta = \dfrac{dS}{S \, d\theta}$

Coefficient of volume expansion: $\gamma = \dfrac{dV}{V \, d\theta}$

James Prescott Joule
(24 December 1818 – 11 October 1889)

Isotropic and anisotropic thermal expansion:

Thermal expansion is isotropic, if coefficients of thermal expansions in all directions within a solid body are equal; otherwise, it is anisotropic.

Suppose coefficients of linear expansion in three mutually perpendicular directions x, y and z within a body are α_x, α_y and α_z.

Coefficient of area expansion in the x-y plane: $\beta_{xy} = \alpha_x + \alpha_y$

Coefficient of volume expansion: $\gamma = \alpha_x + \alpha_y + \alpha_z$

Elasticity

The property of a body, by virtue of which it tends to regain its original size and shape when deforming forces are removed, is known as elasticity and the deformation caused is known as elastic deformation.

Stress: The restoring force per unit area.

Strain: Fractional change in dimensions.

Longitudinal Strain: $\dfrac{dl}{l}$

Shearing strain: Angle through which a hypothetical plane perpendicular to deforming force turns.

Modulus of elasticity:

It is defined as the ratio of stress to strain.

Young's Modulus: $Y = \dfrac{\text{Stress}}{\text{Longitudinal strain}}$

Bulk Modulus: $B = \dfrac{\text{Stress}}{\text{Volumetric strain}}$

Shear Modulus: $\eta = \dfrac{\text{Shear Stress}}{\text{Shearing strain}}$

Elastic potential energy density: $u = \tfrac{1}{2}(\text{stress})(\text{strain})$

Surface Tension

Free surface of liquids has a tendency to shrink. This phenomenon is known as surface tension.

Surface tension σ is the work ∂W required to increase the free surface area by ∂S.

$$\sigma = \dfrac{\partial W}{\partial S}$$

Surface tension gives rise to tangential forces in the surface. On an infinitesimal length dl, force dF due to surface tension is

$$dF = \sigma dl$$

Surface tension gives rise to pressure a difference Δp across the surface of a liquid.

$$\Delta p = \sigma\left(\dfrac{1}{r_1} + \dfrac{1}{r_2}\right)$$

Here r_1 and r_2 are radii of two principal curvatures on the surface.

Viscosity

Phenomenon of viscosity is the resistance to flow due to friction between portions of a liquid having different velocities.

Newton's law of viscosity:

The force F of viscous drag between two layers of a fluid in laminar flow is given by the following equation.

$$F = -\eta A \frac{dv}{dr}$$

Here η is coefficient of viscosity, A is the area in contact between the layers and dv/dr is the velocity gradient across the layers.

Multiple Choice Questions

1. Volumes V_1 and V_2 of a liquid are maintained in two calorimeters at temperatures θ_1 and θ_2 ($\theta_2 > \theta_1$). Coefficient of volume expansion of the liquid is independent of temperature. Now liquids from both the calorimeters are poured into another calorimeter of negligible heat capacity. Heat loss to the surroundings is strictly restricted. Final volume V of the mixture after they are well mixed is best represented by the equation

   (a) $V = V_1 + V_2$
   (b) $V > V_1 + V_2$
   (c) $V < V_1 + V_2$
   (d) Insufficient information

2. Radii of a slightly tapered cylindrical wire of length L at its ends are a and b. It is stretched by two forces each of magnitude F applied at its ends. The forces are uniformly distributed over the end faces. If Young's modulus of material of the wire is denoted by Y, extension produced is

   (a) $\dfrac{4FL}{\pi(a+b)^2 Y}$
   (b) $\dfrac{FL}{\pi(a^2+b^2)Y}$
   (c) $\dfrac{FL}{\pi(a^2-b^2)Y}$
   (d) $\dfrac{FL}{\pi ab Y}$

3. A long capillary tube of radius r is put in contact with the surface of a perfectly wetting liquid of density ρ and very low viscosity. What maximum height h the liquid can rise inside the capillary? Here height is measured above the level of the liquid outside the capillary. Surface tension of the liquid and acceleration due to gravity are denoted by σ and g respectively.

   (a) $h = \dfrac{2\sigma}{\rho g r}$
   (b) $h = \dfrac{4\sigma}{\rho g r}$
   (c) $\dfrac{2\sigma}{\rho g r} < h < \dfrac{4\sigma}{\rho g r}$
   (d) Insufficient information

4. Consider two hollow glass spheres: one of them containing water in approximately 10% of its volume, and the other containing a similar volume of mercury. If the spheres are brought into a zero-gravity environment of a space-shuttle, what will you observe?

   (a) Water and mercury both float in their spheres as spherical drops.
   (b) Water forms a layer on the inner surface of the sphere while mercury floats as a spherical drop.
   (c) Mercury forms a layer on the inner surface of the sphere while water floats like a spherical drop.
   (d) In each case, some amounts of the liquids form layers on inner surfaces of the spheres and remaining amounts float as spherical drops.

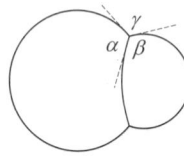

5. When two soap bubbles of different radii coalesce, some portions of their surfaces make a common surface. At any point on the circumference of the common surface, the three surfaces meet at angles α, β and γ. What relation should these angles bear?

   (a) $\alpha > \beta$
   (b) $\alpha > \beta > \gamma$
   (c) $\alpha = \beta < \gamma$
   (d) $\alpha = \beta = \gamma$

6. Air is confined in a thin-walled glass tube with the help of soap films at the ends of the tube. These films on both ends have equal radii of curvatures. By some arrangements not shown here, these soap films are given different shapes. In the first and second columns of the following table, different shapes of the soap films and possible nature of equilibrium of the system are shown respectively. Suggest suitable matches.

   You may need the expression $V = \frac{1}{3}\pi h^2 (3R - h)$. Here V is volume of a spherical cap of height h cut from a sphere of radius R.

	Shape of the soap films	Nature of equilibria
(a)		(p) Stable
(b)		(q) Unstable
(c)	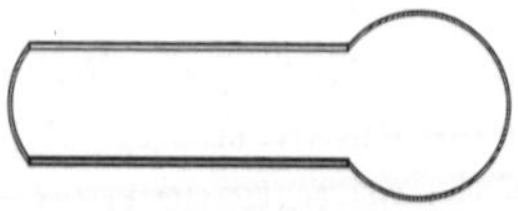	(s) Neutral
(d)	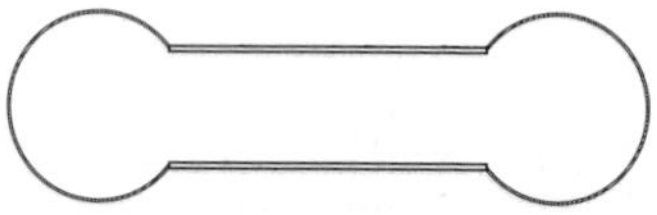	(r) Not in equilibrium

Build up your understanding

1. With the help of some arrangement, different portions of a uniform metal rod of length 1.0 m placed on a frictionless horizontal tabletop are maintained at different temperatures as shown in the given graph. Here $\Delta\theta$ is deviation in temperature of a point from room temperature and x is the distance of the point from the left end of the rod. After a steady state is established, total extension of the rod is found to be Δl.
   (a) Find points on the rod that do not shift.
   (b) Find displacements of both the ends of the rod.

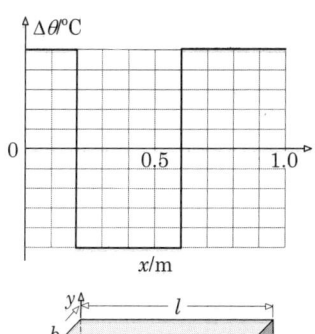

2. A steel plate and an aluminium plate each of length l and width b are welded on each other to make a composite plate. The thickness of the steel plate is t_s and that of the aluminium plate is t_a. Young's moduli of steel and aluminium are Y_s and Y_a respectively. Find force constants of the composite plate along the x, y and z-axes.

3. Consider a real fluid; compressibility of which is β and density at atmospheric pressure p_0 is ρ_0.
   (a) Express density ρ of a real fluid as a function of depth h.
   (b) Express pressure p as a function of depth h in a real fluid that is open to the atmosphere.

4. A capillary made of a glass sheet has length $l = 6$ cm, mass $m = 12$ g, inner sectional area $A_i = 0.2$ mm² and outer perimeter $s_o = 16$ mm. Half-length of this capillary is vertically dipped in water. Surface tension of water is $\sigma = 0.07$ N/m, density of water is $\rho_w = 1.00$ g/cm³, density of glass of the capillary is twice of that of water, and acceleration of free fall is $g = 10.00$ m/s². How much additional force is required to keep the capillary in equilibrium? Assume water a perfect wetting liquid for glass.

5. When a glass capillary of length $l = 1.01$ m is held vertically, touching water surface of a large reservoir at its lower end, water rises in the capillary to a height $h_0 = 1.10$ cm. If the top end of the tube were closed before touching the water surface, what would have been the height of the water column in the capillary? Density of water is $\rho = 1000$ kg/m³, atmospheric pressure is $p_0 = 1.01 \times 10^5$ Pa and acceleration due to gravity is $g = 10$ m/s². Consider water a perfect wetting liquid for glass.

6. A U tube, vertical arms of which have length l and radii r_1 and r_2 ($r_2 > r_1$), is dipped in water with its open ends down to such an extent that the water level in the narrow arm coincides with that of outside the tube. Surface tension and density of water are σ and ρ respectively and atmospheric pressure is p_0. Consider the volume of the horizontal part connecting the vertical arms to be negligible, find water level in the wider arm relative to the water level outside. Assume water is a perfect wetting liquid for glass.

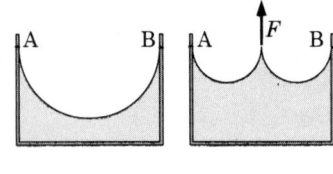

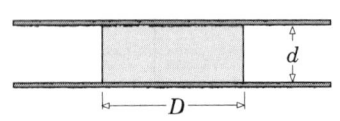

7. A film of a soap solution created in a loop formed by a rectangular wire frame and an inextensible light thread AB of length l, pulls the thread in the shape of a semicircle. If a force F applied at midpoint of the thread perpendicular to line segment AB turns the wire into two semicircles as shown in the figure, calculate surface tension of the soap solution.

8. An amount of water is poured on the top horizontal circular face of a glass cylinder. Excess amount of water spills over the edges and a little amount of water remains there in a thin uniform layer, a portion of which is shown in the figure. If contact angle is θ and surface tension of water is σ, determine thickness of the water layer left.

9. In a zero-gravity region, a drop of a liquid of surface tension σ assumes a cylindrical shape of diameter D between two parallel glass plates that are a distance d apart. If the curved surface of the drop is at right angles to the plates as shown in the figure, find force exerted by the drop on a plate.

10. A bubble of radius r is made of a soap solution at one end of a long capillary tube, the other end of which is closed. If the closed end is opened, the bubble collapses in a time interval Δt_0. Making the following assumptions, estimate time interval taken by another bubble of radius ηr made from the same soap solution at the end of the same tube to collapse.
    - Air is non-viscous and its flow in the capillary is laminar.
    - The process is slow enough to regard it as a quasi-static one and disregard effects of viscosity and time required for liquid in the wall of the bubble to readjust its shape.

11. Two soap bubbles of diameters a and b coalesce to form a larger bubble of diameter c. If surface tension of the soap solution used is σ, find a suitable expression for the atmospheric pressure.

12. An amount of heat is slowly supplied to a bubble of radius r made of a soap solution of surface tension σ. If pressure p_0 outside the bubble remains constant, find an expression for the molar specific heat of the heating process. Molar specific heat of the gas inside the bubble at constant pressure is C_P and universal gas constant is R.

13. A mercury drop on a clean horizontal glass surface and a water drop on a horizontal glass plate coated with a thin layer of talcum powder are similar in shape. If it is known that for a particular shape of a drop, surface energy of surface tension and the gravitational potential energy bear a definite ratio that is independent of the size of the drop, estimate the ratio masses of these drops.

    Density of mercury is $\rho_H = 13.60$ g/cm³, density of water is $\rho_W = 1.00$ g/cm³, surface tension of mercury is $\sigma_H = 0.46$ N/m and surface tension of water is $\sigma_W = 0.07$ N/m.

14. A soap film of thickness $h = 1.0$ μm is formed in a circular wire loop of radius $r = 5.0$ cm. If the soap film is punctured in the center, the hole thus made, spreads symmetrically. How long will the soap film take to

disappear? Assume that the thickness of the soap film remains almost unchanged during the process. Surface tension and density of the soap solution are $\sigma = 0.025$ N/m and $\rho = 1000$ kg/m³ respectively.

15. A balloon filled with helium at the atmospheric pressure p_0 occupying volume V, when released, it rises and bursts at an altitude where atmospheric pressure is $0.5p_0$. Immediately before bursting, the balloon has a volume of $1.25V$. If rubber used in making the balloon has mass m and density ρ, find breaking stress of the rubber. Assume the balloon is always spherical in shape, the density of the rubber is constant and the temperature outside is uniform and constant.

16. An almost inertia-less metal sheet is placed on a horizontal tabletop lubricated with oil. The sheet is a square of side length $l = 1.0$ m and the oil layer has thickness $h = 1.0$ mm. Initially one edge of the sheet coincides with one edge of the table. The sheet is pulled outwards without rotation with a constant force $F = 15$ N. If coefficient of viscosity of the oil is $\eta = 0.2$ N·s/m², how long will it take to pull half of the sheet out of the table?

17. A cylindrical capsule can move inside a long vertical cylindrical tube filled with a viscous Newtonian liquid. The diameter of the capsule is slightly smaller than the inner diameter of the tube and the walls of the capsule have negligible thickness. Drag force on the capsule is proportional to speed of the capsule. If the capsule is empty, it rises with a uniform velocity v_1 and if the capsule is filled completely with the liquid, it moves down with a uniform velocity v_2.

    (a) Find expression of velocity of the capsule if η fraction of its volume is filled with the liquid.
    (b) How will the above relation change if the η fraction of volume of the capsule is filled with another liquid, density of which is k times of that of the liquid in the tube?

Check your understanding

1. A uniform metal rod of length l stays along the line of greatest slope on a roof inclined at an angle θ with the horizontal. Coefficient of friction between the sheet and the roof is μ ($\mu > \tan\theta$) and temperature coefficient of linear expansion of the material of the rod is α. On a particular day, the temperature of the environment increases by an amount ΔT and then decreases by the same amount during a span of 24 h.

    (a) How much and in which direction will the upper edge, the mass center and the lower edge of the rod shift during the period of temperature rise?
    (b) How much and in which direction will the upper edge, the mass center and the lower edge of the rod shift during the period of temperature fall?
    (c) What is the net shift in location of the rod during the complete cycle of temperature rise and fall?

2. Two pieces of equal length of a steel wire cut from a role are used to make two helical springs of identical pitch. Diameter of the coils in the second spring is double of that in the first spring. Find ratio of percentage elongation of the second spring to that of the first spring, if they are stretched by equal forces. Shear strain in both springs remain within the elastic limits.

3. A uniform wire of length $l = 800$ m and cross-sectional area $S = 1.0$ mm² is made of a material of density $\rho = 8.0 \times 10^3$ kg/m³ and Young's modulus $Y = 2.0 \times 10^{11}$ N/m². The wire is placed straight on a frictionless horizontal floor, and an end is pulled by a constant horizontal force $F = 1.0$ N uniformly distributed over the face of the end. Find displacement of this end in a time interval $\Delta t = 0.1$ s after the force is applied.

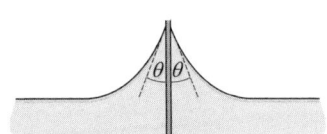

4. When a glass plate is inserted vertically in water, water rises along the plate making its surface close to the plate curved as shown in the figure. Find an expression for the height to which water rises along the plate. Surface tension of water is σ, density of water is ρ and acceleration due to gravity is g.

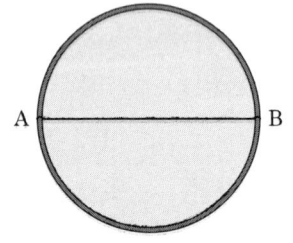

5. A film of soap-solution of surface tension σ is made in a circular wire frame of radius r, two diametrically opposite points A and B of which are connected by a thin and light elastic cord in relaxed state as shown in the figure. Young's modulus of the material of the cord is Y and the area of cross-section is S. If the film on one side of the cord is punctured, find elongation in the elastic thread.

If necessary, you may use the relation $\sin^{-1}\theta \approx \theta + \frac{1}{6}\theta^3$ with an appropriate degree of accuracy.

6. A soap bubble of radius r and wall thickness h is made in vacuum by blowing a diatomic gas in it. Surface tension of the soap solution is σ and density is ρ.

(a) Find molar specific heat of the gas in the bubble in terms of molar gas constant R.

(b) Find expression for angular frequency of radial oscillations of small amplitudes. Consider that the heat capacity of the soap film is much greater than that of the gas in the bubble and that thermodynamic equilibrium establishes in the bubble in a time that is negligible as compared to period of the oscillations.

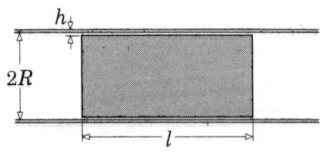

7. A cylinder of length l can move inside a cylindrical pipe of inner radius R. If the cylinder is coaxial to the pipe, clearance between the curved surface of the cylinder and the inner surface of the pipe is h ($h \ll R$). Density of the material of the cylinder is ρ, density of the water is ρ_0 and dynamic viscosity of water is η.

Assume flow of a liquid in this pipe to be laminar and force of viscous friction f on per unit area of the inner surface of the pipe as well as of the curved surface of the cylinder to be expressed by the following expression.

$$f = \eta \frac{v_{av}}{h}$$

Here v_{av} is the average velocity of the fluid flow in the clearance space.

(a) The cylinder is held at rest inside the pipe with the help of a thread and a liquid is made to flow towards the right at a constant rate. If pressures on the flat faces of the cylinder differ by an amount Δp, determine tensile force in the thread and volume flow rate of the liquid in the pipe.

(b) The pipe closed at one end and filled with the liquid is placed on a table. The cylinder is held at the top coaxially with the pipe and fully immersed in the liquid. If the cylinder is denser than the liquid, it will start moving downwards after it is released and in a short time acquires a steady downwards velocity. Deduce suitable expressions for this steady speed of the cylinder.

(c) If cylinder is less dense than the liquid and released from the bottom of the pipe, it will move upwards and acquire a steady upwards velocity in a short time. Deduce suitable expression for this steady speed of the cylinder.

Challenge your understanding

1. With the help of some arrangements, different portions of a uniform metal rod of length 1.0 m placed on a horizontal tabletop are maintained at different temperatures as shown in the given graph. Here $\Delta\theta$ is deviation in temperature of a point from room temperature and x is the distance of the point from the left end of the rod. The tabletop is not frictionless. After a steady state is established, total extension of the rod is found to be Δl. Find displacements of both the ends of the rod.

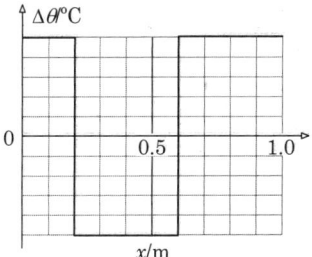

2. When a soap bubble is left in a room, air molecules diffuse out from the bubble. If at an instant, the concentrations of air molecules inside the bubble and in room are n_i and n_o respectively and thickness of the walls of the bubble is h, the rate q of diffusion i.e. number of air molecules coming out of the bubble per second from a unit surface area is given by the following equation.

$$q = D\left(\frac{n_i - n_o}{h}\right)$$

Here D is a positive constant. If the initial radius of the bubble is r_0 and the initial thickness of the walls of the bubble is h_0, find an expression for rate of change in radius r of the bubble. Atmospheric pressure in the room is p_0 and the surface tension of the soap solution is σ. Neglect the evaporation of soap-solution and treat air as an ideal gas.

3. If an elastic film can be modelled as a square grid formed by very small springs each of stiffness k, show that the potential energy U of the film if stretched uniformly and isotropically can be given by $U = k\left(\sqrt{S} - \sqrt{S_0}\right)^2$. Here S_0 is area of unstretched film and S is the area of the stretched film. Now such an elastic film is used to fabricate

a spherical balloon of radius r_0 in relaxed state. Find the dependence of the air pressure p inside the balloon on its radius r. Assume vacuum outside the balloon.

ANSWERS AND HINTS

Multiple Choice Questions

1. (a)
2. (d)
3. (c)
4. (b)
5. (d)
6. (a) → (p)
   (b) → (p)
   (c) → (p)
   (d) → (q)

Build up your understanding

1. (a) The mass centre and a point 0.2 m to the right of the mass centre.

   Hint: Mass centre certainly remains immobile. In addition, some points may also remain immobile, if portion of the rod included between them (including the mass centre) consists of equal lengths of higher and lower temperature regions.

   (b) The right and the left ends, both shift towards the right by amounts $1.5\Delta l$ and $0.5\Delta l$ respectively.

2. $\dfrac{b}{l}(t_s Y_s + t_a Y_a)$, $\dfrac{l}{b}(t_s Y_s + t_a Y_a)$ and $\dfrac{l b Y_s Y_a}{t_a Y_s + t_s Y_a}$ respectively

3. (a) $\rho = \rho_0(1 + \beta \rho_0 g h)$

   (b) $p = p_0 + \rho_0 g h \left(1 + \dfrac{\rho_0 g \beta h}{2}\right)$

4. $\approx \dfrac{3mg}{4} + \dfrac{\rho_w A_1 l g}{2} + \sigma s_0 = 91.24 \times 10^{-3}$ N

   Hint: The water will fill the entire upper half of the capillary.

5. $\approx h_0 \left(1 + \dfrac{p_0}{\rho g l}\right)^{-1} = 1.00$ mm

6. $\dfrac{2\sigma}{\rho g}\left(\dfrac{r_2 - r_1}{r_1 r_2}\right)$ Below the water level outside

7. $\dfrac{\pi F}{2l}$

   Hint: In equilibrium conditions, lateral pull of the soap film on the thread due to surface tension must everywhere be normal to the thread.

8. $\sqrt{\dfrac{2\sigma(1 - \cos\theta)}{\rho g}}$

9. $\dfrac{\pi \sigma D}{2}$ (Inwards)

   Hint: The net force between the drop and a glass plate results from the force of surface tension and the force of excess pressure inside the drop.

10. $\eta^{7/2} \Delta t_0$

11. $\dfrac{8\sigma(a^2 + b^2 - c^2)}{c^3 - a^3 - b^3}$

12. $C_P + R\left(\dfrac{4\sigma}{3p_0 r + 8\sigma}\right)$

    Hint: Apply the first law of thermodynamics on the gas inside the bubble.

13. $\dfrac{m_H}{m_W} = \left(\dfrac{\rho_W}{\rho_H}\right)^{1/2} \left(\dfrac{\sigma_H}{\sigma_W}\right)^{3/2}$

14. $r\sqrt{\dfrac{\rho h}{4\sigma}} = 5.0$ ms

   Hint: The hole spreads symmetrically away from the centre and in this process the surface energy lost by an infinitesimal circular strip disappeared is available as kinetic energy.

15. $\dfrac{9 p_0 V \rho}{16 m}$

16. $\dfrac{3\eta l^3}{8 F h} = 5$ s

17. (a) $v = (1-\eta)v_1 - \eta v_2$

    (b) $v = (1-k\eta)v_1 - k\eta v_2$

Check your understanding

1. (a) Upper edge: $(\mu - \tan\theta)\dfrac{\alpha l \Delta T}{2\mu}$ up

   Mass centre: $\dfrac{\alpha l \Delta T \tan\theta}{2\mu}$ down

   Lower edge: $(\mu + \tan\theta)\dfrac{\alpha l \Delta T}{2\mu}$ down

   (b) Upper edge: $(\mu + \tan\theta)\dfrac{\alpha l \Delta T}{2\mu}$ down

   Mass centre: $\dfrac{\alpha l \Delta T \tan\theta}{2\mu}$ down

   Lower edge: $(\mu - \tan\theta)\dfrac{\alpha l \Delta T}{2\mu}$ up

   (c) $\dfrac{\alpha l \Delta T \tan\theta}{\mu}$ down

   Hint: Try to find a point on the rod that remains immobile.

2. 4:1

3. $\dfrac{F \Delta t}{S\sqrt{\rho Y}} = 2.5$ mm

4. $\sqrt{\dfrac{2\sigma(1 - \sin\theta)}{\rho g}}$

5. $\left(\dfrac{16\sigma^2 r^5}{3 Y^2 S^2}\right)^{1/3}$

   Hint: In equilibrium conditions, lateral pull of the soap film on the thread due to surface tension must everywhere be normal, therefore after pricking the soap film on any one side of the thread, the thread assume shape of an arc of a circle. Furthermore, the pull due to surface tension is very small as compared to the tension force developed in the thread; therefore, the radius of arc made by the thread will be much larger than the radius of the wire frame.

6. (a) $4R$ (b) $\sqrt{\dfrac{8\sigma}{\rho h r^2}}$

7. (a) $\approx \pi \Delta p R^2 \left(1 + \dfrac{h}{R}\right)$ and $\approx \dfrac{\pi \Delta p R h^3}{\eta l}$

   (b) $\approx (\rho - \rho_0) \dfrac{g h^3}{\eta (R + h)}$

   (c) $\approx (\rho_0 - \rho) \dfrac{g h^3}{\eta (R + h)}$

Challenge your understanding

1. The right end towards the right by $\tfrac{5}{6}\Delta l$ and the left end towards the left by $\tfrac{1}{6}\Delta l$.

   Hint: Net impulse of frictional forces on the rod must be zero. In addition, three points on the rod remain immobile during the expansion process.

2. $\dfrac{dr}{dt} = -\dfrac{12\sigma D}{h_0 r_0^3}\left(\dfrac{r^2}{3 p_0 r + 8\sigma}\right)$

Hint: The higher air concentration inside the bubble causes air molecules to diffuse out of the bubble, thus reducing inside air pressure and hence volume of the bubble. Since volume of amount of soap solution remains constant, the thickness must increase as the size of the bubble decreases.

3. $p = 2k\left(\dfrac{r - r_0}{r^2}\right)$

Hint: Consider a square mesh of side l made from springs of length a ($l \gg a$). The springs are parallel to either x-axis or y-axis of a coordinate system. In this mesh $(l/a - 1)$ springs in a line along the x-axis are repeated $(l/a - 1)$ times similarly $(l/a - 1)$ springs in a line along the y-axis are repeated $(l/a - 1)$ times. Therefore total number n of springs are

$$n = 2\left(\dfrac{l}{a} - 1\right)^2$$

For infinitely small springs $a \to 0$, the above relation reduces to

$$n = 2\left(\dfrac{l}{a}\right)^2$$

Chapter 10

Oscillations and Waves

Linear and angular simple harmonic motions, wave motion, wavefront and rays, longitudinal and transverse waves, wave speed, superposition principle, interference of waves, progressive and stationary waves, vibrations in strings and air columns, beats, Doppler's effect.

"Natural science does not simply describe and explain nature; it is a part of the interplay between nature and ourselves."

BACK TO BASICS

Simple Harmonic Motion (SHM)

If a position coordinate varies sinusoidally with time, it is a linear simple harmonic motion and if an angular coordinate varies sinusoidally with time, it is an angular simple harmonic motion.

Linear SHM: $\quad x = A\sin(\omega t + \phi_0)$

Here A is amplitude, ω is angular frequency and ϕ_0 is initial phase angle.

Angular SHM: $\quad \theta = \theta_m \sin(\omega t + \phi_0)$

Here θ_m is amplitude, ω is angular frequency and ϕ_0 is initial phase angle.

Werner Heisenberg
(5 December 1901 – 1 February 1976)

Wave Motion

Wave is a disturbance represented by variation in a physical quantity that travels through a medium and transfers energy progressively in that medium. The disturbance may take the form of an elastic deformation or of a variation of pressure, electric or magnetic intensity, electric potential etc.

Mechanical waves propagate through a material medium (solid, liquid or gas) at a wave speed that depends on elasticity and density of that medium.

Longitudinal waves:

In a longitudinal wave, particle displacement is parallel to the direction of wave propagation.

Transverse waves:

In a transverse wave, particle displacement is perpendicular to the direction of wave propagation.

General equation of wave motion in one dimension:

$$y = f(x \pm vt)$$

Here y is a measure of the disturbance; x is position coordinate of the disturbance at an instant t and v is the wave speed.

Differential equation of wave motion in one dimension:

$$\frac{\partial^2 y}{\partial x^2} = \frac{1}{v^2}\frac{\partial^2 y}{\partial t^2}$$

Equation of harmonic waves in one dimension:

$$y = A\sin(kx \pm \omega t)$$

Here A is amplitude; k is angular wave number and ω is angular frequency.

Superposition of waves:

When two or more waves interfere, the resulting disturbance at a point can be calculated by principle of superposition, which states that the resulting disturbance at that point is algebraic sum individual disturbances of all the interfering waves.

Doppler's effect:

A stationary source emits wavefronts that propagate with constant velocity with constant separation between them and a stationary observer encounters them at regular constant intervals at which they were emitted by the source.

A moving observer will encounter more or lesser number of wavefronts depending on whether he is approaching or receding the source.

A source in motion will emit different wavefronts at different places thus alter wavelength i.e. separation between the wavefronts.

Multiple Choice Questions

1. A particle of mass m can move in a force field. Potential energy U varies on location of the particle according to the following equation.

$$U = -k(x-a)^2(x-b)^2$$

Here k, a and b are positive constants.

What can you conclude about small amplitude oscillations of the particle?

(a) It can oscillate about a specific location with angular frequency $(b-a)\sqrt{2k/m}$.

(b) It can oscillate about two separate locations with angular frequency $(b-a)\sqrt{k/m}$.

(c) It can oscillate about a specific location with angular frequency $(b-a)\sqrt{k/m}$.

(d) It can oscillate about two separate locations with angular frequency $(b-a)\sqrt{2k/m}$.

2. In figure-I, is shown acoustic pressure variation with position in a harmonic sound wave travelling in the positive x-direction. Period of the sound wave is 8 s. Figure-I was recorded at $t = 10$ s. In figure-II are shown variation in acoustic pressure by two curves recorded at two successive instants of time $t = t_1$ and then $t = t_2$. Both the figures are drawn to the same scale.

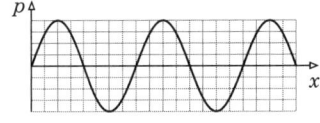

Figure-I

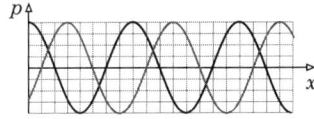

Figure-II

Which of the following sets correctly express possible values of the instants t_1 and t_2?

(a) $t_1 = 0$ s and $t_2 = 3$ s
(b) $t_1 = 11$ s and $t_2 = 16$ s
(c) $t_1 = 8$ s and $t_2 = 11$ s
(d) $t_1 = 16$ s and $t_2 = 19$ s

3. A simple pendulum initially oscillating simple harmonically with angular amplitude α and period T_0 is symmetrically confined between two rigid fixed planes A and B making angle $\beta < \alpha$ with each other as shown in the figure.

(a) If collisions at both the walls are elastic, period is $T_0(1-\beta/\alpha)$.

(b) If collisions at both the walls are inelastic, period is T_0.

(c) If collision at one wall is elastic and at the other is inelastic, the period is T_0.

(d) If collision at one wall is elastic and at the other is inelastic, the period is less then T_0.

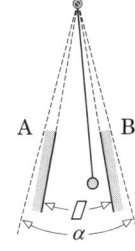

4. Two identical simple pendulums each of length l are suspended from the ceiling. Their bobs each of mass m are connected by a very light relaxed elastic cord of force constant k as shown in the figure. If the bobs are symmetrically pulled apart slightly and released, what is period of the ensuing oscillations?

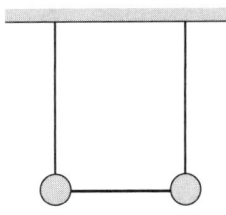

(a) $\pi\left(\dfrac{2k}{m}+\dfrac{g}{l}\right)^{-\tfrac{1}{2}}$

(b) $\pi\left\{\left(\dfrac{2k}{m}\right)^{-\tfrac{1}{2}}+\left(\dfrac{g}{l}\right)^{-\tfrac{1}{2}}\right\}$

(c) $\pi\left\{\left(\dfrac{k}{m}+\dfrac{g}{l}\right)^{-\tfrac{1}{2}}+\left(\dfrac{g}{l}\right)^{-\tfrac{1}{2}}\right\}$

(d) $\pi\left\{\left(\dfrac{2k}{m}+\dfrac{g}{l}\right)^{-\tfrac{1}{2}}+\left(\dfrac{g}{l}\right)^{-\tfrac{1}{2}}\right\}$

5. Consider a fixed highly evacuated cylinder in a gravity free region. Inside the cylinder, a piston of mass M can move without friction. In each part of the cylinder, a ball of mass m ($m \ll M$) is moving back and

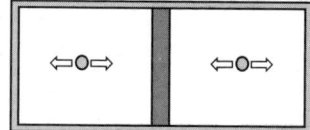

forth with remarkably high frequency and in doing so they are colliding elastically with the ends of the cylinder and with the piston. When the piston is at the centre, it is in equilibrium as shown in the figure. Now the piston is shifted slightly towards one of the ends of cylinder with a negligible speed and then released. What will happen to the piston?

(a) It will stay where it is released.
(b) It will ultimately come at the centre and stop.
(c) It will start oscillating back and forth simple-harmonically.
(d) It will start oscillating back and forth but not simple harmonically.

6. A small bead of mass m can slide on a frictionless fixed ring of radius r. With the help of two identical strings of force constant k, the bead is connected to two nails A and B each on a diameter at a distance $0.5r$ from centre O of the ring. Relaxed length of each string is negligible as compared to the radius of the ring. The bead is given a small velocity at point C. What can you predict about subsequent motion of the bead before any of the string strikes a nail?

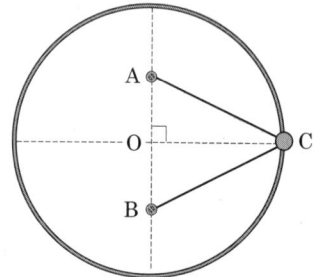

(a) It will keep moving with its initial speed.
(b) It will oscillate simple harmonically about the point C.
(c) Its angular momentum about centre O of the ring is conserved.
(d) Total elastic potential energy stored in both the strings is $1.25kr^2$.

7. Four tunnels are supposed to be bored through the earth between two places on a longitude as shown in the figure. One of them with midpoint at A is straight, whereas other three have bent at their midpoints B, C and D. Both the bent sections are coplanar. A particle released from one end of the tunnels, spends time intervals T_A, T_B, T_C and T_D respectively to reach the other end. If the particle passes the bent smoothly without a change in speed there, which of the following relations will these time intervals bear?

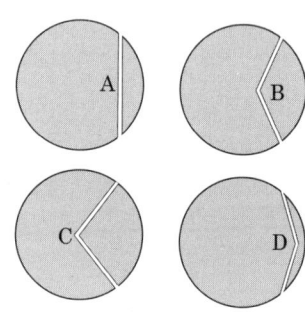

(a) $T_A = T_B = T_C = T_D$
(b) $T_A = T_C > T_B = T_D$
(c) $T_A = T_C < T_B > T_D$
(d) $T_B < T_A = T_C < T_D$

8. On a windless day, rays of the sound waves emanating from an isotropic point source placed close to the ground are shown in the figure. If a horizontal wind starts blowing towards the left with a constant and uniform velocity, which of the following will best represent pattern of the sound rays?

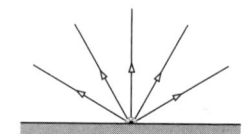

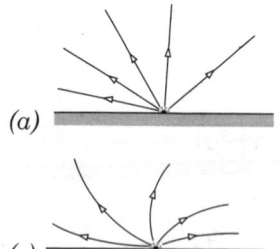
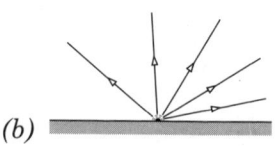
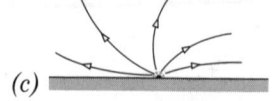
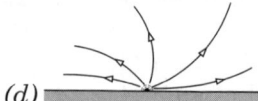

9. A detector receding from a stationary sound source with a speed that increases continuously without a limit. Which of the following statements correctly describes frequency of the sound detected by the

detector? Assume that sound waves propagate indefinitely without attenuation and the detector does not create any air drag.

(a) It first decreases, becomes zero and then increases.
(b) It continuously decreases and eventually no sound is detected.
(c) It continuously decreases and eventually acquires a small value.
(d) It first decreases, becomes zero and then increases and eventually no sound is detected.

10. Three aircrafts A, B and C are flying in a line with the same speed. Another aircraft D is flying on another straight line making an acute angle with the line of motion of the aircrafts A, B and C as shown. If pilots of these aircrafts hear sound of the aircraft D simultaneously, what can you conclude about speed of the aircraft D?

(a) It is possible only when the aircraft D is moving at speed of sound.
(b) It is possible only when the aircraft D is moving at speed lower than speed of sound.
(c) It is possible only when the aircraft D is moving at speed higher than speed of sound.
(d) The pilots of aircrafts A, B and C cannot hear sound of the aircraft D simultaneously.

11. When a boat moves on stagnant water with a speed that is greater than speed of surface waves on water, the surface waves generated due to movement of the boat combine to make a V shape pattern as shown in the figure. This pattern is known as bow-waves. Various bow wave patterns and velocity profile of water flow are shown in the first and the second columns of the following table. Suggest suitable matches.

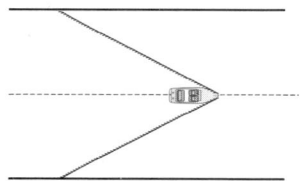

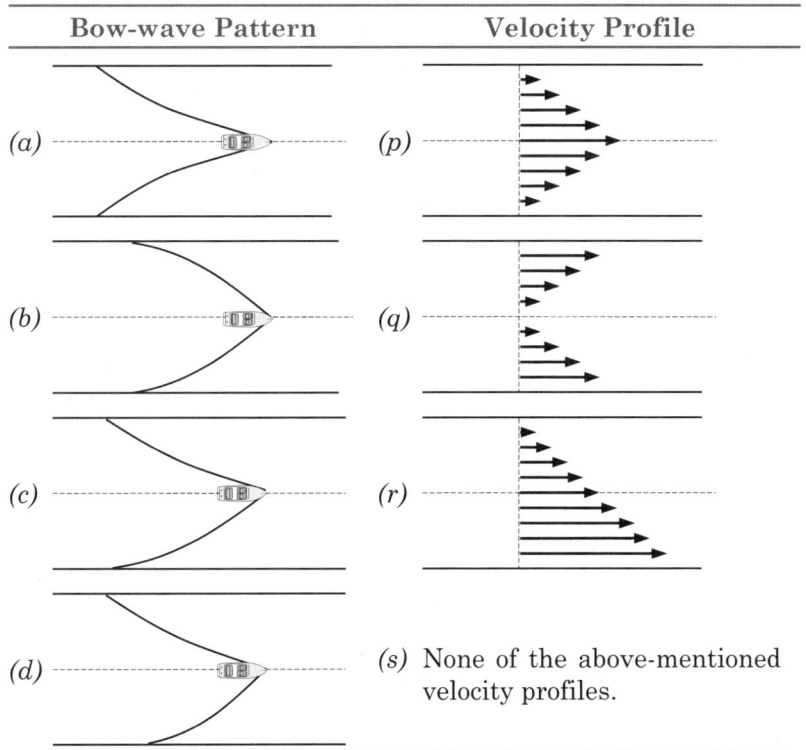

(s) None of the above-mentioned velocity profiles.

Build up your understanding

1. A particle of mass m can move along x-axis of a coordinate frame in a force field of stationary sources. Potential energy U of system varies with position x the particle according to equation $U = k|x|$, where k is a positive constant. If the particle is projected from the origin with a kinetic energy K, find period of its bound motion.

2. A particle of mass m is connected from the origin O of an inertial frame with the help of an elastic cord of force constant k and negligible relaxed length. In addition to the elastic force of the cord, a constant force $\vec{F} = F_0 \hat{i}$ also acts on the particle. The particle is pulled to an arbitrary position (x_0, y_0) as shown in the figure and released. Find the positions between which the particle oscillates and period of the oscillations.

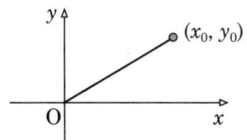

3. A uniform inextensible rope of length l and a light inextensible thread are connected at their ends A and B to make a loop. The thread passes over a fixed ideal pulley and the rope passes under another fixed ideal pulley. The junction B is pulled slightly downwards and then released. Find period of the ensuing oscillations. Acceleration of free fall is g.

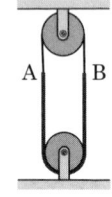

4. A train of length $l = 900$ m running on a horizontal track with its engine off starts moving up a hill of uniform inclination $\theta = 9.2°$ to the horizontal. If $\eta = 0.6$ fraction of length of the train rises the hill before it starts moving back due to gravity, how much time does the train spend on the hill? Assume all the resistive forces negligible, distribution of mass uniform in the train and no impact at the beginning of the hill. Acceleration due to gravity is g. Use $\sin(9.2°) = 0.16$ and $\sqrt{g} = \pi$.

5. A small disc is projected on a horizontal floor with a speed u. Coefficient of friction between the disc and the floor varies according to equation $\mu = \mu_0 + kx$, where μ_0 and k are positive constants and x is distance travelled by the disc. Find distance slid by the disc on the floor and the corresponding time interval. Acceleration of free fall is g.

6. A small ring is threaded on an inextensible frictionless cord of length $2l$. The ends of the cord are fixed to a horizontal ceiling. In equilibrium, the ring is at a depth h below the ceiling. Now the ring is pulled aside by a small distance in the vertical plane containing the cord and released. Find period of small oscillations of the ring. Acceleration of free fall is g.

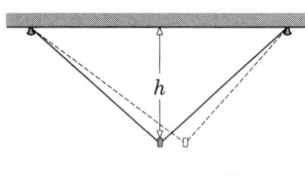

7. Two identical small discs each of mass m placed on a frictionless horizontal floor are connected with the help of a spring of force constant k. The discs are also connected with two light rods each of length l that are pivoted to a nail driven into the floor as shown in the figure by a top view. If period of small oscillations of the system is $2\pi\sqrt{(m/k)}$, find relaxed length of the spring.

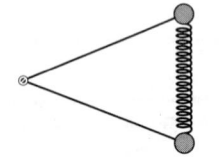

8. A block of mass m, which can slide up and down without rotation between two frictionless walls, is suspended with the help of two light springs and a light inextensible cord that passes over an ideal pulley as shown in the figure. Force constants of the springs are k_1 and k_2. If the bar is pulled down slightly and released, it will oscillate up and down. Find period of these oscillations.

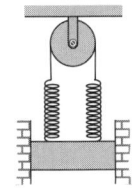

9. When the arrangement shown is in equilibrium, the spring on the right is stretched by an amount x_0. Coefficient of static friction between the blocks is μ and the horizontal floor is frictionless. Both the blocks have equal mass m and force constants of the spring are $3k$ and k as shown in the figure. Find the maximum amplitude of oscillations of the blocks along the springs that does not allow them to slide on each other. Acceleration of free fall is g.

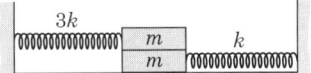

10. A uniform rope is suspended from the ceiling with the help of a spring. The lower end of the rope is in the air. At what distance from the lower end (fraction of the total length of the rope), the rope can be cut so that the portion hanging from the spring oscillates remaining straight?

11. A uniform rope of linear mass density λ is suspended from the ceiling with the help of a light spring of force constant k. In equilibrium, a length l_0 of the rope is in air and rest in a heap on the floor as shown in the figure. Height of the heap is negligible as compared to the length of the rope in air. If the rope is pulled down slightly and released, find angular frequency of ensuing oscillations of the rope. Acceleration due to gravity is g.

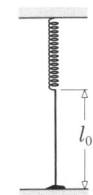

12. A platform of mass M mounted on a vertical spring is made to oscillate up and down with a period T. The very moment, the platform passes its equilibrium position; it collides elastically with a small ball falling from a height. Due to the collision, speeds of the platform and the ball remain unchanged, but their directions are reversed. After the collision, the platform moves downwards a distance H then starts moving up and again collides with the ball at its equilibrium position. If this process repeats indefinitely, find mass of the ball. Acceleration of free fall is g.

13. A light platform is affixed on the top of a vertical spring of force constant k, lower end of which is affixed on the ground. A small ball of mass m falling from a height h above the platform collides with it elastically. Find the maximum velocity and maximum acceleration of the ball in ensuing oscillatory motion. Acceleration of free fall is g.

14. A thin light plate is affixed on the upper end of a spring of force constant k, lower end of which is affixed on the ground. An inverted beaker of mass M is placed on the plate. A putty blob of mass m is stuck inside the beaker at its bottom as shown in the figure. After some time, when the adhesion of the putty becomes too weak to support it, the putty blob falls. The putty hits the plate after the plate has completed exactly one oscillation and sticks there. If the beaker does not lose contact with the plate, find height h of beaker and amplitude A of oscillations of the system after the putty sticks to the plate. Acceleration of free fall is g.

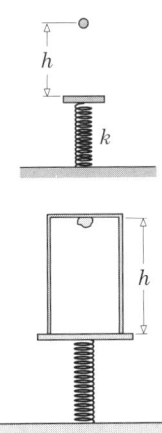

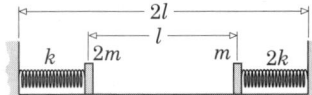

15. In the arrangement shown, two blocks of masses m and $2m$ affixed on the ends of springs of force constant $2k$ and k are held at rest. The other ends of the springs are affixed on fixed supports. Relaxed length of each spring is l, distance between the supports is $2l$, size of the blocks is negligible, and the floor is frictionless. Initially the blocks are held a distance l apart compressing the spring identically. After the blocks are released, they rush towards each other, collide head on and stick to each other. Find maximum speed of the blocks in the ensuing oscillations.

16. A block of mass M can slide without friction on a horizontal frictionless floor. A small ball of mass m is suspended by a light inextensible cord of length l from a hanger fixed on the top of a vertical pole rigidly mounted on the block so that the ball can swing freely in a vertical plane. When the block is held fixed, the period of small amplitude oscillations of the simple pendulum consisting of the ball and the thread is T_0. What would be period of small amplitude oscillations of the simple pendulum, if the block were not held fixed?

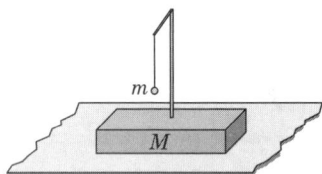

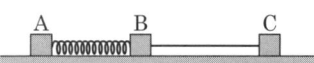

17. Three identical blocks A, B and C are placed in a line on a frictionless horizontal floor. Blocks A and B are connected with a light spring of force constant k and blocks B and C with a light inextensible cord. Initially the system is motionless. Block A is given a velocity u by a sharp hit towards block B. When the blocks B and C collide, a sound bang is created. What should the minimum length of the cord be in order to create a sound bang of maximum loudness?

18. A small ball of mass m is affixed at one end of a light rod of length l, the other end of which is hinged to a fixed pivot on a wall. One end of a spring of force constant k is attached on the rod at a distance d from the hinge and the other end of the spring is attached to a nail on the wall. In equilibrium, the rod stays horizontal and angle between the spring and the rod is θ_0. If the ball is pulled slightly downwards and released, the system begins to oscillate. Find period of these small amplitude oscillations.

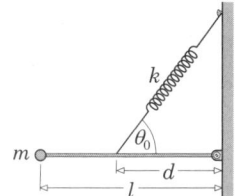

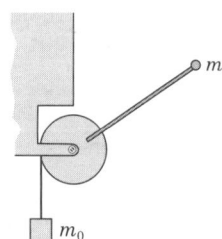

19. In the arrangement shown, a block of mass m_0 is suspended at one end of a light inextensible cord that is wrapped on a light drum of radius r. The drum can rotate without friction about a fixed horizontal axle that coincides with axis of the drum. A light rod is attached radially with the drum and a particle of mass m is affixed at the free end of the rod. Distance between the particle and the axle is l.

(a) Find orientation of the rod when the system is in stable equilibrium.
(b) Find period of small oscillations about this stable equilibrium.
Acceleration of free fall is g.

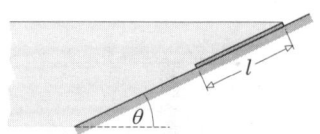

20. One wall of a water tank is inclined at angle θ to the horizontal. On this wall, a thin square plate of mass m and side l is held with its upper edge coinciding with the water level. Coefficient of friction between the plate and the wall is μ. When the plate is released, it slides down the wall and water does not enter between the plate and the wall. How long will the plate keep sliding? Neglect viscosity and turbulence of the water. Density of water is ρ_0 and acceleration of free fall is g.

21. A glass tube of circular section of area S bent in a shape shown, has one arm vertical and the other inclined at an angle θ. A light piston that can slide without friction in the vertical arm is connected at the lower end of a vertical spring of force constant k, the upper end of which is connected to a fixed support. When a mass m of a non-viscous liquid of density ρ is poured in the tube, level of liquid in the inclined arm stays higher than the piston as shown in the figure. Find period of small oscillations of the liquid. There is no friction between the piston and the tube and acceleration due to gravity is g.

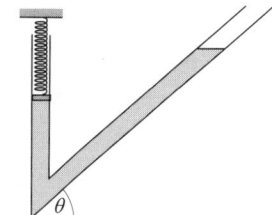

22. A thin vertical U-tube of very long arms contains some amount of mercury. Period of small amplitude oscillations of mercury is $T_1 = 2.0$ s. If in one arm, a mass $m = 100$ g of water is added, period of small oscillation becomes $T_2 = 3.0$ s. Find mass of mercury in the tube. Neglect effects of surface tension.

23. A volleyball can be modelled as a non-stretchable but flexible spherical envelope of mass m and radius R filled with air at excess pressure Δp. The excess pressure remains unchanged with small deformation in the volleyball when it is hit or when its strikes some rigid surface. Mass of the air inside the volleyball can be neglected. If such a volleyball strikes a rigid wall and bounces back without losing speed, how long will the ball remain in contact with the wall?

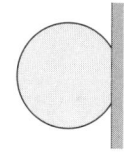

24. A heat-insulating piston of mass m divides a horizontal cylinder into two chambers. Area of a circular section of the cylinder is A. Initially when the piston is in equilibrium, pressure in both the chambers is p and volumes of the chambers are V_1 and V_2. The chambers are maintained at temperatures T_1 and T_2. The piston is given a small horizontal displacement and then released. Find period of its oscillations.

25. Opening of a glass bottle containing an ideal monoatomic gas is tightly closed with a cork fitted with a thin frictionless glass tube of cross-section area S. Inner volume of the tube is negligibly small as compared to volume V of the bottle. A small glass marble of mass m, when dropped in the tube, it starts oscillating up and down in the tube without friction. The marble exactly fits inside the tube so that there is no leakage of air. Denoting atmospheric pressure by p_0, find expression for period of oscillations of the marble. Treat the glass, the cork and the material of the marble as perfect insulator of heat.

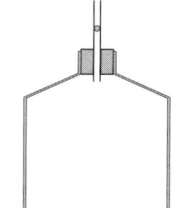

26. A long uniform helical spring of mass m, length l and force constant k is placed straight on a frictionless horizontal floor. One end of the spring is tapped sharply producing a compression pulse. Deduce an expression to find time taken by this pulse to reach the other end.

27. When a stone is dropped at point A in the water near a bank of a river, ripples produced spread in the water. Width of the river is b, water in it flows everywhere at a velocity u and velocity of propagation of surface wave relative to water is v. How long after the stone was dropped, will the ripples reach the point B on the opposite bank in front of A? Consider the conditions $v > u$, $v = u$ and $v < u$.

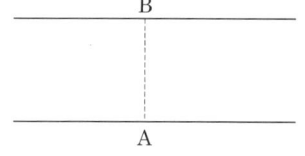

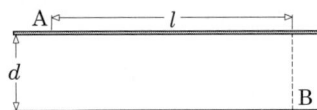

28. Two thin metal rods are arranged in water parallel to each other a distance d apart. Speeds c and v of sound in the water and in the rod respectively are not equal. If one of the rods is tapped at point A, find the shortest time the sound takes to travel from the point A to a point B on the other rod.

29. Walls, floor and the ceiling of a large hall are covered with a perfect sound absorbing coating. A powerful isotropic point source of sound of frequency 2.0 kHz is installed at a height 5.0 cm above the floor. The speed of sound waves in the air is 340 m/s. A small and very sensitive microphone is installed at a horizontal distance of 4.0 m from the source and at a height of 3 m above the floor. The microphone is connected to a very sensitive voltmeter, reading of which is proportional to the amplitude of sound waves received by the microphone. When the sound source is switched on, the voltmeter reads 0.10 V.

    (a) If sound absorbing coating on the floor is completely removed, how much will the voltmeter read?
    (b) Now the floor is again covered with some inferior quality sound absorbing material that absorbs 50% of incident sound energy, how much will the voltmeter read?

30. In a cylindrical vessel of radius r water is filled up to some height. A small iron ball is dropped at the centre of water surface. A time τ after the ball is dropped, water surface starts moving up and down with a portion having amplitude more than any other place on the surface. Explain the reason for this occurrence and find an expression to obtain a best approximate value of the speed of the surface waves.

31. A sound detector is moving with a constant velocity towards a stationary sound source. The source emits a beep of sound of frequency $v_0 = 262$ Hz that propagates with speed $c = 330$ m/s. The detector detects the beep of sound over a distance $\Delta x = 78$ m and registers a frequency $v = 275$ Hz. Find duration of the beep emitted by the source.

Check your understanding

1. A particle of mass m can move along the x-axis in a force field created by stationary sources. Potential energy U of the system varies with position coordinate x of the particle in accordance with the equation $U = kx/(x^2 + x_0^2)$. Find positions of stable equilibrium of the particle and period of small oscillations of the particle about this position.

2. A simple pendulum consists of a bob of mass m and a thread of length l. In an experiment demonstration, your physics teacher pulls the bob aside until the thread makes an angle $(2/\sqrt{3} - 1)$ rad with the vertical and start pushing the bob towards the equilibrium position. While pushing, he continuously applies a force $F = mg$ along the circular path of the bob until the thread becomes vertical and thereafter, he releases the bob. For what length of time did he push the bob? The acceleration of free fall is g.

Oscillations and Waves 10.11

3. Two small balls each of mass m connected by a light rod of length l_0 are suspended by two light inextensible cords of lengths l_1 and l_2. When the system is at rest, the cords are vertical. The system is set into small amplitude oscillations in the vertical plane containing the rod. Find period of these oscillations. Acceleration of free fall is g.

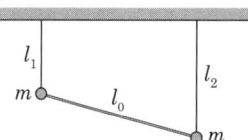

4. Three identical elastic cords each of force constant k and almost zero relaxed lengths are connected at their one end to a particle of mass m and the other ends of the cords are connected to three equally spaced points A, B and C on a rigid ring placed on a frictionless tabletop. Mass of the ring is $\dot{\eta} = 2$ times the mass of the particle. In equilibrium, the system stays at rest with the particle at the centre of the ring.

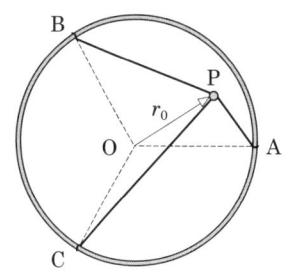

Now the ring is held and the particle is pulled horizontally to a point P at a distance r_0 from the centre O of the ring and then both of them set free simultaneously.

(a) Find period of the oscillatory motion.
(b) Assume initial location of the centre of the ring as origin and the line OP as the x-axis, express position of particle x_p and centre of the ring x_r as function of time t.

5. A block of mass m placed on a frictionless horizontal floor is connected with two identical springs each of force constant k. One end of the left spring is connected to a fixed support and one end of the right spring is free. Initially the block is at rest, the springs are collinear and relaxed. If someone begins to pull the free end of the right spring with a constant velocity u away from the wall, how far will the block move before it acquires a speed equal to u?

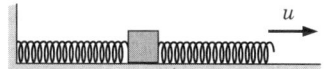

6. A thin rod of mass m is welded on inner surface of a thin cylindrical shell of mass M (M >> m) and radius R parallel to the axis of the cylinder. The composite body thus formed is placed on a horizontal floor. When disturbed slightly from the equilibrium as shown in the figure, it undergoes small amplitude oscillations without sliding on the floor. Find period of these oscillations. The acceleration of free fall is g.

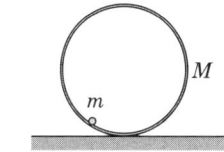

7. A small disc of mass m is attached to one end of a light inextensible cord, which passes through a frictionless hole in a frictionless horizontal tabletop. At the other end of the cord is attached a weight of mass M. Initially the disc is moving on a circle of radius R with an angular velocity ω. If the hanging weight is pulled slightly downwards and then released, it will undergo small amplitude oscillations. Find the angular frequency of these oscillations.

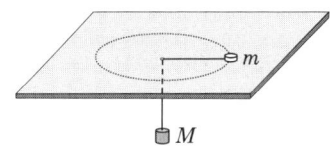

8. Two aircrafts installed with identical pendulum clocks, take off simultaneously from an airport in a city X at the equator. Both the aircrafts fly in opposite directions over the equator and land at an airport in another city Y exactly in 12 hours later according to local time of the city X. If the city Y is situated diametrically opposite to the city X, find ratio of difference, if any, in the times shown by both the clocks to the time taken. Radius of the earth is R, its angular velocity is ω and acceleration of free fall at the equator is g. Assume the aircrafts fly at constant speeds relative to the earth surface.

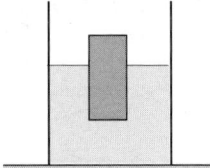

9. A uniform cylinder of mass m and area of a circular section s is floating partially immersed in a non-viscous liquid of density ρ occupying some volume of a beaker of circular section area S as shown in the figure. The beaker rests on a horizontal tabletop. If the cylinder is slightly displaced either up or down and then released, it will oscillate. Find angular frequency of these small amplitude oscillations of the cylinder. The acceleration of free fall is g.

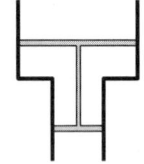

10. A vertical tube made of highly conducting material has two portions of cross-sectional area A_1 and A_2 ($A_2 > A_1$). Two pistons connected by a rod of length l can slide in these portions without friction. Total mass of the pistons and the rod is m. Between the pistons, n moles of an ideal gas is trapped. Atmospheric pressure is p_0, acceleration of free fall is g and universal gas constant is R. If the piston-rod assembly is shifted slightly from its equilibrium position and then released, it starts oscillating. Find angular frequency of these oscillations.

11. Two ships are anchored a distance $l = 3$ km apart in a sea, where seabed between the ships is at a uniform depth $h = 1.0$ km and consists of a flat rock. Speed of sound in the air is $v_a = 333$ m/s, in the water is $v_w = 1.5$ km/s and in the rock is $v_r = 4.5$ km/s. If a gun is fired at a ship, in how much minimum time will the firing be heard at the other ship?

12. Water is continuously flowing at a speed $v = 1.0$ m/s in a steel pipeline of radius $r = 5.0$ cm. A valve installed in the pipeline is closed almost instantaneously, resulting in an abrupt rise in water pressure known as hydrodynamic shock. What should the minimum thickness of the pipe be in order to provide a safety factor of $\eta = 5$? Density of water is $\rho = 1.0 \times 10^3$ kg/m³, speed of sound in water $c = 1.5 \times 10^3$ m/s and tensile strength of steel is $\sigma_b = 0.35$ GPa.

13. If separation between a source and a detector changes due to relative motion between them, the detector detects sound of pitch different from that emitted by the source. This observed change in pitch is known as Doppler's shift and the effect is known as Doppler's effect. Under the conditions when Doppler's shift is observed, intensity of the sound also changes. In this task, we study change in intensity of sound detected by a detector due to relative motion between a source and a detector.

    A point source is emitting sound isotropically at constant power P and the sound travels with velocity c relative to the air.

    (a) A detector is moving with a constant velocity v_d towards a stationary source in still air. Find suitable expression for intensity I of sound received by the detector at a distance r from the source.

    (b) A point source is moving with a constant velocity v_s towards a stationary detector in still air. Find suitable expression for intensity I of sound received by the detector at a distance r from the source.

    (c) A point source is moving in still air with a constant velocity v_s towards a detector that is moving with a constant velocity v_d towards the source. Find suitable expression for intensity I of sound received by the detector at a distance r from the source.

Challenge your understanding

1. Two rubber pads are affixed at the bottom of a box and the assembly thus formed is placed on a uniform slope of inclination $\theta = 0.5°$. Coefficient of friction between the slope and the pads is $\mu = 0.60$. Two electric motors installed in the box can make these pads to move back and forth relative to the box simple harmonically in opposite phase along the line of fastest descent on the slope. Amplitude of these simple harmonic motions is $A = 0.25$ mm and angular frequency is $\omega = 72$ rad/s. Soon after the motors are switched on simultaneously, the box acquires a constant velocity down the slope. Find the magnitude of this constant velocity.

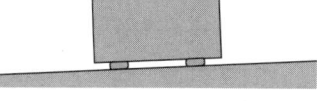

2. A block of mass m placed on a horizontal conveyor belt is attached at one end of a spring of force constant k. The other end of the spring is attached to a support A. Coefficients of static and kinetic friction between the belt and the block are μ_s and μ_k ($\mu_s > \mu_k$). Initially the belt, the block and the support all are moving towards the right with constant velocity u and the spring is relaxed. The support is suddenly stopped.

   (a) Explain qualitatively the mechanism of motion of the block after the support is stopped.
   (b) Find the maximum and minimum deformations of the spring.
   (c) Find period T of the oscillatory motion of the block.

Answers and Hints

Multiple Choice Questions

1. (c)
2. (a), (b), (c) and (d)
3. (b) and (c)
4. (d)
5. (c)
6. (a), (c) and (d)
7. (d)
8. (c)
9. (d)
10. (c)
11. (a)→ (q)
    (b)→ (p)
    (c)→ (s)
    (d)→ (r)

Build up your understanding

1. $\dfrac{8}{k}\sqrt{\dfrac{mK}{2}}$

2. (x_0, y_0) and $\left(\dfrac{2F_0}{k} - x_0,\; -y_0\right)$

   and $2\pi\sqrt{\dfrac{m}{k}}$

3. $2\pi\sqrt{\dfrac{l}{2g}}$

4. $\pi\sqrt{\dfrac{l}{g\sin\theta}} = 75$ s

   Hint: Retardation of the train is proportional to length of the train on the hill.

5. $\dfrac{\sqrt{ku^2 g + (\mu_0 g)^2} - \mu_0 g}{kg}$ and

   $\dfrac{1}{\sqrt{kg}}\left\{\dfrac{\pi}{2} - \tan^{-1}\left(\dfrac{\mu_0}{u}\sqrt{\dfrac{g}{k}}\right)\right\}$

6. $2\pi\sqrt{\dfrac{l^2}{gh}}$

   Hint: You may assume that the shift of ring is almost horizontal for small amplitude oscillations.

7. $l\sqrt{2}$

8. $2\pi\sqrt{\dfrac{(k_1 + k_2)m}{4k_1 k_2}}$

9. $\dfrac{\mu mg}{k} - x_0$

10. Less than half.

11. $\sqrt{\dfrac{1}{l_0}\left(g + \dfrac{k}{\lambda}\right)}$

12. $\dfrac{8\pi HM}{(2n+1)gT^2}$, where $n = 0, 1, 2 \ldots\ldots\ldots$

    Hint: Airtime of the ball must be an odd integral multiple of the half of the period of the oscillations of the platform.

13. $v_m = \sqrt{g\left(2h + \dfrac{mg}{k}\right)}$ and $a_m = g\sqrt{1 + \dfrac{2kh}{mg}}$

    Hint: Motion of the ball while it is in contact with the platform is simple harmonic. Till the ball passes the equilibrium position, its speed increases and acquires its maximum value at the equilibrium position. At the lowest point, spring-force is more than twice of the weight of the ball; therefore, the ball has maximum acceleration at the lowest point.

14. $h = \dfrac{2\pi^2 Mg}{k}$ and $A = \dfrac{2\pi mg}{k}\sqrt{\dfrac{M}{m+M}}$

15. $\dfrac{l}{4}\sqrt{\dfrac{k}{m}}$

    Hint: Both the blocks collide somewhere in the left half region.

16. $T_0\sqrt{\dfrac{M}{m+M}}$

    Hint: For small amplitude oscillations, the ball can be assumed moving almost horizontally without an appreciable loss in accuracy.

17. $\dfrac{\pi u}{2}\sqrt{\dfrac{M}{2k}}$

    Hint: After the ball A is hit, the motion of the balls A and B before B hits C can be conceived as superposition of translation of their mass centre and oscillations about the mass centre.

    Loudness of the sound bang depends on the kinetic energy lost in the collision. More is the loss in kinetic energy; louder is the sound bang. For this condition to fulfill, the ball B must collide with the ball C at the end of the first half time period of the oscillations.

18. $\dfrac{2\pi l}{d\sin\theta_0}\sqrt{\dfrac{m}{k}}$

19. (a) $\cos^{-1}\left(\dfrac{m_0 r}{ml}\right)$ down the horizontal

    (b) $2\pi\sqrt{\dfrac{ml^2 + m_0 r^2}{g\sqrt{m^2 l^2 - m_0^2 r^2}}}$

20. $\pi\sqrt{\dfrac{m}{\mu\rho_0 g l^2 \sin\theta}}$

    Hint: Retardation of the plate increases linearly with its displacement.

21. $2\pi\sqrt{\dfrac{m}{k + \rho g S(1 + \sin\theta)}}$

22. $\dfrac{mT_1^2}{T_2^2 - T_1^2} = 80$ g

   Hint: Since cross-section of the tube is uniform, masses of both the liquids are proportional to the lengths of the spaces individually occupied by them.

23. $\sqrt{\dfrac{\pi m}{2R\Delta p}}$

   Hint: Force of the excess pressure on the flat area in contact with the wall makes the ball move simple harmonically.

24. $2\pi \sqrt{\dfrac{mV_1 V_2}{pA^2(V_1 + V_2)}}$

25. $2\pi \sqrt{\dfrac{3mV}{5S(p_0 S + mg)}}$

26. $\sqrt{\dfrac{m}{k}}$

27. $= \begin{cases} \dfrac{b}{\sqrt{v^2 - u^2}}; & v > u \\ \infty & v \le u \end{cases}$

28. $t = \begin{cases} \dfrac{\sqrt{d^2 + l^2}}{c} & \text{If } \dfrac{c}{v} \ge \dfrac{l}{\sqrt{d^2+l^2}} \\ \dfrac{l}{v} + d\sqrt{\dfrac{1}{c^2} - \dfrac{1}{v^2}} & \text{If } \dfrac{c}{v} < \dfrac{l}{\sqrt{d^2+l^2}} \end{cases}$

29. (a) 0.09 V (b) 0.08 V

30. $v = \dfrac{2r}{\tau}$

31. $\dfrac{v\Delta x}{c(v - v_o)} = 5.0$ s

Check your understanding

1. $x = x_0$ and $2\pi \sqrt{\dfrac{2mx_0^3}{k}}$

2. $\dfrac{\pi}{6}\sqrt{\dfrac{l}{g}}$

3. $2\pi \sqrt{\dfrac{2l_1 l_2}{g(l_1 + l_2)}}$

   Hint: For small amplitude oscillations, both the balls have almost equal horizontal shifts.

4. (a) $2\pi \sqrt{\dfrac{\eta m}{3(1+\eta)k}}$

   (b) $x_p = \left(\dfrac{\eta r_0}{1+\eta}\right)\cos\left\{\left(\sqrt{\dfrac{3(1+\eta)k}{\eta m}}\right)t\right\}$;

   $x_r = -\left(\dfrac{r_0}{1+\eta}\right)\cos\left\{\left(\sqrt{\dfrac{3(1+\eta)k}{\eta m}}\right)t\right\}$

5. $\dfrac{\pi u}{2}\sqrt{\dfrac{m}{2k}}$

6. $2\pi \sqrt{\dfrac{2MR}{mg}}$

7. $\sqrt{\dfrac{3m\omega^2}{(m+M)}}$

   Hint: Since angular momentum of the disc is conserved; its angular velocity will increase on reduction in radius of its path. The increment in angular velocity and decrement in the radius are so related that tension force will not be sufficient to provide required centripetal acceleration, thus causing the disc to increase radius of its path by pulling up the hanging block, setting up oscillations in the system in such a way that the hanging block starts up and down oscillations and the disc radial oscillations.

8. $\approx \dfrac{2\omega^2 R}{g}$

9. $\sqrt{\dfrac{\rho s S g}{m(S-s)}}$

   Hint: Water level shifts in opposite direction of movement of the cylinder. Relation between the shift in the water level and displacement of the cylinder is governed by constancy of volume of the water.

   During the downwards movement of cylinder, the immersed length increases and during the upward movement of the cylinder it decreases. This increment and decrement is the sum of magnitudes of the displacements of the cylinder and of the water level.

10. $\dfrac{p_0(A_2 - A_1) + mg}{\sqrt{nmRT}}$

    Hint: The piston-rod assembly oscillates under the simultaneous actions of gravity, the force applied by atmospheric pressure and the force applied by the pressure of the trapped gas.

11. $\dfrac{l v_w + 2h\sqrt{v_r^2 - v_w^2}}{v_r v_w} = 1.92$ s

    Hint: Sound propagating through water then in the rock and again in the water will take shortest time.

12. $\dfrac{\eta c v \rho r}{\sigma_b} = 1.1 \times 10^{-3}$ m

    Hint: As the valve is closed; water in the pipe first stops at the valve, creating there a compression pulse that propagates in the water away from the valve making flow velocity zero. Obviously, this pulse propagates with the speed of the sound waves in water.

13. (a) $I = \dfrac{P}{4\pi r^2}\left(1 + \dfrac{v_d}{c}\right)$

    Hint: Intensity of spherical waves is proportional to inverse of square of distance from the source. In addition to this idea, you have to consider that energy emitted by the source during a period is received by the detector in a smaller period.

    (b) $I = \dfrac{P}{4\pi r^2}\left(1 - \dfrac{v_s}{c}\right)$

    Hint: Proceed on similar lines as in the previous part, but while using inverse square law, take care of the fact that distance between the source and the detector is not radius of a wavefront received by the detector.

    (c) $I = \dfrac{P}{4\pi r^2}\left(1 + \dfrac{v_d}{c}\right)\left(1 - \dfrac{v_s}{c}\right)$

Challenge your understanding

1. $v \approx \dfrac{\pi A \omega \theta}{2\mu} = 0.4$ mm/s

   Hint: Initially velocities of the pads relative to the slope are in opposite directions; creating frictional forces on them in opposite directions, hence no net frictional force. Therefore, the box starts moving down due to gravity.

   In each cycle of oscillation of the pads while the box is moving down, when velocities of the pads relative to the box are smaller than that of the box, net friction points up the plane and rest of the time net friction is zero.

   Consider the total time interval in a cycle when net friction acts up the plane. This total interval can be divided into four very small subintervals spanning symmetrically about the instants of reversal of direction of motion of the pads relative to the box. This will help you to estimate this total time interval, hence net impulse of frictional forces in a cycle. When the box acquires a constant velocity down the plane, in each cycle of vibrations of the pads, total impulse of frictional forces, cancel the total impulse of component of gravity on the box-pad-motor assembly.

2. (a) Immediately after the support is stopped, the belt pulls the block together with it to a position x_1, where force of limiting friction is balanced by the spring force. At this position, the friction force decreases abruptly into kinetic friction and the block slides further to

a position x_{max} in the positive x-direction due to its inertia. Thereafter the block starts moving back with acceleration, determined by the friction and spring force, to a certain position x_{min}. Then again, its direction of motion changes, the speed starts to increase until it becomes equal to the speed of the belt at position x_2, and then the process repeats.

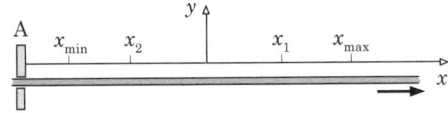

During each cycle, the loss of mechanical energy of the block because of the sliding friction is compensated by the work of the force of static friction.

(b) $x_{max} = \dfrac{\mu_k mg}{k} + \sqrt{\left[\dfrac{(\mu_s - \mu_k)mg}{k}\right]^2 + \left(u\sqrt{\dfrac{m}{k}}\right)^2}$

$x_{min} = \dfrac{\mu_k mg}{k} - \sqrt{\left[\dfrac{(\mu_s - \mu_k)mg}{k}\right]^2 + \left(u\sqrt{\dfrac{m}{k}}\right)^2}$

(c) $T = 2\left\{\pi + \dfrac{(\mu_s - \mu_k)g}{u}\sqrt{\dfrac{k}{m}}\right.$

$\left. - \tan^{-1}\left(\dfrac{(\mu_s - \mu_k)g}{u}\sqrt{\dfrac{k}{m}}\right)\right\}\sqrt{\dfrac{m}{k}}$

Chapter 11

Ray and Wave Optics

Geometrical optics, rectilinear propagation of light, mutual independence of rays, the principle of optical reversibility, laws of reflection, laws of refraction, reflection and refraction at spherical surfaces, total internal reflection, deviation and dispersion of light by a prism, thin lenses, combinations of mirrors and thin lenses and prisms, magnification and magnifying power, wave nature of light, Huygens's principle, interference of light waves.

"All truths are easy to understand once they are discovered; the point is to discover them."

Galileo Galilei
(15 February 1564 – 8 January 1642)

BACK TO BASICS

What is light?

Light is a form of energy, which produces sensation of sight.

We treat light as a ray while studying its interactions with moderate size objects (much larger than wavelength of light), as electromagnetic wave while studying its interactions with small size objects (comparable to wavelength of light) and as photon while studying its interactions with subatomic particle (much smaller than the wavelength of light).

Optics:

Optics is the study of properties and nature of light and vision.

Geometrical Optics:

In geometrical optics, the basic concept is the ray, which depicts the path of light propagation.

Geometrical optics deals with phenomenon like shadow formation and image formation due to reflection and refraction.

Fundamental laws of Geometrical Optics:

Geometrical optics is based on the following five laws.
- Rectilinear propagation of light.
- Mutual independence of rays
- The principle of optical reversibility.
- Laws of reflection.
- Laws of refraction.

Rectilinear propagation of light:

In a homogeneous isotropic medium, light travels on a straight-line path.
Rectilinear propagation explains shadow formation, eclipses of the sun and the moon, image formation by a pinhole camera etc.

Mutual independence of rays:

Light rays do not disturb each other upon intersection.

The principle of optical reversibility:

Light rays retrace their path after their direction is reversed.

Laws of reflection:

The angle of incidence equals the angle of reflection.

The incident ray, the reflected ray and the normal to the surface at the point of incidence all remain in the same plane called the plane of incidence.

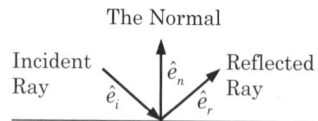

Laws of reflection in vector notations

$$\hat{e}_r = \hat{e}_i - 2(\hat{e}_i \cdot \hat{e}_n)\hat{e}_n$$

Laws of refraction:

When a ray of light passes from a medium 1 to a medium 2, the angles θ_1 and θ_2 that it makes at the point of incidence with the normal to the interface of the mediums bear the following relation, known as Snell's law.

$$\mu_1 \sin\theta_1 = \mu_2 \sin\theta_2$$

Here μ_1 and μ_2 are the respective refractive indices of the mediums.

Refractive index of a medium is defined as the ratio of speed c of light in vacuum and speed v of light in the medium.

$$\mu = \frac{c}{v}$$

If the mediums are isotropic, the rays in the two mediums are in the same plane with the normal and lie on opposite sides of the normal.

Total internal reflection:

When a light ray in a medium of higher refractive index encounters a medium of lower refractive index, the ray will be totally reflected back, if its angle of incidence exceeds the critical angle θ_c given by the following equation.

$$\theta_c = \sin^{-1}\left(\frac{\mu_{\text{Rarer}}}{\mu_{\text{Denser}}}\right)$$

Spherical mirrors:

Under paraxial approximations, the mirror equation relates object distance x_o, image distance x_i with radius of curvature R or focal length f.

$$\frac{1}{x_i} + \frac{1}{x_o} = \frac{2}{R} = \frac{1}{f}$$

Paraxial rays make very small angles with the optical axis and lie close to the optical axis throughout their length. For these rays, spherical aberration is minimal, and a sharp image is obtained.

Refraction at spherical surfaces:

Under paraxial approximations, object distance x_o, image distance x_i, radius of curvature R and refractive indices μ_1 and μ_2 of the mediums containing the incident and the refracted ray respectively bear the following relation.

$$\frac{\mu_2}{x_i} - \frac{\mu_1}{x_o} = \frac{\mu_2 - \mu_1}{R}$$

Lens:

A transparent medium bounded by two refracting surfaces of which at least one must be spherical.

Thin and thick lens:

In thin lenses, the distance between the two refracting surfaces is negligible in comparison to their radii of curvatures; and in thick lenses, this distance is not negligible.

Lens maker's formula:

Under paraxial approximations, focal length of a thin lens is given by the following equation.

$$\frac{1}{f} = \left(\frac{\mu_l}{\mu_s} - 1\right)\left(\frac{1}{R_1} - \frac{1}{R_2}\right)$$

Here R_1 and R_2 are radii of curvatures of the refracting surfaces of the lens, μ_l is refractive index of material of the lens and μ_s is refractive index of the surrounding medium.

Thin lens equation:

Under paraxial approximations, the thin lens equation relates object distance x_o and image distance x_i with focal length f.

$$\frac{1}{x_i} - \frac{1}{x_o} = \frac{1}{f}$$

Transverse magnification:

It is the ratio of the height y_i of the image to the height y_o of the object.

Spherical Mirrors: $\quad m = \dfrac{y_i}{y_o} = -\dfrac{x_i}{x_o}$

Spherical Refracting Surface: $\quad m = \dfrac{y_i}{y_o} = \dfrac{x_i - R}{x_o - R} = \dfrac{\mu_1 x_i}{\mu_2 x_o}$

Thin Lens: $$m = \frac{y_i}{y_o} = \frac{x_i}{x_o}$$

Wave Optics:

In wave optics, light is treated as transverse electromagnetic wave.

Wave optics deals with phenomenon like interference, diffraction, polarization etc.

Huygens's principle:

Each point on a propagating wavefront serves as a source of spherical secondary wavelets. An envelope of all these wavelets is the wavefront at some later instant of time.

Fresnel and Kirchhoff later modified the Huygens's principle by discarding physical existence of backward moving wavefronts.

Multiple Choice Questions

1. When the Sun is behind dark clouds and there are gaps in the clouds, you will often see sunlight "fanning" out from the gaps as shown in the given photograph.

   Though the rays are closely parallel, but we see them diverging as they approach the earth. Which of the following statements most suitably explains this effect?

   (a) Distant objects appear smaller than nearer objects.
   (b) Sunrays are actually radiated from the sun radially.
   (c) Light bends at sharp corners of an opaque object that it encounters.
   (d) The gaps work as light sources at finite distance hence radiate diverging light.

2. Bodies that can be impregnated with water, colours of their surface appear richer after moistening. Which of the following is the most appropriate reason for this effect?

   (a) Due to moistening, surface irregularities are covered with water film, which reduces diffused reflection of light.
   (b) Due to moistening, surface irregularities are covered with water film, which reduces the amount of reflected light.
   (c) Due to moistening, surface irregularities are covered with water film, which increases the amount of reflected light.

3. An arrow object is viewed through a bent metal tube with the help of four plane mirrors A, B, C and D as shown in the figure. Every mirror is inclined at an angle of 45° with the horizontal. Which of the following represents correct images made by these mirrors in sequence?

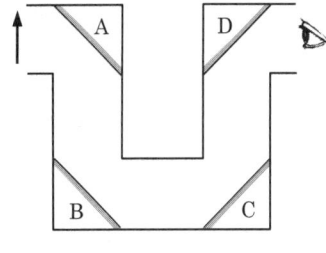

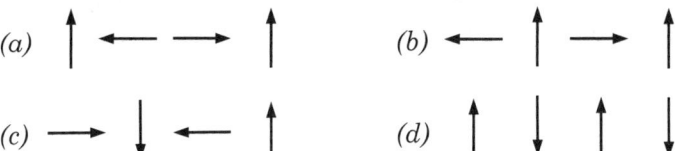

4. While fishing from a dock, you see a fish in the water. For this, you can use either a bow and arrow, or a laser gun. Which of the following strategy you must follow?
   (a) Aim the arrow as well as the laser gun at the fish.
   (b) Aim the arrow below the fish and the laser gun at the fish.
   (c) Aim the arrow below the fish and the laser gun above the fish.
   (d) Aim the arrow above the fish and the laser gun below the fish.

5. Light travelling through three transparent substances follows a path shown in the figure. Arrange their indices of refraction in order from smallest to largest.
   (a) $\mu_3 < \mu_1 < \mu_2$
   (b) $\mu_1 < \mu_3 < \mu_2$
   (c) Neither of the above is possible.
   (d) More information is required.

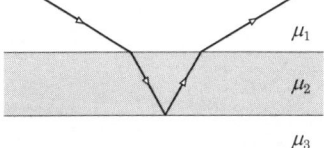

6. A lens held above a coin placed on a table forms an image of the coin. After the lens is moved vertically a distance equal to its focal length, it forms another image of the coin equal in size to the previous image. If diameter of the coin is 2.0 cm, what is the diameter of the image?
   (a) 3.0 cm.
   (b) 4.0 cm
   (c) 5.0 cm
   (d) 6.0 cm

7. A converging lens of focal length f is used to cast an image of an object as shown in the figure. The upper half of the lens is now covered by an opaque coating. Which of the following statements is most appropriate?

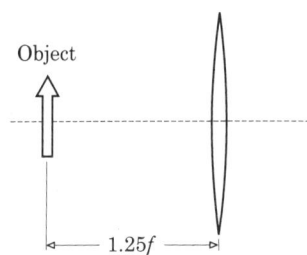

   (a) Upper half of the image is brighter than its lower half.
   (b) Lower half of the image is brighter than its upper half.
   (c) Entire portion of the image appears with uniformly reduced brightness.
   (d) Entire portion of the image appears with reduced brightness but to predict intensity distribution more information is required.

8. It is a common belief that reading in reasonably bright light is more comfortable than reading in dim light. Which of the following is the most appropriate reason for this effect?
   (a) Contraction of ciliary muscles reduces astigmatism.
   (b) Contraction of pupil in bright light reduces spherical aberration.
   (c) In bright light image formed on retina has more intensity than that in dim light.
   (d) This is purely a psychological effect; bright light merely stimulates some more visual neurons that are normally dormant.

9. Refractive indices of two varieties of glass A and B depend on wavelength λ of light according to the following equations.

$$\mu_A = \mu_{A0} - \beta_A(\lambda - \lambda_0) \text{ and } \mu_B = \mu_{B0} - \beta_B(\lambda - \lambda_0)$$

Here λ_0 is wavelength of yellow light. An achromatic combination of lenses is made from these materials. Radii of curvature of two outer surface of this combination are r_1 and r_2. Which of the following is a correct expression for radius of curvature of the common surface?

(a) $\dfrac{r_1 r_2 (\beta_A - \beta_B)}{r_2 \beta_A - r_1 \beta_B}$

(b) $\dfrac{r_1 r_2 (\beta_A - \beta_B)}{r_2 \beta_A + r_1 \beta_B}$

(c) $\dfrac{r_1 r_2 (\beta_A - \beta_B)}{r_2 \beta_A - r_1 \beta_B} + \dfrac{r_1 r_2 (\mu_{A0} - \mu_{B0})}{r_2 \mu_{A0} - r_1 \mu_{B0}}$

(d) $\dfrac{r_1 r_2 (\beta_A - \beta_B)}{r_2 \beta_A - r_1 \beta_B} - \dfrac{r_1 r_2 (\mu_{A0} - \mu_{B0})}{r_2 \mu_{A0} - r_1 \mu_{B0}}$

10. In the middle of a calm lake, a radio receiver is installed on a pole at a height 4.0 m above water level. The receiver is used to track radio signals from a satellite orbiting the earth. As the satellite rises above the horizon, intensity of the signals at the receiver varies periodically. It is maximum, when the satellite is 3° above the horizon and then again when the satellite is 6° above the horizon. Wavelength of the satellite signals is closest to

(a) 24 cm
(b) 36 cm
(c) 42 cm
(d) 48 cm

11. While travelling by train or by bus, if we look outside, we observe some effects. These effects and some facts possibly explaining these effects are given in the first and the second columns of the following table. Suggest suitable matches.

Column I	Column II
(a) Nearby objects appear moving past faster than distant objects.	(p) Human eye senses the direction from which light enters it.
(b) Extremely distant objects appear moving along with us.	(q) It cannot resolve two points if they subtend an angle less than one minute
	(r) Persistence of eye is 0.1 s.

Questions 12 to 14 are based on the following write-up.

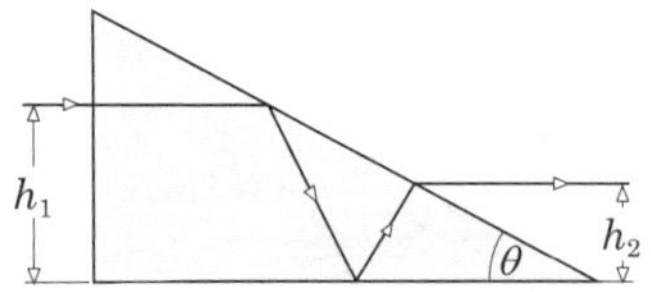

Consider the setup shown in the figure, which uses a right-angled prism to transmit a horizontal incident ray. This device is known as anamorphic de-magnifier. During its passage through the prism, the ray experiences total internal reflection (TIR) twice and then exits as shown in the figure. The prism is made from a glass of refractive index μ.

12. If the emerging ray propagates horizontally, which of the following is a correct expression for refractive index μ?

(a) $\mu = \dfrac{\sin\theta}{\sin 3\theta}$

(b) $\mu = \dfrac{\sin\theta}{\cos 3\theta}$

(c) $\mu = \dfrac{\cos\theta}{\sin 3\theta}$

(d) $\mu = \dfrac{\cos\theta}{\cos 3\theta}$

13. Range of values of tip angle θ for the device to work as anamorphic de-magnifier is

   (a) $\frac{1}{3}\cos^{-1}\left(\frac{1}{\mu}\right) < \theta < \frac{1}{2}\sin^{-1}\left(\frac{1}{\mu}\right)$ (b) $\frac{1}{3}\sin^{-1}\left(\frac{1}{\mu}\right) < \theta < \frac{1}{2}\cos^{-1}\left(\frac{1}{\mu}\right)$

   (c) $\frac{1}{3}\sin^{-1}\left(\frac{1}{\mu}\right) < \theta < \frac{1}{2}\sin^{-1}\left(\frac{1}{\mu}\right)$ (d) $\frac{1}{3}\cos^{-1}\left(\frac{1}{\mu}\right) < \theta < \frac{1}{2}\cos^{-1}\left(\frac{1}{\mu}\right)$

14. Ratio of height of the incoming ray from the base of the prism to that of the emerging ray is defined as the vertical de-magnification ratio. Which of the following is a correct expression for the vertical de-magnification ratio?

   (a) $\dfrac{\sin\theta}{\sin 3\theta}$ (b) $\dfrac{\cos\theta}{\cos 3\theta}$

   (c) $\dfrac{2\mu}{1+\mu}$ (d) $\dfrac{\mu}{1+2\mu}$

Questions 15 to 17 are based on the following write-up.

If Snell's law is found valid for two mediums, whose refractive indices have opposite signs, the incident and the refracted rays must remain on the same side of the normal at the point of incidence. In the figure is shown a ray crossing the interface between two mediums I and II. The ray makes angles θ_1 and θ_2 with normal in the medium-I and II. The refractive indices of the mediums μ_1 and μ_2 have opposite signs.

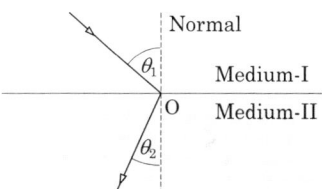

Snell's law is expressed for the above situation as usual by the equation $\mu_1 \sin\theta_1 = \mu_2 \sin\theta_2$. Therefore, to satisfy this equation, the angles θ_1 and θ_2 must also have opposite signs.

15. A self-luminous point object placed at a distance x_o from a slab of transparent material of negative refractive index is viewed through the slab as shown in the figure. Thickness of the slab is d, refractive index of material of the slab with respect to the outside medium is $\mu = -1$.

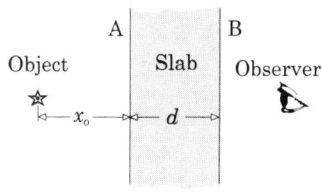

   For different moduli of values of x_o and d the observer may find real or virtual image of the object. Which of the following statements is true?
   (a) If $x_o > d$, image is virtual and for $x_o < d$ image is real.
   (b) If $x_o < d$, image is virtual and for $x_o > d$ image is real.
   (c) If $x_o \leq d$, image is virtual and for $x_o > d$ image is real.
   (d) If $x_o > d$, image is virtual and for $x_o \leq d$ image is real.

16. Suppose a virtual object instead of a real object is at a distance x_o from the surface A of the slab. Now which of the following statements is true?
   (a) For the cases $x_o < d$ and $x_o > d$ a real and erect image is formed outside the slab.
   (b) For the cases $x_o < d$ and $x_o > d$ a real and inverted image is formed outside the slab.
   (c) If $x_o < d$ a real image is formed outside the slab and for $x_o > d$ a virtual image is formed inside the slab.
   (d) If $x_o < d$ a real image is formed and for $x_o > d$ a virtual image is formed and in both the cases the image is outside the slab.

17. Distances x_o and x_i of the object and the final image respectively are measured from the face A of the slab. The Cartesian sign conventions are also followed. Which one of the following graphs correctly represents relationship between x_o as abscissa and x_i as ordinate?

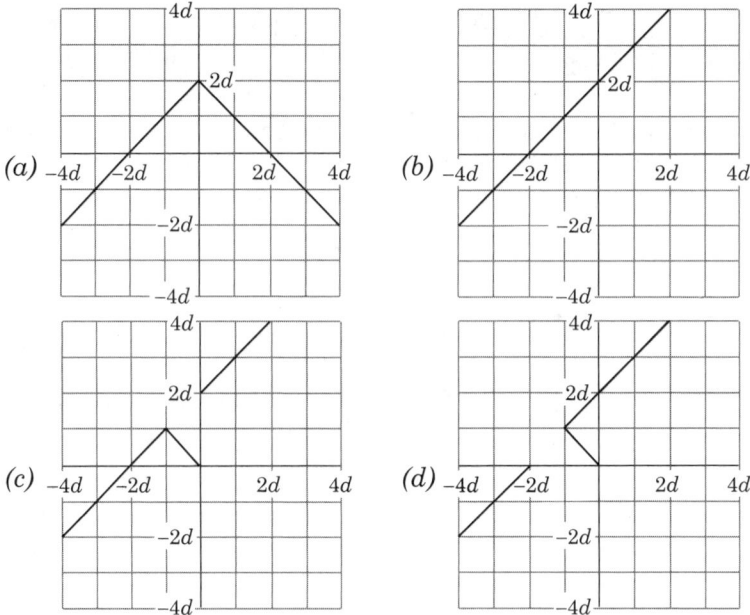

Build up your understanding

1. A pin hole-camera of adjustable length (hole to screen distance) is placed 10 m away from a pole casts image of the pole. If it is shifted 1.0 m farther, find percentage change in its length required to keep the size of image unchanged.

2. A globe of radius $r = 10$ cm is placed on a circular plane mirror touching centre of the mirror with its south pole. Find the minimum radius of the mirror so that image of the latitude $\theta = 37°$ N be visible in the mirror.

3. A large plane mirror with its bottom on the floor is tilted at an angle θ to the vertical (see figure). A boy whose eyes are at a height h above the floor is standing in front of the mirror. At what maximum distance from the mirror should the boy be to see his full image in the mirror?

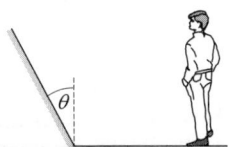

4. One night, a boy of height $h = 1.8$ m is standing on the bank of a straight canal, on the other bank of which a lamp is installed at a height $H = 5.4$ m on a pole. There are no ripples on the water surface so light emanated from the lamp, appears as a flare (bright spot) after reflection from the water surface. When the boy starts walking along the bank, the flare appears to him moving at a constant speed $u = 2.4$ m/s relative to the ground. Find speed of the boy.

5. One end of a cylindrical tube of length l and radius r is covered with an opaque disc having a small hole in the centre and a point light source S is placed at centre of the other end. Inner surface of tube is perfectly reflecting. A white screen is placed normal to the axis of the tube at a distance L from the end covered with the disc as shown in the figure. After the source is switched on, what kind of pattern of light distribution, will you obtain on the screen?

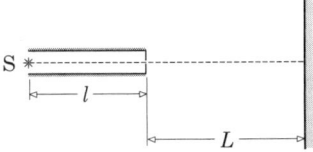

6. In free space, a particle is projected from a point P on axis of a fixed rigid cone AOB, at an angle $\alpha = 37°$ with the axis (see figure). Distance of point P from the apex O is $x = 10$ cm and the apex angle of the cone is $\beta = 20°$. All the collisions of the ball with the cone are perfectly elastic.

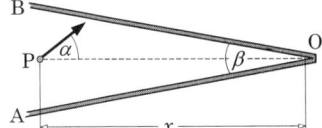

(a) Find the distance of closest approach of the ball from the apex.
(b) How many times will the ball collide with the cone?

7. Parallel beam of light incident normally on a wall illuminates a round spot of radius 4.0 cm on it. When a ball, surface of which is mirrored is placed with its centre on the axis of the beam and at a distance of 11 cm from the wall, a large part of the wall is illuminated, but at the centre a circular shadow of radius 52 cm is formed. Find radius of the ball.

8. If a cylindrical container filled with mercury is rotated with an angular velocity ω about its vertical axis of symmetry, the mercury-air interface takes shape of a paraboloid of revolution. If this surface is used as a mirror, where should a photo film be placed to get a clear picture of a distant star? Acceleration of free fall is g.

9. A wide homogeneous beam of light falls on a concave spherical mirror of radius R parallel to the optical axis. A small opaque disc of radius r ($r \ll R$) made of a perfectly heat insulating material is placed at a distance $R/4$ from the pole of the mirror perpendicular to the optical axis. In steady state, both the surfaces of the disc acquire different temperatures slightly higher than the surroundings. Find the ratio $\Delta T_1/\Delta T_2$, where ΔT_1 and ΔT_2 are the temperature differences of the left and the right surfaces of the disc and the surroundings.

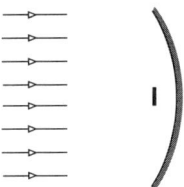

10. If energy reflection coefficient is the same whether light is reflected from glass back into air or from air back into glass and has a value $r = 0.25$. If a narrow beam of light falls obliquely on a large thin glass plate, what fraction of the light energy will be transmitted through the plate?

11. A research submarine has a circular glass window in its bottom to observe the seabed. Radius of the window is $r = 30$ cm, thickness of the glass is $t = 20$ mm, refractive index of water is $\mu_w = 1.25$ and that of the glass is $\mu_g = 1.5$. If the seabed is $d = 6.0$ m beneath the window, estimate radius of portion of the seabed visible through the window.

12. A homogeneous glass cone of half angle 30° is placed inverted on a disc so that its axis is vertical. Radius of the disc is 4.0 cm and the tip of the cone coincides with the centre of the disc. What is the radius of the disc visible through the circular base of the cone from a large height? Refractive index of the glass of the cone is 1.5.

11.10 Chapter-11

13. Refractive index of air depends on temperature and pressure. Within few metres of height difference near the ground, air pressure remains almost uniform but air temperature changes by appreciable amount. Suppose under such conditions, the refractive index μ depends only on the temperature, and this dependence has the form

$$\mu = 1 + \frac{a}{T}$$

Here a is a constant, value of which at normal pressure is 1/6 K.

The sun heats up the air above a road and simultaneous random small movements of air make the dry asphalt appear like a puddle. This phenomenon is called mirage. Suppose that in a thin layer immediately above the road, temperature of air is $\Delta T = 20$ K more than temperature $T_0 = 300$ K of the air elsewhere. From what minimum horizontal distance x an observer of height $h = 1.75$ m can see a puddle on the road. Also plot a rough graph for relation $x(\Delta T)$.

14. A steel wire is coaxially embedded in a glass tube, external diameter of which is much greater than that of the wire. Refractive index of the glass is 4/3. If diameter of the steel wire appears 8/3 mm when looked into the glass tube through its curved surface, find the actual diameter of the steel wire?

15. An isotropic point light source is placed inside a homogeneous sphere of radius R at a distance r from the centre. What should the value of refractive index of the material of the sphere be so that all the light emitted by the source comes out of the sphere?

16. A spider is hanging above the north pole of a transparent globe of diameter d at a distance $d/\sqrt{3}$ from the centre of the globe. Refractive index of the material of the globe is $\mu = 2$. Between which latitudes a fly can sit on the globe so that it cannot be seen by the spider. Treat the spider and the fly both as point objects.

17. A capillary of outer radius r_o made of a glass of refractive index μ is filled with a liquid of refractive index μ_1 ($\mu_1 < \mu$). What should the minimum internal radius of the capillary be so that all the light incident on the capillary enter the liquid?

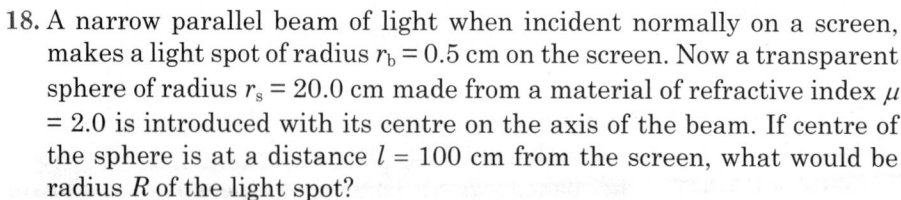

18. A narrow parallel beam of light when incident normally on a screen, makes a light spot of radius $r_b = 0.5$ cm on the screen. Now a transparent sphere of radius $r_s = 20.0$ cm made from a material of refractive index $\mu = 2.0$ is introduced with its centre on the axis of the beam. If centre of the sphere is at a distance $l = 100$ cm from the screen, what would be radius R of the light spot?

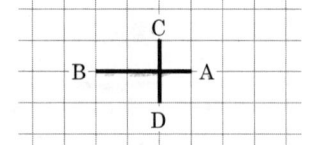

19. Two thin rods AB and CD welded on each other make a frame that is shown on a graph paper. This frame is placed in front of a converging lens of focal length 10 cm with the arm AB coinciding with the optical axis of the lens. By shifting the frame on the optical axis, if an image of exactly the same size as that of the frame can be obtained, find length of the rod AB.

20. A high-speed movie camera is being used to shoot an oscillating simple pendulum at a speed $n = 24$ frames per second and takes $N = 48$ frames to shoot one complete oscillation. Focal length of the lens of the camera is $f = 50$ mm and length of the pendulum in the image on the film is $l = 10$ mm. Find distance of the pendulum from the camera lens. You may use $\pi^2 = g$.

21. In the arrangement shown, S_1 and S_2 are two point-light sources placed on the optical axis PA of a lens L of unknown nature and I_1 is the image of the source S_1. Distances S_2I_1, I_1S_1 and S_1O are equal. Draw a ray diagram to obtain image of the source S_2 and with the help of this diagram determine location of the image.

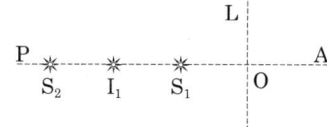

22. In a setup of displacement method experiment, distance between the screen and a light source is 120 cm and the lens used has a small aperture. By moving the lens between the source and the screen, sharp images are obtained on the screen for two different positions of the lens. The ratio of sizes of these two images is 1:9.
   (a) What is the focal length of the lens?
   (b) Which image is the brighter one? Determine the ratio of the brightness of these two images.

23. A thin glass lens is fixed in the wall of an aquarium filled with water. A real inverted image of an object that is in the air at a distance a from the lens is obtained in the aquarium at a distance b. Where will the image of an object be formed, if the object is located in the aquarium at a distance a_1 ($a_1 > b$) from the lens? Refractive index of water with respect to air is n.

24. A point light source S moves on a circular path, centre of which is on one of the foci F of a thin converging lens of focal length f. Radius of the circular path is $r = f/2$ and its plane is perpendicular to the plane of the lens. In the coordinate system shown, find position coordinates of the image of source in terms of the focal length f and the angular position θ of the source. Also, plot the locus of the image.

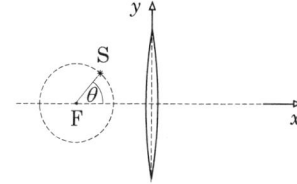

25. A thin converging lens of focal length f makes image of a moving point source of light. When the source is crossing the optical axis of the lens, its velocity vector makes an angle α with the optical axis and velocity vector of the image makes an angle β with the optical axis. At what distance from the lens, does the source cross the optical axis?

26. A converging lens of focal length f is placed in front of and parallel to a plane mirror. An object is placed on the optical axis of the lens on the segment not included between the lens and the mirror. What should be the distance between the lens and the mirror so that final magnification is independent of the distance of the object from the lens?

27. Two converging lenses of focal lengths f_1 and f_2 are placed with their optical axes coinciding. This lens system is used to form image of an object. If it is found that size of the image does not depend on distance between the first lens and the object, find the distance between the lenses.

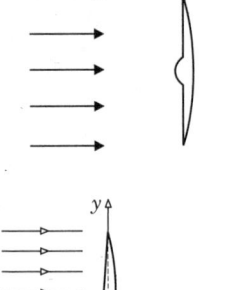

28. A composite lens is placed coaxially in the path of a cylindrical light beam of diameter 5 cm as shown in the figure. The composite lens is made by gluing two plano-convex lenses. Diameters of the first and second lens are 1.0 cm and 5.0 cm and their focal lengths are 10 cm and 20 cm respectively. Where to the right of the lens a screen should be placed to obtain a light spot of smallest diameter on it?

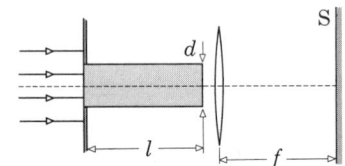

29. Due to manufacturing defect, plane surface of a thin plano-convex lens has been made tilted at a small angle α outwards from its usual place. The spherical surface has radius R and refractive index of the glass used is μ. A parallel beam of light is incident as shown in the figure. Will this defective lens focus the beam and if so, find coordinates of the focus?

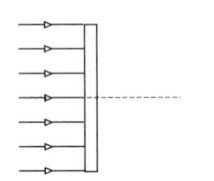

30. A transparent rectangular slab of length $l = 20$ cm and thickness $d = 4.0$ cm is placed in front of a converging lens of focal length $f = 20$ cm. A screen S is placed in the focal plane of the lens. Refractive index of the material of the slab increases linearly from $\mu_0 = 1.5$ at the bottom face by an amount $\delta\mu = 2.0 \times 10^{-4}$ between the bottom and the top faces. A parallel beam is made to incident on the slab as shown in the figure. What kind of light pattern appears on the screen?

31. Refractive index of a material can be adjusted by diffusing impurities; moreover, by adjusting concentration distribution of diffused impurities, a specimen of any desired gradient of refractive index can be obtained. Consider a thin disc of uniform thickness d made of a transparent material, refractive index of which is made to vary with distance r from its centre by suitable diffusion of impurities. If a parallel beam of light incident normally on the disc, converges at a distance f ($f \gg r$) after passing through the disc, find suitable expression for radial variation of its refractive index μ. Assume refractive index at the centre of the disc to be μ_0.

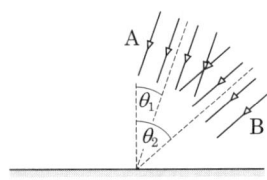

32. Two identical beams A and B of plane coherent waves of the same intensity and wavelength λ fall on a plane screen. The directions of the beam propagations make angles θ_1 and θ_2 with the normal to the screen and lie in the same plane as shown in the figure. Find distance between adjacent interference fringes on the screen.

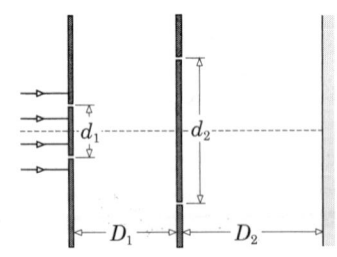

33. In front of a screen, two opaque cardboards are placed parallel to the screen. Distance between the cardboards is D_1 and distance between the middle cardboard and the screen is D_2. Two narrow parallel slits equidistant from the line of symmetry of the setup are cut on each of the cardboard. Distances between the slits in the first and the second cardboards are d_1 and d_2 as shown in the figure. A plane monochromatic light wave of wavelength λ is incident normally on the first set of slits.

Denoting intensity of central maxima on the screen by I_0, find intensity distribution of light on the screen as a function of the coordinate y that is distance from the line of symmetry of the setup to a point on the screen at which intensity is sought.

34. A liquid of refractive index μ is poured on a large horizontal clear glass plate to make a thin layer of it. When a broad light beam is projected on the liquid layer at an angle θ with the vertical, an interference pattern is obtained. Due to evaporation, thickness of the liquid layer decreases making changes in the interference pattern. If in a time interval Δt, intensity of reflected light at a point, decreases from a maxima to a minima and then increases to a maxima, find suitable expression for the time rate at which thickness of the liquid layer decreases.

Check your understanding

1. A three-blade fan, rotating at frequency $n_0 = 20$ Hz is illuminated by a flashing light of a stroboscope. The flash rate, i.e. the number of flashes per second, is an integer from 2 to 200. Assume persistence of human vision to be 1/16 s. Find flash rates for the following conditions.
   (a) The fan appears stationary having three blades.
   (b) The fan appears stationary having six blades.
   (c) The fan appears rotating in the opposite direction with a frequency $n = 4$ Hz.

2. One night, a boy of height h is walking at a constant speed v_0 along the edge of a straight horizontal sidewalk moves past a lamppost. The lamppost is at a distance l, from the edge of the sidewalk and the lamp installed on it is at a height H above the ground. As the boy walks, the position and size of his shadow on the ground continuously change.
   (a) Find the velocity vector of the shadow of his head.
   (b) Find time rate of change in length of his shadow as a function of position (x, y) of the boy.

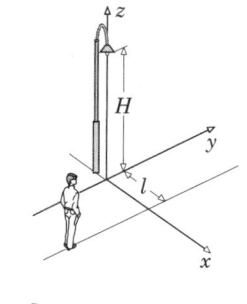

3. A glass plate has a cross-section in the shape of an isosceles trapezium. The top and the bottom slant faces make very small angle $\beta \ll 1°$ from each other. These surfaces are made reflecting from inside. The refractive index of the glass is μ. Find range of values of angle of incidence α at the central plane so that an incident ray of light will pass through the plate.

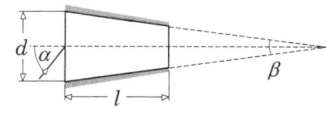

4. A silvered ball of radius $r = 5.0$ cm is so suspended that its centre is $h = 1.0$ m above the floor and $s_0 = 2.0$ m horizontally away from a person of height $h_0 = 2.0$ m. There is also a large plane mirror, which stands vertically at some distance from the person. If the person sees his image in the ball as small as he sees his image in the plane mirror, how far is the plane mirror from the person?

5. Signals in the form of light pulses are fed at one end of an optical fibre of circular cross-section of radius r. All the rays from the source lie within a cone of half angle θ measured from the axis of the optical fibre. The refractive index of the material of the fibre is μ. A light pulse lasts for a duration τ and two pulses are separated by a time interval Δt from each other. What can be the maximum length of the fibre so that the output pulses are still distinguishable?

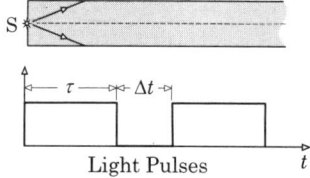

Light Pulses

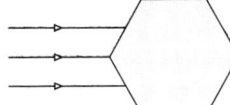

6. A monochromatic light beam is incident on a glass prism, cross section of which is a regular hexagon. The width of the beam is so adjusted that it falls up to middle of two adjacent sides of the prism as shown. For what refractive index of glass, two separate parallel beams emerge out.

7. A transparent cylinder of radius R and height H made from a material of refractive index $\mu = 1.5$ is placed on a horizontal tabletop and a point light source is placed at a height h above the centre of top circular face of the cylinder. Find the unilluminated area on the tabletop outside the cylinder.

8. Refractive index μ of atmosphere around a planet varies with altitude h according to equation $\mu = \mu_0 - kh$. Here μ_0 and k are positive constants. Denoting radius of the planet by R, find the altitude at which a point flash of light spreads around the planet in a spherical layer concentric with the planet in addition to other directions.

9. Two point-sources of light a distance 24 cm apart are placed near a converging lens in the plane containing the optical axis of the lens and a diameter of the lens. In the given figure locations of the sources and their images are shown by four dots. Three dots are on vertices of an equilateral triangle and the fourth dot is on the centroid of this triangle. Find the focal length of the lens.

10. Two converging lenses of focal lengths $f_1 = 20$ cm and $f_2 = 10$ cm are placed with their optical axes coinciding. A rectangle of sides $a_1 = 1$ mm and $b_1 = 2$ mm is placed in front of the first lens with its side a_1 on the common optical axis of the lenses. If the image formed by this system of lenses is real and also a rectangle, find distance l between the lenses and sides a_2 and b_2 of the image.

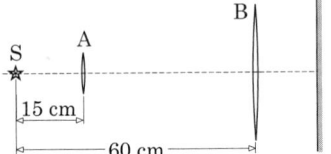

11. Lenses A and B of focal lengths 7.5 cm and 20 cm respectively are placed at distances 15 cm and 60 cm from a point source of light S. The source is on the common principal axis of the lenses. Aperture radii of the lenses are 2.0 cm and 10 cm respectively. If a screen is placed behind the lens B, a circular light spot will be obtained on it. At what distance from lens B should the screen be placed so that the light spot on it has minimum radius? Also, find the radius of this spot.

12. A point light source is located at a distance L from a screen. A thin converging lens of focal length $f > L/4$ and aperture radius R, held parallel to the screen makes a circular spot of light on the screen. If lens is moved from the source towards the screen, the size of the spot varies. Find the radius of the smallest light spot, which can be obtained in this way on the screen.

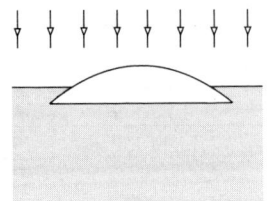

13. A thin plano-convex lens is partially immersed in water with its curved side up. Thickness of the lens in the middle is H. Aperture of the lens is horizontal as shown in the figure. Refractive index of water is μ_0. If there is no reflection at any surface and no absorption in any medium, we obtain two equally bright images at depths d and D ($D > d$). Find expressions for radius of curvature of the curved surface, refractive index μ of material of lens and depth h of the lens immersed in water.

14. A person wearing glasses sees two images of a flower that is 5.0 m behind him. One of these images appears 5.0 m in front of him and the other 0.714 m in front of him. When he turns around and looks directly at the flower, still wearing the glasses, the flower appears 2.5 m in front of him. Find refractive index of material of the glasses.

15. Two broad monochromatic beams A and B of plane coherent waves of the same intensity and wavelength λ propagating at angle θ from each other, simultaneously illuminate a cylindrical screen. Directions of propagation of both the beams are perpendicular to the axis of the screen. Consider a point P on the screen at angular position ϕ from the direction of propagation of the beam A as shown in the figure. Find distance between adjacent interference fringes on the screen near the point P. Assume that the distance between adjacent fringes is much less than the radius of the cylinder.

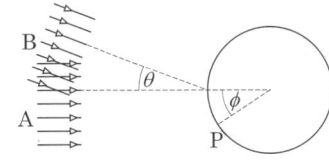

16. Spherical waves emanated from an isotropic point source of light located at a distance l from a plane screen and a broad parallel beam of light emanated from an extended source simultaneously illuminate the screen. The parallel beam falls on the screen at normal incidence. Both the sources are coherent, emit monochromatic light of wavelength λ and the point source is in phase with a wavefront of parallel beam at its location.

    (a) What kind of interference pattern is obtained on the screen?
    (b) Find expression for the spacing between the nth and the $(n-1)^{th}$ bright fringe.

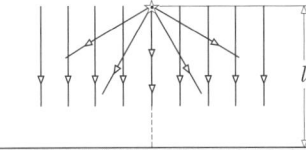

17. Two incoherent line sources S_1 and S_2 each emitting monochromatic light of wavelength λ are placed symmetrically in front of an opaque screen A containing two symmetrically positioned slits. In front of screen A another white screen B is placed as shown schematically in the figure. Distance between the sources is l and that between the slits is d. Distance between the sources and the screen A as well as that between screens A and B is D. The distance D is much larger than the distances l and d. For what values of the distance l between the sources, no stationary interference pattern will be observed on the screen B?

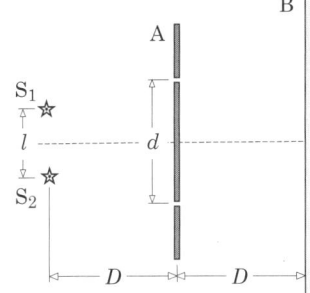

Challenge your understanding

1. A cylindrical rod made of some unknown glass is placed on a ruled white paper of a common exercise book. If the axis of the rod makes an angle θ with the ruled lines, the lines will appear broken and tilted at some angle α as shown in the figure.

    (a) Explain this appearance of the ruled lines shown.
    (b) Find refractive index of the glass, assuming the rod not to be thick and lines are being observed from a height vertically above the rod.

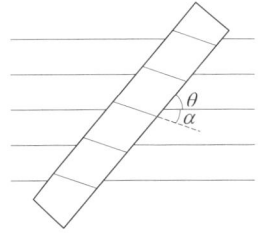

11.16 Chapter-11

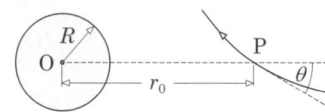

2. A laser beam propagates through a spherically symmetric medium surrounding a metal sphere of radius $R = 10$ cm. Refractive index of the medium varies with distance r from centre O of the sphere according to the law $\mu(r) \propto r$. Here $R \ll r < \infty$.

The laser beam makes angle of $\theta = 30°$ with a radial line at point P, which is $r_0 = 50\sqrt{2}$ cm away from O. What minimum distance from surface of the sphere can the beam reach?

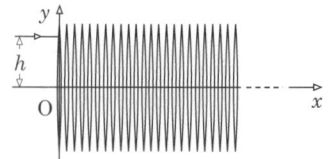

3. A large number of thin converging lenses each of focal length f are placed at equal distances l from each other so that their optical axes coincide. The distance l is negligibly small as compared to the focal length f. An incident light ray is made parallel to the common optical axis on the first lens at a distance h from the optical axis as shown in the figure. Deduce a suitable equation of the path, the ray will trace during its passage through the stack of the lenses.

Answers and Hints

Multiple Choice Questions

1. (a)
2. (a)
3. (b)
4. (b)
5. (a)
6. (b)
7. (a)
8. (b)
9. (a)
10. (c)
11. (a) → (p)
    (b) → (p) and (q)
12. (d)
13. (d)
14. (a) and (d)
15. (d)
16. (a)
17. (b)

Build up your understanding

1. 10% increase

2. $r\{\cos\theta + (1+\sin\theta)\tan\theta\} \approx 20$ cm

3. $h\cot(2\theta)$

4. $\dfrac{(h+H)u}{H} = 3.2$ m/s

5. A central bright spot surrounded by concentric bands of radii

   $2n\dfrac{rL}{l}$ Where $n = 1, 2, 3...$

6. (a) $x \sin\alpha = 6.0$ cm

   (b) Number of collisions =

   Integer part of $\dfrac{360° - 2\alpha + \beta}{2\beta} = 7$

   Hint: Perfectly elastic collision of a particle with a fixed plane is analogous to reflection of a light ray, thus the ball follows a zigzag path inside the cone. Therefore, if the cone is considered to flip each time to account for a collision, the path of the ball will appear a straight line as shown in the figure. The perpendicular distance OQ of this straight line from O is the distance of closest approach of the ball from the apex of the cone.

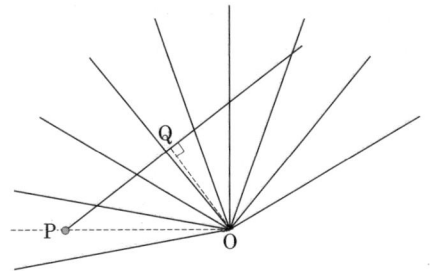

7. 5.0 cm

8. $\dfrac{g}{2\omega^2}$ above the lowest point of the mercury surface

9. $\dfrac{\Delta T_1}{\Delta T_2} = \dfrac{1}{3}$

10. $\dfrac{1-r}{1+r} = 0.6$

11. $\approx r + \dfrac{d}{\sqrt{\mu_w^2 - 1}} = 8.3$ m

12. 2.0 cm

13. $x \approx h\sqrt{\dfrac{T_0(T_0 + \Delta T)}{2a\Delta T}} = 210$ m

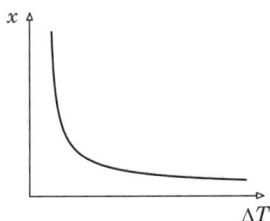

14. 2 mm

15. $\mu \leq \dfrac{R}{r}$

16. Between 60° N and 60° S

17. $\dfrac{r_o}{\mu_1}$

18. $\approx (l - r_s)\dfrac{r_b}{r_s} = 2.0$ cm

19. 15 cm

   Hint:

   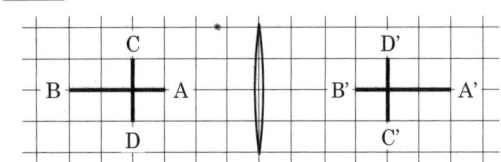

20. $\approx \dfrac{fgN^2}{4\pi^2 n^2 l} = 5$ m

21. $OI_2 = 2OS_2 = 6OS_1$

   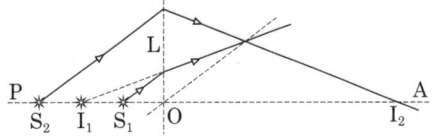

22. (a) 22.5 cm

   (b) The smaller image is 9 times brighter.

23. $\dfrac{aba_1}{a_1 b + na(a_1 - b)}$

24. $x = f\left(1 - \dfrac{2}{\cos\theta}\right)$ and $y = f\tan\theta$

   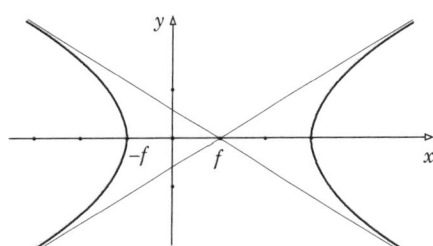

25. $f\left(1 \pm \dfrac{\tan\beta}{\tan\alpha}\right)$

   Here "+" and "–" signs correspond to real and virtual images.

26. f

27. $f_1 + f_2$

28. 15 cm

29. $\left(\dfrac{R}{\mu-1},\ -\alpha R\right)$

30. Image is a sharp light spot shifted up by an amount
$$\approx \dfrac{\delta\mu l f}{d} = 2.0\times 10^{-2}\,\text{cm}$$

   Hint: Speed of light in every layer that is parallel to the optical axis is smaller than that in a lower layer. Therefore, as the beam propagates in the slab, the wavefronts get tilted and this tilt increases as the beam proceeds.

31. $\mu \approx \mu_0 - \dfrac{r^2}{2df}$

   Hint: Refractive index inside the disc should vary with distance from the axis of symmetry of the disc in such a way that wavefronts inside the disc take the desired curvature.

32. $\dfrac{\lambda}{\sin\theta_2 - \sin\theta_1}$

33. $I = I_0 \cos^2\left(\dfrac{2\pi}{\lambda}\dfrac{d_1 d_2}{4D_1}\right)\cos^2\left(\dfrac{2\pi}{\lambda}\dfrac{d_2 y}{2D_2}\right)$

34. $\dfrac{\lambda}{2\Delta t\sqrt{\mu^2 - \sin^2\theta}}$

Check your understanding

1. (a) $\dfrac{3n_0}{k}$ Here $k = 1, 2, 3, 5, 6, 10, 15$ and 30

   (b) $\dfrac{6n_0}{2k+1}$ Here $k = 1$ and 2

   (c) $\dfrac{3(n_0+n)}{k}$ Here $k = 1, 2, 3, 4, 6, 8, 9, 12, 18$ and 36

2. (a) $\left(\dfrac{v_0 H}{H-h}\right)\hat{j}$ (b) $\dfrac{h}{H-h}\dfrac{yv_0}{\sqrt{l^2+y^2}}$

3. $0° \leq \alpha \leq \alpha_{max} \approx \sin^{-1}\left(1 - \dfrac{\beta l}{d}\right)$

   Hint: Consider the section of the plate repeated repeatedly as shown in the figure. This idea allows us to replace zigzag path of propagation of light due to multiple reflections by a straight path.

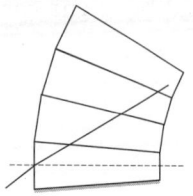

4. $\approx \dfrac{4s_0^2 + h_0^2}{4r} = 100\,\text{m}$

5. $L \leq \dfrac{c\Delta t}{\mu(\sec\theta - 1)}$

   Hint: Difference between time taken by the extreme ray and the axial ray in travelling the whole length of the fibre must be smaller than Δt.

6. $\mu > \dfrac{1+\sqrt{3}}{\sqrt{2}}$

7. $\dfrac{\pi R^2 H(H+2h)}{h^2}$

8. $h = \dfrac{1}{2}\left(\dfrac{\mu_0}{k} - R\right)$

9. 9 cm

10. $l = f_1 + f_2 = 30\,\text{cm}$,

   $a_2 = a_1\left(\dfrac{f_2}{f_1}\right)^2 = 0.25\,\text{mm}$ and

   $b_2 = b_1\left(\dfrac{f_2}{f_1}\right) = 1\,\text{mm}$

11. $35 \text{ cm}, \dfrac{5}{3} \text{ cm}$

12. $R\left(\dfrac{2\sqrt{fL} - L}{f}\right)$

13. $R = \dfrac{dD(\mu_o - 1)}{\mu_o(D-d)}$, $\mu = \dfrac{\mu_o D - d}{D - d}$ and $h = \dfrac{H}{2}$

14. 1.5

    Hint: Lenses of the glasses are plano-concave, having the flat surface inside i.e. towards the eyes and the concave surface outside.

15. $\dfrac{\lambda}{2\sin\left(\dfrac{\theta}{2}\right)\cos\left(\phi + \dfrac{\theta}{2}\right)}$

16. *(a)* The interference pattern consists of circular fringes with the central one a bright spot vertically below the point source.

    (b) $\approx \sqrt{2\lambda l}\left(\sqrt{n} - \sqrt{n-1}\right)$

17. $l = \dfrac{(2n+1)\lambda D}{2d}$

    Here n = 0, 1, 2 ....

Challenge your understanding

1. *(a)* The rod can magnify only those linear dimensions, which are perpendicular to its axis and cannot magnify linear dimensions, which are parallel to its axis. Therefore, a point say P on a ruled line will appear in its virtual image at point Q due to magnification of distance OP as shown in the figure.

   (b) $\dfrac{2\tan(\theta + \alpha)}{\tan\theta + \tan(\theta + \alpha)}$

2. $r_0\sqrt{\sin\theta} - R = 40$ cm

3. $y = h\cos\left(\dfrac{x}{\sqrt{lf}}\right)$

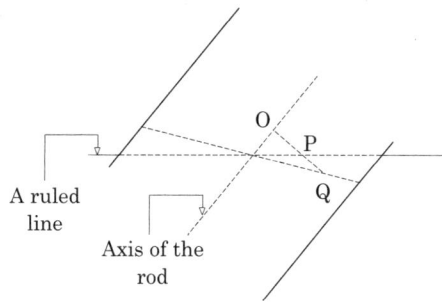

Chapter 12

Electrostatics

Electric charge, electrical properties of materials: conduction, induction and polarization, Coulomb's law, electric field, electric field lines, flux of electric field, Gauss' law and its applications, electrostatic potential and potential energy, electric dipole, electrostatics of capacitors with and without dielectrics; energy stored in electric field.

"A man may imagine things that are false, but he can only understand things that are true."

Sir Isaac Newton
(25 December 1642 – 20 March 1726)

BACK TO BASICS

Electric charge:

A property of matter that is responsible to produce electric and magnetic effects.

It creates a field known as electrostatic field or magnetic field in addition to electric field, depending upon whether it appears stationary or in uniform motion respectively relative to a reference frame. When a charge is in accelerated motion, it also radiates energy in the form of electromagnetic waves.

It is a scalar quantity and exists in two kinds that are called positive and negative charges. Like charges repel and unlike charges attract each other.

It is invariant to a reference frame, exists in quantized amounts and is additive in nature.

For an isolated system, total electric charge is conserved.

Conductors and insulators:

Conductors conduct electricity due to presence of free charge carriers whereas insulators do not conduct electricity.

Induction and polarization:

Induction:
In presence of external electric field, some of the free charges in a conductor appear on the surface. These surface charges are called induced charges, and the phenomenon is called induction. In this process, the net electric field (resultant of the applied electric field and electric field of induced charges) vanishes inside the conductor.

Polarization:
In presence of external electric field, atoms and molecules become individually polarized. This phenomenon is called polarization. In this process, uncompensated charges appear on the surface and the applied electric field is diminished inside the material by an amount equal to the electric field produced by the uncompensated surface charges.

$$\vec{E}_{net} = \vec{E}_{applied} + \vec{E}_{uncompensated\ surface\ charges}$$

Net electric field inside a linear isotropic dielectric is found equal to the ratio of applied electric field and relative permittivity or dielectric constant ε_r.

$$\vec{E}_{net} = \frac{\vec{E}_{applied}}{\varepsilon_r}$$

Coulomb's law:
It is an experimental law and states that the electrostatic force between two point-like charges q_1 and q_2 separated by a distance r is given by the equation

$$F = \frac{Kq_1 q_2}{r^2}$$

Here K is a constant of proportionality.

$$K = \frac{1}{4\pi\varepsilon_0} = 9 \times 10^9 \ \frac{N \cdot m^2}{C^2}$$

$\varepsilon_0 \equiv$ Permittivity of free space $= 8.85 \times 10^{-12} \ \dfrac{C^2}{N \cdot m^2}$ or $\dfrac{F}{m}$

Force of electrostatic interaction between two charges is independent of the medium between the charges.

Electric field:
It is a physical property that exists in surrounding region of a charge, due to which the charge establishes electric interactions with other charges.

A measure of electric field known as electric field intensity is the electrostatic force experienced by a unit test charge with an assumption that the unit test charge does not disturb the original electric field.

$$\vec{E} = \lim_{q \to 0} \frac{\vec{F}}{q}$$

Here $\vec{E}$ is the electric field intensity; and $\vec{F}$ is the force experienced by a test-charge q.

Superposition of electric fields:

Since the field at a point due to one charge is not affected by presence of other charges; therefore, net electric field at any point due to several point charges is the vector sum of individual contributions from all the charge.

$$\vec{E} = \sum_{i=1}^{n} \vec{E}_i$$

Flux of electric field:

Flux ϕ of electric field $\vec{E}$ through a surface S is defined by the following equation.

$$\phi = \int \vec{E} \cdot d\vec{S}$$

Gauss' law:

Net flux of electric field through a closed surface is equal to net charge enclosed by the surface divided by the permittivity of free space.

$$\oint \vec{E} \cdot d\vec{S} = \frac{q_{en}}{\varepsilon_0}$$

Gauss' Law is applicable to inverse square law fields only.

Electrostatic potential:

Like potential energy, electrostatic potential is defined as difference of potentials and equals to negative of work done by the electric field in moving a unit test charge.

$$dV = -\vec{E} \cdot d\vec{r}$$

For electrostatic field $\oint \vec{E} \cdot d\vec{r} = 0$

Electrostatic potential energy:

System of two point-charges:

The potential energy due the mutual electrostatic interaction between two particles of charges q_1 and q_2 at a distance r is given by the equation

$$U_r = \frac{Kq_1q_2}{r}$$

When separation between the particles is infinitely large, the potential energy is arbitrarily assumed zero ($U_\infty = 0$).

System of several point-charges:

Total electrostatic potential energy of a system of several point charges equals the sum of potential energies of all possible pairs of charges within the system.

System of continuous charge distribution:

Total electrostatic potential energy of a system of continuous charge distribution can be calculated by the following two methods.

Considering the system already made:

$$U = \frac{1}{2}\int V dq$$

Here V is potential due to all the charges of the system at the site of charge dq.

Considering the system in making:

$$U = \int V dq$$

Here V is potential at the site of charge dq due to all the charges assembled before the charge dq is brought.

Electric potential and associated field intensity:

Electric field intensity associated with an electric potential is equal to negative of gradient of the potential function.

$$\vec{E} = -\vec{\nabla}V = \begin{cases} -\left(\hat{i}\dfrac{\partial V}{\partial x} + \hat{j}\dfrac{\partial V}{\partial y} + \hat{k}\dfrac{\partial V}{\partial z}\right); & \text{Cartesian Coordinates} \\ -\left(\hat{e}_r\dfrac{\partial V}{\partial r} + \hat{e}_\theta\dfrac{\partial V}{r\partial \theta}\right); & \text{Polar coordinates} \end{cases}$$

Electric field energy density:

When in a region electric field is established, energy is stored in that region. This stored energy per unit volume is given by the equation

$$u = \frac{1}{2}\varepsilon E^2$$

Capacitor:

A device that stores energy by creating electric field. It consists of two conductors that may be of any shape and size. These conductors are usually called plates.

The magnitude of charge Q on either of the plates is proportional to the potential difference V between the plates. The constant of proportionality is known as capacitance C.

$$Q = CV$$

Capacitance of a structure depends upon the geometry of the structure and the permittivity of the medium where electric field is established.

Energy stored in a capacitor:

When a capacitor is charged, it stores energy in its electric field. The energy stored U is

$$U = \frac{Q^2}{2C} = \frac{1}{2}CV^2 = \frac{1}{2}QV$$

Multiple Choice Questions

1. When identical point charges are placed at the vertices of a cube of edge length a, each of them experiences a net force of magnitude F. Now these charges are placed on the vertices of another cube of edge length b. What will magnitude of the net force on any of the charges be? These cubes are simply geometrical constructs and not made of any matter.

   (a) $\dfrac{aF}{b}$
   (b) $\dfrac{bF}{a}$
   (c) $\dfrac{a^2 F}{b^2}$
   (d) $\dfrac{b^2 F}{a^2}$

2. Two charged spheres are kept at a finite centre-to-centre spacing as shown in the figure. The force of electrostatic interaction between them is first calculated assuming them point like charges at their respective centres and then force is measured experimentally. If the calculated and the measured values are F_c and F_m respectively, which of the following conclusion can you certainly draw?

   (a) If $F_c > F_m$ for like charges and $F_c < F_m$ for unlike charges, both the spheres must be made of insulating materials.
   (b) If $F_c > F_m$ for like charges and $F_c < F_m$ for unlike charges, both the spheres must be made of conducting materials.
   (c) Irrespective of their materials, $F_c < F_m$ for like charges and $F_c > F_m$ for unlike charges.
   (d) Irrespective of their materials, $F_c > F_m$ for like charges and $F_c < F_m$ for unlike charges.

3. A thin conducting ring is ruptured when it is given a charge q. Consider another thin conducting ring, radius of which is n times and tensile strength is k times of the former ring. How much maximum charge can this second ring be given without rupturing?

   (a) $< qnk$
   (b) $< qn\sqrt{k}$
   (c) $< qn^2 \sqrt{k}$
   (d) Insufficient information

4. Each of the following figures shows electric field vectors at two points A and B in an electric field. In which figure or figures can the illustrated field be created by a single point charge?

   (a)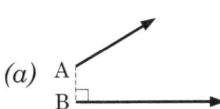
   (b)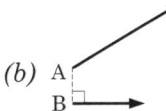

   (c)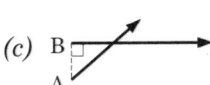
   (d)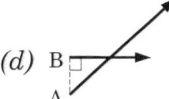

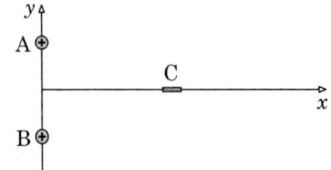

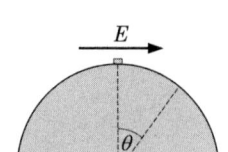

5. Two equal point-like positive charges A and B are fixed on the y-axis equidistant from the origin. What can you say for the net electrostatic force on a small electrically neutral rod placed on the x-axis as shown in the figure?
   (a) No force at all.
   (b) It points away from the origin.
   (c) It points towards the origin.
   (d) Information is insufficient.

6. A positively charged small disc is released on the top of fixed hemispherical frictionless dome in presence of a uniform horizontal electric field. If the disc leaves the dome after an angular displacement $\theta = \sin^{-1}(3/5)$, find ratio of gravitational and electrostatic forces on the disc. Assume that the dome does not exhibit any electrical property.
   (a) 4/3
   (b) 3/4
   (c) 9/2
   (d) 12

7. If a dipole of dipole moment $p\hat{i}$ is placed at point $(0, y)$ and a point charge at the origin of a coordinate system, net electric field at point $(x, x + y)$ vanishes. If both x and y are positive, the coordinate y is equal to
   (a) x
   (b) $2x$
   (c) $2.5x$
   (d) $3x$

8. Two infinitely large planes A and B intersect each other at right angles and carry uniform surface charge densities $+\sigma$ and $-\sigma$. Which of the following figures best represents electric field lines?

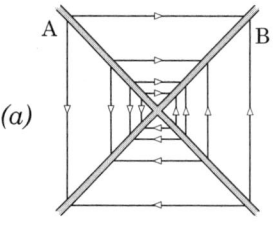
(a)

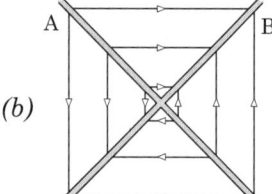
(b)

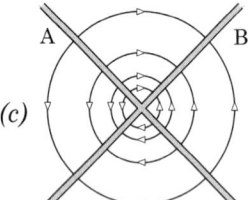
(c)

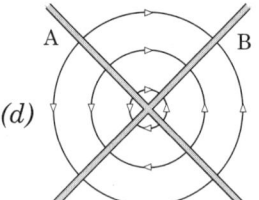
(d)

9. In the following figures, electric field lines of some electrostatic fields are shown. Which of them are incorrect representations?

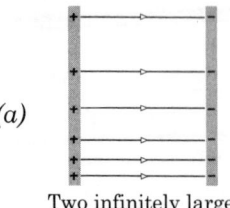
(a) Two infinitely large, charged layers

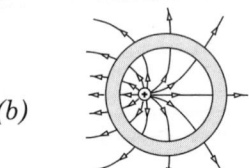
(b) Point charge in a neutral conducting shell

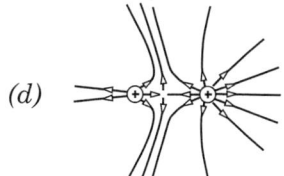

(c) Point charge in a neutral conducting shell

(d) Two unequal point charges

10. Electric field lines of a portion of an electric field that is symmetrical with respect to rotation about y-axis are shown in the figure. A charge particle stays in equilibrium at point (0, 10). If modulus of charge of the particle is changed gradually till it shifts to another equilibrium position (0, 0), estimate fractional change in the charge modulus.

(a) 1/3 (b) 2/3
(c) 1/9 (d) 8/9

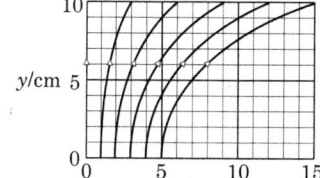

11. In the figure, a line of electric field created by two point-charges q_1 and q_2 is shown. If it is known that $q_1 = 1$ μC, the charge q_2 is closest to

(a) −2 μC (b) −4 μC
(c) −6 μC (d) −8 μC

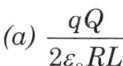

12. A conducting shell of radius R has charge Q. Electrostatic force between two parts of the shell which are on either sides of a plane that is at a distance r ($r < R$) from the centre of the shell is

(a) $\dfrac{Q^2}{32\pi\varepsilon_0 R^2}\left(1+\dfrac{r}{R}\right)$
(b) $\dfrac{Q^2}{32\pi\varepsilon_0 R^2}\left(1-\dfrac{r}{R}\right)$
(c) $\dfrac{Q^2}{32\pi\varepsilon_0 R^2}\left(1+\dfrac{r^2}{R^2}\right)$
(d) $\dfrac{Q^2}{32\pi\varepsilon_0 R^2}\left(1-\dfrac{r^2}{R^2}\right)$

13. A half cylinder of radius R and length $L \gg R$ is formed by cutting a cylindrical pipe made of an insulating material along a plane containing its axis. The rectangular base of the half cylinder is closed by a dielectric plate of length of length L and width $2R$. A charge Q on the half cylinder and a charge q on the dielectric plate are uniformly sprinkled. Electrostatic force between the plate and the half cylinder is closest to

(a) $\dfrac{qQ}{2\varepsilon_0 RL}$
(b) $\dfrac{qQ}{2\pi\varepsilon_0 RL}$
(c) $\dfrac{qQ}{4\varepsilon_0 RL}$
(d) $\dfrac{qQ}{8\varepsilon_0 RL}$

14. A conducting sphere of radius r_1 is surrounded by a dielectric layer of outer radius r_2 and dielectric constant ε_r. If the conducting sphere is given a charge q, determine surface density of polarization charges on the outer surface of the dielectric layer.

(a) $\dfrac{\varepsilon_r q}{4\pi r_2^2}$
(b) $\dfrac{q}{4\pi\varepsilon_r r_2^2}$
(c) $\dfrac{(\varepsilon_r-1)q}{4\pi r_2^2}$
(d) $\dfrac{(\varepsilon_r-1)q}{4\pi\varepsilon_r r_2^2}$

15. Due to a point charge, potential and electric field at a point A are 7 V and 3 V/m respectively and electric field at a point B is less than 3 V/m. Now magnitude of the charge is tripled. If electric field at B becomes 3 V/m, potential at B will become closest to

(a) 7 V
(b) 12 V
(c) 21 V
(d) Insufficient information

16. In another world, instead of the Coulomb's law, electric force $\vec{F}$ on a point like charge q due to another point like charge Q is found to obey the following law.

$$\vec{F} = \frac{Qq(1-\sqrt{\alpha r})}{4\pi\varepsilon_0 r^3}\vec{r}$$

Here α is a positive constant and $\vec{r}$ is the position vector of charge q relative to the charge Q.

(a) Electric field due to a point charge Q is $\vec{E} = \dfrac{Q(1-\sqrt{\alpha r})}{4\pi\varepsilon_0 r^3}\vec{r}$

(b) Line integral of this electric field $\oint \vec{E}\cdot d\vec{l}$ over a closed path is also zero as in our world.

(c) Gauss' law $\oint \vec{E}\cdot d\vec{s} = \dfrac{q_{enclosed}}{\varepsilon_0}$ also holds true for this electric field.

(d) All the above statements are true, but this electric field is not conservative.

17. A cube made of an insulating material has uniform charge distribution throughout its volume. Assuming electric potential due to this charged cube at infinitely distant places to be zero, potential at the centre is found to be V_0. What is electric potential at one of its corners?

(a) V_0
(b) $V_0/2$
(c) $V_0/4$
(d) $V_0/8$

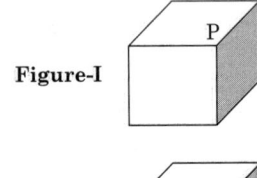

Figure-I

Figure-II

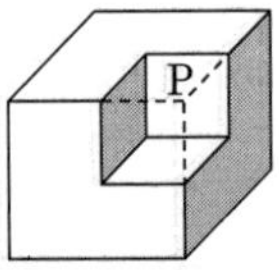

18. Consider a cube as shown in the figure-I, with uniformly distributed charge in its entire volume. Intensity of electrical field and potential at one of its vertex P are E_0 and V_0 respectively. A portion of half the size (half edge length) of the original cube is cut and removed as shown in the figure-II. Find modulus of electric field and potential at the point P in the new structure.

(a) $\dfrac{E_0}{2}$ and $\dfrac{3V_0}{4}$
(b) $\dfrac{3E_0}{4}$ and $\dfrac{V_0}{2}$
(c) $\dfrac{3E_0}{4}$ and $\dfrac{7V_0}{8}$
(d) $\dfrac{7E_0}{8}$ and $\dfrac{7V_0}{8}$

19. Electrostatic potential V has been measured everywhere outside a spherical body of radius R made of unknown material. It was found that the potential is spherically symmetric, i.e. depends only on the distance r from the centre of the sphere as given by the expression $V = A/r$, where A is a constant. No measurement of the potential inside the sphere has been done. What can you conclude for charge distribution of the body?

(a) It must be uniform.
(b) It may be nonuniform but must have spherical symmetry.
(c) It may be uniform or nonuniform without any spherical symmetry.
(d) To predict charge distribution precisely we need to know electric field outside the sphere.

20. Consider a thin conducting shell of radius r carrying total charge q. Two point-charges q and $2q$ are placed on points A and B, which are at distances $0.5r$ and $2r$ from the centre C of the shell, respectively. If the shell is earthed, how much charge will flow to the earth?

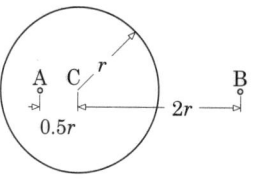

(a) $2q$ \qquad (b) $3q$
(c) $4q$ \qquad (d) More than $2q$ and less then $3q$

21. A straight chain consisting of n identical metal balls is at rest in a region of free space as shown. In the chain, each ball is connected with adjacent balls by identical conducting wires. Length l of a connecting wire is much larger than the radius r of a ball. A uniform electric field E pointing along the chain is switched on in the region. Find magnitude of induced charges on one of the end balls.

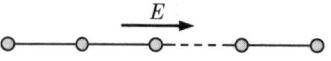

(a) $2\pi\varepsilon_0 rnlE$ \qquad (b) $2\pi\varepsilon_0 r(n-1)lE$
(c) $4\pi\varepsilon_0 r(n-1)lE$ \qquad (d) $4\pi\varepsilon_0 (n-1)^2 l^2 E$

22. Small identical balls are attached at each end of a spring of force constant $k = 200$ N/m and relaxed length $l = 20$ cm. Unknown amount of charges are gradually transferred to the balls in unequal amounts until the spring length becomes twice of its relaxed length. What amount of work must be done by an external agency in slowly compressing the spring back to its relaxed length?

(a) 8 J \qquad (b) 12 J
(c) 16 J \qquad (d) 20 J

23. Electrostatic potential V at a point on circumference of a circular layer of uniform charge and radius r is given by equation $V = 4\sigma r$, here σ is surface charge density in the layer. Which of the following expression correctly represents electrostatic energy stored in the electric field of a similar charge layer of radius R?

(a) $\frac{1}{3}\pi\sigma^2 R^3$ \qquad (b) $\frac{2}{3}\pi\sigma^2 R^3$
(c) $\frac{4}{3}\pi\sigma^2 R^3$ \qquad (d) $\frac{8}{3}\pi\sigma^2 R^3$

24. Three identical electric dipoles are arranged parallel to each other at equal separations as shown in the figure. The separation between the charges of a dipole is negligible as compared to the separation between the dipoles. In the given configuration, total electrostatic interaction energy of these dipoles is U_0. Now one of the end dipoles is gradually reversed, how much work is done by the electric forces?

(a) $\dfrac{17U_0}{18}$ \qquad (b) $-\dfrac{17U_0}{18}$
(c) $\dfrac{18U_0}{17}$ \qquad (d) $-\dfrac{18U_0}{17}$

12.10 Chapter-12

25. A parallel plate capacitor of capacitance C_0 is charged to a voltage V and then the battery is disconnected. A dielectric covering one-third area of each plate is now inserted as shown in the figure. If charges on the capacitor plates get redistributed such that the portions covered with dielectric and not covered with the dielectric share equal amounts of charge, which of the following statements is/are true?

   (a) Dielectric constant of the dielectric is 2.0.
   (b) Charge appearing due to polarization on the surface of the dielectric is $0.25C_0V$.
   (c) Force of electrostatic interaction between portions of the plates covered with dielectric is equal to that between uncovered portions.
   (d) Force of electrostatic interaction between the plates after insertion of the dielectric becomes 9/8 times of its value before insertion of the dielectric.

26. A flat air capacitor C consists of two large plates that are close to each other. Initially, one of the plates was not charged, while the other had charge Q. If entire space between the plates is filled with a slab of finite electrical resistance, estimate total amount of energy lost in the slab.

   (a) $\dfrac{Q^2}{2C}$ (b) $\dfrac{Q^2}{8C}$

   (c) $\dfrac{3Q^2}{8C}$ (d) $\dfrac{7Q^2}{8C}$

27. Two particles each of mass 100 g and charge 10 µC are released on a horizontal plane at a distance 1.0 m from each other. Coefficient of friction between the particles and the plane is 0.1 and acceleration of free fall is 10 m/s². Maximum speed acquired by the particles after they are released is closest to

   (a) 2.0 m/s   (b) 2.8 m/s
   (c) 3.0 m/s   (d) 4.2 m/s

28. Two identical point charges are moving in free space, when they are 60 cm apart; their velocity vectors are equal in moduli and make angles of 45° from the line joining them as shown in the figure. If at this instant, their total kinetic energy is equal to their potential energy, what will be the distance of closest approach between them?

   (a) 20 cm   (b) 30 cm
   (c) 40 cm   (d) 45 cm

29. A thin disk of radius R is held closing the opening of a thin hemispherical shell of the same radius. Both the bodies are made of insulating materials and have uniform charges of surface charge density σ each. The plate is released keeping the shell fixed. How much maximum kinetic energy will the plate acquire after it is released?

   (a) $\dfrac{\pi R^3 \sigma^2}{8\varepsilon_0}$ (b) $\dfrac{\pi R^3 \sigma^2}{4\varepsilon_0}$

   (c) $\dfrac{\pi R^3 \sigma^2}{2\varepsilon_0}$ (d) Insufficient information

Questions 30 to 32 are based on the following write-up.

Electrons (mass m and charge e) can be projected with a certain velocity from a point O between two parallel plate like electrodes separated by a distance d as shown in the figure. The bottom plate is connected to mid-point C of a rheostat, while the upper plate is connected to the rheostat through a sliding jockey J. The end terminals A and B of the rheostat are connected across an ideal battery of electromotive force V. When the jockey is held at C, electrons move along the x-axis that is parallel to the plates and hit a phosphorescent screen S in time T_0.

Distance d between the electrodes is large enough so that none of the electrons strikes the electrodes. Ignore magnetic effects and electromagnetic radiations.

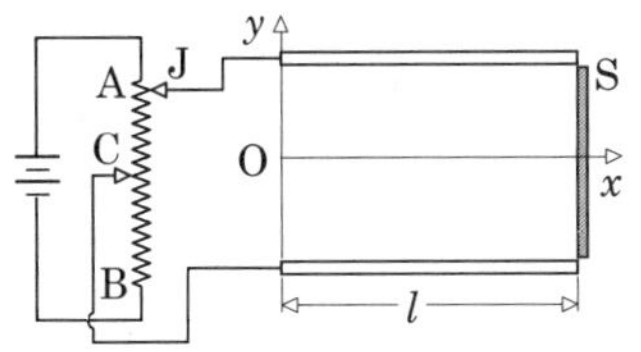

30. In a trial, the jockey J is held at A and an electron is projected. A time interval $0.5T_0$ after the electron is projected, the jockey is suddenly made to jump to the end B. Where on the screen does the electron make a spot?

    (a) On the x-axis.

    (b) $\dfrac{eVT_0^2}{8md}$ above the x-axis.

    (c) $\dfrac{eVT_0^2}{8md}$ below the x-axis.

    (d) None of these

31. In second trial, the jockey J is made to slide from C to A and then back to C with the same speed in a total time interval T_0. Where will the electron hit the screen?

    (a) On the x-axis with velocity $\vec{v} = \dfrac{l}{T_0}\hat{i}$.

    (b) On the x-axis with velocity $\vec{v} = \dfrac{l}{T_0}\hat{i} - \dfrac{eVT_0}{4md}\hat{j}$.

    (c) Above the x-axis with velocity $\vec{v} = \dfrac{l}{T_0}\hat{i} + \dfrac{eVT_0}{4md}\hat{j}$.

    (d) Below the x-axis with velocity $\vec{v} = \dfrac{l}{T_0}\hat{i} - \dfrac{eVT_0}{4md}\hat{j}$.

32. In third trial, the jockey is made to slide from A to B with a constant speed in the time interval T_0. Where will the electron hit the screen?

    (a) On the x-axis with velocity $\vec{v} = \dfrac{l}{T_0}\hat{i}$.

    (b) Above the x-axis with velocity $\vec{v} = \dfrac{l}{T_0}\hat{i}$.

    (c) Below the x-axis with velocity $\vec{v} = \dfrac{l}{T_0}\hat{i}$.

    (d) On the x-axis with velocity $\vec{v} = \dfrac{l}{T_0}\hat{i} + \dfrac{eVT_0}{2md}\hat{j}$.

Build up your understanding

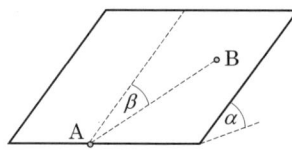

1. A charge particle A is fixed at the base of a uniform slope of inclination α. Another charge particle B is placed on the slope at an angular position β from the line of greatest slope through the position of the first particle. Coefficient of friction between the particle B and the slope is μ ($\mu < \tan\alpha$). For the particle at B to stay in equilibrium, what could be the maximum value of the angle β?

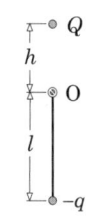

2. One end of an insulating rigid rod of negligible mass and length l is pivoted to a fixed-point O. A small ball of mass m having a negative charge of modulus q is attached to the lower end of the rod. Another small ball carrying a positive charge Q is fixed at a height h above the point O as shown in the figure. What should the range of values of mass m of the lower ball be so that the rod remains in a state of stable equilibrium? Acceleration due to gravity is g.

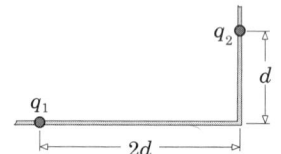

3. Two beads of equal mass m and unlike charges of modulus q_1 and q_2 can slide on a fixed frictionless non-conducting rod, bent at right angle. Initially, the beads are held at rest at distances d and $2d$ from the corner as shown and then released simultaneously. When one of the beads reaches the corner, where will the other bead be? Treat the beads as particles.

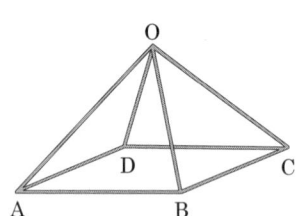

4. A rigid frame in the shape of a right pyramid is made of conducting rods. The base ABCD is a square and the apex O is vertically above the centre of the base. The frame is electrically neutral. When it is placed in a uniform electric field of intensity E pointing from the corner A towards the corner D, total charges induced on the rods DC and OC are known to be q_1 and q_2 respectively. Now the frame is rotated to make the electric field pointing from the corner A towards the corner C. What are the charges induced on each rod?

5. Three identical point charges are placed on the vertices of an equilateral triangle. At how many places within the triangle electric field vanishes.

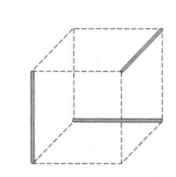

6. Three identical thin uniformly charged filaments are fixed along three sides of a cube as shown in the figure. Length of each filament is l and line charge density on each of them is λ. Determine electric field at the centre of the cube. The cube is a geometrical construct and not made of any matter.

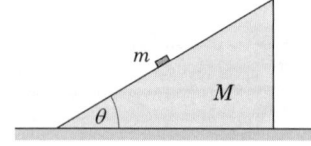

7. In presence of a uniform horizontal electric field E, a small non-conducting disc of mass m and charge q is released on a non-conducting triangular prism of mass M placed on a frictionless horizontal floor as shown in the figure. Slant face of the prism makes an angle θ with the horizontal and coefficient of friction between it and the disc is μ. If the disc accelerates up the slant face, find acceleration of the prism.

8. A particle of mass m and charge q projected with a speed u at an angle θ above the horizontal, after travelling a horizontal distance x_0, enters a region where in addition to gravity a uniform static horizontal electric field also exists. Boundary of this region is vertical. If after some time, the particle returns to the point of projection, find magnitude of the electric field and time of flight of the particle. Acceleration of free fall is g and influence of the air is to be neglected.

9. Two particles of charges and masses $(+q_1, m_1)$ and $(-q_2, m_2)$ are released at different locations in a uniform electric field E in free space. If their separation remains unchanged, find the separation between them.

10. A ring of radius R having a uniformly distributed charge Q is fixed in a horizontal plane. A bead of mass m and an unknown charge stays in equilibrium at such point on the vertical axis of the ring that if it is displaced slightly up or down, it undergoes oscillatory motion. Find charge on the bead. Intensity of gravitational field is g.

11. A thin rod of mass m carrying uniform negative charge $-q$ is placed symmetrically along the axis of a thin ring of radius R carrying uniformly distributed charge Q. The ring is held fixed in free space and length of the rod is $2R$. Find period of the small amplitude oscillations of the rod along the axis of the ring.

12. A thin rigid insulating ring of radius r and mass m has a very small gap of length l ($l \ll r$) and carries a uniformly distributed charge q. The ring is at rest in free space and a uniform electric field E in the plane of the ring and parallel to the gap is switched on as shown in the figure. Find the maximum angular speed of the ring in subsequent motion.

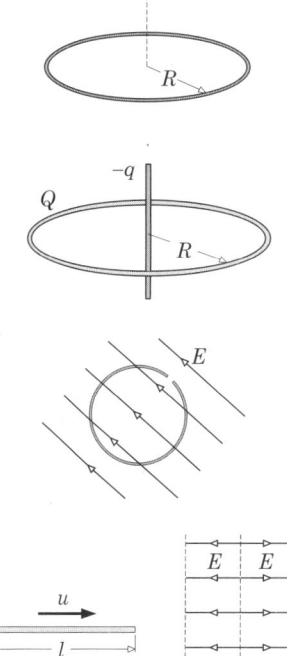

13. A thin dielectric rod of mass m and length l carrying a uniform positive charge q, moving with a velocity u enters a two-section region of electric field. Both the sections are of equal thickness d ($l > 2d$) each and have electric fields of the same magnitudes E that points opposite to the initial velocity of the rod in the first section and in the direction of the initial velocity of the rod in the second section. Assume charge distribution of the rod remains unaffected by the electric fields and ignore electromagnetic induction due to motion of the charged rod.
    (a) What should the minimum velocity u of the rod be so that it will completely pass through both the sections?
    (b) If the rod enters the first section with a velocity, which is double of that obtained in the previous part, with what speed will it emerge out of the second section?

14. A charge q is uniformly distributed on a thin rod of mass m and length l that stays at rest in free space. Two regions of uniform electric field of intensity E are created on both sides of the rod as shown in the figure. In the region of width L where the rod is initially placed, there is no electric field. Now the rod is projected along its length so that it cannot enter completely into any of the regions of electric field. Find period of oscillations of the rod as a function of the maximum distance x_m entered by a leading end of the rod into a region of electric field.

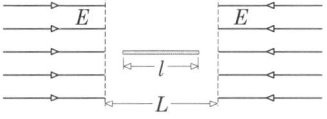

12.14 Chapter-12

15. In an external electric field, a molecule is polarized. The dipole moment thus induced is given by equation $\vec{p} = \alpha \vec{E}$, where α known as polarizability is a positive constant and $\vec{E}$ is the external electric field. Consider a molecule of polarizability α located at a distance r from a dipole of dipole moment p_0 on its axis. Find force of electrostatic interaction between the molecule and the dipole.

16. A particle of charge Q is placed on the axis of a neutral cylinder of volume V at a distance x from one end of the cylinder as shown in the figure. Here the distance x is much larger than the linear dimensions of the cylinder. Using suitable approximations, find force F of electrostatic interaction between the charge particle and the cylinder considering the cases - the cylinder is made of a conducting material, and the cylinder is made of an insulating material of relative permittivity ε_r.

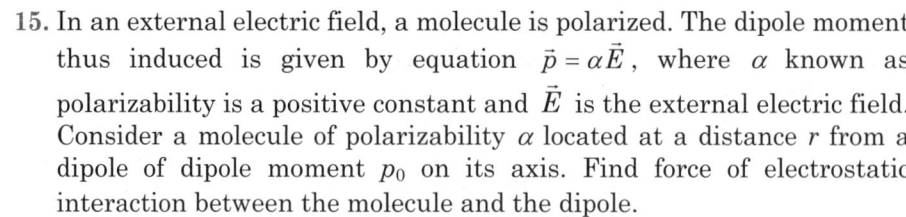

17. Find electric field everywhere on a plane containing the borders of two parallel half-planes extending in opposite directions. Distance between the half-planes is d and they have uniform surface charge density σ each. Angle between the plane and the half-planes is θ.

18. An insulating hollow cube of side l carries uniform charge on all of its surfaces. The surface charge density is σ. Determine the force acting on a face due to all the other faces.

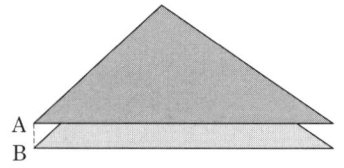

19. Two parallel equilateral triangular plates are placed overlapping each other very close to each other. The plates carry uniformly distributed unlike charges of equal moduli. Deep inside the region between the plates, electric field is uniform but near the edges, it becomes nonuniform. If modulus of electric field deep inside the plates is E_0, find modulus of electric field at the midpoint of line AB. What happens if the plates have the shape of a regular pentagon?

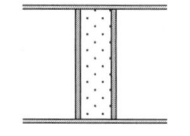

20. An ideal gas is trapped in a thin glass tube of cross section area A between two metallic pistons that can slide without friction. Initially the pistons stay in equilibrium a distance d apart that is small compared to their diameter. If the pistons are given unlike charges each of modulus q, what will the distance between them become? Electrical permittivity of the gas is ε and atmospheric pressure is p_0.

21. Two identical nonconducting triangular plates each of area A carrying uniform positive charges $+3q$ and $-2q$ are kept parallel to each other by inserting three identical insulating rods between their corners as shown in the figure. Distance between the plates is much smaller than their linear dimensions. Assuming the assembly to be isolated from other bodies, find compressive forces developed in the rods.

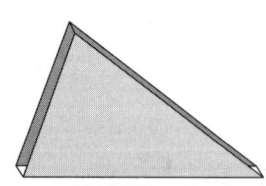

22. An infinitely large layer of charge of uniform thickness t is placed normal to an existing uniform electric field. Presence of this charge layer so alters the electric field that it remains uniform on both the sides and assumes values E_1 and E_2 as shown in the figure. Charge distribution in the layer is not uniform and depends only on distance from its faces. Find expression for the force per unit area experienced by the charge layer.

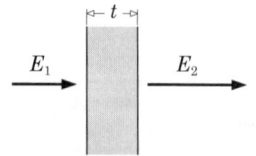

23. A small circular metal disc of mass m and radius r is glued on a heavy porcelain ball of radius R with a special type of glue that loses its strength very quickly. Before the glue loses its strength, a total charge Q is sprinkled uniformly on the surface of the assembly. The metal disc jumps off the ball, immediately after the glue loses its strength. Find acceleration of the metal disc at the time of separation. Neglect effects of gravity and assume area of the disc negligibly small as compared to the surface area of the ball.

24. Two point like charges $q_1 = 4.0$ nC and $q_2 = 1.0$ nC occupy fixed positions in free space. If at every point on a curve surrounding the charges as shown in the figure, net electrostatic potential V created by these charges is 900 V, what should the separation between the charges be?

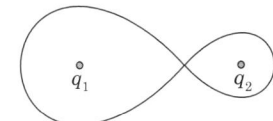

25. A right pyramid of square base and height H has uniform charge distributed everywhere within its volume. Modulus of electric field and potential at the apex P of the pyramid are E_0 and V_0. A symmetrical portion of height h from the apex has been removed. Find modulus of electric field and potential at the apex P of this truncated pyramid.

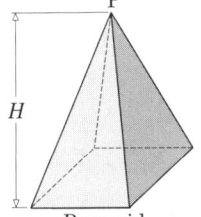 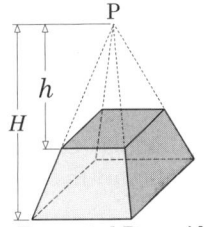

Pyramid   Truncated Pyramid

26. If a charge q is uniformly spread on a thin dielectric square plate, the electric potential at its centre is found to be V_1. If six such charged plates are joined to make a hollow cube, the potential at the centre of the cube is found to be V_2. Find potential at one of the vertices of this cube. In all the cases, potential at infinitely distant points has been assumed zero.

27. A parallel plate capacitor has two sections. In these sections, areas of plates are A_1 and A_2 and distances between the plates are d_1 and d_2 respectively. The distances between the plates are much smaller than their linear dimensions. A uniform electric field E that is perpendicular to the plates is switched on. Neglecting edge effects, deduce expressions for the intensities E_1 and E_2 of electric fields established in both the sections of the capacitor.

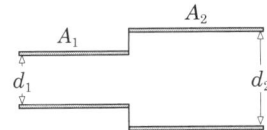

28. Radii of the inner and outer concentric conducting spheres of a spherical capacitor are a and b. One half of the space between the spheres is filled with a linear isotropic dielectric of permittivity ε_1 and the other half with another linear isotropic dielectric of permittivity ε_2 as shown in the figure. The inner and the outer spheres are given charge $+q$ and $-q$ respectively. Find expressions for the electric fields in both the dielectrics and potential difference between the spheres.

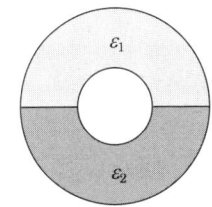

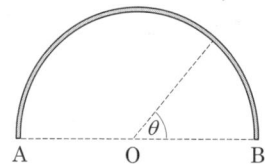

29. Charge distribution on a rod bent as a semicircular arc of radius R follows a function $\lambda = \lambda_0 \sin\theta$. Here λ is line charge density at a point on the rod, λ_0 is a positive constant and θ is angular position of the point as shown in the figure. Find the ratio of electrostatic potentials at the centre O and at a general point on the diameter AB at distance r ($r \leq R$) from the centre O.

30. A conducting sphere of radius $R = 1.0$ m is charged to a potential $V_i = 1000$ V. A thin metal disc of radius $r = 1.0$ cm mounted on an insulating handle is touched with the sphere making contact with one of its flat faces and then separated. After separation the disc is earthed and the process is repeated until the potential of the sphere becomes $V_f = 999$ V. Approximately how many times has this process been repeated?

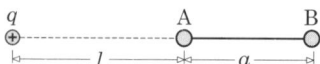

31. Two small metal spheres A and B each of radius r supported on insulating stands, located at a distance a ($a \gg r$) from each other are connected by a thin conducting wire. A point charge q is placed on the line joining centres of the spheres at distance l ($l \gg r$) from the ball A. What are the moduli of charges induced on the spheres?

32. Consider a dumbbell like structure consisting of two conducting balls connected by a conducting rod. Radius r of the balls is much smaller than the length l of the connecting rod. The dumbbell is placed midway between two unlike point charges Q and $-Q$ that are a distance $3l$ apart. Rod of the dumbbell is collinear with the line joining the charges. By what amount will the net force on a charge change after placing the dumbbell?

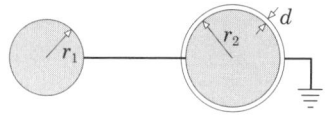

33. Two metal spheres of radius r_1 and r_2 are connected by a thin conducting wire. The second sphere is surrounded by a grounded concentric conducting shell with uniform separation d between their facing surfaces. If the second sphere is given a charge Q, find charges acquired by all the three spheres. Assume that $d \ll r_2$, and the distance between the spheres is much larger than their radii.

34. A large conducing plate of surface area A and thickness d is placed perpendicular to a uniform electric field E. How much heat will be dissipated in the plate after the electric field is switched off?

35. Two conducting spheres of external radii r and $3r$ have wall thickness $0.05r$ each. Point charges q and $2q$ are placed at the centres of these spheres respectively. The spheres are kept at great separation so that they do not affect charge distribution on the surfaces of each other and their interaction energy is negligible. Deduce expression for the minimum amount of work done by an external agency to exchange the position of the charges. The holes made to enable exchange of charges are so small that their size can be neglected.

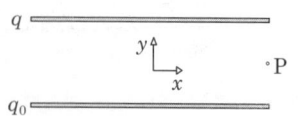

36. A point P is located equidistant from both the plates and near one edge of a parallel plate capacitor as shown in the figure. In an experiment, maintaining charge q_0 on the bottom plate constant, potential V and modulus of electric field E at the point P are measured for different values of the charge q on the upper plate. In the following graphs the

potential for one value of the charge q and modulus of electric field for two values of the charge q are shown as functions of the ratio of the charges $r = q/q_0$.

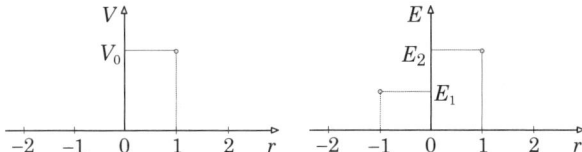

Deduce analytical dependence of the potential V and the electric field vector $\vec{E}$ at point P on the ratio r of the charges.

37. Four uncharged identical metal plates, each of area A are placed parallel to each other in vacuum. The distances d between adjacent plates is much smaller than the linear dimensions of a plate. The inner plates are given unlike charges each of modulus q and then the outer plates are connected through a resistance. Determine total heat dissipated in the resistance. Neglect effects of electromagnetic radiation.

38. Four identical metallic plates are arranged very close and parallel to each other as shown in the figure. Plates A and D are connected across a voltage source, which maintains potential of plate A higher than that of D by an amount V_0. Plates B and C are connected by a short conducting wire for a while and then the wire is removed. Now the voltage source is removed and then plates A and D are connected by another short conducting wire. Find potential differences between the pairs A-B, A-C and B-D.

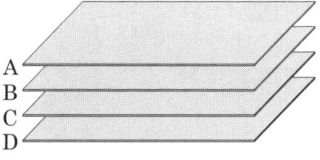

39. Between two thin parallel metal plates having charges $+q$ and $-q$ is inserted a thick metal slab having charge $+q$ so that distance between the upper plate and top face of the slab is $2d$ and the distance between lower plate and bottom face of the slab is d. Adjacent surfaces of the plates and that of the slab are equal in area and parallel to each other. Now the upper and the lower plates are earthed by closing the switches A and B simultaneously. Find amounts of the charges that pass through the switches.

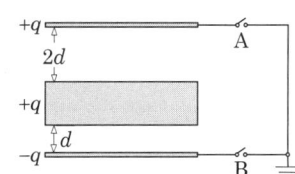

40. Plates of a parallel plate capacitor have area A and distance between them is d. A potential difference V is maintained across the capacitor by a battery. Two identical dielectric slabs D and a metal slab M each of thickness $d/3$ are inserted in the capacitor as shown in the figure. Relative permittivity of each of the dielectric slab is ε_r. Find expression for modulus of the force of electrostatic interaction on either of the plates.

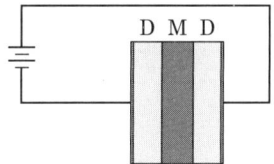

41. Two uncharged thin metal plates A and B each of area A are fixed parallel to each other and earthed. Another identical plate C made of a dielectric material is placed midway between plates A and B. Plate C has a net positive charge Q uniformly distributed in its volume. Determine net electrostatic force on plate C, if it is shifted a distance x towards plate A. Neglect the end effects.

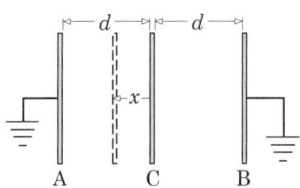

12.18 Chapter-12

42. A device has been suggested to measure charge and electrostatic voltage. It consists of a cylindrical rubber pad with identical circular metal plates coaxially glued on both of its circular faces. Radius of the rubber pad and that of the metal plates are equal. One of the plates is held fixed and the other one can move while remaining parallel to the first one. In this way, a directly measured quantity from this device is the displacement x of the movable plate.

The area of a metal plates is S, the length of the rubber pad in undeformed state is d and its stiffness is k. Electrical permittivity of the free space is ε_0 and dielectric constant of the rubber is ε_r.

Neglect the fringing of the electric field at the edges of the plates, i.e. the electric field between the plates can be considered homogeneous.

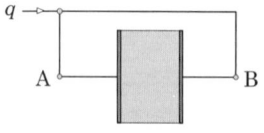

(a) To use the device as a charge meter, the charge q to be measured is fed to the plates through terminals A and B. Find relation between the plate displacement x and the charge q.
(b) In which part of its range, is the device as a charge meter more accurate?

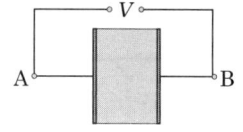

(c) To use the device as an electrostatic voltmeter, the electrostatic voltage V to be measured is applied between the terminals A and B. Find relation between the plate displacement x and the voltage V.
(d) In which part of its range, is the device as an electrostatic voltmeter more accurate?

43. Two small balls of masses m_1 and m_2 having like charges are connected with each other by an insulating light thread of length l. Initially, the balls are at rest and tensile force in the thread is T. After the thread is cut, the balls move apart. Determine distance between the balls, when momentum of the first ball becomes p. Ignore effects of all forces other than the electrostatic forces between the balls.

44. Two particles each of mass $m = 50$ g and charge $q = 10$ µC are at rest on a horizontal plane a distance $r_0 = 10$ m apart. Coefficient of friction between the particles and the plane is $\mu = 0.2$. What is the minimum constant horizontal force that must be applied to one of the particles so that the other one starts sliding?

45. A particle of charge –4.0 µC is fixed at a height 3.0 m above the ground and another particle of mass 0.9 g and charge 1.0 µC is held under the previous particle at a height 2.2 m above the ground. What minimum speed must be given to the second particle so that it reaches the ground? Acceleration of free fall is 10 m/s².

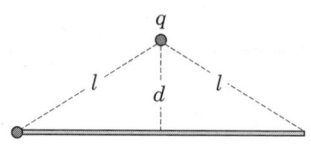

46. A point like positive charge q is fixed at a distance d on the perpendicular bisector of thin electrically neutral nonconducting rod. Ends of the rod are at distance l from the point charge. A bead of mass m having the same charge q is threaded on the rod. The bead is projected from one end of the rod towards the other end. Velocity of the bead at the centre of the rod is observed to be v_1 and at the other end v_2. If coefficient of friction between the bead and the rod is uniform everywhere, find velocity of projection of the bead.

47. A small block carrying a positive charge q_1 is held at rest on an inclined plane. A negative point charge q_2 is fixed somewhere at point O in the vertical plane containing the block. Coefficient of friction between the block and the inclined plane is $\mu = 0.375$. When released, the block acquires a speed $v_0 = 3.0$ m/s after sliding down a height $h = 1.25$ m. If the block has negative charge of the same magnitude (i.e. $-q_1$), what speed will it acquire after sliding down from rest between the same initial and final points. Acceleration due to gravity is $g = 10$ m/s^2.

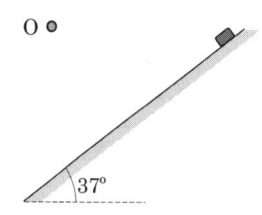

48. Two identical beads each of mass m and charge q can slide on two long parallel insulating frictionless rigid rods that are a distance d apart. Initially the beads are so far from each other that no electrostatic interaction exists between them. With what speed must one of the beads be projected so that it passes over the other bead? Assume radii of the beads negligibly small as compared to the distance between the rods. Neglect effects of gravity.

49. Two small non-conducting balls A and B are rigidly attached at the ends of a light frictionless non-conducting rod. A third non-conducting ball C can slide on the rod like a threaded bead between the balls A and B. All the three balls are of equal mass m and have equal charges q. Initially the balls are held at rest in free space with centre-to-centre spacing as shown in the figure. All the balls are simultaneously released. Find maximum speed of the ball C in subsequent motion. Neglect radii of the balls as compared to the distance d.

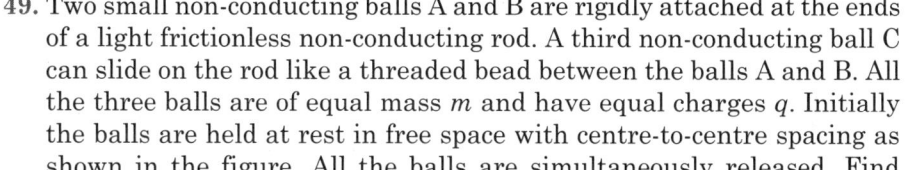

50. Four identical particles A, B, C and D each of mass m and charge q are connected by insulating light inextensible threads of equal length l to make a tetrahedron as shown in the figure.

The thread connecting particles A and B is cut. Find maximum speed acquired by every particle in subsequent motion.

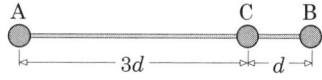

51. Two particles each of mass m and charges $+q$ and $-q$ separated by a distance l are given initial velocities u perpendicular to the line joining them as shown in the figure. Neglect gravitational and magnetic forces between the particles in comparison to Coulombian forces between them.

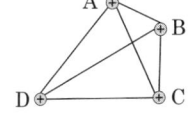

(a) Under what conditions will the masses eventually collide?
(b) Under what conditions will the masses follow circular orbits of diameter l?
(c) Under what conditions will the masses follow closed orbits?
(d) What is the minimum distance between the masses in their subsequent motion?

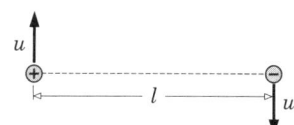

52. An amount Q of positive charge is sprinkled uniformly on surface of a large and massive non-conducting spherical shell of radius R and then a small circular portion of radius r ($r \ll R$) is removed from the shell. Now a particle carrying positive charge q is released from the centre of the shell. Considering only electrostatic interactions, find the kinetic energy of the charged particle when it comes out of the hole.

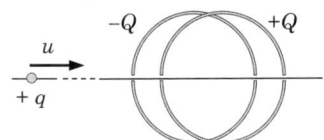

53. Two identical dielectric spherical shells each of radius R carrying uniformly distributed charges $+Q$ and $-Q$ are fixed intersecting each other with their centres at separation $x_0 < R$. A straight thin uncharged insulating rod is fixed along the line joining centres of the shells, on which a small bead of mass m carrying a positive charge q can slide without friction. The holes made in the shells to pass the rod and the bead are so small that their effect on the electric field of the charges of the shells can be ignored. The rod is made of such a material that no charge accumulates on it due to induction or polarization. The bead is projected with an initial velocity u towards the shells from a point that is far away from the shells as shown in the figure. If the bead stops sliding on the rod, where must it stop and what must be the range of its initial velocity u?

To specify your answer, assume centre of the positively charged dielectric sphere at the origin of a coordinate system whose x-axis coincides with the rod.

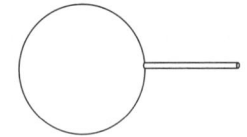

54. A soap bubble of mass m (excluding air inside) blown with the help of a capillary tube is given an unknown amount of charge. Surface tension of the soap solution is σ. When the bubble acquires a stable radius, an additional small amount of air is blown into the bubble from the tube and then the tube is left open. Because of this operation, the soap bubble starts oscillations. If the soap bubble retains its spherical shape during the oscillations, find expression for period of these small amplitude oscillations.

Check your understanding

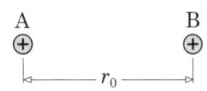

1. Two identical particles A and B each having charge q when released in free space with initial separation r_0 between them, their separation becomes double in time t_0. How long will it take to double the separation, if charge of particle A is made aq, that of particle B is made bq and they are released with initial separation ηr_0?

2. A small block having charge Q placed on a frictionless horizontal table is attached to one end of a spring of force constant k. The other end of the spring is attached to a fixed support and the spring stays horizontally in a relaxed state. Another small block carrying a negative charge $-q$ is brought very slowly from a great distance towards the former block along the line coinciding with the axis of the spring. Find extension in the spring when both the blocks collide.

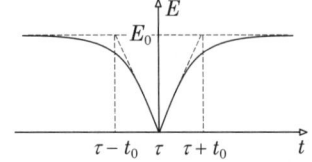

3. Modulus of electric field intensity at a point in space varies with time according to the given graph. This field is created by two identical point charges; one of them is fixed at a distance r_0 from the observation point and the other one is moving with a constant velocity. Find modulus of the charges, the minimum distance of the moving charge from the point of observation and speed of the moving charge. Neglect electromagnetic induction due to motion of the moving charge.

4. Two parallel half-planes are uniformly charged with surface charge densities $+\sigma$ and $-\sigma$. Find magnitude and direction of electric field due to these half planes at a point P located at a height h above the edge of the positively charged half-plane (see figure). Distance d between the half-planes is much smaller than h.

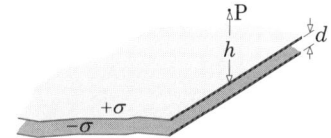

5. Four infinite planes intersect each other forming a tetrahedron. Three adjacent edges meeting on the vertex O of the tetrahedron are of equal length l and the face opposite to the vertex O is an equilateral triangle of edge b. Each plane is uniformly charged with positive surface charge density σ. A particle of mass m and positive charge q is held at rest within the tetrahedron on the line of symmetry through the vertex O at distance d from the lower face as shown in the figure. For better readability, complete planes are not shown. With what speed will the particle collide with the tetrahedron, after it is released? Consider that the charges on the planes remain immobile and neglect gravity.

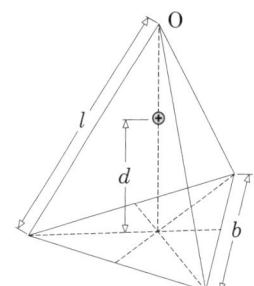

6. Two hemispherical thin shells made of insulating materials are concentrically arranged in a free space as shown. The radii of the larger and the smaller hemispheres are R and r and they carry net positive charges Q and q respectively. The charges are uniformly distributed over the surfaces of the shells. Find the force of electrostatic interaction between the shells.

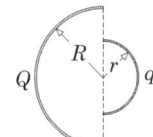

7. A bead of mass m and charge q can slide without friction on an insulating thread tied between two diametrically opposite points on a ring of radius R made of an insulating material. An amount Q of positive charge is uniformly distributed on the ring. Find the period of small oscillations of the bead about its equilibrium position. Mass of the beads is negligible as compared to that of the ring.

8. A uniformly charged right-angled triangular lamina ABC is shown in the figure. Acute angle at vertex A is θ. If the potential of vertices A and B are V_A and V_B respectively, find potential of vertex C.

9. Electrostatic potential at a point close to a charged conducting ball is V. When a very small conducting object (a probe) is brought close to the ball, potential of the ball changes by $|\Delta V|$. Find force of electrostatic interaction between the ball and the probe.

10. A grounded metallic ball of radius r is placed on the centre of a uniformly charged thin insulating disc of radius R ($R \gg r$). If total charge on the disc is Q, find force of electrostatic interaction between the ball and the disc.

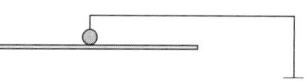

11. Two electrically neutral conducting bodies A and B of arbitrary shapes are placed far away from each other in free space. If A is given a charge q and B being neutral is brought in contact with A, both of them will acquire a potential V and work done by electrical forces in this process is W_1. If B is given charge q and A being neutral is brought in contact with B, work done by electrical forces is W_2. What will be the work done by electrical forces, if both the bodies are given charge q each and then brought in contact with each other?

12.22 Chapter-12

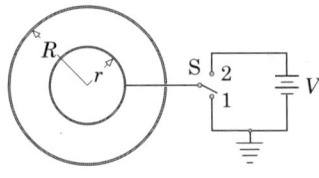

12. A thin dielectric spherical shell of radius R is divided into two equal parts. These parts are held together forming a complete shell and are given uniformly distributed unlike charges Q and $-q$. If work done in making the separation between the shells infinite is W, determine self-energy of a charge q, uniformly distributed on a hemispherical shell of radius r.

13. Consider two concentric conducting spherical shells of radii R and r. The inner shell is connected to a two-way switch S by a long thin insulated conducting wire passing through a small hole in the outer shell. The inner shell can be connected either to the earth or to the positive terminal of a battery of terminal voltage V by throwing the switch in position 1 or 2 respectively. The outer shell is given a charge Q keeping the switch in position 1. Find total amount of heat released after the switch is thrown to position 2.

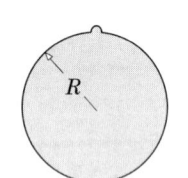

14. Due to nonuniform mechanical strength, when a conducting sphere is given a charge Q, the electrostatic forces make a small hemispherical bulge on its surface. The radius r of the bulge is negligibly small as compared to the radius R of the conducting sphere.

    (a) Can you assume charge on the bulge distributed uniformly?
    (b) Estimate charge q on the bulge.
    (c) Find the change in capacitance ΔC due to this bulge.

15. A dielectric slab of thickness t and relative permittivity ε_r is placed between two fixed parallel metal plates. Faces of the slab and the plates are parallel and distance between the plates is d. Neglecting end effects, find the minimum voltage applied between the plates sufficient to rupture the slab. Breaking stress of the material of the slab is σ_b.

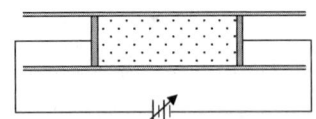

16. An ideal gas is trapped between two metallic pistons A and B inside a thin glass tube. The pistons are connected with the terminals of a variable voltage battery. Relative permittivity of the gas is ε_r. The pistons stay in equilibrium at separation x_0 between them when battery voltage is V_0.

    (a) Is the equilibrium stable, unstable or neutral?
    (b) How will the distance x between the pistons change, if battery voltage is slowly increased?

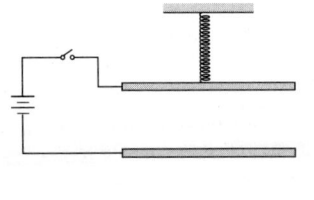

17. Two identical metal plates each of area A are arranged parallel to each other as shown. The lower plate is held fixed, and the upper plate is connected at its middle to one end of a spring of force constant k. The other end of the spring is attached to a fixed support. When either of the plates have no charge, the equilibrium distance between them is d. Now the switch is closed to apply a voltage between the plates. In this way, what maximum voltage can be applied between the plates, so that they will not touch each other? Ignore the force of gravity as compared to the spring force and the force of electrostatic interactions.

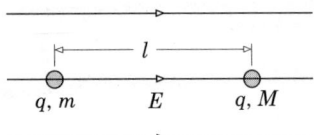

18. Two point-charges each of charge q and masses m and M ($M > m$) are released in a uniform electric field E with initial separation l as shown. Find the maximum separation between them in subsequent motion.

19. Consider a non-conducting ring of radius r and mass m and a particle of equal mass, both at rest in free space. The particle is on the axis of the ring and far away from the ring. An amount Q of positive charge is uniformly distributed on the ring and the particle is given a positive charge q. The particle is imparted a velocity u towards the centre of the ring. Find maximum speed the ring can acquire during the subsequent motion.

20. Three identical particles each of mass m and charge q connected by light inextensible non-conducting threads are held in free space with the threads connecting the central particle to the other two making an angle slightly less than 180° as shown in the figure. Both the threads are of length l. All the particles are simultaneously released. Find period of oscillations in the system.

21. Two identical conducting balls each of radii r, and mass m, connected by a light conducting spring of stiffness k and un-deformed length l_0 ($l_0 \gg r$) are at rest in free space. If a uniform electric field of strength E directed along the spring is switched on, the balls may oscillate.

    (a) What should the value of the stiffness k of the spring be to make oscillations possible?
    (b) Determine the amplitude and period of oscillations.

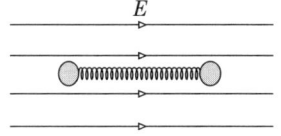

22. A dumbbell-like structure is made by affixing two particles A and B at the ends of a light spring. Both the particles have equal mass m and particle B carries a positive charge q. A uniform electric field of intensity E pointing in the negative x-direction is established in the region $x > 0$ and gravity is absent everywhere in the region of interest. The dumbbell is initially at rest on the x-axis in the region $x < 0$. It is projected with a velocity u in the positive x-direction as shown in the figure. After a while, the dumbbell is observed moving in the negative x-direction with the same speed u. During this interval, particle A never enters the region of electric field, and the spring length becomes minimum only once.

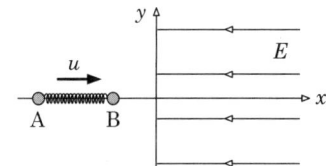

    (a) How much time particle B spends in the electric field?
    (b) If the process takes place exactly in the same way as described, what should the relaxed length l of the spring be?

23. Two identical small elastic conducting balls each of mass m and radius r have charges of opposite signs Q and $-q$. Initially they are held in free space with their centres at separation $l > 2r$ and then released. Find their speeds v long after their collision. Ignore non-uniformity in charge distribution when ball come close to each other, magnetic field produced by motion of charges and the gravitational interaction between them.

24. Two neutral particle-like identical metal balls each of radius r and mass m are connected by a light inextensible conducting thread of length L. The balls are held in free space with separation between their centres l ($r \ll l < L$). Now everywhere a uniform electric field directed along the line joining the centres of the balls is switched on and then the balls are released. Find maximum speeds of the balls in subsequent motion.

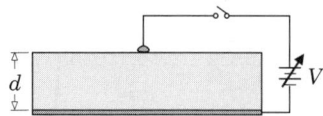

25. Bottom face of a horizontal dielectric slab is coated with a conducting paint and at centre of the top face is placed a small mercury drop, which does not wet the plate. Thickness of the slab is d and relative permittivity is ε_r. Now the switch is closed, and the battery voltage is increased so gradually that the mercury drop spreads on the dielectric slab at negligible rate. At what battery voltage will the mercury drop cover the whole of the upper face of the dielectric? Surface tension of mercury is σ and initial surface area of the drop is negligible as compared to surface area of mercury when spread.

26. A parallel plate capacitor completely filled with a dielectric sheet of thickness d and relative permittivity ε_r is placed on a horizontal tabletop. The lower plate is glued with the tabletop and the dielectric slab is glued with the lower plate. The plates are square of edge length l and mass of the upper plate is m. The plates are given charges $+q$ and $-q$, then the upper plate is shifted horizontally by a small distance x along one of its edges and set free. Find period of oscillation of this plate. Thickness d of the dielectric is much smaller than the edge length l.

27. In a gravity free cabin, a non-conducting liquid of surface tension σ and possessing uniform volume charge density ρ is sprayed into large number of drops. After spraying, the drops float around in the cabin and keep on breaking apart into smaller drops and coalescing into larger drops. While floating, the electrostatic forces between the drops are negligible. Estimate radius of the drops when their number reaches a stable value.

Challenge your understanding

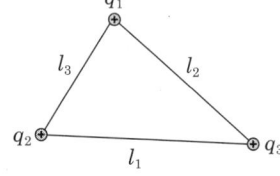

1. A frictionless non-conducting inextensible thread of length l wears three beads of positive charges q_1, q_2 and q_3. The ends of the thread are connected to make a knotless loop. Length of the thread is so large as compared to the size of the beads that the beads can be treated as point particles. The system is in a state of equilibrium with beads at vertices of a triangle.
   (a) Find lengths l_1, l_2 and l_3 of the sides of the triangle.
   (b) What relation the charges q_1, q_2 and q_3 must bear to establish the above-mentioned state of equilibrium?

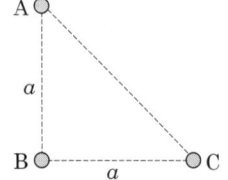

2. Three identical metal spheres each of radius r are fixed at the vertices of an isosceles right triangle, as shown in the figure (assume $r \ll a$). Initially each sphere is individually given a charge q. Spheres A and B are connected for a short while with a conducting wire, and then the wire is taken away. This operation is repeated with the spheres B and C and then with the spheres C and A. What are the electric charges on the spheres after all these operations?

3. Three particles A, B and C of charges q, q and $2q$ and masses $m, 2m$ and $5m$ respectively are held in free space in a straight line at separation r_0 between two adjacent particles as shown in the figure. All the three particles are released simultaneously. Find velocities of all the three particles when they reach so far from each other that electrostatic interactions between them can be neglected

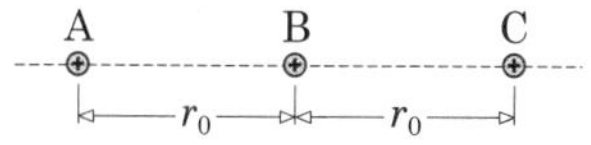

4. Three long frictionless rods are fixed parallel to each other in a horizontal plane with separation d between adjacent rods. The rods wear identical sleeves A, B, C and D each of mass m and charge q. Initially sleeves B, C and D are arranged in a line perpendicular to the rods and sleeve A is far away from them as shown in the figure. In this way, sleeves B, C and D are in a state of unstable equilibrium and have no electrostatic interaction with sleeve A. If sleeve A is launched towards the right with an initial velocity u, find velocities of all the sleeves when they acquire steady motion. Consider all possible cases.

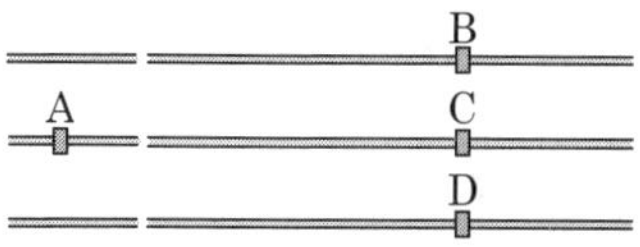

Answers and Hints

Multiple Choice Questions

1. (c)
2. (d)
3. (b)
4. (a) and (c)
5. (d)
6. (c)
7. (b)
8. (b)
9. (a), (b) and (c)
10. (d)
11. (d)
12. (d)
13. (d)
14. (d)
15. (b)
16. (a) and (b)
17. (b)
18. (a)
19. (c)
20. (b)
21. (b)
22. (b)
23. (d)
24. (c)
25. (a), (b) and (d)
26. (b)
27. (a)
28. (c)
29. (c)
30. (b)
31. (c)
32. (b)

Build up your understanding

1. $\sin^{-1}(\mu \cot \alpha)$

2. $m > \dfrac{Qqh}{4\pi\varepsilon_0 g(h+l)^3}$

3. Both reach the corner simultaneously.
   Hint: Ratios of acceleration magnitudes of the beads to their respective distances from the corner are equal.

4. Total charges induced on each of the edges are given in the following table.

AB	BC	CD	DA	OA	OB	OC	OD
$-\dfrac{q_1}{\sqrt{2}}$	$\dfrac{q_1}{\sqrt{2}}$	$\dfrac{q_1}{\sqrt{2}}$	$-\dfrac{q_1}{\sqrt{2}}$	$-\sqrt{2}q_2$	0	$\sqrt{2}q_2$	0

Hint: The electric field along the diagonal is superposition of the two electric fields each along the edges. In addition, modulus of induced charge on a conductor is proportional to the applied electric field intensity.

5. 4

   Hint: There are two such points on each median with the centroid as a common point.

6. Zero newton per coulomb

7. $\dfrac{(qE\sin\theta + mg\cos\theta)(\sin\theta + \mu\cos\theta)}{M + m\sin\theta(\sin\theta + \mu\cos\theta)}$

8. $\dfrac{mg}{q}\left(\dfrac{u^2\cos^2\theta}{u^2\sin\theta\cos\theta - gx_0}\right)$ and $\dfrac{2u\sin\theta}{g}$

9. $\dfrac{1}{2}\sqrt{\dfrac{q_1 q_2 (m_1 + m_2)}{\pi\varepsilon_0 E(q_1 m_2 + q_2 m_1)}}$

10. $< \dfrac{6\sqrt{3}\pi\varepsilon_0 R^2 mg}{Q}$

11. $4\pi R\sqrt{\dfrac{2\sqrt{2}\pi\varepsilon_0 mR}{Qq}}$

12. $\sqrt{\dfrac{qlE}{\pi mr^2}}$

    Hint: Angular velocity acquires its maximum value when angular acceleration vanishes.

13. (a) $u = d\sqrt{\dfrac{2qE}{ml}}$

    (b) $2d\sqrt{\dfrac{2qE}{ml}}$

14. $2\sqrt{\dfrac{ml}{qE}}\left(\pi + \dfrac{L-l}{x_m}\right)$

15. $\dfrac{3\alpha p_0^2}{4\pi^2 \varepsilon_r^2 r^7}$ (Attractive)

    Hint: Force on a dipole of dipole moment $\vec{p}$ in an electric field $\vec{E}$ is given by the following relation.

    $\vec{F} = -\vec{\nabla}(-\vec{p}\cdot\vec{E})$

    In the given situation the above relation reduces to

    $\vec{F} = \left(\vec{p}\cdot\dfrac{\partial \vec{E}}{\partial r}\right)\hat{e}_r$

16. Conducting cylinder: $F = \dfrac{Q^2 V}{8\pi^2 \varepsilon_0 x^5}$ attractive

    Insulating cylinder: $F = \dfrac{(\varepsilon_r - 1)Q^2 V}{8\pi^2 \varepsilon_0 \varepsilon_r x^5}$ attractive

    Hint: Due to electric field of the point charge, the charges appearing on the flat faces of the cylinder constitute an electric dipole. Moreover, the electric field of the point charge can be assumed almost uniform inside the cylinder to calculate charges appearing on its faces.

17. Zero at all points between the half-plane and $\sigma/(2\varepsilon_0)$ outside.

18. $\dfrac{\sigma^2 l^2}{2\varepsilon_0}$

19. In case of triangular plates: $E = \dfrac{E_0}{6}$

    In case of pentagonal plates: $E = \dfrac{3E_0}{10}$

20. $\dfrac{2\varepsilon_0 p_0 A^2 d}{2\varepsilon_0 p_0 A^2 + q^2}$

21. $\dfrac{q^2}{\varepsilon_0 A}$ in each rod

22. $\tfrac{1}{2}\varepsilon_0(E_2^2 - E_1^2)$

23. $\dfrac{Q^2 r^2}{32\pi\varepsilon_0 mR^4}$

    Hint: Since the ball is made of porcelain, the space from where the metal disc flies off will remain devoid of charge.

24. $r = \dfrac{\left(\sqrt{q_1} + \sqrt{q_2}\right)^2}{4\pi\varepsilon_0 V} = 9.0$ cm

    Hint: Electric field intensity must vanish, where the equipotential crisscross itself.

25. $E_0\left\{1 - \dfrac{h}{H}\right\}$ and $V_0\left\{1 - \left(\dfrac{h}{H}\right)^2\right\}$

26. $\dfrac{3V_1}{2}+\dfrac{V_2}{4}$

27. $E_1 = Ed_2\left(\dfrac{A_1+A_2}{A_1d_2+A_2d_1}\right)$ and

   $E_2 = Ed_1\left(\dfrac{A_1+A_2}{A_1d_2+A_2d_1}\right)$

28. $\vec{E}_1 = \vec{E}_2 = \dfrac{q\vec{r}}{2\pi(\varepsilon_1+\varepsilon_2)r^3}$

   $V = \dfrac{q(b-a)}{2\pi(\varepsilon_1+\varepsilon_2)ab}$

   Hint: The potential distribution in both the regions occupied by the dielectrics is identical; therefore, electric field in both the regions can be expressed by the same function.

29. 1:1

   Hint: The given charge distribution is equivalent to charge on a strip S on a uniformly charged spherical shell of radius R.

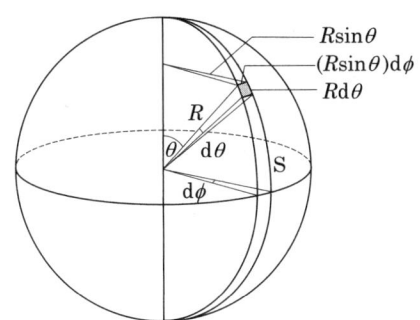

   Since electric field in the sphere is zero, therefore net electric field due to any two diametrically opposite such strips on all points of the common diameter must be zero. It suggests that electric field of a single strip and hence electric field of the given semicircular arc anywhere on their diameter cannot have a component parallel to the diameter.

30. $\approx \dfrac{4R^2(V_i-V_f)}{r^2 V_i} = 40$

   Hint: Each time the disc is separated from the sphere, it removes a charge in proportion to area of its flat face and hence reduces the potential of the sphere in proportion to the removed charge.

31. $\dfrac{arq}{2l(l+a)}$

32. $\dfrac{3Q^2 r}{32\pi\varepsilon_0 l^3}$

33. $\dfrac{r_1 d}{r_1 d + r_2^2} Q$ and $\dfrac{r_2^2}{r_1 d + r_2^2} Q$

34. $\dfrac{1}{2}\varepsilon_0 E^2 Ad$

35. $-\dfrac{q^2}{60\pi\varepsilon_0 r}$

   Hint: The overall electric field in both configurations differs only in the region occupied by the material of the shells where electric field is zero.

36. $V = \dfrac{1}{2}V_0(1+r)$ and

   $\vec{E} = \dfrac{1}{2}\{E_2(1+r)\hat{i} + E_1(1-r)\hat{j}\}$

37. $\dfrac{q^2 d}{6\varepsilon_0 A}$

38. $V_A - V_B = \tfrac{1}{6}V_0$, $V_A - V_C = -\tfrac{1}{6}V_0$ and

   $V_B - V_D = -\tfrac{1}{6}V_0$

39. $4q/3$ through A out of the plate and $q/3$ through B into the plate.

40. $\dfrac{1}{2}\varepsilon_0 A\left(\dfrac{3\varepsilon_r V}{2d}\right)^2$

41. $\dfrac{Q^2}{2\varepsilon_0 A}\cdot\dfrac{x}{d}$ ←

42. (a) $q = \sqrt{8\varepsilon_0 Skx}$

   (b) In the higher portion of the range

   (c) $V = \dfrac{(d-x)}{\varepsilon_r}\sqrt{\dfrac{2kx}{\varepsilon_0 S}}$

   (d) In the higher portion of the range

43. $\dfrac{2m_1 m_2 l^2 T}{2m_1 m_2 lT - p^2(m_1 + m_2)}$

44. $\mu mg + \dfrac{\sqrt{\mu mg K q^2}}{r_0} = 0.13 \text{ N}$

45. 6.0 m/s

46. $\sqrt{2v_1^2 - v_2^2 + \dfrac{q^2}{\pi \varepsilon_0 m}\left(\dfrac{1}{d} - \dfrac{1}{l}\right)}$

47. $\sqrt{4gh(1 - \mu \cot\theta) - v_0^2} = 4.0$ m/s

48. $> \dfrac{q}{\sqrt{\pi \varepsilon_0 md}}$

49. $\dfrac{q}{3}\sqrt{\dfrac{1}{\pi \varepsilon_0 md}}$

Hint: The electrostatic potential energy acquires its least value when ball C passes midpoint between balls A and B.

50. $v_A = v_B = v_C = v_D = \sqrt{\dfrac{q^2}{8\pi \varepsilon_0 ml}\left(1 - \dfrac{1}{\sqrt{3}}\right)}$

51. (a) $u = 0$

(b) $\dfrac{Kq^2}{mlu^2} = 2$

(c) $\dfrac{Kq^2}{mlu^2} > 1$

(d) $= \begin{cases} l; & \text{If } \dfrac{Kq^2}{mlu^2} \le 2 \\ \dfrac{l}{\dfrac{Kq^2}{lu^2} - 1}; & \text{If } \dfrac{Kq^2}{mlu^2} > 2 \end{cases}$

52. $\dfrac{Qqr}{8\pi \varepsilon_0 R^2}$

53. Inside the positive dielectric sphere and outside the negative one i.e. the position x, where the bead will stop satisfies inequality

$(R - x_0) < x < R$

Range of initial velocity of the bead

$u < \sqrt{\dfrac{Qqx_0}{2\pi \varepsilon_0 mR(R + x_0)}}$

Hint: Direction of the net electric field created by charges on the shells on the line of motion of the bead is shown in the following figure.

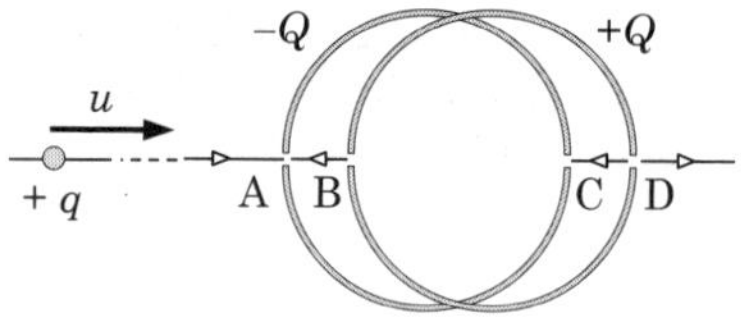

The moving charge experiences retarding force only in regions AB and CD, therefore it can stop only within either of these regions.

Since the potential rise from the initial position of the bead to hole A equals to the potential drop from hole A to hole B, therefore the bead being projected from its initial position with a finite speed cannot stop within region AB and if it stops, it can do so only within region CD.

54. $\sqrt{\dfrac{\pi m}{12\sigma}}$

Check your understanding

1. $t_0 \sqrt{\dfrac{\eta^3}{ab}}$

Hint: For simplicity, you may proceed with dimensional analysis.

2. $l = \dfrac{3}{2}\left(\dfrac{Qq}{2\pi \varepsilon_0 k}\right)^{\frac{1}{3}}$

3. $4\pi\varepsilon_0 r_0^2 E_0$, r_0 and $\dfrac{r_0}{t_0}$

   Hint: The observation point becomes a null point at the instant $t = \tau$ and both the charges have equal modulus, therefore at the instant $t = \tau$, the observation point must be the midpoint of the line joining the charges. In addition, symmetry in the graph suggests that the path of the moving charge is a straight line perpendicular to the line joining the observation point and the stationary charge.

4. $\dfrac{\sigma d}{2\pi\varepsilon_0 h}$ parallel to the planes and outwards

   Hint: You may conceive each of the half planes made of infinitely large numbers of strips like AB and CD each parallel to the left edges of the planes.

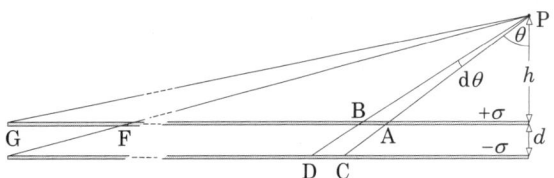

   Electric fields of the strips in every such pair are equal in magnitude and opposite in direction at point P; therefore, they cancel out electric fields of each other. In this way, we reach on a conclusion that it is part FG of the upper plane, which is the only contributor of electric field at point P.

5. $= \begin{cases} \sqrt{\dfrac{\sigma q d}{m\varepsilon_0}\left(\dfrac{b\sqrt{3}}{\sqrt{4l^2 - b^2}} - 1\right)}; & \dfrac{b}{\sqrt{3}} < l < b \quad \text{Hit the bottom} \\ 0; & l = b \quad \text{Stays Immobile} \\ \sqrt{\dfrac{\sigma q}{m\varepsilon_0}\left(\sqrt{l^2 - \dfrac{b^2}{3}} - d\right)\left(1 - \dfrac{b\sqrt{3}}{\sqrt{4l^2 - b^2}}\right)}; & l > b \quad \text{Hit the top corner} \end{cases}$

6. $\dfrac{Qq}{8\pi\varepsilon_0 R^2}$

7. $4\pi\sqrt{\dfrac{2\pi\varepsilon_0 m R^3}{Qq}}$

8. $V_A \sin\theta + V_B \cos\theta$

9. $8\pi\varepsilon_0 V \Delta V$

   Hint: Charges induced on the probe constitute an equivalent electric dipole, field of which is responsible for change in potential of the ball by an amount equal to potential created by the dipole at the centre of the ball.

10. $\dfrac{Q^2 r}{\pi\varepsilon_0 R^3}$

11. $W_1 + W_2 - qV$

12. $\dfrac{q^2}{4\pi\varepsilon_0 r} - \dfrac{qWR}{2rQ}$

13. $2\pi\varepsilon_0 r V^2$

14. (a) No

    Hint: Charge on the bulge accumulates in a negligibly small region as far as possible from the centre of the sphere. Therefore, this charge can satisfactorily be treated as a point charge.

    (b) $q \approx \dfrac{Qr^2}{2R^2}$

    (c) $\Delta C \approx 2\pi\varepsilon_0 \dfrac{r^3}{R^2}$

    Hint: Since the bulge is of negligibly small size, the change in capacitance is also very small. Moreover, the total charge is constant, therefore we can say that the fractional increase in the capacitance equals the fractional decrease in potential or vice versa.

15. $\{\varepsilon_r d - (\varepsilon_r - 1)t\}\sqrt{\dfrac{2\sigma_b}{\varepsilon_0(\varepsilon_r^2 - 1)}}$

16. (a) Unstable
    (b) $x \to 0$

17. $\dfrac{2}{3}\sqrt{\dfrac{2kd^3}{3\varepsilon_0 A}}$

18. $=\begin{cases} l_0; & \text{If } l < l_0 \\ l_0; & \text{If } l = l_0 \\ l; & \text{If } l > l_0 \end{cases}$ Here $l_0 = \sqrt{\dfrac{q(M+m)}{4\pi\varepsilon_0 E(M-m)}}$

19. $=\begin{cases} u; & \text{If } u < \sqrt{\dfrac{Qq}{\pi\varepsilon_0 mr}} \\ \dfrac{u}{2}; & \text{If } u = \sqrt{\dfrac{Qq}{\pi\varepsilon_0 mr}} \\ \dfrac{u}{2}\left(1-\sqrt{1-\dfrac{Qq}{\pi\varepsilon_0 mru^2}}\right); & \text{If } u > \sqrt{\dfrac{Qq}{\pi\varepsilon_0 mr}} \end{cases}$

20. $T = \dfrac{8\pi}{q}\sqrt{\dfrac{\pi\varepsilon_0 ml^3}{3}}$

Hint: During the oscillatory motion, mass centre remains stationary. In the figure, angle between the threads is shown much exaggerated only for the sake of readability. The mass centre is assumed as the origin of the coordinate system, on the y-axis of which the middle particle oscillates. The end particles follow a curved path of so small curvature that their path can be assumed almost straight and perpendicular to the x-axis.

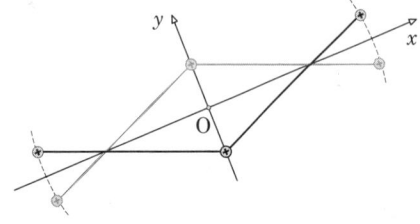

21. (a) $k > 2\pi\varepsilon_0 rE^2$

(b) $\dfrac{\pi\varepsilon_0 r l_0 E^2}{k - 2\pi\varepsilon_0 rE^2}$ and $2\pi\sqrt{\dfrac{m}{2k - 4\pi\varepsilon_0 rE^2}}$

22. (a) $\dfrac{4mu}{qE}$

(b) $l \geq \dfrac{mu^2}{qE}\left\{1+\left(\dfrac{2}{\pi}\right)^2\right\}$

Hint: Interaction with the electric field lasts over the first cycle of oscillation of the dumbbell about its mass centre; thereafter, dumbbell moves backwards with speed u without any residual oscillations.

23. $v = \sqrt{\dfrac{1}{4\pi\varepsilon_0 m}\left\{\dfrac{(Q+q)^2}{8r} - \dfrac{Qq}{l}\right\}}$

Hint: Kinetic energies of the ball can only change due to work done by interaction forces. The loss of energy due to redistribution of charges between the balls at time of contact will dissipate as heat and has nothing to do with change in kinetic energy. Therefore, the balls gain kinetic energy at the expense of interaction energy before the collision, during collision they exchange their velocities and after the collision, they further gain kinetic energy at the expense of their interaction energy.

24. $\approx E\sqrt{\dfrac{\pi\varepsilon_0 r}{m}\{(L^2-l^2)-r(L-l)\}} \approx E\sqrt{\dfrac{\pi\varepsilon_0 r(L^2-l^2)}{m}}$

25. $V = 2\sqrt{\dfrac{\sigma d}{\varepsilon_r \varepsilon_0}}$

Hint: Since the drop is made to spread slowly, all the energy supplied by the battery is utilized in increasing electrostatic potential energy stored in the electric field and in increasing the surface energy of mercury.

26. $\dfrac{8l}{q}\sqrt{\dfrac{\varepsilon_r \varepsilon_0 mlx}{d}}$

27. $r = \left(\dfrac{15\sigma\varepsilon_0}{2\rho^2}\right)^{\frac{1}{3}}$

Hint: Total energy comprising of electrostatic potential energy and surface energy due to surface tension of all the drops eventually acquires a minimum value.

Challenge your understanding

1. (a) $l_1 = \dfrac{l\sqrt{q_2 q_3}}{\sqrt{q_1 q_2} + \sqrt{q_2 q_3} + \sqrt{q_3 q_1}}$,

   $l_2 = \dfrac{l\sqrt{q_1 q_3}}{\sqrt{q_1 q_2} + \sqrt{q_2 q_3} + \sqrt{q_3 q_1}}$ and

   $l_3 = \dfrac{l\sqrt{q_1 q_2}}{\sqrt{q_1 q_2} + \sqrt{q_2 q_3} + \sqrt{q_3 q_1}}$

   (b) $\sqrt{q_1 q_2} < \sqrt{q_2 q_3} + \sqrt{q_3 q_1}$,

   $\sqrt{q_2 q_3} < \sqrt{q_1 q_2} + \sqrt{q_3 q_1}$ and

   $\sqrt{q_3 q_1} < \sqrt{q_1 q_2} + \sqrt{q_2 q_3}$

   Hint: Tension force has same magnitude everywhere on the thread.

2. $q_A \approx q\left\{1 - \dfrac{3r}{2a}\left(\dfrac{2-\sqrt{2}}{4}\right)\right\}$

   $q_B = q_C \approx q\left\{1 + \dfrac{3r}{4a}\left(\dfrac{2-\sqrt{2}}{4}\right)\right\}$

3. $v_A = \dfrac{3}{2}\sqrt{\dfrac{q^2}{2\pi\varepsilon_0 r_0 m}}$ ←,

   $v_B = \dfrac{1}{2}\sqrt{\dfrac{q^2}{2\pi\varepsilon_0 r_0 m}}$ ← and

   $v_C = \dfrac{1}{2}\sqrt{\dfrac{q^2}{2\pi\varepsilon_0 r_0 m}}$ →

4. If $u = 2v_0$, then $v_A = v_B = v_D = 0$ and $v_C = 2v_0$

   If $u > 2v_0$, then $v_A = 2v_0$, $v_B = v_D = -v_0$ and $v_C = u$

   If $u < 2v_0$, then $v_A = -\dfrac{1}{3}(u + 4v_0)$, $v_B = v_D = \dfrac{1}{3}(2u - v_0)$ and $v_C = 2v_0$

   Here $v_0 = \sqrt{\dfrac{q^2}{6\pi\varepsilon_0 m d}}$

Chapter 13

Electric Current

Electric current, current density, Ohm's law: general and circuital forms, series and parallel arrangements of resistances, capacitors and cells, voltage and current sources, equi-valent circuits, Kirchhoff's laws and their applications to resistive and RC circuits, Wheatstone bridge and its applications, heating effect of current, galvanometer, voltmeter, ammeter and other measuring instruments.

"Except our own thoughts, there is nothing absolutely in our power."

René Descartes
(31 March 1596 – 11 February 1650)

BACK TO BASICS

Electric current:

It is defined as time rate of flow of electric charge across a surface.

$$I = \lim_{\Delta t \to 0} \frac{\Delta q}{\Delta t} = \frac{dq}{dt}$$

Conventionally, direction of current is taken along the direction of flow of positive charge or opposite to flow of negative charge.

Current density:

Electric current is a macroscopic description (over a surface), whereas current density is a microscopic description that defines electric current flowing through a surface at a point. It is a vector quantity.

Electric current is defined as flux of current density vector $\vec{J}$.

$$I = \int \vec{J} \cdot d\vec{S}$$

If current flow is everywhere normal to the surface under investigation, the current density is given by

$$J = \frac{dI}{dS}$$

Electric conduction and Ohm's Law:

Electric current density at a point in a conductor of conductivity σ subjected to electric field $\vec{E}$ is given by the equation

$$\vec{J} = \sigma \vec{E}$$

The above equation is known as the generalized Ohm's law.

For a material in which conductivity does not depend on current, the potential difference V across a specimen of length l and cross-section area A is proportional to the current I flowing through it.

$$V = \frac{l}{\sigma A} I = \frac{\rho l}{A} I = RI$$

Here ρ is reciprocal of conductivity and is known as resistivity or specific resistance of a material and R is known as resistance of the specimen.

The above equation is the circuital form of the Ohm's law.

Relation between resistance and capacitance of a medium:

Product of resistance and capacitance between two interfaces of a homogeneous medium equals the product of resistivity and permittivity of the medium.

$$RC = \rho \varepsilon$$

Kirchhoff's laws:

All kinds of electric circuits can be analysed by the following two laws.

> **Current law:**
> Algebraic sum of all branch currents at a junction is zero.
>
> **Voltage law:**
> Algebraic sum of all electromotive forces in a closed loop is equal to algebraic sum of all voltage drops in the loop.

Electric power:

Electric power p consumed or delivered in the circuit by a device equals the product of potential difference V across the device and current I flowing through the device.

$$p = VI$$

A device consumes or delivers power depending on, whether in the device the current flows in the direction of decreasing potential or increasing potential.

For an Ohmic resistance R

$$p = VI = \frac{V^2}{R} = I^2 R$$

Electric Current 13.3

Multiple Choice Questions

1. A constant current I flows in a strip-line conductor, resistivity of which increases monotonically in the direction of the current flow. If resistivities at cross-sections A and B are ρ_A and ρ_B, find excess charge accumulated in section AB. Permittivity of free space is ε_0 and relative permittivity of material of the strip is ε_r everywhere in the strip.

   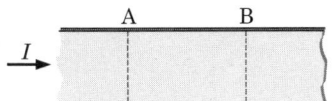

   (a) $\varepsilon_0 (\rho_B - \rho_A) I$
   (b) $\varepsilon_0 \varepsilon_r (\rho_B - \rho_A) I$
   (c) $\varepsilon_0 (\varepsilon_r - 1)(\rho_B - \rho_A) I$
   (d) $\varepsilon_0 (\varepsilon_r^2 - 1)(\rho_B - \rho_A) I$

2. Under which of the following conditions, resistance of a cylindrical specimen of an Ohmic material is least affected by small temperature variations.

   (a) Temperature coefficient of resistivity is greater than that of linear expansion.
   (b) Temperature coefficient of resistivity is lesser than that of linear expansion.
   (c) Temperature coefficient of resistivity is equal to that of linear expansion.
   (d) Temperature coefficient of resistivity is negligible as compared to that of linear expansion.

3. A homogeneous rod AB of uniform cross-section is connected across a battery. By some arrangement (not shown in the figure), section CD of the rod is being uniformly heated. What can you conclude regarding temperature distribution in the rod?

   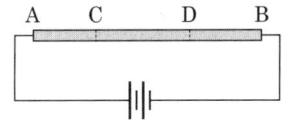

   (a) Temperatures in all the three sections will be uniform with the highest value in section CD and equal lower values in sections AC and DB.
   (b) Temperatures in all the three sections will be uniform with the highest value in section AC, the lowest value in section DB and an intermediate value in section CD.
   (c) Temperatures in all the three sections will be uniform with the highest value in section CD, the lowest value in section DB and an intermediate value in section AC.
   (d) Temperature distribution in all the three sections will be non-uniform with location of the highest temperature nearer to D in section CD.

4. A closed cubical box is made by a thin conducting sheet. When its diagonally opposite corners are connected across a battery, it draws a current I from the battery. Find current flowing across edge BE.

   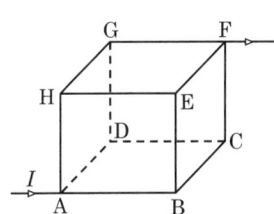

   (a) $\dfrac{I}{3}$
   (b) $\dfrac{I}{6}$
   (c) $\dfrac{I}{9}$
   (d) Between $\dfrac{I}{6}$ and $\dfrac{I}{3}$

13.4 Chapter-13

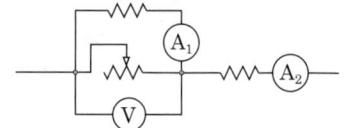

5. In the figure is shown a part of a large network. If resistance of the rheostat is increased, how will the readings I_1 and I_2 of ammeters A_1 and A_2 respectively and the reading of the voltmeter V change?

   (a) I_1 and I_2 will decrease and V increase.
   (b) I_1 will decrease and I_2 and V increase.
   (c) I_2 will decrease and I_1 and V increase.
   (d) It is sure that I_2 will decrease but nothing can be predicted about I_1 and V from the given information.

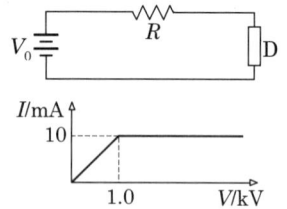

6. Volt-ampere (V-I) characteristics of an unknown device D connected in a circuit in series with a resistance and a battery is shown in the figure. If value of the resistance is $R = 300$ kΩ and terminal voltage of the battery is $V_0 = 5$ kV, find potential drop across the device.

   (a) 1.0 kV   (b) 2.0 kV
   (c) 3.0 kV   (d) 4.0 kV

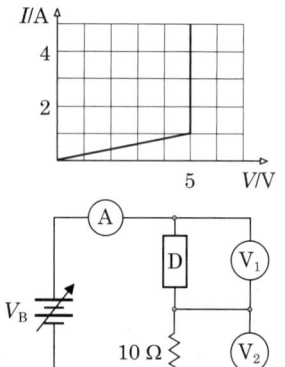

7. Volt-ampere (V-I) characteristic of a nonlinear device D and corresponding circuit used are shown in the adjoining figures. Voltage V_B of the battery is made to vary from zero to 30 V and voltage V_1 across the device D, voltage V_2 across the 10 Ω resistor and current I supplied by the battery are measured by ideal voltmeters V_1 and V_2 and an ideal ammeter A. Which of the following graph/graphs represent correct relationship?

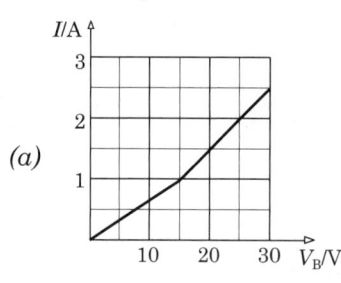
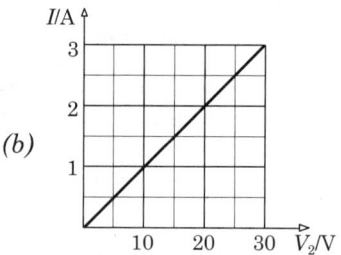
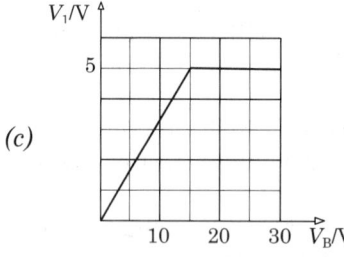
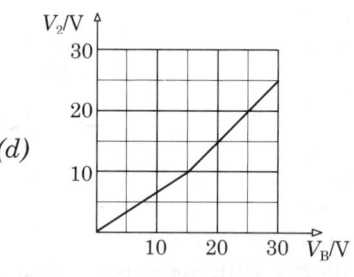

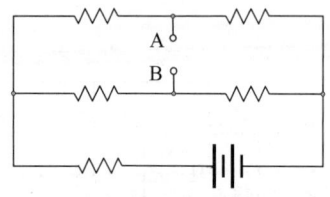

8. A network shown in the figure consists of a battery and five unknown resistors. When an ideal ammeter is connected between terminals A and B, its reading is 4 A and when a resistance of 3 Ω is connected in series with the ammeter its reading becomes 2 A. Now the ammeter and the resistance are disconnected, and an ideal voltmeter is connected between terminals A and B. What would the voltmeter read?

   (a) 6 V   (b) 10 V
   (c) 12 V   (d) 18 V

9. The network shown consists of an ideal battery, an ideal voltmeter V, an ideal ammeter A, several resistors of different values and a rheostat. If resistance of the rheostat is increased by a finite amount, how will the readings of the voltmeter and ammeter change?

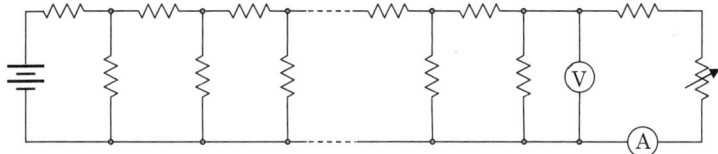

(a) Both will decrease.
(b) Voltmeter reading will decrease, and ammeter reading will increase.
(c) Voltmeter reading will increase, and ammeter reading will decrease.
(d) Voltmeter reading will not change but ammeter reading will decrease.

10. The circuit shown in the diagram extends to the right into infinity. Each branch resistance is denoted by r. What is the resistance between the terminals A and B?

(a) $\dfrac{(\sqrt{5}+1)r}{2}$
(b) $\dfrac{(\sqrt{5}-1)r}{2}$
(c) $(\sqrt{5}+1)r$
(d) $(\sqrt{5}-1)r$

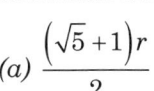

11. The circuit shown in the diagram extends to the right into infinity. Each battery has electromotive force V (unknown) and internal resistance r (known). Each resistor has resistance 4r. Reading of the ideal ammeter shown in the diagram is I. Find the value of V in terms of I and r.

(a) $(2-2\sqrt{2})Ir$
(b) $(2+2\sqrt{2})Ir$
(c) $4.5Ir$
(d) $3.0Ir$

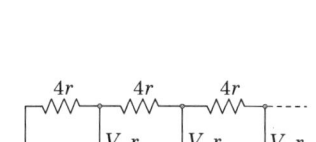

12. An ideal battery of electromotive force $\mathcal{E}$ is connected in series with an ammeter and a voltmeter of unknown internal resistances. If a certain resistance is connected in parallel with the voltmeter, the voltmeter and the ammeter readings becomes $1/\eta$ and η times of their respective initial readings. What is the initial reading of the voltmeter?

(a) $\dfrac{\mathcal{E}}{(\eta+1)}$
(b) $\dfrac{\eta\mathcal{E}}{(\eta+1)}$
(c) $\dfrac{\eta\mathcal{E}}{(\eta-1)}$
(d) $\dfrac{(\eta+1)\mathcal{E}}{\eta}$

13. Two identical conducting spheres each of radius a are placed at centre-to-centre separation d (d >> a). They are kept in a homogeneous medium of permittivity ε and resistivity ρ. Which one of the following is a correct expression of resistance between them?

(a) $\dfrac{\rho}{2\pi a}$
(b) $\dfrac{\rho}{4\pi a}$
(c) $\dfrac{\rho d}{2\pi a^2}$
(d) $\dfrac{\rho d}{4\pi a^2}$

14. An air-filled parallel-plate capacitor with the plate area A is connected to a battery of electromotive force V and negligible internal resistance. One of the plates is made to vibrate so that the distance between the plates varies as $d = d_0 + a\cos(\omega t)$, where $a \ll d_0$. If instantaneous current in the circuit reaches a maximum value of I_0, the maximum possible amplitude of vibrations a is

(a) $\dfrac{aI_0}{VA\omega\varepsilon_0}$
(b) $\dfrac{I_0 d_0}{VA\omega\varepsilon_0}$
(c) $\dfrac{I_0 d_0^2}{VA\omega\varepsilon_0}$
(d) $\dfrac{I_0 d_0}{V\sqrt{A\omega\varepsilon_0}}$

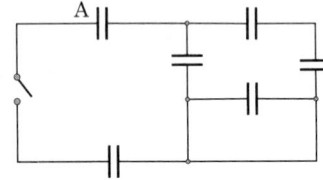

15. In the circuit shown, all capacitors are identical, initially the switch is open and only capacitor A is charged. After the switch is closed and a steady state is established, charge on capacitor A becomes 5.0 μC. Initial charge on this capacitor is closest to

(a) 7.5 μC (b) 8.0 μC
(c) 13.3 μC (d) 15.0 μC

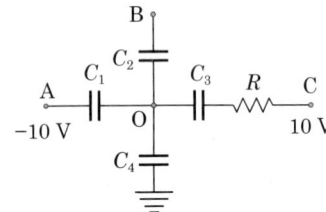

16. The figure shows part of a large network in which potentials of some of the points are shown. Each capacitor has a capacitance 5 μF. Which of the following statements is/are true?

(a) From the given information, potential of point O can be determined but that of B cannot be determined.
(b) From the given information, potential of both points O and B cannot be determined.
(c) If charge on capacitor C_2 were also specified, potential of point O can be determined but that of B cannot be determined.
(d) If charge on capacitor C_2 were also specified, potentials of both points O and B can be determined.

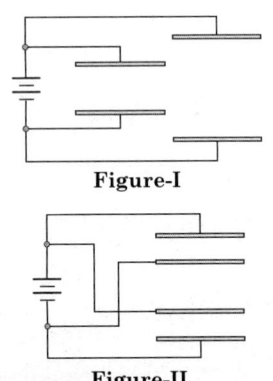

17. Two parallel plate capacitors of capacitances C and $2C$ consisting of plates of identical dimensions are connected with an ideal battery of terminal voltage V as shown in figure-I. Now the capacitor smaller in volume is completely inserted into the larger capacitor and kept in symmetric position and then connection polarities of the plates are reversed as shown in figure-II. Which one of the following statements is correct?

(a) Charge flown through the battery is $8CV$ and it absorbs energy.
(b) Charge flown through the battery is $8CV$ and it delivers energy.
(c) Charge flown through the battery is $7CV$ and it absorbs energy.
(d) Charge flown through the battery is $7CV$ and it delivers energy.

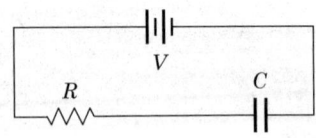

18. An air-filled parallel plate capacitor of capacitance C is connected through a resistance R to an ideal voltage source of electromotive force V. A dielectric plate of dielectric constant k is inserted in the capacitor to occupy whole space between the plates. After a steady state is reached, the plate is quickly pulled out. Which of the following is correct expression for heat generated in the resistance until a steady state is reached again?

(a) $CV^2(k-1)$
(b) $\frac{1}{2}CV^2(k-1)$
(c) $CV^2(k-1)^2$
(d) $\frac{1}{2}CV^2(k-1)^2$

19. In the circuit shown, device D has a property that, if initially non-conducting, it remains non-conducting until voltage across it rises to a value V_1 ($<V_0$). It then rapidly discharges the capacitor until the voltage across it drops to a negligibly small value, where upon it returns to a non-conducting state. The voltage developed across the capacitor is

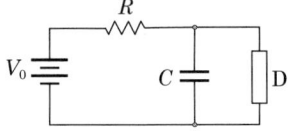

(a) periodic with time period RC.
(b) periodic with time period $RC\ln\left(\dfrac{V_0}{V_1}\right)$.
(c) periodic with time period $RC\ln\left(\dfrac{V_0}{V_0-V_1}\right)$.
(d) periodic with time period $RC\ln\left(\dfrac{V_0^2}{V_1(V_0-V_1)}\right)$.

Questions 20 and 21 are based on the following write-up.

A conducting balloon of radius a is charged to a potential V_0 and held at a large height above the earth surface. The large height of the balloon from the earth ensures that charge distribution on the surface of the balloon remains unaffected by the presence of the earth. It is earthed through a resistance R and a valve is opened. The gas inside the balloon escapes through the valve and the size of the balloon decreases. The rate of decrease in radius of the balloon is controlled in such a manner that potential of the balloon remains constant. Assume electric permittivity of the surrounding air equal to that of free space (ε_0) and charge does not leak to the surrounding air.

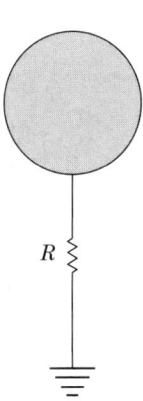

20. Time rate at which radius r of the balloon changes is best represented by the expression

(a) $\dfrac{1}{4\pi\varepsilon_0 R}$
(b) $-\dfrac{1}{4\pi\varepsilon_0 R}$
(c) $\dfrac{r}{4\pi\varepsilon_0 aR}$
(d) $-\dfrac{r}{4\pi\varepsilon_0 aR}$

21. How much heat is dissipated in the resistance R until the radius of the balloon becomes half?

(a) $0.5\pi\varepsilon_0 aV_0^2$
(b) $\pi\varepsilon_0 aV_0^2$
(c) $2\pi\varepsilon_0 aV_0^2$
(d) $4\pi\varepsilon_0 aV_0^2$

Questions 22 and 23 are based on the following write-up.

A parallel plate capacitor is filled with two layers of different materials A and B as shown in the figure on the next page. The material A has dielectric constant k_1 and conductivity σ_1 and the material B has

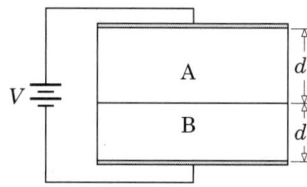

dielectric constant k_2 and conductivity σ_2. The capacitor is connected across an ideal battery of terminal voltage V. Permittivity of free space is ε_0.

22. Electric field in the material A is

(a) $\dfrac{V\sigma_1}{d_1\sigma_1 + d_2\sigma_2}$

(b) $\dfrac{V\sigma_2}{d_1\sigma_1 + d_2\sigma_2}$

(c) $\dfrac{V\sigma_1}{d_1\sigma_2 + d_2\sigma_1}$

(d) $\dfrac{V\sigma_2}{d_1\sigma_2 + d_2\sigma_1}$

23. What is the total surface charge density on the interface of the two materials?

(a) $\dfrac{\varepsilon_0 V(k_1 - k_2)}{d_1 k_2 + d_2 k_1}$

(b) $\dfrac{\varepsilon_0 V(\sigma_1 - \sigma_2)}{d_1\sigma_2 + d_2\sigma_1}$

(c) $\dfrac{\varepsilon_0 V(\sigma_1 k_2 - \sigma_2 k_1)}{d_1\sigma_2 + d_2\sigma_1}$

(d) $\dfrac{V}{\varepsilon_0 d_1 d_2}\left[\dfrac{d_1}{d_1 + d_2} - \dfrac{d_2}{d_1 + d_2}\right]$

Questions 24 and 25 are based on the following write-up.

Consider two electrically neutral concentric conducting thin spherical shells of radii r and $3r$. A particle of positive charge Q is fixed at a distance $2r$ from the common centres of the shells. The inner shell can be electrically connected to the outer shell through a resistance R_1 with the help of a switch S_1 and the outer shell can be grounded through a resistance R_2 with the help of another switch S_2 as shown in the figure.

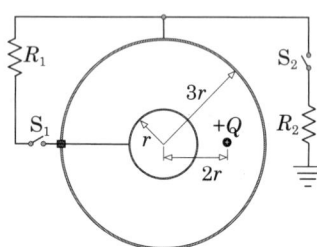

24. How much total heat is dissipated in the resistance R_1 after switch S_1 is closed keeping switch S_2 open until a steady state is reached?

(a) $\dfrac{Q^2}{48\pi\varepsilon_0 r}$

(b) $\dfrac{Q^2}{96\pi\varepsilon_0 r}$

(c) $\dfrac{Q^2}{192\pi\varepsilon_0 r}$

(d) $\dfrac{Q^2}{384\pi\varepsilon_0 r}$

25. When a steady state is reached after closing switch S_1, the other switch S_2 is closed. How much total heat is dissipated after switch S_2 is closed until a new steady state is reached?

(a) Heat-dissipated in each resistor is $\dfrac{Q^2}{48\pi\varepsilon_0 r}$.

(b) Heat-dissipated in R_1 is $\dfrac{Q^2}{24\pi\varepsilon_0 r}$ and no heat is dissipated in R_2.

(c) Heat-dissipated in R_2 is $\dfrac{Q^2}{24\pi\varepsilon_0 r}$ and no heat is dissipated in R_1.

(d) Both the resistors dissipate different amounts of heat, total amount of which is $\dfrac{Q^2}{24\pi\varepsilon_0 r}$.

Build up your understanding

1. An electron gun on a space-probe starts emitting an electron beam into the space. Electrons in the beam have energy $W = 9.0 \times 10^4$ eV, and the beam is equivalent to an electric current $I = 1.0$ mA. If the space-probe is a metal sphere of radius $r = 1.0$ m, find electric field strength at the surface of the space-probe 1.0 min after starting the electron gun. Charge on an electron is $e = -1.6 \times 10^{-19}$ C.

2. A composite spherical shell of radius $r = 10$ cm and wall thickness $t = 0.1$ mm is made of copper except an equatorial strip of width $b = 0.2$ cm, which is made of aluminium. When the poles of the sphere are connected across an ideal battery of terminal voltage $V = 0.1$ mV, a current $I = 5.12$ A flows through it. If the aluminium strip is replaced by an iron strip of identical dimensions and the experiment is repeated with the same battery, what current will flow through the battery? Resistivities of aluminium and iron are $\rho_{Al} = 0.03$ $\Omega \cdot$mm^2/m and $\rho_{Fe} = 0.10$ $\Omega \cdot$mm^2/m.

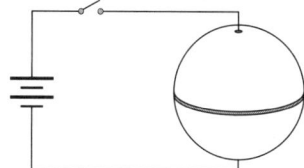

3. A ring of a radius $r = 16$ cm is made of a wire of uniform cross-section of radius $a = 1.0$ mm. Resistivity ρ of the material of the wire is not uniform and varies with angular position θ measured from a fixed radius according to the given graph. How much maximum resistance between a pair of points on this ring can be obtained?

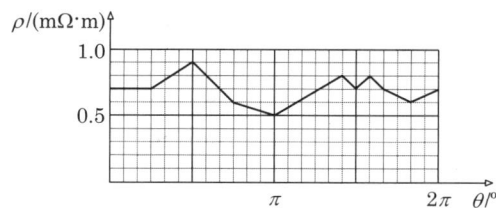

4. Three uncharged metallic balls of radii a, b and a respectively are connected to terminals A, B and C with the help of long thin conductors as shown in the circuit. Find charges established on each of the balls, when a steady state is reached after the switch is closed. Consider the balls to be at great distances from each other as well from the circuit and neglect internal resistance of the battery.

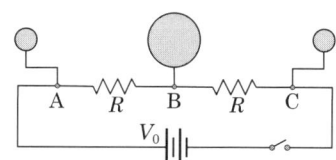

5. A uniform underground cable AB connects two telegraph offices, which are 8 km apart. Due to a fault at a place C, the conductor of the cable comes in contact with the earth. Current flowing to the earth at fault location faces 10 Ω resistance. To locate the fault when an engineer applies 20 V between end A and the earth, his colleague measures 5 V between end B and the earth. Moreover, when his colleague applies 30 V between end B and the earth, the engineer measures 5 V between end A and the earth. What is the distance of the fault location along the cable from end A?

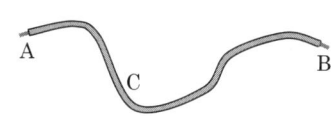

6. The network shown consists of an ideal voltage source, an ideal ammeter and five resistances. Determine reading of the ammeter.

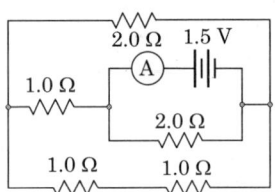

7. An actual battery can be represented as a constant voltage source in series with a resistor, known as internal resistance. Three identical actual batteries A, B and C connected as shown in first figure, cause a current of 3.0 A to flow in the circuit. If the batteries were connected as shown in the second figure, what would the current through batteries A, B and C be?

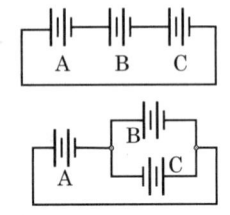

8. A portion of a large network is shown in the figure. Values of the resistances are indicated in the figure and both ammeters A_1 and A_2 are ideal. If reading of ammeter A_1 is 1.0 A, how much will ammeter A_2 read?

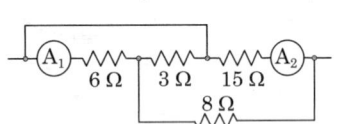

9. When a resistance $R = 100\ \Omega$ is connected across terminals of a battery, a current I flows through it and when an additional unknown resistance is connected in series with R, a current $3I/4$ flows through the battery. If the unknown resistance is connected in parallel with R, the battery current becomes $6I/5$. Find value of the unknown resistance.

10. Resistors R, $2R$, $3R$ .... $100R$ are connected in series and free ends of this series are connected to make a closed loop. An ideal battery is connected between the junction of resistor R and $100R$ and the junction of resistors nR and $(n+1)R$. Find value of n for which a minimum current flows through the battery?

11. A resistance R and a nonlinear device D are connected with an ideal battery as shown in the given network. Current I through the nonlinear device varies with voltage V across the device according to equation $I = kV^2$. Here k is a positive constant. Find expression for the current in the circuit.

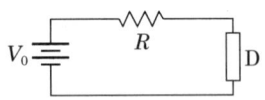

12. In the given circuit, an ideal battery of terminal voltage $V_0 = 200$ V is connected across a network consisting of resistors $R_1 = 20\ \Omega$ and $R_2 = 20\ \Omega$ and a nonlinear device D. Volt-ampere (V-I) characteristic of non-linear device D is also shown in the adjoining figure. Find voltage across resistance R_2.

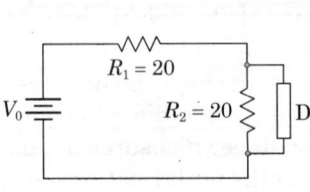
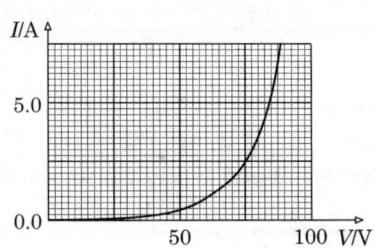

13. Determine equivalent resistance between terminals A and B of the network shown.

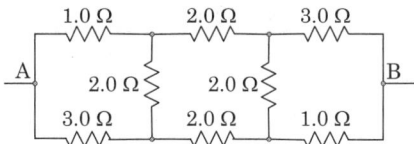

14. Twelve resistances are arranged in the edges of a cube and electrically connected only at the corners of the cube. Find equivalent resistance between corners A and G.

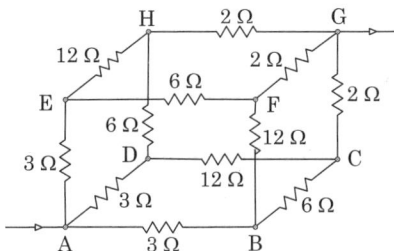

15. A circuit shown in the figure consists of an ideal battery, three resistances R_1, R_2 and R_3 and two ideal ammeters. At present the ammeters read 0.2 A and 0.3 A as shown. If on interchanging places of any two of these resistances, the readings of the ammeters remain unaffected, how much current is the battery supplying?

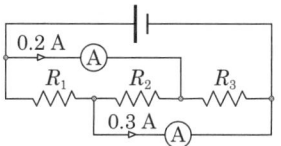

16. A network shown in the figure consists of three ideal batteries each of terminal voltage 100 V, four resistances each of value 4 Ω and a rheostat. Find relationship between current I through the rheostat and voltage V across the rheostat for all values of resistance of the rheostat.

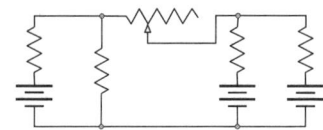

17. A black box (you cannot see what is inside the box) with an unknown electric circuit inside has four terminals A, B, C and D. To know the contents inside the black box, following circuit consisting of an ideal battery, two non-ideal identical voltmeters and two non-ideal identical ammeters is arranged. Terminal voltage of the battery and readings of the instruments are shown in the figure. Suggest the simplest possible circuit in the black box and find its parameters.

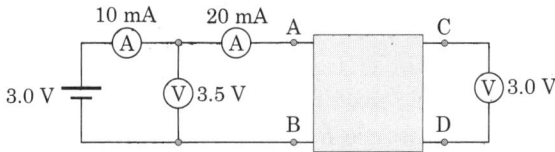

18. In an infinite grid of square cells made of conducting wires, resistance of an edge of a square cell is R. In the figure, point C is midpoint of edge AB. Find resistance of the entire grid as measured between terminal pairs A-B and A-C.

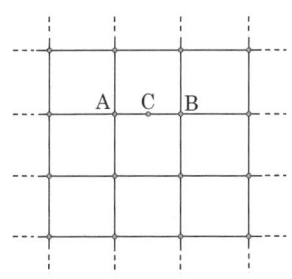

13.12 Chapter-13

19. Find the equivalent resistance between terminals A and B of the following infinite ladder networks.

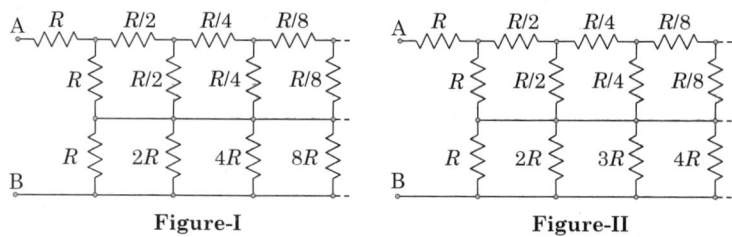

Figure-I   Figure-II

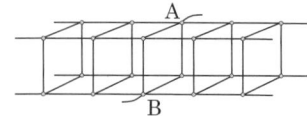

20. The network shown consists of an infinitely large number of identical sections. Resistance of each branch is R. Find resistance of the whole network measured between terminals A and B.

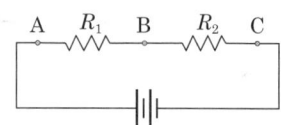

21. A voltmeter of internal resistance 1.0 kΩ reads voltages 1.8 V, 1.8 V and 4.5 V between terminal pairs A-B, B-C and A-C respectively of a circuit consisting of an ideal battery and two unknown resistances R_1 and R_2 as shown. What will another voltmeter of internal resistance 2.0 kΩ read between these terminal pairs?

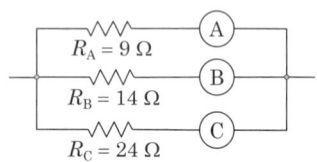

22. The figure shows a portion of an electric circuit. All the resistances R_A, R_B and R_C are known, and their values are indicated in the figure. All the voltmeters A, B and C are identical. If the readings of voltmeters A and B are $V_A = 7.5$ V and $V_B = 5.0$ V respectively, find the reading of voltmeter C.

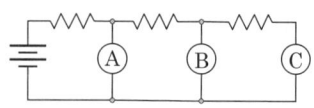

23. The circuit shown consists of three identical resistances and three identical voltmeters A, B and C. If the first voltmeter A reads $V_A = 22$ V and the third voltmeter C reads $V_C = 8$ V, calculate reading of the second voltmeter B.

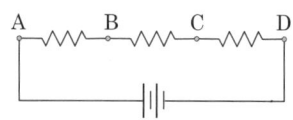

24. Three identical resistances are connected in series and their combination is connected across an ideal battery. If you connect a voltmeter between terminals A and D, the voltmeter reads $V_1 = 3.00$ V and if you connect the voltmeter between terminals A and B, the voltmeter reads $V_2 = 0.96$ V. If you short-circuit terminals A and C and then connect the voltmeter between terminals B and D, how much will it read?

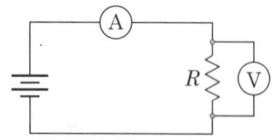

25. In the circuit shown, the voltmeter reads $V_1 = 1.0$ V and the ammeter reads $I_1 = 1.0$ A. On changing the places of the ammeter and the voltmeter, the voltmeter will read $V_2 = 2.0$ V and the ammeter will read $I_2 = 0.5$ A. Find resistance R, resistances R_V of the voltmeter and R_A of the ammeter.

26. To measure electromotive force of a wristwatch battery, you are given two voltmeters. Each of them when connected alone across the battery, read $V_1 = 0.9$ V and $V_2 = 0.6$ V. If the voltmeters are simultaneously connected across the battery, both of them read $V_3 = 0.45$ V. Find the electromotive force of the battery.

27. The circuit shown consists of three identical ideal voltmeters A, B and C, five resistors and an ideal battery. Find readings of all the voltmeters in terms of the terminal voltage V of the battery.

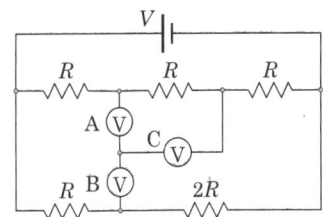

28. A multi-range milli-ammeter is made by providing a set of interchangeable shunts and a microampere range galvanometer. This milli-ammeter is connected in a circuit to measure current. When 1.0 mA range is selected, it reads $I_1 = 1.0$ mA and when 3.0 mA range is selected it reads $I_2 = 1.5$ mA. What is the true current I_0 in the circuit without the milli-ammeter?

29. A homemade Ohmmeter consists of a series connected battery, a resistance and an ammeter. A student constructs two such ohmmeters using non-identical components and calibrates them by measuring the same set of known resistances. These two Ohmmeters are together connected in parallel with an unknown resistance R as shown in the figure. If one of the ohmmeters reads $R_1 = 30\ \Omega$ and other reads $R_2 = 60\ \Omega$, find true value of the unknown resistance R.

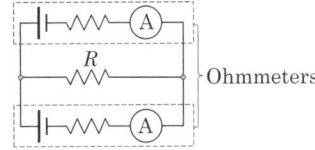

30. When a 50 W bulb is inserted in a table lamp holder, the connecting wires dissipate 1.0 mW. How much power will be dissipated in the connecting wires, if you insert a 100 W bulb in the table lamp holder?

31. The circuit shown, consists of three resistances, an incandescent bulb, a switch and a battery. If bulb B glows equally bright whether the switch is closed or open, find resistance of the bulb and the voltage-drop across it.

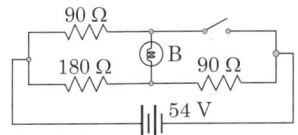

32. In the given circuit when the switch is open, ammeter A reads 2.5 A, two of the four resistances dissipate 50 W each and other two resistances dissipate 200 W each. If the switch is closed and terminal voltage of the battery is so adjusted that the ammeter reading again becomes 2.5 A, find power dissipation in each of the resistances.

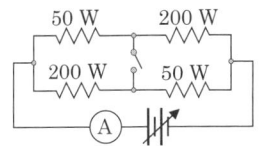

33. The given circuit consists of two ideal batteries, two fixed value resistances and a variable resistance. Terminal voltages V_1 and V_2 of the batteries and resistances R_1 and R_2 are known. Find the resistance R of the variable resistance for which maximum power is developed in it and the corresponding maximum power.

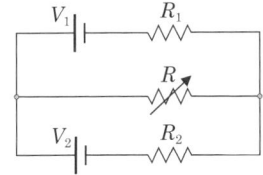

34. Three identical vessels A, B and C containing equal quantities of ice at 0 °C are placed in a room. Identical heating elements placed inside each vessel are connected across batteries of terminal voltages $V_A = 380$ V, $V_B = 220$ V and $V_C = 110$ V respectively. If all the ice of vessel A melts in $t_A = 4$ min and all the ice of vessel B melts in $t_B = 20$ min, how long will it take to melt all the ice of vessel C? Assume that the heating element, the ice and vessels remain in thermal equilibrium.

35. A cylindrical conductor is connected across a battery and when a steady state is reached, temperature of the conductor exceeds the ambient temperature by $\Delta\theta = 16$ °C. If the length of the conductor is reduced to $\eta = 0.8$ times by cutting off extra length and other conditions are kept unaltered, by what amount will the temperature of the conductor change?

36. In a laboratory where room temperature is $\theta_0 = 0$ °C, temperature of a cylindrical conductor connected across a battery reaches a value $\theta = (20\sqrt{2})$ °C in steady state. Now the cylinder is uniformly stretched to $\eta = 2$ times of its initial length and left connected across the same battery in the same surroundings. If resistivity of material of the conductor remains unchanged on stretching, find its temperature when it comes again in a steady state.

37. Two identical metal spheres are immersed in a homogeneous medium of large extent. Radius of each sphere is negligible as compared to the depth of immersion and the distance between the spheres. When one sphere is connected with the positive terminal of a battery and other with the negative terminal of the battery using thin insulated conductors, current $I_0 = 3.0$ A flows through the battery. What current will flow through the battery, if one of these spheres is replaced by another sphere of radius $\eta = 0.5$ times of that of the previous sphere? Resistance of the conductors and the source can be neglected.

38. It is desired to keep current in discharge process of a capacitor constant. For the purpose, following three schemes (a), (b) and (c) are suggested.

(a) In this scheme, after closing the switch you have to vary resistance of the rheostat. The initial charge on the capacitance C_0 is q_0 and range of values of resistance of the rheostat is zero to R_0. Find the law $R(t)$ according to which resistance of the rheostat should be changed with time.

(b) In this scheme, a variable disk capacitor is connected across a fixed resistance R_0. After closing the switch, you have to vary the capacitance by rotating one of its plates. The initial value of capacitance is C_0 and charge on it is q_0. Find the law $C(t)$ according to which capacitance should be changed with time and corresponding angular velocity $\omega(t)$ of one plate relative to the other.

(c) In this scheme, a variable capacitor is used in which one plate can be shifted towards or away from the other fixed plate without changing overlap area. After closing the switch, you have to move the movable plate. The initial value of capacitance is C_0 and charge on it is q_0. Find the law $C(t)$ according to which capacitance and the distance $x(t)$ between the plates should be changed with time.

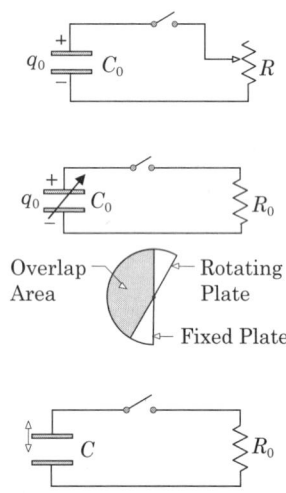

39. Three 1 Ω, three 8 Ω and three 3 Ω resistances and three 5 μF capacitors are connected in the edges of a cube constructed by conducting wires. If an ideal battery of electromotive force 12 V is connected between the two diagonally opposite corners A and B of the cube, find charges on the capacitors.

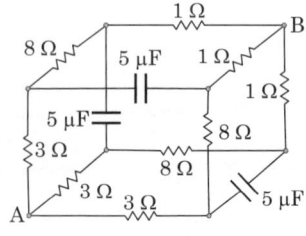

40. In the circuit shown, ratio of capacitors is $C_2/C_1 = 4/3$ and terminal voltage of the battery connected at the left end is V_0. What should be terminal voltage of the battery connected at the right most end so that the potentials of nodes 1, 2, 3, 4, 5 and 6 be in a geometric progression?

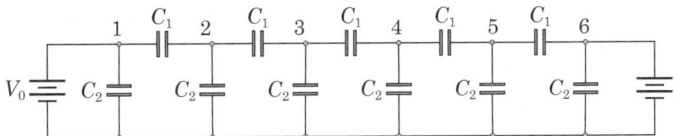

41. The circuit shown consists of two capacitors of capacitances C and $2C$, a resistance R and an ideal battery of terminal voltage V. Initially the switch is open and the capacitors are fully charged. How much total heat will be dissipated in the circuit after the switch is closed?

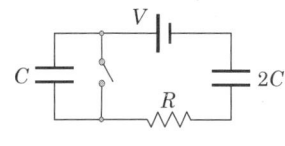

42. Two identical parallel plate capacitors are connected as shown in the figure. Initially both have a total charge q_0 and separation between their plates x_0. At an instant, plates of one capacitor begin to move towards each other and plates of the other capacitor away from each other. If velocity of a plate relative to the other in both the capacitors has the same magnitude v, find current in the circuit.

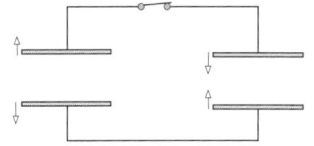

43. A circuit consisting of an uncharged capacitor and a resistance sealed inside a black box and two terminals are taken outside. At time $t = 0$ a capacitor of capacitance $C = 1.0\ \mu F$ having a charge $q_0 = 50\ \mu C$ is connected across the terminals taken outside the black box. A plot of the charge on this capacitor with time is shown in the figure. Find resistance R_{in} and capacitance C_{in} that are inside the black box.

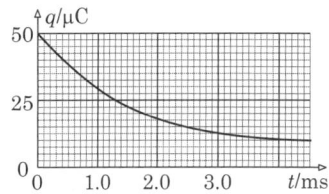

44. A thick spherical shell of inner and outer radii r_1 and r_2 is made of a material of resistivity ρ and dielectric constant ε_r. Initially the shell is electrically neutral and has no charge accumulation anywhere. If at the instant $t = 0$, a point charge q_0 is somehow placed at the centre, find charge on the outer surface of the shell as a function of time t. Ignore any effects due to magnetism or radiation.

45. Space between plates of a parallel plate capacitor is filled by a weakly conducting viscous fluid of resistivity ρ and dielectric constant ε_r. Distance between the plates is d. The capacitor is connected across an ideal battery of terminal voltage V and a small conducting and almost massless ball having a charge q_0 is released in the fluid. Force of viscous drag on the ball in the fluid is $F = \beta v$, where v is velocity of the ball and β is a known factor. If the ball stops before striking any of the plates, find the maximum distance the ball will move. Assume no gravity.

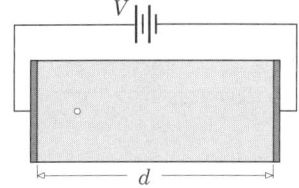

46. In the setup shown, when a particle P of charge q and mass m enters with velocity u in an uncharged parallel plate capacitor of capacitance C, the switch is closed. If time spent by the charge particle inside the capacitor is negligible as compared to the time constant RC of the circuit, find how acceleration of the particle varies with time t. Assume that the particle neither collides with the plates nor affects charge distribution on the plates. Also, neglect the edge effects and gravity.

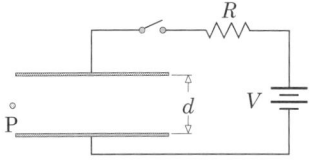

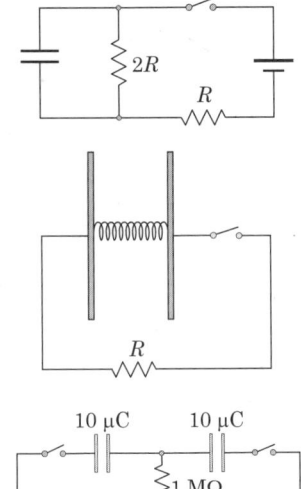

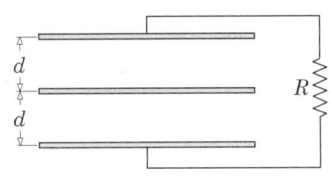

47. In the electric circuit shown, power dissipated in the resistances R and $2R$ at an instant after the switch is closed are 9 W and 2 W respectively. What is the rate of increase in the energy stored in the capacitor at this instant?

48. Midpoints of plates of a parallel plate capacitor are connected with the help of a light spring of stiffness k, relaxed length l and made of an insulating material. Each plate has an area A and mass m. One of the plates of the capacitor is given a charge $+q$ and the other a charge $-q$ and then the capacitor is allowed to discharge through a resistance R. Find expressions for total heat developed in the resistance under the following conditions.
    (a) Resistance R is very high.   (b) Resistance R is very small.

49. The circuit shown consists of two identical capacitor 10 µF each, a 1.0 MΩ resistor, three ideal voltage sources of terminal voltages 100 V, 550 V, 200 V and three switches. Calculate amount of heat dissipated in the resistor over a long time after all the switches are closed simultaneously.

50. One plate of a parallel plate capacitor of capacitance C is connected through a resistance R_1 and a key to a conducting ball of radius r. The other plate of the capacitor is earthed through another resistance R_2 as shown in the figure. The ball is far away from the earth as well as from the rest of the circuit. If the ball is given a charge Q and then the key is closed, what amount of heat will be dissipated in R_1 and R_2?

51. Three identical thin metal plates each of area A are arranged parallel to each other with separation d between adjacent plates and the outer plates are connected through a high resistance R as shown in the figure. A charge Q is given to the middle plate and then the middle plate is quickly shifted towards one of the outer plates by a distance $d/2$. How much heat will be dissipated in the resistor after this shift? Neglect gravity and assume free space conditions.

52. The circuit shown consists of two capacitors of capacitances 1.0 µF and 2.0 µF, two resistors of resistances 10 kΩ and 3 kΩ and two switches. Initially the switches are open and the capacitors are charged to potentials 4.0 V and 6.0 V respectively according to the polarities shown. If both the switches are closed simultaneously, what are amounts of heat dissipated in the 10 kΩ and the 3 kΩ resistors over a time large enough for complete discharge of both the capacitors?

Check your understanding

1. The given circuit consists of an ideal battery, n identical resistors each of resistance R and $n + 1$ identical conducting spheres each of radius r. Assume the balls to be at great distances from each other as well from

the circuit. Find the total charge finally accumulated on all the spheres after the key is closed.

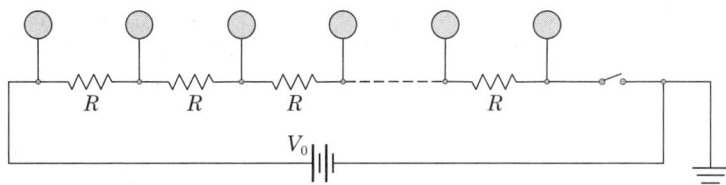

2. A black box has three terminals A, B and C coming out. If across A and B a voltage of 20 V is applied, terminals B and C show 8 V across them. If across terminals B and C a voltage of 20 V is applied, terminals A and C show 15 V across them. If the black box contains only resistances, suggest simplest circuit inside the black box.

3. A black box containing an unknown electric circuit has three terminals A, B and C. Three different experiments were performed with the black box by connecting a battery, a rheostat, an ideal ammeter and an ideal voltmeter. Measurements done in these experiments were recorded in graphs, which are shown together with corresponding circuit used. Suggest the simplest possible circuit or circuits in the black box and find its parameters.

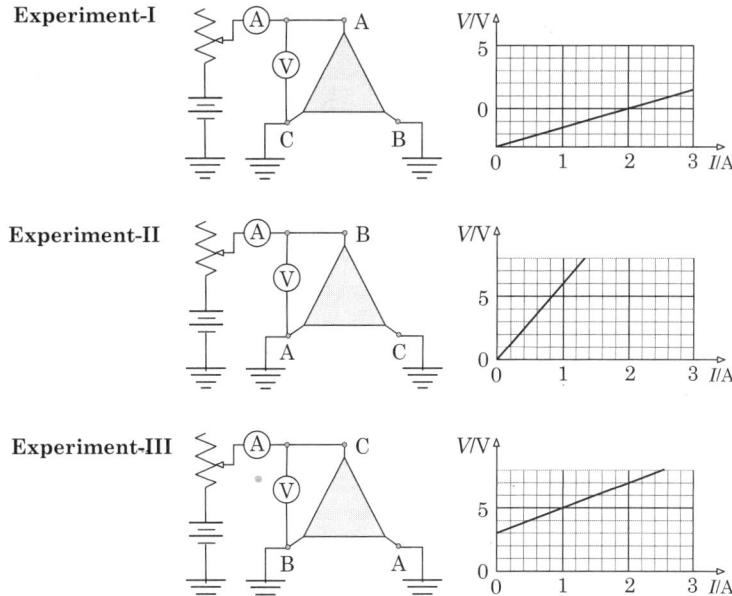

4. A network shown in the figure consists of an ideal battery of terminal voltage $V_0 = 3.00$ V, a milli-ammeter of very low resistance, four fixed value resistances and a rheostat. If on varying resistance of the rheostat from a large value to a vanishingly small value, reading of the milli-ammeter varies between $I_1 = 0.75$ mA to $I_2 = 1.00$ mA, find values of the fixed resistances R_1 and R_2.

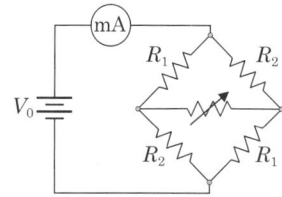

13.18 Chapter-13

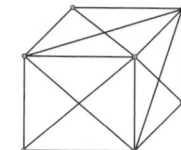

5. In a well-known cube network, each edge contains a 24 Ω resistor and additional 24 Ω resistors along each face diagonal. These resistors are only connected electrically at the corners of the cube. For the sake of readability, in the figure only some of these branches without the resistors are shown. Find equivalent resistance between two terminals connecting a face diagonal.

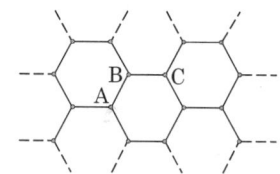

6. In an infinite grid of hexagonal cells, resistance of each branch is R. Determine equivalent resistance of the circuit between terminal pairs A-B and A-C.

7. Find equivalent resistance of the infinite ladder network between terminals A and B.

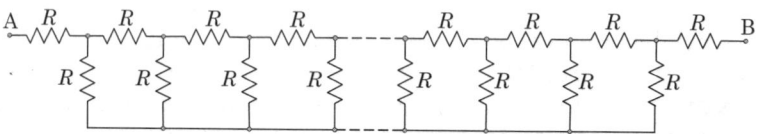

8. An infinite network is composed of identical batteries and identical voltmeters. Reading of the leftmost voltmeter is $V = 15$ V and reading of a voltmeter is $1/\eta$ times of the reading of the adjacent voltmeter to the left. Here $\eta = 1.1$. If the batteries and the voltmeters are not ideal, find the emf of a battery.

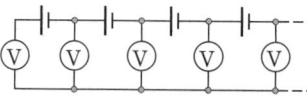

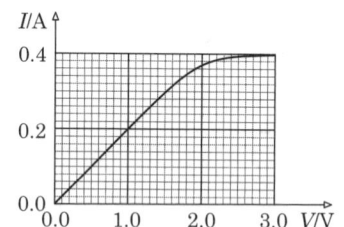

9. Volt-ampere (V-I) characteristics of an incandescent lamp is shown in the adjoining figure. This lamp can withstand a maximum voltage 3.0 V and a maximum current 0.4 A. An infinite ladder network consisting of a large number of these lamps is also shown in the figure given below. How much maximum voltage can be applied between the terminals A and B, so that no lamp gets damaged? (Use $\sqrt{5} \approx 2.2$).

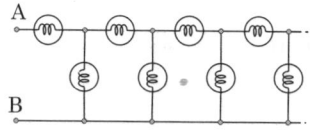

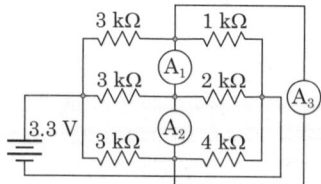

10. In the network shown in the figure, ammeters A_1, A_2 and A_3 are identical and internal resistance of the battery and internal resistances of the ammeters are much smaller than the six resistances connected in the network. Calculate readings of all the ammeters.

11. A nickel wire when connected across an ideal battery, temperature of the wire increases by $\Delta\theta_1 = 100$ °C after a long time. If the wire of half-length is used, by how many degrees will its temperature increase? Specific resistance of nickel depends on temperature θ according to the law $\rho = \rho_0(1 + \alpha\Delta\theta)$, where $\alpha = 0.0050$ K^{-1} and ρ_0 is the resistivity at the initial temperature.

12. Resistance R of a graphite resistor depends on its temperature according to the equation $R = R_0\{1 - \alpha(\theta - \theta_0)\}$, where R_0 and α are positive constants and temperature θ is in degree Celsius. Rate of heat transferred to the surrounding from this resistor is given by the equation $H = \beta(\theta - \theta_0)$, where β is a positive constant and θ_0 is the temperature of the surroundings. When this resistor is connected across an ideal battery and kept in a room maintained at θ_0, how does the steady state value of the following quantities depend on the electromotive force V of the battery?

    (a) Temperature of the resistor.   (b) Current through the resistor.

13. There are four identical resistors each in cylindrical shape. Their curved surfaces are thermally insulated therefore heat transfer can take place through their circular ends only. When one of them is connected across an ideal battery, its steady state temperature becomes $\theta_1 = 38\ °C$. Now the remaining three resistors are connected in series with very good electrical contacts and the pack is connected across the same battery. To what value will the temperature of this pack rise in steady state? Room temperature is $\theta_0 = 20\ °C$ and amount of heat transfer to the surroundings is proportional to the temperature difference between the resistor and the surroundings. Neglect thermal expansion and change in resistivity for the range of temperature involved.

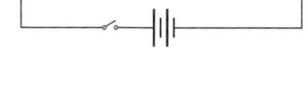

14. A container thermally insulated from the surroundings is divided into two parts by a heat-insulating piston that can slide in the container without friction. On one side of the piston, mass m_1 of gaseous hydrogen occupies volume V_1 and on the other side mass m_2 of gaseous helium occupies volume V_2. Molar masses of these gases are M_{H_2} and M_{He} respectively. The gases can be heated by two series connected heating coils. The resistance of the coil which heats hydrogen gas depends on absolute temperature T according to the law $R_1 = R_0 + AT$. If the piston does not move after closing the switch, find the law describing dependence of resistance of the coil heating the helium gas. The gases always remain in thermal equilibrium with the heating coils.

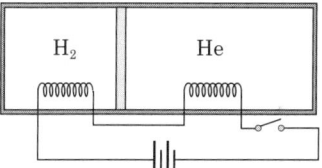

15. In an ice industry following scheme is used to cut ice into blocks of desired size. A large log of ice of thickness h is placed on a moving conveyor belt and a taut vertical steel wire AB of radius r connected across an ideal battery of terminal voltage V, when comes in contact with the ice passes through the ice by melting it. Size and shape of a piece of ice is controlled by controlling motion of the ice-log and of wire AB. In the given arrangement, the belt can carry the ice-log along the x-axis and the wire can move along the y-axis. Consider that the entire amount of heat developed in wire AB is utilized to melt the ice and the ice is at its melting temperature. Specific latent heat of melting of ice is L, the density of ice is d and the resistivity of steel is ρ.

    (a) Find minimum time to cut a stationary rectangular log of length l and width b by moving wire AB with a constant velocity.
    (b) If the log is made to move with constant velocity v_x, with what velocity the wire has to be moved for most energy efficient cutting.

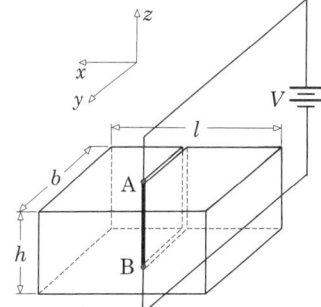

13.20 Chapter-13

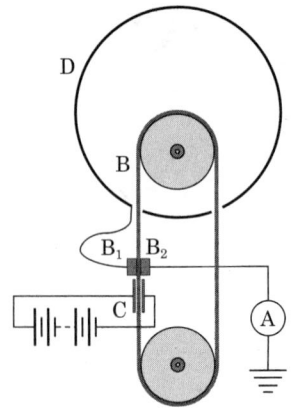

16. A schematic representation of a Van de Graff generator is shown in the figure. A belt B of thickness h and width b made of a material of dielectric constant ε_r running on two fixed wheels is set into motion with the help of a small electric motor (not shown). Linear speed of the belt is v. The belt passes between the plates of a parallel-plate capacitor C connected across an accumulator of terminal voltage V. The plates of the capacitor are a short distance d apart and do not touch the belt. Charges appearing on the outer surface of the belt is collected by brush B_1 and fed to a spherical conducting dome D of radius R to create the desired high electrostatic voltage. The charges on the inner surface of the belt are collected by brush B_2 and discharged to the ground through an ammeter A. Neglect size of the holes cut into the dome at the entrance and the exit of the belt.

Find suitable expressions for the following.

(a) The surface charge density σ_p of polarization charges on the belt when leaving the capacitor.
(b) The charge q collected by the spherical dome after time t measured from the beginning of operation. Assume that all the polarization charges collected by brush B_1 are transferred to the dome and there is no leakage of charge from the surface of the dome.
(c) Current I shown by the ammeter.
(d) Find steady state charge q on the dome considering the air as medium of very high resistivity ρ.
(e) At sufficiently high voltages, the dome loses charge into the surroundings by a faint discharge process known as corona discharge. Find the steady-state charge q on the dome during corona discharge, if current density in air during corona discharge is given by the following relation.

$$\vec{j} = \frac{\vec{E}}{\rho} + \beta |\vec{E}| \vec{E}$$

Here β is a known constant.

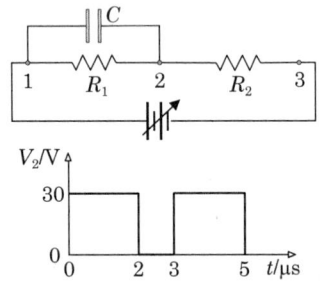

17. A branch of a circuit consists of two series-connected resistors of resistances $R_1 = 10$ kΩ and $R_2 = 5$ kΩ. A capacitor of unknown capacitance C (few microfarads) is connected in parallel with the resistance R_1 as shown in the figure. Voltage applied across this branch i.e. between the terminals 1 and 3 is made to vary periodically with time in such a manner that voltage V_2 across the resistance R_2 varies with time as shown in the graph. When a steady state is reached, fluctuations in capacitor voltage are negligible as compared to the average voltage on the capacitor, find the average voltage across the resistance R_1.

18. Plates of a parallel plate capacitor have area A and distance between them is $2d$. A dielectric slab of area A and of thickness d made of a weak conducting material of resistivity ρ and relative permittivity ε_r is inserted in the capacitor. The plates are connected across an ideal battery of electromotive force V through a switch.

Find the following quantities.

(a) Maximum current within the dielectric.

(b) Initial and final charges on the capacitor plates and on the faces of the dielectric.
(c) Time constant of charge building process on the faces of the dielectric.

19. Linear dimensions of plates of a parallel plate capacitor are $l \times l$ and distance between them d is much smaller than l. Half of the space between the plates is filled with a mica sheet of thickness $d/2$ and dielectric constant ε_r. The plates are connected across an ideal battery of terminal voltage V through a resistance R. The mica sheet is slowly pulled out of the capacitor with a constant velocity v. Find heat developed in the resistance. Permittivity of free space is ε_0.

20. In the circuit shown, initially the switch is open and all the capacitors are uncharged. Consider the first 100 s interval after the switch is closed. Find the total energy stored in the capacitors and the total energy dissipated in the resistance in this 100 s interval. Internal resistance of the battery does not exceed a few ohms.

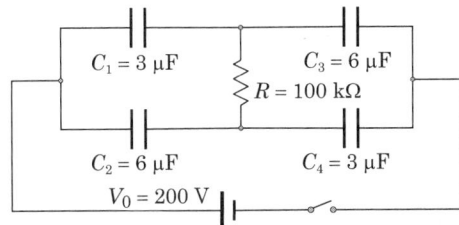

Challenge your understanding

1. A material has anisotropic resistivity such that is its resistivity in one direction say along the x-axis has a maximum value ρ_{max} and a minimum value $\rho_{min} = 0.4\rho_{max}$ in all other directions perpendicular to the x-axis. A strip ABCD of length l = 9.0 cm and width b = 1.0 cm is cut from a specimen of this material in such a manner that the x-axis passes through the strip, making an angle $\theta = \sin^{-1}(3/5)$ with edge AB as shown in the figure. If a constant potential difference V = 196 V is applied between faces AD and BC, how much potential difference will be developed between midpoints P and Q of edges AB and CD respectively?

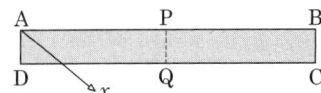

2. In the arrangement shown, a pulley is suspended from a fixed support with the help of a spring. A uniform resistive wire connected between immovable terminals A and B, passes over the pulley. A resistance R connected between terminals A and B is also connected in parallel with the resistive wire. Resistance r of the resistive wire is much larger than load resistance R_L which is also much larger than R i.e. $r \gg R_L \gg R$. The spring supporting the pulley always keeps the resistive wire taut. The pulley wheel and its axle are made of conducting materials to establish electrical contact of the resistive wire with terminal C. When

the switch is closed, the pulley wheel starts rotating very gradually and stops rotating after some time.

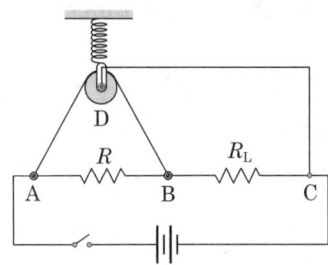

(a) Why does the pulley wheel rotate and why does it stop after some time?
(b) Show that the angular displacement of the disk is approximately proportional to power consumed by the resistance R_L.

3. What maximum potential difference can you obtain with the help of a battery of terminal voltage $V_0 = 1.5$ V and two capacitors $C_1 = 2$ µF and $C_2 = 3$ µF.

ANSWERS AND HINTS

Multiple Choice Questions

1. (a)
2. (c)
3. (d)
4. (b)
5. (c)
6. (b)
7. (a), (b), (c) and (d)
8. (c)
9. (c)
10. (c)
11. (b)
12. (b)
13. (a)
14. (c)
15. (b)
16. (b) and (d)
17. (d)
18. (d)
19. (c)
20. (b)
21. (c)
22. (d)
23. (b)
24. (c)
25. (c)

Build up your understanding

1. $\dfrac{W}{|e|r} = 9 \times 10^4$ V/m

2. $\dfrac{V}{\dfrac{V}{I} + (\rho_{Fe} - \rho_{Al})\dfrac{b}{2\pi rt}} = 5.06$ A

3. $\dfrac{r}{4\pi a^2} \displaystyle\int_0^{2\pi} \rho d\theta = 55\ \Omega$

4. $Q_A = -Q_C = 2\pi\varepsilon_0 a V_0$ and $Q_B = 0$

   Hint: Steady state current circulating in the circuit maintains terminals A, B and C and hence the spheres connected with these terminals at constant potentials. The total charge on the spheres, which is zero, gets redistributed among the spheres in accordance to the potentials acquired by them.

5. 3 km

6. 1.5 A

7. 2.0 A, 4.0 A and 2.0 A

8. 2.0 A

9. 100 Ω

   Hint: This problem cannot be solved under the assumption that the battery has no internal resistance.

10. $n = 71$

11. $I = \dfrac{\left(\sqrt{1+4kRV_0} - 1\right)^2}{4kR^2}$

12. 75 V

    Hint: Express relation between voltage across device D and current through it with the help of the given circuit and then plot it on the given graph.

13. $\dfrac{8}{3}$ Ω

14. 3 Ω

15. If $R_1 \leftrightarrow R_2$, the battery current is 0.35 A.
    If $R_2 \leftrightarrow R_3$, the battery current is 0.4 A.

16. $V = 50 - 4I$

    The terminal to the right is at higher potential.

    Hint: Voltage V across a resistive branch and current I through it can be expressed by a linear equation of the form $V = aI + b$. Here a and b are constants.

17.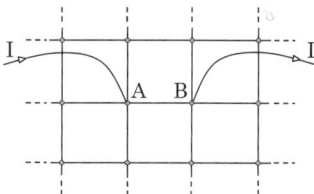

18. $\dfrac{R}{2}$ and $\dfrac{3R}{8}$

    Hint: The situation can easily be handled using superposition theorem together with symmetry considerations. We elucidate the idea here by calculating resistance between terminals A and B.

    Consider two constant current sources or equivalently voltage sources of infinitely large internal resistance; one of the source is connected between terminal A and an infinitely distant point on the grid and the other source between terminal B and an infinitely distant point on the grid. The polarities of the sources are such that the current enters the grid at terminal A and leave the grid at terminal B or vice versa. Let current from each of these sources is I.

    According to the superposition theorem, net current in branch AB of the grid is the algebraic sum of individual contribution of each source. While calculating individual contribution of a source, the other source has to be replaced by its internal resistance.

    In the following two figures distribution of the currents is shown assuming only one source connected at a time. In the branches connected to terminals A and B, currents are distributed equally due to symmetry.

    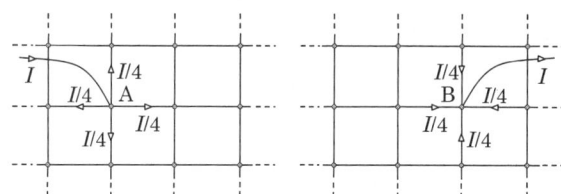

    Now the superposition theorem suggests that the net current is equally divided between branch AB and in rest of the grid. This idea is shown in the following equivalent circuit.

    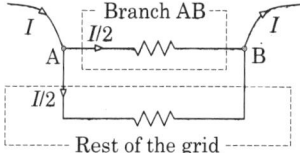

    The above equivalent circuit suggests that resistance of branch AB is equal to the equivalent resistance of the rest of the grid and both of them are in parallel so the net equivalent resistance of the grid between terminals A and B must be $R/2$.

19. Figure-I: $\dfrac{(1+2\sqrt{2})R}{2}$

    Figure-II: $\sqrt{2}R$

20. $\dfrac{R}{\sqrt{3}}$

    Hint: All the nodes on lines CD and EF are at the same potential that is arithmetic mean of the potentials of nodes A and B.

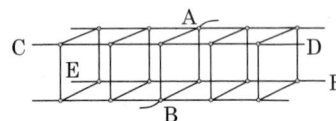

21. 2.0 V, 2.0 V and 4.5 V

22. $\dfrac{V_A V_B (R_B - R_A)}{V_A (R_C - R_A) - V_B (R_C - R_B)} = 3.0$ V

    Hint: Since the voltmeters are identical and read different voltages between same pair of nodes, therefore they cannot be ideal voltmeters.

23. $\dfrac{\sqrt{5V_C^2 + 4V_A V_C} - V_C}{2} = 12$ V

24. $\dfrac{4V_1 V_2}{V_1 + V_2} = 2.91$ V

25. $R = \dfrac{V_1}{I_1 - I_2} = 2.0\ \Omega$

    $R_V = \dfrac{V_1}{I_2} = 2.0\ \Omega$

    $R_A = \dfrac{V_2 - V_1}{I_1 - I_2} = 2.0\ \Omega$

26. $\dfrac{V_1 V_2 V_3}{V_1 V_3 + V_2 V_3 - V_1 V_2} = 1.8$ V

27. $V_A = V_B = \dfrac{V}{9}$ and $V_C = \dfrac{2V}{9}$

    Hint: An ideal voltmeter also draws a negligibly small current to actuate its pointer mechanism.

28. $I_0 = \dfrac{2 I_1 I_2}{3 I_1 - I_2} = 2.0$ mA

29. $R = \dfrac{R_1 R_2}{R_1 + R_2} = 20\ \Omega$

    Hint: The ohmmeter is so calibrated that it reads ratio of potential difference across its terminals and current flowing through it; therefore, current flowing through the ohmmeter can be expressed as ratio of potential difference across its terminals and resistance that it reads.

30. ≈ 4.0 mW

31. 30 Ω, 6 V

32. 128 W and 32 W

33. $R = \dfrac{R_1 R_2}{R_1 + R_2}$ and $\dfrac{(V_1 R_2 + V_2 R_1)^2}{4 R_1 R_2 (R_1 + R_2)}$

34. Never

35. $\left(\dfrac{1-\eta^2}{\eta^2}\right) \Delta\theta = 9.0$ °C

36. $\theta_0 + (\theta - \theta_0)\left(\dfrac{1}{\eta}\right)^{\frac{5}{2}} = 5.0$ °C

37. $\dfrac{2\eta I_0}{\eta + 1} = 2.0$ A

38. (a) $R(t) = R_0 \left(1 - \dfrac{t}{R_0 C_0}\right)$

    (b) $C(t) = C_0 \left(1 - \dfrac{t}{R_0 C_0}\right)$ and $\omega(t) = \dfrac{\pi}{R_0 C_0}$

    (c) $C(t) = C_0 \left(1 - \dfrac{t}{R_0 C_0}\right)$ and $x(t) = \dfrac{x_0 R_0 C_0}{R_0 C_0 - t}$

39. 40 µC on each

40. $3^5 V_0$ or $\dfrac{V_0}{3^5}$

41. $\dfrac{2CV^2}{3}$

42. $\dfrac{q_0 v}{2 x_0}$

Electric Current **13.25**

43. $C_{in} = \left(\dfrac{q_0 - q_\infty}{q_\infty}\right) C = 4.0\ \mu F$

$R_{in} = \dfrac{q_0}{C_0 \left.\dfrac{dq}{dt}\right|_{t=0}} = 2.0\ k\Omega$

44. $q_0 \left\{ 1 - \exp\left(-\dfrac{t}{\rho \varepsilon_r \varepsilon_0}\right) \right\}$

Hint: Product of resistance and capacitance of the medium between the shell and the ground equals the product of resistivity and permittivity of the medium.

$RC = \rho \varepsilon$

45. $\dfrac{\rho \varepsilon_r \varepsilon_0 q_0 V}{\beta d}$

Hint: Charge of the ball leaks due to its own electric field only.

46. $a = \dfrac{qVt}{mdRC}$

47. 4 W

48. (a) $\dfrac{q^2 l}{2\varepsilon_0 A} - \dfrac{q^4}{8\varepsilon_0^2 kA^2}$

(b) $\dfrac{q^2 l}{2\varepsilon_0 A} - \dfrac{q^4}{4\varepsilon_0^2 kA^2}$

Hint: The discharge process is very slow, if the value of the resistance is very high and vice versa.

49. 1.6 J

50. $\dfrac{R_1 CQ^2}{8\pi\varepsilon_0 r (R_1 + R_2)(C + 4\pi\varepsilon_0 r)}$ and

$\dfrac{R_2 CQ^2}{8\pi\varepsilon_0 r (R_1 + R_2)(C + 4\pi\varepsilon_0 r)}$

51. $\dfrac{Q^2 d}{16\varepsilon_0 A}$

52. 20 μJ and 24 μJ

Check your understanding

1. $2\pi\varepsilon_0 r(n+1)V_0$

Hint: In steady state, the terminals of the resistors and hence the spheres connected with them are at constant potentials. Moreover, due to the grounding of the right most terminal, we are not sure that whether the total initial charge of these spheres gets redistributed or some charge transfer takes place between the spheres and the earth. Therefore, the only way remaining to find the total charge is to sum up product terms of capacitances of the spheres and their potentials.

2. 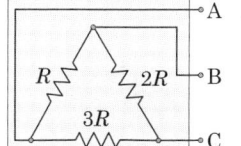 OR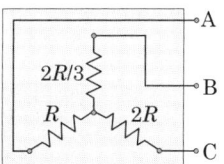

3.
```
        A
   6.0 Ω │ 2.0 Ω   3.0 V
B ──/\/\──/\/\──┤├── C
```

4. $R_1 = \dfrac{V_0}{I_1 I_2}\left(I_2 \pm \sqrt{I_2(I_2 - I_1)}\right) = 6\ k\Omega$ or $2\ k\Omega$

and

$R_2 = \dfrac{V_0}{I_1 I_2}\left(I_2 \mp \sqrt{I_2(I_2 - I_1)}\right) = 2\ k\Omega$ or $6\ k\Omega$

5. 7 Ω

6. $\dfrac{2R}{3}$ and R

7. $R(1 + \sqrt{5})$

8. $(\eta - 1)V = 1.5$ V

9. ≈ 4.2 V

Hint: Current in all the bulbs except the first one is less than 0.25 A.

10. 0.2 mA, 0.1 mA and 0.3 mA

11. $\dfrac{1}{2\alpha}\left\{\sqrt{1+16\alpha(1+\alpha\Delta\theta_1)\Delta\theta_1}-1\right\} \approx 261\ °C$

12. (a) $\theta_0 + \dfrac{1}{2\alpha}\left\{1-\sqrt{1-\left(\dfrac{V}{V_0}\right)^2}\right\}$

(b) $\dfrac{2V}{R_0\left\{1+\sqrt{1-\left(\dfrac{V}{V_0}\right)^2}\right\}}$

Here $V_0 = \sqrt{\dfrac{\beta R_0}{4\alpha}}$

13. $\dfrac{(2\theta_0+\theta_1)}{3} = 26\ °C$

14. $\left(R_0 + AT\dfrac{m_2 M_{H_2} V_1}{m_1 M_{He} V_2}\right)\left(\dfrac{3V_2}{5V_1}\right)$

15. (a) $\dfrac{2L\rho dbh^2}{\pi rV^2}$

(b) $\sqrt{\left(\dfrac{\pi rV^2}{2Ldh^2\rho}\right)^2 - v_x^2}$

Hint: Maximum speed of wire relative to the ice block is

$$v = \dfrac{\pi rV^2}{2Ldh^2\rho}$$

16. (a) $\sigma_p = \dfrac{\varepsilon_0(\varepsilon_r-1)V}{\varepsilon_r(d-h)+h}$ (b) $q = \dfrac{\varepsilon_0(\varepsilon_r-1)Vbvt}{\varepsilon_r(d-h)+h}$

(c) $I = \dfrac{\varepsilon_0(\varepsilon_r-1)Vbv}{\varepsilon_r(d-h)+h}$ (d) $q = \dfrac{\rho bv\varepsilon_0^2(\varepsilon_r-1)V}{\varepsilon_r(d-h)+h}$

(e) $q = \dfrac{2\pi\varepsilon_0 R^2}{\rho\beta}\left\{\sqrt{1+\dfrac{\rho^2\varepsilon_0\beta}{\pi R^2}\left(\dfrac{(\varepsilon_r-1)bvV}{\varepsilon_r(d-h)+h}\right)}-1\right\}$

17. 40 V

18. (a) $\dfrac{VA}{d\rho(\varepsilon_r+1)}$

(b) Initial charge on the plates $= \dfrac{\varepsilon_0\varepsilon_r VA}{d(\varepsilon_r+1)}$

Initial charge on the faces of the dielectric

$$= \dfrac{\varepsilon_0(\varepsilon_r-1)VA}{d(\varepsilon_r+1)}$$

Final charge on the plates $= \dfrac{\varepsilon_0 VA}{d}$

Final charge on the faces of the dielectric

$$= \dfrac{\varepsilon_0 VA}{d}$$

(c) $\tau = 2\rho\varepsilon_0$

19. $\dfrac{\varepsilon_0^2 l^3}{d^2}\left(\dfrac{\varepsilon_r-1}{\varepsilon_r+1}\right)^2 vRV^2$

20. Stored energy: 9.0×10^{-2} J
    Energy dissipated: 1.0×10^{-2} J

Hint: In a negligibly small duration of time immediately after the switch is closed, before an appreciable amount of current starts to flow through the resistance, all the capacitors get charged and the resistance can be treated like an open circuit as shown in the figure.

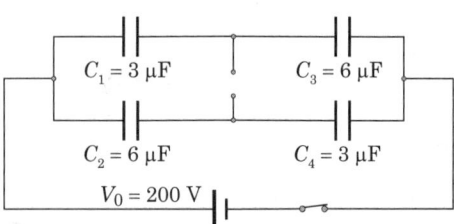

Time constant of the circuit is of the order of milliseconds, therefore 100 s after the switching, it can be assumed that steady state is reached and processes of charging the capacitor is over, making current through the resistance and potential difference across it to vanish. Now the resistance can be treated like a short circuit as shown in the figure.

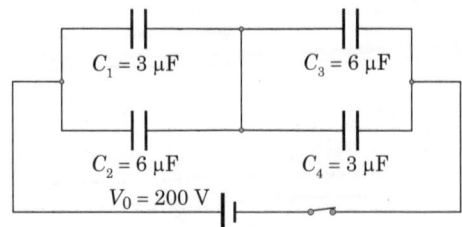

Challenge your understanding

1. $V_P - V_Q = \dfrac{bV(\rho_{max} - \rho_{min})\sin\theta\cos\theta}{l(\rho_{max}\cos^2\theta + \rho_{min}\sin^2\theta)} = 8.0$ V

2. (a) Since current in portion AA_1 of the resistive wire is more than the current in portion B_1B, thermal expansion in AA_1 will be more than that in B_1B. The spring-loaded pulley always keeps these portions taut and the wire does not slide over the pulley wheel, therefore pulley will rotate to compensate the unequal thermal expansions. Moreover, the process will take place very slowly because thermal expansion in the resistive wire is a slow process.

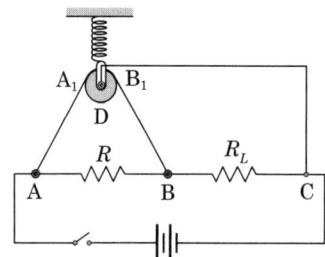

A sufficient time after the key is closed, rate of heat developed in both the portions of the resistive wire becomes equal to the rate of heat dissipated by them, and therefore their temperatures will acquire steady values ceasing any further thermal expansion and hence rotation of the pulley wheel.

3. $2V_0\left(\dfrac{C_1 + 3C_2}{C_1 + C_2}\right) = 6.6$ V

Chapter 14

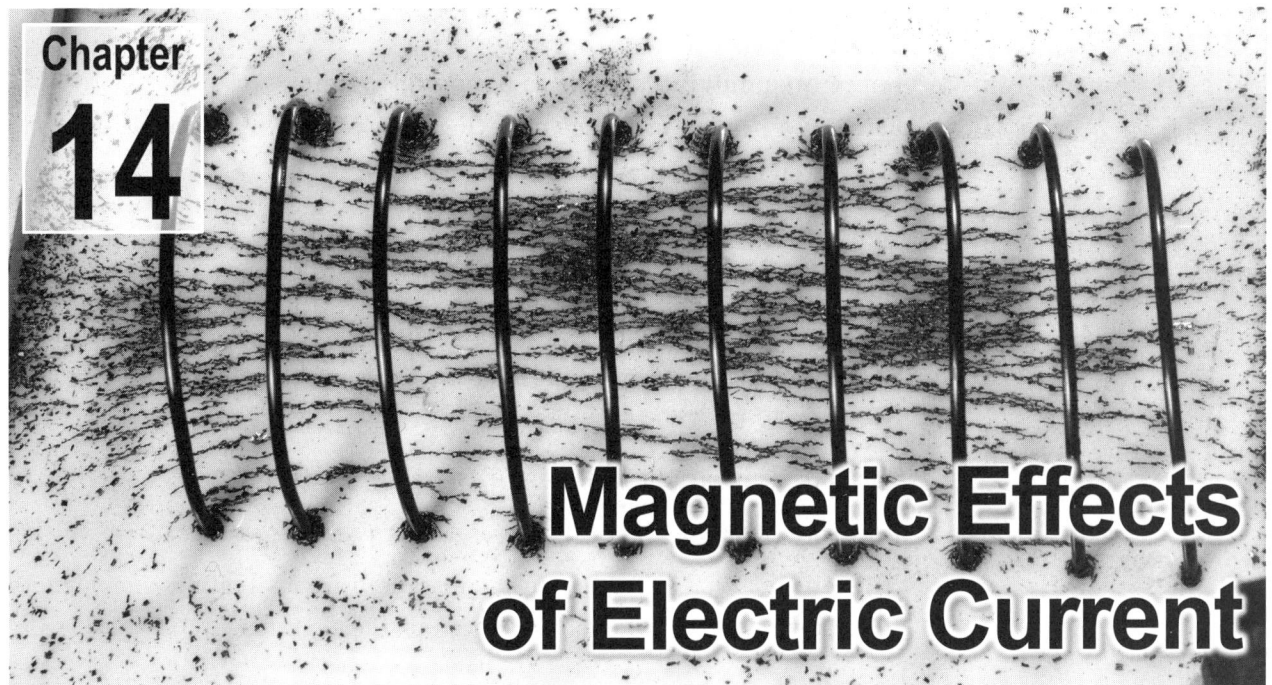

Magnetic Effects of Electric Current

Magnetic field, force on current carrying conductor in magnetic field, force on a moving charge in magnetic field, Lorentz force equation, Biot–Savart's law, Gauss' law, Ampere's law in free space, generalised Ampere's law and magnetic field intensity, magnetisation, the three magnetic field vectors, magnetic energy density.

"I can live with doubt and uncertainty and not knowing. I think it is much more interesting to live not knowing than to have answers that might be wrong."

Richard P. Feynman
(11 May 1918 – 15 February 1988)

BACK TO BASICS

Magnetic field:

A physical property that accounts for magnetic effects existing in the surrounding region of an electric current and magnets or equivalently moving charges.

Force on current carrying wire in a magnetic field:

Force on an infinitesimal length dl of a wire carrying current I in a magnetic field of flux density $\vec{B}$ is given by the equation.

$$\vec{F} = I(\mathrm{d}\vec{l} \times \vec{B})$$

Here the vector d$\vec{l}$ is in direction of current flow and the product term $I\mathrm{d}\vec{l}$ is usually called a current element.

Magnetic flux density also known as magnetic induction is a measure of strength of magnetic field.

A term magnetic field is often used to refer magnetic flux density or magnetic induction.

Force on a moving charge in a magnetic field:

Force on a particle of charge q moving with velocity $\vec{v}$ in a magnetic field $\vec{B}$ is given by the equation

$$\vec{F} = q(\vec{v} \times \vec{B})$$

Lorentz force equation:

Force on a particle of charge q moving with velocity $\vec{v}$ in a region where an electric field $\vec{E}$ and a magnetic field $\vec{B}$ both coexist is given by the equation

$$\vec{F} = q(\vec{E} + \vec{v} \times \vec{B})$$

This force is invariant in all reference frames.

Biot-Savart's law:

Magnetic field $d\vec{B}$ in free space at a distance r from an infinitesimal length $d\vec{l}$ of a wire carrying current I is given by the equation.

$$d\vec{B} = \frac{\mu_0}{4\pi} \frac{I d\vec{l} \times \vec{r}}{r^3}$$

$\mu_0 \equiv$ Permeability of free space $= 4\pi \times 10^{-7} \, \frac{\text{T} \cdot \text{m}}{\text{A}}$ or $\frac{\text{H}}{\text{m}}$

Gauss' law for magnetic field:

Net flux of magnetic field through any closed surface is always zero.

$$\oint \vec{B} \cdot d\vec{S} = 0$$

Ampere's law for free space:

Circulation or line integral of magnetic induction vector $\vec{B}$ on a closed path equals the product of permeability of free space and the net electric current crossing a surface bounded by the closed path.

$$\oint \vec{B} \cdot d\vec{l} = \mu_0 \int \vec{J} \cdot d\vec{S}$$

Magnetic intensity or magnetic field intensity:

Actual current employed to produce magnetic field is the only current, which we can control (switch it on and off, change its intensity or direction, etc.). Therefore, to describe magnetic field, we have to define a vector quantity that depends only on the actual current employed to produce the magnetic field and is independent of the medium. This quantity is the magnetic intensity $\vec{H}$.

$$\vec{H} = \frac{\vec{B}}{\mu}$$

Here μ is the permeability of the medium and $\vec{B}$ is the magnetic induction in the medium.

Generalised Ampere's law and magnetic field intensity:

Magnetic intensity $\vec{H}$ depends only on the actual current employed in producing the magnetic field and is independent of the medium; therefore, its line integral over a closed path depends only on the actual current crossing the surface bounded by the closed path.

$$\oint \vec{H} \cdot d\vec{l} = \int \vec{J} \cdot d\vec{S}$$

Magnetisation:

In a bulk of material, atomic magnetic moments add up vectorially and can give a net non-zero magnetic moment. We define magnetisation $\vec{M}$ of a sample to be equal to its net magnetic moment per unit volume.

The three magnetic field vectors $\vec{B}$, $\vec{H}$ and $\vec{M}$:

$$\vec{B} = \mu_0 (\vec{H} + \vec{M})$$

Magnetic field energy density:

When in a region magnetic field is established, energy is stored in that region. This stored energy per unit volume is given by the equation

$$u = \frac{1}{2}\mu H^2 = \frac{B^2}{2\mu}$$

Multiple Choice Questions

1. Current I flowing along edges of one face of a cube as shown in figure-I, produces magnetic field $\vec{B} = B_0 \hat{j}$ at the centre of the cube. Consider another identical cube, where the current I flows along the path shown in figure-II. How much magnetic field exists at the centre of the second cube?

   Figure-I   Figure-II

   (a) Zero
   (b) $B_0 (\hat{i} + \hat{j} + \hat{k})$
   (c) $B_0 (-\hat{i} + \hat{j} + \hat{k})$
   (d) $B_0 (-\hat{i} + \hat{j} - \hat{k})$

2. A parallel plate capacitor consists of square plates of edge length a separated by a distance d that is much smaller that the edge length. It is charged to a potential V and made to move with a constant velocity v directed along one of its edges. How much magnetic field exists inside the capacitor?

   (a) $\dfrac{\mu_0 \varepsilon_0 v V}{d}$
   (b) $\dfrac{\mu_0 \varepsilon_0 v V}{a}$
   (c) $\dfrac{\mu_0 \varepsilon_0 d v V}{a^2}$
   (d) None of these

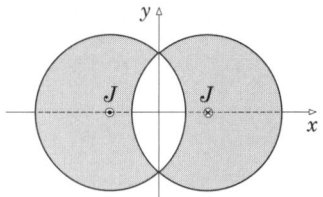

3. A long straight conductor has uniform cross-section in the shape of two identical overlapped circles with centre-to-centre spacing a. Material from overlapped section has been removed from entire length of the conductor and portions to the right and to the left of the y-z plane are insulated from each other. These portions carry uniform currents of current density J in the positive and negative z-directions respectively. Permeability of both the conductors is the same as that of vacuum. Which of the following statements best describes magnetic field in the empty space inside the composite conductor?

   (a) It is nonuniform and points in the positive y-direction everywhere on the y-axis.
   (b) It is nonuniform and points in the positive y-direction everywhere on the x and y-axes.
   (c) It is uniform, points everywhere in the positive y-direction and has magnitude $\frac{1}{2}\mu_0 Ja$.
   (d) It has different directions at different points but the same magnitude $\frac{1}{2}\mu_0 Ja$.

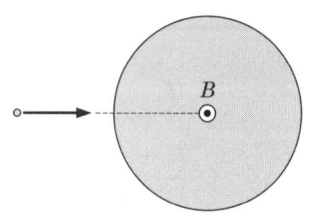

4. Several α-particles of different speeds enter a uniform magnetic field confined into a cylindrical region. If all the α-particles enter the field radially, what can you say about time intervals spent by them in the magnetic field?

   (a) Faster is the particle, lesser is the time.
   (b) Slower is the particle, lesser is the time.
   (c) Slower is the particle, greater is the time.
   (d) The time is same for all the particles.

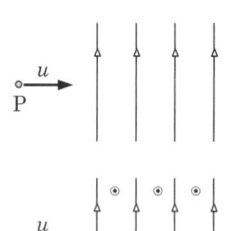

5. A positively charged particle P crosses a region of uniform electric field of intensity E. Velocity u of the particle at the entry on the left side of the region is perpendicular to the electric field as shown in the first figure. Speed of the particle at exit on the right side is v_1. Now the experiment is repeated with a uniform magnetic field of induction B superimposed on the electric field as shown in the second figure, keeping entry velocity of the particle unchanged. In this experiment, speed of the particle at exit on the right side is v_2. What can you conclude regarding the speeds v_1 and v_2?

   (a) If $u < \dfrac{E}{B}$, then $v_2 < v_1$
   (b) If $u = \dfrac{E}{B}$, then $v_2 < v_1$
   (c) If $u = \dfrac{E}{B}$, then $v_2 = v_1$
   (d) If $u > \dfrac{E}{B}$, then $v_2 < v_1$

6. A particle of mass m and charge q is moving with a constant speed in a region of space, where a uniform and constant magnetic field $\vec{B}$ and an electric field $\vec{E}$ coexist in mutually perpendicular horizontal directions in addition to gravitational field of intensity g. After the magnetic and electric fields are switched off, the minimum kinetic energy of the particle is observed to be half of the kinetic energy when all these fields were coexisting. What can you certainly conclude for component of velocity of the particle along the direction of the magnetic field?

(a) $\vec{0}$

(b) $\sqrt{\left(\dfrac{E}{B}\right)^2 - \left(\dfrac{mg}{qB}\right)^2}$ pointing opposite to $\vec{B}$

(c) $\sqrt{\left(\dfrac{E}{B}\right)^2 - \left(\dfrac{mg}{qB}\right)^2}$ pointing in the direction of $\vec{B}$

(d) $\sqrt{\left(\dfrac{E}{B}\right)^2 - \left(\dfrac{mg}{qB}\right)^2}$ pointing either in direction of or opposite to $\vec{B}$

7. In a region of free space, where a uniform and constant electric field of intensity $\vec{E}$ and a magnetic field of induction $\vec{B}$ coexist, an electron projected with speed v in the positive x-direction, moves undeviated without change in speed. In addition, an electron projected with velocity v in the positive y-direction in this region; also, moves undeviated without change in speed. Which of the following conclusions can you make?

(a) $|\vec{E}| < v|\vec{B}|$

(b) $|\vec{E}| = v|\vec{B}|$

(c) The electric field is perpendicular to the x-y plane.

(d) The magnetic field is either at 45° or 135° with the positive x-direction.

8. A rigid square loop of side length l carrying an electric current is held motionless on a frictionless horizontal tabletop. A uniform magnetic field pointing upwards is switched on everywhere to the left of the dashed line as shown in the figure and then the loop is released. Considering different lengths of the side segments x and y ($x < y$), which of the following conclusions can you make?

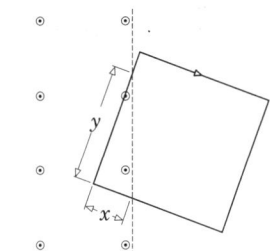

(a) If $x < \dfrac{l}{2}$ and $y = \dfrac{l}{2}$, the loop starts rotating anticlockwise.

(b) If $x < \dfrac{l}{2}$ and $y < \dfrac{l}{2}$, the loop starts rotating anticlockwise.

(c) If $x < \dfrac{l}{2}$ and $y > \dfrac{l}{2}$, the loop starts rotating clockwise.

(d) If $x < \dfrac{l}{2}$ and $y > \dfrac{l}{2}$, more information is required to decide which way the loop starts rotating.

9. Two coaxial circular coils of radii a and b are separated by a large distance x and carry equal currents I. If $a \gg b$, what is the force of mutual interaction between them.

(a) $\dfrac{\mu_0 I^2 a^2 b}{(a^2 + x^2)^{1.5}}$

(b) $\dfrac{3\pi\mu_0 I^2 abx}{(a^2 + x^2)^{1.5}}$

(c) $\dfrac{\pi\mu_0 I^2 a^3 b}{(a^2 + x^2)^2}$

(d) $\dfrac{3\pi\mu_0 I^2 a^2 b^2 x}{2(a^2 + x^2)^{2.5}}$

Questions 10 to 12 are based on the following write-up.

Electric field of a small electric dipole and magnetic field of a small magnetic dipole (a small current loop) have identical patterns. This similarity in field patterns is not only limited to geometrical appearance of the field lines but also extends to mathematical expressions for the fields of both types of dipoles at large distances.

We also know that electric dipole moment and magnetic dipole moment are vector quantities. The electric dipole moment vector $\vec{p}$ points from the negative charge towards the positive charge constituting the dipole. Direction of the magnetic dipole moment vector $\vec{m}$ is decided by the right-hand rule. For this purpose, fingers of right hand are curled along the direction of current flow and the thumb pointing outwards indicates the direction of magnetic dipole moment vector.

If in the expression of electric field due to an electric dipole we replace the constant $(4\pi\varepsilon_0)^{-1}$ by $\mu_0(4\pi)^{-1}$ and electric dipole moment $\vec{p}$ by magnetic dipole moment $\vec{m}$, we obtain expression for magnetic field due to a small magnetic dipole.

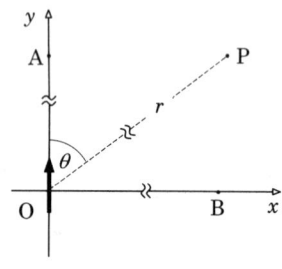

10. In the given figure, dipole moment $\vec{m}$ of a small magnetic dipole placed at the origin is shown by a small, directed line segment. Magnetic induction vectors at distant points A $(0, y)$ on the y-axis and B $(x, 0)$ on the x-axis respectively are

(a) $\dfrac{\mu_0 m}{4\pi y^3}\hat{j}$ and $\dfrac{\mu_0 m}{2\pi x^3}\hat{i}$

(b) $\dfrac{\mu_0 m}{2\pi y^3}\hat{j}$ and $\dfrac{\mu_0 m}{4\pi x^3}\hat{i}$

(c) $\dfrac{\mu_0 m}{4\pi y^3}\hat{j}$ and $-\dfrac{\mu_0 m}{2\pi x^3}\hat{j}$

(d) $\dfrac{\mu_0 m}{2\pi y^3}\hat{j}$ and $-\dfrac{\mu_0 m}{4\pi x^3}\hat{j}$

11. If unit vectors in the radial and the transverse directions are denoted by $\hat{e}_r$ and $\hat{e}_\theta$, magnetic induction vector due to the dipole at a point P shown in the figure is given by

(a) $\dfrac{\mu_0 m}{4\pi r^3}\{(2\cos\theta)\hat{e}_r + (\sin\theta)\hat{e}_\theta\}$

(b) $\dfrac{\mu_0 m}{4\pi r^3}\{(2\cos\theta)\hat{e}_r - (\sin\theta)\hat{e}_\theta\}$

(c) $\dfrac{\mu_0 m}{4\pi r^3}\{(\cos\theta)\hat{e}_r + (2\sin\theta)\hat{e}_\theta\}$

(d) $\dfrac{\mu_0 m}{4\pi r^3}\{(\cos\theta)\hat{e}_r - (2\sin\theta)\hat{e}_\theta\}$

12. A small magnetic dipole of magnetic moment $m_P\hat{j}$ is placed at the point P. Find work done by the forces of magnetic interactions, if this new dipole is rotated to align it along the position vector of the point P.

(a) $\dfrac{\mu_0 m m_P}{4\pi r^3}\cos\theta(2-\sin\theta)$

(c) $\dfrac{\mu_0 m m_P}{4\pi r^3}\sin\theta(2-\cos\theta)$

(b) $\dfrac{\mu_0 m m_P}{4\pi r^3}(1+2\cos\theta-3\cos^2\theta)$

(d) $\dfrac{\mu_0 m m_P}{4\pi r^3}(1+2\cos\theta-3\sin^2\theta)$

Questions 13 to 15 are based on the following physical situation.

In a homogeneous, non-magnetic, highly insulating and viscous medium, a moving particle experiences a viscous drag given by equation

$\vec{f} = -b\vec{v}$. Here b is a positive constant and $\vec{v}$ is velocity of the particle. A particle having charge q projected with an unknown velocity from a point in the medium almost stops (its speed becomes practically negligible) after travelling a distance of 10 m in a straight line.

Now a uniform and constant magnetic field is established in the region and the same particle is again projected with the same velocity directed perpendicular to the magnetic field.

13. In the presence of the magnetic field, the particle moves
    (a) on a circular path.
    (b) on a helical path.
    (c) spiralling into a point.
    (d) spiralling away from a point

14. In the presence of the magnetic field, if the particle practically stops 6 m away from the point of projection, the magnetic field is equal to
    (a) $\dfrac{4b}{3q}$
    (b) $\dfrac{3b}{4q}$
    (c) $\dfrac{3b}{5q}$
    (d) $\dfrac{5b}{3q}$

15. Magnetic induction is now doubled in magnitude without altering its direction. How far from the point of projection will the particle practically stop?
    (a) $\dfrac{\sqrt{73}}{2}$ m
    (b) $\dfrac{8}{\sqrt{73}}$ m
    (c) $\dfrac{20}{\sqrt{73}}$ m
    (d) $\dfrac{30}{\sqrt{73}}$ m

Build up your understanding

1. A lamina made of an insulating material carrying some amount of charge is placed in the x-y plane of a coordinate system as shown in the figure. Electrostatic potential at the origin O due to the charges on the lamina is V_0. Now the lamina is made to rotate with a constant angular velocity ω about the z-axis. Find magnetic field at the origin created by the moving charges of the lamina.

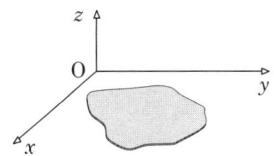

2. A long cylindrical dielectric rod of radius r and length l ($l \gg r$) carrying uniform charge of surface charge density σ on its curved surface is rotating with a constant angular velocity ω about its own axis. Find magnetic induction at the centre of the rod. Relative magnetic permeability of the material of the rod is μ_r.

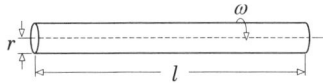

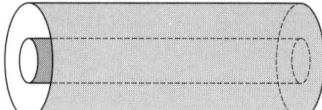

3. Consider two infinitely long coaxial dielectric cylindrical shells. The inner and the outer shells are of radius R_1 and R_2 and carry uniform charges of surface charge densities σ_1 and σ_2 respectively. These shells begin to rotate in the same sense with angular velocities ω_1 and ω_2.

   (a) Find magnetic induction B at a distance r from the common axis.
   (b) Find pressures p_1 and p_2 on the surfaces the inner and the outer cylinders due to magnetic forces.

4. An isolated conducting sphere of radius R maintained at a potential V is being rotated at a constant angular velocity ω about one of its diameters. Find magnetic dipole moment $\vec{m}$ of the sphere and magnetic induction $\vec{B}$ at its centre.

5. A uniform electric field is established inside a long cylindrical straight rod along its axis. Energy density of this electric field is uniform and is equal to $u_E = 2 \times 10^{-17}$ J/m³. Inside the rod, energy density of magnetic field is nonuniform and assumes a value $u_B = 0.4$ J/m³ at a distance $r = 2$ cm from the axis of the rod. Find electrical resistivity of the material of the rod.

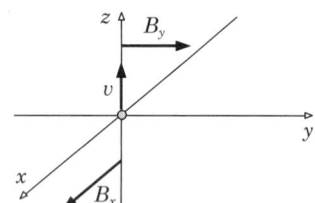

6. A particle of mass m and charge q is projected from the origin with a velocity v in the positive z-direction. Above the plane $z = 0$, a uniform and constant magnetic field of induction B_y exists in the positive y-direction and below the plane $z = 0$, a uniform and constant magnetic field of induction B_x exits in the positive x-direction. Determine coordinates of the point where the particle crosses the plane $z = 0$ third time.

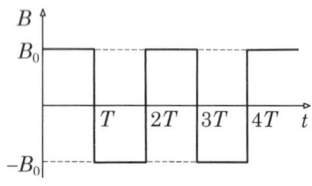

7. In a region of free space, a uniform magnetic field of induction B varies with time t as shown in the graph. At the instant $t = 0$, a particle of charge q and mass m enters the region with a velocity v perpendicular to the direction of the magnetic field. Neglect the influence of the induced electric field and explore motion of the particle. For what values of the charge q, will the particle follow a closed path?

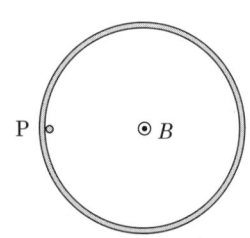

8. In a hollow rigid cylinder of radius R gravity is absent and a uniform magnetic field of induction B is established everywhere parallel to the axis of the cylinder. The cylinder is made of an insulating material and is fixed by some external means. A very small ball of mass m and charge q is projected normally from a point P on the inner surface of the cylinder. If the ball returns to the point P after a certain number of elastic collisions with the cylinder, find range of velocity v of projection of the ball.

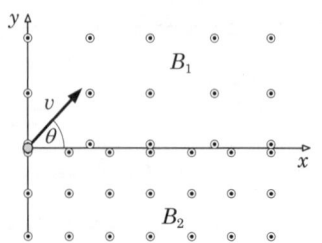

9. In a region of space, a uniform static magnetic field of induction B_1 is established above the x-z plane and another uniform static magnetic field of induction B_2 ($> B_1$) is established below the x-z plane. Both the fields are in the positive z-direction. A particle of mass m and charge q is projected from the origin with velocity v making an angle θ with x-axis as shown in the figure. Find average velocity of the particle in a large time interval.

10. A dumbbell is made by fixing two particles at the ends of a thin rigid rod of length l. The particles carry unlike charges of equal modulus q. The dumbbell is moving in a region of space, where a uniform magnetic field of induction B pointing everywhere in the positive z-direction is present. At a particular instant when the rod of the dumbbell makes an angle θ with positive x-direction, it is rotating with angular velocity $\omega\hat{k}$ and its centre is moving with velocity $\vec{v}_c = v_x\hat{i} + v_y\hat{j}$. Find net force $\vec{F}$ on the dumbbell and net torque $\vec{\tau}$ about the centre of the dumbbell at this instant.

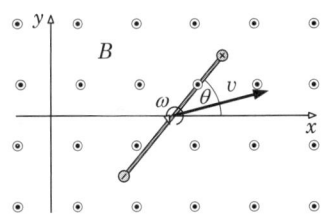

11. A long thin inextensible light thread is wound on a fixed cylinder of radius r and a positively charged bead P of mass m is attached to the free end of the thread. A uniform magnetic field of induction B directed along the axis of the cylinder exists in the region surrounding the cylinder as shown in the figure. Initially the thread is fully wound on the cylinder and the bead touches it. If the bead is projected with a velocity v radially away from the cylinder, it will eventually touch the cylinder tangentially. What should be the magnitude of charge on the bead to fulfil the above-mentioned conditions?

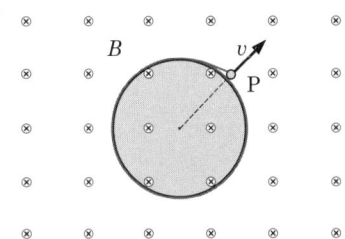

12. An insulating bead of mass M and total charge q spinning with angular momentum $\vec{L}$ enters a region of uniform magnetic field with a velocity that is in the direction of its angular momentum vector. If the velocity vector and the angular momentum vector always remain parallel to each other and the bead moves on a circular path, find magnetic dipole moment vector of the bead associated with its spin.

13. In a uniform magnetic field from a point O, a particle of charge q and mass m is projected with velocity u at an angle θ with the magnetic field. For what value of magnetic induction will the particle pass through the point P that is a distance l apart from the point of projection as shown in the figure?

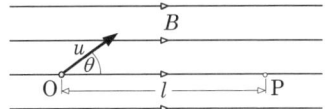

14. In a region of space, a uniform magnetic field of induction B is established everywhere pointing in the positive x-direction. A rigid plane is fixed perpendicular to the x-axis at a certain distance from the origin. A particle of mass m and charge q is projected from the origin with its velocity vector $\vec{u}$ in the x-y plane making an angle θ with the x-axis as shown in the figure. After an elastic collision with the plane, the particle loses half of its charge and then returns to the point of projection crossing the x-axis n times. Find distance of the plane from the origin.

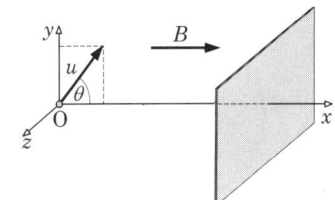

15. Consider the arrangement shown, where distance between the plates of a parallel plate capacitor is d. When a potential difference V is applied between the plates, electrons are emitted from the negative plate with negligible initial velocity. These electrons are attracted towards the positive plate creating a small electric current, which is registered in a micro-ammeter. What minimum magnetic field must be applied perpendicular to the electric field in the capacitor so that the micro-ammeter registers no current? Denote charge and mass of an electron by symbols e and m respectively and neglect effects of gravity.

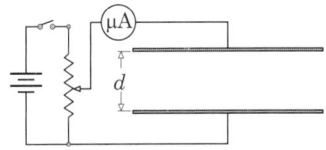

16. A small ball of mass $m = 1.0$ g and charge $q = 2.0$ µC is falling vertically with terminal velocity $u = 0.1$ m/s in a viscous fluid. After a uniform and constant horizontal magnetic field of induction B is switched on, it is observed that the ball acquires another terminal velocity and power dissipated in the viscous fluid becomes $\eta = 0.5$ times of the power dissipated prior to switching on the magnetic field. At what maximum value of magnetic induction is this possible? Dependence of the viscous forces on the velocity is unknown.

17. In a region of space, a uniform electric field of strength E, a uniform magnetic field of induction B and a uniform gravitational field of strength g coexist in mutually perpendicular directions. A charge particle is moving with a uniform velocity in this region. Once the particle leaves this region and begins moving into another region where there is only gravitational field of strength g, its speed begins to decrease. How long after departure from the first region, will the velocity of the particle become minimum?

18. In a region of space, a uniform magnetic field of induction $\vec{B} = -B\hat{k}$ is established. A particle moving with velocity $\vec{v}$ in this region experiences a viscous drag $\vec{f} = -k\vec{v}$, where k is a positive constant. A particle of mass m and charge q is projected with velocity $\vec{u} = u\hat{i}$ in this region. Find its displacement when it practically stops.

19. A particle of mass m and charge q is projected with a velocity v_0 in a viscous medium, where a uniform and constant magnetic field of induction B exists everywhere in a direction perpendicular to the direction of projection of the particle. The force of viscous drag on the particle is given by the law $\vec{f} = -b\vec{v}$, where b is a positive constant and $\vec{v}$ is velocity of the particle. Find distance travelled by the particle during a time interval from the instant of projection until velocity vector turns by 2π radians.

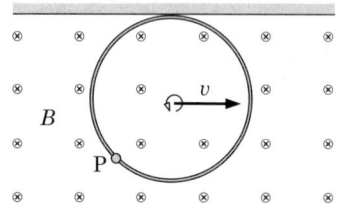

20. A rigid ring is made to roll along the ceiling of a room, where a horizontal uniform and static magnetic field of induction B exists perpendicular to the plane of the ring. Velocity of the centre of the ring is constant and its modulus is v. A charge particle P of mass m is fixed on the ring. What should the charge q on the particle and radius r of the ring be so that there is no force of interaction between the ring and the particle?

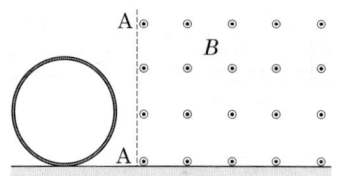

21. A ring of radius r made of an insulating material has mass m and carries uniform charge. Initially it rests on a frictionless horizontal tabletop with its plane vertical. A uniform horizontal magnetic field of induction B pointing everywhere parallel to the axis of the ring is established in the region to the right of a vertical plane AA as shown in the figure. The ring is pushed forward to acquire a velocity v_0 without any rotation. What should the charge on the ring be so that it starts rolling on the tabletop after completely entering the region of the magnetic field?

22. An insulated conducting rod in shape of a five-point star like planar structure carries a current I. In the regions to the left and to the right of a line A_1A_2, uniform magnetic fields each of induction B exist perpendicularly into and out of the plane of the star as shown in the figure. If length of a side of a unit cell of the grid shown is l, find force of interaction between the current and the magnetic field.

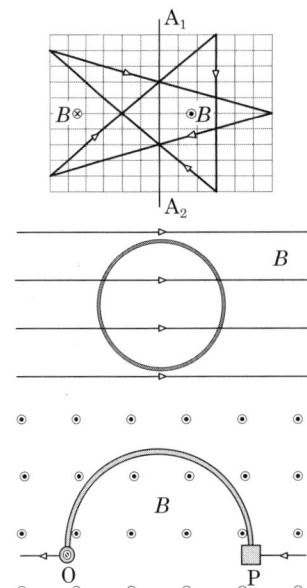

23. A uniform rod of resistance R is bent into a ring of radius r. The ring is placed in a uniform magnetic field of induction B directed parallel to its plane. You have an ideal battery of electromotive force $\mathscr{E}$. How will you connect this battery between two points on the ring to obtain maximum force on the ring and how much is this maximum force F_{max}?

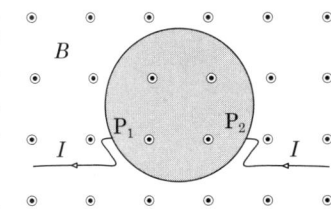

24. A schematic model of a current limiter consists of a conducting half ring of radius r and mass m, one end O of which is hinged while the other rests on a fixed metallic support P. The ring can rotate in a vertical plane without friction in presence of a uniform horizontal magnetic field of induction B pointing perpendicular to the plane of the ring. The ring is connected in series in a branch of a circuit through hinge O and metallic contact P. Find the minimum current, at which the limiter opens the circuit. The acceleration of free fall is g.

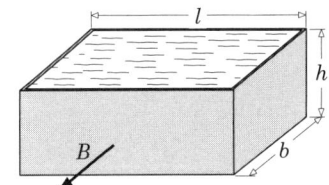

25. A thin uniform conducting disc of radius r and mass m rests on a horizontal tabletop where a uniform magnetic field of induction B pointing vertically upwards exists. Coefficient of friction between the disc and the tabletop is μ. Two points P_1 and P_2 on the rim of the disc are connected with two flexible wires, which facilitate a current to flow through the disc. Contact points P_1 and P_2 subtend an angle θ at the centre of the disc. How much minimum current I must flow through the disc so that it begins to slide? The acceleration of free fall is g.

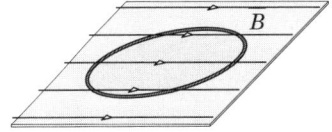

26. A conducting fluid of mass density ρ_m and electrical resistivity ρ_e is kept in an insulating vessel of dimensions $l \times b \times h$. The vessel is placed on a horizontal floor where a uniform horizontal magnetic field of induction B is established perpendicular to the face $l \times h$ as shown in the figure. How much potential difference must be applied across the fluid between the side faces designated by dimensions $b \times h$ so that the fluid pressure at the bottom of the vessel vanishes? The acceleration of free fall is g.

27. A uniform rigid ring of radius r and unknown mass is placed on a nonconducting frictionless horizontal tabletop, where exists a uniform horizontal magnetic field of induction B as shown in the figure. A current I that is double of the minimum current required to flip over the ring is made to circulate in the coil. Find force of normal reaction from the tabletop on the ring immediately after the current is switched on.

28. Two mutually perpendicular infinitely long straight rods each carrying current I are fixed at a distance d apart. One rod is along the z-axis and the other is parallel to the y-axis in x-y plane as shown in the figure.

    (a) Find force experienced by a rod due to magnetic interaction.
    (b) Find torque experienced by a symmetrically located segment of length $2d$ of a rod.

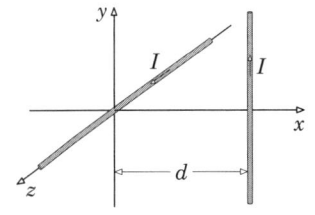

Check your understanding

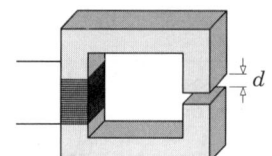

1. An air gap of length d is made in a rectangular iron core of mean perimeter l and cross-sectional area A as shown in the figure. Relative permeability of the iron is μ_r ($\gg \mu_0$). A coil of N turns carrying a current I is wound on the core. Ignore fringing of field at edges of the gap and leakage of magnetic flux. Find magnetic induction in the air gap.

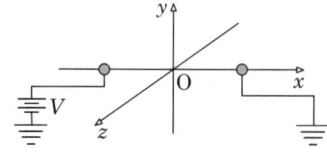

2. Two identical metallic spheres each of radius r are fixed with their centres at points $(d, 0, 0)$ and $(-d, 0, 0)$ in a homogeneous medium of conductivity σ. Here $d \gg r$. One of them is maintained at potential V and the other one is grounded as shown in the figure. Calculate magnetic flux density at a point that is in the y-z plane at a distance R from the origin O.

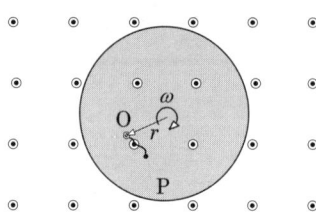

3. A large frictionless disk can rotate about its central vertical axis in a uniform static magnetic field of induction B pointing vertically upward. A particle P of mass m and charge q is connected with the help of an inextensible thread of length l to a nail O fixed at a distance r ($l < r$) from the centre C of the disk as shown in the top view of the situation. The disk is rotated at various constant angular velocities. Draw graph between tension force T in the thread when the particle stops relative to the disk and corresponding angular velocity ω of the disk.

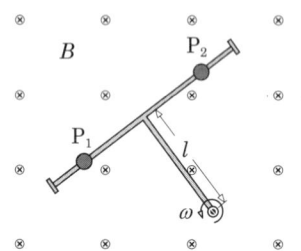

4. In a gravity free region, a T-shape rigid insulating frame is rotating in its plane about the end of the central bar of length l with a constant angular velocity ω. A strong uniform and static magnetic field of induction B exists everywhere pointing into the plane of the frame. Two identical beads P_1 and P_2 each of mass m and charge q can slide without friction on the frame.

   (a) Find the equilibrium position of the beads relative to the frame.
   (b) What can you say about the equilibrium positions, if sign of charge of one of the beads is reversed?

5. Two particles of equal mass m and having unlike charges of modulus q each are placed in free space a distance r_0 apart. A uniform and constant magnetic field of induction B is established everywhere perpendicular to the line joining the particles and the particles are released. If the magnetic field is sufficient to avoid collision of the particles, find the minimum separation between the particles.

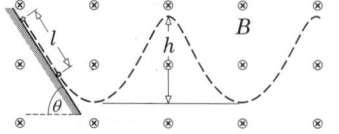

6. A charge particle starts sliding down a frictionless slope of inclination θ in presence of a horizontal uniform and static magnetic field of induction B directed perpendicularly into the plane of the figure and uniform gravitational field of the earth. Intensity of the gravitational field is g. After sliding an unknown distance l, the particle leaves the slope and follows a cycloidal trajectory as shown in the figure. If on the trajectory maximum vertical displacement of the particle is h, find the distance l it had slid on the slope.

7. An elastic conducting wire of length l_0 and force constant k is secured between two nails N_1 and N_2 on a horizontal frictionless tabletop in presence of a strong uniform magnetic field of induction B pointing vertically upwards. Top view of the situation is shown in the figure. Now a constant current I is switched on in the wire that flows from the nail N_1 towards N_2.

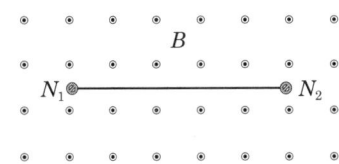

   (a) What stationary shape will the wire assume?
   (b) What should be the range of force constant k of the wire so that the wire assumes a stationary shape?

8. A loop is made by joining the ends of a flexible, inextensible and light conducting wire of length $2l$ with a thin insulating coating. The loop passes through two frictionless hooks, one of the hooks is attached to the ceiling and from the other hook a small rubber block of mass is suspended as shown in the figure. Below the ceiling, a horizontal magnetic field of induction B is established. Now a gradually increasing current is made to circulate in the loop. For all values of current in the loop, forces of magnetic interaction between different parts of the wire are negligible as compared to other forces.

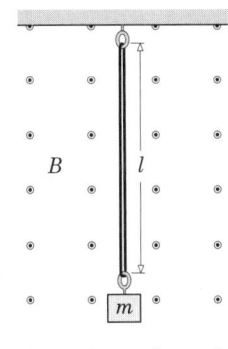

   (a) What shape will the wire loop assume for a particular value of current in the loop?
   (b) Find the maximum height up to which the block can be lifted.
   (c) Find the current in the loop to lift the block to a height $h = l\left(1 - \dfrac{3}{\pi}\right)$.

9. A load is connected across the terminals of a battery of terminal voltage $V_0 = 2$ kV with the help of two long conducting strips each of width $b = 4$ cm and connecting wires. The strips are arranged parallel to each other such that separation between their inner flat faces is $d = 4.0$ mm. For a certain value of load resistance, the net force of electrostatic and magnetic interactions between the strips vanishes. What will be the net force of electrostatic and magnetic interaction between unit lengths of the strips, if the load resistance is made $\eta = \sqrt{3}$ times of the value at which the interaction forces vanished.

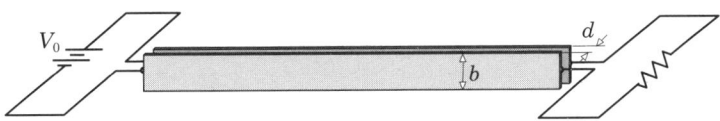

10. A single layer conducting coil is wound with no gap between adjacent turns on a cylindrical frame of radius R. Diameter of cross-section of the wire used is d ($d \ll R$). If breaking stress of the material of the wire is σ_b, at what magnitude of current will the coil rupture?

Challenge your understanding

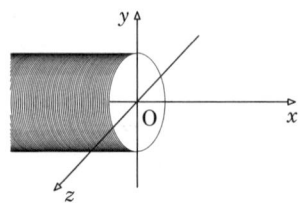

1. A tightly wound thin wire semi-infinite solenoid of radius R and n turns per unit length carries a current I. Magnetic field well inside the solenoid is uniform but near the end it fans out. Find the magnetic induction vector $\vec{B}$ in terms of radial and axial components at a point outside the solenoid and at a distance x from the end and a very small distance r from the axis. You may denote unit vector in the positive x-direction by $\hat{e}_x$ and unit vector away from the x-axis in y-z plane (radial direction) by $\hat{e}_r$.

2. Consider a long current carrying cylindrical conductor of radius r. Current density j inside the conductor is uniform over its cross-section. Deduce suitable expression for force of interaction per unit length between two halves that are obtained by dividing the conductor by a plane containing the axis of the conductor.

ANSWERS AND HINTS

Multiple Choice Questions

1. (c)
2. (a)
3. (c)
4. (a), (c)
5. (a), (b) and (d)
6. (d)
7. (a), (c) and (d)
8. (a), (b) and (d)
9. (d)
10. (d)
11. (a)
12. (b)
13. (c)
14. (a)
15. (d)

Build up your understanding

1. $\mu_0 \varepsilon_0 \omega V_0$

2. $\mu_r \mu_0 \sigma r \omega$

3. (a) $B = \begin{cases} \mu_0(\sigma_1\omega_1 R_1 + \sigma_2\omega_2 R_2); & r < R_1 \\ \mu_0 \sigma_2 \omega_2 R_2; & R_1 < r < R_2 \\ 0; & r > R_2 \end{cases}$

   (b) $p_1 = \mu_0 \sigma_1 \omega_1 R_1 \left(\dfrac{\sigma_1 \omega_1 R_1}{2} + \sigma_2 \omega_2 R_2 \right)$

   $p_2 = \dfrac{\mu_0 \sigma_2^2 \omega_2^2 R_2^2}{2}$

4. $\vec{B} = \dfrac{2\varepsilon_0 \mu_0 V}{3} \vec{\omega}$ and $\vec{m} = \dfrac{4\pi\varepsilon_0 R^3 V}{3} \vec{\omega}$

5. $\dfrac{r}{2}\sqrt{\dfrac{\mu_0 u_E}{\varepsilon_0 u_B}} = 2.6 \times 10^{-8}\,\Omega\cdot\text{m}$

Magnetic Effects of Electric Current 14.15

6. $\left(-\dfrac{4mv}{qB_y}, -\dfrac{2mv}{qB_x}\right)$

7. Trajectory of the particle will be in the shape similar to digit 8, if charge q has values given by the following equation.

   $q = \dfrac{2n\pi m}{BT}$ Here $n = 1, 2, 3$ ....

8. Any speed

   Hint: $v = \dfrac{qBR}{m}\tan\left(\dfrac{a\pi}{b}\right)$

   Where a and b can assume a value from the set of whole numbers and therefore the ratio a/b can assume any positive value.

9. $\hat{i}\,\dfrac{v(B_2 - B_1)\sin\theta}{\pi B_1 + \theta(B_2 - B_1)}$

10. $\vec{F} = q\omega Bl\left(\hat{i}\cos\theta + \hat{j}\sin\theta\right)$

    $\vec{\tau} = -qBl\left(v_x \cos\theta + v_y \sin\theta\right)\hat{k}$

    Hint: Net force depends only on the rotational motion and the net torque depends only on the translational motion.

11. $\dfrac{mv}{2rB}$

    Hint: The bead moves with a constant speed. In addition, to fulfil the given condition, the bead must move on a circular path of radius $2r$ after the thread becomes slack.

12. $\dfrac{q\vec{L}}{M}$

    Hint: The angular momentum vector rotates with the angular velocity of the circular motion while its modulus remains constant.

13. $\dfrac{2\pi nmu\cos\theta}{ql}$, here $n = 1, 2, 3$ ......

14. $\dfrac{4\pi nmu\cos\theta}{qB}$

15. $\dfrac{1}{d}\sqrt{\dfrac{2mV}{e}}$

16. $\dfrac{mg}{2q\eta u} = 5.0 \times 10^4 \dfrac{\text{Wb}}{\text{m}^2}$

17. $\dfrac{E}{gB}$

18. $\hat{i}\left\{\dfrac{kmu}{(qB)^2 + k^2}\right\} + \hat{j}\left\{\dfrac{qBmu}{(qB)^2 + k^2}\right\}$

19. $\dfrac{mv_0}{b}\left\{1 - \exp\left(-\dfrac{2\pi b}{qB}\right)\right\}$

20. $q = \dfrac{mg}{Bv}$, $r = \dfrac{v^2}{g}$

21. $\dfrac{\sqrt{2}mv_0}{Br}$

22. $16IBl$ towards the left

23. Between two points at the ends of a diameter perpendicular to the magnetic field.

    $F_{max} = \dfrac{8rB\mathscr{E}}{R}$

24. $\dfrac{mg}{2Br}$

25. $\dfrac{\mu mg}{2Br\sin(\theta/2)}$

26. $\dfrac{\rho_m \rho_e gl}{B}$

27. $\dfrac{5\pi rIB}{6}$

28. (a) $\vec{0}$

    (b) $\hat{j}\,\dfrac{\mu_0 I^2 d}{4\pi}(4 - \pi)$

Check your understanding

1. (a) $\dfrac{\mu_0 \mu_r NI}{l+(\mu_r-1)d}$

   (b) $\dfrac{\mu_0 \mu_r^2 N^2 I^2 A}{2\{l+(\mu_r-1)d\}^2}$

   Hint: In presence of a medium, generalised Ampere's law should be used.

2. $\dfrac{\mu_0 \sigma Vrd}{R}\left(\dfrac{1}{d} - \dfrac{1}{\sqrt{R^2+d^2}}\right)$

   Hint: Electric field created by potential difference between the spheres, cause conduction currents to flow, which is responsible for the magnetic field.

3. $T = \begin{cases} (q\omega B - m\omega^2)(r-l); & 0 \le \omega \le \dfrac{qB}{m} \\ (m\omega^2 - q\omega B)(r+l); & \dfrac{qB}{m} \le \omega \end{cases}$

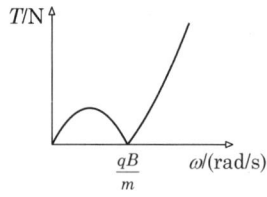

4. (a) $\theta = \tan^{-1}\left\{\dfrac{q^2}{16\pi\varepsilon_0 \omega l^3 (qB-m\omega)}\right\}^{\frac{1}{3}}$

   Here θ is the angular position of the beads measured from the central rod.

   The equilibrium is stable.

   (b) Depending upon initial locations of the beads, it is possible that both the beads move apart and stop at the ends of the bar, or the positively charged bead stops at the junction of the bars and the negatively charged bead stops at the end of the bar, or both the balls stop at the junction of the bars.

5. $\dfrac{r_0}{2}\left(1 + \sqrt{1 - \dfrac{4m}{\pi\varepsilon_0 r_0^3 B^2}}\right)$

6. $l = \dfrac{h\cot^2\theta}{4}$

7. (a) Circular arc (b) $k > \dfrac{IB}{2\pi}$

8. (a) Each straight segment will assume shape of a circular arc.

   (b) $l\left(1 - \dfrac{2}{\pi}\right)$ (c) $\dfrac{\pi mg}{3\sqrt{3}Bl}$

9. $\dfrac{\varepsilon_0 b V_0^2}{2d^2}\left(1 - \dfrac{1}{\eta^2}\right) = 2.9 \times 10^{-2}\,\text{N}$

10. $\sqrt{\dfrac{\sigma_b \pi d^3}{2\mu_0 R}}$

Challenge your understanding

1. $\vec{B} = \dfrac{\mu_0 nI}{2}\left\{\left(1 + \dfrac{x}{\sqrt{R^2+x^2}}\right)\hat{e}_x + \dfrac{rR^2}{2(R^2+x^2)^{3/2}}\hat{e}_r\right\}$

2. $\tfrac{1}{3}\mu_0 j^2 r^3$

Chapter 15

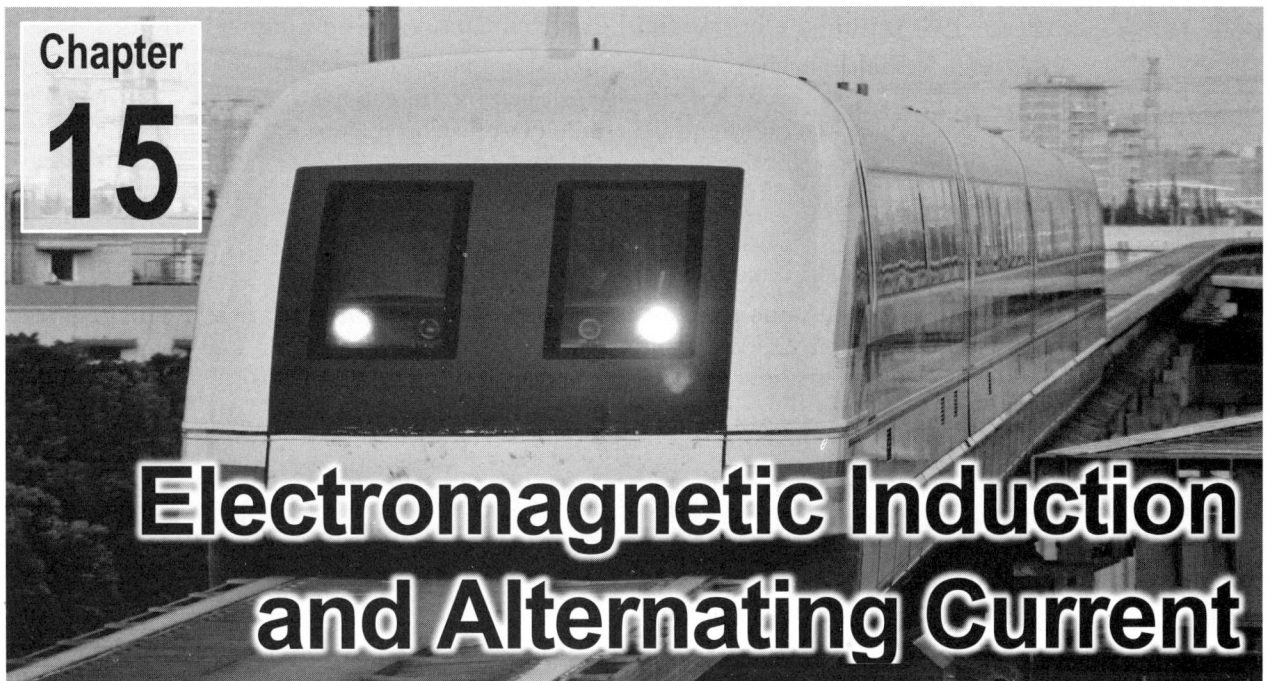

Electromagnetic Induction and Alternating Current

Faraday's Law of electromagnetic induction, Lenz's law, general case of electromagnetic Induction – motional emf and emf due time varying magnetic field, eddy current, self and mutual induction, RC, LR and LC circuits with direct current and alternating current sources.

"I am not a poet, but if you think for yourselves, as I proceed, the facts will form a poem in your minds."

BACK TO BASICS

Electromagnetic Induction

Faraday's law of electromagnetic induction:

Magnitude $\mathcal{E}$ of the induced electromotive force (emf) in a circuit is equal to the time rate of change in total magnetic flux ϕ through the circuit.

$$\mathcal{E} = -\frac{d\phi}{dt}$$

Here the minus sign is in accordance with the **Lenz's Law**, which suggests that the polarity of induced emf must be such that the current, if produced by it, will oppose the change in magnetic flux that produced it.

Electromotive force induced in a moving conductor in a static magnetic field:

A conductor cutting across a magnetic field $\vec{B}$ with a velocity $\vec{v}$ generates an emf producing electric field $\vec{E}$.

$$\vec{E} = \vec{v} \times \vec{B}$$

An emf appearing across an infinitesimal conductor length $d\vec{l}$ is given by

$$d\mathcal{E} = (\vec{v} \times \vec{B}) \cdot d\vec{l}$$

Michael Faraday
(22 September 1791 – 25 August 1867)

Induced electric field due to a time varying magnetic field:

Time varying magnetic field in space induces electric field whose line integral around a closed path equals the time rate of change in magnetic flux crossing the area bounded by the closed loop.

$$\oint \vec{E} \cdot dl = -\int \frac{\partial \vec{B}}{\partial t} \cdot d\vec{S}$$

General case of electromagnetic induction:

Flux through a circuit can change either by time variation of magnetic field or by mechanical motion of the circuit as a whole or some part of it in a magnetic field or by both these modes simultaneously.

$$\mathcal{E} = -\int \frac{\partial \vec{B}}{\partial t} \cdot d\vec{S} \quad + \quad \oint (\vec{v} \times \vec{B}) \cdot d\vec{l}$$

$$\text{Time variation} \qquad \text{Motion}$$

Self and mutual induction

Self-induction:

A time varying current in a device leads to appearance of an induced emf in the device, which in accordance with the Lenz's law opposes the variation in the current. This phenomenon is called self-induction and the emf so induced is called the self-induced emf.

Self-flux linkage λ_{self} of a device due to magnetic field of its own current I is given by the equation

$$\lambda_{self} = LI$$

Here the term L is a constant of proportionality and is known as self-inductance.

If in a coil of total number of turns N, the same flux ϕ due to magnetic field of the current I in the coil passes through every turn of the coil, the self-flux linkage λ_{self} is defined by equation

$$\lambda_{self} = N\phi = LI$$

The self-induced electromotive force $\mathcal{E}_{self}$ is given by

$$\mathcal{E}_{self} = -\frac{d\lambda_{self}}{dt} = -N\frac{d\phi}{dt} = -L\frac{dI}{dt}$$

Mutual induction:

If magnetic flux of a time varying current in a circuit links with some other device, an emf is induced in that device. This phenomenon is called mutual induction.

If in a coil of total number of turns N_1, the same flux ϕ (that is whole or a part of the magnetic flux produced by some other coil carrying current I_2) passes through every turn, the mutual-flux linkage λ_{mutual} is defined by equation

$$\lambda_{mutual} = N_1\phi = MI_2$$

Here the term M is a constant of proportionality and is known as mutual inductance.

The net induced electromotive force $\mathcal{E}$ in presence of mutual induction is given by

$$\mathcal{E} = -\frac{d}{dt}\left(\lambda_{self} \pm \lambda_{mutual}\right) = -\left(L_1 \frac{dI_1}{dt} \pm M \frac{dI_2}{dt}\right)$$

Alternating Current

The usual waveform of current and voltage in alternating power circuits is a sine wave.

Resistance in AC circuits

Voltage across a resistance R: $v_R = V_R \sin(\omega t + \phi_0)$

Current in the resistance R: $i = \dfrac{V_R}{R} \sin(\omega t + \phi_0)$

Inductance in AC circuits

Voltage across a inductance L: $v_L = V_L \sin(\omega t + \phi_0)$

Current in the inductance L: $i_L = \dfrac{V_L}{\omega L} \sin\left(\omega t + \phi_0 - \dfrac{\pi}{2}\right)$

Inductive Reactance: $X_L = \omega L$

Capacitance in AC circuits

Voltage across a capacitance C: $v_C = V_C \sin(\omega t + \phi_0)$

Current in the capacitance C: $i_C = \omega C V_C \sin\left(\omega t + \phi_0 + \dfrac{\pi}{2}\right)$

Capacitive Reactance: $X_C = \dfrac{1}{\omega C}$

Power in AC circuits

If voltage across and current through a device are $v = V \sin(\omega t)$ and $i = I \sin(\omega t \pm \phi)$ respectively, for this device

Instantaneous Power: $p = vi$

Real Power: $P = V_{rms} I_{rms} \cos\phi$
Unit: Watt (W)

Power Factor: $\cos\phi$

Reactive Power: $Q = V_{rms} I_{rms} \sin\phi$
Unit: Volt-Ampere Reactive (VAR)

Apparent Power: $S = V_{rms} I_{rms}$
Unit: Volt-Ampere (VA)

15.4 Chapter-15

Multiple Choice Questions

1. An aircraft is flying at a level height in presence the magnetic field of the Earth. If an electric bulb is connected between the two extreme ends of the wings,

   (a) a voltage will induce across the wings and the bulb will glow.
   (b) no voltage will induce across the wings, but the bulb will glow.
   (c) a voltage will induce across the wings, but the bulb will not glow.
   (d) no voltage will induce across the wings and the bulb will not glow.

2. A wire of uniform cross-section is drawn from a piece of mass m of a metal of density d and resistivity ρ. The ends of the wire are joined to make a planar closed loop, and the loop is placed in a uniform magnetic field that varies with time t according to equation $B = \beta t$, where β is a positive constant. What maximum current can you obtain in the loop by properly selecting shape and dimensions of the loop?

   (a) $\beta m/(\pi \rho d)$
   (b) $\beta m/(2\pi \rho d)$
   (c) $\beta m/(4\pi \rho d)$
   (d) $\beta m/(8\pi \rho d)$

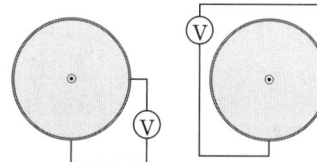

Figure-I   Figure-II

3. In a cylindrical region that is encircled by a uniform metallic ring, a uniform magnetic field perpendicular to the plane of the ring varies with time in such a manner that a constant electromotive force of 12 V is induced in ring. A voltmeter of very high resistance is used to measure potential difference between two points on the ring separated by one quarter of ring. For the purpose, the voltmeter is connected in two different manners as shown in figures. In both the arrangements, the ring and connecting wires are in the same plane.

   Which of the following conclusion can you draw regarding readings V_I and V_{II} of the voltmeters in the first and the second arrangement respectively?

   (a) $V_I = V_{II} = 3$ V
   (b) $V_I = V_{II} = 9$ V
   (c) $V_I = 3$ V and $V_{II} = 9$ V
   (d) $V_I = 9$ V and $V_{II} = 3$ V

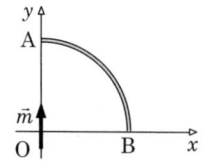

4. Consider a quarter circular conducting ring of large radius r with its centre at the origin, where a magnetic dipole of moment $\vec{m}$ is placed as shown in the figure. If the ring rotates at a constant angular velocity ω about the y-axis, electromotive force induced between its ends is

   (a) Zero
   (b) $\mu_0 m\omega/(2\pi r)$
   (c) $\mu_0 m\omega/(4\pi r)$
   (d) $\mu_0 m\omega/(8\pi r)$

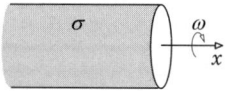

5. A long thin wooden cylindrical pipe of radius R carrying a uniform surface charge density σ, is rotating about its axis with an angular velocity ω that increases slowly with time t as $\omega = kt$, where k is a positive constant. Which of the following statements is/are correct for the region inside the pipe?

(a) Both the magnetic and the electric fields are uniform and constant.
(b) The magnetic field is uniform but not constant and the electric field is constant but not uniform.
(c) The magnetic field is constant but not uniform and the electric field is uniform but not constant.
(d) Total energy density u due to both the fields varies with time as $u = a + bt^2$, where a and b are positive constants.

6. The top and bottom faces of a rigid insulating box of dimensions $a \times b \times h$ and mass m are charged with uniform surface charge densities σ and $-\sigma$ respectively and the box is placed in a uniform horizontal magnetic field $\vec{B} = B_0 \hat{j}$. Assuming free space conditions and h negligibly small as compared to the dimensions a and b, find how much velocity will the box acquire after the magnetic field is switched off?

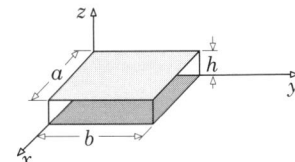

(a) $\dfrac{\sigma a b h B_0}{m} \hat{j}$ (b) $\dfrac{2\sigma a b h B_0}{m} \hat{j}$

(c) $\dfrac{\sigma a b h B_0}{m} \hat{i}$ (d) $\dfrac{2\sigma a b h B_0}{m} \hat{i}$

7. A superconducting rigid planar loop of area A and self-inductance L carrying a current is held motionless in a region of free space. Now a uniform magnetic field of induction B pointing everywhere parallel to the magnetic moment $\vec{m}$ of the loop is switched on. Current in the loop after the magnetic field is switched on is given by

(a) $\dfrac{AB}{L}$ (b) $\dfrac{m}{A}$

(c) $\dfrac{m}{A} - \dfrac{AB}{L}$ (d) $\dfrac{m}{A} + \dfrac{AB}{L}$

8. Three identical lamps A, B and C and two identical inductive coils L_1 and L_2 are connected to a DC power supply through a switch S as shown in the figure. Initially the switch is closed for a long time and steady state is reached. Now the switch S is opened. Which of the following statements correctly describes order of brightness of the bulbs immediately after the switch is opened?

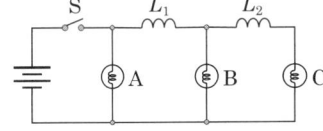

(a) Brightness of A suddenly increases but that of B and C remains unchanged.
(b) Brightness of B suddenly increases but that of A and C remains unchanged.
(c) Brightness of C suddenly increases but that of A and B remains unchanged.
(d) Brightness of all the bulbs suddenly increases equally.

9. A circuit shown consists of a coil of inductance L, an unknown resistance R, a switch and an ideal current source of current I_0. Find total heat dissipated in the resistance after the switch is closed.

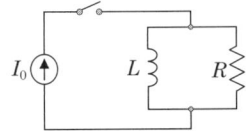

(a) Zero   (b) $\frac{1}{4} L I_0^2$

(c) $\frac{1}{2} L I_0^2$ (d) $L I_0^2$

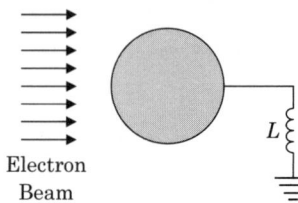

Electron Beam

10. An uncharged conducting ball of radius r is earthed through an inductor L as shown in the figure. A horizontal electron beam swoops on the ball from a great distance. The density of electrons in the incident beam is n and all these electrons are moving with velocity v that is much smaller than the speed of light so the relativistic effects can be neglected. Which of the following statements is/are correct?

(a) Maximum charge on the ball is equal to $2ne\pi r^2 v\sqrt{\pi\varepsilon_0 rL}$

(b) Maximum charge on the ball is equal to $4ne\pi r^2 v\sqrt{\pi\varepsilon_0 rL}$

(c) Maximum current through the inductor is equal to $2ne\pi r^2 v$

(d) Maximum current through the inductor is equal to $4ne\pi r^2 v$.

11. Consider a series combination of a resistance R, an inductance L, and a capacitance C undergoing electromagnetic oscillations. During a certain period, amplitude of current through the resistance drops from I to $0.5I$. What is the amount of heat dissipated by the resistance in this period?

(a) $0.375 LI^2$
(b) $0.375 I^2 CR^2$
(c) $0.375 I^2 (L + CR^2)$
(d) $0.375 LI^2 + 0.75 I^2 CR^2$

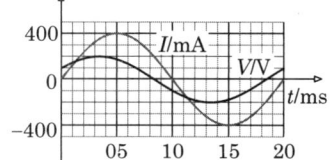

12. The given graph shows variation with time in the source voltage V and steady state current I drawn by a series RLC circuit. Which of the following statements is/are correct?

(a) Current lags the voltage.
(b) Resistance in the circuit is $250\sqrt{3}\ \Omega$.
(c) If capacitive reactance is $74\ \Omega$, inductance in the circuit is approximately 560 mH.
(d) Average power dissipation in the circuit is $20\sqrt{3}$ W.

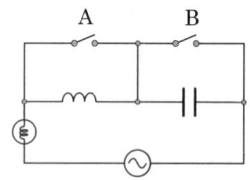

13. A series combination of an incandescent lamp, an inductor and a capacitor is connected across an alternating voltage source. Two switches A and B are provided to short circuit the inductor or the capacitor or both. Initially both the switches are open and the lamp glows with a certain brightness. If switch A is closed keeping B open, brightness of the lamp remains unchanged. How does the brightness of the lamp change, if switch B were closed keeping A open?

(a) Decreases
(b) Increases
(c) Remain unchanged
(d) Insufficient information to decide.

14. If an AC ammeter, an AC voltmeter and a resistor are connected in series and the combination is connected across an AC voltage source, the instruments read A and V respectively. The instruments are purely resistive in nature. If a capacitor is now connected across the voltmeter

(a) both A and V will increase
(b) both A and V will decrease
(c) A will decrease, V will increase
(d) A will increase, V will decrease

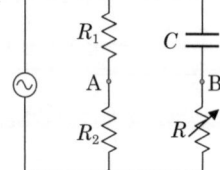

15. A circuit shown consists of two resistances R_1 and R_2 of equal and fixed values, a variable resistance R, a capacitor of capacitance C and an alternating voltage source. If the variable resistance is made to vary over a wide range, how does the peak voltage between terminals A and B change?

(a) First decreases then increases. (b) First increases then decreases.
(c) Decreases to a constant value. (d) Remains unchanged.

16. Consider the following series RLC circuit. Here the symbols R, L and C denote resistance, inductance and capacitance respectively. If frequency of the supply voltage is increased from a very low value to a very high value, the maximum voltages across L and C are measured at frequencies f_L and f_C respectively. Which of the following statements is correct?

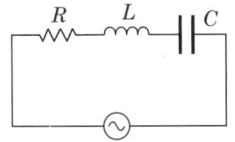

(a) $f_C < \dfrac{1}{2\pi\sqrt{LC}}$ and $f_L < \dfrac{1}{2\pi\sqrt{LC}}$ (b) $f_C > \dfrac{1}{2\pi\sqrt{LC}}$ and $f_L > \dfrac{1}{2\pi\sqrt{LC}}$

(c) $f_C > \dfrac{1}{2\pi\sqrt{LC}}$ and $f_L < \dfrac{1}{2\pi\sqrt{LC}}$ (d) $f_C < \dfrac{1}{2\pi\sqrt{LC}}$ and $f_L > \dfrac{1}{2\pi\sqrt{LC}}$

Build up your understanding

1. A metal rod of length L, attached to a vertical shaft by a non-conducting thread of length l is rotating in a horizontal plane with a constant angular velocity ω. Find potential difference between the ends of the rod. Now a uniform magnetic field in vertically upward direction is switched on. What should the magnitude of the flux density of the magnetic field be so that the potential difference between the ends of the rod becomes double? Neglect gravity and denote the mass and the charge on an electron by m and e respectively.

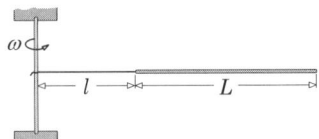

2. A bar of thickness d is made to move with a velocity v perpendicular to a uniform magnetic field of induction B. Top and bottom faces of the bar are parallel to the lines of magnetic field as shown in the figure.

   (a) Find surface charge densities on the upper and the bottom faces of the bar, assuming material of the bar to be a perfect conductor.
   (b) Find the surface charge densities on the upper and the bottom faces of the bar, assuming material of the bar to be a dielectric of dielectric constant ε_r.

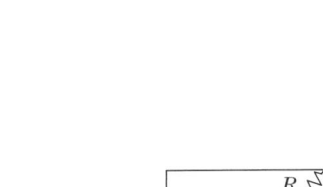

3. The basic principle of magneto-hydrodynamic (MHD) generators used for generating electricity is described here by a simple model that consists of a parallel plate capacitor immersed in a stream of a conducting liquid in presence of a uniform magnetic field of induction B pointing perpendicular to the stream and parallel to the plates. Area of each plates is A, distance between the plates is d and electrical conductivity of the liquid is σ. The liquid flows between the plates with a constant velocity v towards the left. If a resistance R is connected across the capacitor plates how much power will it dissipate? From where does this power come?

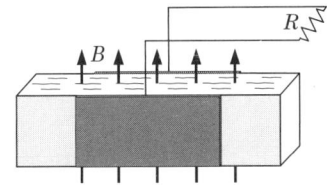

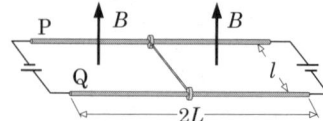

4. Two parallel rails P and Q each of length $2L$ and resistance per unit length ρ are fixed in a horizontal plane a distance l apart in presence of a uniform vertical magnetic field of induction B and two ideal batteries each of terminal voltage V_0 are connected between the ends of the rails as shown in the figure. Two light sleeves rigidly connected by a conducing rod of length l and resistance R and mass m can slide without friction on the rails. The rod is slightly displaced from mid position and then released. Find the period of small oscillations of the rod. Neglect potential drop at the contacts and damping.

5. In a region of space, a radial magnetic field is established, flux density B of which varies with distance r from the origin of a coordinate system according to the law $B = \beta/r^2$. Here β is a positive constant. A small conducting ring of radius a and resistance R is placed parallel to the y-z plane with its centre at point $(x, 0, 0)$. Find the force that must be applied on the ring to move it with a constant velocity $v\hat{i}$.

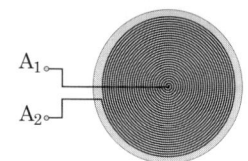

6. A planar spiral coil of outer radius R consisting of N closely wound turns of a thin conducting wire is placed in a uniform magnetic field with its plane perpendicular to the field. The magnetic field is confined in a circular region shown by shaded area in the figure. If flux density B of the magnetic field varies with time t as $B = B_0 \cos(\omega t)$, find electromotive force induced between the terminals A_1 and A_2 of the coil.

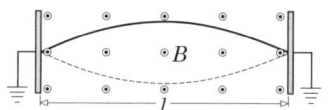

7. A conducting wire of length l and cross-section area A taut between two fixed grounded metallic supports is vibrating in its fundamental mode with a frequency ν and amplitude a in presence of a uniform magnetic field of induction B pointing normal to the plane of vibration of the string. Find an expression for electromotive force induced in the wire as a function of time t assuming the wire straight at $t = 0$.

8. A metal disc of radius r is affixed coaxially on a thin conducting shaft that is mounted along the axis of a long solenoid. One end of the solenoid is electrically connected to the periphery of the disc with the help of a graphite brush through an ideal ammeter and a resistance R; the other end of the solenoid is electrically connected with one end of the shaft. A uniform magnetic field of induction B pointing along the axis of the solenoid towards the right is switched on.

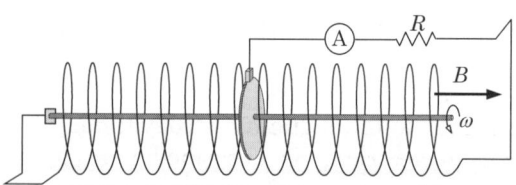

Consider the solenoid an ideal one having n turns per unit of its length, find an expression for the reading of the ammeter in a steady state for the direction of rotation of the disc shown as well as its opposite one.

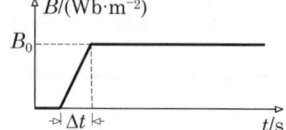

9. A particle of mass m and charge q is at rest at a point $(a, 0, 0)$ of a coordinate system in free space. A uniform magnetic field that varies with time t according to the given graph and points in the negative z-

direction is switched on in a cylindrical region of radius R ($R > a$) coaxial with the z-axis. If the time interval Δt is negligibly small, find equation of path of the particle long time after the magnetic field is switched on.

10. A thin light insulating rod of length l is free to rotate in a horizontal plane about a vertical axle passing through its centre. Two small balls each of mass m and charge q are affixed at the ends of the rod. This assembly is symmetrically placed between cylindrical poles N and S of an electromagnet that have established a uniform vertical magnetic field of induction B_0. The electric supply to the coils of the electromagnet is switched off. Find the angular velocity acquired by the rod long time after the magnetic field vanishes. Assume that the field was only between the poles of the magnet.

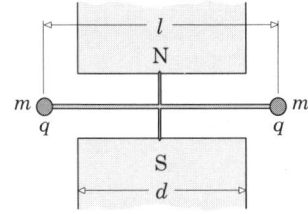

11. Curved surface of a very long hollow cylinder of radius R (much smaller than its length) is uniformly charged with surface charge density σ. At the centre of this cylinder, a small insulating ring of radius r, mass m and charge q is coaxially placed. The arrangement is in a gravity free space. If the cylinder is given an angular velocity ω_0 about its axis, how much maximum angular velocity will the ring acquire and in which direction relative to angular velocity of the cylinder?

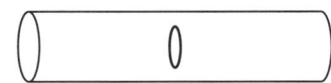

12. A rectangular loop of width b, length l, mass m and resistance R is placed close to and coplanar with a very long fixed straight conductor carrying current I. One side of the loop is parallel to the straight conductor as shown in the figure. The current in the conductor is suddenly switched off. Neglecting gravity find velocity acquired by the loop.

13. A thin conducting disc of mass m, thickness d and radius r ($r \gg d$) is released in a uniform horizontal magnetic field of induction B. The magnetic induction vector is in the plane of the disc as shown in the figure. Denoting acceleration due to gravity by g, find expression for acceleration of the disc.

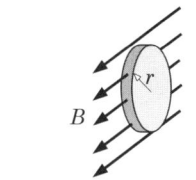

14. A conducting coil held coaxially near one pole of a cylindrical permanent magnet as shown in the figure, if made to vibrate up and down simple harmonically with a frequency $f = 100$ Hz and an amplitude $a = 1.0$ mm, much smaller than the linear dimensions of the magnet, the voltage induced in the coil has amplitude $V_0 = 5\pi$ V. If the coil is held stationary at the mean position of the oscillations and a current $I = 200$ mA is made to flow through it, how much force will it experience?

15. A long solenoid of radius r having n turns per unit length carries a constant current I. Consider two situations, in the first an inertia-less paper cylinder of radius r_p ($r_p < r$) and length l is inserted coaxially at the middle of the solenoid and in the second case another inertia-less paper cylinder of radius r_p ($r_p > r$) and length l surrounds coaxially the solenoid in the middle as shown in the figures. The paper cylinders carry uniform charge Q over their curved surfaces. If current in the solenoid is suddenly reduced to I/η, find angular velocity ω acquired by the paper cylinders. Ignore effects of gravity.

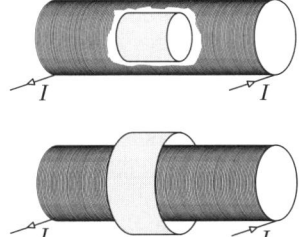

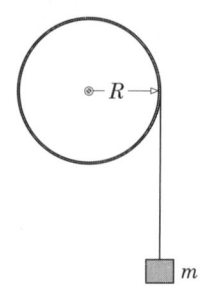

16. A uniform dielectric hollow cylinder of mass M, radius R, length l carrying uniform charge of surface charge density σ can rotate without friction about a fixed horizontal axle that coincides with the axis of the cylinder. Several turns of a light thin insulating cord are wrapped on the cylinder and a block of mass m is suspended from the free end of the cord. Initially the block is held at rest as shown in the figure. Find acceleration of the block after it is released. Neglect charge transferred to the cord and fringing of magnetic field at the ends of the cylinder. Acceleration due to gravity is g and permeability of the medium inside the cylinder is μ_0.

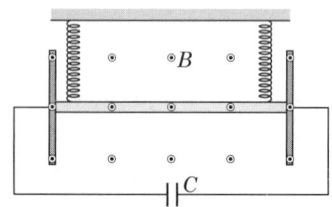

17. A conducting rod of mass m and length l is suspended horizontally with the help of two identical non-conducting springs each of stiffness k in a uniform horizontal magnetic field B. The rod can slide between two fixed frictionless vertical conducting guides and an uncharged capacitor of capacitance C is connected between the guides as shown in the figure. Find the period of oscillations of the rod. Neglect resistance and inductance in the circuit and assume acceleration of free fall to be g.

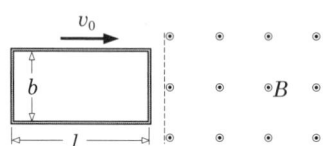

18. A rectangular perfectly conducting coil of mass m, width b, length l and inductance L moving with a velocity v_0 along its length in a region of no magnetic field enters a region of uniform magnetic field B that is everywhere perpendicular to the plane of the coil. How does position x of the leading edge of the coil measured from the entry point into the magnetic field varies with time t.

19. A perfectly conducting square frame of mass m, side l and inductance L with a small gap cut in one of its arms is placed on a frictionless horizontal floor where a nonuniform magnetic field that is given by equation $\vec{B} = \hat{j} B_0 (1 + kx)$ exists. Here k is a positive constant. Centre of frame initially coincides with the origin of coordinate system attached to the floor as shown in the figure.

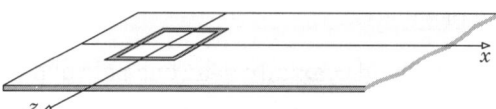

If the gap is closed with a perfectly conducting material and then the frame is imparted a velocity v_0 in the positive x-direction without any rotation, how will its displacement x vary with time t.

20. A cable consists of coaxial conducting cylindrical shells, radii of the inner and the outer shells of which are a and b respectively. Magnetic permeability of insulation between the shells is equal to that of the free space. Find inductance of a unit length of the cable.

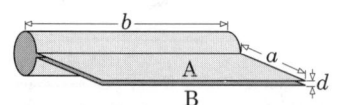

21. A rectangular copper foil of width b is bent into a shape consisting of a cylindrical portion of radius r ($r \ll b$) and two parallel identical flat portions each of length a as shown in the figure. A current enters uniformly into the edge A, flows uniformly over the whole width and comes uniformly out of the edge B. Find the inductance between edges A and B for a slowly varying current.

22. A coil is wound on a hollow insulating cylinder, which contains in it a laminated iron core. How the inductance L of the coil varies with the displacement x of the iron core is shown in the figure. In the initial state $x = 0$ (the core is fully inserted into the coil), the current in the coil is 1.0 A. Find current in the coil immediately after the core is quickly taken out of the coil.

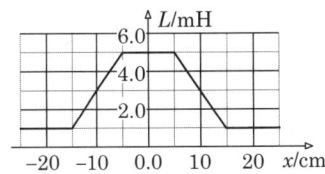

23. Three identical coils A, B and C are wound symmetrically on a toroidal iron core in the same sense. An alternating voltage source is connected across coil A and an ideal voltmeter is connected across coil C. If coil B is left open, the voltmeter reads half of the source voltage. How much will the voltmeter, if coil B is short-circuited?

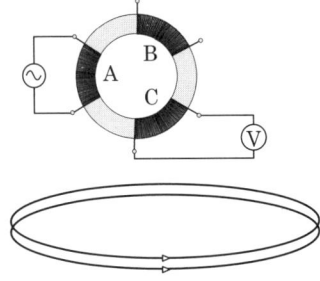

24. Two identical perfectly conducting rings are coaxially placed very close (infinitesimally small separation) to each other. Each of the coils has of inductance L and carries a current I_0 in the same direction. How much minimum amount of work has to be done in making their separation infinitely large?

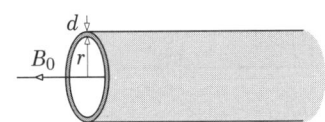

25. A uniform magnetic field of induction B_0 exists everywhere in a long hollow thin walled metallic cylinder along its axis as shown in the figure. Length l of the cylinder is much larger than its radius r that is much larger than its wall thickness d ($l \gg r \gg d$). Resistivity of the material of the cylinder is ρ. Neglecting flux linkage with the material of the cylinder, find how the magnetic induction B inside the cylinder will decay with time t after the magnetic field is switched off.

26. A coil is made by winding a large number of turns of a thin wire on a hollow plastic cylinder. A magnet is inserted in the coil and its ends are short-circuited. The magnet is suddenly removed. Immediately after removal of the magnet, if in first two consecutive time intervals of 0.1 s each, amounts heat dissipated in the coil are $\Delta W_1 = 0.01$ J and $\Delta W_2 = 0.006$ J respectively, find total amount of heat dissipated in the coil.

27. A circuit consists of two inductances L_1 and L_2, a resistance R, a two-way switch, a battery of electromotive force $\mathscr{E}$ and internal resistance r. The switch was in position 2 for a long time and at the instant $t = 0$, it is thrown to position 3.

(a) Find current through the switch as a function of time t after the switching.
(b) Find total heat dissipated in resistance R after the switching.

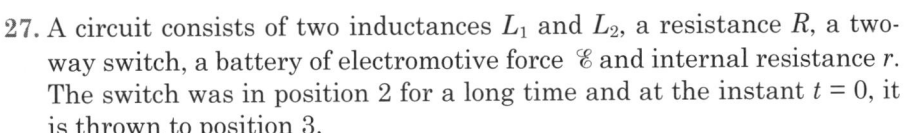

28. In the circuit shown, a parallel combination of a coil of inductance L and a resistance R can be connected across a battery of electromotive force $\mathscr{E}$ and internal resistance r through a switch. Find total heat dissipated in the resistance R after the switch is closed.

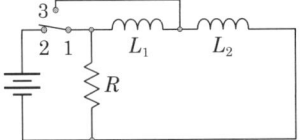

29. A parallel combination of an inductance L and a resistance R can be connected to either of the two ideal current sources of current I_0 and ηI_0 through a switch as shown. Initially the switch is in position 1 for a long time. Now the switch is thrown to position 2. Find amount of charge that will pass through the resistance and heat dissipated in it after the switching until a steady state is established.

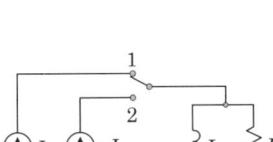

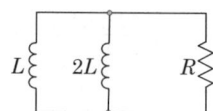

30. A parallel circuit consists two ideal inductances L and $2L$ and a resistance R. At an instant the same current I_0 is flowing in both the inductances in the same direction. How much charge will flow and how much heat will be dissipated in the resistance after this instant.

31. A conducting ball of radius $3r$ having charge Q is at a great distance from a neutral conducting ball of radius r. They are connected with a thin perfectly conducting wire of inductance L through a switch. What will the maximum current in the wire be after the switch is closed?

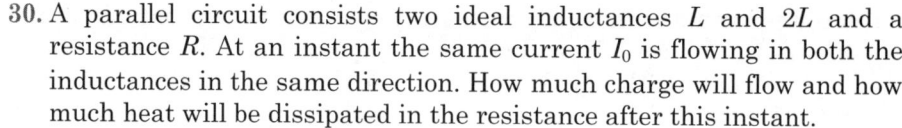

32. A circuit shown consists of two inductances L_0 and L, a resistance R, a battery of electromotive force $\mathcal{E}$ and internal resistance r and two switches 1 and 2. Initially switch 1 is closed for a long time. Find total charge that will flow through the resistance after the switch 2 is closed.

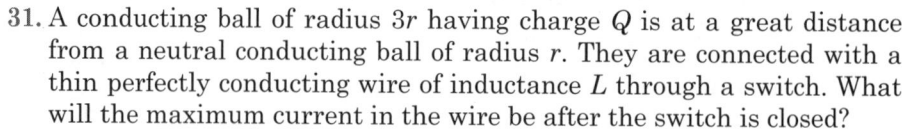

33. A circuit shown consists of two resistances R and $3R$, two capacitors each of capacitance C, two inductors each of inductance L, an ideal battery of electromotive force $\mathcal{E}$, an ideal voltmeter and a switch. Initially the switch is closed and the circuit is in steady state.

    (a) Find the voltmeter reading.

    Now, the switch is opened.

    (b) Find the voltmeter reading immediately after the switching.
    (c) Find the total heat dissipated in the resistors after the switching.

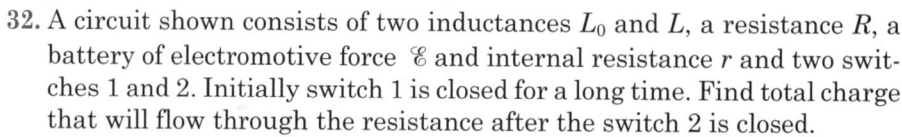

34. A circuit shown consists of three coils of inductances 1.0 H each and a 1.0 μF capacitance. At an instant, when charge on the capacitor is zero, currents of 1.0 A, 2.0 A and 4.0 A are flowing through the coils in the same direction.

    (a) Find the maximum charge on the capacitor.
    (b) Find the maximum currents through each of the coils.

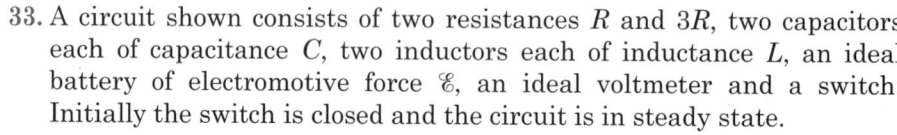

35. A circuit shown consists of two identical capacitors each of capacitance C, a coil of inductance L, two ideal batteries of electromotive force $\mathcal{E}$ and $2\mathcal{E}$ and a switch. The switch is open for a long time. Find maximum current through the coil after the switch is closed.

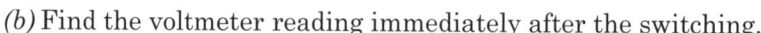

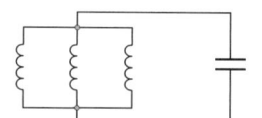

36. The circuit shown consists of four capacitors, an ideal battery of electromotive force $\mathcal{E}$, a switch and an inductance L. Capacitance of three of these capacitors is C and that of the fourth is $3C$. Find maximum current through the coil after the switch is closed.

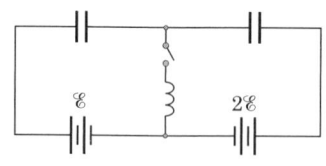

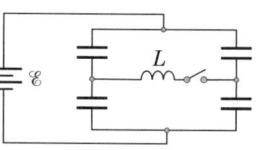

37. A circuit shown consists of two inductors of inductances L_1 and L_2, a capacitor of capacitance C, a battery of electromotive force $\mathcal{E}$ and internal resistance r and a switch. Initially the switch was in position 1 for a long time. Find the maximum charge on the capacitor and maximum current in the inductor L_2 after the switch is thrown to position 2.

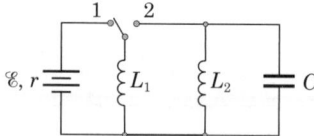

38. A capacitor of unknown capacitance and an induction coil of inductance 1.0 H are connected in series and then the series combination is connected across a source of alternating voltage 220 V and frequency 50 Hz. Now an ideal voltmeter is connected across the capacitor. For what

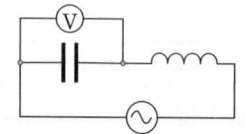

value of capacitance, the voltmeter will read 220 V. What value of capacitance can never be used in this circuit? Use $\pi^2 = 10$.

39. A circuit shown consists of two identical coils each of inductance L, two identical capacitors each of capacitance C and a variable frequency alternating voltage source. Find expression for the angular frequency of the source at which the peak voltage between the terminals A and B becomes η ($\eta \geq 1$) times of the peak voltage of the source.

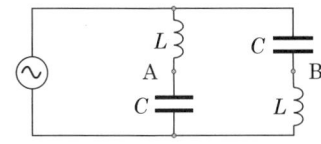

40. An alternating voltage source of peak voltage V_0 and angular frequency ω is connected across a series combination of a capacitance C and a variable resistance R as shown in the figure. Find the maximum power that can be obtained on the load resistance in this circuit.

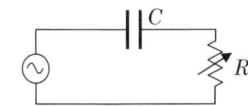

41. A fluorescent lamp (commonly known as tube light) employs a choke coil (an inductor) and a starter. In normal operating mode, the choke coil is in series with the tube that behaves as a resistance and the starter as an open switch in parallel with the tube. In a particular fluorescent lamp, the voltage drop on the choke coil is η times of that on the tube. If the choke coil is an ideal inductor of inductance L, how much capacitance should you connect in parallel with lamp assembly to make power factor unity? Angular frequency of the supply mains is ω.

42. A loop of resistance R is placed near a coil excited by a source of unknown alternating voltage. The phase shift between the current in the coil and induced current in the loop is 45° and power dissipated in the loop is p. The loop is replaced by another loop of identical shape and size. If resistivity of material of the new loop is η times of that of the previous loop, how much power will be dissipated in the new loop?

43. Two straight parallel diametrically opposite thin grooves are cut on an insulating cylinder parallel to its axis. A metal of density same as that of material of the cylinder is filled in the groove making two parallel conducting rods. The ends of these rods are short circuited by light wires to make a coil. Mechanically the assembly is a uniform cylinder of radius r, length l and mass m and electrically it is a coil of length l, width $2r$ and resistance R. This assembly is released on a slope of uniform inclination θ with the horizontal in a vertical magnetic field B. If the cylinder rolls down the slope without slipping, it acquires a constant velocity soon after it has been released. Neglect inductance and capacitance of the coil and find an expression for this constant velocity.

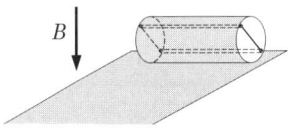

44. A rubber-coated wire is bent in the shape of a rigid sinusoid and then its ends P and Q are electrically connected with the help of a straight conducting wire making a closed loop of total resistance R and inductance L. The amplitude of the sinusoid is a_0. On the right of line AA is a region of uniform magnetic field of induction B pointing perpendicular to the plane of the wire loop. The loop is made to move along line PQ with a constant velocity v to enter the magnetic field. If one cycle of the sinusoid enters the region of magnetic field in time T, find average thermal power generated in the loop while it is entering the region of magnetic field.

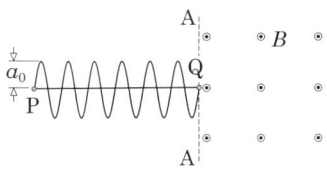

Check your understanding

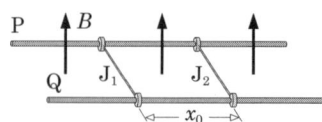

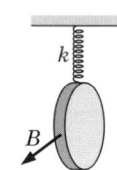

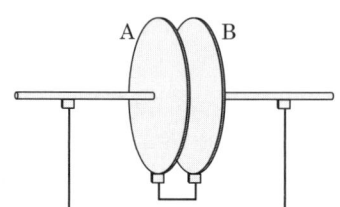

1. Two long conducting bars P and Q are fixed parallel to each other in a horizontal plane some distance apart. On these bars, two parallel jumpers J_1 and J_2 each of resistance R are arranged at separation x_0 as shown in the figure. The jumpers can slide on the bars without friction. If a uniform vertical magnetic field of induction B is switched on, find final separation between the jumpers. Force between the jumpers due to their currents is negligible as compared to the force of interaction between current in a jumper and the magnetic field.

2. A conducting disc of mass m and volume V is suspended with the help a light spring of force constant k from a fixed support. Thickness of the disc is much smaller than its radius. A uniform magnetic field of induction B parallel to the plane of the disc is established and the disc is pulled down slightly and released. Find period of the small amplitude oscillations of the disc.

3. Two identical metallic discs A and B each of radius r are affixed coaxially at the ends of two coaxial metallic shafts. The discs and the shafts are electrically connected with the help of conducting wires and sliding contacts as shown in the figure. A uniform magnetic field of induction B is established everywhere perpendicular to the plane of the discs. Assume the shafts and the discs to be perfectly conducting and all the resistance that is equal to R is concentrated in the connecting wires. Disc A is driven by a motor and disc B is connected to a mechanical load of constant torque τ. How does efficiency of power transfer from disc A to disc B depend on angular speed ω_B of disc B?

4. A wooden bobbin consists of two coaxial cylinders, the inner cylinder is of radius r and the outer is of radius R. A conducting wire PQ wrapped on the outer cylinder passes through a small hole in it and then it is wrapped on the inner cylinder in the same sense. Now the bobbin is placed on a horizontal table, where a uniform and constant magnetic field B exists parallel to the axis of the bobbin. If one end P of the wire is fixed on the tabletop and the other end Q is pulled horizontally with a constant velocity u as shown in the figure, the bobbin rolls without slipping. An ideal voltmeter is connected between end P and a stationary sliding contact S.

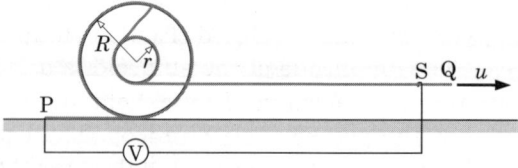

(a) Find the moduli of electromotive forces induced in each of the coils wrapped on the bobbin.
(b) Hence or otherwise, find the reading of the voltmeter.

5. A small bar magnet P is moving with a constant velocity v towards a fixed conducting ring of radius a along its axis as shown in the figure. Electrical resistance of the ring is R and its self-inductance is vanishingly small. The bar magnet can be modelled as magnetic dipole of dipole moment m. Find force of interaction between the bar magnet and the ring.

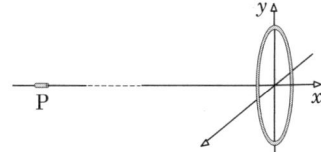

6. A conducting rod of mass m and length l is suspended horizontally with the help of two identical non-conducting springs each of stiffness k in presence of a uniform horizontal magnetic field of induction B. The ends of the rod are connected in a circuit consisting of an ideal battery of electromotive force $\mathcal{E}$, a capacitor of capacitance C and a switch as shown in the figure. Initially the switch was at position 1 for a long time. Describe motion of the rod after the switch is thrown to position 2. Neglect resistance and inductance in the circuit. Consider the wires connecting the rod extremely flexible and denote acceleration due to gravity by g.

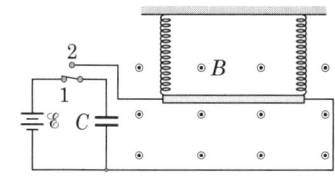

7. It is known that when a superconductor is brought into a magnetic field, surface currents are induced that make net magnetic field inside the superconductor zero. Due to this, a superconductor is repelled by the magnetic field.

A superconducting cube is made to hover in a uniform vertical magnetic field by suitably adjusting magnetic induction. Now if we gently place a nonmagnetic cube of the same mass as that of the superconducting cube on the superconducting cube, how many times the magnetic induction has to be increased to make the loaded cube hover.

8. A perfectly conducting rectangular frame of sides a and b can rotate without friction about a horizontal axis A_1A_2 in a weak uniform magnetic field of induction B pointing vertically upward and uniform gravitational field of intensity g of the earth. Mass of the frame is m and its inductance is L. Viscous drag of air is not negligible. Consider the following experiments.

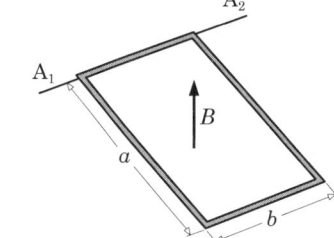

   (a) Initially the frame is hanging motionless with its plane vertical, and then it is slowly tilted to a horizontal orientation and released. In which orientation will the frame eventually stop?
   (b) Initially a small gap is cut in the frame when the frame is hanging motionless with its plane vertical. Now the frame is slowly tilted to a horizontal orientation, the gap is closed by the same conducting material and then the frame is released. In which orientation will the frame eventually stop?

9. A ring of mean radius r and cross-sectional area A is made of a perfectly conducting wire. Inductance L of the ring is so small that inertia of free electrons cannot be neglected in the current building process. The free electron density in the conductor is n, mass of an electron is m and modulus of charge on an electron is e. Initially the ring is placed in a uniform magnetic field with its plane parallel to induction vector $\vec{B}$ of the field as shown in the figure. Find the current in the ring after it is turned through an angle of $90°$.

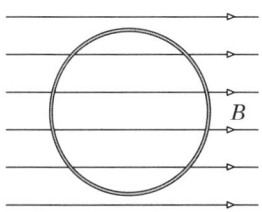

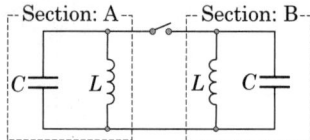

10. A circuit shown consists of two identical sections A and B, each of them is a parallel combination of a capacitor of capacitance C and an inductor of inductance L. Initially the voltage of capacitor in the section A is V_0, the capacitor in the section B has no charge and none of the inductors carry current. When voltage on the capacitor in section A drops to half of its initial value, the switch is closed. Find the maximum current through the inductor of section B after the switching.

11. The circuit shown consists of seven identical coils each of inductance L, one capacitor of capacitance C, two batteries and two switches with a common handle shown by dashed double lines. The common handle operates both the switches simultaneously. Initially the switch is in position 1 for a long time and currents I_1 and I_2 are flowing in the coils. After the switch is thrown to position 2, find the maximum charge acquired by the capacitor and corresponding current in the right-most coil.

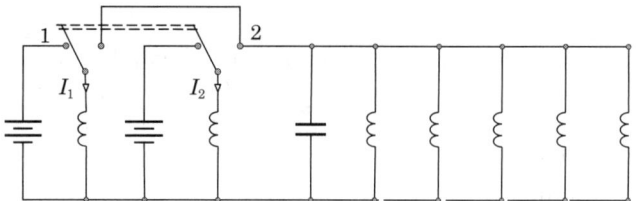

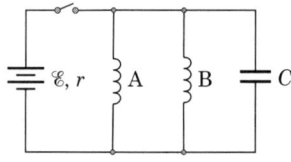

12. Two coils A and B are made by winding a conducting wire in one layer without gap between adjacent turns on two identical cores of very high magnetic permeability and very high electrical resistivity. Inductance of coil A is L, number of turns in coil B is double of that in coil A and the wire used has so small resistance that the resistive voltage drop on the inductors can be neglected as compared to self-induced voltages. A circuit is arranged by connecting parallel combination of these coils and a capacitor of capacitance C across a battery of electromotive force $\mathcal{E}$ and internal resistance r as shown in the figure.

    The switch is opened after keeping it closed for a long time. Calculate the following quantities when charge on the capacitor acquires its maximum value after the switching.

    (a) Currents in both the coils.
    (b) The maximum charge on the capacitor.

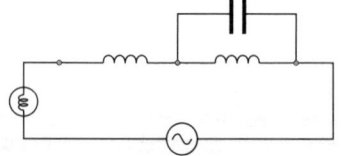

13. Two ideal inductors each of inductance L are connected in series and then a capacitor of capacitance C is connected in parallel to one of the inductors. This combination is connected across a series combination of an incandescent lamp and a variable frequency alternating voltage source as shown in the figure. It has been observed that the lamp glows with minimum brightness at an angular frequency ω. At what angular frequency will the lamp glow with maximum brightness?

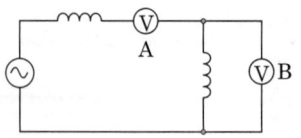

14. A circuit shown consists of two identical inductors, two identical voltmeters A and B and a source of alternating voltage $v = V_0 \sin(2\pi ft)$. The voltmeters offer only resistances in the circuit. If the frequency of the voltage source is changed over a wide range, what maximum reading will voltmeter B show?

15. Consider a network shown in the figure consisting of a resistance, a capacitor, an inductor and three alternating voltage sources 1, 2 and 3. Terminal voltages of the sources 1, 2 and 3 are $v_1 = V\sin(\omega t)$, $v_2 = V\sin(\omega t + 120°)$ and $v_3 = V\sin(\omega t + 240°)$ respectively and moduli of the reactances of the capacitor and the inductor are equal to the resistance. Find the voltage of the junction P.

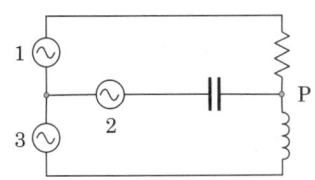

Challenge your understanding

1. Two ideal inductors each of inductance L are connected in series and a capacitor of capacitance C is connected in parallel to one of the inductors. This combination is connected across a battery of electromotive force $\mathcal{E}$ through a switch. Initially the switch was open for a long time and the capacitor was uncharged. How will the voltage on the capacitor vary with time t after the switch is closed?

2. A tuned circuit consisting of an inductor and a parallel plate capacitor of capacitance C with plate separation d has a resonating frequency v_0. What will be the resonating frequency, if a particle P of mass m and charge q is inserted in the middle of the capacitor plates? Neglect effects of gravity, fringing of electric field and electrostatic images.

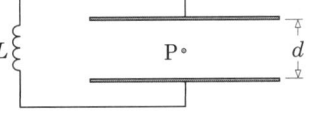

ANSWERS AND HINTS

Multiple Choice Questions

1. (c)
2. (c)
3. (c)
4. (c)
5. (b) and (d)
6. (c)
7. (c)
8. (a)
9. (c)
10. (a) and (c)
11. (c)
12. (a), (b) and (d)
13. (a)
14. (d)
15. (d)
16. (d)

Build up your understanding

1. $\dfrac{m\omega^2(2l+L)L}{2e}$ and $\dfrac{m\omega}{e}$

2. (a) $\varepsilon_0 Bv$, positive on the lower face and negative on the upper face

   (b) $\varepsilon_0 vB\left(\dfrac{\varepsilon_r - 1}{\varepsilon_r}\right)$, positive on the lower face and negative on the upper face

3. $\dfrac{(vBd)^2 \sigma^2 A^2 R}{(\sigma AR + d)^2}$

This power comes from the agency that maintains flow of the liquid.

4. $2\pi\sqrt{\dfrac{mL(\rho L + R)}{BlV_0}}$

5. $\dfrac{4\pi^2 a^4 \beta^2 v}{R(x^2 + a^2)^3}$

6. $\tfrac{1}{3}\pi\omega NR^2 B_0 \sin(\omega t)$

7. $4avBl\cos(2\pi vt)$

8. For the given direction of angular velocity:
$\dfrac{\omega r^2 B}{2R + \omega\mu_0 r^2 n}$

For angular velocity opposite to the given one:
$\dfrac{\omega r^2 B}{2R - \omega\mu_0 r^2 n}$

9. $\left(x - \dfrac{a}{2}\right)^2 + y^2 = \dfrac{a^2}{4}$

10. $\dfrac{qd^2 B_0}{2ml^2}$

11. $\dfrac{\mu_0 \sigma Rq\omega_0}{2m}$

Opposite to the angular velocity of the cylinder

12. $\dfrac{\mu_0^2 bl^2 I^2}{8\pi^2 mRa(a+b)} \ln\left(\dfrac{a+b}{a}\right)$ towards the straight conductor

13. $\dfrac{mg}{m + \pi\varepsilon_0 r^2 dB^2} \downarrow$

Hint: After the disc is released, it moves down cutting the horizontal magnetic field with an increasing speed. The time varying emf induced between the faces of the disc in this way makes the faces of the disc behave as a parallel plate capacitor, charge on which is increasing continuously. The force of interaction of the charging current with the magnetic field and the force of gravity together decide the acceleration of the disc.

14. $\dfrac{IV_0}{2\pi fa} = 5.0$ N

Hint: Only the component of the magnetic field of the magnet, which is in the plane of the coil is responsible for the induced emf as well as for the force.

15. $\omega = \begin{cases} \dfrac{2\pi nIl(\eta - 1)}{\eta Q}; & r_p < r \\ \dfrac{2(\eta - 1)\pi nIl}{\eta Q}\left(\dfrac{r}{r_p}\right)^2; & r_p > r \end{cases}$

Hint: The paper cylinders are inertia-less so they offer no resistance to change their state of motion and hence to change in state of motion of charges on them. Thus, we can treat each of them as a special case of superconductor in which charges instead of flowing move together with the cylinder.

16. $\dfrac{mg}{m + M + \pi\mu_0\sigma^2 R^2 l}$

17. $2\pi\sqrt{\dfrac{m + CB^2 l^2}{2k}}$

18. If $v_0 < \dfrac{bBl}{\sqrt{mL}}$, $x = \dfrac{v_0\sqrt{mL}}{bB}\sin\left(\dfrac{bBt}{\sqrt{mL}}\right)$

If $v_0 > \dfrac{bBl}{\sqrt{mL}}$

$\begin{cases} \dfrac{v_0\sqrt{mL}}{bB}\sin\left(\dfrac{bBt}{\sqrt{mL}}\right); & 0 < t < \dfrac{\sqrt{mL}}{bB}\sin^{-1}\left(\dfrac{bBl}{v_0\sqrt{mL}}\right) \\ \left(\sqrt{v_0^2 - \dfrac{b^2 B^2 l^2}{mL}}\right)t; & \dfrac{\sqrt{mL}}{bB}\sin^{-1}\left(\dfrac{bBl}{v_0\sqrt{mL}}\right) < t \end{cases}$

19. $x = \dfrac{v_0\sqrt{mL}}{B_0 kl^2}\sin\left(\dfrac{B_0 kl^2}{\sqrt{mL}}t\right)$

20. $\dfrac{\mu_0}{2\pi}\ln\left(\dfrac{b}{a}\right)$

21. $\dfrac{\mu_0(\pi r^2 + ad)}{b}$

22. 5.0 A

23. 1/3

   Hint: Take care of mutual induction in addition to the self-induction.

24. $2LI_0^2$

25. $B = B_0 \exp\left(-\dfrac{2\rho t}{\mu_0 rd}\right)$

26. $\dfrac{\Delta W_1^2}{\Delta W_1 - \Delta W_2} = 0.025\,\text{J}$

27. (a) $\dfrac{\mathcal{E}}{r}\left\{1 - \exp\left(-\dfrac{Rt}{L_2}\right)\right\}$

   (From the terminal 3 towards the terminal 1)

   Hint: Current through the first inductor will remain unchanged and circulate in the loop containing the switch, where decaying current through the second inductor will be superimposed.

   (b) $\dfrac{L_2 \mathcal{E}^2}{2r^2}$

28. $\dfrac{L\mathcal{E}^2}{2r(r+R)}$

29. $\dfrac{(\eta-1)LI_0}{R}$ and $\dfrac{(\eta-1)^2 LI_0^2}{2}$

30. $\dfrac{4LI_0}{3R}$ and $\dfrac{4LI_0^2}{3}$

   Hint: Since the inductors are in parallel, voltage across each of them must always be the same.

31. $\dfrac{Q}{4}\sqrt{\dfrac{1}{3\pi\varepsilon_0 LR}}$

32. $\dfrac{\mathcal{E}}{R}\left(\dfrac{L}{r+R} + \dfrac{L_0}{r}\right)$

33. (a) $\mathcal{E}$ (b) $-2\mathcal{E}$

   (c) Heat dissipated in R: $\dfrac{C\mathcal{E}^2}{2} + \dfrac{L\mathcal{E}^2}{2R^2}$

   Heat dissipated in $3R$: $\dfrac{L\mathcal{E}^2}{2R^2}$

34. (a) $\dfrac{7}{\sqrt{3}}$ mC

   (b) $-\dfrac{11}{3}$ A, $-\dfrac{8}{3}$ A and $-\dfrac{2}{3}$ A

35. $3\mathcal{E}\sqrt{\dfrac{C}{2L}}$

36. $\dfrac{\mathcal{E}}{2}\sqrt{\dfrac{C}{3L}}$

37. $\dfrac{\mathcal{E}}{r}\sqrt{\dfrac{CL_1 L_2}{L_1 + L_2}}$ and $\dfrac{2\mathcal{E}}{r}\left(\dfrac{L_1}{L_1 + L_2}\right)$

   Hint: Since the inductors are in parallel, voltage across each of them must always be the same.

   When charge on the capacitor is maximum, current through it is zero. Thus, the same current circulates in the inductors at this instant.

   When current through the inductor L_2 is maximum, voltage across it as well as on the capacitor is zero and hence charge on the capacitor is zero.

38. Zero, 20 µF,   Forbidden capacitance 10 µF

   Hint: The given condition is possible when voltage drop on the inductor is double of that on the capacitor or when the reactance of the capacitor is so high that it works as an open circuit.

39. $\sqrt{\dfrac{(\eta-1)}{(\eta+1)LC}}$ and $\sqrt{\dfrac{(\eta+1)}{(\eta-1)LC}}$

40. $\dfrac{\omega C V_0^2}{4}$

41. $\dfrac{\eta^2}{\omega^2 L(\eta^2+1)}$

42. $\dfrac{2\eta p}{\eta^2+1}$

   Hint: Since geometrical configuration of the system remains the same in both the cases, equal emfs are induced in the old and the new loop.

15.20 Chapter-15

43. $\dfrac{Rmg\sin\theta}{2B^2l^2}$

44. $\dfrac{(Bva_0)^2 RT^2}{2(T^2R^2+4\pi^2L^2)}$

Check your understanding

1. $\dfrac{x_0}{2}$

   Hint: Initially when the magnetic field is building up, impulses of the force of interaction between the currents induced in the jumpers due to the time varying magnetic field and the magnetic field provide each of the jumpers an inward momentum. Thereafter, each jumper will eventually stop by losing its momentum due to the impulse of force of interaction between the static magnetic field and the current caused by motional emf in the jumper.

2. $2\pi\sqrt{\dfrac{m+\varepsilon_0 VB^2}{k}}$

3. $\dfrac{\omega_B}{\omega_B + \dfrac{4R\tau}{B^2 r^4}}$

4. (a) $\mathcal{E}_{\text{Outer Coil}} = \dfrac{BuR^2}{2(R-r)}$, $\mathcal{E}_{\text{Inner Coil}} = \dfrac{Bur^2}{2(R-r)}$

   Hint: The flux linkages of the outer and the inner coil change respectively due to un-wrapping and wrapping of the wire, thus emfs are induced in these coils.

   (b) $\dfrac{B(R-r)u}{2}$

5. $\dfrac{9\mu_0^2 a^4 m^2 x^2 v}{4R(a^2+x^2)^5}$ (Repulsive)

6. Simple harmonic oscillation:

   $y = \dfrac{BlC\mathcal{E}}{\sqrt{2km}} \sin\left(\sqrt{\dfrac{2k}{m}}\,t\right)$

   Here y is displacement of the rod in vertical direction from its equilibrium position.

   Hint: Absence of resistance makes discharge process of the initially charged capacitor almost instantaneous, and absence of inductance suppresses possibilities of LC oscillations. During the instantaneous discharge process of the capacitor, the instantaneous flow of charge through the bar imparts it an initial velocity at the mean position of the oscillations.

7. $\sqrt{2}$

8. (a) Vertical

   Hint: There is always a current in the loop when it is in any orientation other than the vertical. Torque due to interaction of this current with the magnetic field as well as the torque of gravity will always try to bring the loop in the vertical orientation. Thus, the net torque of magnetic forces and gravity can be zero only when the loop is in vertical orientation.

   Forces of air resistance are velocity dependent and so is their torque; therefore, the loop can stop only in vertical orientation where the net torque on it is zero.

   (b) Angular position $\approx \dfrac{2B^2 ab^2}{mgL}$ from the vertical.

   Hint: There is always a current in the loop when it is in any orientation other than the horizontal. Torque due to interaction of this current with the magnetic field and the torque of gravity will always in opposition to each other.

   Since the magnetic field is very weak, the equilibrium is achieved at such a small angular position from the vertical for which you can use small angle approximations.

9. $\dfrac{\pi r^2 B}{L + \dfrac{2\pi rm}{nAe^2}}$

   Hint: During the process of turning of the coil, the free electrons are being accelerated because of the net electric field inside the ring, which is an outcome of the difference of motional emf, and voltage drop by self-induction.

10. $\left(\dfrac{2+\sqrt{3}}{4}\right)\sqrt{\dfrac{CV_0^2}{L}}$

Hint: After the switching, charge sharing between the capacitors takes place almost instantaneously, moreover, during this charge sharing process currents in the inductors remain practically unchanged.

11. $(I_1+I_2)\sqrt{\dfrac{LC}{7}}$ and $\dfrac{I_1+I_2}{7}$

12. (a) $I_A=I_B=0$ (b) $\dfrac{\mathcal{E}}{r}\sqrt{\dfrac{2LC}{3}}$

13. $\omega\sqrt{2}$

14. $\dfrac{1}{3}V_0$

Hint: You may need the following phasor diagram.

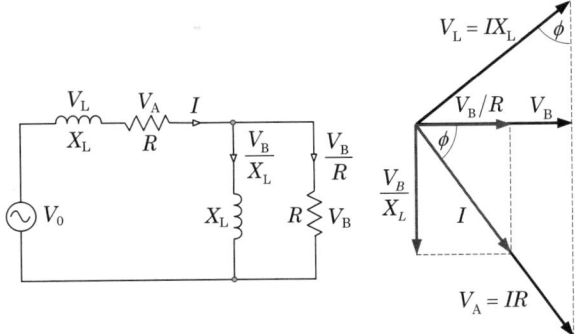

15. $V(\sqrt{3}-1)\sin(\omega t+180°)$

Challenge your understanding

1. $\dfrac{1}{2}\mathcal{E}\left\{1-\cos\left(t\sqrt{\dfrac{2}{LC}}\right)\right\}$

2. $v=\sqrt{\dfrac{v_0^2}{2}+\sqrt{\left(\dfrac{v_0^2}{2}\right)^2+\dfrac{q^2v_0^2}{4\pi^2d^2mC}}}$

Chapter 16

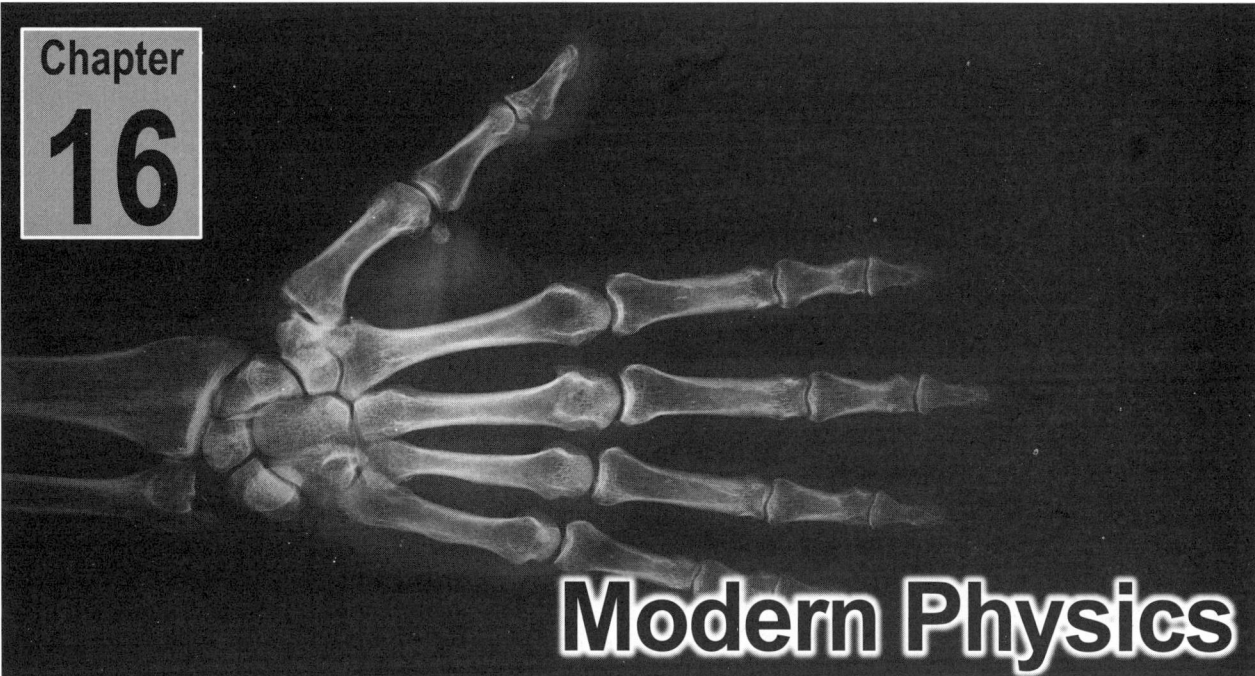

Modern Physics

Photon, photoelectric effect – Einstein's photoelectric equation, De Broglie hypothesis, Bohr's atomic model for Hydrogen atom or hydrogen-like ions, the atomic nucleus, binding energy of a nucleus, radioactivity, alpha, beta and gamma radiation, Q-value of a nuclear reaction.

"It's not that I'm so smart, it's just that I stay with problems longer."

Albert Einstein
(March 14, 1879 – April 18, 1955)

BACK TO BASICS

Photon:

Photons are quanta of electromagnetic energy.

Energy E and frequency ν of an electromagnetic radiation are related by the Planck's equation that is

$$E = h\nu$$

$h \equiv$ Planck's constant $= 6.63 \times 10^{-34}$ J·s

For a photon moving in a specific direction with velocity c, the energy E and momentum p are related by the equation

$$E = pc$$

The rest of a photon is zero.

Photoelectric effect:

It is emission of electrons from a metal surface resulting from absorption of electromagnetic radiations.

Einstein's photoelectric equation:

Maximum kinetic energy K_{max} of emitted photoelectrons equals the difference between energy E of incident photon and work function ϕ of the metal.

$$K_{max} = E - \phi$$

De Broglie hypothesis:

Wavelength λ assigned to a particle of mass m moving with velocity v is

$$\lambda = \frac{h}{mv}$$

Bohr's atomic model for hydrogen atom or hydrogen like ions:

- An electron in an atom can revolve in certain stable orbits without emission of radiant energy.
- An electron might make a transition from one of its non-radiating orbits to another. In a transition from a higher energy orbit to a lower one, a photon is emitted and in a transition from a lower energy orbit to a higher one, a photon is absorbed. These emitted or absorbed photons have energy equal to the energy difference between the initial and final states.

$$h\nu = |E_{final} - E_{initial}|$$

- Only those orbits are possible for which the angular momentum L of the orbiting electrons is quantized.

$$L = \frac{nh}{2\pi}$$

Energy level in a hydrogen-like atom:

$$E_n = -13.6 \frac{Z^2}{n^2} \text{ eV}$$

Here Z is the atomic number, and n is the principal quantum number.

Radioactivity:

In any radioactive sample, the rate of decay or activity at an instant is proportional to the number N of nuclei of the radioactive material present in the sample at that instant.

$$\frac{dN}{dt} = -\lambda N$$

Here λ is known as decay constant.

Binding energy of a nucleus:

The total energy of a nucleus is less than the combined energy of the separated nucleons. This difference in energy is called the binding energy of the nucleus and can be thought of as the minimum energy that must be added to a nucleus to break it apart into its constituents.

$$E_b = \{Zm_{protons} + (A-Z)m_{neutrons} - m_{nucleus}\}c^2$$

Here Z is atomic number and A is mass number.

Q-Value of a nuclear reaction:

It is the total energy liberated in a nuclear reaction.

$$Q = \left(\Sigma m_{\text{Reactants}} - \Sigma m_{\text{Products}}\right)c^2$$

Multiple Choice Questions

1. If photoelectrons emitted by a metal irradiating it by a light of wavelength λ cannot move away farther than a distance d in presence of a retarding electric field E, find threshold wavelength of the metal.

   (a) $\dfrac{hc}{eEd}$

   (b) $\lambda - \dfrac{hc}{eEd}$

   (c) $\lambda + \dfrac{hc}{eEd}$

   (d) $\left(\dfrac{1}{\lambda} - \dfrac{eEd}{hc}\right)^{-1}$

2. How much power must a light beam of wavelength λ_2 have to produce the same saturation current on irradiating a metal plate as produced by a light beam of wavelength λ_1 and power W_1? Quantum yield of photoelectric effect for these wavelengths are η_1 and η_2 respectively.

   (a) $W_1 \dfrac{\eta_1 \lambda_2}{\eta_2 \lambda_1}$

   (b) $W_1 \dfrac{\eta_2 \lambda_2}{\eta_1 \lambda_1}$

   (c) $W_1 \dfrac{\eta_2 \lambda_1}{\eta_1 \lambda_2}$

   (d) $W_1 \dfrac{\eta_1 \lambda_1}{\eta_2 \lambda_2}$

3. An isolated zinc bead of radius r charged to a negative potential V_0 (assuming potential at infinitely distant points to be zero) placed in free space is being continuously irradiated by ultraviolet light of wavelength λ. Photoelectric threshold wavelength for zinc is λ_0, speed of light is c, Denoting Planck's constant by h, permittivity of free space by ε_0, charge and mass of an electron by $-e$ and m, select correct statements from the following?

   (a) Maximum speed of a photoelectron immediately after emission is $\sqrt{\dfrac{2hc}{m}\left(\dfrac{1}{\lambda} - \dfrac{1}{\lambda_0}\right)}$.

   (b) Maximum speed of a photoelectron at a great distance from the bead is $\sqrt{\dfrac{2hc}{m}\left(\dfrac{1}{\lambda} - \dfrac{1}{\lambda_0}\right) + \dfrac{2eV_0}{m}}$.

   (c) Potential of the bead after prolonged irradiation is $-\dfrac{hc}{e}\left(\dfrac{1}{\lambda} - \dfrac{1}{\lambda_0}\right)$.

   (d) Total number of photoelectrons emitted from the bead is $\dfrac{4\pi\varepsilon_0 r}{e}\left\{\dfrac{hc}{e}\left(\dfrac{1}{\lambda} - \dfrac{1}{\lambda_0}\right) + V_0\right\}$.

4. What is the principal quantum number of the highest energy level for which the lines in the Balmer series of emission spectra of atomic hydrogen will just be resolved by a spectrometer of resolving power $\lambda/d\lambda = 8 \times 10^3$?

(a) 30 (b) 40
(c) 50 (d) 60

5. A moving neutron collides with a singly ionized stationary helium atom that is in ground state. What should be the minimum speed of the moving neutron for the collision to be perfectly inelastic?

(a) 2.50×10^4 m/s (b) 4.25×10^4 m/s
(c) 6.25×10^4 m/s (d) 9.89×10^4 m/s

6. A dose containing radioactive ^{18}F is scheduled to be prepared at 6.10 AM and 1.00 mL of it is to be given to a patient at 8.00 AM. If the patient reaches clinic late and takes the dose at 8.55 AM, how much quantity of the dose should be given to the patient? Half-life of ^{18}F is 110 min.

(a) 1.41 ml (b) 2.00 ml
(c) 2.82 ml (d) None of these

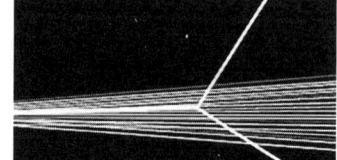

7. A stream of α-particles encounters a stationary unknown nucleus in a cloud chamber. After a collision, the nuclei are scattered in mutually perpendicular directions. If some kinetic energy is lost in the collision, the unknown nucleus must be

(a) a proton (b) a nucleus lighter than an α-particle
(c) an α-particle (d) a nucleus heavier than an α-particle

8. In a protonium atom, a proton and an antiproton orbit each other. What is the energy of a photon emitted in transition of a protonium atom from the first excited state to the ground state?

(a) 5.1 eV (b) 9.37 keV
(c) 12.5 keV (d) 18.74 keV

9. A proton collides with a stationary deuteron and a ^{3}He nucleus is formed. For this reaction to take place, the proton must have minimum kinetic energy 1.4 MeV. If instead, a deuteron collides with a stationary proton to make a ^{3}He nucleus, how much minimum kinetic energy must it possess?

(a) 0.7 MeV (b) 1.4 MeV
(c) 2.1 MeV (d) 2.8 MeV

Questions 10 to 12 are based on the following write-up.

A narrow beam of monochromatic light of wavelength λ emitted from a source of power P is propagating in the positive x-direction. After being reflected from a perfectly reflecting plane mirror of area vector $\vec{A} = A(-\hat{i} + \hat{j})$, the beam falls on a metal plate of surface area A placed parallel to the x-z plane. The work function of the metal is ϕ and photoelectric efficiency is η. Photoelectrons emitted from the metal plate are immediately removed from the vicinity of the plate.

10. Reflection from the mirror changes the momentum of photons and exerts force on the mirror. Which of the following statements is/are correct?

(a) Change in momentum of each photon is $\dfrac{h}{\lambda}(-\hat{i}+\hat{j})$.

(b) Change in momentum of each photon is $\dfrac{h}{\lambda}(\hat{i}-\hat{j})$.

(c) The force exerted by light beam on the mirror is $\dfrac{P}{c}(\hat{i}-\hat{j})$.

(d) The force exerted by light beam on the mirror is $\dfrac{P}{c}(-\hat{i}+\hat{j})$.

11. After a time interval Δt from the instant light falls on the metal plate, an electric field at a point very close to the metal plate and far away from its edges is explored. Which of the following statements is/are true

(a) The modulus of electric field is $\dfrac{\eta P \lambda e \Delta t}{4\varepsilon_0 hcA}$.

(b) The modulus of electric field is $\dfrac{\eta P \lambda e \Delta t}{2\varepsilon_0 hcA}$.

(c) The modulus of electric field is $\dfrac{\eta P \lambda e \Delta t}{\varepsilon_0 hcA}$.

(d) Electric field increases linearly with time in starting and reaches saturation after a short while.

12. If power of the source, wavelength of light, surface area and photoelectric efficiency of the metal of the plate are adjusted to 60 W, 6000 Å, 0.04 m² and 10^{-4} respectively. Which of the following statements are correct? Use $hc = 12420$ eV·Å.

(a) Range of kinetic energy of photoelectrons does not depend on photoelectric efficiency of the metal used.
(b) If the work function of the metal of the ball is 1.9 eV, the maximum kinetic energy of the photoelectrons is 0.17 eV.
(c) If material of metal plate has work function 2.1 eV, no photoelectrons are observed.
(d) The number of photoelectrons emitted per second is 1.82×10^{16}.

Questions 13 to 15 are based on the following write-up.

Consider a classic experiment on the photoelectric effect in which a monochromatic plane wave of light falls on a metal plate of area 66.3 cm² at an angle 30° as shown in the figure. Electric field in the light wave varies according to equation $E = E_0 \cos(\omega t + \varphi_0)$, where amplitude is $E_0 = 15$ V/m, angular frequency is $\omega = 9.5 \times 10^{15}$ rad/s and φ_0 is some initial phase angle. For a plane wave, the density u of electromagnetic energy is given by the equation $u = \tfrac{1}{2}\varepsilon_0 E_0^2$. Dependence of photoelectric current I on voltage V applied between the electrodes is shown by a graph.

Speed of light is $c = 3.0 \times 10^8$ m/s, Planck's constant is $h = 6.63 \times 10^{-34}$ J·s, electrical permittivity of free space is $\varepsilon_0 = 8.85 \times 10^{-12}$ F/m and charge on an electron is $e = -1.6 \times 10^{-19}$ C.

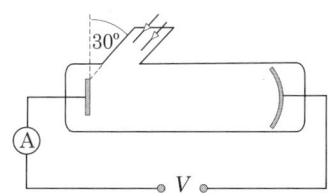

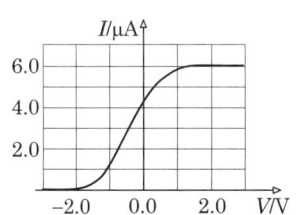

16.6 Chapter-16

13. What is quantum yield in this experiment?
    (a) 0.019
    (b) 0.038
    (c) Unity when saturation current flows otherwise less than unity.
    (d) It has no unique value as it depends on photoelectric current registered.

14. If amplitude of electric field in the incident light is made 25 V/m, how much will the saturation current become?
    (a) 8.00 µA
    (b) 10.00 µA
    (c) 16.67 µA
    (d) None of these

15. Instead of a simple plane wave, a complex plane wave of light governed by the following equation falls on the metal plate.
    $$E = E_0 \{1 + \cos(\omega t + \varphi_0)\} \cos(\omega t + \varphi_0)$$
    Stopping potential and saturation current respectively are
    (a) 6.27 V and 6.75 µA
    (b) 6.27 V and 7.50 µA
    (c) 8.27 V and 6.75 µA
    (d) 8.27 V and 7.50 µA

Build up your understanding

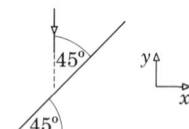

1. In a thought experiment, an evacuated tube of mass m and length l closed at its ends by two discs of masses m_1 and m_2 stay at rest in free space. If a photon of frequency ν is emitted from one disk and absorbed at the other, find the displacement of the tube in this process. Denote the Planck's constant by h and the speed of light by c.

2. Two thin partially silvered glass plates are rigidly joined at an angle 45°. The structure is placed in gravity free region and a short light pulse is made to incident on the structure as shown. The reflection of light from each plate is ρ for all angles of incidence. Find the direction of the total force of light pressure on the plate.

3. How many photons of wavelength λ = 450 nm does it take to achieve pressure p = 10⁵ Pa in an empty cubical box of edge length l = 10 cm? The inner surfaces of all the faces of the box are perfectly reflecting. Plank's constant is $h = 6.67 \times 10^{-34}$ J·s and speed of light is $c = 3 \times 10^8$ m/s.

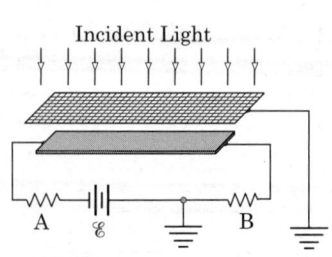

4. A plate of area S connected to a battery of electromotive force $\mathscr{E}$ through two identical resistors A and B each of resistance R is uniformly illuminated by a monochromatic light of wavelength λ. The photoelectrons emitted from the plate are collected by an earthed wire grid as shown in the figure. The intensity of the light that reaches the plate after passing through the grid is I_0. Resistance of the plate to current flow along its length is R_0. Quantum efficiency of the photoelectric emission is η. Find the strength of currents through each of resistors A and B. Denote modulus of charge on an electron by e and the Planck's constant by h.

5. A neutron beam of initial kinetic energy E_0 is divided into two beams at point O by some mechanism. Thereafter the beams proceed on the path OAC and OBC without a phase change at the corners A and B to interfere with each other at point C. Here OACB is a square of side l tilted at an angle θ above the horizontal. Mass of a neutron is m, Planck's constant is h and acceleration of free fall is g. Find an expression for the angle θ at which a maxima is detected at point C.

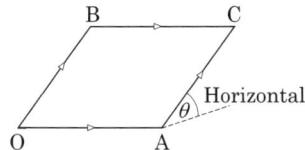

6. In a glass bulb filled with gaseous neon two metal plates are used as electrodes separated by a distance $d = 4$ mm that is much smaller than the linear dimensions of the plates. Ionization energy for neon atom is $E_0 = 21.5$ eV, average distance travelled by an electron between two consecutive collisions with neon atoms is $l = 0.4$ mm and charge on an electron is $e = -1.6 \times 10^{-19}$ C. How much potential difference between the electrodes should be applied to initiate a discharge process?

7. A Hydrogen molecule in an excited state travelling in the x-direction with kinetic energy of 1.0 eV dissociates into two hydrogen atoms. If one of them moves perpendicular to the x-direction with a kinetic energy 0.8 eV, calculate the energy released in the dissociation reaction.

8. If a gaseous sample consisting of identically excited hydrogen like ions is irradiated by a stream of photons each of energy $144E_0/225$, ten distinct lines are observed in the emission spectrum. Some of the lines correspond to energy lower than, some higher than and some equal to the energy of the incident photons. Here E_0 is the ionization energy of a hydrogen atom in ground state.

   (a) In which excited state were the ions in the gaseous sample before interaction with the incident photons?
   (b) To which highest state were the ions in the gaseous sample excited?
   (c) Identify the element in the gaseous sample.

9. A small spherical pellet of a β-radioactive element affixed at one end of a thin metallic rod is concentrically enclosed by a metallic sphere and the rod extends out of the sphere through a small opening. The rod and the sphere are well insulated from each other. There are n radioactive decays per second and the energy in eV of the emitted electrons is uniformly distributed in the interval [W_{min}, W_{max}]. For which range of values of external load resistance R does this device behave as

   (a) a constant current source?   (b) a voltage source?

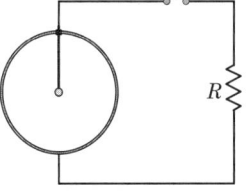

10. A point-like radioactive sample of decay constant λ initially at a distance r_0 from a radiation counter starts moving towards the counter. If the count number recorded by the counter remains constant with time, express speed of the radioactive sample as function of time.

11. Plutonium ^{239}Pu is an unstable nuclei and decays with a half-life $\tau = 2.4 \times 10^4$ years by producing smaller nuclei including an alpha particle. Find the alpha particle flux density (number of the alpha particles per unit area per unit time) near the surface of a large plate of ^{239}Pu having thickness $d = 1$ mm. Density of plutonium is $\rho = 19800$ kg/m^3 and mass of an atom of ^{239}Pu is $m_0 = 3.84 \times 10^{-25}$ kg.

12. At present, concentrations of ^{238}U and ^{235}U in natural uranium are η_1 and η_2 and their half-lives are τ_1 and τ_2 respectively. Assuming concentrations of each of these isotopes were identical at the time of the birth of the earth; find the approximate age of the earth.

13. A free motionless nucleus of tin [^{119}Sn] emits a γ-photon of energy 22.6 keV, which is absorbed by another tin nucleus approaching the γ-photon. Find velocity of the moving nucleus, if in the emission and absorption of γ-photon, transitions of the nuclei take place between the same energy states. The rest energy of the tin nucleus is 113 GeV.

14. When an α-particle collides with a stationary lithium nucleus, the following nuclear reaction may take place.

$$^4\text{He} + {^7\text{Li}} \rightarrow {^{10}\text{B}} + \text{n}$$

If Q-value of this reaction is E = −2.87 MeV, find the minimum value of kinetic energy of incoming α-particles required for the reaction.

15. Nuclei of deuterium D (^{2}H) and tritium T (^{3}H) can fuse according to the following reaction to produce a neutron and an alpha particle.

$$\text{D} + \text{T} \rightarrow {^4\text{He}} + {^1\text{n}}$$

Calculate energies carried away by the neutron and the alpha particle in the above nuclear reaction.

Assume binding energies per nucleon of deuterium, tritium and helium to be 1.00 MeV, 2.80 MeV and 7.00 MeV respectively and neglect kinetic energy of the nuclei before the fusion.

Check your understanding

1. An isotropic point light source S of power P located a distance d from a specially designed non-absorbing, non-dispersing and non-reflecting lens. This lens converges all the radiant energy coming from the source into a beam parallel to its optical axis. Find magnitude of the force of radiation pressure on the lens.

2. Five faces of a homogeneous cube of mass m = 4.0 g are painted in white (reflects all wavelengths) and one face in black (absorbs as well as radiates wavelengths) and the cube is placed in vacuum in free space at a very low temperature (near absolute zero). Initially, when the cube is at rest, it is given Q = 900 J of heat. As it cools down due to heat radiation, it starts moving slowly. Estimate its terminal speed. The speed of light is $c = 3 \times 10^8$ m/s.

3. In the emission spectrum of hydrogen-like ions, energies of the spectral lines range from a minimum value 1.224 eV to a maximum value 52.244 eV. Now the photons of the second line of the Balmer series are filtered and made to incident on the surface of a metal of work function 2.20 eV. If the most energetic photoelectrons emitted pass un-deviated through

a cross-field region (magnetic field 1.0 mT and unknown electric field perpendicular to the magnetic field), calculate the intensity of the electric field.

4. The energy radiated by the Sun is generated primarily by the fusion of hydrogen into ^{4}He. In stars of size in the order of that of the Sun, the primary mechanism by which fusion takes place is the proton-proton chain. The chain begins with the following reactions:

$$2p \to X_1 + e^+ + X_2 \quad (0.42 \text{ MeV}) \quad \text{(R-1)}$$

$$p + X_1 \to X_3 + \gamma \quad (5.49 \text{ MeV}) \quad \text{(R-2)}$$

The amounts listed in parentheses in the above reactions are the total kinetic energy carried by the products, including gamma rays. Here p denotes a proton, e^+ denotes a positron, γ denotes gamma rays and X_1, X_2 and X_3 are unknown particles.

The density of electrons in the core of the Sun is sufficient so that a positron is annihilated almost immediately, releasing energy x.

$$e^+ + e^- \to 2\gamma \quad (x) \quad \text{(R-3)}$$

Subsequently, two major processes occur simultaneously that we call pp-I and pp-II branches.

The pp-I branch is the following single reaction, which releases energy y.

$$2X_3 \to {}^4\text{He} + 2X_4 \quad (y) \quad \text{(R-4)}$$

The pp-II branch consists of the following three reactions:

$$X_3 + {}^4\text{He} \to X_5 + \gamma \quad \text{(R-5)}$$

$$X_5 + e^- \to X_6 + X_7 \quad (z) \quad \text{(R-6)}$$

$$X_6 + X_4 \to 2 \, {}^4\text{He} \quad \text{(R-7)}$$

Here z is energy released in step R-6.

(a) Identify the particles X_1 through X_7. Here X_2 and X_7 are neutral particles of negligible masses.

(b) Find the energy released during the production of one helium-4 nucleus, including the kinetic energy of all products and all energy carried by gamma rays.
Mass of an electron is 0.51 MeV/c^2, mass of a proton is 938.27 MeV/c^2 and mass of a ^{4}He nucleus is 3727.38 MeV/c^2.

(c) Find the energies x and y released in reactions R-3 and R-4.

(d) Reaction (R-6) does not proceed as follows because there is insufficient energy.

$$X_5 \to X_6 + e^+ + X_7$$

What constraint does this fact place on values of z?

(e) In which of the above reactions, energy carried by any given product has unique value every time the reaction occurs. Assume that kinetic energy carried in by the reactants in each step is negligible, and that the products are in the ground state.

Answers and Hints

Multiple Choice Questions

1. (d)
2. (d)
3. (a), (b) and (d)
4. (b)
5. (d)
6. (a)
7. (d)
8. (b)
9. (d)
10. (a) and (c)
11. (b)
12. (a), (b), (c) and (d)
13. (b)
14. (c)
15. (c)

Build up your understanding

1. $\dfrac{h\nu}{c^2}\left(\dfrac{l}{m+m_1+m_2}\right)$

   Along the tube opposite to the direction of the photon emission

2. $\tan^{-1}\left\{\dfrac{1-(1-\rho)^3}{\rho(1-\rho+\rho^2)}\right\}$ from the x-axis towards the negative y-axis.

3. $\dfrac{3p\lambda l^3}{hc} = 6.79 \times 10^{20}$

4. $I_A = \dfrac{\mathscr{E}}{R_0 + 2R} + \dfrac{e\eta\lambda I_0 S}{2hc}$ and

   $I_B = \dfrac{\mathscr{E}}{R_0 + 2R} - \dfrac{e\eta\lambda I_0 S}{2hc}$

5. $\theta = \sin^{-1}\left(\dfrac{2nhl\sqrt{2mE_0} - n^2h^2}{2m^2gl^3}\right)$

   Here $n = 1, 2, 3 \ldots$

6. $\dfrac{E_0 d}{el} = 135$ V

7. 2.6 eV

8. (a) First excited state
   (b) Fourth excited state
   (c) Lithium

9. (a) $0 \le R \le \dfrac{W_{min}}{ne^2}$ (b) $\dfrac{W_{min}}{ne^2} \le R \le \dfrac{W_{max}}{ne^2}$

10. $\dfrac{r_0 \lambda}{2}\exp\left(-\dfrac{\lambda t}{2}\right)$

11. $\dfrac{\rho d \ln 2}{2\tau m_0} \approx 2.36 \times 10^{13}$ m$^{-2} \cdot$ s^{-1}

12. $\left(\dfrac{\tau_1 \tau_2}{\tau_1 - \tau_2}\right)\left\{\dfrac{\ln\left(\dfrac{\eta_1}{\eta_2}\right)}{\ln 2}\right\}$

13. ≈ 60 m/s

14. $-E\left(1 + \dfrac{m_\alpha}{m_{Li}}\right) = 4.51$ MeV

15. 14.08 MeV and 3.52 MeV

Check your understanding

1. $\dfrac{P}{2c}\left(\dfrac{r^2}{2(r^2+d^2)} + \dfrac{d}{\sqrt{r^2+d^2}} - 1\right)$

2. $\approx \dfrac{Q}{3mc} = 0.25$ mm/s

3. 1.68 kV/m

4. (a) $X_1 \equiv {}^2H$, $X_2 \equiv$ neutrino, $X_3 \equiv {}^3He$, $X_4 \equiv {}^1H$, $X_5 \equiv {}^7Be$, $X_6 \equiv {}^7Li$, $X_7 \equiv$ neutrino

   (b) 26.72 MeV

   (c) $x = 1.02$ MeV and $y = 12.86$ MeV

   (d) $z < 1.02$ MeV

   (e) R-2, R-3, R-5, R-6 and R-7

   Hint: Reactions with two products have a single set of product energies, whereas those with three or more products produce a spectrum of output energies.